Handbook of Research on New Challenges and Global Outlooks in Financial Risk Management

Mara Madaleno
University of Aveiro, Portugal

Elisabete Vieira
University of Aveiro, Portugal

Nicoleta Bărbuță-Mișu
University of Galati, Romania

A volume in the Advances in Finance, Accounting, and Economics (AFAE) Book Series

Published in the United States of America by
IGI Global
Business Science Reference (an imprint of IGI Global)
701 E. Chocolate Avenue
Hershey PA, USA 17033
Tel: 717-533-8845
Fax: 717-533-8661
E-mail: cust@igi-global.com
Web site: http://www.igi-global.com

Copyright © 2022 by IGI Global. All rights reserved. No part of this publication may be reproduced, stored or distributed in any form or by any means, electronic or mechanical, including photocopying, without written permission from the publisher. Product or company names used in this set are for identification purposes only. Inclusion of the names of the products or companies does not indicate a claim of ownership by IGI Global of the trademark or registered trademark.
    Library of Congress Cataloging-in-Publication Data

Names: Madaleno, Mara, 1981- editor. | Vieira, Elisabete S., editor. |
   Barbuta-Misu, Nicoleta, 1978- editor.
Title: Handbook of research on new challenges and global outlooks in financial
   risk management / Mara Madaleno, Elisabete Vieira, and Nicoleta
   Barbuta-Misu, editors.
Description: Hershey, PA : Business Science Reference, 2022. | Includes
   bibliographical references and index. | Summary: "This book discusses
   the financial instruments firms use to manage the different kind of
   financial risks, such as interest rate risk, corporate risk, credit
   risk, liquidity and default risk and is intended to help the reader
   understand the risk management practices in different countries, and
   their relationship to firms' performance, and other dimensions of
   companies"-- Provided by publisher.
Identifiers: LCCN 2021035411 (print) | LCCN 2021035412 (ebook) | ISBN
   9781799886099 (hardcover) | ISBN 9781799886112 (ebook)
Subjects: LCSH: Business enterprises--Finance. | Risk management. |
   Organizational effectiveness. | Organizational behavior.
Classification: LCC HG4026 .N488 2022 (print) | LCC HG4026 (ebook) | DDC
   658.15/1--dc23
LC record available at https://lccn.loc.gov/2021035411
LC ebook record available at https://lccn.loc.gov/2021035412

This book is published in the IGI Global book series Advances in Finance, Accounting, and Economics (AFAE) (ISSN: 2327-5677; eISSN: 2327-5685)

British Cataloguing in Publication Data
A Cataloguing in Publication record for this book is available from the British Library.

All work contributed to this book is new, previously-unpublished material. The views expressed in this book are those of the authors, but not necessarily of the publisher.

For electronic access to this publication, please contact: eresources@igi-global.com.

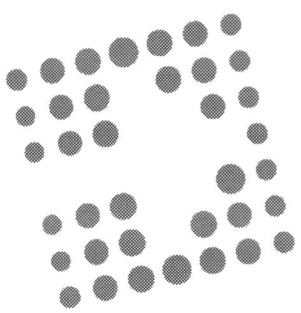

Advances in Finance, Accounting, and Economics (AFAE) Book Series

Ahmed Driouchi
Al Akhawayn University, Morocco

ISSN:2327-5677
EISSN:2327-5685

Mission

In our changing economic and business environment, it is important to consider the financial changes occurring internationally as well as within individual organizations and business environments. Understanding these changes as well as the factors that influence them is crucial in preparing for our financial future and ensuring economic sustainability and growth.

The **Advances in Finance, Accounting, and Economics (AFAE)** book series aims to publish comprehensive and informative titles in all areas of economics and economic theory, finance, and accounting to assist in advancing the available knowledge and providing for further research development in these dynamic fields.

Coverage

- E-Accounting
- Economics of Migration and Spatial Mobility
- Health Economics
- Economic Downturn
- Wages and Employment
- Microeconomics
- Fiscal Policy
- Behavioral Economics
- Managerial Accounting
- Economic Indices and Quantitative Economic Methods

IGI Global is currently accepting manuscripts for publication within this series. To submit a proposal for a volume in this series, please contact our Acquisition Editors at Acquisitions@igi-global.com or visit: http://www.igi-global.com/publish/.

The Advances in Finance, Accounting, and Economics (AFAE) Book Series (ISSN 2327-5677) is published by IGI Global, 701 E. Chocolate Avenue, Hershey, PA 17033-1240, USA, www.igi-global.com. This series is composed of titles available for purchase individually; each title is edited to be contextually exclusive from any other title within the series. For pricing and ordering information please visit http://www.igi-global.com/book-series/advances-finance-accounting-economics/73685. Postmaster: Send all address changes to above address. © © 2022 IGI Global. All rights, including translation in other languages reserved by the publisher. No part of this series may be reproduced or used in any form or by any means – graphics, electronic, or mechanical, including photocopying, recording, taping, or information and retrieval systems – without written permission from the publisher, except for non commercial, educational use, including classroom teaching purposes. The views expressed in this series are those of the authors, but not necessarily of IGI Global.

Titles in this Series

For a list of additional titles in this series, please visit: http://www.igi-global.com/book-series/advances-finance-accounting-economics/73685

Transitioning From Globalized to Localized and Self-Reliant Economies
Ruchika Gupta (Amity University, India) Priyank Srivastava (Amity University, India) Shiv Ranjan (Amity University, India) and M. Affan Badar (Indiana State University, USA)
Business Science Reference • © 2022 • 256pp • H/C (ISBN: 9781799887058) • US $195.00

COVID-19 Pandemic Impact on New Economy Development and Societal Change
Cristina Raluca Gh. Popescu (University of Bucharest, Romania & The Bucharest University of Economic Studies, Romania & The National Institute for Research and Development in Environmental Protection (INCDPM), Romania & National Research and Development Institute for Gas Turbines (COMOTI), Romania)
Business Science Reference • © 2022 • 425pp • H/C (ISBN: 9781668433744) • US $195.00

Microfinance and Sustainable Development in Africa
Yahaya Alhassan (University of Sunderland in London, UK) and Uzoechi Nwagbara (University of the West of Scotland, UK & Cardiff Metropolitan University, UK)
Business Science Reference • © 2022 • 368pp • H/C (ISBN: 9781799874997) • US $195.00

Redefining Global Economic Thinking for the Welfare of Society
Md Mashiur Rahman (Bank Asia Ltd., Bangladesh) Richa Goel (Amity University, Noida, India) Anthony P. Gomes (TeamPeople, USA) and Md Almas Uzzaman (Independent Researcher, Australia)
Business Science Reference • © 2022 • 268pp • H/C (ISBN: 9781799882589) • US $225.00

FinTech Development for Financial Inclusiveness
Muhammad Anshari (Universiti Brunei Darussalam, Brunei) Mohamad Nabil Almunawar (Universiti Brunei Darussalam, Brunei) and Masairol Masri (Universiti Brunei Darussalam, Brunei)
Business Science Reference • © 2022 • 269pp • H/C (ISBN: 9781799884477) • US $225.00

Evaluating Trade and Economic Relations Between India and Southeast Asia
Anita Medhekar (Central Queensland University, Australia) and Harpreet Kaur (Central Queensland University, Australia)
Business Science Reference • © 2022 • 347pp • H/C (ISBN: 9781799857747) • US $195.00

Handbook of Research on Global Aspects of Sustainable Finance in Times of Crises
Ibrahim Yasar Gok (Süleyman Demirel University, Turkey & Freie Universität Berlin, Germany)
Business Science Reference • © 2022 • 442pp • H/C (ISBN: 9781799885016) • US $285.00

701 East Chocolate Avenue, Hershey, PA 17033, USA
Tel: 717-533-8845 x100 • Fax: 717-533-8661
E-Mail: cust@igi-global.com • www.igi-global.com

Editorial Advisory Board

Ishaq Bhatti, *La Trobe University, Australia*
Petre Brezeanu, *The Bucharest University of Economic Studies, Romania*
Maria do Céu Cortez, *School of Economics and Management, University of Minho, Portugal*
Luis Miguel da Mata Artur Dias Pacheco, *Departamento de Economia e Gestão, Universidade Portucalense, Portugal*
Júlio Fernando Seara Sequeira da Mota Lobão, *Faculty of Economics, University of Oporto, Portugal*
Elisabete Neves, *CETRAD, Polytechnic Institute of Coimbra, Portugal*
Fernando Oliveira Tavares, *Instituto Superior de Ciências Empresariais e do Turismo, Portugal*
Rúben M. T. Peixinho, *Faculty of Economics and CEFAGE, University of Algarve, Portugal*
Manuel Rocha Armada, *School of Economics and Management, University of Minho, Portugal*
Luís Miguel Serra Coelho, *Faculdade de Economia da Universidade do Algarve, Portugal*
Florinda Silva, *Research Centre and School of Economics and Management, University of Minho, Portugal*
Piotr Staszkiewicz, *Warsaw School of Economics, Poland*
Florina Oana Virlanuta, *Department of Economics, Dunarea de Jos University of Galati, Romania*
Frédéric Vrins, *Louvain Finance Center, France & CORE, Université catholique de Louvain, Belgium*

List of Contributors

Agyekum Addae, John / *Ghana Communication Technology University, Ghana & University of Aveiro, Portugal* 99
Ahmed, Ezaz / *Columbia College, USA* 204
Bakar Türegün, Feride / *Bursa Uludag University, Turkey* 250
Barbuta-Misu, Nicoleta / *University of Galati, Romania* 1
Borelli, Alberto / *University of Verona, Italy* 270
Brandão, Fábio / *University of Aveiro, Portugal* 116
Canguende-Valentim, Cláudio Félix / *University of Aveiro, Portugal* 316
Casalinho, Cristina / *Portuguese Treasury and Debt Management Agency, Portugal* 231
Ceylan, Özcan / *Özyeğin University, Turkey* 384
Cortez, Maria Céu / *NIPE, Portugal & School of Economics and Management, University of Minho, Portugal* 178
Deari, Fitim / *South East European University, Macedonia* 25
Di Persio, Luca / *University of Verona, Italy* 270
Gerçek, Adnan / *Bursa Uludag University, Turkey* 250
Grable, John E. / *University of Georgia, USA* 293
Gyamfi, Emmanuel Numapau / *Ghana Institute of Management and Public Administration, Accra, Ghana* 99
Hasan, Md. Mahadi / *Anwer Khan Modern University, Bangladesh* 204
Heo, Wookjae / *Purdue University, USA* 293
Horváthová, Jarmila / *Faculty of Management and Business, University of Prešov, Slovakia* 148
Irfan, Mohammad / *CMR Institute of Technology, India* 204
Jungo, João / *University of Aveiro, Portugal* 83
Kwak, Eun Jin / *University of Georgia, USA* 293
Leite, Joana / *Coimbra Business School Research Centre, ISCAC, Polytechnic of Coimbra, Coimbra, Portugal* 354
Lobão, Júlio / *University of Porto, Portugal* 64
Luzendo, Wilson / *Banco de Desenvolvimento de Angola, Angola* 83
Madaleno, Mara / *GOVCOPP, University of Aveiro, Portugal* 1, 38, 83, 116
Maurício, Germano / *Coimbra Business School, ISCAC, Instituto Politécnico de Coimbra, Portugal* 340
Mokrišová, Martina / *Faculty of Management and Business, University of Prešov, Slovakia* 148
Mota, Jorge / *GOVCOPP, University of Aveiro, Portugal* 116
Neves, Maria / *Coimbra Business School Research Centre, ISCAC, Polytechnic of Coimbra, Coimbra, Portugal & CETRAD, University of Trás-os-Montes and Alto Douro, Portugal* 354

Neves, Maria Elisabete / *Coimbra Business School Research Centre, ISCAC, Polytechnic of Coimbra, Coimbra, Portugal & CETRAD, University of Trás-os-Montes and Alto Douro, Portugal* 340
Neves, Renato / *Coimbra Business School Research Centre, ISCAC, Polytechnic of Coimbra, Coimbra, Portugal* 354
Pena, Joana / *School of Economics and Management, University of Minho, Portugal* 178
Quixina, Yuri / *Instituto Superior Politécnico de Tecnologias e Ciências (ISPTEC), Angola* 83
Rodrigues, Lucas / *Coimbra Business School, ISCAC, Instituto Politécnico de Coimbra, Portugal* 340
Saraiva, Helena I. B. / *Guarda's Polytechnic Institute, Portugal* 231
Shaikh, Zakir Hossen / *Bahrain Training Institute, Bahrain* 204
Teodósio, João / *Polytechnic Institute of Santarém, Portugal* 38
Trinh, Hai Hong / *Massey University, New Zealand* 25
Vieira, Elisabete / *GOVCOPP, University of Aveiro, Portugal* 1, 38

Table of Contents

Preface xviii

Acknowledgment xxii

Chapter 1
Financial Risk and Corporate Governance: A Bibliometric Analysis 1
    Elisabete Vieira, GOVCOPP, University of Aveiro, Portugal
    Nicoleta Barbuta-Misu, University of Galati, Romania
    Mara Madaleno, GOVCOPP, University of Aveiro, Portugal

Chapter 2
The Relationship Between Risk and Firm Performance: A Review 25
    Fitim Deari, South East European University, Macedonia
    Hai Hong Trinh, Massey University, New Zealand

Chapter 3
Gender Diversity and Financial Risk: A Bibliometric Analysis 38
    João Teodósio, Polytechnic Institute of Santarém, Portugal
    Elisabete Vieira, GOVCOPP, University of Aveiro, Portugal
    Mara Madaleno, GOVCOPP, University of Aveiro, Portugal

Chapter 4
Gender Differences in Risk Tolerance: New Evidence From a Survey of Postgraduate Students 64
    Júlio Lobão, University of Porto, Portugal

Chapter 5
Corruption, Credit Risk, and Bank Profitability: Evidence of Angolan Banks 83
    João Jungo, University of Aveiro, Portugal
    Wilson Luzendo, Banco de Desenvolvimento de Angola, Angola
    Yuri Quixina, Instituto Superior Politécnico de Tecnologias e Ciências (ISPTEC), Angola
    Mara Madaleno, GOVCOPP, University of Aveiro, Portugal

Chapter 6
Risk Governance and Bank Performance: Do Risk Committee Activism and Finance Experts on the Risk Committee Matter? 99
    John Agyekum Addae, Ghana Communication Technology University, Ghana & University of Aveiro, Portugal
    Emmanuel Numapau Gyamfi, Ghana Institute of Management and Public Administration, Accra, Ghana

Chapter 7
Loss Aversion in Companies Whose Location Is Affected by Fire 116
    Mara Madaleno, GOVCOPP, University of Aveiro, Portugal
    Jorge Mota, GOVCOPP, University of Aveiro, Portugal
    Fábio Brandão, University of Aveiro, Portugal

Chapter 8
Risk of Business Bankruptcy: The Application of DEA Method – Case Study of Slovak Businesses 148
    Jarmila Horváthová, Faculty of Management and Business, University of Prešov, Slovakia
    Martina Mokrišová, Faculty of Management and Business, University of Prešov, Slovakia

Chapter 9
The Impact of Social Screening on the Performance of US and European Funds 178
    Joana Pena, School of Economics and Management, University of Minho, Portugal
    Maria Céu Cortez, NIPE, Portugal & School of Economics and Management, University of Minho, Portugal

Chapter 10
Stock Market Volatility: A Pre- to Post-COVID-19 Analysis of Emerging Markets 204
    Ezaz Ahmed, Columbia College, USA
    Md. Mahadi Hasan, Anwer Khan Modern University, Bangladesh
    Zakir Hossen Shaikh, Bahrain Training Institute, Bahrain
    Mohammad Irfan, CMR Institute of Technology, India

Chapter 11
Environmental, Social, and Governance Assets: Recent History of Green Bonds – Genesis and Current Perspectives 231
    Helena I. B. Saraiva, Guarda's Polytechnic Institute, Portugal
    Cristina Casalinho, Portuguese Treasury and Debt Management Agency, Portugal

Chapter 12
Managing the Current Risks of Companies: The Applicability of Tax Risk Management 250
    Feride Bakar Türegün, Bursa Uludag University, Turkey
    Adnan Gerçek, Bursa Uludag University, Turkey

Chapter 13
Boosted Decision Trees for Credit Scoring 270
    Luca Di Persio, University of Verona, Italy
    Alberto Borelli, University of Verona, Italy

Chapter 14
The Role of Big Data Research Methodologies in Describing Investor Risk Attitudes and
Predicting Stock Market Performance: Deep Learning and Risk Tolerance 293
    Wookjae Heo, Purdue University, USA
    Eun Jin Kwak, University of Georgia, USA
    John E. Grable, University of Georgia, USA

Chapter 15
Determining Consumer Purchase Intention Toward Counterfeit Luxury Goods Based on the
Perceived Risk Theory 316
    Cláudio Félix Canguende-Valentim, University of Aveiro, Portugal

Chapter 16
Insider Transactions and Performance: The Portuguese Case 340
    Maria Elisabete Neves, Coimbra Business School Research Centre, ISCAC, Polytechnic of
        Coimbra, Coimbra, Portugal & CETRAD, University of Trás-os-Montes and Alto Douro,
        Portugal
    Germano Maurício, Coimbra Business School, ISCAC, Instituto Politécnico de Coimbra,
        Portugal
    Lucas Rodrigues, Coimbra Business School, ISCAC, Instituto Politécnico de Coimbra,
        Portugal

Chapter 17
Does Technical Analysis Win? Evidence From the Period Between Donald Trump's Campaign
and the First Date for Brexit.. 354
    Maria Neves, Coimbra Business School Research Centre, ISCAC, Polytechnic of Coimbra,
        Coimbra, Portugal & CETRAD, University of Trás-os-Montes and Alto Douro, Portugal
    Joana Leite, Coimbra Business School Research Centre, ISCAC, Polytechnic of Coimbra,
        Coimbra, Portugal
    Renato Neves, Coimbra Business School Research Centre, ISCAC, Polytechnic of Coimbra,
        Coimbra, Portugal

Chapter 18
Hedging Effectiveness of the VIX ETPs: An Analysis of the Time-Varying Performance of the
VXX 384
    Özcan Ceylan, Özyeğin University, Turkey

Compilation of References 402

About the Contributors 461

Index 467

Detailed Table of Contents

Preface xviii

Acknowledgment xxii

Chapter 1
Financial Risk and Corporate Governance: A Bibliometric Analysis 1
    Elisabete Vieira, GOVCOPP, University of Aveiro, Portugal
    Nicoleta Barbuta-Misu, University of Galati, Romania
    Mara Madaleno, GOVCOPP, University of Aveiro, Portugal

This chapter intends to contribute to the analysis of the influence of corporate governance (CG) practices on company financial risk (FR) to understand the current state of CG and FR research. Although there is extensive research on CG and FR, to the best of the authors' knowledge, no recent study tries to update the current state of the research over the influence of CG practices on FR. To do so, the authors will conduct a bibliometric analysis focused on financial risk and CG studies resorting to different online available libraries. The study describes the evolutional research studies published in the digital libraries Scopus and Web of Science between 2010 and 2020 and compares the results obtained in evolutionary terms. The study ends up concentrating the bibliometric analysis in the Scopus and Web of Science databases and the keyword "financial risk," leading to a total of 14,942 and 3,760 documents, respectively.

Chapter 2
The Relationship Between Risk and Firm Performance: A Review 25
    Fitim Deari, South East European University, Macedonia
    Hai Hong Trinh, Massey University, New Zealand

The relationship between risk and return is a crucial point in typical decision making, and empirical previous studies can help related stakeholders in this process. Henceforth, this chapter aims to present some fundamental theoretical concepts and interpretations of the relationship between risk and firm performance. Accordingly, this chapter offers a review of some highlighted studies in this field by presenting methodologies used and developed by several scholars. The chapter provides a timely reference source for a range of target audience from both academia and industry who have common interests to decompose and examine the relationship between risk and firm performance.

Chapter 3
Gender Diversity and Financial Risk: A Bibliometric Analysis... 38
    João Teodósio, Polytechnic Institute of Santarém, Portugal
    Elisabete Vieira, GOVCOPP, University of Aveiro, Portugal
    Mara Madaleno, GOVCOPP, University of Aveiro, Portugal

This chapter intends to contribute to the analysis of gender diversity and financial risk through a bibliometric review of the existent literature to understand the current state of financial risk research as well as to contribute to the analysis of the influence of gender diversity on financial risk. Although there is extensive research on financial risk, no recent study tries to update the current state of the research over the influence of gender on financial risk practices. This chapter describes the evolutional research studies published in the digital library Scopus, between 2010 and June 2021, and compares the results obtained in evolutionary terms. When the research is concentrated on the bibliometric analysis in the Scopus database and the keyword "financial risk," it leads to a total of 15,979 documents. Regarding the analysis concentrated on the keywords "gender diversity" and "financial risk" for the period between 2010 and June 2021, the authors end with a final sample of 96 documents. Proposals for further research are provided based on the current state of the art.

Chapter 4
Gender Differences in Risk Tolerance: New Evidence From a Survey of Postgraduate Students 64
    Júlio Lobão, University of Porto, Portugal

In this chapter, the author examines the influence of gender on financial risk tolerance. The risk tolerance is assessed by the instrument developed by Grable and Lytton in a sample that includes 272 postgraduate students of the University of Porto (Portugal). The results show that males are significantly more risk-tolerant than females, even after controlling for factors such as the economic status and educational levels of the respondents' parents. The gender differences seem to be essentially driven by a higher proportion of males with high levels of risk tolerance. Moreover, belonging to a household with a high level of annual income contributes to increase the likelihood of exhibiting high levels of risk tolerance. In the total sample, the levels of risk tolerance are lower than those reported in similar studies. Overall, the author documents that there are significant gender differences in financial risk perception.

Chapter 5
Corruption, Credit Risk, and Bank Profitability: Evidence of Angolan Banks 83
    João Jungo, University of Aveiro, Portugal
    Wilson Luzendo, Banco de Desenvolvimento de Angola, Angola
    Yuri Quixina, Instituto Superior Politécnico de Tecnologias e Ciências (ISPTEC), Angola
    Mara Madaleno, GOVCOPP, University of Aveiro, Portugal

The economies of African countries are generally characterized by inefficient management of resources, strong heterogeneity in the rate of economic growth, as well as high levels of corruption and embezzlement of public funds, clearly highlighting the need to consider the role of government in the performance of the economic environment. Corruption is characterized by three key behaviors—bribery, embezzlement, and nepotism—characteristics that can influence the performance of any financial system. The objective is to examine the effect of corruption on credit risk in Angola. The result of the feasible generalized least squares (FGLS) estimation suggests that corruption increases non-performing loans in the Angolan economy; additionally, the authors find that the larger the bank's assets (bank size), the more averse to credit risk they become, and the smaller the state's stake in the banking system, the lower the non-performing loans.

Chapter 6
Risk Governance and Bank Performance: Do Risk Committee Activism and Finance Experts on the Risk Committee Matter? 99
    John Agyekum Addae, Ghana Communication Technology University, Ghana & University
        of Aveiro, Portugal
    Emmanuel Numapau Gyamfi, Ghana Institute of Management and Public Administration,
        Accra, Ghana

Global discourse is geared towards greater accountability and regulatory oversight of banks to promote sound financial systems and charter value. The authors applied dynamic pool panel analysis to investigate the relationship between risk governance and financial performance among African global banks spanning the years 2015 to 2020. They find significant positive association between financial experts on risk committee and bank profitability. The results further reveal that risk committee activism as a proxy for risk committee effectiveness significantly increase bank profitability. Therefore, stakeholders must prioritize regular risk committee meetings and attach importance to risk committee compositions with finance experts on the majority. Additionally, this study offers policy implications for regulators and bank mangers to clearly define risk committee financial experts and minimum financial experts required to serve on the risk committee.

Chapter 7
Loss Aversion in Companies Whose Location Is Affected by Fire 116
    Mara Madaleno, GOVCOPP, University of Aveiro, Portugal
    Jorge Mota, GOVCOPP, University of Aveiro, Portugal
    Fábio Brandão, University of Aveiro, Portugal

In Portugal, fires have originated a big debate not only because of the environmental damages they cause but also because of the material damages they provoke to families and companies. This way, it is important to understand how these events impact companies' cash holdings, not because of the direct damages caused by them, but because of managers' loss aversion. The empirical evidence, mainly documented by Dessaint and Matray and Kahneman and Tversky, were the main sources to this empirical study, where the authors have chosen to work with panel data analysis using a sample of 38,574 small and medium enterprises during the period from 2009 to 2015. About the obtained results, there is evidence that cash holdings increase when managers of a company located in a region close to a fire, but not directly damaged by it, perceive a salient event of a future fire. In other words, when they anticipate the occurrence of an identical event, cash holdings are increased to protect the company against it.

Chapter 8
Risk of Business Bankruptcy: The Application of DEA Method – Case Study of Slovak
Businesses 148
    Jarmila Horváthová, Faculty of Management and Business, University of Prešov, Slovakia
    Martina Mokrišová, Faculty of Management and Business, University of Prešov, Slovakia

Recently, the demand of business owners to ensure the sustainability of their businesses has come to the fore. It results in a focus on identifying the risks of businesses' financial failure. Several prediction models can be applied in a given area. Which of these models is most suitable for Slovak companies? The aim of this chapter was to point out the possibility of applying the DEA method in measuring the financial health of companies and predicting the risk of their possible bankruptcy. The research was carried out on a sample of companies operating in the field of heat supply. The indicators were selected using related empirical studies, a univariate Logit model, and a correlation matrix. In this chapter, two main models were applied: the DEA model and the Logit model. The main conclusion of the paper is that the DEA method is a suitable alternative in assessing businesses' financial health.

Chapter 9
The Impact of Social Screening on the Performance of US and European Funds 178
    Joana Pena, School of Economics and Management, University of Minho, Portugal
    Maria Céu Cortez, NIPE, Portugal & School of Economics and Management, University of
      Minho, Portugal

This chapter investigates the relationship between the performance and the screening strategies of US and European socially responsible funds. For the full sample and, in particular, for US funds, the results show a curvilinear relationship between screening intensity and fund performance. Continental European funds exhibit a positive relationship between the number of screens and performance. Furthermore, for the full sample and US funds, screening on governance impacts performance positively. In turn, environment and products screens have a negative impact on US fund performance. Finally, funds certified with social labels tend to yield higher performance. Overall, the geographical differences in the impact of the screening process on SRI fund performance are consistent with the contextual nature of socially responsible investments.

Chapter 10
Stock Market Volatility: A Pre- to Post-COVID-19 Analysis of Emerging Markets 204
    Ezaz Ahmed, Columbia College, USA
    Md. Mahadi Hasan, Anwer Khan Modern University, Bangladesh
    Zakir Hossen Shaikh, Bahrain Training Institute, Bahrain
    Mohammad Irfan, CMR Institute of Technology, India

Researchers examine stock volatility in emerging (E7) nations prior to and during COVID-19 announcements using multiple volatility estimations. The correlation coefficient matrix indicates that there is a strong positive correlation between the specified volatility estimators in the pre-COVID-19 and post-COVID-19 periods. Rogers-Satchell standard deviation has the first rank, and Garman-Klass has the last position in the pre-post-COVID-19 analysis volatility estimators. However, the authors discover a considerable influence of pre-post COVID-19 on the world's E7 countries. The findings' primary implication is that post-COVID-19 volatility is greater than pre-COVID-19 volatility. This means that investors' financial portfolios should be rebalanced to favor industries that are less impacted by COVID-19. Additionally, it serves as an early warning signal for investors and the government to take preventative measures in the event that it occurs again in the future.

Chapter 11
Environmental, Social, and Governance Assets: Recent History of Green Bonds – Genesis and
Current Perspectives 231
Helena I. B. Saraiva, Guarda's Polytechnic Institute, Portugal
Cristina Casalinho, Portuguese Treasury and Debt Management Agency, Portugal

This chapter presents a historical overview of the emergence and evolution of ESG assets and, in particular, analyses the main market trends that have been observed in recent years in relation to these assets. The authors intend to present a summary of the main moments and phases that these assets have gone through, from the moment of their appearance in 2007, the year in which the European Investment Bank carried out its Climate Awareness Bond as a test issuance. The movement associated with the issue of these assets is initiated by supranational entities with little homogeneity and no fixed conventions. To overcome this impasse, the green bond principles emerged and a process of defining the characteristics of these assets began, with a particular focus on transparency and the governance process. From this stage onwards, the market showed interest in these financial products and hence the emergence of a harmonising movement regarding green bond standards in which Europe seems to have taken a leading role.

Chapter 12
Managing the Current Risks of Companies: The Applicability of Tax Risk Management................250
Feride Bakar Türegün, Bursa Uludag University, Turkey
Adnan Gerçek, Bursa Uludag University, Turkey

The taxation power of governments affects companies' business activities. For this reason, the legal limit of tax law must be known by taxpayers. Uncertainty, frequent changes, and interpretation differences in the tax field and reporting reveal tax risks. Today, companies, especially large ones, accept tax risk as a part of the risk management process. Focusing on tax risk management, this chapter presents the discussions on various definitions of tax risk and on the tax risk categories, factors that affect tax risk. The applicability of tax risk management is evaluated from the following perspectives in the chapter: empirical analyses conducted in different countries, tax control framework, and tax risk management practice in various countries. As a result, tax risks are manageable with the support of cooperative compliance models of revenue administrations in countries, the necessity of corporate governance principles, the situation of legal regulations, and the increasing risk management experience of especially large companies.

Chapter 13
Boosted Decision Trees for Credit Scoring 270
Luca Di Persio, University of Verona, Italy
Alberto Borelli, University of Verona, Italy

The chapter developed a tree-based method for credit scoring. It is useful because it helps lenders decide whether to grant or reject credit to their applicants. In particular, it proposes a credit scoring model based on boosted decision trees which is a technique consisting of an ensemble of several decision trees to form a single classifier. The analysis used three different publicly available datasets, and then the prediction accuracy of boosted decision trees is compared with the one of support vector machines method.

Chapter 14
The Role of Big Data Research Methodologies in Describing Investor Risk Attitudes and
Predicting Stock Market Performance: Deep Learning and Risk Tolerance 293
 Wookjae Heo, Purdue University, USA
 Eun Jin Kwak, University of Georgia, USA
 John E. Grable, University of Georgia, USA

The purpose of this chapter is to compare the performance of a deep learning modeling technique to predict market performance compared to conventional prediction modeling techniques. A secondary purpose of this chapter is to describe the degree to which financial risk tolerance can be used to predict future stock market performance. Specifically, the models used in this chapter were developed to test whether aggregate investor financial risk tolerance is of value in establishing risk and return market expectations. Findings from this chapter's examples also provide insights into whether financial risk tolerance is more appropriately conceptualized as a predictor of market returns or as an outcome of returns.

Chapter 15
Determining Consumer Purchase Intention Toward Counterfeit Luxury Goods Based on the
Perceived Risk Theory 316
 Cláudio Félix Canguende-Valentim, University of Aveiro, Portugal

This study aims to understand the impact of financial, psychological, and social risk dimensions on attitude and intention to purchase counterfeit luxury goods. Data were collected through a questionnaire conducted with 116 Angolan consumers and were treated with structural equation modeling. The results revealed that only financial risk and social risk were influential in attitude toward counterfeit luxury goods. Attitude had a significant influence on the intention to purchase counterfeit luxury goods. The research contributes to the literature because there has been no previous study in an African country that seeks to understand the purchase intention of counterfeit luxury goods according to risk perception theory. On the other hand, this study is one of the few to report that social risk perception positively impacts attitudes towards counterfeit luxury goods.

Chapter 16
Insider Transactions and Performance: The Portuguese Case 340
 Maria Elisabete Neves, Coimbra Business School Research Centre, ISCAC,Polytechnic of
  Coimbra, Coimbra, Portugal & CETRAD, University of Trás-os-Montes and Alto Douro,
  Portugal
 Germano Maurício, Coimbra Business School, ISCAC, Instituto Politécnico de Coimbra,
  Portugal
 Lucas Rodrigues, Coimbra Business School, ISCAC, Instituto Politécnico de Coimbra,
  Portugal

This study investigates the relevance of stock buy/sell transactions by insiders in Portuguese companies' performance. To achieve this aim, the sample covers the period from 2013 to 2017. The data from buy/sell transactions by insiders were collected in the internal transaction reports delivered by the companies to the Portuguese Securities Market Commission for the same time interval. The results, using panel data methodology, suggest a negative relationship between the long/short positions and the companies' performance, although the volume traded is not significant. Therefore, the increased control of Portuguese companies by their managers signals the existence of conflicts of interest of the managers, whether due to financial reasons or to strengthen their continuity in the position. As far as the authors are aware, this is the first time that a study has been carried out using insider transactions for Portuguese companies and their influence on corporate performance.

Chapter 17
Does Technical Analysis Win? Evidence From the Period Between Donald Trump's Campaign
and the First Date for Brexit..354
    Maria Neves, Coimbra Business School Research Centre, ISCAC,Polytechnic of Coimbra,
        Coimbra, Portugal & CETRAD, University of Trás-os-Montes and Alto Douro, Portugal
    Joana Leite, Coimbra Business School Research Centre, ISCAC,Polytechnic of Coimbra,
        Coimbra, Portugal
    Renato Neves, Coimbra Business School Research Centre, ISCAC,Polytechnic of Coimbra,
        Coimbra, Portugal

The main goal of this chapter is to analyze the performance of four investment strategies within a recent period of international political uncertainties. RSI and MACD supported three competing investment strategies, which were compared to the conservative Buy and Hold strategy. Euro Stoxx 50 Index was selected through the Markowitz Theory, and the DAX index was established as a benchmark. The period considered was between the start of Donald Trump's official campaign to the US elections and the first date set for Brexit. Two subsequent additional studies were performed to evaluate their profitability. The entry and exit points were determined by international economic reports. Alternative time lengths for the RSI window were considered. The results suggest that, when the market is bear or undefined, the investor should have a strategy supported on technical analysis and he should consider more than one indicator to increase the information that is taken from the market. The passive Buy and Hold strategy should be considered when the market is considered a bull market.

Chapter 18
Hedging Effectiveness of the VIX ETPs: An Analysis of the Time-Varying Performance of the
VXX..384
    Özcan Ceylan, Özyeğin University, Turkey

This study introduces basic concepts about hedging and provides an overview of common hedging practices. This theoretical introduction is followed by an empirical application in which the hedging effectiveness of the VIX ETPs is evaluated. The iPath Series B S&P 500 VIX Short Term Futures ETN (VXX) and the SPDR S&P 500 Trust ETF (SPY) are taken for the empirical application. Dynamic conditional correlations between the VXX and SPY are obtained from DCC-GARCH framework. Based on the estimated conditional volatilities of the SPY and the hedged portfolio, a hedging effectiveness index is constructed. Results show that the hedging effectiveness of the VXX increases in turbulent periods such as the last three months of 2018 marked by the plummeting oil prices, increasing uncertainties about the Brexit deal, and rising federal funds rates and the month of March 2020 when the COVID-19 pandemic became a global concern.

Compilation of References 402

About the Contributors 461

Index 467

Preface

ABOUT THE SUBJECT

The topic of financial risk management has gained a huge international relevance. Financial risk management has become increasingly important in the last years and a profound understanding of this subject is vital for managers, practitioners, investors, and students of finance and related areas.

The book intends to provide the major trends regarding the research on financial risk management, as well as the practices of different countries and economies. The idea of this book is to be a compilation of the state of the art, pointing new trends, theoretical and empirical studies on the domain of enterprise risk. It presents a variety of crucial issues of risk management domain (interest rate risk, corporate risk, credit risk, liquidity risk, operational risk, corporate governance, and risk management), collecting several chapters that are coherent with each other and that allow, on a scientific basis, to know what the practices of risk management are. In addition, this book shows evidence on the motivations to risk management practices and shows the tendency of these subjects at the international level. Moreover, the book provides evidence to understand how risk affects different types of institutions, and how risk is managed.

It is fruitful to investigate and disseminate the results of theoretical and empirical studies that reveal different aspects of the financial risk management phenomenon, to obtain insightful knowledge on how to promote effectively the financial decision-making process.

This book folds several coherent chapters which allow, on a scientific basis, to discuss at an international level the new directions in financial risk management, mainly associated with corporate governance, corruption, loss aversion, business bankruptcy, stock market volatility, as well as banks and companies performance.

EXPECTATIONS

The editors intend this book to be useful for regulatory authorities and researchers in the field of financial risk, capital markets, investments, corporate finance, economics, and accounting.

Through dissemination of the research findings on the rigor of finance, this publication could also be valuable to develop and inspire further studies by researchers and students in postgraduate courses, whose research interests are related to financial risk and risk management.

The book intends to provide a state of art in what respects the major trends regarding financial risk management, showing similarities and striking differences in the practices of different countries and

Preface

economies. The idea of this book is to be a compilation of ideas in new trends that are currently shaping modern corporate finance.

This book aims to achieve the following main objectives:

- Document the state of the art related to financial risk;
- Document the relationship between financial risk management and corporate governance;
- Document the relationship between financial risk and firm performance;
- Analyze the main market trends of Environmental, Social, and Governance assets:
- Analyze the loss aversion;
- Consider specific cases, such as the COVID-19 effects and the analysis of big data;
- Analyze the gender effect on financial risk;
- Analyze the effects of corruption on credit risk;
- Analyze the tax risk management;
- Construct a hedging index.

ORGANIZATION OF THE BOOK

Eighteen chapters organize this book.

The first two chapters are focused on the literature review of the financial risk phenomenon. Thus:

- Chapter 1, "Financial Risk and Corporate Governance: A Bibliometric Analysis," offers a literature review on financial risk and corporate governance based on the bibliometric analysis methodology.
- Chapter 2, "The Relationship Between Risk and Firm Performance: A Review," offers a review of some highlighted studies concerning the relationship between risk and firm performance.

The next two chapters provide studies analyzing the issue of gender phenomenon and its effects on financial risk. In this way:

- Chapter 3, "Gender Diversity and Financial Risk: A Bibliometric Analysis," offers a bibliometric review of the existent literature, to understand the current state of financial risk research, as well as to contribute to the analysis of the influence of gender diversity on financial risk.
- Chapter 4, "Gender Differences in Risk Tolerance: New Evidence From a Survey of Postgraduate Students," examines the influence of gender on financial risk tolerance, considering a sample of postgraduate students.

Chapters 5 and 6 analyze the risk issues on specific financial organizations: banks. Thus:

- Chapter 5, "Corruption, Credit Risk, and Bank Profitability: Evidence of Angolan Banks," examine the effect of corruption on credit risk in Angola, since corruption is characterized by key behaviors, bribery, embezzlement, and nepotism, characteristics that can influence the performance of any financial system.

- Chapter 6, "Risk Governance and Bank Performance: Do Risk Committee Activism and Finance Experts on Risk Committee Matter?" investigates the relationship between risk governance and financial performance among African global banks, applying dynamic pool panel analysis.

The following eight chapters cover diverse topics, such as loss aversion, business bankruptcy, and the impact of social screening on the funds' performance. Thus:

- Chapter 7, "Loss Aversion in Companies Whose Location Is Affected by Fire," intends to understand how this kind of event, such as fires, impacts companies' cash holdings, because of managers' loss aversion.
- Chapter 8, "Risk of Business Bankruptcy: The Application of DEA Method – Case Study of Slovak Businesses," points out the possibility of applying the DEA method in measuring the financial health of companies and predicting the risk of their possible bankruptcy, considering a sample of companies operating in the field of heat supply.
- Chapter 9, "The Impact of Social Screening on the Performance of US and European Funds," investigates the relationship between the performance and the screening strategies of the American and the European socially responsible funds.

Chapter 10 covers the most recent pandemic: COVID-19, which poses new challenges in all types of risk, in this case, in the stock market volatility. In this way:

- Chapter 10, "Stock Market Volatility: A Pre- to Post-COVID-19 Analysis of Emerging Markets," contributes to the debate on stock market volatility by exploring stock volatility in emerging nations before and during COVID19 announcements, using multiple volatility estimations.

The following chapter covers a recent topic, with sustainability horizon: the environmental, social, and governance assets: Thus:

- Chapter 11, "Environmental, Social, and Governance Assets: Recent History of Green Bonds, Its Genesis, and Current Perspectives," proceeds to a historical overview of the emergence and evolution of ESG assets and, in particular, analyses the main market trends that have been observed in recent years concerning these assets.

The following six chapters cover diverse topics, such as tax risk management, the role of big data, insider transactions, and technical analysis. In this way:

- Chapter 12, "Managing the Current Risks of Companies: The Applicability of Tax Risk Management," focuses on tax risk management, this chapter presents the discussions on various definitions of tax risk and on the tax risk categories, factors that affect tax risk. The applicability of tax risk management is evaluated from distinct perspectives: empirical analyses conducted in different countries, tax control framework, and tax risk management practice in various countries.
- Chapter 13, "Boosted Decision Trees for Credit Scoring," develops a tree-based method for credit scoring since it is useful because it helps lenders decide whether to grant or reject credit to their

Preface

applicants. In particular, it will be proposed a credit scoring model based on boosted decision trees.
- Chapter 14, "The Role of Big Data Research Methodologies in Describing Investor Risk Attitudes and Predicting Stock Market Performance: Deep Learning and Risk Tolerance," compares the performance of a deep learning modeling technique to predict market performance compared to conventional prediction modeling techniques. Moreover, it describes the degree to which financial risk tolerance can be used to predict future stock market performance.
- Chapter 15, "Determining Consumer Purchase Intentions Toward Counterfeit Luxury Goods Based on the Perceived Risk Theory," helps to understand the impact of financial, psychological, and social risk dimensions on attitude and intention to purchase counterfeit luxury goods, using a questionnaire conducted with Angolan consumers.
- Chapter 16, "Insider Transactions and Performance: The Portuguese Company Case," explores the relevance of stock buy and sell transactions by insiders in Portuguese companies' performance, considering a Portuguese sample.
- Chapter 17, "Does Technical Analysis Win? Evidence From the Period Between Donald Trump's Campaign and the First Date for Brexit," helps to understand the performance of four investment strategies within a recent period of international political uncertainties, using competing investment strategies, and comparing them to the conservative Buy and Hold strategy.

Finally, the last chapter constructed a hedging index. Thus:

- Chapter 18, "Hedging Effectiveness of the VIX ETPs: An Analysis of the Time-Varying Performance of the VXX," helps to understand hedging strategies, provides an overview of common hedging practices, and then, uses an empirical application in which the hedging effectiveness of the VIX ETPs is evaluated. In addition, a hedging effectiveness index is constructed.

Mara Madaleno
GOVCOPP, University of Aveiro, Portugal

Elisabete Vieira
GOVCOPP, University of Aveiro, Portugal

Nicoleta Barbuta-Misu
University of Galati, Romania

Acknowledgment

The editors would like to thank all the people involved in this project for all the help provided, especially to the authors and reviewers. We sincerely appreciate the contributions provided by all of you. It was an excellent and relevant input to the publication process. Without your support, this project would not be possible to achieve.

The editors would like to thank each of the authors of the chapters who contributed deeply dispending their time and expertise to this book, making it so special.

It is never too much to thank and recognize the valuable work of the members of the IGI Editorial Advisory Board in improving the quality, consistency, and presentation of the content of the chapters, which has ensured the highest accuracy in the double-blind review process. We would like to thank the Editorial Advisory Board for its precise collaboration, as well as to some of the authors who have taken on a double task, serving as well as referees for their pairs.

Thanks are also due to FCT/MCTES for the financial support to GOVCOPP (Research Unit on Governance, Competitiveness and Public Policy (UIDB/04058/2020), through national funds.

To all, our most sincere thank you.

Mara Madaleno
GOVCOPP, University of Aveiro, Portugal

Elisabete Vieira
GOVCOPP, University of Aveiro, Portugal

Nicoleta Bărbuță-Mișu
University of Galati, Romania

Chapter 1
Financial Risk and Corporate Governance:
A Bibliometric Analysis

Elisabete Vieira
https://orcid.org/0000-0003-3593-368X
GOVCOPP, University of Aveiro, Portugal

Nicoleta Barbuta-Misu
University of Galati, Romania

Mara Madaleno
https://orcid.org/0000-0002-4905-2771
GOVCOPP, University of Aveiro, Portugal

ABSTRACT

This chapter intends to contribute to the analysis of the influence of corporate governance (CG) practices on company financial risk (FR) to understand the current state of CG and FR research. Although there is extensive research on CG and FR, to the best of the authors' knowledge, no recent study tries to update the current state of the research over the influence of CG practices on FR. To do so, the authors will conduct a bibliometric analysis focused on financial risk and CG studies resorting to different online available libraries. The study describes the evolutional research studies published in the digital libraries Scopus and Web of Science between 2010 and 2020 and compares the results obtained in evolutionary terms. The study ends up concentrating the bibliometric analysis in the Scopus and Web of Science databases and the keyword "financial risk," leading to a total of 14,942 and 3,760 documents, respectively.

INTRODUCTION

No bibliometric research should start without previously defining what the main subject under analysis is. The study concentrates on financial risk (FR) and corporate governance (CG) articles published in

DOI: 10.4018/978-1-7998-8609-9.ch001

the recent years of 2010-2020. Companies are experiencing many different types of risk, such as risks associated with the business environment, laws and regulations, operational efficiency, the organization's reputation, as well as with financial risks. As well, what is FR? Financial risks create the possibility of losses arising from the failure to achieve financial objectives. Companies are exposed to financial risk in their day-by-day activities, and the respective consequences, that can affect their earnings, returns, and value. Several types of risk, such as market risk, model risk, credit risk, liquidity risk, operational risk, and risk of disclosure compose the financial risk.

Market risk is the risk of loss due to unexpected changes in market prices or liquidity, including all balance sheet risks (Schroeck, 2002). Also, it refers to the unpredictable price changes of the different commodities, goods, stocks, or other financial instruments that may determine possible losses. The market risk, caused by the overall change in market conditions, is composed of four factors of risk: the equity risk, the interest rate risk, the currency risk, and commodity risk (Salomons & Grootveld, 2003). The model risk quantifies the consequences of using the wrong models in risk measurement, pricing, or portfolio selection (Jokhadze & Schmidt, 2018). The credit risk arises when there is a potential that a borrower may be unable to fulfill their obligations to repay funds borrowed from the financial institution (Putri, Bunga & Rochman, 2021). Liquidity risk is associated with the inability of banks to fulfill their maturing obligations that come from funding sources of cash flows or from high-quality liquid assets and, consequently, the assets cannot be converted immediately into cash. The operational risk is the risk that a company faces due to their operational activities, internal systems, and processes that are not perfect, meaning no way could eliminate the operational risks (Girling, 2013). Finally, companies face disclosure risks when readers of firms' reports are informed about opportunities or prospects, hazards, losses, threats, or exposures that will affect the company (Linsley & Shrives, 2006).

This chapter intends to analyze the state-of-art in what concerns the FR and their consequences on firms, by trying to understand how the literature has researched the topic in recent years. By doing this through a bibliometric analysis, the authors can find the current stage of this phenomenon.

In addition, and respecting the book title, the authors have an additional section relating to FR and CG's present state of research. As such, it is intended to present the state of the current literature regarding research on FR and CG. In this context, this chapter intends to contribute to the analysis of the influence of CG practices on companies' FR, namely financial risk disclosure and financial distress risk, conducting a bibliometric analysis focused on FR risk and CG studies resorting to different online available libraries, offering proposals for further research considering what is the current state-of-the-art. Indeed, the bibliometric analysis allows us to analyze the scientific evolution in a certain topic of research, while it enlightens us on emerging subjects in the same field of investigation (Donthu et al., 2021). The first document researching under the keyword "financial risk" was published in 1964 according to our bibliometric research.

The rest of this chapter is organized as follows. Section two presents a brief literature review on the FR and CG topics. Section three presents the general status of FR and CG research from 2010 to 2020. Section four concludes this chapter.

BRIEF LITERATURE REVIEW ON FINANCIAL RISK AND CORPORATE GOVERNANCE

FR includes several types of risk, such as market risk, model risk, credit risk, liquidity risk, operational risk, and risk of disclosure compose the financial risk, and some of these types of FR are also divided into various classes of risk. For example, market risk (Schroeck, 2002) is composed of four kinds of risk: the equity risk, the interest rate risk, the currency risk, and commodity risk (Salomons & Grootveld, 2003). From the different types of FR, risk disclosure is related to good CG practices, making companies more transparent in disclosing risks, helping investors to make a better decision in their portfolio investment, creating benefits to firms and shareholders, and, consequently, improving the competitiveness of companies (Solomon et al., 2000). Thus, we can see that it is expected an influence of CG on firms FR.

The CG practices are determinant to protect investors' and other stakeholders' interests (Soltani & Maupetit, 2015). Indeed, CG proposes a set of practices to reduce the conflicts between managers and shareholders (Vieira & Neiva, 2019). The most concise definition of CG was provided by the Cadbury Report in 1992, "Corporate governance is the system by which companies are directed and controlled", and all the responsibility is placed over their leaders. For most companies, those leaders are the directors, responsible for the decision of the long-term strategy of the company, to serve the best interests of all the stakeholders.

The CG rules and practices present different stages of development, according to the economic characteristics of countries. For example, the Western Continental European firms present higher levels of ownership concentration and the dominance of family owners (Aganin & Volpin, 2002; Högfeldt, 2003). Developing countries characterize Central Europe, being now consolidating their CG systems to improve investor protection and transparency (Svejnar, 2002). Eastern Europe exposes diverse CG characteristics, with strong ownership concentration and poor investor protection. For example, the United Kingdom (UK) is characterized by dispersed ownership, liquid capital market, transparency, and high investors' protection, while France, Germany, and Italy are making efforts to improve the stock market efficiency, the investor protection, as well as best practice codes (Aluchna, 2016). Consequently, we expect that different CG practices will influence differently the firm's financial risk.

The economic failures over the past, as well as the current economic changes, show the need for efficient CG practices and financial risk disclosure approaches (Luo, 2016). Indeed, various studies analyze how CG affects the level of FR disclosure, such as the ones of Alnabsha et al. (2018), Elamer and Benyazid (2018), Solomon et al. (2000), Ettredge et al. (2011), Ntim et al. (2013), Bufarwa et al. (2020) and Putri et al. (2021).

Bufarwa et al. (2020) analyze the impact of CG mechanisms on FR reporting in the UK, considering a sample of 50 non-financial firms listed on the London Stock Exchange in the period between 2011 and 2015. The authors find that CG has a significant influence on FR disclosure. Board gender diversity has a positive effect on the level of corporate financial risk disclosure, which adds to the results of previous studies, such as the ones of Barako and Brown (2008), Ntim et al. (2012), and Ntim et al. (2013). Block ownership has also a positive impact on FR disclosure, suggesting that the UK firms will engage in a high level of financial disclosure, including voluntary disclosures. This result is in agreement with the findings of Abraham and Cox (2007) and Oliveira et al. (2011). However, the authors find no significant relationship between board size and corporate FR disclosure, which is consistent with the results of Elzahar and Hussainey (2012), but inconsistent with the findings of Ntim et al. (2013), who find a positive relationship between these variables.

More recently, Putri et al. (2021) study the effect of CG on risk financial disclosure, considering a sample of 20 companies from 2015 to 2017. The authors' results show that the size of the board of commissioners and the frequency of audit committee meetings have a positive effect on financial risk disclosure. However, the results do not show a significant influence of the number of audit committees and the number of boards of commissioner meetings on the degree of FR disclosure.

CG and its impact on the firms' distress risk is one of the most researched topics in contemporary corporate finance (Younas et al., 2021). Indeed, a vast number of studies are carried to analyze the relationship between CG and financial distress (Lee & Yeh, 2004; Lajili & Zeghal, 2010; Al-Tamimi, 2012; Dhamija et al., 2014; Mgammal et al., 2018; Awan et al., 2020; Handriania et al., 2021; Younas et al., 2021).

Ud-Din et al. (2020) investigate the relationship between CG and the likelihood of financial distress for a sample of non-financial firms listed on the Pakistan Stock Exchange, covering the period from 2005 to 2019. The results show that the board size and board independence have a negative relationship with the probability of financial distress. Handriania et al. (2021) analyze a sample of 300 manufacturing companies listed on the Indonesia Stock Exchange from 2011 through 2018, finding that institutional ownership and board independence had a positive relationship to avoid financial distress. However, they find no evidence that board size influences financial distress risk.

Younas et al. (2021) investigate the impact of CG on firm financial distress, considering a sample of 152 non-financial firms listed at the Pakistan Stock Exchange, for the period between 2003 and 2017. The results show a positive impact of CG on the risk of firms' financial distress, suggesting that good CG practices have an important role in the reduction of financial distress. The outcomes indicate a negative impact of block holders on financial distress, suggesting that the concentrated block ownership takes monopolistic decisions to protect their interests, consistent with the results of Udin et al. (2017). The authors find a positive association between institutional ownership and distress risk. The study also reveals a negative relationship between CEO duality and distress risk, which is consistent with the results of Ali and Nasir (2018). In what concerns the control variables, firm size and firm growth are positively associated with financial distress, suggesting that large companies have a low risk of default due to their experiences and operational efficiency (Udin et al., 2017).

GENERAL BIBLIOMETRIC ANALYSIS ON FINANCIAL RISK AND CORPORATE GOVERNANCE: 2010-2020

Bibliometric analysis is a method that turns easier the research of the relationship between research criteria and variables related to the research and environment of that research. During this research, it was applied the exploratory, descriptive, and bibliographic research methodology, performing a content analysis through the keywords "financial risk" and "corporate governance". Provided the authors wanted a recent analysis period, they concentrate the chapter research during the period 2010-2020. Just by searching for the keyword earnings management in the Scopus database, it was found a total of 14,942 documents (from all types), while in the Web of Science database only 4,542 documents, also from all types. Regarding the analysis concentrated on the keywords "financial risk" and "corporate governance" for the 2010-2020 period, the authors end with a final sample of 138 documents in the Scopus database and 50 documents in the Web of Science database.

Another classification performed in our study is the kind of quantitative and qualitative research that takes on its basis a content analysis. The acquired data has on its basis several sources which are found in Scopus (https://www.scopus.com/search/), a database with a huge quantity of articles and Web of Science (https://www.webofscience.com/wos/woscc/basic-search). The process of data collection in this platform is divided into several parameters: the choice of the database, the definition of keywords, the identification of the article, the journal identification, and the classification of the articles. The study performed and presented next will follow over some of these parameters.

Figure 1 presents the evolution of the documents collected during 2010 and 2020, after applying the parameters defined in the Scopus and Web of Science databases, leading us to a total database of 138 documents, and 50 documents, respectively.

Figure 1. Number of documents published during 2010-2020, by year
Source: Scopus and Web of Science

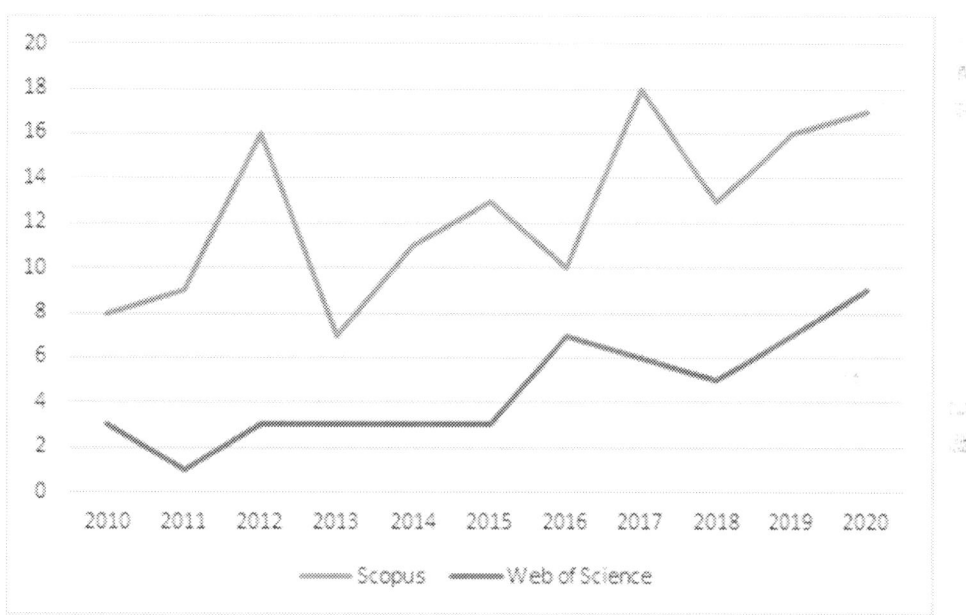

Although there is some instability of published papers in both databases in the 2010-2020 period, it is visible a growing trend in the number of published documents, with 8 documents in 2010, and 17 documents in 2020 in Scopus and with 3 documents in 2010 and 9 documents in 2020 in the Web of Science. It is visible two peaks, in 2017 and 2020, with 18 and 17 documents published in Scopus, respectively in 2016 and 2019 with 7 documents and 2020 with 9 documents in the Web of Science. In the last five years, the published documents represent more than 50% of the total documents (53.6%) in Scopus and more than 60% of total documents (68%) in Web of Science, which leads the authors to argue that this continues to be a hot topic on the subject areas of research.

Figure 2.a and 2.b shows the journals to which correspond the major sources of publishing journals in Scopus and respectively Web of Science.

Figure 2. Documents published in 2010-2020 by source title in Scopus
Source: Scopus

As it can be observed, the major sources of publishing journals associated with the 138 documents published during the analysis period in Scopus, are the Corporate Ownership and Control, Economic Research Ekonomska Istrazivanja, Journal of Banking and Finance, Managerial Finance, and the Accounting and Finance Journal. However, the papers are very dispersed, with 138 documents being published in 88 journals. From the top five journals, the documents are published in the rhythm of one per year (or none), except for Corporate Ownership and Control, which has two publications in the year 2016.

Related to the Web of Science database (Figure 2.b), the major sources of publishing journals associated with the 50 documents published during the analysis period, are the Advances in Social Science Education and Humanities Research, Corporate Governance The International Journal of Business in Society, Journal of Applied Accounting Research, Journal of Corporate Finance, Life Science Journal Acta Zhengzhou University Overseas Edition, and Managing and Modelling of Financial Risks. However, the papers are very dispersed, with 50 documents being published in 51 journals. From the top six journals, where are published 2 papers in the analyzed period, the documents are published in the rhythm of one per year (or none), except for Life Science Journal Acta Zhengzhou University Overseas Edition, which has two publications in the year of 2013.

Figure 3. Documents published in 2010-2020 by source title in Web of Science
Source: Web of Science

Figure 3 highlights the authors who most published in the field of FR and CG during 2010 and 2020. All the ten authors have published 2 documents during this period.

Figures 3.a and 3.b highlights the authors who most published in the field of FR and CG during 2010 and 2020. In the Scopus database, all the ten authors have published 2 documents during this period. In the Web of Science database, only 3 authors published 2 documents during the period analyzed, the other authors published only one paper. In the Web of Science were found 129 authors that contributed to those 50 documents.

Even if about the same thematic, no common author's names are presented in Figures 3.a and 3.b. Still, no more than 2 articles per author have been published in neither bibliographic database. Even so, it is highlighted that these are the authors appearing during the search and for the specific period analyzed. If the period under analysis had been broadened, more publications per author would have emerged.

From a brief analysis of the literature collected, regulations, liquidity, profitability, innovation, internationalization, company size, company maturity, debt, leverage, dual listing, conflicts of interest, industry, investment projects, listing status, among others, are just some of the several factors have been identified in the literature as major drivers of the relationship between CG and FR.

Several differences distinguish corporate entities. These vary considerably in terms of the levels of asset base, annual profit, profitability, assets growth, size, life cycle, cash flows, turnover, location, governance, financial architecture, among other distinguishing factors and characteristics. A great number of studies were conducted in both developed and emerging economies. In terms of methodologies employed, content analysis and regression methods were used as evaluation methods. More sophisticated econometric methodologies are being employed more recently since there is the need to control for issues like multicollinearity, endogeneity, and heteroscedasticity. All these employed methods depend on the nature of the dependent variables used, the number of companies analyzed, and the period.

Figure 4. Documents published during 2010-2020 by author in Scopus
Source: Scopus

Figure 5. Documents published during 2010-2020 by author in Web of Science
Source: Web of Science

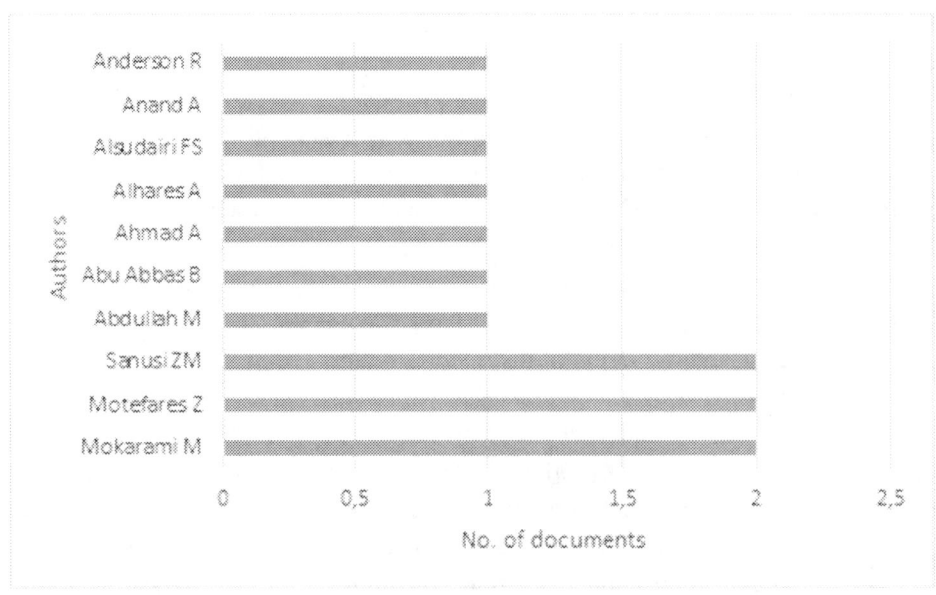

Figure 4.a and 4.b shows the documents by affiliation, considering the top 10 affiliations with more

authors and co-authors, during the 2010-2020 period, one figure for each bibliographic database consulted.

Figure 6. Documents published by affiliation during 2010-2020 in Scopus
Source: Scopus

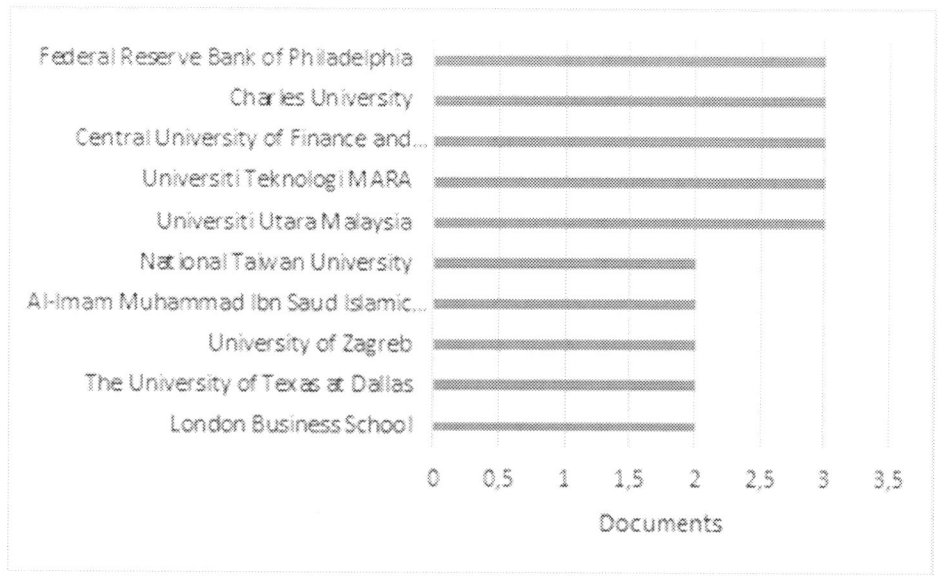

Figure 7. Documents published by affiliation during 2010-2020 in Web of Science
Source: Web of Science

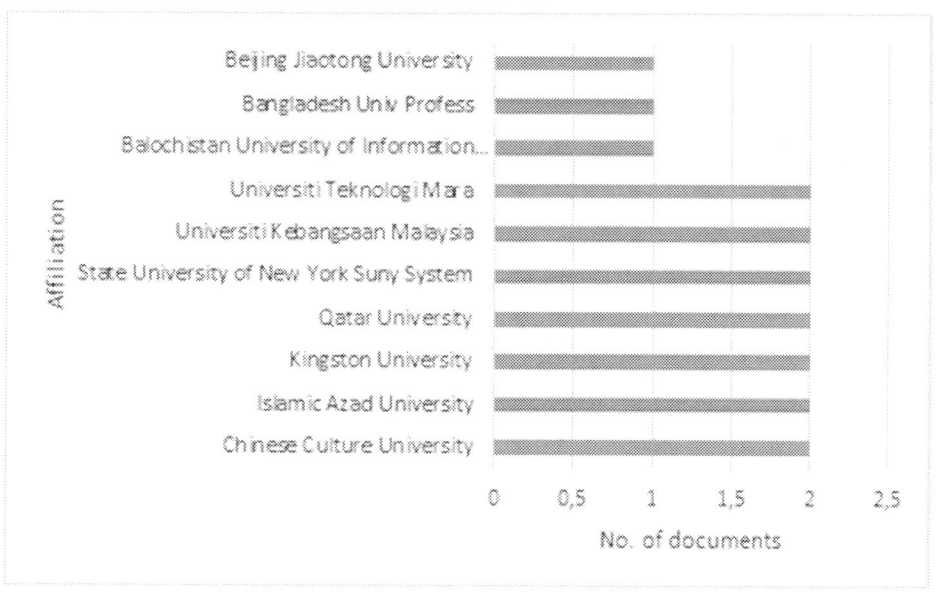

Regarding the affiliation of the authors for the Scopus database, Figure 4.a exposes that there are five Institutions with the highest number of affiliated authors and co-authors publishing during 2010 and 2020, which are the Federal Reserve Bank of Philadelphia, Charles University (Czech Republic), Central University of Finance and Economics (China), Universiti Teknologi MARA (Malaysia), and the Universiti Utara Malaysia. These are followed by the National Taiwan University, Al-Imam Muhammad Ibn Saud Islamic University, University of Zagreb, The University of Texas at Dallas, and the London Business School. These institutions belong to the North of America (two), Europe (three), and Asia (five).

Related to the affiliation of the authors for the Web of Science database, Figure 4.b exposes that there are seven Institutions with 2 affiliated authors and co-authors publishing during 2010 and 2020, which are the Chinese Culture University, Islamic Azad University, Kingston University, Qatar University, State University Of New York Suny System, Universiti Kebangsaan Malaysia, and Universiti Teknologi Mara. These are followed by the Balochistan University of Information Technology Engineering Management Sciences Buitems, Bangladesh Univ Profess, Beijing Jiaotong University. In Web of Science were found 103 institutions of affiliated authors contributed to those 50 documents. Even so, there is a clear discrepancy among the affiliation of the authors and no clear networks are built for example between developing and developed countries, losing some valuable flows of information able to build effective policies to control for some of the issues emerging in corporate governance and financial risk-taking behavior analysis.

Figure 5.a and 5.b displays the documents by country or territory during 2010-2020 in both databases analyzed.

Figure 8. Documents by country or territory during 2010-2020 in Scopus
Source: Scopus

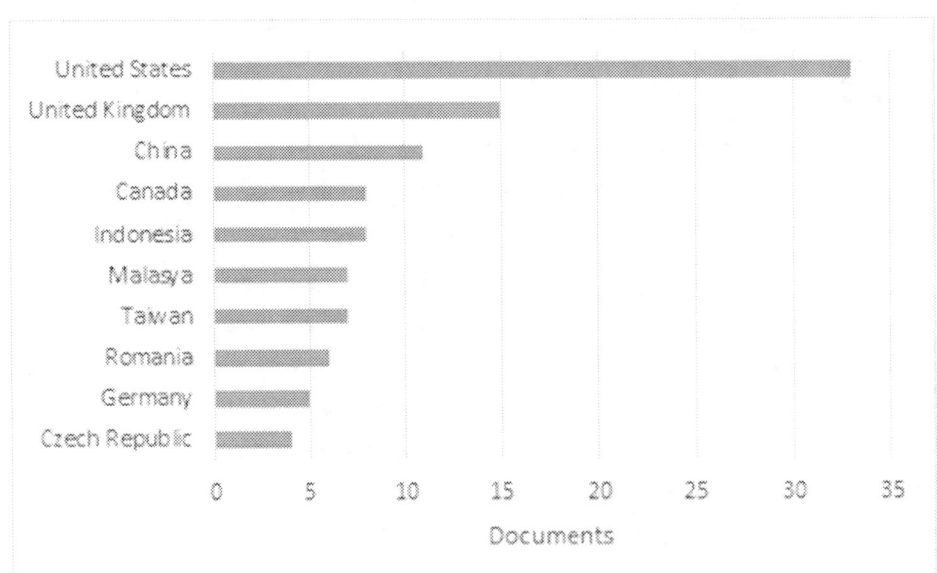

Regarding the number of documents published in Scopus by country or territory, it can be seen that research on FR and CG is being focused on the United States (33), countries in Asia (33), Europe (30), and Canada (8). At least, these are the home countries identified where the authors belong to. In what concerns the publications from the European countries, two countries belong to Central Europe, one to Eastern Europe and another from Western Europe. This would mean that more research is needed on European countries, namely Eastern and Western Europe.

Regarding the number of documents published in the Web of Science by country or territory, it can be seen that research on FR and CG is being focused on the United States (8), countries in Asia (17), Europe (13), and Canada (2). In what concerns the publications from the European countries, one country belongs to Central Europe, and four from Western Europe. This would mean that more research is needed on European countries, namely Eastern and Central Europe, as identified previously. Data accessibility issues and database management may be a possible explanation for these presented numbers.

Figure 9. Documents by country or territory during 2010-2020 in Web of Science
Source: Web of Science

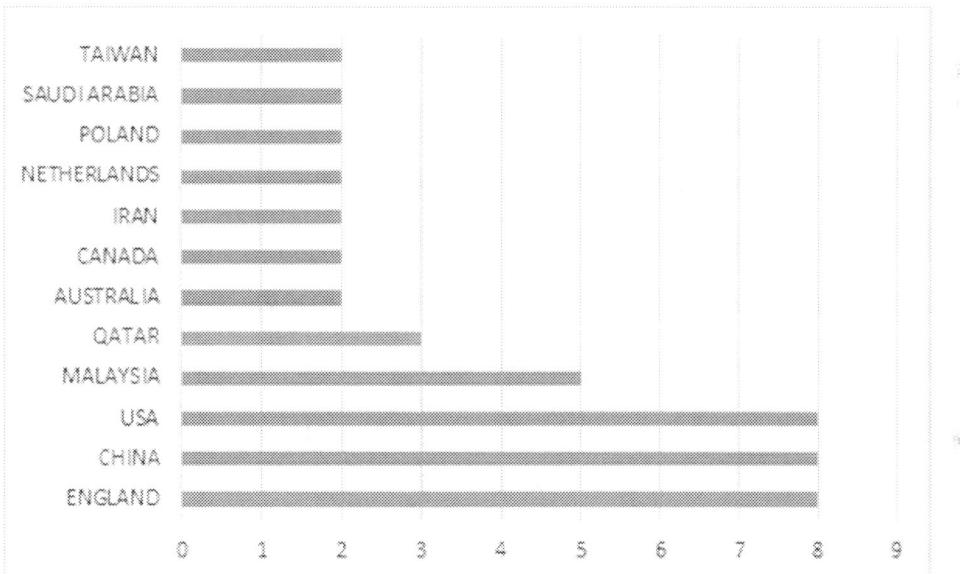

Figure 6.a and 6.b displays the documents published during the analysis period, by type. The most published documents during this period in Scopus were made in the form of scientific articles (75.4%). Conference papers represent 15.9% of the publications, while Book Chapters represent only 5.8%. Other types of publications, such as Review and Editorial are residual.

The most published documents during this period in Web of Science were made in the form of scientific articles (76%). Conference papers represent 20% of the publications, while Book Chapters and Review articles represent only 2%. As such, both bibliographic databases are similar in the type of documents published in relative terms.

Figure 11. Documents published during 2010-2020 by type in Web of Science
Source: Web of Science

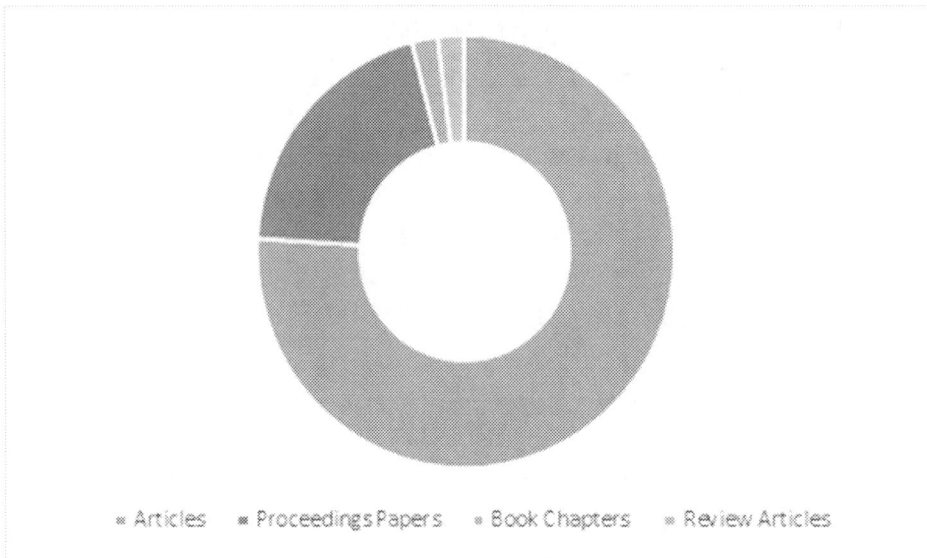

Regarding the main subject areas of publication in Scopus, Figure 7.a shows that most are within the Econometrics and Finance (33.0%) and Business, Management and Accounting (31.2%) areas, with a total of 64.2% of the publications. However, it is visible that FR and CG are being explored in other knowledge areas, such as Social Sciences (8.8%), Computer Science (7.4%), as well as Decision Sciences (5.1%). The other subjects' areas of publication are residual.

Regarding the main subject areas of publication in Web of Science, Figure 7.b shows that most are within the Business Economics, respectively 60.32% of the publications. However, it is visible that FR and CG are being explored in other knowledge areas, such as Engineering (6.35%), Government Law and Mathematical Methods in Social Sciences (4.76%), International Relations, Life Sciences Biomedicine Other Topics, Operations Research Management Science, Social Sciences Other Topics (3.17%). The other subjects' areas of publication are residual, with 1.59%.

Figure 12. Documents by subject area published during 2010-2020 in Scopus
Source: Scopus

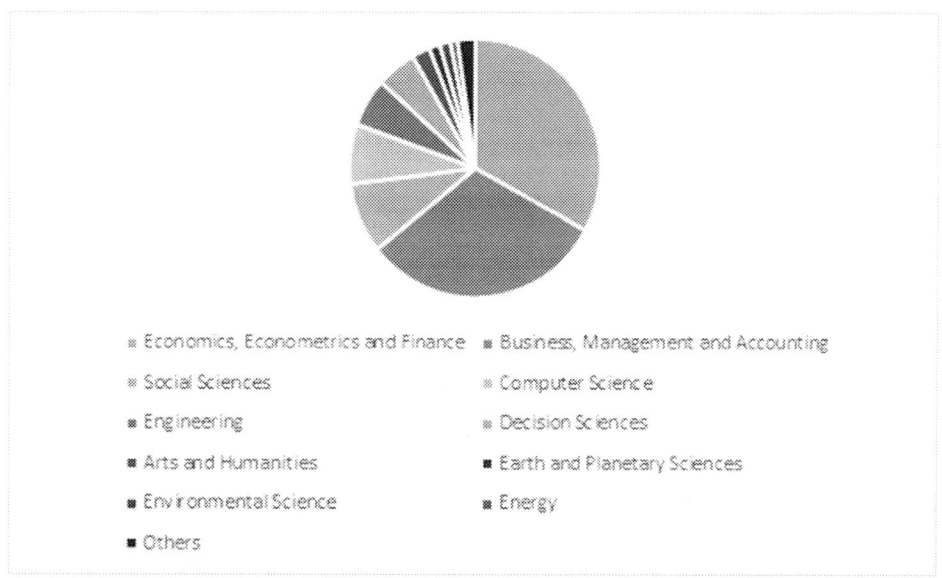

Figure 13. Documents by subject area published during 2010-2020 in Web of Science
Source: Web of Science

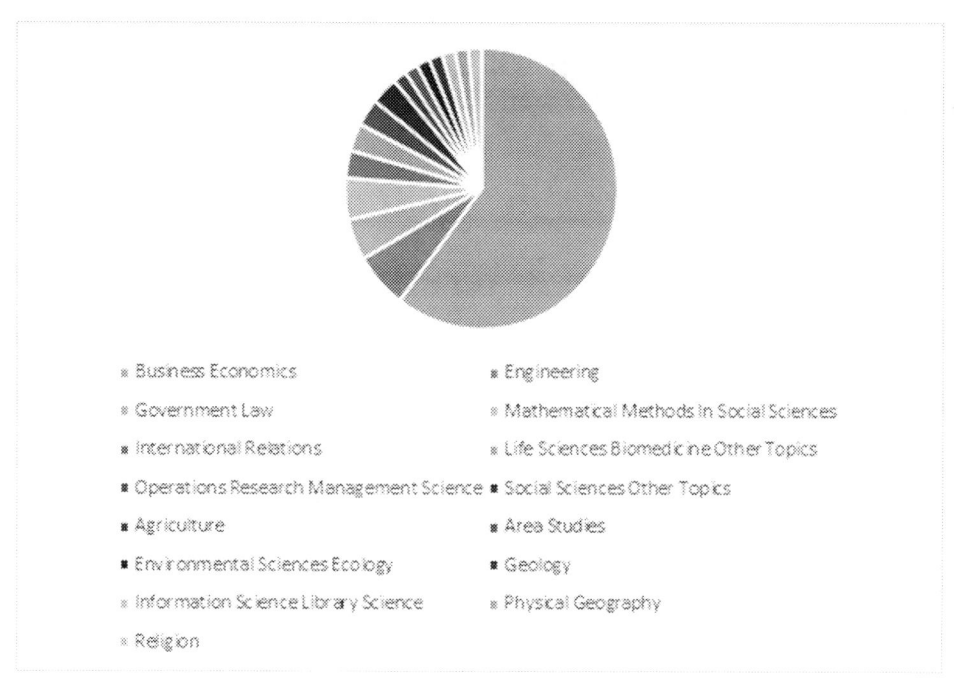

Regarding the funding sponsor of these documents in Scopus, it can be observed that during 2010-2020 the Universiti Utara Malaysia and the National Natural Science Foundation of China are those which mostly sponsored the documents under analysis. Related to the funding sponsor of these documents in Web of Science, it can be observed that only 14 documents mention the funding sponsor from those 50 documents published during 2010-2020: research institutes, universities, ministers, foundations, schools of economics, etc.

The 10 most cited articles from those 138 documents indexed in Scopus are described in Table 1. Those from the WoS are presented in Table 2. Based on the titles of the articles of both Tables 1 and 2, Figure 9 has been created using WordCloud software.

Table 1. Top 10 cited articles during 2010-2020 in Scopus

	Document title	Authors	Year	Source	Cited by
1	Risk management, corporate governance, and bank performance in the financial crisis	Aebi, V., Sabato, G., Schmid, M.	2012	Journal of Banking and Finance, 36(12), pp. 3213-3226	345
2	Corporate governance and risk reporting in South Africa: A study of corporate risk disclosures in the pre-and post-2007/2008 global financial crisis periods	Ntim, C.G., Lindop, S., Thomas, D.A.	2013	International Review of Financial Analysis, 30, pp. 363-383	129
3	A support vector machine-based model for detecting top management fraud	Pai, P.-F., Hsu, M.-F., Wang, M.-C.	2011	Knowledge-Based Systems, 24(2), pp. 314-321	66
4	Size, leverage, and risk-taking of financial institutions	Bhagat, S., Bolton, B., Lu, J.	2015	Journal of Banking and Finance, 59, pp. 520-537	54
5	The effect of the Rana Plaza disaster on shareholder wealth of retailers: Implications for sourcing strategies and supply chain governance	Jacobs, B.W., Singhal, V.R.	2017	Journal of Operations Management, 49-51, pp. 52-66	53
6	Committee Independence and Financial Institution Performance during the 2007-08 Credit Crunch: Evidence from a Multi-country Study	Yeh, Y.-H., Chung, H., Liu, C.-L.	2011	Corporate Governance: An International Review, 19(5), pp. 437-458	51
7	Internationalization and bank risk	Berger, A.N., El Ghoul, S., Guedhami, O., Roman, R.A.	2017	Management Science, 63(7), pp. 2283-2301	50
8	Boards of Directors and Financial Risk during the Credit Crisis	Mcnulty, T., Florackis, C., Ormrod, P.	2013	Corporate Governance: An International Review, 21(1), pp. 58-78	47
9	Directors' and officers' liability insurance and stock price crash risk	Yuan, R., Sun, J., Cao, F.	2016	Journal of Corporate Finance, 37, pp. 173-192	45
10	The effect of corporate governance on auditor-client realignments	Cassell, C.A., Giroux, G.A., Myers, L.A., Omer, T.C.	2012	Auditing, 31(2), pp. 167-188	43

Source: Own Development

The article gathering more citations was published in 2012 in the Journal of Banking and Finance, with 345 citations at the moment of this chapter writing (June/July 2021). The citations of the 10 studies more cited range between 345 and 43 and the year of publication are comprised between 2011 and 2017. Therefore, within the subject of analysis, the authors Aebi, V., Sabato, G., Schmid, M., have been those receiving more citations among all the others. They even received more citations than those identified in the WoS as being the most cited authors/article during the same period (Jan Fichtner, Eelke M. Heemskerk, and Javier Garcia-Bernardo). From the topics of interest between CG and FR, we may mention that the highly cited article in Scopus refers to the study of "Risk management, corporate governance, and bank performance in the financial crisis", whereas in WoS the most mentioned publication refers to a completely different subject, namely "Hidden Power of the Big Three? Passive index funds, re-concentration of corporate ownership, and new financial risk". Whereas the former refers to banks' risk assessment and CG, the latter respect investment funds, ownership, and financial risk.

As stated previously, the most cited articles from those 50 documents included in our data sample indexed in Web of Science are described in Table 2.

Table 2. Top 10 cited articles during 2010-2020 in Web of Science

	Document title	Authors	Year	Source	Cited by
1	Hidden Power of the Big Three? Passive index funds, re-concentration of corporate ownership, and new financial risk	Fichtner, J., Heemskerk, F.M., Garcia-Bernardo, J.	2017	Business and Politics, 19 (2), pp. pp. 298 - 326	93
2	The Effect of Corporate Governance on Auditor-Client Realignments	Cassell, C.A., Giroux, G.A., Myers, L.A., Omer, T.C.	2012	AUDITING: A Journal of Practice & Theory, 31 (2), pp. 167–188.	44
3	Boards of Directors and Financial Risk during the Credit Crisis	McNulty, T., Florackis, C., Ormrod, P.	2013	Corporate Governance: An International Review, 21 (1), pp. 58-78	40
4	Currency hedging and corporate governance: A cross-country analysis	Lel, U.	2012	Journal of Corporate Finance, 18(2), pp. 221-237	38
5	Corporate communication of financial risk	Taylor, G., Tower, G., Neilson, J.	2010	Accounting and Finance, 50 (2), pp. 417-446	29
6	Corporate Governance and Risk-Taking: Evidence From the U.K. and German Insurance Markets	Eling, M., Marek, S.D.	2013	Journal of Risk and Insurance, 81 (3), pp. 653-682	26
7	Corporate social responsibility and firm financial risk reduction: On the moderating role of the legal environment	Benlemlih, M., Girerd-Potin, I.	2017	Journal of Business Finance and Accounting, 44 (7-8), pp. 1137-1166	24
8	Risk management disclosure: A study on the effect of voluntary risk management disclosure toward firm value	Abdullah, M., Shukor, Z.A., Mohamed, Z.M., Ahmad, A.	2015	Journal of Applied Accounting Research, 16 (3), pp. 400-432	20
9	Option incentives, leverage, and risk-taking	Kim, K., Patro, S., Pereira, R.	2017	Journal of Corporate Finance, 43, pp. 1-18	14
10	Corporate risk-taking and performance in Malaysia: the effect of board composition, political connections and sustainability practices	Chong, L.-L., Ong, H.-B., Tan, S.-H.	2018	Corporate Governance, 18 (4), pp. 635-654	14

Source: Own Development

The article gathering more citations was published in 2017 in the Journal Business and Politics, with 93 citations in documents indexed in Web of Science at the moment of this chapter writing (June/July 2021). The citations of the 10 studies mostly cited range between 93 and 14 and the year of publication is comprised between 2010 and 2018.

Through an analysis of proxy vote records, Fichtner et al. (2017) found that the Big Three (the passive index fund industry that is dominated by BlackRock, Vanguard, and State Street) do utilize coordinated voting strategies and hence follow a centralized corporate governance strategy. Also, they found that the Big Three may exert "hidden power" through private engagements with the management of invested companies and because company executives could be prone to internalizing the objectives of the Big Three. Lel (2012) examined the impact of the strength of governance on firms' use of currency derivatives, using a sample of firms from 30 countries over the period 1990 to 1999. He found that weakly governed firms use derivatives mostly for managerial reasons and strongly governed firms tend to use derivatives to hedge currency exposure and overcome costly external financing.

Figure 14. Word cloud of article titles of tables 1 and 2 - 2010-2020
Source: Web of Science and Scopus. https://www.wordclouds.com/

Several authors focus their studies on CG characteristics, such as Pai et al. (2011), Cassell et al. (2012), Ntim et al. (2013), and Yuan et al. (2016). Pai et al. (2011) propose a model to detect top management fraud, providing a set of comprehensible decision rules for auditors. The authors suggest that it will be important to consider the influence of audit committees, boards with a significant proportion of outside members, CPA tenure, and CEO duality (corporate governance characteristics), to enhance the model effectiveness in analyzing financial statement data, to detect the risk of fraud. Cassell et al. (2012) extend prior research analyzing the effect of CG on downward (from Big N to non-Big N auditors) switching activity. Developing a CG index comprised of governance characteristics, such as board and audit committee independence, diligence, and expertise, the authors find evidence that Big N auditors consider client CG mechanisms when making client portfolio decisions. Ntim et al. (2013) explore whether the quality of firm-level CG has any effect on the quality and extent of corporate risk disclosures in South Africa for the period between 2002 and 2011. The results show that block ownership and institutional ownership are negatively associated with the extent of corporate risk disclosures, while board diversity, board size, and independent non-executive directors are positively related to the extent of corporate risk disclosures. Finally, the authors find that dual board leadership structure has no significant relationship with the extent of corporate risk disclosures. Yuan et al. (2016) investigate the impact of Chinese directors' and officers' insurance on stock price crash risk, finding a negative relationship between the variables. The empirical evidence shows that the impact of directors' and officers' insurance on crash risk is more pronounced in firms with lower board independence, non-Big 4 auditors, lower institutional shareholdings, and weaker investor protection. The authors conclude that directors' and officers' insurance appears to improve CG.

Other studies focus on the effects of the 2007-2008 financial crisis (Yeh et al., 2011; Aebi et al., 2012; Mcnulty et al.. 2013). Yeh et al. (2011) analyze whether the performance of financial institutions is higher with more independent directors on different committees during the 2007–08 financial crisis, considering a sample of financial institutions from G8 countries (Australia, Canada, France, Germany, Italy, Japan, United Kingdom, and the United States). The results show that the performance during the crisis period is higher for financial institutions with more independent directors on auditing and risk committees, being the influence particularly stronger for civil law countries. The evidence also suggests that the performance relationships are more significant in institutions with excessive risk-taking behaviors. Aebi et al. (2012) examine whether risk management-related with CG mechanisms is associated with a better bank performance during the period of the financial crisis of 2007-2008, concluding that CG variables, such as CEO ownership, the board size, and board independence, are mostly insignificantly or even negatively related to the banks' performance during the crisis period, indicating that banks were pressured by their boards of directors to maximize shareholder wealth before the crisis, taking risks that supposedly provided wealth. However, this goal was not achieved during the credit crisis. Mcnulty et al. (2013) analyze the relationship between board processes and corporate FR in the UK, during the 2008-2009 crisis, based on a questionnaire. The empirical evidence shows that the boarding process is an important determinant of financial risk during the crisis. FR is lower in firms where non-executive directors have high effort norms and where board decision processes are characterized by a degree of cognitive conflict.

Analyzing the impact of factors related to corporate governance (i.e., compensation, monitoring, and ownership structure) on risk-taking in the insurance industry, Eling and Marek (2013) found that higher levels of compensation, increased monitoring (more independent boards with more meetings), and more block holders are associated with lower risk-taking. Benlemlih and Girerd-Potin (2017) show that Corporate Social Responsibility (CSR) significantly reduces firms' idiosyncratic risk in civil law countries but not in common law countries and that the relationship between CSR and financial risk is moderated by the institutional context of the firm. Kim et al. (2017) found that firm leverage is associated with a significant weakening of the positive relationship between option incentives in flow compensation and managerial risk-taking. This result holds after accounting for the endogeneity of the firm leverage and incentive compensation decisions and is robust across alternative measures of managerial risk-taking and to using the firm's credit ratings instead of leverage. Chong et al. (2018) show that a larger board size contributes to greater financial risk, and this risk can be reduced with more independent directors in the boardroom.

Bhagat et al. (2015) examine the relationship between firm size and risk-taking among US financial institutions, for the 2002-2012 period, finding that size is positively related to risk-taking measures. Considering the risk of failure, measured by the Z-score, the results show that financial firms engage in excessive risk-taking, mainly through increased leverage. The authors conclude that banks that enjoy better CG practices engage in less risk-taking. Taylor et al. (2010), using a sample with Australian listed resource companies for the 2002–2006 period show that the introduction of IFRS changes a corporation's willingness to communicate risk information. Also, they demonstrated that corporate governance and capital raisings of firms are significant and positively associated with Financial Risk Management Disclosure (FRMD) patterns, while overseas stock exchange listing of firms is significantly negatively associated with FRMD patterns.

Jacobs and Singhal (2017) analyze the effect of the Rana Plaza disaster on the shareholder wealth of retailers in Bangladesh, finding no evidence of significant stock market reaction during the 11 trading days (approximately two weeks in calendar time) following the disaster.

Berger et al. (2017) documents a positive relationship between internationalization and bank risk, due to market-specific factors in foreign markets, which is consistent with the market risk hypothesis, and find evidence that the magnitude of this effect is more pronounced during financial crises. According to the authors, the results seem to be explained by agency problems related to poor CG.

Among the possible avenues of future research, we may include, derived from the analysis performed previously, that the current COVID19 pandemic opens room for deeper analysis in the relationship between CG and FR. As was evident from the financial crisis, a pandemic with worldwide effects as the current one poses challenges to managers that are dealing presently with increased financial risk, of all types. From a quick search in the Scopus bibliographic database, it was found five recent articles relating to financial risk, corporate governance, and COVID. Demers et al. (2021) present robust evidence during the COVID crisis that controlling industry affiliation, market-based measures of risk, and accounting-based measures of performance, financial position, and intangibles investments, environmental, social, and governance ("ESG") scores offer no such positive explanatory power for returns. They conclude that ESG did not immunize stocks during the COVID-19 crisis, but those investments in intangible assets did. Chandra and Walton (2020) argue that a top-down economic nationalist stance, state-driven action, political resistance to reforms, and attacks on accountability institutions, will continue to threaten long-run development dynamics in India. This places challenges not only at the companies governance level but as well highlights the need to control for political risk, which will impact economic growth and firms growth, even more, problematic during the pandemic period. Fassas et al. (2021) try to assess the management responses and intentions of 3,279 US firms from all industries, before and after the coronavirus outbreak. The goal was to identify the level of managerial concern about specific financial issues and potential economic costs of the COVID-19 pandemic. The conclusions of the authors point that firm managers are rather swift to provide coronavirus-related information in the US Securities and Exchange Commission (SEC) corporate filings. The formulation of appropriate government policies in the corresponding sectors, able to mitigate the economic risks related to the pandemic, are pointed. They call attention to the need for flow information given that disseminated knowledge can assist firms either in the same sector or in similar/related sectors (adjust or align strategies and decisions) to surpass the pandemic. Finally, Jebran and Chen (2021) focus on how corporate governance practices can help firms to survive during the COVID-19 crisis. The authors provide a literature review highlighting several governance mechanisms that may help firms to cope with the COVID-19 crisis. Among the governance attributes found by the authors, we may mention risk management committees, board diversity, independent directors, foreign investors, institutional ownership, ownership concentration, CEO's dual roles, block ownership, and family ownership. From there, they point to independent risk management committees, institutional ownership, board independence, block holders, and family ownership as essential and effective governance mechanisms, as compared to other governance attributes, during the pandemic period.

CONCLUSION

Financial risks create the possibility of losses arising from the failure to achieve financial objectives. Companies are exposed to financial risk in their day-by-day activities, and the respective consequences, that can affect their earnings, returns, and value. Several types of risk, such as market risk, model risk, credit risk, liquidity risk, operational risk, and risk of disclosure compose the financial risk.

Corporate governance is a system that provides instructions to protect all the firms' stakeholders. According to the literature, an inefficient system of corporate governance has a significant effect on performance, fraud, misappropriation of assets, and dissatisfied shareholders. In addition, there is evidence that forensic accounting affects corporate governance effectiveness, leading to transparency and honesty in corporate governance and corporate reporting.

Based on the evidence that there is a relation between CG characteristics and firms FR, this study proposes to contribute to the analysis of the influence of CG on FR, by conducting a bibliometric analysis focused on FR and CG for the period between 2010 and 2020, making a point of situation in what concerns the current state-of-the-art.

The publications on these subjects leave space for new developments in research terms. In addition, European markets exploration, namely Eastern and Western Europe, is still in deeper need of analysis. Exploring deeper CG attributes and sociodemographic characteristics and their corresponding influence over FR, in its various fields, is as well found to still require research.

Corporate governance can be used as a tool to control several types of risk, such as the risk of disclosure, internationalization, and the risk of failure, just to mention a few. Thus, one of the limitations of the current study is the fact that it concentrates on financial risk rather than a specific type, and after analyzing the state of the art of relationship between the type of FR and CG. Further bibliometric and bibliographic analysis of more specific types of risk and CG is as well necessary.

A deeper understanding of corporate governance beyond the audit committees, the institutional and market pressures, legal environments, macroeconomic conditions, and many others are still in need of research or deserve more understanding. Cross-country comparisons, regional and local analysis, inter and intra-economic activity sector analysis, and behavioral aspects of the relationship between CG, governance mechanisms, governance characteristics and behavior, and financial risk management is a field that still deserves attention. It would as well be useful to concentrate analysis on small and medium enterprises, family firm's, and industrial clusters.

REFERENCES

Abdullah, M., Shukor, Z. A., Mohamed, Z. M., & Ahmad, A. (2015). Risk management disclosure: A study on the effect of voluntary risk management disclosure toward firm value. *Journal of Applied Accounting Research*, *16*(3), 400–432. doi:10.1108/JAAR-10-2014-0106

Abraham, S., & Cox, P. (2007). Analysing the determinants of narrative risk information in UK FTSE 100 annual reports. *The British Accounting Review*, *39*(3), 227–248. doi:10.1016/j.bar.2007.06.002

Aebi, V., Sabato, G., & Schmid, M. (2012). Risk management, corporate governance, and bank performance in the financial crisis. *Journal of Banking & Finance*, *36*(12), 3213–3226. doi:10.1016/j.jbankfin.2011.10.020

Aganin, A., & Volpin, P. (2002). The History of Corporate Ownership in Italy. In A History of Corporate Governance Around the World. The University of Chicago Press.

Al-Tamimi, H. A. (2012). The effects of corporate governance on performance and financial distress. *Journal of Financial Regulation Compliance*, *20*(2), 169–181. doi:10.1108/13581981211218315

Ali, M. M., & Nasir, N. M. (2018). Corporate governance and financial distress: Malaysian perspective. *Asian Journal of Accounting Perspectives*, *11*(1), 108–128. doi:10.22452/AJAP.vol11no1.5

Alnabsha, A., Abdou, H. A., Ntim, C. G., & Elamer, A. A. (2018). Corporate boards, ownership structures and corporate disclosures: Evidence from a developing country. *Journal of Applied Accounting Research*, *19*(1), 20–41. doi:10.1108/JAAR-01-2016-0001

Aluchna, M. (2016). Applying Corporate Governance in Europe. In Global Perspectives on Corporate Governance and CSR. Routledge.

Awan, T., Shah, S. Z. A., Khan, M. Y., & Javeed, A. (2020). Impact of corporate governance, financial and regulatory factors on firms' acquisition ability. *Corporate Governance: The International Journal of Business in Society*, *20*(3), 461–484. doi:10.1108/CG-07-2019-0214

Barako, D. G., & Brown, A. M. (2008). Corporate social reporting and board representation: Evidence from the Kenyan banking sector. *The Journal of Management and Governance*, *12*(4), 309–324. doi:10.100710997-008-9053-x

Benlemlih, M., & Girerd-Potin, I. (2017). Corporate social responsibility and firm financial risk reduction: On the moderating role of the legal environment. *Journal of Business Finance & Accounting*, *44*(7-8), 1137–1166. doi:10.1111/jbfa.12251

Berger, A. N., El Ghoul, S., Guedhami, O., & Roman, R. A. (2017). Internationalization and bank risk. *Management Science*, *63*(7), 2283–2301. doi:10.1287/mnsc.2016.2422

Bhagat, S., Bolton, B., & Lu, J. (2015). Size, leverage, and risk-taking of financial institutions. *Journal of Banking & Finance*, *59*, 520–537. doi:10.1016/j.jbankfin.2015.06.018

Bufarwa, I. M., Elamer, A. A., Ntim, C. G., & AlHares, A. (2020). Gender diversity, corporate governance and financial risk disclosure in the UK. *International Journal of Law and Management*, *62*(6), 521–538. doi:10.1108/IJLMA-10-2018-0245

Cassell, C. A., Giroux, G. A., Myers, L. A., & Omer, T. C. (2012). The effect of corporate governance on auditor-client realignments. *Auditing*, *31*(2), 167–188. doi:10.2308/ajpt-10240

Cassell, C. A., Giroux, G. A., Myers, L. A., & Omer, T. C. (2012). The effect of corporate governance on auditor-client realignments. *Auditing*, *31*(2), 67–188.

Chandra, R., & Walton, M. (2020). Big potential, big risks? Indian capitalism, economic reform and populism in the BJP era. *India Review*, *19*(2), 176–205. doi:10.1080/14736489.2020.1744997

Chong, L.-L., Ong, H.-B., & Tan, S.-H. (2018). Corporate risk-taking and performance in Malaysia: The effect of board composition, political connections and sustainability practices. *Corporate Governance*, *18*(4), 635–654.

Demers, E., Hendrikse, J., Joos, P., & Lev, B. (2021). ESG did not immunize stocks during the COVID-19 crisis, but investments in intangible assets did. *Journal of Business Finance & Accounting*, *48*(3-4), 433–462. doi:10.1111/jbfa.12523 PMID:34230747

Dhamija, A., Yadav, S. S., & Jain, P. (2014). The impact of corporate governance on the financial performance: A study of nifty companies. *International Research Journal of Finance and Economics*, *121*, 60–75.

Donthu, N., Kumar, S., Mukherjee, D., Pandey, N., & Lim, W. M. (2021). How to conduct a bibliometric analysis: An overview and guidelines. *Journal of Business Research*, *133*, 285–296. doi:10.1016/j.jbusres.2021.04.070

Elamer, A. A., & Benyazid, I. (2018). The impact of risk committee on financial performance of UK financial institutions. *International Journal of Accounting and Finance*, *8*(2), 161–180. doi:10.1504/IJAF.2018.093290

Eling, M., & Marek, S. D. (2013). Corporate governance and risk taking: Evidence from the U.K. and German insurance markets. *The Journal of Risk and Insurance*, *81*(3), 653–682. doi:10.1111/j.1539-6975.2012.01510.x

Elzahar, H., & Hussainey, K. (2012). Determinants of narrative risk disclosures in UK interim reports. *The Journal of Risk Finance*, *13*(2), 133–147. doi:10.1108/15265941211203189

Ettredge, M., Johnstone, K., Stone, M., & Wang, Q. (2011). The effects of firm size, corporate governance quality, and bad news on disclosure compliance. *Review of Accounting Studies*, *16*(4), 866–889. doi:10.100711142-011-9153-8

Fassas, A., Bellos, S., & Kladakis, G. (2021). *Corporate liquidity, supply chain and cost issues awareness within the covid-19 context: Evidence from US management reports' textual analysis*. Corporate Governance. doi:10.1108/CG-09-2020-0399

Fichtner, J., Heemskerk, E. M., & Garcia-Bernardo, J. (2017). Hidden power of the Big Three? Passive index funds, re-concentration of corporate ownership, and new financial risk. *Business and Politics*, *19*(2), 298–326. doi:10.1017/bap.2017.6

Girling, P. (2013). *Operational risk management: a complete guide to a successful operational risk framework*. Wiley. doi:10.1002/9781118755754

Handriania, E., & Ghozalib, I. (2021). Corporate governance on financial distress: Evidence from Indonesia. *Management Science Letters, 11*, 1833–1844. doi:10.5267/j.msl.2021.1.020

Högfeldt, P. (2003). The History and Politics of Corporate Ownership in Sweden. In History of Corporate Governance around the World. The University of Chicago Press.

Jacobs, B. W., & Singhal, V. R. (2017). The effect of the Rana Plaza disaster on shareholder wealth of retailers: Implications for sourcing strategies and supply chain governance. *Journal of Operations Management, 49-51*(1), 52–66. doi:10.1016/j.jom.2017.01.002

Jebran, K., & Chen, S. (2021). Can we learn lessons from the past? COVID-19 crisis and corporate governance responses. *International Journal of Finance & Economics*, ijfe.2428. Advance online publication. doi:10.1002/ijfe.2428

JokhadzeV.SchmidtW. M. (2018). Measuring model risk in financial risk management and pricing. SSRN. doi:10.2139/ssrn.3113139

Kim, K., Patro, S., & Pereira, R. (2017). Option incentives, leverage, and risk-taking. *Journal of Corporate Finance, 43*, 1–18. doi:10.1016/j.jcorpfin.2016.12.003

Lajili, K., & Zeghal, D. (2010). Corporate governance and bankruptcy filing decisions. *Journal of General Management, 35*(4), 3–26. doi:10.1177/030630701003500401

Lee, T. S., & Yeh, Y. H. (2004). Corporate governance and financial distress: Evidence from Taiwan. *Corporate Governance, 12*(3), 378–388. doi:10.1111/j.1467-8683.2004.00379.x

Lel, U. (2012). Currency hedging and corporate governance: A cross-country analysis. *Journal of Corporate Finance, 18*(2), 221–237. doi:10.1016/j.jcorpfin.2011.12.002

Linsley, P. M., & Shrives, P. J. (2006). Risk reporting: A study of risk disclosure in the annual reports of UK Companies. *Journal The British Accounting Review, 38*(4), 387–404. doi:10.1016/j.bar.2006.05.002

Luo, D. (2016). Changes in corporate governance practice of the Chinese commercial banks. In The Development of the Chinese Financial System and Reform of Chinese Commercial Banks. Palgrave Macmillan. doi:10.1057/9781137454669_3

Mcnulty, T., Florackis, C., & Ormrod, P. (2013). Boards of directors and financial risk during the credit crisis. *Corporate Governance, 21*(1), 58–78. doi:10.1111/corg.12007

Mgammal, M. H., Bardai, B., & Ismail, K. N. I. K. (2018). Corporate governance and tax disclosure phenomenon in the Malaysian listed companies. *Corporate Governance: The International Journal of Business in Society, 18*(5), 779–808. doi:10.1108/CG-08-2017-0202

Ntim, C. G., Lindop, S., & Thomas, D. A. (2013). Corporate governance and risk reporting in South Africa: A study of corporate risk disclosures in the pre-and post-2007/2008 global financial crisis periods. *International Review of Financial Analysis, 30*, 363–383. doi:10.1016/j.irfa.2013.07.001

Ntim, C. G., Opong, K. K., & Danbolt, J. (2012). The relative value relevance of shareholder versus stakeholder corporate governance disclosure policy reforms in South Africa. *Corporate Governance: An International Review, 20*(1), 84-105.

Oliveira, J., Rodrigues, L. L., & Craig, R. (2011). Risk-Related disclosures by Non-Finance companies: Portuguese practices and disclosure characteristics. *Managerial Auditing Journal, 26*(9), 817–839. doi:10.1108/02686901111171466

Pai, P.-F., Hsu, M.-F., & Wang, M.-C. (2011). A support vector machine-based model for detecting top management fraud. *Knowledge-Based Systems, 24*(2), 314–321. doi:10.1016/j.knosys.2010.10.003

Putri, A., Bunga, M., & Rochman, E. (2021). Financial risk disclosure and corporate governance: Empirical evidence on banking companies in Indonesian Stock Exchange. *Advances in Economics, Business and Management Research, 161*, 32–39.

Salomons, R., & Grootveld, H. (2003). The equity risk premium: Emerging vs. developed markets. *Emerging Markets Review, 4*(2), 121–144. doi:10.1016/S1566-0141(03)00024-4

Schroeck, G. (2002). *Risk management and value creation in financial institutions*. John Wiley & Sons, Inc.

Solomon, J. F., Solomon, A., Norton, S. D., & Joseph, N. L. (2000). A conceptual framework for corporate risk disclosure emerging from the agenda for corporate governance reform. *The British Accounting Review, 32*(4), 447–478. doi:10.1006/bare.2000.0145

Soltani, B., & Maupetit, C. (2015). Importance of core values of ethics, integrity and accountability in the European corporate governance codes. *The Journal of Management and Governance, 19*(2), 259–284. doi:10.100710997-013-9259-4

Svejnar, J. (2002). Transition economies: Performance and challenges. *The Journal of Economic Perspectives, 16*(1), 1, 3–28. doi:10.1257/0895330027058

Taylor, G., Tower, G., & Neilson, J. (2010). Corporate communication of financial risk. *Accounting and Finance, 50*(2), 417–446. doi:10.1111/j.1467-629X.2009.00326.x

Ud-Din, S., Khan, M. Y., Javeed, A., & Pham, H. (2020). Board structure and likelihood of financial distress: An emerging Asian market perspective. *Journal of Asian Finance. Economics and Business, 7*(11), 241–250.

Udin, S., Khan, M. A., & Javid, A. Y. (2017). The effects of ownership structure on likelihood of financial distress: An empirical evidence. *Corporate Governance: The International Journal of Business in Society, 17*(4), 589–612. doi:10.1108/CG-03-2016-0067

Vieira, E., & Neiva, J. (2019). Corporate Governance Board of Directors and Firm Performance in Portugal. In Handbook of Board of Directors and Company Performance: An International Outlook. Virtus Interpress.

Yeh, Y.-H., Chung, H., & Liu, C.-L. (2011). Committee independence and financial institution performance during the 2007-08 credit crunch: Evidence from a multi-country study. *Corporate Governance, 19*(5), 437–458. doi:10.1111/j.1467-8683.2011.00884.x

Younas, N., UdDin, S., Awan, T., & Khan, M. Y. (2021). Corporate governance and financial distress: Asian emerging market perspective. *Corporate Governance*.

Yuan, R., Sun, J., & Cao, F. (2016). Directors' and officers' liability insurance and stock price crash risk. *Journal of Corporate Finance, 37,* 173–192. doi:10.1016/j.jcorpfin.2015.12.015

KEY TERMS AND DEFINITION

Bibliometric Analysis: Is the attempt to quantitatively assess the academic quality of journals or authors by statistical methods such as citation rates.

Content Analysis: Is the study of documents and communication artifacts, which might be texts of various formats, pictures, audio, or video. Social scientists use content analysis to examine patterns in communication in a replicable and systematic manner.

Corporate Governance: Is the system of rules, practices, and processes by which a firm is directed and controlled. Corporate governance essentially involves balancing the interests of a company's many stakeholders, such as shareholders, senior management executives, customers, suppliers, financiers, the government, and the community. Since corporate governance also provides the framework for attaining a company's objectives, it encompasses practically every sphere of management, from action plans and internal controls to performance measurement and corporate disclosure.

Financial Crisis of 2007-2008: The global financial crisis of 2007-2008 was a severe worldwide economic crisis. Financial institutions worldwide suffered severe damage, reaching a peak with the bankruptcy of Lehman Brothers on September 15, 2008, with a subsequent international banking crisis. It was the most serious financial crisis since the Great Depression.

Financial Risk: Is the possibility of losing money on an investment. Financial risk can result in the loss of capital to interested parties. It includes several types of risk, such as credit risk, liquidity risk, and operational risk.

Chapter 2
The Relationship Between Risk and Firm Performance:
A Review

Fitim Deari
South East European University, Macedonia

Hai Hong Trinh
Massey University, New Zealand

ABSTRACT

The relationship between risk and return is a crucial point in typical decision making, and empirical previous studies can help related stakeholders in this process. Henceforth, this chapter aims to present some fundamental theoretical concepts and interpretations of the relationship between risk and firm performance. Accordingly, this chapter offers a review of some highlighted studies in this field by presenting methodologies used and developed by several scholars. The chapter provides a timely reference source for a range of target audience from both academia and industry who have common interests to decompose and examine the relationship between risk and firm performance.

INTRODUCTION

Viewed from a historical retrospective and nowadays, the role of risk management to business decision-makers is indisputable and especially in times of crisis as it is the ongoing pandemic COVID-19. This role is increasingly reinforced because of the influence of several factors that affect the business directly and indirectly.

Risk management helps managers to measure and estimate risk and return of investments. This role remains crucial in finding a proper solution toward maximizing shareholders' value. However, estimating and composing an efficient risk-return relationship is not easy due to finding the probability or likelihood that an event is going to happen and have an influential impact on the expected outcome, e.g., firm performance.

DOI: 10.4018/978-1-7998-8609-9.ch002

Hence, risk managers will be faced with forecasting accuracy because there is no such a certain business environment in which operate investors. Consequently, risk managers often are not able to precisely forecast the risk-return relationship due to several unknown factors influencing it.

Given a broad range of risks that a firm might face including interest rate, credit risk, bankruptcy, liquidity, default risk, corporate risk, political risk, and other risks. However, given the past and merging different shocks of global uncertainties such as the 2008 Global Financial Crisis (GFC) and the emerging 2019/20 Global Health Pandemic (GHP) that have put great challenges faced by firms across countries and regions putting big questions on "How different kinds of risk emerge and volatile during the Global Crises (GCs)?" and "How can firms overcome those challenges and deal with several kinds of emerging risks to avoid going bankrupt?". Those questions are especially important to small and medium enterprises (SMEs) with lower market capitalization, quicker human resources, corporate governance, financial and operational management compared with higher market capitalization firms[1].

Further, by deploying risk management, managers, shareholders, and other related decision-makers can turn opportunities into real returns. Obviously, there are no so ready-made and general recipes on how to minimize the risk and maximize the return. Investors would composite such a risk-return relationship according to their own preferences. For example, Kukeli, Deari and Rocşoreanu (2019) show the composition of an efficient portfolio using the Lagrange multiplier method (short sales are allowed) and Kuhn-Tucker system (short sales are not allowed) in the light of the investor's risk tolerance.

Given the established motives and in this light of importance, this chapter is prepared as a timely reference source to synthesis previous literature in the field ideally for a range of target audiences such as corporate stakeholders, directors, policymakers, analysts, researchers, and students bringing experts from both academia and industry who have common interests in risk management and firm performance optimization.

The chapter aims to investigate the relationship between risk management and firm performance by covering theoretical and empirical studies. These studies are selected by no preferences to any article/author/journal and are collected in the context of problem definition. The chapter is oriented toward the research question if risk management affects firm performance by presenting a plenty number of empirical studies. Further, Enterprise Risk Management (ERM, hereafter) is expected to influence firm performance, and a significant relationship between risk and firm performance exists.

Based on the arguments above, the study provides the following hypotheses for the relation between risk management and firm performance:

Hypothesis 1: There is a relationship between risk management and firm performance. In other words, the better the risk management the higher the firm performance.

Hypothesis 2: Implementing ERM leads to better firm performance.

Motivated by those critical hypotheses, this chapter contributes to the existing literature by revisiting the relationship between risk management and firm performance that is associated with several financial and economic disciplines from the theoretical perspective. It presents a systematic review of some empirical studies realized in the field of risk management.

This book chapter is structured as follows. Section 1 provides a gentle introduction of the context, background, different kinds of risks, emerging trends in risk management and firm performance. Section 2 provides a systematic literature review on risk management with a strong focus on liquidity, default, and bankruptcy risk. Section 3 synthesizes the methodology and approaches that can be used to hedge, manage, and mitigate different types of risks mentioned in Section 2. Sections 4 and 5 present insightful discussion, conclusions, and further research needed.

LITEREATURE REVIEW

The relationship between risk and return is well known in the finance literature. This relationship has been examined by extensive studies and there is still room for future research. The dynamic changes on business risk environment make this relationship quite difficult to predict, even both practitioners and academicians, have putted efforts to decompose this relationship over the past decades.

It was Knight (1921) who made a significant contribution by introducing the distinction between risk and uncertainty. Several empirical studies are done after that and the relationship between risk and firm performance has attracted the interest of scholars among other views of the risk investigation. For example, Wiseman and Bromiley (1996) in their study examine variables such as: (1) performance, (2) slack, (3) aspirations, (4) expectations, (5) risk, and (6) organization size. The authors among other findings reveal that risk reduces performance. Also, Bromiley (1991) by examining risk, performance, performance expectations and aspirations, slack, and industry performance suggests a model wherein low performance and lack of slack drive risk-taking, but the risks taken have poor returns.

Berman, Wicks, Kotha and Jones (1999) in their study provide evidence that supports a strategic stakeholder management model but no support for an intrinsic stakeholder commitment model.

McNamara and Bromiley (1997) in their study examine the risk assessments bankers assigned to commercial borrowers and reveal that organizational and cognitive factors influenced risky decision making.

Further, Adams and Jiang (2016) investigate the relationship between outside board directors and six measures of financial performance such as: (1) profit margin, (2) return on assets, (3) return on equity, (4) solvency position, (5) loss ratio, and (6) combined operating ratio. By examining panel data for 1999–2012 drawn from the UK's property-casualty insurance industry, the authors among other findings highlight that the implied understanding of risk management is a core competence.

Gordon, Loeb and Tseng (2009) investigate whether the relation between ERM and firm performance is contingent upon the proper match between ERM and variables such as: environmental uncertainty, industry competition, firm size, firm complexity, and monitoring by the board of directors. By examining 112 US firms, the authors confirm that argument.

Psillaki, Tsolas and Margaritis (2010) examine whether productive inefficiency measured as the distance from the industry's 'best practice' frontier is an important ex-ante predictor of business failure in the case of French textiles, wood and paper products, computers, and R&D firms. The authors reveal that productive efficiency has significant explanatory power in predicting the likelihood of default over and above the effect of standard financial indicators.

Florio and Leoni (2017) in the context of Italy show that listed firms with advanced levels of ERM implementation present higher performance, both as financial performance and market evaluation. The authors introduce new and more complete measures for ERM implementation, concerning not only corporate governance bodies dedicated to risk management, but also the characteristics of the risk assessment process.

Zhang, Tadikamalla and Shang (2016) in their paper propose a comprehensive method of credit-risk evaluation based on dynamic incentives. By examining 12 publicly traded firms, the authors reveal that the proposed integrated evaluation model outperforms the conventional models by better reflecting the key credit-risk management concept of "motivation and guidance".

Chang, Yu and Hung (2015) by examining the data of listed firms from 2008–2012 in the case of Taiwan among other results reveal that firms with higher levels of corporate governance report high performance and low risk.

Recently, Dang and Nguyen (2020) investigate whether and how ex-ante liquidity risk affects realized stock returns during the global financial crisis of 2008–2009 in international equity markets across 41 countries. The authors reveal that that stocks with higher pre-crisis return exposure to global market liquidity shocks experience larger price reductions.

In addition, Huang, Kerstein and Wang (2018) examine the consequences of climate-related risk on financing choices by publicly listed firms across 55 countries for the period 2006-2012. The authors reveal that due to the likelihood of loss, there are lower and more volatile earnings and cash flows. Further, the authors reveal that firms located in countries characterized by more severe weather tend to have less short-term debt but more long-term debt and to be less likely to distribute cash dividends.

Further, an empirical decomposition of the default, liquidity, and tax factors that determine expected corporate bond returns is provided by Driessen (2005) by estimating the risk premium associated with a default event. Davydenko, Strebulaev and Zhao (2012) propose a novel method of extracting the cost of default from the change in the market value of a firm's assets upon default and estimated it to be 21.7%.

Franzoni, Nowak and Phalippou (2012) find that the unconditional liquidity risk premium is about 3% annually and the inclusion of this liquidity risk premium reduces alpha to zero.

He and Xiong (2012) by their model demonstrate that deterioration in debt market liquidity leads to an increase in not only the liquidity premium of corporate bonds but also credit risk. Also, Ozerturk (2006) reveals that the manager's optimal hedge depends on the liquidity of the market.

Lee and Lee (2012) examine panel data from the 1999 to 2009 period of the property-liability insurance industry in Taiwan and among other findings they find that managers have to strike a balance between decreasing insolvency risk and reducing potential profitability.

Han, Mittal and Zhang (2017) by investigating data of 2,403 firms from 2000 to 2014 reveal that firm's strategic accent on value appropriation versus value creation reduces firm risk.

In addition, Goyal and Wang (2013) in their study reveal that short-term debt issuance leads to a decline in borrowers' asset volatility and an increase in their distance to default, whilst the contrary is true for long-term debt issues.

Chen and Lee (2013) among other findings show that the book-to-market ratio, rather than the liquidity effect, plays a crucial role in explaining the default risk in equity returns.

Further, Herranz, Krasa and Villamil (2015) find that more risk-averse entrepreneurs run smaller, more highly leveraged firms and less default, because running a smaller firm with higher debt reduces personal funds at risk in the firm.

Barinov (2014) reveals that neither liquidity nor liquidity risk explains why higher turnover predicts lower future returns. Further, the author shows that the aggregate volatility risk factor explains why higher turnover predicts lower future returns.

Moreover, Chava and Purnanandam (2010) in their study show a positive cross-sectional relationship between expected stock returns and default risk.

Charitou, Lambertides and Theodoulou (2011) by examining data for firms that either increased or initiated cash dividend payments during the period 1986-2008 reveal a reduction in default risk and that is a significant factor in explaining the 3-year excess returns following dividend increases and initiations.

Alderson and Betker (1999) examine the post-bankruptcy cash flows for a sample of firms for the period 1983–1993 and evaluate the rate of return available to investors who owned all of the debt and equity claims on the firm as it emerged from bankruptcy. However, Dichev (1998) proves that bankruptcy risk is not rewarded by higher returns.

Miller and Chen (2003) by applying various model specifications and risk measures provide evidence for positive risk-cost relations. Further, the authors reveal that the relation of distance from bankruptcy to firms' costs depends on whether relations are contemporaneous or lagged and whether bankruptcy is an immediate threat or not.

McAlister, Srinivasan and Kim (2007) by using panel data on 644 publicly listed firms between 1979 and 2001, reveal that advertising/sales and R&D/sales lower a firm's systematic risk.

Lim and McCann (2014) examine panel data from 1992 to 2006 on the research and development spending of U.S. manufacturing firms and develop a theoretical framework that predicts the differential interaction effects of performance feedback and values of stock option grants of multiple agents on firm risk-taking.

Audia and Greve (2006) in their study show that performance below the aspiration level reduces risk-taking in small firms, but either does not affect risk-taking or increases risk-taking in large firms.

Matta and McGuire (2008) examine 208 U.S. CEOs for the period 1997–1999 and support the role of downside risk and firm performance in CEO equity reductions.

Further, some empirical studies investigate whether short selling affects and predicts stock returns–performance. In this line, Deshmukh, Gamble and Howe (2015) advocate that short interest may reflect private information about firm fundamentals rather than other factors that may drive stock price changes, whilst Kelley and Tetlock (2017) show that retail short-selling predicts negative stock returns.

METHODOLOGY

This section presents popular empirical models used by previous studies in risk literature and variables construction. Different authors use different risk classifications as assessing and evaluation methodologies as well (see e.g., Brunnermeier, Gorton and Krishnamurthy, 2012) by studying not just the firm-investor level (see e.g., Vassalou and Xing, 2004) but also including macroeconomic factors (see e.g., Arellano, 2008). For example, Beck (2019) illustrate liquidity risk with a specific example and revealed a statistical test for market efficiency.

Holmström and Tirole (2000) propose a theoretic framework by integrating: (1) liquidity management, (2) risk management, and (3) capital structure.

Gordon, Loeb and Tseng (2009) by examining the relationship between ERM and firm performance, measured firm performance as by the one-year excess stock market return to shareholders.

Table 1 presents the study by Adams and Jiang (2016) investigating six variables, whilst Florio and Leoni (2017) use the operating income to total assets and sum of market capitalization and the book value of liabilities to book value of total assets as measurements of firm performance.

Table 1. Firm performance measurements

Authors and year	Variable name	Variable definition
Adams and Jiang (2016)	Profit margin	Earnings (after interest & taxes) / Gross premiums
	Return on assets (ROA)	Net operating income before interest and taxes / Total assets
	Return on equity (ROE)	Net operating income before interest and taxes / Issued (& paid-up) equity
	Solvency position (Leverage)	1- surplus (capital + reserves) / Total assets
	Loss ratio	Total incurred (paid + reserved) claims / Total earned premiums
	Combined operating ratio	Total incurred (paid + reserved) claims + expenses (acquisition & management) / Total earned premiums
Florio and Leoni (2017)	ROA	Operating income to total assets at the end of the year expressed in percentages
	Tobin's Q	Sum of market capitalization and book value of liabilities / Book value of total assets

Source: Authors' preparation based on the literature.

As Table 1 shows, common firm performance proxies typically include ratios such as: Return on Assets (ROA), Return on Equity (ROE), Tobin's Q ratio (Q), profit margin, etc. and they usually are quantitative variables. However, González, Santomil and Herrera (2020) except ROA, ROE, and Q, use Quantitative Financial Health Distance to Default, Value at Risk (VaR), Systematic risk, Volatility, and Z-score as dependent variables. On the other hand, risk measurements typically are dummy variables.

In addition, Table 2 shows risk variables definition/construction and used approaches. Florio and Leoni (2017) use six binary variables representing the ERM components and multivariate OLS regressions as the estimation approach. González, Santomil and Herrera (2020) use five variables related to the presence of a risk management system which also is defined as dummy (binary) ones.

Table 2. Risk measurements and approaches

Authors and year	Variable name and definition	Approach
Florio and Leoni (2017)	Chief Risk Officer: dummy	Multivariate OLS regressions clustered by firm
	Risk Committee: dummy	
	Reporting frequency between risk committee or internal control and risk committee and the board of directors: dummy	
	The frequency of the assessment: dummy	
	The depth of the procedure: dummy	
	The methodology for the assessment: qualitative/quantitative	
González, Santomil and Herrera (2020)	Risk Committee: dummy	Panel data multiple regression models
	Chief Executive Officer: dummy	
	Risk map: dummy	
	ISO: dummy	
	Committee of Sponsoring Organizations of the Treadway: dummy	

Source: Authors' preparation based on the literature.

RESULTS AND DISCUSSION

The previous literature has documented the importance of asset liquidity in association with firm innovation (Pham, Vo, Le, & Le, 2018), capital structure (Morellec, 2001; Sibilkov, 2009), the cost of capital (Ortiz-Molina & Phillips, 2010), portfolio choice (Geromichalos & Simonovska, 2014); asset prices (Lester, Postlewaite, & Wright, 2012) and among others (Amihud & Mendelson, 1988; Amihud, Mendelson, & Pedersen, 2006; Gavazza, 2010; Geromichalos, Jung, Lee, & Carlos, 2021; Herrenbrueck & Geromichalos, 2017; Kruse, 2002; Nejadmalayeri, 2021). Prior studies capture asset liquidity as the liquidity scores for firms' major asset classes in their balance sheets including (1) cash and cash equivalents, (2) other non-current assets, (3) tangible fixed assets, and other assets (Gopalan, Kadan, & Pevzner, 2012) and the non-cash assets (Pham et al., 2018).

For several types of liquidity risk, stock market liquidity has been continuously attractive to international scholars in investigating its relation to several themes of corporate finance as well as the real economy. For instance, Vivian W. Fang, Tian, and Tice (2014) find that higher stock liquidity induces a decrease in future firm innovation, the authors explain by the two possible mechanisms including (1) greater subjection to hostile takeovers and (2) increased attendance of institutional investors who might not actively collect information or keep track of information.

Stock liquidity negatively affects firm default risk via the two possible mechanisms: enhancing informational efficiency in stock prices and promoting corporate governance quality by blockholes (Brogaard, Li, & Xia, 2017); furthermore, the authors document that the channel of information efficiency presents better explanatory ability than the channel of corporate governance in the negative effects of stock liquidity on default risk.

By employing the 2001 Securities and Exchange Commission decimalization regulation event in the US and difference-in-differences approach, the authors provide that the firms with the lowest change in stock liquidity (treatment group) experience a higher decrease in default risk after the decimalization in comparison with the firms with the highest change in stock liquidity (control group) surrounding the event year.

For an international context, Nadarajah, Duong, Ali, Liu, and Huang (2020) also find the same negative relation between stock liquidity and default risk; using the event of the Directive on Markets in Financial Instruments (MiFID), the authors document a decrease in default risk after the 2007 MiFID event as an exogenous shock to stock liquidity.

Besides firm innovation and default risk, the importance of stock liquidity have been documented in associated with stock returns (Cakici & Zaremba, 2021), bond-stock liquidity and capital structure choices (Nguyen, Alpert, & Faff, 2021), earning management (Li & Xia, 2021), investment efficiency (Quah, Haman, & Naidu, 2021), cash holdings (Nyborg & Wang, 2021), dividend pay-outs (Jiang, Ma, & Shi, 2017) and among others (Ahmed & Ali, 2017; Chang, Chen, & Zolotoy, 2017; Dou, Ji, Reibstein, & Wu, 2021; Vivian W Fang, Noe, & Tice, 2009; Gu, Wang, Yao, & Zhang, 2018; Jiang et al., 2017; Odders-White & Ready, 2006).

In addition, as it was presented above, there is plenty number of variables that are examined by different authors by applying generally different methodological approaches. For instance, González, Santomil and Herrera (2020) in addition to ROA, ROE, and Tobin's Q as measures of performance, use Value at Risk, Beta, Volatility of Return, Z-score, and Distance to Default as dependent variables. Thus, research studies deploy numerous models, techniques, methods, and approaches to decompose and investigate the fundamental relation between several types of risk and return. For instance, studies such as: Dang and Nguyen (2020), González, Santomil and Herrera (2020), Huang, Kerstein and Wang (2018), Florio and Leoni (2017), Adams and Jiang (2016), Psillaki, Tsolas and Margaritis (2010), Gordon, Loeb and Tseng (2009), Chang, Yu and Hung (2015), Wiseman and Bromiley (1996) use regression models. Yang, Ishtiaq and Anwar (2018) use Confirmatory Factor Analysis (CFA) and structural models. Also, the recent article by Saeidi et al. (2021) uses a structural model. Walls and Dyer (1996) develop a decision-theoretic model and a new risk propensity measure which is the Risk Tolerance Ratio (RTR).

Despite common divergences in the methodological view, empirical studies prove that there is a relationship between risk and firm performance (Matta and McGuire, 2008; Walls and Dyer, 1996, Wiseman and Bromiley, 1996; Bromiley, 1991, etc.).

Further, studies such as Saeidi et al. (2021), Yang, Ishtiaq and Anwar (2018), Florio and Leoni (2017), prove that there is a positive relationship between ERM and firm performance. However, other studies offer different results. For instance, González, Santomil and Herrera (2020) show that the adoption of ERM is neither associated with a change in the performance of Spanish firms nor reduces the probability of bankruptcy. Onsongo, Muathe and Mwangi (2020) show that credit and operational risk have an insignificant effect on ROE ratio, whilst liquidity risk has a significant effect.

CONCLUSION

Risk management as a discipline is developed by advancing both theoretical and practical approaches. Methodological approaches are advanced over the past decades. Theoretical foundation shows that the relationship between risk and firm performance remains a crucial role of risk management. Hence, the relationship between risk management and firm performance has been a motivating topic that is attractive to intentional scholars and experts come from both academia and industry. Because there are different investors' risk perceptions, the solutions proposed for risk hedging and return maximization of a company need further research works. However, the better the relationship between risk and firm performance is investigated, the better the strategic plans for business decision-makers. The fundamental knowledge and further empirical examinations by using different methodologies can be implemented relying on the previous literature. In this function, this chapter provides a general review of both theoretical and empirical backgrounds of the relation between firm performance and risk management.

REFERENCES

Adams, M., & Jiang, W. (2016). Do outside directors influence the financial performance of risk-trading firms? Evidence from the United Kingdom (UK) insurance industry. *Journal of Banking & Finance*, *64*, 36–51. doi:10.1016/j.jbankfin.2015.11.018

Ahmed, A., & Ali, S. (2017). Boardroom gender diversity and stock liquidity: Evidence from Australia. *Journal of Contemporary Accounting & Economics*, *13*(2), 148–165. doi:10.1016/j.jcae.2017.06.001

Alderson, M., & Betker, B. (1999). Assessing Post-Bankruptcy Performance: An Analysis of Reorganized Firms' Cash Flows. *Financial Management*, *28*(2), 68–82. doi:10.2307/3666196

Amihud, Y., & Mendelson, H. (1988). Liquidity and asset prices: Financial management implications. *Financial Management, 17*(1), 5–15. doi:10.2307/3665910

Amihud, Y., Mendelson, H., & Pedersen, L. H. (2006). *Liquidity and asset prices*. Now Publishers Inc.

Arellano, C. (2008). Default Risk and Income Fluctuations in Emerging Economies. *American Economic Review, 98*(3), 690–712. doi:10.1257/aer.98.3.690

Audia, P., & Greve, H. (2006). Less Likely to Fail: Low Performance, Firm Size, and Factory Expansion in the Shipbuilding Industry. *Management Science, 52*(1), 83–94. doi:10.1287/mnsc.1050.0446

Barinov, A. (2014). Turnover: Liquidity or Uncertainty? *Management Science, 60*(10), 2478–2495. doi:10.1287/mnsc.2014.1913

Beck, K. (2019). A Note on Teaching Liquidity Risk. *Journal of Financial Education, 45*(1), 94–100. Retrieved June 17, 2021, from https://www.jstor.org/stable/26918028

Berman, S., Wicks, A., Kotha, S., & Jones, T. (1999). Does Stakeholder Orientation Matter? The Relationship between Stakeholder Management Models and Firm Financial Performance. *Academy of Management Journal, 42*(5), 488–506. Retrieved April 3, 2021, from https://www.jstor.org/stable/256972

Brogaard, J., Li, D., & Xia, Y. (2017). Stock liquidity and default risk. *Journal of Financial Economics, 124*(3), 486–502. doi:10.1016/j.jfineco.2017.03.003

Bromiley, P. (1991). Testing a Causal Model of Corporate Risk Taking and Performance. *Academy of Management Journal, 34*(1), 37–59. Retrieved April 3, 2021, from https://www.jstor.org/stable/256301

Brunnermeier, M., Gorton, G., & Krishnamurthy, A. (2012). Risk Topography. *NBER Macroeconomics Annual, 26*(1), 149–176. doi:10.1086/663991

Cakici, N., & Zaremba, A. (2021). Liquidity and the cross-section of international stock returns. *Journal of Banking & Finance, 127*, 106123. doi:10.1016/j.jbankfin.2021.106123

Chang, Ch., Yu, Sh., & Hung, Ch. (2015). Firm risk and performance: The role of corporate governance. *Review of Managerial Science, 9*(1), 141–173. doi:10.100711846-014-0132-x

Chang, X., Chen, Y., & Zolotoy, L. (2017). Stock liquidity and stock price crash risk. *Journal of Financial and Quantitative Analysis, 52*(4), 1605–1637. doi:10.1017/S0022109017000473

Charitou, A., Lambertides, N., & Theodoulou, G. (2011). Dividend Increases and Initiations and Default Risk in Equity Returns. *Journal of Financial and Quantitative Analysis, 46*(5), 1521–1543. doi:10.1017/S0022109011000305

Chava, S., & Purnanandam, A. (2010). Is Default Risk Negatively Related to Stock Returns? *Review of Financial Studies, 23*(6), 2523–2559. doi:10.1093/rfs/hhp107

Chen, C., & Lee, H. (2013). Default Risk, Liquidity Risk, and Equity Returns: Evidence from the Taiwan Market. *Emerging Markets Finance & Trade, 49*(1), 101–129. doi:10.2753/REE1540-496X490106

Dang, T. L., & Nguyen, Th. M. H. (2020). Liquidity risk and stock performance during the financial crisis. *Research in International Business and Finance, 52*, 101165. doi:10.1016/j.ribaf.2019.101165

Davydenko, S., Strebulaev, I., & Zhao, X. (2012). A Market-Based Study of the Cost of Default. *Review of Financial Studies*, *25*(10), 2959–2999. doi:10.1093/rfs/hhs091

Deshmukh, S., Gamble, K., & Howe, K. (2015). Short Selling and Firm Operating Performance. *Financial Management*, *44*(1), 217–236. doi:10.1111/fima.12081

Dichev, I. (1998). Is the Risk of Bankruptcy a Systematic Risk? *Journal of Finance*, *53*(3), 1131–1147. doi:10.1111/0022-1082.00046

Dou, W. W., Ji, Y., Reibstein, D., & Wu, W. (2021). Inalienable customer capital, corporate liquidity, and stock returns. *Journal of Finance*, *76*(1), 211–265. doi:10.1111/jofi.12960

Driessen, J. (2005). Is Default Event Risk Priced in Corporate Bonds? *Review of Financial Studies*, *18*(1), 165–195. doi:10.1093/rfs/hhi009

Fang, V. W., Noe, T. H., & Tice, S. (2009). Stock market liquidity and firm value. *Journal of Financial Economics*, *94*(1), 150–169. doi:10.1016/j.jfineco.2008.08.007

Fang, V. W., Tian, X., & Tice, S. (2014). Does Stock Liquidity Enhance or Impede Firm Innovation? *Journal of Finance*, *69*(5), 2085-2125. . doi:10.1111/jofi.12187

Florio, C., & Leoni, G. (2017). Enterprise risk management and firm performance: The Italian case. *British Accounting Review*, *49*(1), 56–74. doi:10.1016/j.bar.2016.08.003

Franzoni, F., Nowak, E., & Phalippou, L. (2012). Private Equity Performance and Liquidity Risk. *Journal of Finance*, *67*(6), 2341–2373. doi:10.1111/j.1540-6261.2012.01788.x

Gavazza, A. (2010). Asset liquidity and financial contracts: Evidence from aircraft leases. *Journal of Financial Economics*, *95*(1), 62–84. doi:10.1016/j.jfineco.2009.01.004

Geromichalos, A., Jung, K. M., Lee, S., & Carlos, D. (2021). A model of endogenous direct and indirect asset liquidity. *European Economic Review*, *132*, 103627. doi:10.1016/j.euroecorev.2020.103627

Geromichalos, A., & Simonovska, I. (2014). Asset liquidity and international portfolio choice. *Journal of Economic Theory*, *151*, 342–380. doi:10.1016/j.jet.2014.01.004

González, L. O., Santomil, P. D., & Herrera, A. T. (2020). The effect of Enterprise Risk Management on the risk and the performance of Spanish listed companies. *European Research on Management and Business Economics*, *26*(3), 111–120. doi:10.1016/j.iedeen.2020.08.002

Gopalan, R., Kadan, O., & Pevzner, M. (2012). Asset Liquidity and Stock Liquidity. *Journal of Financial and Quantitative Analysis*, *47*(2), 333–364. doi:10.1017/S0022109012000130

Gordon, L. A., Loeb, M. P., & Tseng, Ch. (2009). Enterprise risk management and firm performance: A contingency perspective. *Journal of Accounting and Public Policy*, *28*(4), 301–327. doi:10.1016/j.jaccpubpol.2009.06.006

Goyal, V., & Wang, W. (2013). Debt Maturity and Asymmetric Information: Evidence from Default Risk Changes. *Journal of Financial and Quantitative Analysis*, *48*(3), 789–817. doi:10.1017/S0022109013000240

Gu, L., Wang, Y., Yao, W., & Zhang, Y. (2018). Stock liquidity and corporate diversification: Evidence from China's split share structure reform. *Journal of Empirical Finance*, *49*, 57–80. doi:10.1016/j.jempfin.2018.09.002

Han, K., Mittal, V., & Zhang, Y. (2017). Relative Strategic Emphasis and Firm-Idiosyncratic Risk: The Moderating Role of Relative Performance and Demand Instability. *Journal of Marketing*, *81*(4), 25–44. doi:10.1509/jm.15.0509

He, Z., & Xiong, W. (2012). Rollover Risk and Credit Risk. *Journal of Finance*, *67*(2), 391–429. doi:10.1111/j.1540-6261.2012.01721.x

Herranz, N., Krasa, S., & Villamil, A. (2015). Entrepreneurs, Risk Aversion, and Dynamic Firms. *Journal of Political Economy*, *123*(5), 1133–1176. doi:10.1086/682678

Herrenbrueck, L., & Geromichalos, A. (2017). A tractable model of indirect asset liquidity. *Journal of Economic Theory*, *168*, 252–260. doi:10.1016/j.jet.2016.12.009

Holmström, B., & Tirole, J. (2000). Liquidity and Risk Management. *Journal of Money, Credit and Banking*, *32*(3), 295–319. doi:10.2307/2601167

Huang, H. H., Kerstein, J., & Wang, Ch. (2018). The impact of climate risk on firm performance and financing choices: An international comparison. *Journal of International Business Studies*, *49*(5), 633–656. doi:10.105741267-017-0125-5

Jiang, F., Ma, Y., & Shi, B. (2017). Stock liquidity and dividend payouts. *Journal of Corporate Finance*, *42*, 295–314. doi:10.1016/j.jcorpfin.2016.12.005

Kelley, E., & Tetlock, P. (2017). Retail Short Selling and Stock Prices. *Review of Financial Studies*, *30*(3), 801–834. doi:10.1093/rfs/hhw089

Knight, F. H. (1921). *Risk, Uncertainty and Profit*. Houghton Mifflin Company.

Kruse, T. A. (2002). Asset liquidity and the determinants of asset sales by poorly performing firms. *Financial Management*, *31*(4), 107–129. doi:10.2307/3666176

Kukeli, A., Deari, F., & Rocşoreanu, C. (2019). Portfolio composition and critical line: A methodological approach. *International Journal of Risk Assessment and Management*, *22*(2), 195–211. doi:10.1504/IJRAM.2019.101289

Lee, H., & Lee, C. (2012). An Analysis of Reinsurance and Firm Performance: Evidence from the Taiwan Property-Liability Insurance Industry. *Geneva Papers on Risk and Insurance. Issues and Practice*, *37*(3), 467–484. doi:10.1057/gpp.2012.9

Lester, B., Postlewaite, A., & Wright, R. (2012). Information, Liquidity, Asset Prices, and Monetary Policy. *Review of Economic Studies*, *79*(3), 1209–1238. doi:10.1093/restud/rds003

Li, D., & Xia, Y. (2021). Gauging the effects of stock liquidity on earnings management: Evidence from the SEC tick size pilot test. *Journal of Corporate Finance*, *67*, 101904. doi:10.1016/j.jcorpfin.2021.101904

Lim, E., & McCann, B. (2014). Performance Feedback and Firm Risk Taking: The Moderating Effects of CEO and Outside Director Stock Options. *Organization Science*, *25*(1), 262–282. doi:10.1287/orsc.2013.0830

Matta, E., & McGuire, J. (2008). Too Risky to Hold? The Effect of Downside Risk, Accumulated Equity Wealth, and Firm Performance on CEO Equity Reduction. *Organization Science*, *19*(4), 567–580. doi:10.1287/orsc.1070.0334

McAlister, L., Srinivasan, R., & Kim, M. (2007). Advertising, Research and Development, and Systematic Risk of the Firm. *Journal of Marketing*, *71*(1), 35–48. doi:10.1509/jmkg.71.1.035

McNamara, G., & Bromiley, P. (1997). Decision Making in an Organizational Setting: Cognitive and Organizational Influences on Risk Assessment in Commercial Lending. *Academy of Management Journal*, *40*(5), 1063–1088. Retrieved April 3, 2021, from https://www.jstor.org/stable/256927

Miller, K., & Chen, W. (2003). Risk and firms' costs. *Strategic Organization*, *1*(4), 355–382. doi:10.1177/14761270030014001

Morellec, E. (2001). Asset liquidity, capital structure, and secured debt. *Journal of Financial Economics*, *61*(2), 173–206. doi:10.1016/S0304-405X(01)00059-9

Nadarajah, S., Duong, H. N., Ali, S., Liu, B., & Huang, A. (2020). Stock liquidity and default risk around the world. *Journal of Financial Markets*, 100597.

Nejadmalayeri, A. (2021). Asset liquidity, business risk, and beta. *Global Finance Journal*, *48*, 100560. doi:10.1016/j.gfj.2020.100560

Nguyen, T., Alpert, K., & Faff, R. (2021). Relative bond-stock liquidity and capital structure choices. *Journal of Corporate Finance*, *69*, 102026. doi:10.1016/j.jcorpfin.2021.102026

Nyborg, K. G., & Wang, Z. (2021). The effect of stock liquidity on cash holdings: The repurchase motive. *Journal of Financial Economics*, *142*(2), 905–927. doi:10.1016/j.jfineco.2021.05.027

Odders-White, E. R., & Ready, M. J. (2006). Credit ratings and stock liquidity. *Review of Financial Studies*, *19*(1), 119–157. doi:10.1093/rfs/hhj004

Onsongo, S. K., Muathe, S. M. A., & Mwangi, L. W. (2020). Financial Risk and Financial Performance: Evidence and Insights from Commercial and Services Listed Companies in Nairobi Securities Exchange, Kenya. *Int. J. Financial Stud*, *8*(51), 51. Advance online publication. doi:10.3390/ijfs8030051

Ortiz-Molina, H., & Phillips, G. M. (2010). *Asset liquidity and the cost of capital*. National Bureau of Economic Research. doi:10.3386/w15992

Ozerturk, S. (2006). Managerial Risk Reduction, Incentives and Firm Value. *Economic Theory*, *27*(3), 523–535. doi:10.100700199-004-0569-2

Pham, L. T. M., Vo, L. V., Le, H. T. T., & Le, D. V. (2018). Asset liquidity and firm innovation. *International Review of Financial Analysis*, *58*, 225–234. doi:10.1016/j.irfa.2017.11.005

Psillaki, M., Tsolas, I. E., & Margaritis, D. (2010). Evaluation of credit risk based on firm performance. *European Journal of Operational Research*, *201*(3), 873–881. doi:10.1016/j.ejor.2009.03.032

Quah, H., Haman, J., & Naidu, D. (2021). The effect of stock liquidity on investment efficiency under financing constraints and asymmetric information: Evidence from the United States. *Accounting and Finance*, *61*(S1), 2109–2150. doi:10.1111/acfi.12656

Saeidi, P., Saeidi, S. P., Gutierrez, L., Streimikiene, D., Alrasheedi, M., Saeidi, S. P., & Mardani, A. (2021). The influence of enterprise risk management on firm performance with the moderating effect of intellectual capital dimensions. *Economic Research-Ekonomska Istraživanja*, *34*(1), 122–151. doi:10.1080/1331677X.2020.1776140

Sibilkov, V. (2009). Asset liquidity and capital structure. *Journal of Financial and Quantitative Analysis*, *44*(5), 1173–1196. doi:10.1017/S0022109009990354

Vassalou, M., & Xing, Y. (2004). Default Risk in Equity Returns. *Journal of Finance*, *59*(2), 831–868. doi:10.1111/j.1540-6261.2004.00650.x

Walls, M. R., & Dyer, J. S. (1996). Risk Propensity and Firm Performance: A Study of the Petroleum Exploration Industry. *Management Science*, *42*(7), 1004–1021. doi:10.1287/mnsc.42.7.1004

Wiseman, R. M., & Bromiley, P. (1996). Toward a Model of Risk in Declining Organizations: An Empirical Examination of Risk, Performance and Decline. *Organization Science*, *7*(5), 524–543. doi:10.1287/orsc.7.5.524

Yang, S., Ishtiaq, M., & Anwar, M. (2018). Enterprise Risk Management Practices and Firm Performance, the Mediating Role of Competitive Advantage and the Moderating Role of Financial Literacy. *J. Risk Financial Manag*, *11*(35), 35. Advance online publication. doi:10.3390/jrfm11030035

Zhang, F., Tadikamalla, P. R., & Shang, J. (2016). Corporate credit-risk evaluation system: Integrating explicit and implicit financial performances. *International Journal of Production Economics*, *177*, 77–100. doi:10.1016/j.ijpe.2016.04.012

ENDNOTE

[1] For the 100 largest firms by market capitalization as of 2021, please see: https://www.statista.com/statistics/263264/top-companies-in-the-world-by-market-capitalization/.

Chapter 3
Gender Diversity and Financial Risk:
A Bibliometric Analysis

João Teodósio
https://orcid.org/0000-0002-7877-1564
Polytechnic Institute of Santarém, Portugal

Elisabete Vieira
https://orcid.org/0000-0003-3593-368X
GOVCOPP, University of Aveiro, Portugal

Mara Madaleno
https://orcid.org/0000-0002-4905-2771
GOVCOPP, University of Aveiro, Portugal

ABSTRACT

This chapter intends to contribute to the analysis of gender diversity and financial risk through a bibliometric review of the existent literature to understand the current state of financial risk research as well as to contribute to the analysis of the influence of gender diversity on financial risk. Although there is extensive research on financial risk, no recent study tries to update the current state of the research over the influence of gender on financial risk practices. This chapter describes the evolutional research studies published in the digital library Scopus, between 2010 and June 2021, and compares the results obtained in evolutionary terms. When the research is concentrated on the bibliometric analysis in the Scopus database and the keyword "financial risk," it leads to a total of 15,979 documents. Regarding the analysis concentrated on the keywords "gender diversity" and "financial risk" for the period between 2010 and June 2021, the authors end with a final sample of 96 documents. Proposals for further research are provided based on the current state of the art.

DOI: 10.4018/978-1-7998-8609-9.ch003

INTRODUCTION

No bibliometric research should start without previously defining what the main subject under analysis is. The study concentrates on Financial Risk (FR) and Gender Diversity (GD) articles published in the recent years of 2010 and June 2021.

FR is present in the day-by-day activities of companies all over the world. It is usually referred to as the possibility that a firm's cash flow will prove to be inadequate to meet its obligations, and is related to the odds of losing money, which can result in the loss of capital to interested parties. There are several forms of FR, such as market risk (Salomons & Grootveld, 2003), model risk (Jokhadze & Schmidt, 2020), credit risk (Putri, Bunga & Rochman, 2021), operational risk (Girling, 2013), disclosure risk (Linsley & Shrives, 2006) and financial distress risk (Altman, 1968).

One of the factors that can influence the management decisions, and, consequently, the firms' risk, is GD. There is evidence that women have different characteristics in what concerns the understanding of market conditions, creativity and public image (Smith et al., 2006), the communication and listening skills (Julizaerma & Sori, 2012), and the decision-making process (Bart & McQueen, 2013). Additionally, Singh et al. (2008) argue that females are more likely to bring international diversity to the board of directors and Huse and Solberg (2006) posit that women are better prepared than men for board meetings and Adams and Ferreira (2007) conclude that they have better attendance records. From a psychological perspective, Barber and Odean (2001) held that men are more overconfident than women and Olsen and Cox (2001) conclude that females are more risk-averse than men. The conclusions of Barber and Odean (2001) and Olsen and Cox (2001) suggest that men tend to make riskier financial decisions. However, Olsen and Cox (2001) also conclude that females are more prone to emotional conflicts than men.

Thus, we can see that it is expected an influence of gender diversity on a firm's financial risk. In this context, this chapter intends to contribute to the analysis of the influence of GD on companies' FR, conducting a bibliometric analysis focused on FR and GD studies, highlighting possible future avenues of research identified, opening room for more research needed within the field.

The rest of this chapter develops as follows. The next section presents a brief literature review on the FR topic and its relationship with GD. After, the chapter presents the general status of FR and GD research from 2010 to June 2021, first in global terms and then concentrating on the top seventeen articles, considering the number of citations. The last section concludes the chapter and provides some insights for possible future research regarding GD and FR.

BRIEF LITERATURE REVIEW ON FINANCIAL RISK AND GENDER DIVERSITY

FR is normally referred to as the possibility that a firm's cash flow will prove to be inadequate to meet its obligations, and is related to the odds of losing money, which can result in the loss of capital to interested parties. There are several types of FR, like financial distress risk (Altman, 1968), market risk (Salomons & Grootveld, 2003), operational risk (Girling, 2013), disclosure risk (Linsley & Shrives, 2006), model risk (Jokhadze & Schmidt, 2020), and credit risk (Putri, Bunga & Rochman, 2021). Many factors have been reported in the literature to explain firms' risk. One of the reported factors, influencing management decisions, and, consequently, the firms' risk, is GD. Other recently studied factors include economic policy uncertainty (Wen et al., 2021), policy and corporate financing (Lee et al., 2021), Knowledge management (Hock-Doepgen et al., 2021), cash reserves, and financial constraints

(Lee and Wang, 2021), corporate social responsibility (Kuo et al., 2021), gender diversity (Cho et al., 2021), just to mention a few.

Indeed, previous studies find evidence that women have different characteristics in what concerns firms management decisions, because of their different understanding of market conditions, creativity and public image (Smith et al., 2006), communication and listening skills (Julizaerma & Sori, 2012), and the decision-making process (Bart & McQueen, 2013). In addition, Singh et al. (2008) argue that females are more likely to bring international diversity to the board of directors. Huse and Solberg (2006) posit that women are better prepared than men for board meetings and Adams and Ferreira (2007) conclude that they have better attendance records. From a psychological perspective, Barber and Odean (2001) held that men are more overconfident than women and Olsen and Cox (2001) conclude that females are more risk-averse than men. The conclusions of Barber and Odean (2001) and Olsen and Cox (2001) suggest that men tend to make riskier financial decisions. However, Olsen and Cox (2001) also conclude that females are more prone to emotional conflicts than men. Consequently, we expect that GD influences a firm's FR.

There is plenty of evidence on gender differences in management decisions that affect firms' FR, such as Jianakoplos and Bernasek (1998), Byrnes et al. (1999), Croson and Gneezy (2009), Ahern and Dittmar (2012), Huang and Kisgen (2013), Berger et al. (2014), Lenard et al. (2014), Faccio et al. (2016), Filippin and Crosetto (2016), Sila et al. (2016), Jeong and Harrison (2017), Bernile et al. (2018), L'Haridon and Vieder (2019), Li and Zeng (2019), Bufarwa et al. (2020), Hurley and Choudhary (2020) and Saeed et al. (2021).

Within the U.S. context, Huang and Kisgen (2013) posit a negative association between executive women positions and leverage. In the same line, Faccio et al. (2016) report that firms with female CEOs present lower leverage levels. Concomitantly, Hurley and Choudhary (2020) show that the impact of female CFOs on firms' financial risk is mixed, depending on risk measures used. However, the evidence shows that increasing the female percentage of board members reduces firms' risk. Li and Zeng (2019) argue for an insignificant relationship between female CEO and stock price crash risk that turns negative for female CFOs.

Lenard et al. (2014) investigate gender diversity effect on risk management, based on a sample of firms obtained in the Risk Metrics database for the period between 2007 and 2011, finding evidence that more gender diversity on the board of directors' impacts firm risk by contributing to lower variability of the stock market return. Moreover, the results show that the higher the percentage of female directors on the board of directors, the lower the variability of corporate performance. Sila et al. (2016), document a negative relationship between total risk and women's appointments. Additionally, the authors conclude a non-significant association between the fraction of female directors on board and firm market risk. Bernile et al. (2018) present a positive association between the fraction of women directors and firm market volatility.

Outside the U.S. context, Ahern and Dittmar (2012) analyze a sample of Norwich financial and non-financial firms and conclude that a higher fraction of women directors on the board increase leverage and debt/assets ratio but decreases the level of cash holdings. Berger et al. (2014) studied the impact of executive women on the ratio of risk-weighted assets (RWA) of German listed and non-listed banks and demonstrate a positive association between the fraction of women executive directors and portfolio risk. Moreover, Saeed et al. (2021) analyze the effect of board gender diversity on the firm risk-taking level, comparing the influence of board gender diversity on the firm risk-taking level in high-tech and non-high-tech sectors in the Indian market. The results show that women executives operating in high-

Gender Diversity and Financial Risk

tech sectors take more risk in their management decisions than their counterparts that operate in the non-high sector. The evidence reveals that family ownership negatively moderates the impact of female executives on risk-taking in high-tech firms. Moreover, the authors conclude that the influence of female executives on firm outcomes is not always straightforward. In a cross-country perspective, Jeong and Harrison (2017) provide a meta-analysis based on 33 countries and document a negative relationship between executive women directors and all measures of risk-taking studied (leverage, standard deviation of stock returns, capital expenditures).

In what concerns financial risk disclosure, Bufarwa et al. (2020) analyze the impact of corporate governance (CG) mechanisms on financial risk reporting in the UK, considering a sample of 50 non-financial firms listed on the London Stock Exchange in the period between 2011 and 2015. The authors find that CG has a significant influence on financial risk disclosure. Board gender diversity has a positive effect on the level of corporate financial risk disclosure, which adds to the results of previous studies, such as the ones of Barako and Brown (2008), Ntim et al. (2012), and Ntim et al. (2013). Block ownership has also a positive impact on financial risk disclosure, suggesting that the UK firms will engage in a high level of financial disclosure, including voluntary disclosures. This result is in agreement with the findings of Abraham and Cox (2007) and Oliveira et al. (2011). However, the authors find no significant relationship between board size and corporate financial risk disclosure, which is consistent with the results of Elzahar and Hussainey (2012), but inconsistent with the findings of Ntim et al. (2013), who find a positive relationship between these variables.

More recently, Putri, Bunga, and Rochman (2021) study the effect of CG on risk financial disclosure, considering a sample of 20 companies from 2015 to 2017. The authors' results show that the size of the board of commissioners and the frequency of audit committee meetings have a positive effect on financial risk disclosure. However, the results do not show a significant influence of the number of audit committees and the number of boards of commissioner meetings on the degree of financial risk disclosure.

GENERAL BIBLIOMETRIC ANALYSIS ON FINANCIAL RISK AND GENDER DIVERSITY: 2010-2021 (JUNE)

Bibliometric analysis is a method that turns easier the research of the relationship between research criteria and variables related to the research and environment of that research. During this research, it was applied the exploratory, descriptive, and bibliographic research methodology, performing a content analysis through the keyword "financial risk". The search was performed at the end of June 2021. The authors consider the period between January and June 2021, since the research on the relationship between GD and FR is recent, and 2021 has a significant number of publications, compared with the other years. Provided the authors wanted a recent analysis period, they concentrate the chapter research during the period 2010-2021 (June). Even so, just by searching for the title/abstract/keywords "financial risk" in the Scopus database, it was found 15,979 documents (of all types) published from 2010 until June 2021. Regarding the analysis concentrated on the keywords "gender diversity" and "financial risk" for the analyzed period, the authors end with a final sample of 96 documents. The research was focused on Scopus since by crossing it with other sources like WoS findings were similar, as to the main documents available and published in indexed journals.

The six months of the last year of the sample (2021) was the period with more documents published (20), representing 20.8% of the articles published during the period in analysis. The period between

2010 and 2020 (11 years) represents 79.2% of the publications (76), which shows that it is a recent topic of research. Indeed, the first paper published that relates GD and FR registered in Scopus is dated from 2001. The acquired data has on its basis several sources which are found in Scopus (https://www.scopus.com/search/), a database with a huge quantity of articles. The process of data collection in this platform is divided into several parameters: the choice of the database, the definition of keywords, the identification of the article, the journal identification, and the classification of the articles. The study performed and presented next will follow over some of these parameters.

Figure 1 presents the evolution of the documents collected for the period between 2010 and June 2021, after applying the parameters defined in the Scopus database, and looking for the title/abstract/keywords "gender diversity" and "financial risk", which relation we want to analyze, leading us to a total database of 96 documents, proving that this is a new topic in the financial research.

The growing trend in the publication of the article from 2010 (two) to June 2021 (20) is visible, with the exponential growth from 2018 (five) to 2021 being noteworthy, representing 56.3% of all publications in the considered period. The high growth of publications after 2018 reflects the growing and progressive research interest in the GD and FR subjects.

Figure 2 shows the documents published by source title.

As it can be seen in Figure 2, the two journals that registered the highest number of publications about the relationship between GD and FR are the Journal of Business Ethics and the Managerial Auditing Journal, both with three publications. There are several journals with just two papers published during the period of the study, namely Accounting and Finance, Corporate Governance: An International Review, and the Corporate Governance Bingley. The years with more than one publication in the top five journals are 2015, 2019, 2020, and 2021. The articles published on these subjects are concentrated in the last years, showing again that these topics are a recent tendency of research.

Figure 3 highlights the authors who most published in the field of GD and FR during the 2010-2021 period (June).

Figure 1. Number of documents published during 2010-June 2021, by year
Source: Own elaboration based on Scopus

Figure 2. Documents published in 2010-June 2021 period, by source title
Source: Own elaboration based on Scopus

Figure 3. Documents published during 2010-June 2021 by author
Source: Own elaboration based on Scopus

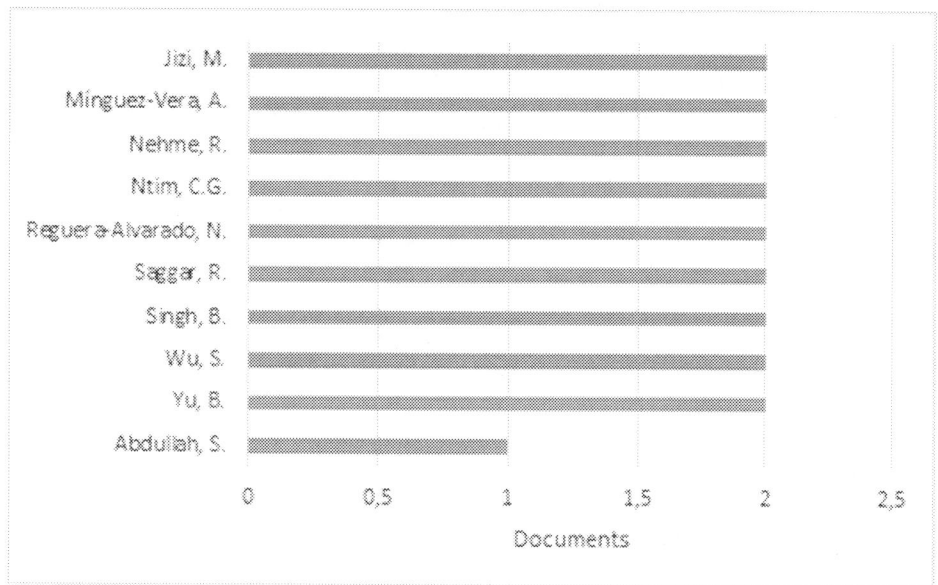

Figure 3 shows that none author stands up from the others. Nine of the 10 authors that have more publications in the period under review have published two documents (Jizi, M.; Mínguez-Vera, A.;

Nehme, R.; Ntim, C.G.; Reguera-Alvarado, N.; Saggar, R.; Singh, B.; Wu, S.; Yu, B.). Abdullah, S. has one study published. The authors want to highlight that up to this phase they are considering all kinds of published documents under the GD and FR keywords for the period of analysis. The low number of published papers on this subject shows that the research on the relationship between GD and FR is still in its initial stage, or infancy, with high research potential, that we intended to highlight.

Figure 4 shows the documents published by affiliation under the keywords gender diversity and financial risk, for the period between 2010 and June 2021.

Figure 4. Documents published by affiliation during 2010-June 2021 under the keywords gender diversity and financial risk
Source: Own elaboration based on Scopus

Regarding the affiliation of the authors, the University of Southampton (United Kingdom) and the Bucharest University of Economic Studies (Romania) are the two with the highest number of affiliated authors publishing during 2010 and June 2021, with four publications. This is followed by the Universidad de Murcia (Spain) and the Lebanese American University (Lebanon), with three publications. The lowest top ten universities of affiliations are composed by the Guru Nanak Dev University (India), the University of Essex (United Kingdom), the University Utara Malaysia, the Zhejiang University (China), the University Alexandru Ioan Cuza (Romania), and the Texas Wesleyan University (USA), with two studies published each one.

Figure 5 displays the documents by country or territory during the period under review.

Figure 5. Documents by country or territory during 2010-June 2021
Source: Own elaboration based on Scopus

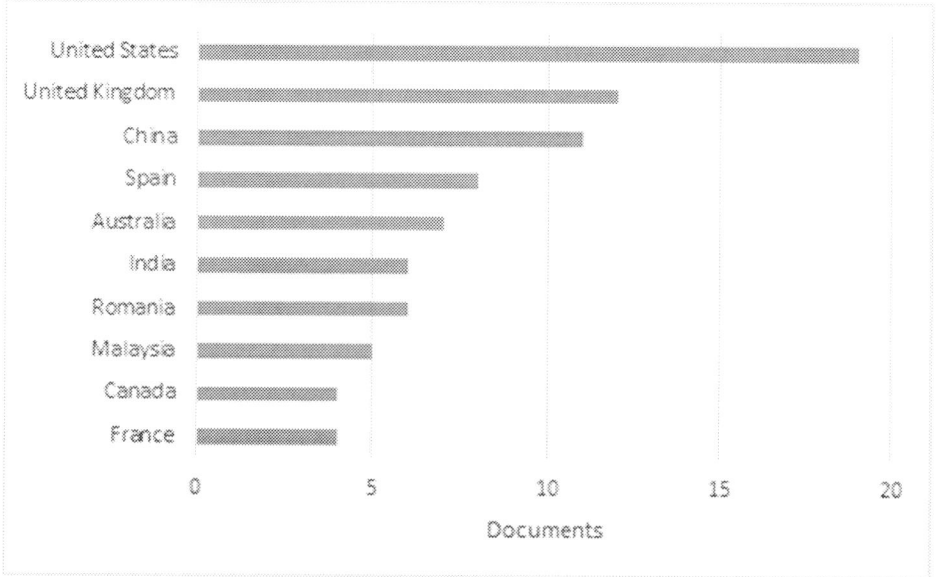

In what concerns the documents published by country or territory, it is clear that the research on GD and FR is concentrated on the Anglo-Saxon countries. The country with more publications is the United States (19), followed by the United Kingdom (12). China has 11 publications, followed by Australia, with seven published studies. The rest of the countries in the top ten documents by country are from Asian countries (India and Malaysia), Europe (Romania and France), and the North of America (Canada). More research is needed, namely on European countries beyond the UK, where there is still a scarcity of research under the GD and FR subjects. Moreover, a comparative analysis within regions and among regions is valuable, to compare results and conclusions.

Figure 6 shows the published documents by type.

As it can be seen in Figure 6, the most published documents during this period in the analysis were made in the form of Scientific Articles (83.3%). Conference Reviews represent 5.2% of the published documents. Conference papers and reviews are responsible for 4.2% of the publications each one, while Book Chapters and Books represent 2.1% and 1% of the publications, respectively.

Figure 6. Documents published by type during 2010-June 2021
Source: Own elaboration based on Scopus

■ Article ■ Conference Review ■ Conference Paper ■ Review ■ Book Chapter ■ Book

Figure 7 shows the documents by subject area published during the period in review.

Figure 7. Documents by subject area published during 2010-June 2021
Source: Own elaboration based on Scopus

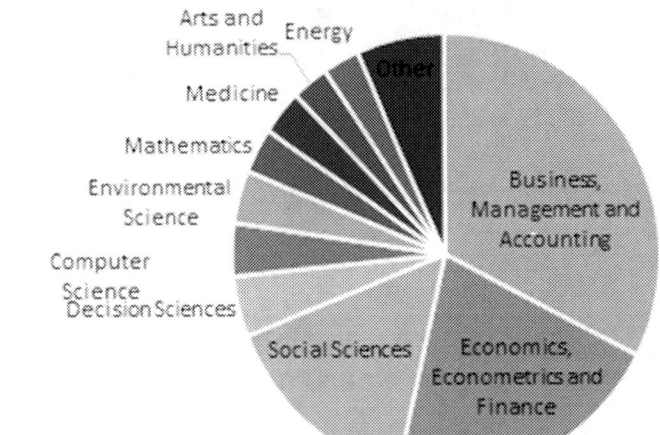

Regarding the main subject areas of publication, it can be seen that most are within the Business, Management and Accounting area (32.6%), followed by the area of Economics, Econometrics and Finance (21.5%) and Social Sciences with 15.5%. However, it is visible that GD and FR research is being explored in other knowledge areas, such as Decision Sciences, Computer Science, Environmental Science, Mathematics, and Medicine. Arts and Humanities and Energy are both associated with 2.8% of the published studies. Finally, 6.6% of the publications are associated with other subject areas, such as Psychology and Nursing. Although there is some dispersion in the subject areas of publication, there is a concentration in the areas of Accounting, Finance, Economics, and Management.

Then, the authors narrow the search, sorting the publications by those that are most cited. To do so, the researchers reach the h-index (Hirsch, 2005), an analysis that conjugates the number of publications and the number of citations (it were excluded the self-citations), in the option "view citation overview". The results are shown in Figure 8.

Figure 8. H-index during the period 2010-June 2021
Source: Own elaboration based on Scopus

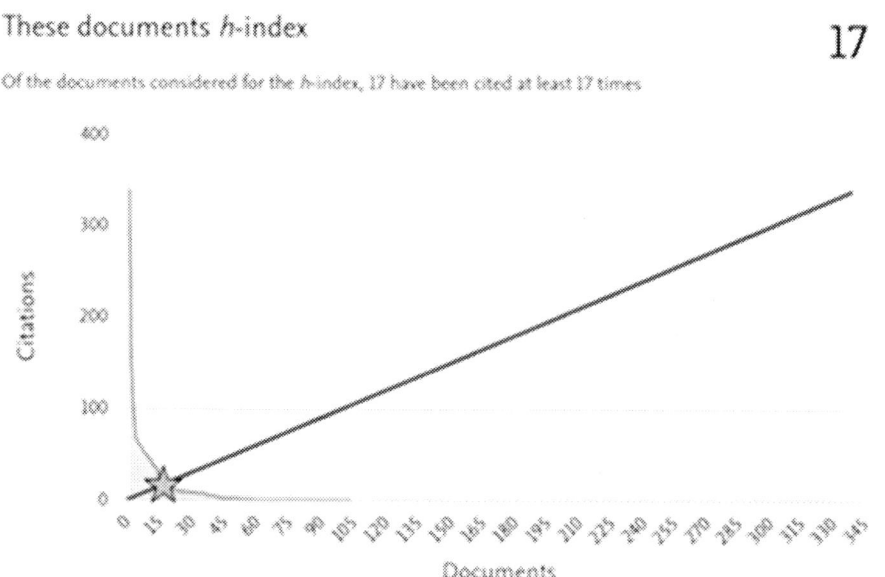

It was reached an h-index of 17, meaning that of the 96 articles examined, 17 have at least 17 citations.

Consequently, our bibliometric analysis is concentrated on the 17 published documents which were more cited between 2010 and the first six months of 2021.

Table 1 shows the articles ranked by citations.

Concerning the article gathering, by far, more citations were published in 2008 in the Journal of Business Ethics, with 342 citations at the data bibliometric analysis (Francoeur, Labelle, & Sinclair-Desgagné, 2008). The third article with more citations has been published in 2015, in the same Journal (Ho et al., 2015), having 101 citations. The second publication at the top of citations is from the area subject of medicine, published in 2011, in the International Journal of Epidemiology, with 207 citations (von Wagner et al., 2011). Another publication about medicine subjects is the one of Ng'ang'a et al. (2009). The papers of Startiene and Remeikiene (2019), Werbel and Danes (2010), and Demey et al. (2013) are associated with social sciences subjects.

Table 1. Top 17 cited articles during 2010-June 2021

	Document title	Authors	Year	Source	Cited by
1	Gender diversity in corporate governance and top management	Francoeur, C., Labelle, R., Sinclair-Desgagné, B.	2008	Journal of Business Ethics, 81(1), 83-95	342
2	Inequalities in participation in an organized national colorectal cancer screening programme: Results from the first 2.6 million invitations in England	von Wagner, C., Baio, G., Raine, R., (...), Halloran, S., Wardle, J.	2011	International Journal of Epidemiology, 40(3), 712-718	207
3	CEO Gender, Ethical Leadership, and Accounting Conservatism	Ho, S.S.M., Li, A.Y., Tam, K., Zhang, F.	2015	Journal of Business Ethics, 127(2), 351-370	101
4	The effects of board characteristics and sustainable compensation policy on carbon performance of UK firms	Haque, F.	2017	British Accounting Review, 49(3), 347-364	72
5	Women on boards, sustainability reporting and firm performance	Arayssi, M., Dah, M., Jizi, M.	2016	Sustainability Accounting, Management and Policy Journal, 7(3), 376-401	65
6	Gender and management on Spanish SMEs: An empirical analysis	Mínguez-Vera, A., Martin, A.	2011	International Journal of Human Resource Management, 22(14), 2852-2873	64
7	Work family conflict in new business ventures: The moderating effects of spousal commitment to the new business venture	Werbel, J.D., Danes, S.M.	2010	Journal of Small Business Management, 48(3), 421-440	60
8	Did Board Configuration Matter? The Case of US Subprime Lenders	Muller-Kahle, M.I., Lewellyn, K.B.	2011	Corporate Governance: An International Review, 19(5), 405-417	55
9	Who selects the 'right' directors? An examination of the association between board selection, gender diversity and outcomes	Hutchinson, M., Mack, J., Plastow, K.	2015	Accounting and Finance, 55(4), 1071-1103	51
10	Impact of board gender diversity on firm risk	Jane Lenard, M., Yu, B., Anne York, E., Wu, S.	2014	Managerial Finance, 40(8), 787-803	46
11	Environmental policy, environmental performance, and financial distress in China: Do top management team characteristics matter?	Shahab, Y., Ntim, C.G., Chengang, Y., Ullah, F., Fosu, S.	2018	Business Strategy and the Environment, 27(8), 1635-1652	45
12	Bed net use and associated factors in a rice farming community in Central Kenya	Ng'ang'a, P.N., Jayasinghe, G., Kimani, V., (...), Githure, J., Mutero, C.	2009	Malaria Journal, 8(1), 64	45
13	Opening the black box of upper echelons: Drivers of poor information processing during the financial crisis	Rost, K., Osterloh, M.	2010	Corporate Governance: An International Review, 18(3), 212-233	42
14	Does gender diversity on corporate boards increase risk-taking?	Loukil, N., Yousfi, O.	2016	Canadian Journal of Administrative Sciences, 33(1), 66-81	35
15	Corporate governance and risk reporting: Indian evidence	Saggar, R., Singh, B.	2017	Managerial Auditing Journal, 32(4-5), 378-405	24
16	Pathways into living alone in mid-life: Diversity and policy implications	Demey, D., Berrington, A., Evandrou, M., Falkingham, J.	2013	Advances in Life Course Research, 18(3), 161-174	23
17	The influence of demographical factors on the interaction between entrepreneurship and unemployment	Startiene, G., Remeikiene, R.	2009	Engineering Economics, 4(64), 60-70	19

Source: Own Development

The citations of the other publications vary between 19 and 72. In what concerns the year of the publications, it ranges from 2008 to 2018. Although nine of the 17 publications are comprised between

2013 and 2018, corresponding to about 53% of the articles (the more recent ones), it only represents 35.6% of the citations. The thematics under research include besides GD and FR, corporate governance, firm performance, leadership, and entrepreneurship.

Several studies analyze the effects of the presence of women on firm performance and risk, finding evidence that the GD contributes positively to firms' performance and/or to moderate the firms' risk (Francoeur et al., 2008; Jane Lenard et al., 2014; Hutchinson et al., 2015; Arayssi et al., 2016; Loukil and Yousfi, 2016; Haque, 2017). However, Mínguez-Vera and Martin (2011) find evidence that the presence of women on boards generates a negative impact on firm performance.

Francoeur et al. (2008) analyze whether the participation of women in the firm's board of directors and senior management enhances financial performance, considering the level of risk and considering a sample of Canadian firms. The results show that firms operating in riskier environments generate positive and significant abnormal returns when they have a high proportion of women officers. Although the participation of women as directors does not seem to make a difference in this regard, firms with a high proportion of women in both their management and governance systems generate enough value to keep up with normal stock-market returns, which reinforces the idea that the presence of women in business is beneficial to firms. Jane Lenard et al. (2014) examine the effect of gender diversity on the board of directors on corporate risk and performance, using a sample of US firms for the period between 2007 and 2011. This database contains information on the corporate board of directors. The results reveal that the higher the percentage of female directors on the board, the lower the variability of corporate performance, which results in lower firms' risk. Hutchinson et al. (2015) analyze whether gender diversity on the board affects firm risk and financial performance, considering a sample of Australian listed firms, finding that greater gender diversity moderates excessive firm risk and improves firms' financial performance. Thus, the authors find evidence that supports the business case for board gender diversity.

Arayssi et al. (2016) study the effect of gender-diverse boards on the relationship between sustainability reporting and shareholders' welfare, considering the listed firms in the Financial Times Stock Exchange 350 index between 2007 and 2012. The results indicate that the presence of women directors on corporate boards influences favorably the firm's risk and performance, contributing to the increase of risk-adjusted abnormal returns and the reduction of the firms' volatility of returns and systematic risk. Loukil and Yousfi (2016) analyze the impact of board gender diversity on firm risk-taking in Tunisia, a developing market, for the 1997-2010 period. The results indicate that women have a risk perception that leads to risk avoidance behavior. However, the results show no significant relationship between board gender diversity and the propensity to take strategic or financial risk-taking. Haque (2017) explore the effects of board characteristics and sustainable compensation policy on carbon reduction initiatives and greenhouse gas (GHG) emissions of a firm, considering a sample of UK firms and covering the period from 2002 to 2014. The results indicate that board independence and board gender diversity have positive effects on climate risk and firm performance. However, Mínguez-Vera and Martin (2011) study the presence of women on the boards of directors of companies. Considering that previous studies that have been written have focused on large firms, the authors used a sample of Spanish SMEs. The results suggest that the presence of women on boards generates a negative impact on firm performance. According to the authors, this is due to less risky strategies implemented by women directors. Moreover, the authors find evidence that firms with more women as directors have less debt, more assets, and larger boards.

Rost and Osterloh (2010) examine whether executives' characteristics affect strategic choices due to bounded rationality, in the context of Switzerland. The authors show that under conditions of uncertainty, the processing of information by financial experts and men is worse than by non-financial experts and women. In addition, the authors conclude that banks with a higher percentage of financial experts within top management teams perform better in stable environments, but are more badly affected by the financial crisis.

Muller-Kahle and Lewellyn (2011) analyze if board configuration plays a relevant role in determining whether a financial institution specialized in subprime lending, considering a sample of US financial institutions for the period 1997-2005. They find that the board configurations of the institutions that engaged in subprime lending were significantly different from those that did not. Indeed, subprime lenders had busier boards, had less tenure, and were less diverse concerning gender.

Ho et al. (2015) study the effects of CEO gender on accounting conservatism, considering a sample of US firms for the 1996-2008 period. The authors find evidence that firms with female CEOs report more conservative earnings. The association between female CEOs and accounting conservatism is significant in companies exposed to high rather than low litigation and takeover risks. Finally, the results reveal that the effects of gender are more pronounced in smaller firms and firms with stronger corporate governance.

Considering the risk of disclosure, Saggar and Singh (2017) quantify the extent of voluntary risk disclosure and examine the relationship between corporate governance and ownership concentration's impact on risk disclosure in the annual reports of Indian listed firms, collecting data from the period 2013-2014. The findings show that corporate governance characteristics, such as board size and gender diversity have a positive effect on risk disclosure, whereas ownership concentration in the hands of the largest shareholder has no significant impact on risk disclosure.

In the context of environmental performance, Shahab et al. (2018) explore the impact of a firm's environmental performance that is driven by good environmental policies, regulations, and management on financial distress, using a sample of Chinese firms for the period between 2009 and 2014. The results reveal that increased environmental performance that is driven by good environmental policies tends to reduce the extent of firm financial distress, being this relation moderated by gender diversity, foreign exposure, and political connection.

Looking for the subjects addressed in the majority of the papers, it can be seen that GD and FR are related to each other.

RESULTS DISCUSSION

To deepen and narrow our results further, we went back to the Scopus database using the research words available in title-abstract-keywords of gender, diversity, risk, management, limiting once more the findings to the period 2010 and June 2021. This time we limited the search to articles published in peer-reviewed journals and to the research areas of "Business, Management and Accounting" and "Economics, Econometrics and Finance". A total of 46 documents have emerged from the refined search. We made this additionally, to identify better the future research opportunities we believe still provide valuable opportunities within the context of GD and FR.

To help us in this analysis we have used VOS viewer to be able to identify clusters starting with Keywords cluster analysis. In total from the 46 documents identified, 17 clusters may be identified (see Figure 9) through different colored links (co-occurrence and author keywords were the type of analysis followed, with full counting). The most frequent occurrence of keywords refers to gender diversity (15), followed by gender (8), corporate governance (7), risk and diversity (4 times each), China, board of directors, risk management, and women (3 times each), and 2 times each we have the keywords financial performance, audit committees, diversity management, human capital, inclusion, performance, top management, critical mass theory, firm performance, impression management, R&D, sustainability disclosure and risk-taking. Finally, appearing one time each in the set of the 46 papers scrutinized, we have the words in Figure 10.

Figure 9. VOSviewer cluster analysis of keywords (46 articles; 2010-June2021)
Source: Own development based over VOSviewer and Scopus collected data

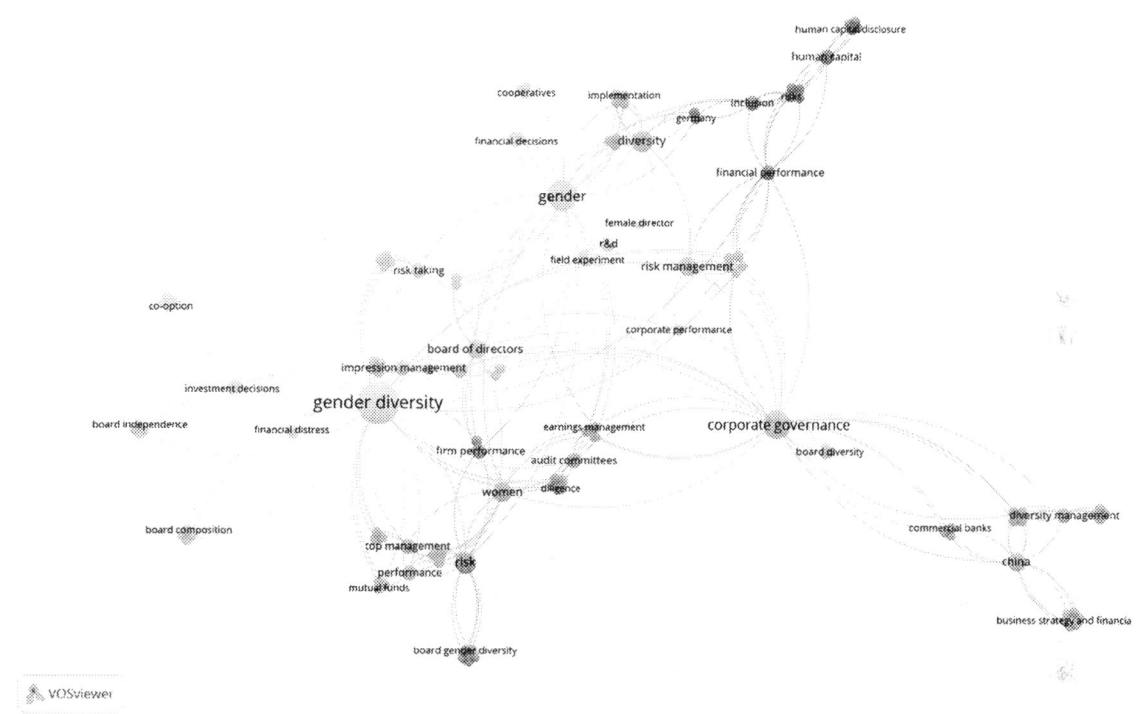

From the 17 clusters identified in Figure 9, cluster 1 in red includes 13 items/keywords, namely, econometric procedures, financial performance, gender and cultural diversity, Germany, human capital, human capital disclosure, human resource management, inclusion, intellectual capital, organizational performance, risks, strategies and talent management. In darker green, we have cluster 2 with 12 items (bank risk profile, European acquiring banks, feminism, feminist theories, M&A, mutual funds, performance, quantile regression, stability, timing, top management, women). In dark blue cluster 3 with 10 items, from which China, commercial banks, and business strategy and finance emerge as the most cited keywords. Both clusters 4 (in dark yellow) and 5 (in purple) have 9 items, while 6, 7, 8, and the 9th clusters contain 8 keywords each. The latter includes the keywords diversity, equal opportunities, human resources (HR) and cross-cultural management, HR metrics, implementation, mixed-methods, process evaluation, and training, identified in pink in Figure 9.

Cluster 11, in light green, includes debt, small firms, start-ups, and cooperatives, whereas cluster 10, including in total 7 keywords as well, refers to risk management, corporate performance, size, and supervision. Issues like financial distress, gender diversity, investment decisions, loss aversion, risk aversion, and risk management committee are included in cluster 12 (blue-grey). Cluster 13 includes 5 keywords (entrepreneurship, female director, field experiment, new venture tmt, and R&D (in light yellow), and clusters 14, 15, 16, and 17 all have 4 keywords included solely. Cluster 14 refers to sustainability issues (light purple) like board independence, carbon reduction initiatives, ESG-based compensation, and GHG emissions. In light blue, cluster 15 includes co-option, crash risk, independent director, and state-owned enterprises. In orange, cluster 16 includes board composition, financial risk, reputation management, and tax avoidance. Finally, in brown, we have cluster 17 including the keywords board diversity, coinsurance effect, corporate governance, and stock price risk. Therefore, despite the 126 keywords identified in the 46 articles analyzed, many more can be identified as possible avenues for future research. For example, the USA, Germany, and China are countries included as keywords in the published articles, while other countries and regions are still in the need of research.

Figure 10. VOSviewer keywords (46 articles; 2010-June2021) – appearing once
Source: Own Development based on VOSviewer and Scopus collected data

Gender Diversity and Financial Risk

Table 2. Gender, risk, COVID cited articles during 2020-June 2021

Publ. Year	Document Title	Authors	Journal Title	2020	2021	total
				7	113	120
2021	People's responses to the COVID-19 pandemic during its early stages and factors affecting those responses	Zhang J.	Humanities and Social Sciences Communications	0	5	5
2021	SportsCenter: A case study of media framing U.S. sport as the COVID-19 epicenter	Bell T.R.	International Journal of Sport Communication	0	0	0
2021	Shining the light on women's work, this time brighter: Let's start at the top	Schultheiss D.E.	Journal of Vocational Behavior	0	1	1
2021	Socio-demographic factors associated with self-protecting behavior during the Covid-19 pandemic	Papageorge N.W., Zahn M.V., Belot M., van den Broek-Altenburg E., Choi S., Jamison J.C., Tripodi E.	Journal of Population Economics	0	12	12
2021	Restaurants and COVID-19: What are consumers' risk perceptions about restaurant food and its packaging during the pandemic?	Byrd K., Her E., Fan A., Almanza B., Liu Y., Leitch S.	International Journal of Hospitality Management	0	6	6
2021	Strategic assessment of COVID-19 pandemic in Bangladesh: comparative lockdown scenario analysis, public perception, and management for sustainability	Shammi M., Bodrud-Doza M., Islam A.R.M.T., Rahman M.M.	Environment, Development and Sustainability	3	16	19
2021	Building Emotional Resilience with Big Five Personality Model Against COVID-19 Pandemic	Sahni S., Kumari S., Pachaury P.	FIIB Business Review	0	0	0
2021	COVID-19 and the immediate impact on young people and employment in Australia: A gendered analysis	Churchill B.	Gender, Work and Organization	0	3	3
2021	Patients' perceptions of teleconsultation during COVID-19: A cross-national study	Baudier P., Kondrateva G., Ammi C., Chang V., Schiavone F.	Technological Forecasting and Social Change	0	3	3
2021	Problematic use of ICTS in trainee teachers during COVID-19: A sex-based analysis	Magana E.C., Ariza A.C., Palmero J.R., Rivas E.S.	Contemporary Educational Technology	0	0	0
2021	Trust in Government and Social Isolation during the Covid-19 Pandemic: Evidence from Brazil	da Silva C.R.M., Aquino C.V.M.G., Oliveira L.V.C., Beserra E.P., Romero C.B.A.	International Journal of Public Administration	0	0	0
2021	Information seeking, personal experiences, and their association with COVID-19 risk perceptions: demographic and occupational inequalities	Brown R., Coventry L., Pepper G.	Journal of Risk Research	0	0	0
2021	COVID-19 risk perception: a longitudinal analysis of its predictors and associations with health protective behaviours in the United Kingdom	Schneider C.R., Dryhurst S., Kerr J., Freeman A.L.J., Recchia G., Spiegelhalter D., van der Linden S.	Journal of Risk Research	0	0	0
2021	Leading the Fight Against the Pandemic: Does Gender Really Matter?	Garikipati S., Kambhampati U.	Feminist Economics	0	1	1
2021	COVID-19 and the Pivotal role of Grandparents: Childcare and income Support in the UK and South Africa	Cantillon S., Moore E., Teasdale N.	Feminist Economics	0	3	3
2021	Working and Caring at Home: Gender Differences in the Effects of Covid-19 on Paid and Unpaid Labor in Australia	Craig L., Churchill B.	Feminist Economics	0	4	4
2021	The effect of coronavirus disease-19 (COVID-19) risk perception on behavioural intention towards 'untact' tourism in South Korea during the first wave of the pandemic (March 2020)	Bae S.Y., Chang P.-J.	Current Issues in Tourism	1	38	39
2021	Reflections on front-line medical work during COVID-19 and the embodiment of risk	Yarrow E., Pagan V.	Gender, Work and Organization	2	5	7
2020	Gender equality and public policy during COVID-19	Profeta P.	CESifo Economic Studies	0	0	0
2020	Gender Equality and Public Policy	Profeta P.	CESifo Forum	0	0	0
2020	Working from Home and COVID-19: The Chances and Risks for Gender Gaps	Arntz M., Ben Yahmed S., Berlingieri F.	Intereconomics	0	3	3

Continued on following page

Table 2. Continued

Publ. Year	Document Title	Authors	Journal Title	2020	2021	total
				7	113	120
2020	Who Wears a Mask? Gender Differences in Risk Behaviors in the Covid-19 Early Days in Taiwan	Chuang Y., Chung-En Liu J.	Economics Bulletin	0	2	2
2020	Disparate disruptions: Intersectional COVID-19 employment effects by age, gender, education, and race/ethnicity	Moen P., Pedtke J.H., Flood S.	Work, Aging and Retirement	0	8	8
2020	Moonlighting to survive in a pandemic: multiple motives and gender differences in Ghana	Asravor R.K.	International Journal of Development Issues	0	0	0
2020	Covid-19, gender inequality, and the responsibility of the state	Fortier N.	International Journal of Wellbeing	1	3	4

Source: Own Development based over VOSviewer and Scopus collected data

One of the hottest topics nowadays is the COVID or pandemic effects. From this additional restriction (gender, risk, COVID), we can find 25 published articles between 2020 and 2021. Table 2 summarizes the number of citations of these recent articles, where self-citations of all authors are excluded. This time, the h-index = 6 (meaning that of the 25 documents considered for the h-index, 6 have been cited at least 6 times).

In Figure 11 we register the keywords of the 25 articles identified in Table 2. From this analysis, several important findings may be highlighted. First of all, there is ample scope for a deeper understanding of the relationship between gender effects, risk management, firm performance, risk behavior, sustainability, corporate social responsibility, and perceptions. The pandemic recently lived highlights the potential for further enhancing research in GD and FR. Besides, there is reported evidence in the literature as to specific issues that still emerge to require exploration. For example, gender and SMEs. This field's knowledge grew exponentially during the last decade (Nguyen et al., 2021). The authors identify three major research lines: "Women's challenges and opportunities in the family business", "Gender diversity in the family business corporate board", and "Gender and family SMEs management." The temporal co-word analysis performed by Nguyen et al. (2021) reveals that "Gender diversity in the family business corporate board" is the latest research line to which attention has been devoted.

Moreover, we would as well point out the need to develop bibliometric indicators to measure women's contribution to financial risk, in their multiple areas. It has well seemed that a lot more needs to be done in the financial sector, especially in bank risk management and its relationship with gender issues. There is still an imbalance between the methodologies employed, and data gathering seems to be one of the main issues pointed out in the literature. Additionally, although research activity onboard diversity occurs globally, a lack of collaboration exists across country lines, especially between authors of developed and developing countries as also pointed out by Baker et al. (2020).

Figure 11. VOSviewer keywords (25 articles; 2020-June2021) – Gender, Risk, COVID
Source: Own Development based over VOSviewer and Scopus collected data

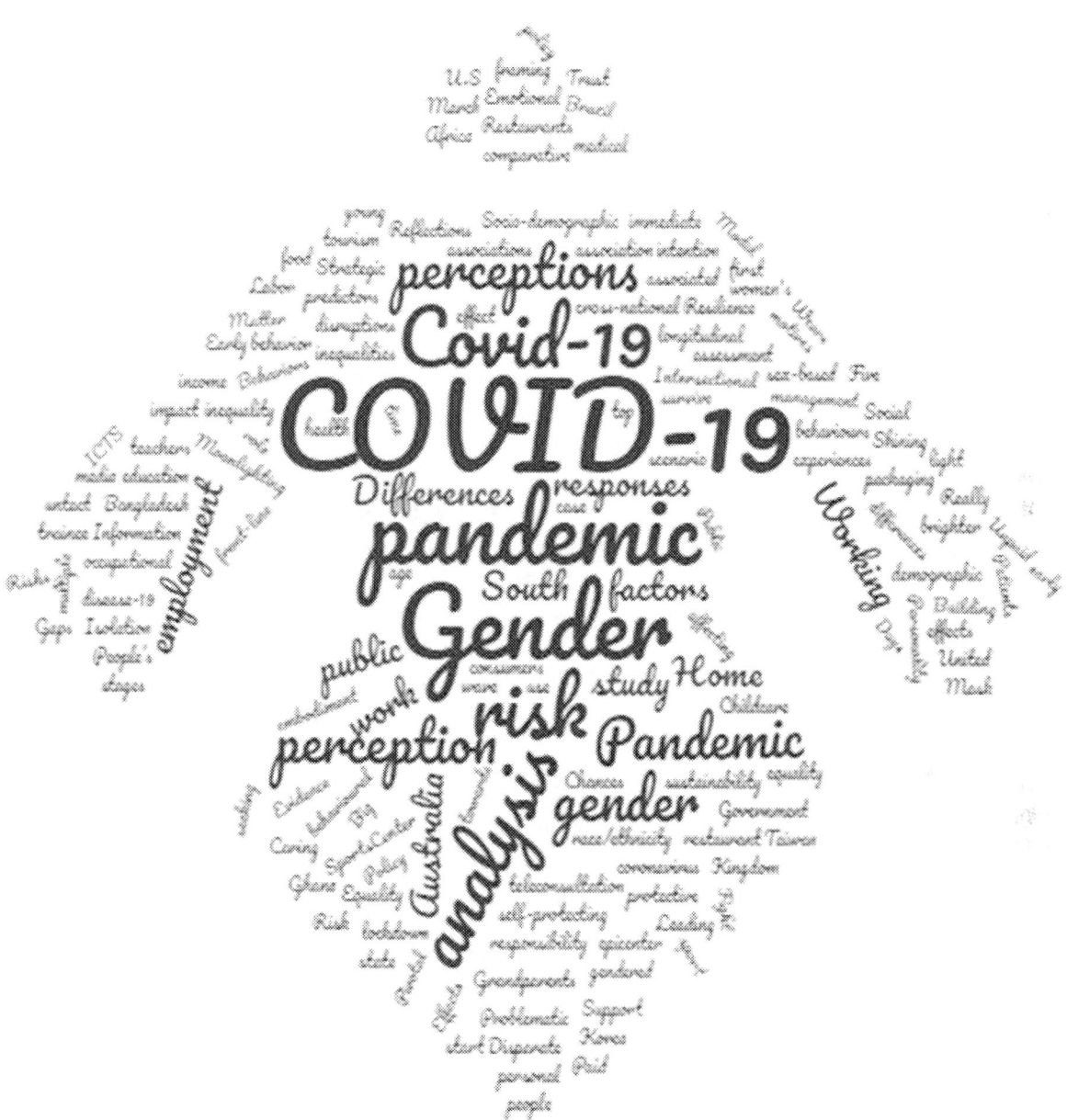

More research relating to board diversity, gender diversity, and financial risk is still necessary as well as studies relying on sociodemographic data like age, nationality, ethnicity, education, literacy (in its three dimensions: knowledge, behavior, and attitude), professional background, and cognition. As well, there is still a lack of regional studies analyzing the relationship between GD and FR, as joint and separate sector analysis, for individual and comparison purposes, is also in need. Previously, it is also mentioned the need to focus on special groups of firms like SMEs (Nguyen et al., 2021). Family firms are also in need of research, at least concerning the GD-FR relationship. An appropriate theoretical background is also necessary, and a lack of academic collaboration could impede the flow of information, especially between developing and developed countries/regions. The culture within the firm (country) can also be an interesting demographic and geographic element to be included in the analysis of GD and FR, as well as cognitive diversity could promote or impel GD, and solve or reduce many of the problems related to risk. Especially at the cognitive diversity level, Baker et al. (2020) point to it as an important topic.

CONCLUSION

FR consists of the possibility that a firm's cash flow will prove to be inadequate to meet its obligations, and is related to the odds of losing money, which can result in the loss of capital to interested parties.

Corporate governance is a system that provides instructions to protect all the firms' stakeholders. According to the literature, one of the corporate governance characteristics, gender diversity, has a significant effect on several types of firm's financial risk, namely the disclosure risk and the risk of failure, as well as on firm's performance. In addition, there is evidence that gender diversity affects accounting conservatism.

Based on the evidence that gender diversity contributes significantly to financial risk, this study contributes to a better understanding of whether gender diversity influences the firm's financial risk. To do so, the authors conduct a bibliometric analysis, describing the evolutional research studies published in digital libraries, between 2010 and June 2021, making a point of situation in what concerns the current state-of-the-art.

The publications on these subjects are still in their infancy, leaving space for new developments in research terms. In addition, European markets exploration is still in deeper need of analysis. Further pointed directions for future research are as well derived from the bibliometric search here presented.

Gender diversity can be used as a tool for a firm's risk control. A deeper understanding of corporate governance beyond the audit committees, the institutional and market pressures, legal environments, macroeconomic conditions, and many others are still in need of research or deserve more understanding. Relating these two themes with the economic value of the firm is still in its infancy even though much research has emerged in recent years, especially that related to COVID effects and the pandemic impacts.

This study has some limitations, namely the fact that the Bibliometric analysis is performed based solely on Scopus and other bibliometric sources could as well be used. More future research lines could have been as well highlighted but it was evidenced during the discussion of results that future works could rely on other sociodemographic diversity issues besides gender, as well as deeper analysis concerning ESG, CSR, and GD-FR analysis is still needed.

REFERENCES

Abdullah, S. (2012). Risk Management via Takaful from a Perspective of Maqasid of Shariah. *Procedia: Social and Behavioral Sciences*, *65*(3), 535–541. doi:10.1016/j.sbspro.2012.11.161

Adams, R. B., & Ferreira, D. (2007). A theory of friendly boards. *The Journal of Finance*, *62*(1), 217–250. doi:10.1111/j.1540-6261.2007.01206.x

Ahern, K. R., & Dittmar, A. K. (2012). The changing of the boards: The impact on firm valuation of mandated female board representation. *The Quarterly Journal of Economics, 127*(1), 137–197. doi:10.1093/qje/qjr049

Altman, E. I. (1968). Financial ratios, discriminant analysis and the prediction of corporate bankruptcy. *The Journal of Finance, 23*(4), 589–609. doi:10.1111/j.1540-6261.1968.tb00843.x

Arayssi, M., Dah, M., & Jizi, M. (2016). Women on boards, sustainability reporting and firm performance. *Sustainability Accounting. Management and Policy Journal, 7*(3), 376–401.

Arntz, M., Ben Yahmed, S., & Berlingieri, F. (2020). Working from home and COVID-19: The chances and risks for gender gaps. *Inter Economics, 55*(6), 381–386. doi:10.100710272-020-0938-5 PMID:33281218

Asravor, R. K. (2020). Moonlighting to survive in a pandemic: Multiple motives and gender differences in ghana. *International Journal of Development Issues, 20*(2), 243–257. doi:10.1108/IJDI-08-2020-0180

Bae, S. Y., & Chang, P. (2021). The effect of coronavirus disease-19 (COVID-19) risk perception on behavioural intention towards 'untact' tourism in south korea during the first wave of the pandemic (march 2020). *Current Issues in Tourism, 24*(7), 1017–1035. doi:10.1080/13683500.2020.1798895

Baker, H. K., Pandey, N., Kumar, S., & Haldar, A. (2020). A bibliometric analysis of board diversity: Current status, development, and future research directions. *Journal of Business Research, 108*, 232–246. doi:10.1016/j.jbusres.2019.11.025

Barber, B., & Odean, T. (2001). Boys will be boys: Gender, overconfidence and common stock investment. *The Quarterly Journal of Economics, 116*(1), 261–292. doi:10.1162/003355301556400

Bart, C., & McQueen, G. (2013). Why women make better directors. *International Journal of Business Governance and Ethics, 8*(1), 93–99. doi:10.1504/IJBGE.2013.052743

Baudier, P., Kondrateva, G., Ammi, C., Chang, V., & Schiavone, F. (2021). Patients' perceptions of teleconsultation during COVID-19: A cross-national study. *Technological Forecasting and Social Change, 163*, 120510. Advance online publication. doi:10.1016/j.techfore.2020.120510 PMID:33318716

Bell, T. R. (2021). SportsCenter: A case study of media framing U.S. sport as the COVID-19 epicenter. *International Journal of Sport Communication, 14*(2), 298–317. doi:10.1123/ijsc.2020-0258

Berger, A. N., Kick, T., & Schaeck, K. (2014). Executive board composition and bank risk taking. *Journal of Corporate Finance, 28*, 48–65. doi:10.1016/j.jcorpfin.2013.11.006

Bernile, G., Bhagwat, V., & Yonker, S. (2018). Board diversity, firm risk, and corporate policies. *Journal of Financial Economics, 127*(3), 588–612. doi:10.1016/j.jfineco.2017.12.009

Brown, R., Coventry, L., & Pepper, G. (2021). Information seeking, personal experiences, and their association with COVID-19 risk perceptions: Demographic and occupational inequalities. *Journal of Risk Research, 24*(3-4), 506–520. doi:10.1080/13669877.2021.1908403

Bufarwa, I. M., Elamer, A. A., Ntim, C. G., & AlHares, A. (2020). Gender diversity, corporate governance and financial risk disclosure in the UK. *International Journal of Law and Management, 62*(6), 521–538. doi:10.1108/IJLMA-10-2018-0245

Byrd, K., Her, E., Fan, A., Almanza, B., Liu, Y., & Leitch, S. (2021). Restaurants and COVID-19: What are consumers' risk perceptions about restaurant food and its packaging during the pandemic? *International Journal of Hospitality Management, 94*, 102821. Advance online publication. doi:10.1016/j.ijhm.2020.102821 PMID:34866742

Byrnes, J. P., Miller, D. C., & Schafer, W. D. (1999). Gender differences in risk taking: A meta-analysis. *Psychological Bulletin, 125*(3), 367–383. doi:10.1037/0033-2909.125.3.367

Cantillon, S., Moore, E., & Teasdale, N. (2021). COVID-19 and the pivotal role of grandparents: Childcare and income support in the UK and south africa. *Feminist Economics, 27*(1-2), 188–202. doi:10.1080/13545701.2020.1860246

Cho, E., Okafor, C., Ujah, N., & Zhang, L. (2021). Executives' gender-diversity, education, and firm's bankruptcy risk: Evidence from China. *Journal of Behavioral and Experimental Finance, 30*, 100500. doi:10.1016/j.jbef.2021.100500

Chuang, Y., & Chung-En Liu, J. (2020). Who wears a mask? gender differences in risk behaviors in the covid-19 early days in taiwan. *Economic Bulletin, 40*(4), 2619–2627. www.scopus.com

Churchill, B. (2021). COVID-19 and the immediate impact on young people and employment in australia: A gendered analysis. *Gender, Work and Organization, 28*(2), 783–794. doi:10.1111/gwao.12563 PMID:33230375

Craig, L., & Churchill, B. (2021). Working and caring at home: Gender differences in the effects of covid-19 on paid and unpaid labor in australia. *Feminist Economics, 27*(1-2), 310–326. doi:10.1080/13545701.2020.1831039

Croson, R., & Gneezy, U. (2009). Gender differences in preferences. *Journal of Economic Literature, 47*(2), 1–27. doi:10.1257/jel.47.2.448

da Silva, C. R. M., Aquino, C. V. M. G., Oliveira, L. V. C., Beserra, E. P., & Romero, C. B. A. (2021). Trust in government and social isolation during the covid-19 pandemic: Evidence from brazil. *International Journal of Public Administration, 44*(11-12), 974–983. doi:10.1080/01900692.2021.1920611

Demey, D., Berrington, A., Evandrou, M., & Falkingham, J. (2013). Pathways into living alone in midlife: Diversity and policy implications. *Advances in Life Course Research, 18*(3), 161–174. doi:10.1016/j.alcr.2013.02.001 PMID:24796556

Faccio, M., Marchica, M. T., & Mura, R. (2016). CEO gender, corporate risk-taking, and the efficiency of capital allocation. *Journal of Corporate Finance, 39*, 193–209. doi:10.1016/j.jcorpfin.2016.02.008

Filippin, A., & Crosetto, P. (2016). A reconsideration of gender differences in risk attitudes. *Management Science, 62*(11), 3138–3160. doi:10.1287/mnsc.2015.2294

Fortier, N. (2020). Covid-19, gender inequality, and the responsibility of the state. *International Journal of Wellbeing, 10*(3), 77–93. doi:10.5502/ijw.v10i3.1305

Francoeur, C., Labelle, R., & Sinclair-Desgagné, B. (2008). Gender diversity in corporate governance and top management. *Journal of Business Ethics, 81*(1), 83–95. doi:10.100710551-007-9482-5

Garikipati, S., & Kambhampati, U. (2021). Leading the fight against the pandemic: Does gender really matter? *Feminist Economics*, *27*(1-2), 401–418. doi:10.1080/13545701.2021.1874614

Girling, P. (2013). *Operational risk management: a complete guide to a successful operational risk framework*. Wiley. doi:10.1002/9781118755754

Haque, F. (2017). The effects of board characteristics and sustainable compensation policy on carbon performance of UK firms. *The British Accounting Review*, *49*(3), 347–364. doi:10.1016/j.bar.2017.01.001

Hirsch, J. E. (2005). An index to quantify an individual's scientific research output. *Proceedings of the National Academy of Sciences of the United States of America*, *102*(46), 16569–16572. doi:10.1073/pnas.0507655102 PMID:16275915

Ho, S. S. M., Li, A. Y., Tam, K., & Zhang, F. (2015). CEO Gender, Ethical Leadership, and Accounting Conservatism. *Journal of Business Ethics*, *127*(2), 351–370. doi:10.100710551-013-2044-0

Hock-Doepgen, M., Clauss, T., Kraus, S., & Cheng, C.-F. (2021). Knowledge management capabilities and organizational risk-taking for business model innovation in SMEs. *Journal of Business Research*, *130*, 683–697. doi:10.1016/j.jbusres.2019.12.001

Huang, J., & Kisgen, D. J. (2013). Gender and Corporate Finance: Are Male Executives Overconfident Relative to Female Executives? *Journal of Financial Economics*, *108*(3), 822–839. doi:10.1016/j.jfineco.2012.12.005

Hurley, D., & Choudhary, A. (2020). Role of gender and corporate risk taking. *Corporate Governance*, *20*(3), 383–399. doi:10.1108/CG-10-2018-0313

Huse, M., & Solberg, A. G. (2006). Gender-related boardroom dynamics: How scandinavian women make and can make contributions on corporate boards. *Women in Management Review*, *21*(1), 113–130. doi:10.1108/09649420610650693

Hutchinson, M., Mack, J., & Plastow, K. (2015). Who selects the 'right' directors? An examination of the association between board selection, gender diversity and outcomes. *Accounting and Finance*, *55*(4), 1071–1103. doi:10.1111/acfi.12082

Jane Lenard, M., Yu, B., Anne York, E., & Wu, S. (2014). Impact of board gender diversity on firm risk. *Managerial Finance*, *40*(8), 787–803. doi:10.1108/MF-06-2013-0164

Jeong, S., & Harrison, D. A. (2017). Glass breaking, strategy making, and value creating: Meta analytic outcomes of women as CEOs and TMT members. *Academy of Management Journal*, *60*(4), 1219–1252. doi:10.5465/amj.2014.0716

Jianakoplos, N. A., & Bernasek, A. (1998). Are women more risk averse? *Economic Inquiry*, *36*(4), 620–630. doi:10.1111/j.1465-7295.1998.tb01740.x

Jokhadze, V., & Schmidt, W. M. (2020). Measuring model risk in financial risk management and pricing. *International Journal of Theoretical and Applied Finance*, *23*(02), 2050012. Advance online publication. doi:10.1142/S0219024920500120

Julizaerma, M. K., & Sori, Z. M. (2012). Gender diversity in the boardroom and firm performance of Malaysian public listed companies. *Procedia: Social and Behavioral Sciences*, *65*(1), 1077–1085. doi:10.1016/j.sbspro.2012.11.374

Kuo, Y.-F., Lin, Y.-M., & Chien, H.-F. (2021). Corporate social responsibility, enterprise risk management, and real earnings management: Evidence from managerial confidence. *Finance Research Letters*, *41*, 101805. doi:10.1016/j.frl.2020.101805

L'Haridon, O., & Vieider, F. M. (2019). All over the map: A worldwide comparison of risk preferences. *Quantitative Economics*, *10*, 185–215. doi:10.3982/QE898

Lee, C.-C., Lee, C.-C., & Xiao, S. (2021). Policy-related risk and corporate financing behavior: Evidence from China's listed companies. *Economic Modelling*, *94*, 539–547. doi:10.1016/j.econmod.2020.01.022

Lee, C.-C., & Wang, C.-W. (2021). Firms' cash reserve, financial constraint, and geopolitical risk. *Pacific-Basin Finance Journal*, *65*, 101480. doi:10.1016/j.pacfin.2020.101480

Lenard, M. J., Yu, B., York, E. A., & Wu, S. (2014). Impact of board gender diversity on firm risk. *Managerial Finance*, *40*(8), 787–803. doi:10.1108/MF-06-2013-0164

Li, Y., & Zeng, Y. (2019). The impact of top executive gender on asset prices: Evidence from stock price crash risk. *Journal of Corporate Finance*, *58*, 528–550. doi:10.1016/j.jcorpfin.2019.07.005

Linsley, P. M., & Shrives, P. J. (2006). Risk Reporting: A Study of Risk Disclosure in the Annual Reports of UK Companies. *Journal The British Accounting Review*, *38*(4), 387–404. doi:10.1016/j.bar.2006.05.002

Loukil, N., & Yousfi, O. (2016). Does gender diversity on corporate boards increase risk-taking? *Canadian Journal of Administrative Sciences*, *33*(1), 66–81. doi:10.1002/cjas.1326

Magaña, E. C., Ariza, A. C., Palmero, J. R., & Rivas, E. S. (2021). Problematic use of ICTS in trainee teachers during COVID-19: A sex-based analysis. *Contemporary Educational Technology*, *13*(4), ep314. Advance online publication. doi:10.30935/cedtech/10988

Mínguez-Vera, A., & Martin, A. (2011). Gender and management on spanish SMEs: An empirical analysis. *International Journal of Human Resource Management*, *22*(14), 2852–2873. doi:10.1080/09585192.2011.599948

Moen, P., Pedtke, J. H., & Flood, S. (2020). Disparate disruptions: Intersectional COVID-19 employment effects by age, gender, education, and race/ethnicity. *Work, Aging and Retirement*, *6*(4), 207–228. doi:10.1093/workar/waaa013 PMID:33214905

Muller-Kahle, M. I., & Lewellyn, K. B. (2011). Did Board Configuration Matter? The Case of US Subprime Lenders. *Corporate Governance*, *19*(5), 405–417. doi:10.1111/j.1467-8683.2011.00871.x

Ng'ang'a, P. N., Jayasinghe, G., Kimani, V., Shililu, J., Kabutha, C., Kabuage, L., Githure, J., & Mutero, C. (2009). Bed net use and associated factors in a rice farming community in Central Kenya. *Malaria Journal*, *8*(1), 64. doi:10.1186/1475-2875-8-64 PMID:19371407

Nguyen, M.-H., Nguyen, H.T.T., Le, T.-T., Luong, A.-P. & Vuong, Q.-H. (2021), Gender issues in family business research: A bibliometric scoping review. *Journal of Asian Business and Economic Studies*. ahead-of-print. . doi:10.1108/JABES-01-2021-0014

Olsen, R. A., & Cox, C. M. (2001). The influence of gender on the perception and response to investment risk: The case of professional investors. *The Journal of Psychology and Financial Markets*, 2(1), 29–36. doi:10.1207/S15327760JPFM0201_3

Papageorge, N. W., Zahn, M. V., Belot, M., van den Broek-Altenburg, E., Choi, S., Jamison, J. C., & Tripodi, E. (2021). Socio-demographic factors associated with self-protecting behavior during the covid-19 pandemic. *Journal of Population Economics*, 34(2), 691–738. doi:10.100700148-020-00818-x PMID:33462529

Profeta, P. (2020). Gender equality and public policy during COVID-19. *CESifo Economic Studies*, 66(4), 365–375. doi:10.1093/cesifo/ifaa018 PMID:34191928

Profeta, P. (2020). Gender equality and public policy. *CESifo Forum*, 21(4), 37-40. Retrieved from www.scopus.com

Putri, A., Bunga, M., & Rochman, E. (2021). Financial Risk Disclosure and Corporate Governance: Empirical Evidence on Banking Companies in Indonesian Stock Exchange. *Advances in Economics, Business and Management Research*, 161, 32–39.

Rost, K., & Osterloh, M. (2010). Opening the black box of upper echelons: Drivers of poor information processing during the financial crisis. *Corporate Governance*, 18(3), 212–233. doi:10.1111/j.1467-8683.2010.00796.x

Saeed, A., Mukarram, S. S., & Belghitar, Y. (2021). Read between the lines: Board gender diversity, family ownership, and risk-taking in Indian high-tech firms. *International Journal of Finance & Economics*, 26(1), 185–207. doi:10.1002/ijfe.1784

Saggar, R., & Singh, B. (2017). Corporate governance and risk reporting: Indian evidence. *Managerial Auditing Journal*, 32(4-5), 378–405. doi:10.1108/MAJ-03-2016-1341

Sahni, S., Kumari, S., & Pachaury, P. (2021). Building emotional resilience with big five personality model against COVID-19 pandemic. *FIIB Business Review*, 10(1), 39–51. doi:10.1177/2319714520954559

Salomons, R., & Grootveld, H. (2003). The equity risk premium: Emerging vs. developed markets. *Emerging Markets Review*, 4(2), 121–144. doi:10.1016/S1566-0141(03)00024-4

Schneider, C. R., Dryhurst, S., Kerr, J., Freeman, A. L. J., Recchia, G., Spiegelhalter, D., & van der Linden, S. (2021). COVID-19 risk perception: A longitudinal analysis of its predictors and associations with health protective behaviours in the united kingdom. *Journal of Risk Research*, 24(3-4), 294–313. doi:10.1080/13669877.2021.1890637

Schultheiss, D. E. (2021). Shining the light on women's work, this time brighter: Let's start at the top. *Journal of Vocational Behavior*, 126, 103558. Advance online publication. doi:10.1016/j.jvb.2021.103558

Shahab, Y., Ntim, C. G., Chengang, Y., Ullah, F., & Fosu, S. (2018). Environmental policy, environmental performance, and financial distress in China: Do top management team characteristics matter? *Business Strategy and the Environment*, *27*(8), 1635–1652. doi:10.1002/bse.2229

Shammi, M., Bodrud-Doza, M., Islam, A. R. M. T., & Rahman, M. M. (2021). Strategic assessment of COVID-19 pandemic in bangladesh: Comparative lockdown scenario analysis, public perception, and management for sustainability. *Environment, Development and Sustainability*, *23*(4), 6148–6191. doi:10.100710668-020-00867-y PMID:32837281

Sila, V., Gonzalez, A., & Hagendorff, J. (2016). Women on board: Does boardroom gender diversity affect firm risk? *Journal of Corporate Finance*, *36*, 26–53. doi:10.1016/j.jcorpfin.2015.10.003

Singh, V. S., Terjesen, S., & Vinnicombe, S. (2008). Newly appointed directors in the boardroom: How do women and men differ? *European Management Journal*, *2*(3), 48–58. doi:10.1016/j.emj.2007.10.002

Startiene, G., & Remeikiene, R. (2009). The influence of demographical factors on the interaction between entrepreneurship and unemployment. *The Engineering Economist*, *4*(64), 60–70.

von Wagner, C., Baio, G., Raine, R., Snowball, J., Morris, S., Atkin, W., Obichere, A., Handley, G., Logan, R. F., Rainbow, S., Smith, S., Halloran, S., & Wardle, J. (2011). Inequalities in participation in an organized national colorectal cancer screening programme: Results from the first 2.6 million invitations in England. *International Journal of Epidemiology*, *40*(3), 712–718. doi:10.1093/ije/dyr008 PMID:21330344

Wen, F., Li, C., Sha, H., & Shao, L. (2021). How does economic policy uncertainty affect corporate risk-taking? Evidence from China. *Finance Research Letters*, *41*, 101840. doi:10.1016/j.frl.2020.101840

Werbel, J. D., & Danes, S. M. (2010). Work family conflict in new business ventures: The moderating effects of spousal commitment to the new business venture. *Journal of Small Business Management*, *48*(3), 421–440. doi:10.1111/j.1540-627X.2010.00301.x

Yarrow, E., & Pagan, V. (2021). Reflections on front-line medical work during COVID-19 and the embodiment of risk. *Gender, Work and Organization*, *28*(S1), 89–100. doi:10.1111/gwao.12505 PMID:32837018

Zhang, J. (2021). People's responses to the COVID-19 pandemic during its early stages and factors affecting those responses. *Humanities and Social Sciences Communications*, *8*(1), 37. Advance online publication. doi:10.105741599-021-00720-1

KEY TERMS AND DEFINITIONS

Bibliometric Analysis: Is the attempt to quantitatively assess the academic quality of journals or authors by statistical methods such as citation rates.

Content Analysis: Is the study of documents and communication artifacts, which might be texts of various formats, pictures, audio, or video. Social scientists use content analysis to examine patterns in communication in a replicable and systematic manner.

Financial Risk: Is the possibility of losing money on an investment. Financial risk can result in the loss of capital to interested parties. It includes several types of risk, such as credit risk, liquidity risk, and operational risk.

Gender Diversity: Consists of a fair and equitable representation of people of different genders, usually referred to as an equitable ratio of men and women. Gender diversity on corporate boards studies and promotes gender diversity in fields traditionally dominated by men. It helps firms attracting and retaining talented women, being especially relevant as more women join the labor force all over the world.

Measurement: Is the numerical quantitation of the attributes of an object or event, which can be used to compare with other objects or events. The scope and application of measurement are dependent on the context and discipline.

Chapter 4
Gender Differences in Risk Tolerance:
New Evidence From a Survey of Postgraduate Students

Júlio Lobão
University of Porto, Portugal

ABSTRACT

In this chapter, the author examines the influence of gender on financial risk tolerance. The risk tolerance is assessed by the instrument developed by Grable and Lytton in a sample that includes 272 postgraduate students of the University of Porto (Portugal). The results show that males are significantly more risk-tolerant than females, even after controlling for factors such as the economic status and educational levels of the respondents' parents. The gender differences seem to be essentially driven by a higher proportion of males with high levels of risk tolerance. Moreover, belonging to a household with a high level of annual income contributes to increase the likelihood of exhibiting high levels of risk tolerance. In the total sample, the levels of risk tolerance are lower than those reported in similar studies. Overall, the author documents that there are significant gender differences in financial risk perception.

INTRODUCTION

When dealing with financial decision-making, females are usually regarded as being less risk-tolerant than men. This stereotype carries important implications. For example, Johnson and Powell (1994) argue that the perception that female managers are less risk-tolerant than men is a major explanation for the "glass ceilings" observed in corporate promotion ladders. Thus, statistical discrimination may arise as women tend to be viewed as less able to make the risky decisions that may be necessary for a firm's success. Moreover, as shown by Bajtelsmit and Bernasek (1996) and Roszkowski and Grable (2005), women are likely to be perceived by brokers and financial advisors as more prudent investors and therefore offered investments with lower-risk/lower expected returns.

DOI: 10.4018/978-1-7998-8609-9.ch004

Gender Differences in Risk Tolerance

Is this widespread belief supported by empirical evidence? Although empirical research has found in general that women are, on average, less risk tolerant in their financial decisions than men (e.g., Hawley and Fujii, 1993; Palson, 1996; Jianakoplos and Bernasek, 1998; Byrnes *et al.*, 1999; Grable and Lytton, 2001; Olsen and Cox, 2001; Gibson *et al.*, 2013), these results have been recently challenged (e.g., Nelson, 2015, 2016; Boulu-Reshef *et al.*, 2016; Filippin and Crosetto, 2016; Shropshire *et al.*, 2021).

This ongoing debate motivates the present study, which explores the gender differences in risk perception recurring to a survey administered to 272 Master students of management and finance at the University of Porto (Portugal). To measure the degree of financial risk tolerance of the individuals, the instrument developed by Grable and Lytton (1999) was employed.

The results of this study indicate that women are less risk-tolerant than men, even after controlling by such factors as the economic status and educational level of the respondents' parents. The individuals in the sample exhibited an average score of 26.01 in the risk tolerance scale, which signals that they were less risk-tolerant than those reported by Grable and Lytton (2003). It is also documented that individuals belonging to households with high economic status are more likely to exhibit high levels of risk tolerance.

In the following sections, this chapter reviews the related literature, describes the data and the methodology used in the study, presents the empirical findings, and offers some conclusions.

LITERATURE REVIEW

Risk tolerance can be defined as the level of risk exposure with which an individual is comfortable and that reflects the individual's willingness to accept the negative changes in the value of investment or an adverse outcome that differs from the expected one. Risk tolerance is the inverse of risk aversion, that is, a lower risk tolerance implies a higher risk aversion (Grable and Lytton, 1999; Adhikari and O'Leary, 2011; Gibson *et al.*, 2013).

Existing empirical research on the influence of gender on risk tolerance focus on behavior in three domains: health and physical safety, strategic decision-making in a professional work context, and finance (including investment and gambling).

In general, the empirical evidence indicates that females tend to be more risk-averse than men in the fields of physical health and safety and that that seems to translate into differences in risk behaviors (Barsky *et al.*, 1997; Pacula, 1997; Finucane *et al.*, 2000; Harris *et al.*, 2006; Harrant and Vaillant, 2008).

However, research focused on managerial contexts has not found, in general, significant gender differences in risk attitudes. For example, Maxfield *et al.* (2010) used the results of the Simmons Gender and Risk Survey database to conclude that there is gender neutrality in risk propensity in specific managerial contexts. Moreover, Yordanova and Alexandrova-Boshnakova (2011) applied a survey to a sample of Bulgarian entrepreneurs and found that female and male entrepreneurs have similar risk perceptions. Other authors, such as Masters and Meier (1988), Johnson and Powell (1993), Corman (2001), and Castillo and Cross (2008), among others, report similar results.

Some empirical findings seem to support the claim that women are more risk-averse than men in the financial domain (investment and gambling). In the investment realm, Olsen and Cox (2001) administered a survey to professional investment managers to conclude that women weigh risk attributes more heavily than their male colleagues. Consistent with this result, there is abundant evidence that wealth holdings of non-professional women investors are less risky than those of men of similar economic status (Riley and Chow, 1992; Bajtelsmit *et al.*, 1996; Embrey and Fox, 1997; Hinz *et al.*, 1997; Jianakoplos and Bernasek, 1998; Sundén and Surette, 1998; Hallahan *et al.*, 2004; Faff *et al.*, 2008; Grable *et al.*, 2009; Neelakantan, 2010). In experiments with risky gambles, women tend more strongly to avoid risks than do their male counterparts (Levin *et al.*, 1988; Johnson and Powell, 1994; Powell and Ansic, 1997, 1999; Sarin and Wieland, 2016). Women are also been found to be more risk-sensitive than men in the context of losses (Hanson, 1989; Yates and Stone, 1992; He *et al.*, 2007; Eriksson and Simpson, 2010) and to have lower expectations of enjoyment for risk-taking (Harris *et al.*, 2006). Other studies (e.g., Hawley and Fujii, 1993; Palson, 1996; Jianakoplos and Bernasek, 1998; Byrnes *et al.*, 1999; Grable and Lytton, 2001; Weber *et al.*, 2002; Xie *et al.*, 2003; Garbarino and Strahilevitz, 2004; Eckel and Grossman, 2008; Croson and Gneezy, 2009; Adhikari and O'Leary, 2011; Gibson *et al.*, 2013) corroborate these conclusions.

However, there is some conflicting evidence. For example, Schubert *et al.* (1999) found no gender differences in an experiment in which undergraduates from Swiss universities were confronted with decisions embedded in an investment or insurance context. In addition, Grable and Joo (1999) and Hanna *et al.* (1998) did not find gender to be a significant predictor of financial risk tolerance. Looking at the assets owned by individuals, Zhong and Xiao (1995) report no gender difference in the dollar holding of stocks and Arano *et al.* (2010) conclude that the proportion of stocks held in retirement accounts is not explained by gender. More recently, Fisher and Yao (2017) used a large dataset from the Survey of Consumer Finances to document that the gender differences of financial risk tolerance do not result from gender in and of itself, but rather from the moderating of individuals' net worth. In the same vein, Atkinson *et al.* (2003) argue that differences in behavior misleadingly attributed to gender may be related to factors such as wealth constraints. Thus, the contributions of Atkinson *et al.* (2003) and Fisher and Yao (2017) highlight the importance of controlling the determinants of risk tolerance by the individuals' economic status. Finally, Nelson (2015, 2016) criticizes the existing research on methodological grounds concluding that, in general, "[t]he data do not reveal 'strong evidence' of a 'fundamental' difference in risk preferences [based on gender]" (Nelson, 2015, p. 137).

Regardless of the empirical findings, some literature explains the possible discrepancies in risk tolerance of women and men as the product of biological and evolutionary factors (Zuckerman, 1994; Buss, 1999; White *et al.*, 2007; Coates and Herbert, 2008; Levy, 2015). For example, Sapienza *et al.* (2009) tested the assertion that risk perception has a biological basis concluding that higher levels of testosterone are associated with lower risk aversion among women, but not among men. Other theories emphasize the role played by social and cultural influences in risk-taking (Prince, 1993; Deaux and Ennsuiller, 1994; Barke *et al.*, 1997; Beyer and Bowden, 1997; Meier-Pesti and Goetz, 2005; Booth *et al.*, 2014).

Besides gender, other factors that have been argued to influence risk tolerance are age (Wang and Hanna, 1997; Grable, 2000; Finke and Huston, 2003; Hallahan *et al.*, 2003; Jianakoplos and Bernasek, 2006; Levy, 2015), education (Heliassos and Bertaut, 1995; Boholm, 1998; Sjoberg, 2000; Grable and Joo, 2004; Al-Aimi, 2008) and the economic status of the individuals (Dowling and Staelin, 1994; Grable and Lytton, 1998; Chaulk *et al.*, 2003; Cho and Lee, 2006; Watson and McNaughton, 2007).

DATA AND METHODOLOGY

As mentioned before, this research follows the standard survey method. The questionnaires were administered to students of the Master in Finance and Master in Management at the School of Economics and Management of the University of Porto (FEP) in Portugal. The questionnaire was written in English

– the language in which the referred masters were taught – and was made available in three consecutive academic years (2018/2019, 2019/2020, and 2020/2021).

The choice of finance students as an object of inquiry is not new in the literature. For example, Sjöberg and Engelberg (2009) used a survey with 93 students to conclude that individuals expressed a positive attitude towards risk-taking and gambling behaviors. And Cagle and Baucus (2006) and Friehs and Craig (2008) conducted surveys to Finance students using the responses of 86 individuals and 140 individuals, respectively.

A total of 272 survey responses were gathered, of which 112 (=41.2% of the total) were completed by males and 160 (=58.8%) by females. The survey form which was developed to gather research data is comprised of two parts. In part A of the survey, the respondents were asked a variety of control questions, including their age, chosen major, and their parents' economic status and education level. In part B of the survey, the students were asked to answer the 13-item risk tolerance assessment instrument developed by Grable and Lytton (1999). For reference, the survey used in this study is included in the Appendix to this chapter.

The next step after the gathering of the surveys is the computation of the numerical value in the risk tolerance scale provided by Grable and Lytton (1999). These authors recurred to a principal component factor analysis to develop their scale, being able to extract three relevant constructs: a) investment risk (items 4, 5, 8, 11, and 12), b) risk comfort and experience (items 1, 3, 6, 7 and 13), and c) speculative risk (items 2, 9 and 10). These constructs reflect the multidimensional nature of the financial risk tolerance as emphasized by the authors. The risk tolerance scale varies from zero to 47. Higher values in the scale imply a higher risk tolerance. The external validity of the instrument was assessed by comparing scale scores to the Survey of Consumer Finances risk-assessment item. The validity was confirmed since it was found that individuals who were categorized as having low risk tolerance were, in general, less confident and more likely to avoid making risky financial decisions than those who were categorized in higher risk tolerance categories. In a follow-up study, Grable and Lytton (2003) corroborated their scale's validity showing a significant positive relationship between the scores of risk tolerance measured by the instrument and the level of equity assets owned by individuals. Moreover, lower scale scores were negatively associated with fixed income and cash ownership. Grable and Lytton (1999) and Gilliam *et al.* (2010) show that the abovementioned survey is better at accurately assessing risk tolerance than the single question asked in the context of the Survey of Consumer Finances.

After conducting a bivariate analysis on the differences between the subsamples of male and female respondents, this research explores the results in a multivariate context recurring to the following ordinary least squares regression model:

$$Score\_RiskTolerance = \alpha + \beta_1 Male + \beta_2 Parent\_LowEd \\ + \beta_3 Parent\_HighEd + \beta_4 High\_Income + \beta_5 Low\_Income + \varepsilon$$

where *Score_RiskTolerance* is the variable that reflects the risk tolerance of the individuals included in the sample. *Male* is a binary variable that equals unity if the respondent is male, and zero otherwise. *Parent_LowEd* and *Parent_HighEd* capture the educational level of the respondents' parents. Thus, *Parent_LowEd* is a binary variable that equals unity if neither the respondent's father nor mother holds at least an undergraduate degree, and zero otherwise. *Parent_HighEd* is a binary variable that equals unity if either the respondent's mother or father holds more than an undergraduate degree, and zero otherwise.

High_Income and *Low_Income* are two variables that reflect the economic status of the respondents' parents. Thus, *High_Income* is a binary variable that equals unity if the respondent's parents earned more than 100,000 euros, and zero otherwise. *Low_Income* is a binary variable that equals unity if the respondent's parents earned less than 50,000 euros, and zero otherwise.

Since there is interest in knowing the determinants of exhibiting a high level of risk tolerance, the following logistic model will be applied:

$$Higher\_Tolerance = \alpha + \beta_1 Male + \beta_2 Parent\_LowEd + \beta_3 Parent\_HighEd + \beta_4 High\_Income + \beta_5 Low\_Income + \varepsilon$$

where *Higher_Tolerance* is defined as a binary variable that equals unity if the individual exhibits a high level of risk tolerance (i.e., score above 28), and equals zero otherwise, and the remaining variables have the meaning mentioned above.

EMPIRICAL FINDINGS

Table 1 presents summary statistics for the entire sample, as well as subsamples for the male and female respondents. The data includes 272 responses, of which 112 were from male students and 160 from female students. The mean age of the respondents was 21.67 years. Of the students surveyed, 63% reported having completed their undergraduate degree in the field of Management (this included courses on Management, Finance, and Marketing) and 32% had obtained a degree in Economics. Almost half of the individuals (46%) report having a mother with at least an undergraduate degree. This figure is somewhat similar in the case of the respondents' fathers. The individuals whose parents hold an undergraduate degree are about 30%. For about one-third of the individuals, neither the father nor the mother holds at least an undergraduate degree, but in 21% of the cases at least one of the parents holds more than an undergraduate degree. The vast majority of students (81%) reported having parents who earned less than 50,000 euros in annual income. Only 5% of respondents indicate having parents who earned more than 100,000 euros per year.

Table 1 presents the summary statistics for the whole sample, as well as subsamples segmented by gender. The final column presents the p-values from associated difference tests. The z-test was used to assess the statistical significance of the difference between the proportions of respondents in the two subsamples. The t-test was used to assess the statistical significance of the difference in the mean age of the respondents of the two subsamples. Age represents the mean age of the respondents. Economics (Management) is the proportion of respondents with a major in the field of Economics (Management, Finance or Marketing). Others stand for the percentage of respondents with majors in other fields of study. Dad_CollPlus (Mom_CollPlus) is the proportion of respondents whose father (mother) holds at least an undergraduate degree. Dad_Grad (Mom_Grad) is the proportion of respondents whose father (mother) holds a graduate degree. Parent_LowEd is the proportion of respondents in which neither their father nor mother holds at least an undergraduate degree. Parent_HighEd is the proportion of respondents in which either their father or mother holds more than an undergraduate degree. High_Income is the proportion of respondents whose parents earned more than 100,000 euros. Low_Income is the proportion of respondents whose parents earned less than 50,000 euros. ** and *** represent significance at the 5% and 1% levels, respectively.

Table 1. Summary statistics

	Total	Male	Female	p-value
N	272	112	160	-
Age	21.67	21.93	21.46	0.1027
Economics	0.32	0.40	0.26	0.0111**
Management (including Finance and Marketing)	0.63	0.54	0.70	0.0089***
Others	0.05	0.05	0.04	0.7183
Dad_CollPlus	0.41	0.43	0.39	0.5382
Mom_CollPlus	0.46	0.45	0.47	0.7519
Dad_Grad	0.26	0.28	0.25	0.6839
Mom_Grad	0.30	0.30	0.30	0.9891
Parent_LowEd	0.33	0.32	0.34	0.7010
Parent_HighEd	0.21	0.21	0.22	0.7907
High_Income	0.05	0.06	0.04	0.3618
Low_Income	0.81	0.76	0.83	0.1358

The differences between the male and female subsamples are, in general, not significant at conventional levels of statistical significance, which indicates that the two groups are relatively similar in their socio-economic characteristics. The exception relates to the chosen major: 70% of females obtained a degree in Management, Finance or Marketing while for men this figure was only 54%. Although statistically significant, it is likely that this difference does not translate into dissimilar levels of risk tolerance since the literature, as far as the author knows, does not predict a connection between having a major in these two fields of study (Management vs. Economics) and individual decisions.

The examination of the data proceeds with Table 2 which presents the bivariate analyses. Similar to Table 1, the data is reported in total as well by male and female subsamples.

Table 2 presents the bivariate analysis for the whole sample, as well as subsamples segmented by male and female respondents. The final column presents the p-values from associated difference tests. The z-test was used to assess the statistical significance of the difference between the proportions of respondents in the two subsamples. The t-test was used to assess the statistical significance of the difference in the mean score of risk tolerance in each of the two subsamples. Score_RiskTolerance is the mean risk tolerance score observed in the whole sample and in the two subsamples of respondents. Low_Tolerance represents the proportion of respondents with low-risk tolerance (i.e., scores lower or equal to 18) in the sample and in the two subsamples. BelowAv_Tolerance represents the proportion of respondents with below-average risk tolerance (i.e., scores between 19 and 22) in the sample and in the two subsamples. Av_Tolerance represents the proportion of respondents with average risk tolerance (i.e., scores between 23 and 28) in the sample and in the two subsamples. AboveAv_Tolerance represents the proportion of respondents with above-average risk tolerance (i.e., scores between 29 and 32) in the sample and in the two subsamples. High_Tolerance represents the proportion of respondents with a high level of risk tolerance (i.e., scores higher or equal to 33) in the sample and in the two subsamples. ** and *** represent significance at the 5% and 1% levels, respectively.

Table 2. Bivariate analyses

	Total	Male	Female	p-value
Score_RiskTolerance	26.01	26.70	25.53	0.0286**
Low_Tolerance (0-18)	0.03	0.04	0.02	0.6004
BelowAv_Tolerance (19-22)	0.18	0.18	0.17	0.9208
Av_Tolerance (23-28)	0.53	0.44	0.59	0.0130**
AboveAv_Tolerance (29-32)	0.18	0.19	0.17	0.7735
High_Tolerance (33-47)	0.09	0.16	0.04	0.0004***

The average score (*Score_RiskTolerance*) in the sample is 26.01 with a standard deviation of 4.16. The values reported by Grable and Lytton (2003) in their research are 28.83 and 4.49, respectively, which suggests that the individuals in the sample of the current study were relatively less risk-tolerant. Male individuals seem to be more tolerant to risk than women since the difference in the values obtained in the score is shown to be significantly different at the 5% level.

The breakdown of results by the risk tolerance categories that was established - low tolerance for risk (score between 0 and 18), below-average tolerance for risk (score between 19 and 22), moderate/average tolerance for risk (score between 23 and 28), above-average tolerance (score between 29 and 32) and a high tolerance for risk (score higher than 32) - allows one to understand the drivers of the differential score. The evidence suggests that much of the gender difference in the risk tolerance scores are driven by the percentage of individuals who exhibit a higher level of risk tolerance (scores higher than 32). While the proportion of the male respondents in this situation is 16%, the respective proportion in the female subsample is just 4%. This difference is statistically significant at the 1% significance level. In addition, the vast majority of female respondents (59%) are in the moderate risk tolerance category while the respective proportion for the male respondents is only 44%. This difference is also statistically significant at the conventional levels of significance.

Figure 1 exhibits the difference between the risk tolerance scores of males and females in each of the percentiles of the respective subsamples.

Figure 1. Difference between the risk tolerance scores of males and females in each percentile of the respective subsamples

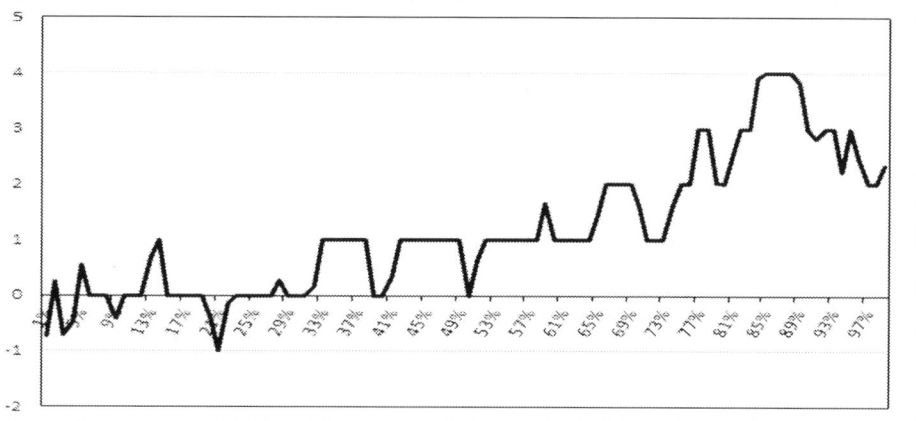

It is possible to observe that the differences in risk tolerance scores between men and women are, in general, positive, which corroborates the idea that men are relatively more tolerant to risk. However, and most importantly, the data indicates that these differences are not evenly distributed across the distribution of the risk tolerance indicator. In fact, the difference appears to widen as one approaches the higher-end of the quantile spectrum. For example, the difference in the indicator in the 87th percentile between the two samples indicates that in this percentile the level of risk tolerance for male respondents is four points higher than that observed at that same point in the distribution of female respondents. This means that there is a group of very risk-tolerant males that represents a significantly higher proportion in the respective subsample than that observed in the subsample of female respondents.

The existence of a greater proportion of male individuals with a high level of risk tolerance suggests that it is important to investigate the determinants of being in this category.

However, before that, the determinants of having a certain risk tolerance level are to be scrutinized in the context of multivariate analysis through the computation of model (1). The results are shown in Table 3.

The dependent variable represents the risk tolerance score exhibited by each respondent. Male is a binary variable that equals unity if the respondent is male, and zero otherwise. Parent_LowEd is a binary variable that equals unity if neither the respondent's father nor mother holds at least an undergraduate degree, and zero otherwise. Parent_HighEd is a binary variable that equals unity if either the respondent's mother or father holds more than an undergraduate degree, and zero otherwise. High_Income is a binary variable that equals unity if the respondent's parents earned more than 100,000 euros, and zero otherwise. Low_Income is a binary variable that equals unity if the respondent's parents earned less than 50,000 euros, and zero otherwise. P-values in parenthesis. ** and *** represent significance at the 5% and 1% levels, respectively.

Table 3. Regressions regarding the tolerance levels

Const.	25.528*** (<0.01)	25.653*** (<0.01)	26.452*** (<0.01)
Male	1.168** (0.022)	1.158** (0.024)	1.030** (0.043)
Parent_LowEd	-	−0.246 (0.669)	0.008 (0.988)
Parent_HighEd	-	−0.026 (0.970)	−0.521 (0.470)
High_Income	-	-	2.009 (0.135)
Low_Income	-	-	−1.053 (0.164)
Adj. R-square	0.015	0.009	0.026

The results indicate that male individuals are more risk-tolerant, even after controlling for the educational level and the economic status of the respondents' parents. This result seems to go against the findings of Fisher and Yao (2017) who argue that gender differences tend to vanish when the results are controlled by the economic status of individuals.

We now recur to model (2) to examine the determinants of the likelihood of exhibiting a high-risk tolerance. Table 4 presents the results.

The dependent variable is defined as a binary variable that equals unity if the individual exhibits a high-risk tolerance (i.e., score above 28), and equals zero otherwise. Male is a binary variable that equals unity if the respondent is male, and zero otherwise. Parent_LowEd is a binary variable that equals unity if neither the respondent's father nor mother holds at least an undergraduate degree, and zero otherwise. Parent_HighEd is a binary variable that equals unity if either the respondent's mother or father holds more than an undergraduate degree, and zero otherwise. High_Income is a binary variable that equals unity if the respondent's parents earned more than 100,000 euros, and zero otherwise. Low_Income is a binary variable that equals unity if the respondent's parents earned less than 50,000 euros, and zero otherwise. P-values in parenthesis. *, ** and *** represent significance at the 10%, 5% and 1% levels, respectively.

Table 4. Logit regressions regarding the likelihood of exhibiting a high-risk tolerance (score above 28)

Const.	−1.317*** (<0.01)	−1.561*** (<0.01)	−1.098** (0.011)
Male	0.691** (0.012)	0.710** (0.010)	0.649** (0.022)
Parent_LowEd	-	0.319 (0.327)	0.517 (0.132)
Parent_HighEd	-	0.374 (0.337)	0.038 (0.928)
High_Income	-	-	1.201* (0.082)
Low_Income	-	-	−0.669 (0.101)
Adj. R-square	0.007	-0.001	0.016

The results of the logit regression confirm that the male respondents are more likely to have a higher level of risk tolerance, even after controlling for factors such as the educational level and the economic status of the respondents' parents. In addition, belonging to a household with a high economic status, which is reflected in the variable *High_Income*, seems to be associated with a higher probability of belonging to the group of respondents with high levels of risk tolerance. This may be explained by the fact that upper-income individuals can more easily afford to incur losses resulting from a risky investment (Grable and Lytton, 1998; Hallahan *et al.*, 2004; Watson and McNaughton, 2007). The findings of the current chapter go in accordance with the results of previous studies that conclude that individuals with higher income and wealth are more likely to exhibit higher levels of financial risk tolerance (e.g., Grable, 2000; Chaulk *et al.*, 2003; Fink and Huston, 2003; Hallahan *et al.*, 2004). In contrast, the evidence collected here goes against those studies that found a negative relationship between wealth and risk tolerance (e.g., Hawley and Fujii, 1993).

CONCLUSION

This chapter examined the widespread belief that when confronted with risk decisions women choose low-risk alternatives, whereas men select alternatives with higher risks. For that purpose, the author recurred to the administration of a survey to 272 postgraduate students, based on the risk assessment instrument developed by Grable and Lytton (1999). The current research confirmed the stereotype as the results reveal that male respondents exhibited, on average, a significantly higher level of risk tolerance. This finding is robust to the introduction of controls regarding the economic status and the educational level of the respondents' parents. Furthermore, it is shown that gender differences are concentrated at the high-end of the risk tolerance spectrum as the proportion of individuals with high levels of risk tolerance was significantly higher in the male subsample than in the female subsample. However, for the total sample, the level of risk tolerance found was lower than those reported in the literature on the topic.

The conclusions of this research may be of interest to financial advisors and investment managers since they can make use of demographic characteristics addressed by the author for classifying investors into different risk tolerance categories.

There is much to know about the topic addressed in this chapter. For example, it would be interesting to identify the biological and sociopolitical drivers of gender differences in financial decision-making.

ACKNOWLEDGMENT

This research has been financed by Portuguese public funds through FCT - Fundação para a Ciência e a Tecnologia, I.P., in the framework of the project with reference UIDB/04105/2020

REFERENCES

Adhikari, B. K., & O'Leary, V. E. (2011). Gender Differences in Risk Aversion: A Developing Nation's Case. *Journal of Personal Finance*, *10*(2), 122–147.

Al-Ajmi, J. Y. (2008). Risk Tolerance of Individual Investors in an Emerging Market. *International Research Journal of Finance and Economics, 17*, 15–26.

Arano, K., Parker, C., & Terry, R. (2010). Gender-based risk aversion and retirement asset allocation. *Economic Inquiry, 48*(1), 147–155. doi:10.1111/j.1465-7295.2008.00201.x

Atkinson, S., Samantha, B., & Frye, M. (2003). Do female fund managers manage differently? *Journal of Financial Research, 26*(1), 1–18. doi:10.1111/1475-6803.00041

Bajtelsmit, V., & Bernasek, A. (1996). Why do women invest differently than men? *Financial Counseling and Planning, 7*, 1–10.

Bajtelsmit, V., Bernasek, A., & Jianakopolos, N. A. (1996). Gender effects in pension investment allocation decisions. Center for Pension and Retirement Research, 145–156.

Barke, R., Jenkins-Smith, H., & Slovic, P. (1997). Risk Perceptions of Men and Women Scientists. *Social Science Quarterly, 78*, 167–176.

Barsky, R. B., Juster, T., Kimball, M. S., & Shapiro, M. D. (1997). Preference parameters and behavioral heterogeneity. *The Quarterly Journal of Economics, 112*(2), 537–579. doi:10.1162/003355397555280

Beyer, S., & Bowden, E. (1997). Gender Differences in Self-perceptions: Convergent Evidence from Three Measures of Accuracy and Bias. *Personality and Social Psychology Bulletin, 23*(2), 157–172. doi:10.1177/0146167297232005

Boholm, A. (1998). Comparative studies of risk perception: A review of 20 years of research. *Journal of Risk Research, 1*(2), 135–163. doi:10.1080/136698798377231

Booth, A., Cardona-Sosa, L., & Nolen, P. (2014). Gender differences in risk aversion: Do single-sex environments affect their development? *Journal of Economic Behavior & Organization, 99*, 126–154. doi:10.1016/j.jebo.2013.12.017

Boulu-Reshef, B., Comeig, I., Donze, R., & Weiss, G. D. (2016). Risk aversion in prediction markets: A framed-field experiment. *Journal of Business Research, 69*(11), 5071–5075. doi:10.1016/j.jbusres.2016.04.082

Buss, D. (1999). *Evolutionary Psychology*. Allyn and Bacon.

Byrnes, J. P., Miller, D. C., & Schafer, W. D. (1999). Gender differences in risk taking: A meta-analysis. *Psychological Bulletin, 125*(3), 367–383. doi:10.1037/0033-2909.125.3.367

Cagle, J. A. B., & Baucus, M. M. (2006). Case Studies of Ethics Scandals: Effects on Ethical Perceptions of Finance Students. *Journal of Business Ethics, 64*(3), 213–229. doi:10.100710551-005-8503-5

Castillo, M. E., & Cross, P. J. (2008). Of mice and men: Within gender variation in strategic behavior. *Games and Economic Behavior, 64*(2), 421–432. doi:10.1016/j.geb.2008.01.009

Chaulk, B., Johnson, P. J., & Bulcroft, R. (2003). Effects of Marriage and Children on Financial Risk Tolerance: A Synthesis of Family Development and Prospect Theory. *Journal of Family and Economic Issues, 24*(3), 257–279. doi:10.1023/A:1025495221519

Cho, J., & Lee, J. (2006). An integrated model of risk and risk-reducing strategies. *Journal of Business Research, 59*(1), 112–120. doi:10.1016/j.jbusres.2005.03.006

Coates, J. M., & Herbert, J. (2008). Endogenous steroids and financial risk taking on a London trading floor. *Proceedings of the National Academy of Sciences of the United States of America, 105*(16), 6167–6172. doi:10.1073/pnas.0704025105 PMID:18413617

Corman, J. (2001). Gender comparisons in strategic decision-making: An entrepreneurial analyses of the entrepreneurial strategy mix. *Journal of Small Business Management, 39*(2), 165–173. doi:10.1111/1540-627X.00015

Croson, R., & Gneezy, U. (2009). Gender differences in preferences. *Journal of Economic Literature, 47*(2), 448–474. doi:10.1257/jel.47.2.448

Deaux, K., & Ennsuiller, T. (1994). Explanations of Successful Performance on Sex Linked Traits: What is Skill for the Male is Luck for the Female. *Journal of Personality and Social Psychology, 29*(1), 80–85. doi:10.1037/h0035733

Dowling, R., & Staelin, R. (1994). A model of perceived risk and intended risk-handling activity. *The Journal of Consumer Research, 21*(1), 119–125. doi:10.1086/209386

Eckel, C. C., & Grossman, P. J. (2008). Forecasting risk attitudes: An experimental study using actual and forecast gamble choices. *Journal of Economic Behavior & Organization, 68*(1), 1–17. doi:10.1016/j.jebo.2008.04.006

Embrey, L., & Fox, J. (1997). Gender differences in the investment decision-making process. *Financial Counseling and Planning, 8*(2), 33–40.

Eriksson, K., & Simpson, B. (2010). Emotional reactions to losing explain gender differences in entering a risky lottery. *Judgment and Decision Making, 5*(3), 159–163.

Faff, R., Mulino, D., & Chai, D. (2008). On the linkage between financial risk tolerance and risk aversion. *Journal of Financial Research, 31*(1), 1–23. doi:10.1111/j.1475-6803.2008.00229.x

Filippin, A., & Crosetto, P. (2016). A Reconsideration of Gender Differences in Risk Attitudes. *Management Science, 62*(11), 3138–3160. doi:10.1287/mnsc.2015.2294

Finke, M. S., & Huston, S. J. (2003). The Brighter Side of Financial Risk: Financial Risk Tolerance and Wealth. *Journal of Family and Economic Issues, 24*(3), 233–256. doi:10.1023/A:1025443204681

Finucane, M. L., Slovic, P., Mertz, C. K., Flynn, J., & Satterfield, T. A. (2000). Gender, race, and perceived risk: The 'white male' effect. *Health Risk & Society, 2*(2), 159–172. doi:10.1080/713670162

Fisher, P. J., & Yao, R. (2017). Gender Differences in financial risk tolerance. *Journal of Economic Psychology, 61*, 191–202. doi:10.1016/j.joep.2017.03.006

Friehs, C. G., & Craig, C. L. (2008). Assessing the Effectiveness of Online Library Instruction with Finance Students. *Journal of Web Librarianship, 2*(4), 493–509. doi:10.1080/19322900802484438

Garbarino, E., & Strahilevitz, M. (2004). Gender differences in the perceived risk of buying online and the effects of receiving a site recommendation. *Journal of Business Research*, *57*(7), 768–775. doi:10.1016/S0148-2963(02)00363-6

Gibson, R., Michayluk, D., & Van de Venter, G. (2013). Financial risk tolerance: An analysis of unexplored factors. *Financial Services Review*, *22*(1), 23–50.

Gilliam, J., Chatterjee, S., & Grable, J. (2010). Measuring the perception of financial risk tolerance: A tale of two measures. *Financial Counseling and Planning*, *21*, 30–43.

Grable, J. (2000). Financial Risk Tolerance and Additional Factors that Affect Risk Taking in Everyday Money Matters. *Journal of Business and Psychology*, *14*(4), 25–63. doi:10.1023/A:1022994314982

Grable, J., & Joo, S. (1999). Factors related to risk tolerance: A further examination. *Consumer Interests Annual*, *45*, 53–58.

Grable, J., & Joo, S. (2004). Environmental and Biopsychosocial Factors Associated with Financial Risk Tolerance. *Financial Counseling and Planning*, *15*(1), 73–82.

Grable, J., & Lytton, R. H. (1998). Investor Risk Tolerance: Testing the Efficacy of Demographics as Differentiating and Classifying Factors. *Financial Counseling and Planning*, *9*(1), 61–73.

Grable, J., & Lytton, R. H. (1999). Financial risk revisited: The development of a risk assessment instrument. *Financial Services Review*, *8*(3), 163–181. doi:10.1016/S1057-0810(99)00041-4

Grable, J., & Lytton, R. H. (2001). Investor risk tolerance: Testing the efficacy of demographics as differentiating and classifying factors. *Financial Counseling and Planning*, *9*, 61–74.

Grable, J., & Lytton, R. H. (2003). The Development of a Risk Assessment Instrument: A Follow-Up Study. *Financial Services Review*, *12*, 257–274.

Grable, J., McGill, S., & Britt, S. (2009). Risk tolerance estimation bias: The age effect. *Journal of Business & Economics Research*, *7*(7), 1–12.

Haliassos, M., & Bertaut, C. C. (1995). Why Do So Few Hold Stocks? *Economic Journal (London)*, *105*(432), 1110–1129. doi:10.2307/2235407

Hallahan, T. A., Faff, R. W., & McKenzie, M. D. (2003). An Exploratory Investigation of the Relation between Risk Tolerance Scores and Demographic Characteristics. *Journal of Multinational Financial Management*, *13*(4-5), 483–502. doi:10.1016/S1042-444X(03)00022-7

Hallahan, T. A., Faff, R. W., & McKenzie, M. D. (2004). An empirical investigation of personal financial risk tolerance. *Financial Services Review*, *13*, 57–78.

Hanna, S. D., Gutter, M., & Fan, J. (1998). A theory-based measure of risk tolerance. *Proceedings of the Academy of Financial Services*, 10–11.

Hansson, S. O. (1989). Dimensions of risk. *Risk Analysis*, *9*(1), 107–112. doi:10.1111/j.1539-6924.1989.tb01225.x

Harrant, V., & Vaillant, N. G. (2008). Are women less risk averse than men? *Evolution and Human Behavior, 29*(6), 396–401. doi:10.1016/j.evolhumbehav.2008.05.003

Harris, C., Jenkins, M., & Glaser, D. (2006). Gender differences in risk assessment. *Judgment and Decision Making, 1*(1), 48–63.

Hawley, C. B., & Fujii, E. T. (1993). An empirical analysis of preferences for financial risk: Further evidence on the Friedman-Savage model. *Journal of Post Keynesian Economics, 16*(2), 197–204. doi:10.1080/01603477.1993.11489978

He, X., Inman, J. J., & Mittal, V. (2007). Gender jeopardy in financial risk taking. *JMR, Journal of Marketing Research, 44*, 414–424.

Hinz, R. P., McCarthy, D. D., & Turner, J. A. (1997). Are women more conservative investors? Gender differences in participant-directed pension investments. In M. S. Gordon, O. S. Mitchell, & M. M. Twinney (Eds.), *Positioning pensions for the twenty-first century* (pp. 91–103). University of Pennsylvania Press.

Jianakoplos, N. A., & Bernasek, A. (1998). Are women more risk averse? *Economic Inquiry, 36*(4), 620–630. doi:10.1111/j.1465-7295.1998.tb01740.x

Jianakoplos, N. A., & Bernasek, A. (2006). Financial Risk Taking by Age and Birth Cohort. *Southern Economic Journal, 72*(4), 981–1001.

Johnson, J. E. V., & Powell, P. L. (1993). Decision making, risk and gender: Are managers different? *British Journal of Management, 5*(2), 123–138. doi:10.1111/j.1467-8551.1994.tb00073.x

Johnson, J. E. V., & Powell, P. L. (1994). Decision Making, Risk and Gender: Are Managers Different? *British Journal of Management, 5*(2), 123–138. doi:10.1111/j.1467-8551.1994.tb00073.x

Levin, I. P., Snyder, M. A., & Chapman, D. P. (1988). 'The interaction of experiential and situational factors and gender in a simulated risky decision-making task. *The Journal of Psychology, 122*(2), 173–181. doi:10.1080/00223980.1988.9712703

Levy, M. (2015). An evolutionary explanation for risk aversion. *Journal of Economic Psychology, 46*, 51–61. doi:10.1016/j.joep.2014.12.001

Masters, R., & Meier, R. (1988). Sex-differences and risk-taking propensity of entrepreneurs. *Journal of Small Business Management, 26*(1), 31–35.

Maxfield, S., Shapiro, M., Gupta, V., & Hass, S. (2010). Gender and risk: Women, risk taking and risk aversion. *Gender in Management, 7*(7), 586–604. doi:10.1108/17542411011081383

Meier-Pesti, K., & Goetze, E. (2005). Masculinity and femininity as predictors of financial risk-taking: evidence from a priming study on gender salience. In K. M. Ekstrom & H. Brembeck (Eds.), *European Advances in Consumer Research* (Vol. 7, pp. 45–46). Association for Consumer Research.

Neelakantan, U. (2010). Estimation and impact of gender differences in risk tolerance. *Economic Inquiry, 48*(1), 228–233. doi:10.1111/j.1465-7295.2009.00251.x

Nelson, J. A. (2015). Are Women Really More Risk-Averse than Men? A Re-Analysis of the Literature Using Expanded Methods. *Journal of Economic Surveys, 29*(3), 566–585. doi:10.1111/joes.12069

Nelson, J. A. (2016). Not-So-Strong Evidence for Gender Differences in Risk Taking. *Feminist Economics*, *22*(2), 114–142. doi:10.1080/13545701.2015.1057609

Olsen, R. A., & Cox, C. M. (2001). The influence of gender on the perception and response to investment risk: The case of professional investors. *The Journal of Psychology and Financial Markets*, *2*(1), 29–36. doi:10.1207/S15327760JPFM0201_3

Pacula, R. L. (1997). Women and substance use: Are women less susceptible to addiction? *The American Economic Review*, *87*, 454–459.

Palsson, A. M. (1996). Does the degree of risk aversion vary with household characteristics? *Journal of Economic Psychology*, *18*(6), 605–628. doi:10.1016/S0167-4870(96)00039-6

Powell, M., & Ansic, D. (1997). Gender differences in risk behaviour in financial decision making: An experimental analysis. *Journal of Economic Psychology*, *18*(6), 605–627. doi:10.1016/S0167-4870(97)00026-3

Powell, M., & Ansic, D. (1999). Gender differences in financial decision-making: A new approach for experimental economic analysis. *Economia, Societa, E Instituzioni*, *11*(1), 71–89.

Prince, M. (1993). Women, Men and Money Styles. *Journal of Economic Psychology*, *14*(1), 175–182. doi:10.1016/0167-4870(93)90045-M

Riley, W. B. Jr, & Chow, K. V. (1992). Asset allocation and individual risk aversion. *Financial Analysts Journal*, *48*(6), 32–37. doi:10.2469/faj.v48.n6.32

Roszkowski, M. J., & Grable, J. (2005). Gender stereotypes in advisors' clinical judgments of financial risk tolerance: Objects in the mirror are closer than they appear to be. *Journal of Behavioral Finance*, *6*(4), 181–191. doi:10.120715427579jpfm0604_2

Sapienza, P., Zingales, L., & Maestripieri, D. (2009). Gender differences in financial risk aversion and career choices are affected by testosterone. *Proceedings of the National Academy of Sciences of the United States of America*, *106*(36), 15268–15273. doi:10.1073/pnas.0907352106 PMID:19706398

Sarin, R., & Wieland, A. (2016). Risk aversion for decisions under uncertainty: Are there gender differences? *Journal of Behavioral and Experimental Economics*, *60*, 1–8. doi:10.1016/j.socec.2015.10.007

Schubert, R., Brown, M., Gysler, M., & Brachinger, H. W. (1999). Financial Decision-Making: Are Women Really More Risk-Averse? *The American Economic Review*, *89*(2), 381–385. doi:10.1257/aer.89.2.381

Shropshire, C., Peterson, S., Bartels, A. L., Amanatullah, E. T., & Lee, P. M. (2021). Are Female CEOs Really More Risk Averse? Examining Economic Downturn and Other-Orientation. *Journal of Leadership & Organizational Studies*, *28*(2), 185–206. doi:10.1177/1548051821997404

Sjoberg, L. (2000). Factors in risk perception. *Risk Analysis*, *20*(1), 1–11. doi:10.1111/0272-4332.00001

Sjöberg, L., & Engelberg, E. (2009). Attitudes to Economic Risk Taking, Sensation Seeking and Values of Business Students Specializing in Finance. *Journal of Behavioral Finance*, *10*(1), 33–43. doi:10.1080/15427560902728712

Sunden, A. E., & Surette, B. J. (1998). Gender Differences in the Allocation of Assets in Retirement Savings Plans. *The American Economic Review, 88*(2), 207–211.

Wang, H., & Hanna, S. (1997). Does Risk Tolerance Decrease with Age? *Financial Counseling and Planning, 8*(2), 27–31.

Watson, J., & McNaughton, M. (2007). Gender Differences in Risk Aversion and Expected Retirement Benefits. *Financial Analysts Journal, 63*(4), 52–62. doi:10.2469/faj.v63.n4.4749

Weber, E., Blais, A., & Betz, E. (2002). A domain specific risk-attitude scale: Measuring risk perceptions and risk behaviors. *Journal of Behavioral Decision Making, 15*(4), 263–290. doi:10.1002/bdm.414

White, R. E., Thornhill, S., & Hampson, E. (2007). A biosocial model of entrepreneurship: The combined effects of nurture and nature. *Journal of Organizational Behavior, 28*(4), 451–466. doi:10.1002/job.432

Xie, X., Wang, M., & Xu, L. (2003). What risks are Chinese people concerned about? *Risk Analysis, 23*(4), 685–695. doi:10.1111/1539-6924.00347 PMID:12926562

Yates, J. F., & Stone, E. R. (1992). The risk construct. In J. F. Yates (Ed.), *Risk-Taking Behavior* (pp. 1–25). John Wiley.

Yordanova, D. I., & Alexandrova-Boshnakova, M. I. (2011). Gender effects on risk-taking of entrepreneurs: Evidence from Bulgaria. *International Journal of Entrepreneurial Behaviour & Research, 17*(3), 272–295. doi:10.1108/13552551111130718

Zhong, L. X., & Xiao, J. J. (1995). Determinants of family bond and stock holdings. *Financial Counseling and Planning, 6*, 107–114.

Zuckerman, M. (1994). *Behavioral Expressions and Biosocial Bases of Sensation Seeking*. Cambridge University Press.

KEY TERMS AND DEFINITIONS

Risk Aversion: The reluctance of people to choose investment alternatives with an uncertain payoff rather than another investment alternative with a more certain but possibly lower expected payoff. The inverse of risk tolerance.

Risk Tolerance: The capacity of people to choose investment alternatives with an uncertain payoff rather than another investment alternative with a more certain but possibly lower expected payoff. The inverse of risk aversion.

APPENDIX

This is the survey that was directed to students in the current study.

Part A.

Please indicate your gender: ___ Male ___ Female
Please identify your major (example: Economics, Management, Physics, etc.): _____
Please indicate the level of education completed by your father and mother:
Father
___ Less than High School Degree
___ High School Degree ("Ensino Secundário")
___ Undergraduate Degree ("Licenciatura")
___ Master's Degree
___ Doctorate Degree
Mother
___ Less than High School Degree
___ High School Degree ("Ensino Secundário")
___ Undergraduate Degree ("Licenciatura")
___ Master's Degree
___ Doctorate Degree
Please indicate the range of your parents combined annual income:
___ less than €20,000
___ between €20,000 and €50,000
___ between €50,000 and €100,000
___ between €100,000 and €250,000
___ over €250,000
Please check the type (all that apply) of accounts/investments you presently or have previously owned:
___ Checking or Savings
___ Bonds (individual or as part of mutual fund)
___ Stocks (individual or as part of mutual fund)

Part B.

1. In general, how would your best friend describe you as a risk taker?
   ___ A real gambler
   ___ Willing to take risks after completing adequate research
   ___ Cautious
   ___ A real risk avoider
2. You are on a TV game show and can choose one of the following. Which would you take?

___ €1000 in cash
___ A 50% chance of winning €5000
___ A 25% chance of winning €10,000
___ A 5% chance of winning €100,000

3. You have just finished saving for a "once-in-a-lifetime" vacation. Three weeks before you plan to leave, you lose your job. You would:
___ Cancel the vacation
___ Take a much more modest vacation
___ Go as scheduled, reasoning that you need the time to prepare for a job search
___ Extend your vacation, because this might be your last chance to go first-class.

4. If you unexpectedly received €20,000 to invest, what would you do?
___ Deposit it in a bank account
___ Invest it in safe high-quality bonds or bond mutual funds
___ Invest it in stocks or stock mutual funds

5. In terms of experience, how comfortable are you investing in stocks or mutual funds?
___ Not at all comfortable
___ Somewhat comfortable
___ Very comfortable

6. When you think of the word "risk" which of the following words come to mind first?
___ Loss
___ Uncertainty
___ Opportunity
___ Excitement

7. Some experts are predicting prices of assets such as gold, jewels, collectibles, and real estate (hard assets) to increase in value; although bond prices may fall, experts tend to agree that government bonds are relatively safe. Most of your investment assets are now in high-interest government bonds. What would you do?
___ Hold the bonds
___ Sell the bonds, put half the proceeds into bank accounts, and the other half into hard assets.
___ Sell the bonds and put the total proceeds into hard assets.
___ Sell the bonds, put all the money into hard assets, and borrow additional money to buy more.

8. Given the best and worst case returns of the four investment choices below, which would you prefer?
___ €200 gain best case; €0 gain/loss worst case
___ €800 gain best case; €200 loss worst case
___ €2600 gain best case; €800 loss worst case
___ €4800 gain best case; €2400 loss worst case

9. In addition to whatever you own, you have been given €1000. You are now asked to choose between:
___ A sure loss of €500
___ A 50% chance to lose €1000 and a 50% chance to lose nothing.

10. In addition to whatever you own, you have been given €2000. You are now asked to choose between:
___ A sure loss of €500
___ A 50% chance to lose €1000 and a 50% chance to lose nothing.

11. Suppose a relative left you an inheritance of €100,000, stipulating in the will that you invest ALL the money in ONE of the following choices. Which would you select?
    ___ A savings account or money market mutual fund
    ___ A mutual fund that owns stocks and bonds
    ___ A portfolio of 15 common stocks
    ___ Commodities like gold, silver, and oil
12. If you had to invest €20,000, which of the following investment choices would you find the most appealing?
    ___ 60% in low-risk investments, 30% in medium-risk investments, and 10% in high-risk investments
    ___ 30% in low-risk investments, 40% in medium-risk investments, and 30% in high-risk investments
    ___ 10% in low-risk investments, 40% in medium-risk investments, and 50% in high-risk investments.
13. Your trusted friend and neighbor, an experienced geologist, is putting together a group of investors to fund an exploratory gold mining venture. The venture could pay back 50 to 100 times the investment if successful. If the mine is a failure, the entire investment is worth nothing. Your friend estimates the chance of success is 20%. If you had the money, how much would you invest?
    ___ Nothing
    ___ One month's salary
    ___ Three month's salary
    ___ Six month's salary

Chapter 5
Corruption, Credit Risk, and Bank Profitability:
Evidence of Angolan Banks

João Jungo
https://orcid.org/0000-0002-2681-4075
University of Aveiro, Portugal

Wilson Luzendo
Banco de Desenvolvimento de Angola, Angola

Yuri Quixina
Instituto Superior Politécnico de Tecnologias e Ciências (ISPTEC), Angola

Mara Madaleno
https://orcid.org/0000-0002-4905-2771
GOVCOPP, University of Aveiro, Portugal

ABSTRACT

The economies of African countries are generally characterized by inefficient management of resources, strong heterogeneity in the rate of economic growth, as well as high levels of corruption and embezzlement of public funds, clearly highlighting the need to consider the role of government in the performance of the economic environment. Corruption is characterized by three key behaviors—bribery, embezzlement, and nepotism—characteristics that can influence the performance of any financial system. The objective is to examine the effect of corruption on credit risk in Angola. The result of the feasible generalized least squares (FGLS) estimation suggests that corruption increases non-performing loans in the Angolan economy; additionally, the authors find that the larger the bank's assets (bank size), the more averse to credit risk they become, and the smaller the state's stake in the banking system, the lower the non-performing loans.

DOI: 10.4018/978-1-7998-8609-9.ch005

INTRODUCTION

The economies of African countries are generally characterized by inefficient resource management, strong heterogeneity in the rate of economic growth, as well as, high levels of corruption and embezzlement of public funds (Igharo et al., 2020; Kunieda, 2014; Sector et al., 2021). Corruption is defined as the use of public office for private gain (Bai et al., 2013; Jalles, 2016; Kunieda, 2014; Sector et al., 2021). Corruption is a problem that affects all economies, however, it is higher in poor countries, regardless of how it is calculated (Kunieda, 2014; Setor et al., 2021), therefore, Angola does not escape this reality.

Corruption causes negative effects on the financial performance of any organization (Van Vu et al., 2018). In the study conducted by Kunieda (2014) aiming to investigate the effect of capital account liberalization on corruption, the author found that more corrupt countries impose higher tax rates and thus, increase the negative impacts on economic growth. In parallel to this, Trabelsi and Trabelsi (2020) evidenced that both high levels of corruption and low levels of corruption can decrease economic growth.

Due to the poor access to credit in emerging countries, bribing banks or turning to relatives and friends to obtain financing has been the alternative solution found by entrepreneurs. Thus, corruption proves to be a strong barrier to entrepreneurship in emerging countries, mainly due to its ability to increase the cost of doing business (Hanoteau et al., 2021).

The economic reality of developing countries forces them to reconsider the role of governments in explaining economic performance (Jalles, 2016), since the personal interests of policymakers in the financial system cause distortions in the market, driving the inefficient allocation of resources. These include, for example, allocation of public resources to meet political needs or even personal interests (Huggard et al, 1993; Jalles, 2016), granting bank loans only to clients who belong to the party in power, appointing bank managers or financial institutions individuals because they belong to political affiliation and overlapping political objectives with the objectives of banking institutions.

Corruption is characterized by three key behaviors, bribery, embezzlement, and nepotism (Bai et al., 2013; Hewa Wellalage et al., 2020). However, these three characteristics can influence the performance of any financial system, since the financial system is very sensitive to any non-transparent behavior, i.e., in an environment where high levels of corruption prevail, financial systems are more fragile and unstable, in addition to the excessive number of defaulting credit risk and the strong inability of banks to intermediate financial resources and stimulate entrepreneurial activity (Jenkins et al., 2021; Mohamad & Jenkins, 2020). Therefore, the quality of access to formal credit, weak institutions, and mainly led by bureaucrats willing to extort, are strong factors for increased corruption and failure of entrepreneurial activity (Hanoteau et al., 2021). Among the various risks existing in the banking sector, credit risk is the main risk that banks face, being the main source of bank failures, able to indicate the beginning of a banking crisis, with the ability to infect all sectors of the economy (Mpofu & Nikolaidou, 2018).

Adequate capitalization, low leverage, excess liquidity, and weak dependence on external funding were the key factors for the non-aggravation of the 2008 global financial crisis in the banking system of Sub-Saharan African countries. Contrary to this, the banking systems of African countries were affected by the financial crisis through trade integrations and sharp exchange rate depreciation, which aggravated the financial problems of borrowers. Consequently, there was an increase in defaulted loans (Nikolaidou & Vogiazas, 2017). The theoretical and empirical literature points to macroeconomic factors and institutional or bank-specific factors as the main determinants for explaining defaulted loans. Regarding macroeconomic factors it is justified by the increase in real GDP and improvement in the country's economic conditions, which can increase the ability of borrowers to meet their credit obligations, on the other hand, institutional factors such as poor management, weakness in risk management and control, low capital and excess lending can increase the defaulted loans (Beck, 2011; Nikolaidou & Vogiazas, 2017). Therefore, corruption can influence macroeconomic factors and institutional or bank-specific factors.

The success of any measure to mitigate credit risk must be supported by knowledge of its determinants, to be able to fight the causes and not the effects. However, we set out to analyze the effects of corruption and government transparency on credit risk and the stability of Angolan banks. The economic and financial crisis has awakened to policymakers and the academic community the need for research on the probable causes of banking instability. Thus, there are several theoretical and empirical studies on this approach, applied in developed and developing countries (Albaity et al, 2019; Batuo et al., 2018; Mengistu & Saiz, 2018; Mpofu & Nikolaidou, 2018; Musau et al., 2018b, 2018a; Nikolaidou & Vogiazas, 2017). Even faced with this need, the literature on this approach applied to the Angolan reality is quite scarce and the existing studies do not consider the role of corruption on credit risk and banking stability. We cogitate with this study to answer the following research question:

- What is the effect of corruption on the credit risk management and stability of Angolan banks?

We intend with this study to contribute to (1) fill the existing gap on empirical studies of the determinants of credit risk, applied in Angolan banks; (2) relate three relevant and current topics such as corruption, credit risk, and bank stability, which are in fact problems experienced particularly by the Angolan financial system and in general the African continent; (3) discuss and compare the experiences of other African countries and outside Africa and present solid conclusions about the effects of corruption on credit risk and banking stability, and finally, awaken policymakers to the urgent need to combat corruption to improve the effectiveness of measures aimed at financial development and economic growth.

BACKGROUND OF THE STUDY

Research articles on corruption, credit risk, and bank stability in the developing economies have increased since the global financial crisis of 2008-9. Jenkins *et al.* (2021) measured the impact of corruption on credit risk in 191 commercial banks in 18 countries and found that corruption aggravated banks' defaulted loans, regardless of whether it does not affect all banks at the same level, i.e.banks in higher quantiles (with higher credit risk) are the most affected. Also, Mohamad and Jenkins (2020) investigated the impact of corruption on defaulted loans from Middle Eastern and North African countries (MENA), noting that corruption increases credit risk even in high-risk aversion banks. Liu *et al.* (2020) tested empirically the hypotheses of the corruption on credit companies in China, finding that low levels of corruption increase access to credit and high levels of corruption prevent access to bank credit. Yet, Liu *et al.* (2020), noted that the link between corruption and access to credit can be explained by government guarantees. Toader *et al.* (2018) analyzed the effect of corruption on banking stability using data from banks in emerging markets, concluding that corruption has a serious impact on bank stability and corruption significantly deteriorates the quality of loans, being associated with moderate growth in bank credit growth.

Son *et al.* (2020) studied the impact of corruption on the banking sector and economic growth, noting that there were positive achievements of corruption on credit risk and negative impacts on economic growth. Wellalage *et al.* (2020), studying the effects of paying bribes on access to credit for Indian small and medium-sized enterprises (SMEs), found that corruption negatively affected access to credit in SMEs.

Rehman et al. (2020) analyzed the relationship between corruption and credit risk in commercial banks in Pakistan, finding a negative and significant link between corruption control and credit risk, indicating that rigidity in the control of corruption can reduce credit risk.

Some researchers briefly explain credit risk as a factor of bank instability. For example, Ali et al. (2019) explored the impact of liquidity risk, credit risk, financing risk, and corruption on banking stability in the banking system in Pakistan, and concluded that the size of the bank, liquidity risk, financing risk, and corruption had a positive impact on the stability of the bank. In addition, the authors found a negative relationship between credit risk and bank stability. Also, Kamran et al. (2019) while examining stability trends in Pakistan's commercial banks, considering the country's governance, market concentration, and financial market dynamics, concluded that both stability measures in the form of ROA, ROE, and Z-Score are affected negatively and significantly because of insufficient control of corruption, regulatory quality, market concentration, financial market development and increased defaulting loans. Additionally, Kamran et al. (2019) dividing the sample into conventional banks and Islamic banks found that in the conventional banking system, the main determinants of financial stability are control over corruption, political instability, market structure, and credit risk. For Islamic banks, corruption and government effectiveness, capital adequacy index, market structure, and financial market development are significant determinants, affecting Z stability measures.

For Gozgor (2018), income and currency supply are positively associated with domestic credits. In a study conducted in 61 developing countries, the author inferred negative effects of the current account balance and differences in interest rates on domestic credit. Additional analyses for the subcomponents of general political risk measures indicate that better socioeconomic conditions (lower poverty, lower unemployment, and higher consumer confidence) and lower corruption positively affect domestic credit. Also, according to Gozgor (2018), the high credit granted in various emerging markets depended on domestic monetary policy (captured by domestic policy rates) and the global liquidity conditions (captured by global interest rates), that have become the main drivers of domestic credit growth in emerging markets.

The investigation of the diversification of the credit portfolio and its effect on the performance of central banks and credit risk was the main objective of a study conducted by Ayesha et al. (2020). In this study, the authors found that economic factors and corruption influence the risks associated with loan portfolios.

In general, the studies presented in this section address two interesting topics (credit risk and corruption) and which constitute real problems in developing countries, in addition, studies converge by proving that corruption is evil for financial stability, increasing credit risk, and reducing access to financing for future projects.

HISTORICAL EVOLUTION OF THE ANGOLAN BANKING SECTOR

The first banking institution established in Angola was Banco Nacional Ultramarino (BNU) on August 21, 1865, during the colonial era. The financial unsustainability and the economic reforms that the environment demanded in that period led to the closure of the BNU in October 1926 and consequently the creation of Banco de Angola in the same year. The commercial activity in the banking sector was reserved exclusively to Banco de Angola, and it maintained this exclusivity until 1957, the year in which Banco Comercial de Angola was created, thus initiating for the first time competing in the Angolan banking sector (Peres, 2017). Prior to Angola's independence, the banking market consisted of six banks, namely

Banco de Angola which performed the functions of issuing bank and commercial bank; and the remaining five were commercial banks (Banco Comercial de Angola (BCA), Banco de Crédito Comercial e Industrial (BCCI), Banco Totta Standard de Angola (BTSA), Banco Pinto & Sotto Mayor (BPSM) and the Inter-Unido Bank); and four credit institutions (Instituto de Crédito de Angola, Banco de Fomento Nacional, Caixa de Crédito Agro-Pecuária and the Montepio de Angola) (Peres, 2017). In 1976, after the independence of Angola, Banco de Angola and Banco Comercial de Angola were confiscated and Banco Nacional de Angola (BNA) and Banco Popular de Angola (BPA) were created to replace them. Therefore, the banking activity became a monopoly of the State, where BNA assumed the functions of a central bank, issuing bank, and commercial bank, and BPA functioned only as a savings bank, without, however, exercising credit activity. The opening of the banking sector to the private sector in Angola only took place in 1991. Thus, from 1993 onwards, the first private national and foreign banking institutions appeared. The first foreign banks to emerge were branches of Portuguese banks such as Banco Totta & Açores (BTA), Banco de Fomento e Exterior (BFE), later private banks under Angolan law such as Banco Africano de Investimento (BAI) in 1997, Banco Comercial Angolano (BCA) in 1999, Banco Sol (BS) in 2001, Banco Espirito Santo Angola (BESA) in 2002, Banco Regional Keve in 2003 (Peres, 2017).

The first registered acquisition in the Angolan financial system was on October 1, 2009, when bank BAI bought Novo Banco, which was specialized in micro-credit and was renamed as BAI-Microfinanças (BMF). Around 25 banks are currently authorized to operate in the banking sector[1]. The National Bank of Angola revoked licenses of 5 Banks, namely:

- Banco BESA, for insolvency issues, caused mainly by excessive undue credit;
- Postal Bank; insufficient regulatory own funds;
- Bank More; insufficient regulatory own funds;
- BANC Bank; insufficient regulatory own funds;
- Kwanza Investment Bank; regulatory own fund insufficiency.

It should be noted that after Banco BESA was declared bankrupt, the shareholders decided to found Banco Economico in 2014, increasing equity and continuing the activities of BESA. Although the failed banks are private, they have in common in their shareholder structure influential people strongly linked to the regime in power.

COMBATING AND CONTROLLING CORRUPTION IN ANGOLA

Corruption is a social problem that affects all sectors of the economy and all members of society, despite the fight against corruption being considered a national and international priority (Bai et al., 2013; Jalles, 2016; Kunieda, 2014). The fight against corruption should be the main design of policymakers, especially when they are committed to reducing inefficiencies and the widespread well-being of economic actors. On the other hand, the first step towards solving any problem is to admit the existence of it and then think of possible solutions for resolution, however, it is not by chance that the fight against corruption was established as one of the main objectives of the current Angolan government.

According to *Transparency International*[2], in 2018 Angola, Chad, and Congo Brazzaville are the countries of sub-Saharan Africa that shared the 165th position among the 180 countries analyzed in the fight against corruption in the world, presenting the corruption perception rates of 0.19, below the average (0.32) of the sub-Saharan Africa region. These results indicate that the levels of corruption in these countries are quite high.

After recognizing the existence of corruption in Angola, the government approved two capital repatriation laws, namely Law No. 9/18 of 26 July-law on repatriation voluntarily and Law No. 15/18 of 26 December, Law on the coercive repatriation of capital (CEDESA, 2021). These Laws aim to ensure the return of funds to the Angolan State. In parallel to these Laws, the National Assembly approved the new Penal Code, where there is a specific chapter reserved for crimes committed in the performance of public functions and to the detriment of public functions in Articles 357º to 375º (CEDESA, 2021). Matters relating to corruption are dealt with in Articles 358º to 361º, trafficking of influence Article 366, and embezzlement article 362º.

To ensure the implementation of anti-corruption policies, the government has the following organs of the Attorney General's Office (PGR), Banco Nacional de Angola (BNA), Financial Information Unit, Criminal Investigation Service (SIC), in addition to having various support and international legal cooperation. Regarding the results of the fight against corruption, some 1522 criminal proceedings, charges, and seizure of persons connected and with responsibility in the government were opened, as well as recovery of money and seizure of property (CEDESA, 2021).

The steps taken to combat corruption are visible, however, much more and especially the awareness of all members of society is still needed, as well as encouraging the culture of social denunciation. No country in the world is free from the phenomenon of corruption, however, the characteristics of countries such as poor governance, poor quality of institutions, freedom of the press, independence of the legal system, weak level of education and education of the population, and impunity, are determining factors in mitigating the effects of corruption. From another perspective, when corruption is systematic, the effectiveness of measures aimed at combating it is greatly reduced, as economic operators consent to abnormal events as normal.

CHARACTERIZATION OF THE FINANCIAL SOUNDNESS OF ANGOLAN BANKS

The data presented in Table 1 originate from the website of the National Bank of Angola and was prepared by the Banking Supervision Department, reflecting the financial soundness of Angolan banks in the period 2017-2020, the data refer to the December months of their respective years.

During the period in reference, the capacity of Angolan banks to provide liquidity to the economy was reduced, that is, in 2017 banks granted loans in the order of 49.3% of the deposits raised and after three years (2020) the banks granted loans of only 32.72% of the deposits raised. Similar behavior is also visible when we analyze the distribution of credit by the public and private sector, for example, the granting of private sector credit decreased from 90.8% in 2017 to 89.78% in 2020.

In 2019, the undue credit recorded by Angolan banking was 32.5% and in the following year (2020), the undue credit decreased to 18.41%, while in previous years (2017 and 2018) the difference in the non-performing loan was greatly reduced, i.e. 28.8% and 28.3%, respectively. It presupposes understanding that the credit risk in Angolan banks during the years 2017-2020 was higher in 2019, and the theoretical literature evaluates credit risk by the relationship between defaulted loans by total loans (Albaity et al., 2019; Jenkins et al., 2021; Klapper & Lusardi, 2020).

Table 1. Financial soundness of Angolan banks.

Variables		2017	2018	2019	2020
liquidity	Credit/Deposit	49.3	44.2	41.85	32.72
Credit by sector	Public	10.9	11.6	9.74	10.22
	Private	90.8	88.5	90.26	89.78
Asset quality	Non-performing loans	28.8	28.3	32.5	18.41
Profitability	ROA[3]	2,1	4,4	1	-2.91
	ROE[4]	14.5	26.6	7.78	-29.79
	Cost/Profit	99.8	99.6	105.6	121.51
	Spread	23,8	27.3	20.35	8.41

Source: BNA-Departamento de Supervisão Bancária, values in (%).

Regarding profitability, we note that returns on assets and return on equity were positive only from 2017 to 2019. These profitability indicators performed negatively and there was a loss in returns on assets of 2.91% and 29.79% in returns on equity in 2020. These indicators show that Angolan banks in 2020 were less profitable, so they were more likely to be more risk-avid or use more flexible credit assessment methods (Mohamad & Jenkins, 2020; Rehman et al., 2020).

The total cost and total income ratio of Angolan banks had a slight reduction in the years 2017 and 2018, i.e. 99.8% to 99.6%. In the following years, it had an increasing behavior, where total costs reached about 121.51%. The overall bank cost is a measure of the bank's efficiency and represents mismanagement when the cost is higher than revenue (Jenkins et al., 2021; Rehman et al., 2020; Son et al., 2020). Therefore, the values that are shown in Table 1 allow us to conclude that Angolan banks were inefficient in the years 2019 and 2020, and the costs are higher than the income of about 105.6% and 121.51%, respectively.

The spread of the interest rate reveals the behavior of the banking environment, as it expresses the difference between deposit rates and loan rates, and reflects the profit margin of banks, able to affect banks' lending decisions. When the deposit rates are higher than the loan rates the spread is positive and soon banks have less interest in lending, for reduced profits (Anarfo et al., 2020; Ugwuanyi, 2015). By the absolute values of bank spread in the years 2017 to 2019, we can conclude that there is a strong difference between the rates of deposits and loans, and in the year 2020, this margin was reduced up to 8.41%.

DATA AND METHODOLOGY

Data Description

The study of the effect of corruption on credit risk lacks greater attention, especially in underdeveloped countries, where the financial system in particular banks are struggling against the high volume of bad-debts credit. Generally, these countries are characterized by high rates of corruption (Jenkins et al., 2021; Mohamad & Jenkins, 2020). To support our study, we collected information on national and international data sources for a sample composed of 32 banks operating in the Angolan[5] economy, from 2004 to 2019. The bank-specific data were collected from the annual reports of each bank included in the sample and on the Website of the National Bank of Angola, and macroeconomic data and corruption indicators were extracted from the World Development Indicators (WDI) database. Several studies use the same databases to support their analyses (Anarfo et al., 2019a; Elsherif, 2019; Jenkins et al., 2021; Rehman et al., 2020; Son et al., 2020).

The main variables of interest in the present study are credit risk and corruption. Credit risk is measured by banks' defaulted loans concerning total loans and the higher the amount resulting from this ratio, the higher the credit risk and the likelihood of bank insolvency (Albaity et al., 2019; Jenkins et al., 2021; Klapper & Lusardi, 2020; Mohamad & Jenkins, 2020). To measure corruption, we use the indicator provided by the world bank, transparency, accountability, and corruption in the public sector. This index assesses the extent to which the executive can be held responsible for the misuse of funds and the results of its actions in the management of resources. When the index is equal to 1 it means a low level of corruption and an index value of 6 represents high corruption in the country.

According to recent studies on the same approach in regions such as Central and Eastern Europe, Pakistan, India, China, and in the countries of the Middle East and North Africa conducted by authors such as Hewa Wellalage et al. (2020), Jenkins et al. (2021), Liu et al. (2020), Mohamad and Jenkins (2020), Rehman et al. (2020) and Son et al. (2020), we select the following control variables: bank ownership, bank size, bank profitability, bank experience in the market, gross domestic product growth rate, and inflation rate. The structure of the property and the size of the bank were used as control variables because we believe that when a bank is composed mostly of public capital, pressure on the satisfaction of the political interests of the ruling party is more easily ceded and may affect its ability to control its loan portfolio. Besides, the hypothesis of moral risk suggests that the dependence of large banks on state intervention during difficult times, motivates banks to assume excessive risks and greater tolerance in lending (Albaity et al., 2019; Jenkins et al., 2021; Mohamad & Jenkins, 2020; Toader et al., 2018).

Profitability is represented in this study by the variables return on capital (ROE) and return on assets (ROA). Several pieces of evidence show that the most profitable banks are more averse and are more rigid in the evaluation of loans (Jenkins et al., 2021; Mohamad & Jenkins, 2020; Rehman et al., 2020; Song et al., 2021). The bank's experience was measured by the time banks existed in the market and we understand that the older the bank in the market the more experienced it becomes and has greater and better technical capacity for credit assessment and customer portfolio management, therefore, we expect the bank's experience in the market to reduce credit risk. For macroeconomic variables such as inflation and the growth rate of gross domestic product, the literature confirms that the less inflation and increases in the economic growth rate, the greater the repayment capacity of borrowers, and consequently there is a considerable reduction in credit risk (Gozgor, 2018; Song et al., 2021).

Property variables and activity time (experience) are dummy variables. They assume value "1" (one) if the bank is composed mostly of private capital and when the bank has more than 10 years of experience in the Angolan market; otherwise these variables assume a value equal to "0" (zero).

Specification of the Model

Authors such as Jenkins et al. (2021), Mohamad and Jenkins (2020), Rehman et al. (2020), Son et al. (2020), and Toader et al. (2018), while studying the effect of corruption on credit risk, have used the quantile regression, fixed effects, and OLS regression models. Our analysis uses the feasible generalized least squares (FGLS) model, based on the fact that the results are free of the problem of autocorrelation and heteroscedasticity (Greene, 2018; Miller, 2017; Saha et al., 1997; Umoru & Osemwegie, 2016). Equation (1) describes the regression model assumed.

$$Y_{it} = X_{it}\beta i_t + u \tag{1}$$

Where Y_{it} represents the dependent variable credit risk (npl) for bank i in time t; the X_{it} is the matrix of the explanatory variables of the model, namely corruption (corrup), returns on bank assets, return on equity (roe), bank size (size), economic growth rate (gdp), inflation rate (inf), proprietary Funds (fprop), bank experience in the market (exp); property. The βi_t are parameters of the vector of explanatory variables and u *is* the vector of random errors.

RESULTS AND DISCUSSION OF RESULTS

Descriptive Statistic

The variables under study and their descriptive statistics are found in Table 2. Table 2shows that in the period under analysis, on average, 3.6% of the credit granted by the banks was not repaid, as well as the maximum amount of credit risk for this period, reached about 79.75%. Regarding corruption, descriptive statistics indicate that the average rate of corruption in this period was 2.5 and the maximum corruption rate was about 3.5.

Table 2. Descriptive statistics

description	abbreviation	count	mean	sd	min	max
Credit risk	npl	319	0.036	0.578	3.908	7.975
Return on assets	roa	319	0.016	0.078	-0.667	0.239
Return on Equity	roe	319	0.159	0.632	-7.905	4.929
Proprietary Funds	fprop	319	0.167	0.166	-1.553	0.846
Bank size	size	319	11.262	1.863	6.201	14.787
Carruption	corrup	319	2.748	0.432	2.500	3.500
GDP growthrate	gdp	319	3.328	5.554	-5.400	15.029
Rate of inflation	inf	319	15.623	8.174	5.365	32.378
Property	property	319	0.859	0.349	0.000	1.000
Bank Experience	expe	319	0.897	0.305	0.000	1.000

Correlation Matrix

To ensure that the model used in the study is free from the problem of multicollinearity, we performed the correlation test, the results of which can be verified in Table 3 From the results presented, we can conclude that there are no indications of multicollinearity problems, once it is verified that we did not find any strong correlation between the main variables included in the study.

Nothing can be measured in terms of the correlation between credit risk and corruption because it does not reveal statistical significance, however, we highlight the positive and significant correlations between return on equity and credit risk, inflation, and credit risk. We can also see the negative and significant correlations between corruption and economic growth, inflation, and economic growth.

Table 3. Correlation between the variables under study.

	npl	roa	roe	size	corrup	gdp	inf
npl	1.00						
roa	0.19***	1.00					
	(0.00)						
roe	0.14**	0.44***	1.00				
	(0.01)	(0.00)					
size	-0.09	0.25***	0.21***	1.00			
	(0.12)	(0.00)	(0.00)				
corrup	-0.09	0.22***	0.13**	0.24***	1.00		
	(0.11)	(0.00)	(0.02)	(0.00)			
gdp	0.00	-0.01	-0.03	-0.29***	-0.52***	1.00	
	(0.94)	(0.79)	(0.56)	(0.00)	(0.00)		
inf	0.11*	-0.08	0.06	-0.01	-0.10*	-0.37***	1.00
	(0.06)	(0.15)	(0.26)	(0.85)	(0.07)	(0.00)	

Note: P-values in parentheses * $p < 0.10$, ** $p < 0.05$, *** $p < 0.01$

Unit Root Tests

In the analysis of panel data, it is important to examine the stationarity of the variables, to avoid spurious regressions (Anarfo et al., 2019). Therefore, we conducted the Augmented Fisher-Dickey Fuller (Fisher-ADF) and Fisher-Phillips Perron (Fisher-PP) stationarity tests, since the respective tests allow us to estimate the unitary root for unbalanced panels[6].

The result suggests that the variables included in the study are integrated of order zero, I(0), except for the variable corruption, which is integrated of order one, I(1). This result suggests that we should use in the analysis the first difference of the corruption variable (Anarfo et al., 2019b; Breitung, 2000; Breitung and Pesaran, 2005; Levin et al., 2002).

Table 4. Panel unit root test

	npl	roa	roe	size	gdp	inflation	corrup
Fisher-ADF	19,85***	22,59***	11,64***	27,14***	22,497***	8,28***	-4,80
Fisher-PP	23,45***	24,91***	14,42***	35,07***	25,82***	8,90***	-4,84
First Difference							
ADF-Fisher							12,01***
Fisher-PP							12,03***

Source: Own elaboration, ***, **, * significance levels of 1%,5% and 10% respectively.

Estimation of the Effect of Corruption on Credit Risk in Angola

Table 5. Effect of corruption over credit risk.

	(1) npl	(2) npl	(3) npl	(4) npl
corrup	0.190	0.661***	0.870***	0.866***
	(0.154)	(0.000)	(0.000)	(0.000)
roa	-0.569**	-0.0260	-0.0458	-0.0658
	(0.016)	(0.937)	(0.889)	(0.843)
roe	0.121***	-0.0640*	-0.0687**	-0.0668*
	(0.000)	(0.063)	(0.046)	(0.051)
size		-0.0219**	-0.0187**	-0.0104
		(0.017)	(0.047)	(0.393)
gdp		0.00386	0.00135	0.00676
		(0.836)	(0.942)	(0.721)
inf			0.0892	0.117*
			(0.163)	(0.082)
exp				8.143
				(0.106)
property				-0.103**
				(0.045)
fprop				0.0879
				(0.400)
_cons	-0.0607	-0.589*	-1.169**	-63.15
	(0.782)	(0.063)	(0.025)	(0.100)
N	319	220	220	220
wch2	20.44	25.97	28.14	34.02
p	0.000	0.000	0.000	0.000

Note: P-values in parentheses * $p < 0.10$, ** $p < 0.05$, *** $p < 0.01$.

To measure the robustness of the effect of corruption on credit risk we considered four models, where we were adding variables as we moved from one model to another. Table 5 presents the result of estimating the effect of corruption on credit risk. In the first model, beyond corruption, we used as an explanatory variable two indicators of profitability, the return on assets and the return on equity. However, in this model we can not measure the effect of corruption on credit risk, for the reason that we do not verify statistical significance, even so, the first model indicates that credit risk can be explained by profitability indicators.

Models (2) to (4) suggest that corruption produces positive effects on credit risk and in dimensional terms, we can see that by keeping the rest constant, the levels of corruption in Angola have the capacity to increase up to about 87% of credit risk or poor credit. The positive relationship between corruption and credit risk indicates that increases in corruption lead to increased credit risk, which affects bank stability and the ability to finance investment in the economy, on the other hand, interest rates for bank loans accompany the same behavior, specifically high to offset the high credit risk. The result found regarding the effect of corruption on credit risk corresponds to the expected result and is in line with recent evidence presented in some studies, like those of Jenkins et al. (2021), Mohamad and Jenkins (2020), and Son et al. (2020) which confirmed in their studies that corruption increases defaulted loans.

Parallel to these results, authors such as Hewa Wellalage et al. (2020), Liu et al. (2020), and Rehman et al. (2020) confirmed in their studies that low levels of corruption increase access to credit, as well as strict control of corruption significantly reduces credit risk in India, China, and Pakistan, respectively.

Regarding the control variables, we found that, in addition to corruption, the factors capable of influencing credit risk in Angola are the variable's return on assets, size of the bank, and the structure of bank ownership. Nothing can be inferred about the effect of macroeconomic variables on credit risk given that the variables economic growth rate and inflation rate did not present statistical significance in our study.

The FGLS estimation results suggest that by keeping the other factors constant, the increase in returns on equity reduces up to about 68.7% of the banks' unchanged credit in Angola. The inverse relationship between return on capital and credit risk indicates that the most profitable banks in Angola are more risk-averse and use more rigorous methods in the assessment of loans. These results corroborate those found by previous studies as Jenkins et al. (2021), Mohamad and Jenkins (2020), Rehman et al. (2020), and Song et al. (2021).

The scarce theoretical and empirical literature that examined the relationship between corruption and credit risk use the logarithm of assets to measure the size of the bank (Ali et al., 2019; Jenkins et al., 2021; Mohamad & Jenkins, 2020; Rehman et al., 2020; Toader et al., 2018). Therefore, we proceeded in the same way to assess the effect of the size of the bank on credit risk and found that the size of the bank in Angola has negative effects on credit risk, indicating that the larger the bank in terms of assets, it becomes less avid to credit risk. This result may be justified by the availability of financial resources and human capital that large banks have to cope with good business management and in particular the use of more sophisticated methods and techniques of credit portfolio management. This is therefore not to say that large banks are immune to the negative effects of corruption and especially when corruption is systematized, as is the case with African countries. For example, Jenkins et al. (2021) have shown that corruption does not affect all banks at the same level in the countries of the Middle East, North Africa, Afghanistan, and Pakistan (MENAP). Our result is in line with that found by Ali et al. (2019) when the authors found that the increase in the size of the bank has a positive relationship with bank stability.

Regarding the structure of banking ownership, the theory is based on the assumption that public banks have on average lower levels of stability compared to private banks, because they more easily satisfy political interests, as well as greater risk-taking because of the strong dependence on state intervention in times of crisis or bankruptcy. Toader et al. (2018) found no evidence of the property on credit risk. Our result suggests that the bank's private ownership considerably reduces credit risk.

CONCLUSION

In countries where the stock market is underdeveloped, access to finance is usually guaranteed by banks (Toader et al., 2018), as is the case with the Angolan reality. Therefore, the banking system in these economies plays a key role in allocating resources from surplus agents to deficit agents. On the other hand, several factors contribute to the risk-taking behavior of banking institutions, among them, we highlight financial regulation, good corporate governance, monetary policy, the structure of the market competition, and the levels of corruption existing in the country.

The quality and quantity of loans can be strongly influenced by corruption, mainly because it allows the discrimination of the most efficient and productive projects, to finance bad projects and safeguard personal interests. The result of our study suggests that default credit in Angola is positively influenced by corruption and negatively influenced by the size of the bank and the structure of the property.

Our result suggests that there is a positive relationship between corruption and credit risk, indicating that the high low-risk in the Angolan economy is the result of high levels of corruption, which has affected the way scarce financial resources have been allocated, i.e. banks ignore efficient projects and prioritize clients who pay bribes, who belong to the same political party or affiliation, family or friends, etc. The result in our study justifies the adoption and implementation of more serious and effective anti-corruption measures, to achieve banking stability and consequently greater and better financing of projects that can contribute to poverty reduction and foster economic growth. Additionally, we found that the size of the bank and the structure of the property contribute to a significant reduction in non-domestic credit in the Angolan economy, however, these results arouse the need to adopt good corporate governance, less public sector presence in the banking system and strict financial regulation.

REFERENCES

Albaity, M., Mallek, R. S., & Noman, A. H. M. (2019). Competition and bank stability in the MENA region: The moderating effect of Islamic versus conventional banks. *Emerging Markets Review*, *38*(January), 310–325. doi:10.1016/j.ememar.2019.01.003

Ali, M., Sohail, A., Khan, L., & Puah, C. H. (2019). Exploring the role of risk and corruption on bank stability: Evidence from Pakistan. *Journal of Money Laundering Control*, *22*(2), 270–288. doi:10.1108/JMLC-03-2018-0019

Anarfo, E. B., Abor, J. Y., & osei, K. A. (2019, July). Financial regulation and financial inclusion in Sub-Saharan Africa: Does financial stability play a moderating role? *Research in International Business and Finance*, *51*, 101070. doi:10.1016/j.ribaf.2019.101070

Anarfo, E. B., Abor, J. Y., Osei, K. A., & Gyeke-Dako, A. (2019a). Financial inclusion and financial sector development in Sub-Saharan Africa: A panel VAR approach. *International Journal of Managerial Finance*, *15*(4), 444–463. doi:10.1108/IJMF-07-2018-0205

Anarfo, E. B., Abor, J. Y., Osei, K. A., & Gyeke-Dako, A. (2019b). Monetary Policy and Financial Inclusion in Sub-Sahara Africa: A Panel VAR Approach. *Journal of African Business*, *20*(4), 549–572. doi:10.1080/15228916.2019.1580998

Ayesha, S., Fatima, S. A., & Krishnadas, L. (2020). Impact of loan portfolio diversification on central bank performance and risk mitigation. *International Journal of Management*, *11*(5), 644–661. doi:10.34218/IJM.11.5.2020.058

Bai, J., Malesky, E., Jayachandran, S., & Olken, A. B. (2013). Does economic growth reduce corruption? Theory and evidence. In The Bureau of economic research (No. 19483). doi:10.3386/w19483

Barone, A. (2021). *Bank*. Investopedia. Retrieved from https://www.investopedia.com/terms/b/bank.asp

Breitung, J. (2000). The Local Power of Some Unit Root Tests for Panel Data. In B. Baltagi (Ed.), Non-stationary Panels, Panel Cointegration, and Dynamic Panels Advances in Econometrics. JAI. doi:10.1016/S0731-9053(00)15006-6

Breitung, J., & Pesaran, M. (2005). *Unitroots and Cointegration in Panels* (No. 1565). https://www.ifo.de/DocDL/cesifo1_wp1565.pdf

CEDESA. (2021). Combate à corrupção em Angola: Radiografia para investidores. *Dinheiro Vivo*. https://www.dinheirovivo.pt/opiniao/combate-a-corrupcao-em-angola-radiografia-para-investidores-13714984.html

Education, C. F. I. (n.d.). *Credit Risk*. Retrieved from https://corporatefinanceinstitute.com/resources/knowledge/finance/credit-risk/

Elsherif, M. (2019). *The Relationship Between Financial Inclusion and Monetary Policy Transmission: the Case of Egypt.* doi:10.20472/IAC.2019.045.014

Gozgor, G. (2018). Determinants of the domestic credits in developing economies: The role of political risks. *Research in International Business and Finance*, *46*(May), 430–443. doi:10.1016/j.ribaf.2018.05.002

Greene, W. H. (2018). Econometric Analysis (8th ed.). Stern School of Business.

Hewa Wellalage, N., Locke, S., & Samujh, H. (2020). Firm bribery and credit access: Evidence from Indian SMEs. *Small Business Economics*, *55*(1), 283–304. doi:10.100711187-019-00161-w

Horton, M. (2021). *The Difference Between Profitability and Profit*. Investopedia. Retrieved from https://www.investopedia.com/ask/answers/012715/what-difference-between-profitability-and-profit.asp

Jalles, J. T. (2016). *A new theory of innovation and growth: The role of banking intermediation and corruption.* doi:10.1108/SEF-01-2016-0017

Jenkins, H., Alshareef, E., & Mohamad, A. (2021). The impact of corruption on commercial banks' credit risk: Evidence from a panel quantile regression. *International Journal of Finance and Economics*, 1–12. doi:10.1002/ijfe.2481

Kamran, H. W., Arshad, S. B. B. M., & Omran, A. (2019). Country governance, market concentration and financial market dynamics for banks stability in Pakistan. *Research in World Economy*, *10*(2), 136–146. doi:10.5430/rwe.v10n2p136

Klapper, L., & Lusardi, A. (2020). *Financial literacy and financial resilience : Evidence from around the world*. doi:10.1111/fima.12283

Kunieda, T. (2014). *Corruption, Globalization, and Economic Growth : Theory and Evidence*. Academic Press.

Levin, A., Lin, C. F., & Chu, C. S. J. (2002). Unit root tests in panel data: Asymptotic and finite-sample properties. *Journal of Econometrics*, *108*(1), 1–24. doi:10.1016/S0304-4076(01)00098-7

Liu, P., Li, H., & Guo, H. (2020). The impact of corruption on firms' access to bank loans: Evidence from China. *Economic Research-Ekonomska Istrazivanja*, *33*(1), 1963–1984. doi:10.1080/1331677X.2020.1768427

Miller, S. (2017). Feasible Generalized Least Squares Using Machine Learning. SSRN *Electronic Journal*, 1–25. doi:10.2139/ssrn.2966194

Mohamad, A., & Jenkins, H. (2020). Corruption and banks' non-performing loans: Empirical evidence from MENA countries. *Macroeconomics and Finance in Emerging Market Economies*, *00*(00), 1–14. doi:10.1080/17520843.2020.1842478

OECD. (n.d.). *Competition*. Retrieved from https://stats.oecd.org/glossary/detail.asp?ID=3163

Rehman, A., Adzis, A. A., & Mohamed-Arshad, S. B. (2020). The relationship between corruption and credit risk in commercial banks of Pakistan. *International Journal of Innovation, Creativity and Change*, *11*(1), 701–715.

Saha, A., Havenner, A., & Talpaz, H. (1997). Stochastic production function estimation: Small sample properties of ML versus FGLS. *Applied Economics*, *29*(4), 459–469. doi:10.1080/000368497326958

Setor, T. K., Senyo, P. K., & Addo, A. (2021). Do Digital Payment Transactions Reduce Corruption? Evidence from Developing Countries. *Telematics and Informatics, 60*(November), 101577. doi:10.1016/j.tele.2021.101577

Son, T. H., Liem, N. T., & Khuong, N. V. (2020). Corruption, nonperforming loans, and economic growth: International evidence. *Cogent Business and Management*, *7*(1), 1735691. Advance online publication. doi:10.1080/23311975.2020.1735691

Song, C. Q., Chang, C. P., & Gong, Q. (2021). Economic growth, corruption, and financial development: Global evidence. *Economic Modelling, 94*(December), 822–830. doi:10.1016/j.econmod.2020.02.022

Toader, T., Onofrei, M., Popescu, A. I., & Andrieș, A. M. (2018). Corruption and Banking Stability: Evidence from Emerging Economies. *Emerging Markets Finance & Trade*, *54*(3), 591–617. doi:10.1080/1540496X.2017.1411257

Transparency International. (n.d.). *What is Corruption?* Retrieved from https://www.transparency.org/en/what-is-corruption

Ugwuanyi, G. O. (2015). Regulation of Bank Capital Requirements and Bank Risk-Taking Behaviour: Evidence from the Nigerian Banking Industry. *International Journal of Economics and Finance*, *7*(8), 31–37. doi:10.5539/ijef.v7n8p31

Umoru, D., & Osemwegie, J. O. (2016). Capital Adequacy and Financial Performance of Banks in Nigeria: Empirical Evidence Based on the Fgls Estimator. *European Scientific Journal, ESJ, 12*(25), 295. doi:10.19044/esj.2016.v12n25p295

Wikipedia. (2021). *Developing Country*. Retrieved from https://en.wikipedia.org/wiki/Developing_country

ENDNOTES

[1] https://www.bna.ao/Conteudos/Artigos/lista_artigos_medias.aspx?idc=834&idl=1

[2] Transparency International is an organization dedicated to combating corruption worldwide, measures the perception of corruption in different countries through the annual publication of a Corruption Perception Index (CPI), ranging from 0 (Zero) to 10 (Ten), with 0 (Zero) corresponding to high levels of corruption and 10 (Ten) low levels of corruption. For more details, see: www.transparency.org/cpi.

[3] Return on assets or return over liquid assets is a profitability indicator used in finance to measure bank capacity in aggregate value with its own resources.

[4] Indicates the amount of revenue that a bank's asset is able to generate, and is calculated by the ratio of operating profits to total assets of the company.

[5] For convenience we decided not to expose the names of the banks analyzed in our study.

[6] Additional informations may be found in https://www.stata.com/manuals13/xtunitroot.pdf.

Chapter 6
Risk Governance and Bank Performance:
Do Risk Committee Activism and Finance Experts on the Risk Committee Matter?

John Agyekum Addae
https://orcid.org/0000-0002-6374-5195
Ghana Communication Technology University, Ghana & University of Aveiro, Portugal

Emmanuel Numapau Gyamfi
https://orcid.org/0000-0002-9829-3977
Ghana Institute of Management and Public Administration, Accra, Ghana

ABSTRACT

Global discourse is geared towards greater accountability and regulatory oversight of banks to promote sound financial systems and charter value. The authors applied dynamic pool panel analysis to investigate the relationship between risk governance and financial performance among African global banks spanning the years 2015 to 2020. They find significant positive association between financial experts on risk committee and bank profitability. The results further reveal that risk committee activism as a proxy for risk committee effectiveness significantly increase bank profitability. Therefore, stakeholders must prioritize regular risk committee meetings and attach importance to risk committee compositions with finance experts on the majority. Additionally, this study offers policy implications for regulators and bank mangers to clearly define risk committee financial experts and minimum financial experts required to serve on the risk committee.

DOI: 10.4018/978-1-7998-8609-9.ch006

INTRODUCTION

Risk Governance has been introduced as another layer to solidify corporate governance. Latent studies have bemoan that the global financial crisis was caused by weak risk governance (Chen et al., 2021). According to Bley et al., (2019), the global financial crisis exploded due to unwarranted risk build-up. Global financial crisis aftermath lessons place premium on risk governance. To forestall future global financial crisis, The Committee of Sponsoring Organizations of the Treadway Commission (COSO) recommended robust risk oversight at the board level (COSO, 2010). On the regulatory front, financial firms are subject to stricter risk governance through Pillar 3 Basel II (Nahar et al., 2016). Moreover, International Financial Reporting Standard (IFRS) 7 was also promulgated to strength risk governance reporting(Nahar & Azim, 2020). The Dodd-Frank Act 2010 also mandates financial holding companies to establish a stand-alone risk committee (Chen et al., 2021; Erin et al., 2020).

Plethora of studies on risk governance and bank performance abound in the developed economics to the neglect of emerging markets (Jia & Bradbury, 2021). However, Agoraki, Delis, and Pasiouras (2011) opine that empirical results from developed market may not be applicable to transition economies because their system, institutional setting and regulatory regime is quantitatively and qualitatively different (Agoraki et al., 2011, p. 39). African context evidence is critical because corporate governance practices is weak in emerging economies(Nahar et al., 2016; Nahar & Azim, 2020; Oradi & E-Vahdati, 2021). African banking system contextualization study have become imperative for several reasons. First, Banks predominately remain the source of fund in Africa. Africa financial system is dominated by banks due to underdeveloped capital market(Nahar & Azim, 2020). Secondly, ineffective rules and regulations, higher levels of corruption and political exploitation are pervasive in developing countries (Nahar et al., 2016, p. 251). Third, financial liberalization fashioned out in the 80s has breeze competition and open up the continent for more bank with some underlying cooperate governance challenges. To fill the African banking sparse studies, prior research examines Africa banking system in Nigeria (Erin et al., 2018, 2020; Kakanda et al., 2018); and Tunisia (Moussa, 2019). Cross-country evidence is the missing link in the literature that merit this studies. Therefore, this research contributes to knowledge with cross-country evidence to evaluate the association between risk governance and performance among African banks.

Financial acumen of board membership and board committee is important especially highly regulated financial intermediation industry (Apergis, 2019, p. 243). According to Malik et al., (2021), Board members that are more financially savvy are better placed to understanding company's risk profile. Moreover, Huang & Zhang, (2020) show that CEO with financial expert sign-up to better disclosure practices. Empirical evident exist for CEO financial expert (Custódio & Metzger, 2014; Gounopoulos & Pham, 2018); audit committee financial expert (Abbasi et al., 2020; Bilal et al., 2018; Defond et al., 2005; Hsu et al., 2018; Krishnan & Lee, 2009; Sultana & Mitchell Van der Zahn, 2015; Tanyi & Smith, 2015; Zalata et al., 2018); board members financial expert (Adams & Jiang, 2020; Apergis, 2019); male financial expert (Abbasi et al., 2020; Zalata et al., 2018) and female financial expert (Abbasi et al., 2020; Oradi & E-Vahdati, 2021; Zalata et al., 2018). However, studies on the role of finance expert on the risk committee are rarely and remain unexplored. Finance expert matter because tapping into financial expertise help to comply with financial policies; better position to handle sophisticated transactions; better able to raise external funding. (Apergis, 2019). According to Oradi & E-Vahdati, (2021) finance expert on audit committee establish more mechanism for effective internal control; and prudently manage risk and improve better monitoring.

Using bank level panel data extracted from 34 global banks with African origin spanning 2015-2020 accounting for 204 bank year observations, our dynamic pool panel analysis show a significant positive relationship between risk committee members financial expert and bank profitability. Our results further reveal that risk committee activism as a proxy for risk committee effectiveness significantly increase bank profitability. Our study contribute to literature severally. First, our study shed light on the factors associated with risk committee effectiveness. Second, we provide further evidence that examine the association between the risk committee attributes and financial outcome . Finally, provide evidence to guide policy direction on rules governing the role and composition of risk committee.

The rest of the study are organized as follows; section 2 discusses the literature review followed by the methodology section in section 3. The results and conclusions for the study are in section 4 and 5 respectively.

LITERATURE

Link between Risk Governance and Bank Performance

Risk Governance focuses on rules, methods and procedures that assist in risk identification and their appropriate mitigation. According to Aljughaiman & Salama, (2019), risk governance is assigned with the outmost oversight responsibility of overseeing all risk confronting the bank. Erin et al., (2020), posit that risk governance essentially deals with board members direct involvement in the risk process, risk implementation, risk reporting, and risk disclosure. Purposefully, risk governance focus on instituting risk culture, alignment of strategic objectives to risk framework, strengthening risk practices and alienate banking sector systematic risk. Extant literature have investigated the relationship between risk governance and bank performance. Nahar et al., (2016) results confirm that risk governance characteristics are significantly and positively associated with bank performance measures among African banks. The results Nahar et al., (2016) further confirm that risk disclosures, number of risk committees and presence of a risk management unit are positively associated with accounting-based and market-based performance. Likewise, Battaglia & Gallo, (2015) affirms positive relationship between size of risk committee and ROE and ROA suggests that banks with larger risk committee perform profitably better among Chinese and Indian banks. Additionally, among Mexican banks, Chavarín, (2020) show that risk governance impact significantly on bank profitability. Using FTSE350 listed Banks in UK, Farhan et al., (2020) finds that strong board-level risk committee increases the firm performance. Interestingly, Ames et al., (2018), reported that although the presence of board risk committees is positively related to financial performance, however they assert that five years presence of the board risk committees are effective and beneficial for long-term financial performance. Erin et al., (2020), empirical evidence show that strong Chief Risk Officer (CRO) presence, effective board risk committee, and inclusion of independent directors in the risk committee pivotally improve financial performance. In terms of risk governance expertise, Bailey, (2019), reported that actuarial expertise, CRO expertise, financial expertise, supervisory expertise and MBA degree are associated financial performance.

RISK GOVERNANCE DETERMENTS

Stand-Alone-Risk Committee

The establishment of a stand-alone risk committee has been sanctioned by many regulators (Aldhamari et al., 2020; Iselin, 2020).Traditionally, boards of banks mandates audit committee to be responsible for risk management functions. Under the current banking practice, risk management and risk governance duties have been entrusted into the care of stand-Alone risk committee. Bhuiyan et al., (2021)and Aldhamari et al., (2020) justify that it is necessary and good practice to separate risk committee from audit committee because these committees offers distinct roles. Bhuiyan et al., (2021) also advocated for stand-alone risk committee because skillset for risk management are distinct from audit functions. Further, while a joint audit and risk committee places a backward-looking emphasis on risk assessment, a stand-alone risk committee takes a forward-looking approach. The existence of risk committee improve monitoring. Operationalization of stand-alone risk committee enables the bank to determine its risk tolerance level as well as identify pursuing risk mitigation to tame inherent risk. Aldhamari et al., (2020) contend that creation of risk committee facilitates effective risk assessment and lowers financial risk. The studies of Teknologi et al., (2019) reveal that bank with stand-alone risk committee alienate incidences of financial crime. Bhuiyan et al., (2021), also reports that stand-alone risk committee drawdown risk-taking behavior and improve firm value compared with banks with joint audit and risk committee. In view of earlier studies, our study will thus test the following hypothesis:

H1: There is a positive relationship between stand-alone risk committee and bank performance

Risk Committee Size

Drawing on the resource dependency theory, larger risk committee membership is expected to enrich the committee with diverse expertise. Extant studies have affirm that majority of risk committee members must be independent directors (Aldhamari et al., 2020). However, concerns have been raised about the optimum risk committee size. Policy framework and prior studies have recommended a minimum 3-member audit committee size (Abdullah et al., 2017; Aldhamari et al., 2020). Proponents of large risk committee size orate that the committee would draw its strength from diversity of opinion(Aldhamari et al., 2020; Farhan et al., 2020).Conversely, advocates of small risk committee size also hold the view that small committees are efficient and more effective in decision-making. Prior empirical results have found that the risk committee size could either have positive or negative impact on performance. Battaglia & Gallo, (2015), affirms positive relationship between size of risk committee and bank performance. This means that, banks with larger risk committee perform profitably better. On the contrary, risk committee size was found to have a negative association with performance (Aldhamari et al., 2020; Malik et al., 2021). The following hypothesis is to be tested:

H2: There is a positive relationship between risk committee size and bank performance

Risk Committee Meeting and Activism

The frequency of risk committee meeting demonstrate the level of oversight. Higher meeting frequency also reflect risk committee extent of monitory. Regular risk committee meeting afford the committee an opportunity to streamline risk control mechanism and risk management communications. According to Farhan et al., (2020), risk committee frequency reflect the committee level of diligence. Usually, inactive committee increase the risk profile. To address agency problem, higher risk committee meeting is recommended(Aldhamari et al., 2020). Empirical results of Kakanda et al., (2018) show positive association between risk committee meeting and market performance.

The effectiveness of risk committee depends on the meeting frequency. . Risk committee activism also demonstrate the committee effectiveness. Jia et al., (2019) suggest that higher risk committee meeting indicates better monitoring. A committee is considered active if it meets more than 4 times in a year. Erin et al., (2018), provide empirical evidence that risk committee activism positively and significantly drive better performance of banks. Also empirical results of Kakanda et al., (2018) show positive association between risk committee meeting and market performance. moreover results of (Jia et al., 2019) found support for positive and significant association between risk effectiveness and firm performance(Farhan et al., 2020). The following hypothesis is thus tested:

H3: There is a positive relationship between the number of annual meetings of the risk committee and bank performance.
H4: There is a positive relationship between the frequency risk committee meeting and bank performance

Risk Committee Financial Expertise

Strong financial acumen of risk committee members optimize the committee effectiveness to address inherent risk in both internal and external operating environment. Financial expertise on the risk committee is highly important to the banking sector due to the financial complexity inherent in banking operations (Apergis, 2019, p. 243). According to Malik et al., (2021), more financially savvy members are better placed to understanding of the company's risk profile. Risk committee with rich financial expertise help to comply with financial policies; better position to handle sophisticated transactions; better able to raise external funding(Apergis, 2019). According to Oradi & E-Vahdati, (2021), finance expert on audit committee establish more mechanism for effective internal control; and prudently manage risk and improve better monitoring. Thus the presence of one financial expertise increase shareholders wealth, improve earnings management and significantly reduce risk. Comparatively women with financial expertise on risk committee are more effective at reducing financial distress likelihood than men with financial experience on risk committee.(Jia, 2019). We thus test the hypothesis that:

H5: There is a positive relationship between the financial expertise of risk committee member bank performance

Risk Committee Independence

Inclusion of independent director on risk committee is desirable. Prior evidence show that majority of risk committee members must be independent directors(Bhuiyan et al., 2021; Hoque et al., 2013; Jia

& Bradbury, 2020). Further, the appointment of independent director as chairman of risk committee is highly recommended(Jia & Bradbury, 2020). As a remedial action, (Chen et al., 2021) show that lower performing banks resort to maintain more independent risk committee members more than higher-performing counterparts. Using Australian listed firms, Jia & Bradbury, (2020) found that risk committee independence significantly leads to improvement of banks profitability. Low risk-taking behavior was recorded with risk committee with higher independent directors (Bhuiyan et al., 2021). That is to say that:

H6: There is a positive relationship between the independence of risk committee members and bank performance

Presence of Women on Risk Committee and Risk Committee Chair Gender

Women representation on the board and sub-committee offer value despite low representation. Women are risk-averse than men(Wang, 2020) and proven to be better decision makers(Moussa, 2019). Comprehensive review of Teodosia et al., (2021) concluded that women representation on the board and top management team reduce litigation risk. Using 2SLS regression to analyze 300 Australian listed firms from 2007-2014, Jia, (2019) show that women are better at monitoring and effective in controlling excessive risk-taking compared to men. Further, women devote more efforts to build strong procedures to detect risk and mitigate against losses. Firms with more women representation on top management team and board positions have competitive edge over those without (Busru et al., 2020).Women are ethical and trustworthy to protect stakeholder's interest(Aldhamari et al., 2020, p. 1288). Contrary evidence documented by Malik et al., (2021) show that presence of women on risk committee negatively influence performance.

In this study, risk committee chair gender is denoted as when the risk committee chair is a woman. The chair role is vested with authority. The chair drives the agenda and tone of the committee meeting discussions as well as establishment of committee practices and procedures. Palvia et al., (2020) finds that risk committee chair gender is relevant to predict bank performance. Similarly, Ud Din et al., (2021) finds that female chairs improve corporate governance mechanisms . In view of this, we test the following:

H7: There is a positive relationship between the number of women serving on the risk committee and bank performance

H8: There is a positive relationship between the chair of the risk committee being a woman and bank performance

CONTROLLING MECHANISMS

BIG4 Auditors, total asset, risk committee independent ratio and ratio of risk committee size to board size were used as control variables. Auditors quality was measured to denote if the bank is been audited by one of the big four audit firms namely PricewaterhouseCoopers, Deloitte & Touche, Ernst & Young, and KPMG. Big four auditing firms are capable at controlling risk taking behaviors. Big Four auditors maintain the ability to curb bank risk in countries characterized by weak institutions (Bley et al., 2019). We followed (Jia, 2019) to model risk committee independent ratio and finds significant and positive association with higher risk corporate performance. Finally, ratio of risk committee size to board size and natural log of total assets was modelled similar to a study conducted by (Chen et al., 2021). The following hypotheses are tested:

H9: There is a positive relationship between a BIG 4 auditor and bank performance
H10: There is a positive relationship between risk committee independent ratio and bank performance
H11: There is a negative relationship between risk committee size to board and bank performance
H12: There is a negative relationship between total assets and bank performance

METHODOLOGY

Sampling and Data Collection

Bank level panel data were employed spanning 2015-2020. African global banks with presence beyond their home country of incorporation constitute our sample. To be included in this study, the bank needed to have a risk committee. Further, to avoid sample duplication, data was extracted from consolidated group annual report. We followed studies that hand-collected data using annual reports (Erin et al., 2018, 2020; Jia & Bradbury, 2021; Kakanda et al., 2018; Nahar et al., 2016; Nahar & Azim, 2020; Rimin et al., 2020). After dropping banks with missing observations, the final sample made up of 34 banks with 204 yearly observations. Study sample details are presented in Tables 2 and 3.

Model Estimates Specification

The study estimation model specified in equation (1) below was tested using the Arellano-Bover/Blundel-Bond dynamic Generalized Method of Moments (GMM) to address any endogeneity and heterogeneity. Stata 16.1 software was used for the analysis.

$$PROFIT_{it} = a + bRISKGOV\ VARIABLES_{it} + cCONTROLS_{it} + \rho PROFITi_{t-1} + \epsilon it \quad (1)$$

Where a, b, c and ρ are coefficients, ϵ is the error term, i and t are indices for bank and time. The dependent variable PROFIT is proxied by ROA Ratio, RISKGOV VARIABLES are RCUniQExist, RCSIZE, RCMEET, RCFinXP, RCIND, RCActiv, RCofWomen and RCChairGen. The Control variables are BIG4, RC_IndRatio, RCBOD Ratio and Log TA. See Table 1 for a description of the variables under study.

Variable Description

Table 1 summaries the study variable, its operational definition, data sources and associated prior studies

Table 1. Model variable description

Variables	Symbol	Operationalization	Expected sign	Latent Studies	Data source
Dependent					
	ROA_Ratio	Net Income/Total Asset		Erin et al., (2020); Iselin, (2020); Nahar et al., (2016)	Annual report
Independent					
	RCUniQExist	1=RC UniQExist; 0=RC Co-Exist	+	Iselin, (2020)	Annual report
	RCSIZE	Number of Risk committee members	+	Erin et al., (2020)	Annual report
	RCMEET	Numbers of Risk committee meetings	+	Nahar et al., (2016)	Annual report
	RCFinXP	Independent director meeting the one of the following criteria: has been an executive of a bank, an executive of a non-bank financial institution, holds a financial position within a non-financial corporation, holds an academic position related to the field, or works in fund or investment management as a professional investor	+	Gontarek & Belghitar, (2018)	Annual report
	RCIND	the percentage of independent directors on the risk committee	+	Jia, (2019)	Annual report
	RCActiv	1= if the number annual meeting is equal or more than four times, otherwise 0	+	Erin et al., (2018)	Annual report
	RCofWomen	Number of women serving on Risk committee	+	Jia, (2019)	Annual report
	RCChairGen	1=if the Risk Committee chairman is female, or 0 otherwise	+	Jia, (2019)	Annual report
	BIG4	1=Bank is audited by one of the big four audit firms (i.e. PricewaterhouseCoopers, Deloitte & Touche, Ernst & Young, or KPMG), or 0 otherwise	+	Nahar et al., (2016)	Annual report
	RC_IndRatio	RCSIZE/ RCIND	+	Jia, (2019)	Annual report
	RCBOD_Ratio	RCSIZE/ BODSIZE	-	Chen et al., (2021)	Annual report
	Log_TA	Natural Logarithm of total assets	-	Chen et al., (2021)	Annual report

Results

The breakdown of banks that make up our sample are displayed in table 2 and 3. The final sample is made up of 34 banks with 204 yearly observations. The tables indicate that nine banks were drawn from South Africa. Followed by Nigeria with eight banks whereas Mauritius make up seven banks in our sample. The remaining banks originate from Ghana, Kenya, Egypt, Togo and Oman.

Table 2. Tabulation of bank

Bank ID	Bank name	Country	Freq.	Percent	Cum.
1	African Bank	South Africa	6	2.94	2.94
2	Al Baraka	South Africa	6	2.94	5.88
3	Capitech	South Africa	6	2.94	8.82
4	First Rand	South Africa	6	2.94	11.76
5	ABSA	South Africa	6	2.94	14.71
6	Stanbic	South Africa	6	2.94	17.65
7	NedBank	South Africa	6	2.94	20.59
8	Access Bank	Nigeria	6	2.94	23.53
9	Ecobank	Togo	6	2.94	26.47
10	GTBank	Nigeria	6	2.94	29.41
11	UBA	Nigeria	6	2.94	32.35
12	Zenith	Nigeria	6	2.94	35.29
13	Fidelity Bank	Nigeria	6	2.94	38.24
14	First City Bank	Nigeria	6	2.94	41.18
15	Union Bank	Nigeria	6	2.94	44.12
16	First Bank	Nigeria	6	2.94	47.06
17	Bidvest	South Africa	6	2.94	50.00
18	SASFIN	South Africa	6	2.94	52.94
19	CIB	Egypt	6	2.94	55.88
20	Bank Muscat	Oman	6	2.94	58.82
21	Mauritius ComB	Mauritius	6	2.94	61.76
22	Kenya ComBank	Kenya	6	2.94	64.71
23	Equity Bank	Kenya	6	2.94	67.65
24	Windhoek	Namibia	6	2.94	70.59
25	Calbank	Ghana	6	2.94	73.53
26	GCB	Ghana	6	2.94	76.47
27	Afrasia	Mauritius	6	2.94	79.41
28	SBM	Mauritius	6	2.94	82.35
29	Bank One	Mauritius	6	2.94	85.29
30	ABC Bank	Mauritius	6	2.94	88.24
31	BCP	Mauritius	6	2.94	91.18
32	SBI	Mauritius	6	2.94	94.12
33	Fidelity GH	Ghana	6	2.94	97.06
34	NBM	Malawi	6	2.94	100.00
Total			204	100.00	

Table 3. List of country

Country	Freq.	Percent	Cum.
Egypt	6	2.94	2.94
Ghana	18	8.82	11.76
Kenya	12	5.88	17.65
Malawi	6	2.94	20.59
Mauritius	42	20.59	41.18
Namibia	6	2.94	44.12
Nigeria	48	23.53	67.65
Oman	6	2.94	70.59
South Africa	54	26.47	97.06
Togo	6	2.94	100.00
Total	204	100.00	

Descriptive Statistics

Table 4 shows that the average ROA Ratio was 2.2%. Impressively, about 92.2% of banks maintain a stand-alone risk committee. On average, membership of risk committee is 5.5 whereas average risk committee meeting was 4.6 times, thus 93.1% of the risk committee meets the threshold of risk committee effectiveness recommended by prior studies. On average women were represented on the risk committee whilst woman as chairperson of risk committee was 13.7%. About 95.1% of banks engage the services of BIG4 auditing firms namely PricewaterhouseCoopers, Deloitte & Touche, Ernst & Young, KPMG for audit engagement. Moreover, about four members on risk committee have expertise in finance whereas four members are always independent directors on the risk committee. Descriptive statistics are presented in table 4.

Table 4. Descriptive statistics

Variable	Obs	Mean	Std. Dev.	Min	Max
ROA Ratio	204	.022	.047	-.011	.66
RCUniQExist	204	.922	.27	0	1
RCSIZE	204	5.529	1.918	3	13
RCMEET	204	4.623	1.317	1	11
RCFinXP	204	4.711	1.628	2	10
RCIND	204	4.412	1.642	2	12
RCActiv	204	.931	.253	0	1
RCofWomen	204	1	1.055	0	6
RCChairGen	204	.137	.345	0	1
BIG4	204	.951	.216	0	1
RC IndRatio	204	1.298	.343	1	3.5
RCBOD Ratio	204	.461	.117	.167	.833
Log TA	204	15.901	3.033	7.263	22.884

Table 5. Pairwise correlations

Variables	(1)	(2)	(3)	(4)	(5)	(6)	(7)	(8)	(9)	(10)	(11)	(12)	(13)
(1) ROA_Ratio	1.000												
(2) RCUQExist	0.031	1.000											
(3) RCSIZE	-0.100	0.252*	1.000										
(4) RCMEET	-0.188*	-0.042	0.039	1.000									
(5) RCFinXP	-0.096	0.296*	0.838*	0.073	1.000								
(6) RCIND	-0.086	0.118	0.797*	0.129	0.647*	1.000							
(7) RCActiv	-0.215*	-0.079	0.106	0.453*	0.083	0.092	1.000						
(8) RCWomen	-0.045	0.156*	0.504*	0.018	0.373*	0.469*	0.111	1.000					
(9) RCChairGen	0.012	0.063	-0.088	0.115	-0.192*	-0.065	0.052	0.217*	1.000				
(10) BIG4	-0.234*	-0.066	0.217*	0.142*	0.169*	0.265*	0.028	0.194*	0.091	1.000			
(11) RCIndR	-0.040	0.227*	0.236*	-0.156*	0.273*	-0.349*	-0.038	0.010	-0.082	-0.134	1.000		
(12) RCBD_R	0.012	0.253*	0.487*	-0.134	0.378*	0.391*	0.167*	0.154*	-0.074	-0.141*	0.099	1.000	
(13) Log_TA	-0.238*	-0.211*	-0.029	-0.070	-0.152*	-0.096	0.197*	0.070	0.051	-0.056	0.055	0.088	1.000

*** $p<0.01$, ** $p<0.05$, * $p<0.1$

A pairwise correlation test was carried out between the variables under study. It was observed that RCSIZE, RCMEET, RCFinXP, RCIND, RCActiv, RCofWOMEN, BIG4, RCIndRatio and LogTA were negatively related to ROARatio. This means that ROARatio move in opposite direction as these variables. Thus when ROARatio is increasing, the variables are decreasing and vice versa

Also, RCUniQExist, RCChairGen and RCBod Ratio was positively related to ROARatio. This means RCUniQExist, RCChairGen and RCBod Ratio move in the same direction as ROARatio.

In addition, to ensure the validity of the analysis, tests including correlation test as shown in table 5 and the Hausman test were conducted to ensure that the most robust method is employed. In deciding between which of the two models is most preferable, results of the Hausman test shows a Chi-square value of 86.84 with a p-value of 0.000. This means the fixed effect model is preferred for our data analysis

The results from the fixed effects model presented in Table 6 shows that only BIG4 and Log TA were significant in predicting profitability. This observation could be misleading because of endogeneity bias. There could either be unobserved heterogeneity, simultaneity and dynamic endogeneity. To address the issue of endogeneity bias, a generalized method of moments (GMM) model as in Equation 1 was employed in analyzing the data.

The results from Table 7 as compared to Table 6 shows differences in the number of variables that were significant in predicting profitability. It was observed from Table 7 that LROARatio significantly affect ROARatio, an indication of the momentum presence in predicting banks profitability. The results also revealed that risk committee activism as a proxy for risk committee effectiveness, RCMEET, RCFinXP and RC Bod Ratio significantly affect bank profitability. On the contrary, RCUniQExist, RCSIZE, RCIND, RCofWomen, RCChairGen, BIG 4, RC_IndRatio and LogTA do not have an effect in predicting banks profitability

Table 6. Fixed effect regression results

ROA_Ratio	Coef.	St.Err.	t-value	p-value	[95% Conf	Interval]	Sig
RCUniQExist	.028	.018	1.52	.13	-.008	.063	
RCSIZE	0	.009	0.04	.967	-.018	.019	
RCMEET	-.002	.003	-0.80	.426	-.008	.003	
RCFinXP	-.001	.005	-0.13	.898	-.011	.01	
RCIND	-.005	.01	-0.51	.613	-.024	.014	
RCActiv	-.018	.013	-1.41	.16	-.044	.007	
RCofWomen	.002	.004	0.55	.58	-.006	.01	
RCChairGen	-.005	.01	-0.50	.618	-.024	.014	
BIG4	-.074	.017	-4.36	0	-.107	-.04	***
RC_IndRatio	-.012	.023	-0.50	.62	-.057	.034	
RCBOD_Ratio	-.001	.044	-0.02	.986	-.088	.086	
Log_TA	-.074	.008	-9.20	0	-.09	-.058	***
Constant	1.313	.124	10.60	0	1.068	1.558	***
Mean dependent var		0.022		SD dependent var		0.047	
R-squared		0.548		Number of obs		204.000	
F-test		15.995		Prob > F		0.000	
Akaike crit. (AIC)		-857.068		Bayesian crit. (BIC)		-813.932	
*** p<.01, ** p<.05, * p<.1							

Table 7. GMM regression results

ROA_Ratio	Coef.	St.Err.	t-value	p-value	[95% Conf	Interval]	Sig
L.ROA_Ratio	-.022	.006	-3.78	0	-.034	-.011	***
RCUniQExist	-.012	.006	-1.91	.056	-.023	0	*
RCSIZE	-.002	.003	-0.67	.504	-.008	.004	
RCMEET	-.002	.001	-2.14	.033	-.004	0	**
RCFinXP	.002	.001	2.58	.01	.001	.004	***
RCIND	.004	.002	1.66	.097	-.001	.008	*
RCActiv	.006	.002	2.69	.007	.002	.011	***
RCofWomen	0	.001	0.23	.819	-.002	.003	
RCChairGen	.003	.003	1.19	.235	-.002	.009	
BIG4	0	.011	0.04	.965	-.02	.021	
RC_IndRatio	.009	.005	1.91	.056	0	.018	*
RCBOD_Ratio	-.035	.016	-2.19	.028	-.067	-.004	**
Log_TA	-.004	.002	-1.88	.06	-.008	0	*
Constant	.08	.031	2.61	.009	.02	.141	***
Mean dependent var		0.019		SD dependent var		0.014	
Number of obs		170.000		Chi-square		263.482	
*** p<.01, ** p<.05, * p<.1							

DISCUSSION

From Table 7, it was observed that activism is positively related and highly significant in predicting profitability. This means that the number of times the committee meets offer value to grow the bank's profitability. This result is in agreement with H4 and the works of (Erin et al., 2018). Moreover, our results reveal that the presence of finance experts improve bank profitability. Therefore, expert knowledge from members with specialization in finance and risk management on the committee go a long way to mitigate risk inherent in banking operations and therefore inure to the benefit of the bank in terms of profit. Thus, we fail to reject H5. Similar results were documented by (Aldhamari et al., 2020) aver risk committee qualification attributes are significantly and positively influence accounting performance. Additionally, we found that there is a negative relationship between risk committee meetings and bank performance. We thus reject H3 and conclude that the more risk committee meets to execute their functions including appraising delinquent loans, accessing the banks risk profile among others they are able to diligently carry out their risk related mandate which are beneficial to the bank. The observation on the frequency of risk committee meetings does not conform to the studies by Hoque et al., (2013) who found that frequencies of risk committee meetings do not show any significant effects on the financial performance among Australian firms. Stand-alone risk committee lessen bank profitability due to the cost of maintaining distinct risk committee instead of combining it with audit committee. This implies that more meetings of the risk committee attract extract operational cost such as sitting allowances and other related cost associated with the committee draw down the profitability of the bank. Our finding contradicts H1 and that of several studies.. For example, studying Australian and Asia–Pacific banks, Bhuiyan et al., (2021), reported that the presence of stand-alone risk committee positively induce better performance. Jia & Bradbury, (2021) further shows that banks with risk committee separately constituted perform better. Rimin et al., (2020) collaborated latent literature and show that separating risk committee as a stand-alone committee significantly and positively increase bank profitability. As expected, we document that if risk committee members are independent, the more profitability the bank. This is because, independent committee members are not biased, they offer independent opinions and fresh ideas unto the committee. They also offer value not existing within the bank management team which eventually leads to bank profitability. The positive relationship follows similar studies conducted by Kweh and Lu (2018) who found out that higher independent directors on risk committee yield high profit among dual banking system. The results of Rimin et al. (2020) affirm that a risk committee with majority of independent directors would significantly improve the firm's performance. Also, Dupire & Slagmulder, (2019) documented evidence that state controlled banks are more likely to have more directors that are independent on the risk committee. Similarly, the higher proportion of independent members on the risk committee induce better performance. There was an inverse relationship between profitability and natural log of total assets.

CONCLUSION

Banks are the primary providers of financing in African countries due to weak capital markets and they play a critical role in bridging the gap between the financial system and the real economies. We applied GMM to analyze the relationship between risk governance and financial performance among African global banks spanning 2015-2020. Our results revealed that risk committee member's financial expertise and frequency of risk committee meeting significantly increase bank profitability. Therefore, improvement in risk committee effectiveness boost the capacity of the bank to achieve more profit. Further, our results highlight the importance of appointing financial expert to serve on banks risk committees. Policy implication for banks is that constituting risk committee with financial expert contrary to appointing non-finance expert will give the bank a mileage in improving their profitability. Stakeholders have yelling about interferences in bank managers appointments especially in Africa. Therefore, banks in emerging markets must solidify their risk governance with finance experts rather than the practice of appointing politically connected directors. The study results support financial services regulators to implement necessary risk governance reforms to optimize bank performance. We consider that our study contributes to literature on corporate governance and financial performance through the lenses of risk governance.

REFERENCES

Abbasi, K., Alam, A., & Bhuiyan, M. B. U. (2020). Audit committees, female directors and the types of female and male financial experts: Further evidence. *Journal of Business Research*, *114*(February), 186–197. doi:10.1016/j.jbusres.2020.04.013

Abdullah, M., Shukor, Z. A., & Rahmat, M. M. (2017). The Influences of Risk Management Committee and Audit Committee towards Voluntary Risk Management Disclosure. *Jurnal Pengurusan*, *50*, 83–95. doi:10.17576/pengurusan-2017-50-08

Adams, M., & Jiang, W. (2020). Do Financial Experts on the Board Matter? An Empirical Test From the United Kingdom's Non-Life Insurance Industry. *Journal of Accounting, Auditing & Finance*, *35*(1), 168–195. doi:10.1177/0148558X17705201

Agoraki, M. E. K., Delis, M. D., & Pasiouras, F. (2011). Regulations, competition and bank risk-taking in transition countries. *Journal of Financial Stability*, *7*(1), 38–48. doi:10.1016/j.jfs.2009.08.002

Aldhamari, R., Nor, M. N. M., Boudiab, M., & Mas'ud, A. (2020). The impact of political connection and risk committee on corporate financial performance : Evidence from financial firms in Malaysia. *Corporate Governance*, *20*(7), 1281–1305. doi:10.1108/CG-04-2020-0122

Aljughaiman, A. A., & Salama, A. (2019). Do banks effectively manage their risks? The role of risk governance in the MENA region. *Journal of Accounting and Public Policy*, *38*(5), 106680. doi:10.1016/j.jaccpubpol.2019.106680

Ames, D. A., Hines, C. S., & Sankara, J. (2018). Board risk committees: Insurer financial strength ratings and performance. *Journal of Accounting and Public Policy*, *37*(2), 130–145. doi:10.1016/j.jaccpubpol.2018.02.003

Apergis, N. (2019). Financial Experts on the Board: Does It Matter for the Profitability and Risk of the U.K. Banking Industry? *Journal of Financial Research*, *42*(2), 243–270. doi:10.1111/jfir.12168

Bailey, C. (2019). The Relationship Between Chief Risk Officer Expertise, ERM Quality, and Firm Performance. *Journal of Accounting, Auditing & Finance*, •••, 1–25. doi:10.1177/0148558X19850424

Battaglia, F., & Gallo, A. (2015). Risk governance and Asian bank performance : An empirical investigation over the fi nancial crisis. *Emerging Markets Review*, *25*, 53–68. doi:10.1016/j.ememar.2015.04.004

Ben Moussa, F. (2019). The Influence of Internal Corporate Governance on Bank Credit Risk: An Empirical Analysis for Tunisia. *Global Business Review*, *20*(3), 640–667. doi:10.1177/0972150919837078

Bhuiyan, B. U., Cheema, M. A., & Man, Y. (2021). Risk committee, corporate risk-taking and firm value. *Managerial Finance*, *47*(3), 285–309. doi:10.1108/MF-07-2019-0322

Bilal, C., Chen, S., & Komal, B. (2016, November). Audit committee financial expertise and earnings quality: A meta-analysis. *Journal of Business Research*, *84*, 253–270. doi:10.1016/j.jbusres.2017.11.048

Bley, J., Saad, M., & Samet, A. (2019). Auditor choice and bank risk taking. *International Review of Financial Analysis*, *61*(December), 37–52. doi:10.1016/j.irfa.2018.11.003

Busru, S. A., Shanmugasundaram, G., & Bhat, S. A. (2020). Corporate Governance an Imperative for Stakeholders Protection : Evidence from Risk Management of Indian Listed Firms. *Business Perspectives and Research*, *8*(2), 89–116. doi:10.1177/2278533719886995

Chavarín, R. (2020). Risk governance, banks affiliated to business groups, and foreign ownership. In Risk Management (Vol. 22, Issue 1). Palgrave Macmillan UK. doi:10.105741283-019-00049-9

Chen, J., Cheng, C., Ku, C. Y., & Liao, W. (2021). Are Banks Improving Risk Governance After the Financial Crisis? *Journal of Accounting, Auditing & Finance*, *36*(3), 540–556. doi:10.1177/0148558X19870099

COSO. (2010). *Board Risk Oversight-A progress report*. https://www.coso.org/pages/erm.aspx

Custódio, C., & Metzger, D. (2014). Financial expert CEOs: CEO's work experience and firm's financial policies. *Journal of Financial Economics*, *114*(1), 125–154. doi:10.1016/j.jfineco.2014.06.002

Defond, M. L., Hann, R. N., Xuesong, H. U., & Engel, E. (2005). Does the market value financial expertise on audit committees of boards of directors? *Journal of Accounting Research*, *43*(2), 153–193. doi:10.1111/j.1475-679x.2005.00166.x

Dupire, M., & Slagmulder, R. (2019). Risk governance of financial institutions : The effect of ownership structure and board independence. *Finance Research Letters*, *28*, 227–237. doi:10.1016/j.frl.2018.05.001

Erin, O., Adebola, D. K., & Abdurafiu, O. N. (2020). Risk governance and cybercrime : The hierarchical regression approach. *Future Business Journal*, *6*(1), 1–15. doi:10.118643093-020-00020-1

Erin, O., Asiriuwa, O., Olojede, P., Ajetunmobi, O., & Usman, T. (2018). Does Risk Governance Impact Bank Performance? Evidence from the Nigerian Banking Sector. *Academy of Accounting and Financial Studies Journal*, *22*(4), 1–15.

Farhan, M., Zaman, M., & Buckby, S. (2020). Enterprise risk management and firm performance : Role of the risk committee. *Journal of Contemporary Accounting & Economics*, *16*(1), 100178. doi:10.1016/j.jcae.2019.100178

Gontarek, W., & Belghitar, Y. (2018). Risk governance : Examining its impact upon bank performance and risk-taking. *Financial Markets, Institutions and Instruments*, *27*(5), 187–224. doi:10.1111/fmii.12103

Gounopoulos, D., & Pham, H. (2018). Financial Expert CEOs and Earnings Management Around Initial Public Offerings. *The International Journal of Accounting*, *53*(2), 102–117. doi:10.1016/j.intacc.2018.04.002

Hoque, M. Z., Islam, M. R., & Azam, M. N. (2013). Board Committee Meetings and Firm Financial Performance : An Investigation of Australian Companies. *International Review of Finance*, *13*(4), 503–528. doi:10.1111/irfi.12009

Hsu, P. H., Moore, J. A., & Neubaum, D. O. (2018). Tax avoidance, financial experts on the audit committee, and business strategy. *Journal of Business Finance & Accounting*, *45*(9–10), 1293–1321. doi:10.1111/jbfa.12352

Huang, H., & Zhang, W. (2020). Financial expertise and corporate tax avoidance. *Asia-Pacific Journal of Accounting & Economics*, *27*(3), 312–326. doi:10.1080/16081625.2019.1566008

Iselin, M. (2020). Estimating the potential impact of requiring a stand-alone board-level risk committee. *Journal of Accounting and Public Policy*, *39*(5), 106709. doi:10.1016/j.jaccpubpol.2019.106709

Jia, J. (2019). Does risk management committee gender diversity matter? A financial distress perspective. *Managerial Auditing Journal*, *34*(8), 1050–1072. doi:10.1108/MAJ-05-2018-1874

Jia, J., & Bradbury, M. E. (2020). Complying with best practice risk management committee guidance and performance. *Journal of Contemporary Accounting & Economics*, *16*(3), 100225. doi:10.1016/j.jcae.2020.100225

Jia, J., & Bradbury, M. E. (2021). Risk management committees and firm performance. *Australian Journal of Management*, *46*(3), 369–388. doi:10.1177/0312896220959124

Jia, J., Li, Z., & Munro, L. (2019). Risk management committee and risk management disclosure : Evidence from Australia. *Pacific Accounting Review*, *31*(3), 438–461. doi:10.1108/PAR-11-2018-0097

Kakanda, M. M., Salim, B., & Chandren, S. A. (2018). Risk Management Committee Characteristics and Market Performance: Empirical Evidence from Listed Review financial service firms in Nigeria. *International Journal of Management and Applied Science*, *4*(2), 6–10. http://www.iraj.in/journal/journal_file/journal_pdf/14-440-15230079706-10.pdf

Krishnan, J., & Lee, J. E. (2009). Audit committee financial expertise, litigation risk, and corporate governance. *Auditing*, *28*(1), 241–261. doi:10.2308/aud.2009.28.1.241

Kweh, Q. L., & Lu, W. (2018). Risk management and dynamic network performance : An illustration using a dual banking system. *Applied Economics*, *50*(30), 3285–3299. doi:10.1080/00036846.2017.1420889

Malik, M., Shafie, R., & Ku Ismail, K. N. I. (2021). Do risk management committee characteristics influence the market value of firms? *Risk Management*, *23*(1–2), 172–191. doi:10.105741283-021-00073-8

Nahar, S., Azim, M. I., & Hossain, M. M. (2020). Risk disclosure and risk governance characteristics : Evidence from a developing economy. *International Journal of Accounting & Information Mangement*, *28*(4), 577–605. doi:10.1108/IJAIM-07-2019-0083

Nahar, S., Jubb, C., & Azim, M. I. (2016). Risk governance and performance : A developing country perspective. *Managerial Auditing Journal, 31*(3), 250–268. doi:10.1108/MAJ-02-2015-1158

Oradi, J., & E-Vahdati, S. (2021). Female directors on audit committees, the gender of financial experts, and internal control weaknesses: Evidence from Iran. *Accounting Forum, 0*(0), 1–34. doi:10.1080/01559982.2021.1920127

Palvia, A., Vähämaa, E., & Vähämaa, S. (2020). Female leadership and bank risk-taking: Evidence from the effects of real estate shocks on bank lending performance and default risk. *Journal of Business Research, 117*(January), 897–909. doi:10.1016/j.jbusres.2020.04.057

Rimin, F., Bujang, I., Wong, A., & Chu, S. (2020). The effect of a separate risk management committee (RMC) towards firms' performances on consumer goods sector in Malaysia. *Business Process Management Journal*. Advance online publication. doi:10.1108/BPMJ-06-2020-0265

Sultana, N., & Mitchell Van der Zahn, J. L. W. (2015). Earnings conservatism and audit committee financial expertise. *Accounting and Finance, 55*(1), 279–310. doi:10.1111/acfi.12042

Tanyi, P. N., & Smith, D. B. (2015). Busyness, expertise, and financial reporting quality of audit committee chairs and financial experts. *Auditing, 34*(2), 59–89. doi:10.2308/ajpt-50929

Teknologi, U., Cawangan, M., & Kampus, K. (2019). Audit and risk committee in financial crime prevention. *Journal of Financial Crime, 26*(1), 223–234. doi:10.1108/JFC-11-2017-0116

Teodosia, J., Veira, E., & Madaleno, M. (2021). Gender diversity and corporate risk-taking : A literature review. *Managerial Finance, 47*(7), 1038–1073. Advance online publication. doi:10.1108/MF-11-2019-0555

Ud Din, N., Cheng, X., Ahmad, B., Sheikh, M. F., Adedigba, O. G., Zhao, Y., & Nazneen, S. (2021). Gender diversity in the audit committee and the efficiency of internal control and financial reporting quality. *Economic Research-Ekonomska Istrazivanja, 34*(1), 1170–1189. doi:10.1080/1331677X.2020.1820357

Wang, Y. H. (2020). Does board gender diversity bring better financial and governance performances? An empirical investigation of cases in Taiwan. *Sustainability, 12*(8), 1–14. doi:10.3390u12083205

Zalata, A. M., Tauringana, V., & Tingbani, I. (2018). Audit committee financial expertise, gender, and earnings management: Does gender of the financial expert matter? *International Review of Financial Analysis, 55*(November), 170–183. doi:10.1016/j.irfa.2017.11.002

Chapter 7
Loss Aversion in Companies Whose Location Is Affected by Fire

Mara Madaleno
https://orcid.org/0000-0002-4905-2771
GOVCOPP, University of Aveiro, Portugal

Jorge Mota
GOVCOPP, University of Aveiro, Portugal

Fábio Brandão
University of Aveiro, Portugal

ABSTRACT

In Portugal, fires have originated a big debate not only because of the environmental damages they cause but also because of the material damages they provoke to families and companies. This way, it is important to understand how these events impact companies' cash holdings, not because of the direct damages caused by them, but because of managers' loss aversion. The empirical evidence, mainly documented by Dessaint and Matray and Kahneman and Tversky, were the main sources to this empirical study, where the authors have chosen to work with panel data analysis using a sample of 38,574 small and medium enterprises during the period from 2009 to 2015. About the obtained results, there is evidence that cash holdings increase when managers of a company located in a region close to a fire, but not directly damaged by it, perceive a salient event of a future fire. In other words, when they anticipate the occurrence of an identical event, cash holdings are increased to protect the company against it.

DOI: 10.4018/978-1-7998-8609-9.ch007

INTRODUCTION

Tversky and Kahneman (1974) state that one of the heuristics that corporate managers use is to attribute the frequency of occurrence of a given event based on the ease with which this event arises in their minds (imminence). Thus, events that occurred relatively recently appear in the mind more easily and are likely to overestimate their occurrence (Dessaint and Matray, 2017). There is also a possibility that these managers may be more loss-averse, as their perceived risk may be temporarily higher, although the actual risk does not change.

Fires are considered to be a good source of information for the study of loss aversion. First of all, when a fire occurs, it does not provide any information on whether or not another fire may occur shortly. According to Dessaint and Matray (2017), the estimation of the increased occurrence of a hurricane at the same location based on the occurrence of another during the last two years results in a statistically non-significant coefficient. This statement, while applied to another type of disaster, could also be applied in the context of fires.

Moreover, the occurrence of a fire is nothing related to the characteristics of a company and its manager (considering that neither agent has any kind of fault in the formation of it). Fires can cause extensive damage to affected areas. Thus, these are considered imminent events, not only for companies directly located in the area but also for their neighborhood. Finally, fires allow a certain identification strategy to be used, as this imminence of danger decreases as the distance to it increases.

This study will analyze the Portuguese Small and Medium Enterprises (SMEs), trying to understand the behavior of their managers regarding the imminence of fire concerning cash, to understand if their aversion to loss affects or not those same amounts. According to Dessaint and Matray (2017), risk perception can be demonstrated through the treasury amounts of a given company, based on the studies by Froot et al. (1993) and Hölmstrom and Tirole (1998), who state that Treasury is used by companies as a liquidity security mechanism when the use of external financing is limited.

From the results obtained, evidence was found that fires have an impact on the change in the companies' cash amounts, and their increase, as Dessaint and Matray (2017) conclude about hurricanes. Thus, our results seem to indicate that managers are trying to anticipate these events by increasing their reserves to prevent disasters. These reserves are increased by an average of 0.15% to protect against these events.

On the other hand, the results are different from those obtained by Dessaint and Matray (2017) regarding the timing of this increase. This difference is explained by the fact that the nature and frequency of these events are different. While there are several fires per year in Portugal (17,607 occurrences on average per year between January 1 and October 31, 2007, to 2017, where 3,444 correspond to forest fires and the rest to hot flushes with a burned area of less than 1 hectare, according to the Institute for Nature Conservation and Forests (2017a)), in the United States there is only an average of 11.7 named storms per year, with only 6.3 being hurricanes and 1.7 touching the ground of the country (National Oceanic & Atmospheric Administration, 2017).

Recently, the literature got more concerned about special events' impacts on a firm's cash flows. Brown et al. (2021) examine firms' use of credit lines when they face a liquidity shock that is not directly related to fundamentals, namely considering abnormally heavy winter snowfall. The authors provide novel evidence of direct effects that firms use credit lines as liquidity insurance against cash flow volatility that is unrelated to firm fundamentals. Gill (2020) explores whether and under which conditions firms hoard cash holdings to address natural disaster risk (Acts of God), technological disaster risk (Human related), or both. Results point that firms do not have a trade-off between these two types of disasters in determining their cash policy, but prioritize the preparedness of possible natural disaster strikes above possible technological accidents. In the same year, Javadi et al. (2020) used data from 41 different countries including the United States, to conclude that firms increase their cash holdings as a response to climate risk. This effect is driven by financially constrained firms and fits consistently within the precautionary motive framework. The authors suggest that firms have been trying to hedge against climate risk by holding more cash. Previously, Noth and Rehbein (2019) investigate firm outcomes after a major flood in Germany in 2013, finding that firms located in the disaster regions have significantly higher turnover, lower leverage, and higher cash in the period after 2013. The authors find evidence that this effect can be partially explained by learning from a previous disaster, that of 2002. Thus, results document a positive net effect on firm performance in the direct aftermath of a natural disaster.

This work is organized as follows: Section 2 presents a review of the literature on the subject, addressing the different theories and biases, and heuristics in decision making, as well as the state of fires in Portugal and how they are treated compared to what happens in the United States of America. This is followed by Section 3, where the methodology used is presented, encompassing the description of all variables used in the study, as well as all filtering criteria used to export the company's database, so that there are no errors. Already in Section 4, the collected data are treated statistically to analyze the impact of the fires on the cash amounts of the companies. Moreover, these results are interpreted and compared with the results obtained by the authors analyzed in the literature review. Finally, the conclusions and some limitations to this study are exposed in section 5, as well as some suggestions for future research.

LITERATURE REVIEW

This section discusses the theoretical framework that supports this study, based on the existing theory on the subject, as well as presents the other studies that analyzed the theme empirically.

Several recent studies are addressing behavioral finance that will underlie this paper. However, it will be necessary to address other older studies focusing, on the one hand, on Kahneman and Tversky's (1979) Prospect Theory, which states that investors are irrational at the time of decision making, as it states that earnings and losses are assessed differently and individuals decide based on perceived gains rather than based on perceived losses; and, on the other hand, the Markowitz Portfolio Theory (1952), which assumes that investors are rational so that they can use the principle of diversification to optimize returns on their investment portfolios.

Finally, there will be a discussion of the different points of view to be made an empirical analysis of the objects under study, directed to a perspective of loss aversion in companies located in areas affected by the fire.

Portfolio Theory

The study of investor rationality when making a decision is relatively recent and one of the first theories to emerge was Portfolio Theory (Markowitz 1952). This theory is not related to the theme of loss aversion; on the contrary, the theory assumes that investors and markets are rational when making a decision. Thus, the intention was to create a mathematical model that could predict the risk of an investment portfolio.

According to the author, this risk cannot be given simply by averaging the individual risk of each of the assets that compose it, thus emerging the concepts of "diversification" and "efficient frontier" created by the same. According to Markowitz (1952), a portfolio should never be composed of just one asset or similar assets. On the other hand, the lower the positive correlation between its assets, the greater the diversification effect, and the lower the portfolio risk. Thus, it is necessary to speak of the second concept referred to.

Looking at the portfolio frontier plot, assuming that E(r) - expected return; σ - Risk (standard deviation); and taking into account that each point corresponds to investing only in one stock and that the area within the curve shows all possible combinations of expected return and risk if investing in a stock portfolio, investors will want, given their degree of risk aversion, to choose portfolios that are on the efficiency frontier.

As will be apparent, it is impossible for an investor to always be rational, and from then on other theories began to emerge to counteract this and to come up with specific terms related to investor irrationality, such as "overreaction", "overconfidence" and "loss aversion". One of the first and most important studies on this subject was that of Tversky and Kahneman (1974), which eventually gave rise to Kahneman and Tversky's Prospect Theory (1979).

Biases and Heuristics in Decision Making

Kahneman and Tversky's Prospect Theory (1979) was one of the first to emerge in contrast to the Markowitz Portfolio Theory (1952) and states that gains and losses are assessed differently, with individuals deciding based on perceived gains rather than deciding based on perceived losses. This calls into question the concept of rationality accepted by Markowitz (1952).

By the way, Abdellaoui et al. (2013) emphasize this phrase, even stating that professionals behave differently from students when making a decision, and there may be several reasons for this, such as that professionals receive feedback by their choices or receive training to diversify the risks and contribution of a particular asset in their portfolio, while students do not receive it.

According to Robbins (2000), managers should use a rational decision-making process as follows: 1) Problem definition; 2) Identification of decision criteria and their weights; 3) Creation of alternatives and classification of them according to each of the criteria; 4) Choice of the best alternative. Also, the author states that the following characteristics are necessary for good use of the model: 1) Clarity of the problem (if the information is complete); 2) Known options (criteria and alternatives); 3) Clear preferences (weight of each of the criteria); 4) Maximum compensation of the chosen alternative.

Now, these kinds of models are designed to simplify all the complexity that a problem can handle since human capacity is too small to understand all that complexity (Robbins 2000). Thus, there may be several biases and heuristics in decision-making.

The studies by Kahneman and Tversky (1979) and Tversky and Kahneman (1986) produced certain results (effects), namely:

1. Certainty effect - is present when there are risky options with known probability and right options. Thus, agents typically exhibit a disproportionate reaction to a decrease in probability when it turns the right option into just probable and/or a probable option into a less likely one;
2. Reflection effect - reflects a change in the preferred order when betting losses replace gains of the same magnitude, as evidenced by the change in the utility curve when bets go from winnings to losses, from concave to convex, meaning from risk aversion to taste for risk (risk lover);

3. Probabilistic insurance effect - changes in the question formulation may influence the decision of the agents;
4. Isolation Effect - Agents do not consider what is in common between the two alternatives, but only the differences. Besides, this makes people consider changes only related to the reference point and not the final effect.

Thus, it is verified that the decision-making process is not as rational as Markowitz's (1952) study suggests, so that there may be several biases and heuristics in decision making. Tversky and Kahneman (1974) highlight three heuristics that can be used to assess probabilities and predict values: representativeness, availability and adjustment, and anchoring.

The first heuristic, the heuristic of representativeness, makes decision-makers evaluate the probability of occurrence of a certain event based on descriptive information rather than on accepted mathematical models. According to Kahneman (2012), this heuristic enhances the occurrence of some biases, such as insensitivity to sample size or regression to the mean. The availability heuristic is related to the tendency of people to calculate the probability of occurrence of a certain event based on how easy it is brought to mind (Tversky and Kahneman 1974). Finally, the adjustment and anchoring heuristic is considered a bias today. Tversky and Kahneman (1974) state that anchoring occurs when people make estimates from an initial value, which is later adjusted to give the final answer. Thus, anchoring is treated as bias, deriving from the confirmation heuristic that, according to Bazerman and Moore (2009), is the search that people make for information that can serve as a basis for validating their beliefs.

These heuristics and biases may also differ depending on the stage of the decision-making process in which the person is, as shown in table 1.

Table 1. Heuristics and biases associated with each step of the decision-making process

Decision-making stage	Heuristic and/or bias	Potential consequences
Definition of the problem	Availability Heuristic.	A strict definition of the problem.
Alternatives creation	The heuristic of representativeness and bias of overconfidence.	Exaggerated optimism about the possibility of success of the alternatives raised, created by previous successful alternatives.
Goal setting	Anchor bias.	Anchors can limit the goals to be set.
Handling of information	Adverse risk behavior.	Risk exposure in loss situations and risk aversion in gain contexts.
Evaluation of Alternatives	Curse of Confirmation and Avoidance of Regret.	Limitation or expansion of time during the evaluation of alternatives, causing difficulty in the choices.
Decision implementation	Procrastination bias.	Negative delay in affecting the decision.
Decision outcome evaluation	Curse of knowledge and self-centered bias.	The tendency to validate positive or negative results based on past results and seeking an explanation of failures in external factors.
Serial decisions	Escalating commitment and bias of the status quo.	Excessive commitment to an originally chosen plan, beyond rational fundamentals, increasing losses.

Source: Adapted from Rodrigues and Russo (2011).

The Aversion to Loss

One of the first studies in this field was that of Thaler (1980) to analyze a person's willingness to pay a certain amount for a good and the willingness to accept selling the same. Thus, the author has concluded that the possession of a good by a person makes them value their good more. This effect is called the "disposition effect". However, the most discussed study today is that of Kahneman and Tversky (1979), which gave rise to the Prospect Theory.

According to Kahneman and Tversky (1979), loss aversion refers to an aspect referred to in Prospect Theory, where losses are perceived differently than gains, leading investors to like losses less than they like the gains in the same proportion. Thus, the decision is often made based on perceived gains rather than perceived losses.

Odean (1998a) also applies the Prospect Theory to explain the "disposition effect", which translates into investors' inclination to sell "winning" stocks too early and to keep "losing" stocks too long in their portfolio. One of the reasons for this is that pointed out by Simon (1960). The author argues that investors, at the moment of decision making, always have limited information and never the ability to evaluate all possible and existing variables and, to try to measure what is not measurable, create mental schemes that are called "mental accounting" (Kahneman and Tversky 1997). This type of study was initiated by Edwards (1954) and Simon (1955), who discussed the principles of Bernoulli's utility theory discussed earlier, stating that there is no indicator for which utility function can be maximized. Also, thoughts influence everyone's decisions in their life and the way people think and look at their plans and the results they get (Baron 2008).

Tversky and Kahneman (1991) demonstrate that for the same amount of gains and losses, people feel losses more intensely than gains. Guthrie (2003) states that people are willing to risk to avoid losses, but are less willing or even unwilling at all to take risks to accumulate gains. Thus, it is noted that the slope of losses is steeper, reflecting the empirical finding that losses outweigh gains (Kahneman et al. 1991).

As can be seen, the authors agree. Thus, Bernstein (1997) states that modern finance predicts investor expectations to be balanced (rational), although the concept of rationality is somewhat different here. The author states that the rational investor will underestimate one part of the time and overestimate another part of the time, and will not underestimate or overestimate all the time, thus there is a balance. However, this does not mean that investors should sometimes not expect to lose in the risks they take since, usually, if someone thinks how well they feel right now and how much better or worse they might feel, some things could make her feel better, but the number of things that could make her feel worse is much larger (Bernstein 1997).

Berejikian and Early (2013) complete the author's idea, stating that the $ 1000 gain produces fewer pleasure units than the number of pain units produced by the loss of the same $ 1000. In addition to the stated disposition effect, loss aversion can explain three more phenomena: i) Maintaining the current situation is a favorite in many decision situations; ii) Preference is given to options that encompass only benchmark improvements; iii) Greater weight given to options defined as disadvantages as opposed to options defined as advantages.

In addition to these, there are also studies in the area of neuroscience to understand the origin and reasons for the existence of loss aversion. Thus, several discoveries were made, namely: i) Gains and losses are recorded and produced in different networks - gains are processed through a neural "reward system" that includes zones such as the midbrain and orbitofrontal cortex (Breiter et al. 2001), while losses they are processed through a pain-associated aversion system and include regions such as the amygdala (Livet 2009); ii) The degree of dopamine decrease in the brain associated with loss consideration is greater than the degree of increase in dopamine associated with reward (Tom et al. 2007); iii) Unrealized gain expectations are considered as losses, while unrealized loss expectations are considered as gains. As demonstrated by Breiter et al. (2001), when a return is much lower than expected, a person considers this as a loss, although this has not been the case, and vice versa.

New Models Based on Prospect Theory

Although Prospect Theory may constitute a major advance in the field of socio-economic sciences, it has some weaknesses that even the authors themselves point out, namely the extension of the theory to cases where there are more than two possibilities of choice, the application of theory in situations where returns are not financial and still for cases where the odds are not explicit. For these reasons, several authors have carried out studies and were refining the existing models to fill these gaps.

Quiggin (1982) developed a cumulative probability distribution model because Prospect Theory is predicted only for situations where one option is preferred to another only stochastically, that is, when situations are equally likely to happen. To refine their model and address some of the flaws pointed out by other authors, Tversky and Kahneman (1992) created a more advanced model of prospect theory. Thus, the theory can now be applied in a situation where there is a finite number of possible outcomes and be used in continuous distributions, addressing the previous failure that it could only be used in situations where there were only two possible outcomes.

Besides, the irregularity in the applicability of the model in situations where the probabilities are not explicit has also been overcome and can now be used when the results are probable or only uncertain. Finally, the new model, called the Cumulative Prospect Theory, allows different probabilities to be defined for gains and losses, thus satisfying the stochastic dominance property, unlike the previous one where the probabilities would have to be equal.

Gächter, Johnson, and Herrmann (2010) developed another model from Thaler's (1980) model - featuring risk-free betting - and from the Köbberling and Wakker (2005) loss aversion index - featuring risky betting - and, based on the Tversky and Kahneman (1991) model, empirically demonstrated that both measurements are homogeneous and that this can be explained by sociodemographic factors and demonstrated that the risk-free measures are on average, larger than risky measures.

Recently, a new concept has been under discussion - aversion to nearsighted loss. This concept was created by Benartzi and Thaler (1995) and combines two concepts discussed earlier - loss aversion and mental accounting. According to the authors, loss aversion, as mentioned above, considers the greater weighting of losses than gains, and short-sightedness in short-term results to the detriment of higher outcomes in also a longer time horizon.

The Problem of Forest Fires and Their Influence on Investor Rationality

On August 25, 1988, the city of Lisbon suffered one of the most violent fires in the history of Portugal, called "Chiado Fire", causing the loss of about 2,000 jobs and the destruction of 18 buildings, some of them emblematic: Chiado warehouses, Eduardo Martins establishment, Ferrari pastry shop, Casa Batalha, among other traditional shops, offices, and dwellings. Also, approximately 1150 men and 275 vehicles were involved in fighting the flames, resulting in the registration of two fatalities and 73 injured, mostly firefighters (Lisbon City Council 2017).

Although this event was a starting point for the statistical treatment of fires in Portugal, it is still relatively late compared to other countries in the world.

Statistical Treatment of Fires in Other Countries

In the United States (US), data collected by the National Fire Incident Reporting System (NFIRS) has several benefits, such as (U.S. Fire Administration (USFA) 2017a): i) Support in analyzing the severity and scope of a specific fire, as well as the use of this information to develop national public education campaigns, to make recommendations regarding national codes and standards, to identify research focuses and to support the national legislation; ii) Management by fire departments of the means and personnel at their disposal, as well as the possibility of documenting the full activity of the department and justifying their budgets with statistical information; iii) Use fire department information to focus on current community issues, predict future issues and measure program performance; iv) NFIRS modular design makes the system easy to use because it only captures the information needed to describe an incident; v) States and fire departments can choose to operate their databases free of charge using the free applications available on the national website.

Besides, the National Fire Data Center (NFDC) also periodically publishes a document entitled "Fire in the United States" with a set of statistics related to US fires. This document may be extremely important for several types of analysis, as it focuses on the most relevant factors for the occurrence of such disasters. Thus, regarding fires abroad, in 2015, the factors were as described in table 2.

As can be seen from the data in Table 2, although most outdoor fires are involuntary (24.0%), there is a large percentage of fires whose cause cannot be determined after the investigation. Thus, although all these fires, regardless of the cause, may influence the rational behavior of an agent, if directly or indirectly affected by one of these, the fires whose cause is not determinable may have a greater impact on them.

Table 2. Causes of external fires (2015)

Cause	Reported	Unknown
Cause non-determined after research	14.4	25.9
Cause under research	2.7	4.8
Nature act	2.6	4.7
Equipment or heat source failure	2.2	3.9
Involuntary	24.0	43.1
Intentional	9.5	17.1
Exposition	0.3	0.5
Unknown	44.3	0.0
Total	100.0	100.0

Source: USFA (2017b, p. 76).

In addition to these causes, a range of other information may be assessed, including the race, age, and gender of the characteristics of the fire victims. According to USFA (2017b), some of the most relevant statistical data for this type of information in the US is as follows: Males are 1.7 times more likely to die in fires than females; Most male deaths in forest fires occur (41%) when they are between 50 and 69 years old; Most fire-related injuries occur between 20 and 59 years of age in both sexes; Individuals with cognitive and physical limitations, especially people over 65, are at increased risk of death from fires. In 2015, this age group accounts for 40% of all deaths and 15% of all estimated fire injuries; Finally, a dramatic change in US demographics is expected, where the volume of the older population will increase and the number of fires expected to follow this trend.

Statistical Treatment of Fires in Portugal

As mentioned above, the "Chiado fire" was the starting point for the statistical treatment of fires in Portugal and, therefore, some work has started to be done in this area.

One of them was the one carried out by Paulo Pereira (1993) called "Fires in Buildings in the City of Porto" who, after collecting information from the archives of the Porto Firefighters Battalion (BSB), developed a computer application to treat the same. This information was provided according to the following significant variables: Parish; Date; Hour; Location; Building Function; Causes of the fire; Damage or death of occupants and/or firefighters; and Fire Spread.

In 2008, as a continuation of this work, Vítor Primo (2008) grouped the information differently from his predecessor into the following groups: Annual and total summaries for all fires occurred; Annual and total summaries for residential buildings, as they constitute the most significant part of recorded occurrences; Fire summaries of non-residential buildings; Summary of information on fires resulting in personal injury.

With this study, it was then possible to draw some conclusions about the spread of fires in each zone; the way the fires were extinguished; the distribution of the number of fires per hectare of the gross area; the number of dead and wounded; the types of people who cause the fires (eg homeless people and/or drug addicts); and the type of establishments where there is a higher incidence of fires.

However, this type of work does not allow measuring the impact of this type of occurrence on companies that are located in these locations and that may have been directly or indirectly affected by them. Also, it can be seen that the likelihood that agents - who belong to these companies and who are in charge of certain important decision-making - in the face of being affected by these kinds of disasters is high. Therefore, it is important to carry out a study on their impact on the decision-making of investors and/or managers of these companies.

The Reality of Fires in Portugal

Portugal has been, in recent years, one of the countries in Europe that have been hit hardest by the fire problem (Harris 2017; Minder 2017; Jones 2017), and although this is a reality, 2017 has been much more problematic than average from 2007 to 2016, becoming even in the year with a total burned area, in hectares, larger in the same period, as shown in table 3.

Thus, although there are 3.6% fewer occurrences in 2017 compared to the annual average of the period under review, there is a further 428% of the burned area compared to that period. Besides, the distribution of burnt areas in Portugal in 2017 varies widely from district to district, as expected. Thus, analyzing Figure 1, where the color represents the burned area, it can be seen that, from January 1 to October 31, 2017, the districts most affected by this problem were the districts of Coimbra (113,839 hectares corresponding to 26% of the total burnt area), Guarda (60,038 hectares corresponding to 14%

of the total burnt area) and Castelo Branco (52,721 hectares corresponding to 12% of the total burnt area) (ICNF 2017a).

Table 3. Number of occurrences and burned area in mainland Portugal, by year, from 1 January to 31 October

Anos	Occurrences			Resettlement (nº)	Burned area (ha)		
	Hot flushes (area <1 ha)	Forest fires	Total		Populations	Matos	Total
2007	12,204	2,286	14,490	315	7,658	15,140	22,798
2008	11,564	2,391	13,955	288	5,335	11,116	16,451
2009	20,172	5,828	26,000	1,244	24,092	63,216	87,308
2010	17,924	3,942	21,866	2,687	46,064	86,924	132,988
2011	19,953	5,008	24,961	3,693	20,028	53,687	73,715
2012	16,694	4,418	21,112	1,977	48,063	62,155	110,218
2013	14,859	3,536	18,395	2,355	54,922	94,816	149,738
2014	5,947	1,066	7,013	305	8,726	11,193	19,919
2015	12,217	3,276	15,493	1,496	23,685	40,524	64,209
2016	10,089	2,693	12,782	1,328	77,442	83,016	160,458
2017	13,328	3,653	16,981	1,446	264,951	177,467	442,418
Average 2007-2016	14,162	3,444	17,607	1,569	31,602	52,179	83,780

Source: Institute for Nature Conservation and Forests (ICNF) (2017a, p. 3).

Although these are the districts that have the largest burned area, three facts are important to note: i) The largest number of occurrences is not found in any of these districts, but in Porto (4,336), Braga (1,743), and Viseu (1,698) (ICNF 2017a). However, most of these occurrences are hot flushes (occurrences that do not exceed 1 hectare of burnt area) and have no major impact on this variable; ii) In addition to the previous information, the highest number of forest fire incidents (ie excluding hot flushes) is in Vila Real (561), Porto (556) and Braga (548) districts; iii) except for Guarda District, none of the other two districts mentioned with the largest area burned between January 1, 2017, and October 31, 2017, has a relatively large area burned between January 1, 2007, and December 31, 2015, as can be analyzed in Table 4.

Thus, although the district of Guarda continues to be one of the districts most affected by fire (116,453 hectares of burned area, with an average of 23,291 hectares per year), the other two districts most affected are, in decreasing order of total burned area, Viseu (with 104,796 hectares of burned area and an annual average of 20,959 hectares) and Vila Real (with 93,581 hectares of burned area and an annual average of 18,716 hectares). Thus, when analyzing the information provided here, it should be noted that it needs to be used with great care.

Using Vila Real district as an example, this is the one with the highest number of occurrences related to forest fires between January 1, 2017, and October 31, 2017. However, when analyzing the total occurrences (including those related to hot flushes), it appears that this district is not in the top 3 districts with the most occurrences. Also, this figure does not guarantee that this is the district with the largest burned area. On the contrary, it is only in third place for the districts with the largest burned area in the 2017 year under review.

Now adopting a monthly periodic analysis and based on the Daily Severity Index (DSR), it is noted that 2017 is the most severe year of the last 15 years, with values similar to 2005, as shown in Figure 2.

Figure 1. Distribution of burned areas in Portugal in 2017 (reported to 31 October)
Source: ICNF (2017a, p. 4).

Table 4. Distribution of burned areas in Portugal from January 1, 2007, to December 31, 2015

	Total Burned Area (ha)										
District	2007	2008	2009	2010	2011	2012	2013	2014	2015	Total	Average
Aveiro	475	324	1,516	8,304	2,683	2,695	3,238	322	3,521	23,079	4,616
Beja	3,043	721	1,378	833	1,076	1,230	2,824	1,332	1,938	14,374	2,875
Braga	4,837	1,445	11,670	14,446	7,561	8,951	12,083	769	7,178	68,939	13,788
Bragança	1,560	2,578	8,198	4,971	11,435	15,123	24,302	2,349	5,300	75,816	15,163
Castelo Branco	553	2,048	720	1,405	3,754	2,157	3,775	387	3,113	17,912	3,582
Coimbra	200	628	382	1,530	613	5,660	3,189	1,312	1,739	15,253	3,051
Évora	1,127	266	256	1,082	779	585	757	656	1,569	7,077	1,415
Faro	272	305	1,796	188	168	25,608	585	848	479	30,248	6,050
Guarda	4,604	4,086	22,199	31,619	13,135	10,718	11,399	5,779	12,915	116,453	23,291
Leiria	2,805	295	422	1,277	2,172	2,554	2,378	104	1,078	13,084	2,617
Lisboa	1,419	1,481	827	946	1,669	1,937	1,049	310	1,080	10,717	2,143
Portalegre	1,881	198	141	537	447	1,289	1,629	3,379	508	10,011	2,002
Porto	1,431	579	9,191	8,621	4,802	3,693	14,186	1,366	2,546	46,414	9,283
Santarém	3,545	1,071	276	1,364	691	10,767	797	350	2,709	21,569	4,314
Setúbal	1,172	401	448	2,353	297	429	594	438	424	6,556	1,311
Viana do Castelo	1,985	811	5,864	24,268	5,652	2,935	12,455	931	10,044	64,946	12,989
Vila Real	3,243	1,603	18,236	18,759	14,293	7,150	23,457	1,222	5,619	93,581	18,716
Viseu	2,368	1,167	9,229	19,336	7,405	15,463	42,181	1,075	6,573	104,796	20,959
Total	36,517	20,009	92,748	141,840	78,630	118,945	160,876	22,929	68,332	740,826	148,165

Source: (ICNF, 2017b).

Looking at the different curves in Figure 2, it can be seen that the line slopes usually change around mid-September. However, in 2017 (as in 2005), this slope is unchanged, which means that conditions have continued to be severe.

Thus, it is important to understand to what extent the managers of companies are affected or not by this type of problem, i.e., if they can exercise rational decision-making being under the influence of this type of event, directly or indirectly.

Figure 2. Daily severity index, accumulated since 1 January, between 2003 and 2017
Source: ICNF (2017a, p. 6).

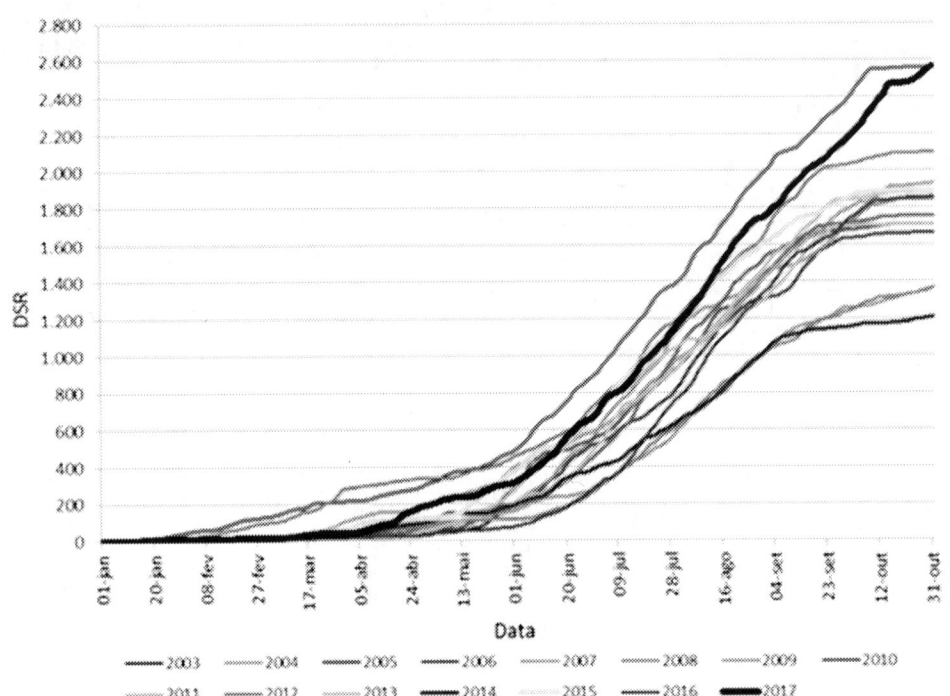

The Probability and Risk Assessment

Kahneman and Tversky (1979) state that, especially events that are unlikely to happen are often ignored or otherwise overvalued. In a study conducted by Whitmarsh (2008), which sought to understand whether or not flood victims care more about climate change than others through a questionnaire conducted in England, it is stated that these victims do not behave very differently from others in understanding climate change. However, victims of air pollution reveal quite different perceptions about this issue, and they are more likely to regard climate change as an imminent risk and to take certain actions in response to it (Whitmarsh 2008). Thus, it can be seen that there is an overestimation of risk by air pollution victims compared to the others.

Tversky and Kahneman (1974) state that people make use of a heuristic, called the "availability heuristic", to simplify the task of assigning probabilities. This is no more than people think that frequent events are much easier to remember or imagine than those that are infrequent. Thus, a discrepancy can be generated here between perceived risk and actual risk, since the availability of a particular event may not only be related to its frequency, but also other factors such as proximity or your imminence. Although the actual risk does not change, there may be temporary changes in perceived risk in response to imminent shock (Dessaint and Matray 2017).

To test this hypothesis, Dessaint and Matray (2017) assumed that risk perception can be demonstrated through the treasury amounts of a given company, based on the studies by Froot et al. (1993) and Hölmstrom and Tirole (1998), which claim that cash is used by companies as a liquidity security mechanism when the use of external financing is limited. Also, these authors use hurricanes to test whether or not corporate managers are affected by these events. A common topic in this type of research is the relationship between treatment and effect, and several studies conclude that exposure to a particular macroeconomic, personal or professional event has a unidirectional effect on risk exposure by a manager and, consequently, in corporate policies. For example, Bernile et al. (2017) test how the intensity of certain childhood experiences impact a manager's attitudes toward risk and corporate policies influenced by them. Froot (2001) analyzes financial claims that are linked to losses associated with natural disasters such as hurricanes and earthquakes and how policyholders behave and protect themselves against such events; Gallagher (2014) assesses the learning process that economic agents use to update their expectations about an uncertain and infrequent event, using flood-related events to compare residents in flooded areas with residents in non-flooded areas.

In this study, the occurrence of fires will be used to verify whether or not managers in Portugal are affected by these events. Thus, larger cash amounts in a post-fire period compared to a pre-fire period will indicate that managers will be influenced by the occurrence of this type of disaster.

DATA AND METHODOLOGY

This study uses two types of information, related to fires and companies affected by them, to identify situations where the risk of liquidity shocks becomes evident. The fact that fires are used as a source for study results from several beliefs. First, a fire is seen as an imminent risk as it causes great impact and catches people's attention, depending on its size, leaving marks on their minds. Then, this attention that is aroused varies depending on how close businesses are to the affected locations, the greater the closer they are. Finally, fires are phenomena that can affect a large number of companies.

According to Yin (2003), various sources of evidence are used when collecting data about a company, levels of analysis, and contextual elements. In this case, a quantitative methodology was used, based on the use of information available in mainly two databases.

Information on fires was obtained from the ICNF database by extracting their locations, dates, and impacts in terms of burnt area for the period from 1 January 2009 to 31 December 2015. There is also information regarding the affected companies through the SABI database, encompassing a set of variables such as total assets, cash amounts, debt levels, and current assets, among others, to assess the impact of fires in the same period.

Regarding information about companies, filters were applied to the results. First, companies were withdrawn from regulated sectors such as the financial, education, health, and public administration, and defense sectors. Then companies were chosen only with an independence indicator level between B- and A + (high), which is necessary for financial decision making. In this case, a level of B- to B + means that in the companies there is no registered shareholder with more than 50% direct, indirect, or full participation, and one or more registered shareholders with more than 25% direct or total participation. An A- to A + level encompasses companies where there is no shareholder with more than 25% direct or full ownership, being classified as "independent companies".

Finally, only small and medium-sized enterprises (SMEs) will be analyzed which, according to the definition of the European Commission (2003), are those that 1. Have a total number of workers less than 250; 2. Have an annual turnover of less than or equal to EUR 50 million or a total balance sheet of less than or equal to EUR 43 million. In this case, companies that do not exceed these limits are considered in any of the years under review. This group of companies also excluded micro-enterprises, which are those with a total number of employees of less than 10 and an annual turnover of less than or equal to EUR 2 million or a total balance sheet of less than EUR 2 million.

Microenterprises were excluded because, due to their size and consequent low number of employees (some may be sole proprietorships), they did not initially, in principle, have someone dedicated specifically to the treatment of accounting and financial information, which could result in the submission of this information not as correct or complete as would be desirable. On the other hand, large companies have been excluded because they have financial resources that others do not have (such as easier access to external financing sources compared to SMEs) and as such can address the issue analyzed by other avenues, than not the change in cash amounts. Besides, some of these are quoted on the stock exchange, which would require the use of a different analysis model (such as that used by Dessaint and Matray (2017) or that used by Ferreira and Vilela (2004), which consider as variable the market-to-book ratio, which is calculated taking into account the companies' market value).

Subsequently, all companies with the items' business volume, bank deposits, and cash or net income for the year with zero values for more than two consecutive years were eliminated. All companies with negative amounts in the balance sheet items used (bank deposits and cash, short-term financial debt, non-current financing, medium, and long-term liabilities, and short-term liabilities) and amortization were also deleted, as well as those which have values in Equity, Total Assets and Total Liabilities equal to zero since they could bias the results of the estimates.

After applying the above criteria, there was a decrease from 65,261 companies in the initial sample to 38,574 companies in the final sample. Also excluded from the sample were the companies in which the following facts were evident: Amounts in Bank and Cash Deposits greater than Total Assets; Amounts in Bank Deposits and Cash equal to Total Assets; Amounts in Current Liabilities, Non-Current Liabilities, Non-Current Loans or Short-Term Financial Debts greater than Total Liabilities; and Negative equity values. Finally, the following modifications were made to bridge missing values: Copy of the amounts from Non-Current Financing and Retained Earnings items from 2010 to 2009 for all companies, as there are no values available for that year; All Business Volume item cells equal to 0 were averaged over the following two years, except for the last two years, where this was averaged over the previous two years.

For both fires and businesses, annual information is used since, although the ICNF database provides information on fire events per minute, the Sabi database only provides annual information.

Regarding the companies' geography, they were divided into three categories, depending on their proximity to the fire zone: disaster zone, neighborhood zone, and rest of Portugal. The first concerns companies located in municipalities whose total burned area is over 10,000 hectares (Table 5). The second concerns municipalities bordering the municipalities referred to in the disaster zone. Finally, the rest of Portugal is the set of all locations not affected by the fires.

Companies located in the vicinity were designated as the treatment group, as the occurrence of a fire is an imminent event in these. Companies located in the disaster zone were not defined as a treatment group as changes in their liquidity amounts may differ for reasons other than the irrationality of decision-makers (e.g. the destruction of some factories and/or warehouses) and resulting in variation of negative direct cash flow (repair and/or replacement costs of damaged assets) or positive cash flow (insurance activation). Also, the companies located in the neighborhood are important because they could also be affected by this event, but they were not by chance, which makes the managers' attention directed to this event. Finally, it is not expected that the attention of managers whose companies are located in the rest of the country will be diverted by the occurrence of a fire at a great distance, which can even be completely ignored.

In short, the effect of fires is examined by taking into account managers' perceptions of risk through changes in their companies' cash amounts. Thus, the model used will be based on that of Dessaint and Matray (2017), resulting in the following estimated regression:

$$Cash_{iym} = \alpha_i + \delta_y + \gamma X_{iym} + \beta Neighbor_{ym} + \varepsilon_{iym} \qquad (1)$$

where i refers to companies, y refers to years, m encompasses the location of municipalities, $Cash_{iym}$ is the amount of cash as a percentage of total assets at the end of the year y, α_i are the annual effects of companies, δ_y are the temporal effects, X_{iyc} is the vector of the control variables, $\beta Neighbor_{ym}$ is a dummy variable that is equal to one, if the company is in the neighborhood zone and zero if this is not true, and ε_{iym} is an error variable.

Table 5. Municipalities with a total area burnt over 10,000 hectares

Concelho	\multicolumn{11}{c}{Total Burned Area (> 10.000 hectares)}										
	2007	2008	2009	2010	2011	2012	2013	2014	2015	Total	Average
Tavira	47	10	10	11	4	24,856	10	38	17	25,003	2,778
Sabugal	596	264	10,836	1,174	1,841	1,237	549	167	6,376	23,040	2,560
Guarda	220	382	5,378	5,598	1,094	873	1,206	203	1,096	16,049	1,783
Alfândega Da Fé	71	74	215	30	382	329	14,378	109	38	15,625	1,736
Arcos de Valdevez	617	165	1,136	6,957	835	886	3,009	129	1,161	14,896	1,655
Montalegre	866	264	4,164	2,904	3,435	939	674	154	1,437	14,838	1,649
Seia	149	62	193	9,131	167	2,747	585	455	50	13,539	1,504
Valpaços	242	227	1,837	928	3,610	379	4,149	588	825	12,785	1,421
Chaves	177	246	2,004	1,427	3,105	1,536	2,874	137	1,170	12,674	1,408
Gouveia	281	254	955	3,719	1,730	1,930	102	28	2,640	11,640	1,293
Fafe	1,077	152	2,161	3,480	954	903	2,045	131	727	11,631	1,292
Vila Pouca de Aguiar	185	131	1,090	1,415	1,806	574	5,714	70	286	11,272	1,252
Ribeira de Pena	136	100	879	8,297	228	421	708	20	352	11,142	1,238
Terras de Bouro	868	221	1,277	5,403	227	808	840	35	1,343	11,021	1,225
Castro Daire	518	194	1,173	2,674	597	1,212	4,223	65	285	10,940	1,216
Mangualde	105	177	1,556	2,364	783	1,656	882	71	2,727	10,321	1,147
Figueira de Castelo Rodrigo	1,121	528	650	3,046	1,383	613	869	1,252	777	10,238	1,138

Source: (ICNF 2017b).

The proximity effect to the fire is β, which measures changes in cash amounts in companies in the neighborhood compared to a control group of companies in more distant municipalities.

To discuss the results obtained, we will use the model also used by Dessaint and Matray (2017) that was described. However, these authors use a set of control variables (X_{iyc}) that applies to listed companies. As this is not the case, the variables present in the study by García-Teruel and Martínez-Solano

(2008) on the determinants of cash amounts in SMEs will serve as the basis for this analysis. The control variables used are described in Table 6, which also presents the calculation formula used in the present study to determine the value of each variable annually.

The first control variable used concerns growth opportunities (GROWP) and is used to the detriment of the market-to-book ratio as these companies are not listed. This variable is expected to be positively related to cash as external financing is more expensive due to information asymmetries and agency problems.

The second and third variables concern company size and are calculated using the natural logarithm of sales (SALES) and the log of total assets (ASSETS), respectively. A negative relationship between the two variables and the cash amount is expected as the information asymmetry and the likelihood of bankruptcy are higher in small companies (García-Teruel and Martínez-Solano 2008).

Relationships with financial institutions were calculated taking into account the levels of indebtedness that companies maintain in their banks. Thus, a negative relationship of this variable (BANKD) with the companies' cash amounts is expected, since the easier it is to finance with a financial institution, the smaller the cash amounts of a company (Dessaint and Matray 2017).

Table 6. Description of control variables used

Name	Definition
Growth Opportunities (GROWP)	$Sales_n / Sales_{n-1}$
Sales (SALES)	ln(Sales)
Assets (ASSETS)	ln(Assets)
Bank Debt (BANKD)	Short-term Financing Obtained / Total Liabilities
Insolvency probability (ZSCORE)	ZSCORE = 0,104 * X1 + 0,010 * X2 + 0,106 * X3 + 0,003 * X4 + 0,169 * X5 where X1 = Working capital / Total assets; X2 = Retained Earnings / Total Assets; X3 = EBIT / Total assets; X4 = Equity / Total liabilities; X5 = Sales / Total Assets
Leverage (LEV)	Total Remunerated Liabilities / Equity
Debt maturity structure (LDEBT)	Medium to long run Financing Obtained / Total Liabilities
Cash Flow (CFLOW)	(EBT + Depreciation) / Total Assets
Other Net Assets (LIQ)	(Working Capital - (Cash + Securities)) / Total Assets
Opportunity Cost (RSPREAD)	Operating Results / Total Assets – 1 Year Treasury Bills Interest Rate
Interest Rates (INT)	1 Year Treasury Bills Interest Rate

Source: García-Teruel and Martínez-Solano (2008)

The likelihood of a financial crisis in a company (ZSCORE) was calculated using the Begley et al. (1996) model. This is a more recent proposal than the original Altman (1968) model, as follows:

$$ZSCORE = 0{,}104 * X_1 + 0{,}010 * X_2 + 0{,}106 * X_3 + 0{,}003 * X_4 + 0{,}169 * X_5 \qquad (2)$$

where X_1 = Working capital / Total assets; X_2 = Retained Earnings / Total Assets; X_3 = EBIT / Total assets; X_4 = Equity / Total liabilities; X_5 = Sales / Total Assets. The X_4 ratio is still changing from the original model, using the equity in the numerator instead of market capitalization, as the companies under study are not listed, according to Scherr and Hulburt (2001). The higher the ZSCORE, the lower the risk of bankruptcy.

Leverage (LEV) is measured through the debt-to-equity ratio and is expected to have a negative relationship with the companies' cash amounts. The following variable refers to the debt maturity structure (LDEBT) and is calculated by the ratio of long-term debt to total liabilities. Thus, it is expected that this variable will have a negative relationship with cash amounts, since the more a company finances itself in the long run, the lower the risk of refinancing and information asymmetry.

Cash flow is calculated by dividing pre-tax income and depreciation by asset (CFLOW). A positive relationship of these variables with the cash amounts is expected. The LIQ ratio is calculated by dividing the working capital (excluding cash) by the asset, thus measuring the existence of other liquid assets that could replace cash and thus a negative relationship is expected between this variable and the dependent variable.

The opportunity cost of capital invested in net assets (RSPREAD) was measured by the difference between the return on the company's assets and the return on Treasury Bonds. Thus, a negative relationship of this variable with the amount of cash is expected as it measures how attractive is the investment in a company's activities compared to the investment in liquid assets. Besides, the short-term interest rate, as measured by 1-year Treasury Bills (INT), is also used to derive temporal changes in interest rates.

The dependent variable will be analyzed as follows: Cash - through the ratio (Bank deposits and cash) / (Total assets); To begin the discussion of results, the sample under study will be analyzed in general so that it can be studied in more detail later. For this, the panel data format (or longitudinal data) will be used, as the information used contains time-series observations for several companies, involving at least two dimensions: transverse dimension and time series dimension (Hsiao 2005).

RESULTS DISCUSSION

About the sample under study, it is made up of SMEs, with average total assets of 1,175.84 thousand euros and an average turnover of 849.25 thousand euros, with 38,574 companies and 270,018 observations in Portugal (Table 7). These companies have a liability 3.61 times greater than the amount of Equity (LEV), and this liability is 7.9% for short-term debt to financial institutions (BANKD). Thus, most external financing is long-term, as it constitutes 29.5% of the total liabilities (LDEBT). The average cash amounts of Portuguese SMEs are 17.7% of total assets (Cash).

To analyze whether or not the companies studied are similar before the fire events, Table 8 was constructed. This table presents, in the first part, the average values of the variables one year before the fire events, to verify if these are similar or not before the effect of the 'treatment' of the fires, leading to the loss of one year in the sample period. Later, hypothesis tests were performed to test if there are differences between the variables of the two zones studied, whether or not they are statistically significant. Thus, if there are no statistically significant differences, it can be argued that the disparities between companies located in the neighborhood and companies located in the rest of Portugal are caused by the effect of the fire treatment. Also, this analysis makes it possible to verify whether these differences have recurred over the years of the sample period or only in some of the years.

Thus, companies are defined taking into account the location of their headquarters. The last columns of Table 8 show, for each year, the t-statistics of a two-sample test for equality of means between treatment and control group companies and the z-values of a median test. This first analysis will then further analyze the effect of the imminence of an event on the risk perceived by the managers of a company through the cash held after the occurrence of a fire.

Table 7. Descriptive Statistics for Portugal - Panel A

Variable	Observations	Average	Standard Deviation	Median	Perc. 10%	Perc. 90%
CASH	270,018	0.17668	0.20715	0.09243	0.00699	0.48697
GROWP	270,018	1.49314	41.33363	0.99576	0.71356	1.37211
SALES	270,018	12.43295	1.52551	12.37636	10.58130	14.40452
ASSETS	270,018	12.63415	1.42592	12.54977	10.86283	14.51326
BANKD	270,018	0.07923	0.17177	0.00000	0.00000	0.30271
ZSCORE	270,018	0.26779	0.27472	0.22338	0.08954	0.46487
LEV	270,018	3.61355	41.01012	1.27008	0.20215	5.88965
LDEBT	270,018	0.29470	0.31498	0.19101	0.00000	0.80059
CFLOW	270,018	0.07184	0.15242	0.05847	-0.02657	0.20551
LIQ	270,018	0.18486	0.40259	0.20167	0.34844	0.69448
RSPREAD	270,018	0.00710	0.14973	0.00814	-0.10004	0.12560

Source: Own elaboration.

The cash amounts are already different between the companies located in the different areas studied. Looking at the t-statistics, we observed statistically significant differences in the Cash variable in almost the entire sample period, with 2012 having the highest statistical significance. On the other hand, looking at z, this happens only in 2012 and 2015, with the remaining years not being statistically significant in terms of cash amounts. The fact that companies have these differences before the treatment effect to be studied may be due to two factors:

1. It is not possible to study the year before the sample period, which means that the cash amounts could already be changing due to the 'treatment' effect of fires not included in the study;
2. The impact of the financial crisis. According to Trejo-Pech et al. (2015), companies changed their cash amounts in the context of the financial crisis.

Thus, it is important to analyze the trends in the evolution of these amounts over the sample period, without the effect of treating 'fires', i.e. encompassing all companies regardless of their area. Looking at figure 3, it can be seen that, overall and without distinguishing between the zones where the companies are located, cash amounts decrease until 2013 and increase after 2013 until 2015. As in Table 8, the values used here are those of previous years, i.e. 2010 uses the cash amounts of 2009 and so on.

Table 8. Descriptive statistics for Portugal - Panel B

Company Location	Neighbor zone		t-statistic					
Group	Treatment							
	Average	Median	2010	2011	2012	2013	2014	2015
Cash	0.168	0.089						
GROWP	2.024	0.974	1.87*	-1.48	6.95***	2.27**	-1.20	-2.36**
SALES	12.460	12.402	0.87	0.78	-2.63***	-0.05	0.22	-0.37
ASSETS	12.614	12.523	-4.08***	6.04***	0.41	-4.64***	4.49***	2.38**
BANKD	0.083	0.000	0.09	3.72***	-2.40**	-0.65	1.92*	2.31**
ZSCORE	0.262	0.223	2.01**	4.77***	-1.61	1.37	1.10	2.01**
LEV	3.740	1.390	0.60	3.69***	5.43***	0.49	2.76***	0.57
LDEBT	0.285	0.186	1.04	-0.69	0.52	1.19	-0.21	-2.36**
CFLOW	0.074	0.059	-2.63***	-6.25***	-4.11***	-1.62	-0.94	-2.71***
LIQ	0.186	0.210	2.45**	1.80*	3.80***	-3.42***	2.57	2.53
RSPREAD	-0.009	-0.008	-1.10	3.13***	-6.09***	-1.13	1.64	3.25***
N	19,273	19,273	2.31**	1.82*	3.33***	-2.44	2.08**	2.15**
Company Location	Rest of Portugal		z					
Group	Control		2010	2011	2012	2013	2014	2015
	Average	Median						
Cash	0.176	0.091	-1.63	-0.94	6.63***	-1.50	-1.35	-2.92***
GROWP	1.497	0.992	-2.04**	-0.85	0.38	-6.32***	0.89	2.95***
SALES	12.435	12.377	-3.61***	6.14***	-0.36	-4.84***	4.34***	2.32**
ASSETS	12.630	12.546	-0.19	3.40***	-3.01***	-0.88	1.77*	2.27**
BANKD	0.080	0.000	-0.82	7.85***	-1.41	0.86	2.87***	2.71***
ZSCORE	0.269	0.224	-2.56**	6.49***	6.13***	-2.69***	4.84***	2.84***
LEV	3.591	1.300	-4.49***	4.10***	-0.29	-3.89***	2.34**	1.59
LDEBT	0.289	0.178	-5.40***	-6.15***	-5.13***	-3.56***	-0.65	-3.38***
CFLOW	0.073	0.059	1.47	2.55**	4.17***	-4.05***	3.71***	3.39***
LIQ	0.185	0.203	-0.77	2.94***	-6.22***	-0.91	1.52	2.96***
RSPREAD	0.003	0.004	1.97**	3.85***	3.93***	-1.31	3.80***	3.53***
N	210,721	210,721						

Source: Own elaboration. Note: t-statistics of a two-sample test for equality of means between treatment and control group companies. The z values of a median test. ***, ** and * denote significance at the 1%, 5% and 10% levels, respectively.

As mentioned, these changes in cash amounts may be due to the financial crisis and these amounts could already be changed by fire but before the sample period, which cannot be included in this study.

To explain, in the first phase, these verified trends, we take the municipality of Tavira as an example. This municipality is very peculiar as regards the burned area since, as shown in table 5, 2012 is the only year in which its burned area exceeds 10,000 hectares (24,856 hectares), and the average of remaining years of the analyzed period does not exceed 19 hectares. Thus, table 9 shows the average of the cash amounts of the companies of the neighboring municipalities of Tavira during that same period.

There are two different trends: a decrease in cash amounts from 2009 to 2012 and an increase from 2012 to 2015. Besides, it is also noted that 2012 is the year in which the total of cash amounts is substantially smaller, being the year in which the burnt area in the municipality of Tavira was larger. Combining the information in table 9 with that in figure 3, it can be seen that the same trends, in this case, may be due to different variables. That is, if, on the one hand, in Table 9 it is presumed that the changes occurred due to the effect of the fires, in Figure 3 the same trends occur regardless of the area where the companies are located, thus excluding their effect. Thus, the values presented are not necessarily justified by the existing fires, and there may have been a set of other variables that may have caused these disparities, such as the effect of the crisis that was felt in Portugal from 2008 to 2012.

Figure 3. Evolution of dependent variable (cash)
Source: Own elaboration.

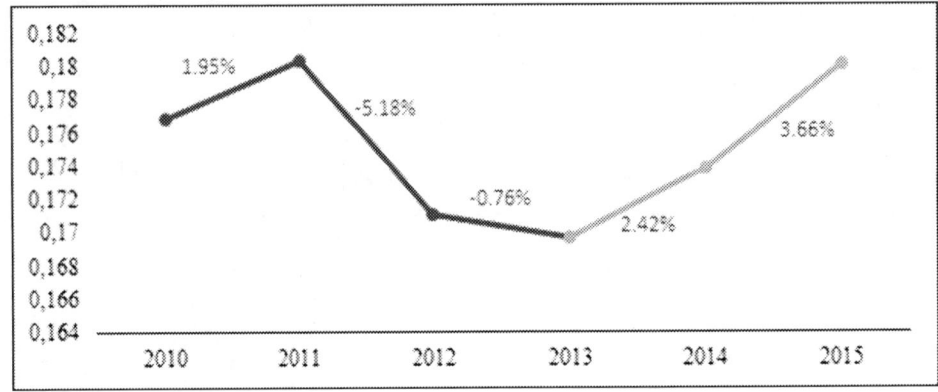

Table 9. Average of the cash amounts of the companies in the Tavira municipality neighborhood in the period 2009-2015

Municipality	Number Companies	2009	2010	2011	2012	2013	2014	2015
Alcoutim	8	459	555	638	789	804	1,301	1,146
Castro Marim	20	676	527	597	571	589	674	577
Loulé	326	29,191	26,951	26,833	23,469	25,961	26,297	30,816
Olhão	114	8,652	10,143	7,449	7,761	9,176	11,007	10,641
São Brás de Alportel	36	2,693	3,660	3,349	2,658	2,395	2,876	3,008
Vila Real de Santo António	64	4,341	5,485	5,577	5,167	4,104	5,374	5,687
Total	568	46,014	47,322	44,444	40,415	43,029	47,528	51,874
Average		7,669	7,887	7,407	6,736	7,172	7,921	8,646

Source: Own elaboration.

To analyze this question, two types of models can be used: a fixed-effects model and a random-effects model. The first concerns a model whose coefficients may vary from individual to individual or overtime, while the second assumes that the specific behavior of individuals and periods is unknown and cannot be observed or measured (Marques, 2000). To verify which model to use, the Hausman test should first be used, where the null hypothesis is that the preferential model is the random-effects model, through the test of the existence (or not) of correlation between error and the regressors. Thus, the result of your p-value may determine which model to use: if less than 0.05, use the fixed effects model; if not, use the random-effects model.

Table 10. Hausman test

Variable	Fixed	Variable	Difference
Neighbor	-0.0058	-0.0058	0.0001
GROWP	-8.49e-08	-4.86e-07	1.44e-07
SALES	-0.0011	0.0004	0.0002
ASSETS	-0.0114	-0.0216	0.0005
BANKD	0.0329	0.0290	0.0003
ZSCORE	0.0295	0.0308	0.0003
LEV	-0.0000	-0.0000	3.05e-07
CFLOW	-0.0207	-0.0383	0.0005
LIQ	-0.3761	-0.3759	0.0003
RSPREAD	0.0797	0.0994	0.0004

Source: Own elaboration. Test *p value* =0.0000.

As can be seen, the result obtained for the p-value is 0.0000, which will indicate at the outset that the model to be used should be the fixed effects model. However, the following test indicates the opposite. The Breusch-Pagan test is another test that helps to decide on whether to choose a simple Ordinary Least Squares (OLS) model or a random-effects model, where the null hypothesis is that variances between entities are equal to zero. Thus, unlike the previous test, a p-value less than 0.05 indicates that the random-effects model should be used; if not, use the simple OLS template. The results obtained are presented in Table 11.

Table 11. Breusch-Pagan test

	Variance	Standard Deviation
Cash	0.0426	0.2065
e	0.0043	0.0656
u	0.0115	0.1075

Source: Own elaboration. Test *p value* =0.0000.

In this case, the p-value is equal to 0.0000, which indicates that the random-effects model should be used, and thus there is no consensus in the two tests previously performed.

According to Marques (2000), the random-effects model is used in large longitudinal samples and, assuming that firm-specific behavior cannot be observed or measured, these individual or temporal effects can be represented as a normal random variable. Given the indecision pointed out by the tests mentioned above, we chose to use the random-effects model.

It is still necessary to verify if there is the presence of heteroscedasticity in the data. For this, the modified Wald test was used, where the null hypothesis indicates that there is no heteroscedasticity. Using the xttest3 command on Stata, a p-value of 0.0000 was obtained, which indicates the presence of heteroscedasticity, which may be because there may be some extreme values in the sample.

Finally, we need to check for autocorrelation in the panel data. For this, two tests were performed: the Wooldridge test, to verify if there is this autocorrelation, where the null hypothesis is that there is no autocorrelation; and a second test with the xtregar command to calculate rho, that is, how much the variables are correlated. Thus, the first test was performed giving a p-value of 0.0000, which indicates that there is indeed autocorrelation. Besides, the second test indicated the results presented in table 12.

Table 12. Estimation of the autocorrelation coefficient

Cash (dependent variable)	Coefficient
Neighbor	-0.0046***
GROWP	-1.14e-06***
SALES	0.0009***
ASSETS	-0.0223***
BANKD	0.0286***
ZSCORE	0.0289***
LEV	-0.0000***
CFLOW	-0.0207***
LIQ	-0.3743***
RSPREAD	0.0837***

Source: Own elaboration.. rho = 0.4234

As can be seen, the correlation coefficient rho is equal to 0.4234, indicating the presence of autocorrelation. Since this coefficient may range from -1 to 1, this value refers to a positive weak level to moderate autocorrelation. Because there is heteroscedasticity in the data and autocorrelation, the regressions used hereinafter include the robust component in Stata, to reinforce errors and dispel these problems.

Table 13 below shows the effects of a company being in the vicinity of a given fire from 2010 to 2015. Random effects panel data estimation was used to produce the results presented. To avoid multicollinearity effects on LEV and LDEBT variables, two columns with different combinations of these variables were used.

As can be seen, the coefficient for the Neighbor variable is negative and statistically significant for the entire sample period, which could indicate that the fact that a company is in the vicinity of a given fire decreases its cash amounts. However, based on the previous information and the corresponding analysis, there were two situations: 1) a downward trend of these amounts from 2009 to 2013 and subsequently an increase, regardless of whether or not the companies are in the vicinity of fire; 2) a downward trend from 2009 to 2012 of these amounts in the case of neighboring companies in the municipality of Tavira and their subsequent increase. Thus, both situations may influence the constructed linear regression and, as such, it is not possible to understand why this negative relation of the Neighbor variable with the dependent variable is due. Given the results presented, the analysis is limited to the period 2013-2015, which is characterized by a period of the end of the financial crisis in Portugal to remove this effect from the analysis, which is presented below (Table 14).

Table 13. Proximity to fires and cash holdings from 2010 to 2015

Dependent variable: Bank deposits and cash / Total assets (cash)		
Linear Regression	Coefficients	
Neighbor	-0.0058***	-0.0053***
GROWP	-4.86e-07	-1.04e-06
SALES	0.0004	0.0016**
ASSETS	-0.0216***	-0.0236***
BANKD	0.0290***	0.0487***
ZSCORE	0.0308***	0.0315***
LEV	-0.0000***	
LDEBT		0.0306***
CFLOW	-0.0383***	-0.0390***
LIQ	-0.3759***	-0.3792***
RSPREAD	0.0994***	0.1039***

Source: Own elaboration. Note: Neighbor is a dummy variable of 1 if the location of the company headquarters is in the vicinity of a location whose burned area exceeds 10,000 hectares and equal to 0 if that location is in the rest of Portugal (excluding areas of disaster); GROWP, SALES, ASSETS, BANK, ZSCORE, LEV, LDEBT, CFLOW, LIQ, RSPREAD are control variables; ***, ** and * denote statistical significance at 1%, 5%, and 10%, respectively.

Using the Neighbor dummy variable, companies in the vicinity of a fire increase their cash amounts on average by 0.15% (as a percentage of total assets), which is a group of companies with an average cash amount of 94.77 thousand euros, corresponds to about 1.4 thousand euros.

As the values used are from previous years, as in figure 3, this means that a company in the neighborhood area in 2014 is using the 2013 cash amounts and so on. Thus, when performing the regression and eliminating the years from 2010 to 2012 in the Neighbor variable (corresponding to the years 2009 to 2011 in the remaining variables), there is an impact of when a company moves from another zone to the neighborhood zone. For example, when a company moves to the neighborhood in 2013, the impacts on cash amounts are verified in 2012 as a result of managers' prediction and anticipation of the imminent risk of fire. To put it in context, there are around 1,000 new businesses in the neighborhood in 2013 compared to 2012 and, as they increase their cash amounts, this gives a positive and statistically significant relationship between the Neighbor variable and the dependent variable Cash.

Thus, the availability heuristic is confirmed as managers respond to the imminence of the fire hazard by increasing their cash amounts, although there is no indication that the risk to them is greater now than it was previously. These managers think that frequent events are much easier to remember than those that are not, which leads to a discrepancy between perceived risk and actual risk (Tversky and Kahneman

1974). Such a discrepancy also exists because the availability of a particular event is not only related to its frequency, but also other factors such as its proximity or imminence, and although the actual risk remains unchanged, there may be temporary changes in perceived risk in response to the imminence-related shock (Dessaint and Matray 2017). Thus, according to Froot et al. (1993) and Hölmstrom and Tirole (1998), who claim that cash is used by companies as a liquidity security mechanism and similar to what happened in the Dessaint and Matray (2017) study, where it has been assumed that risk perception can be demonstrated through a company's treasury amounts, managers increase their cash amounts to guard against future events that may affect them.

Table 14. Proximity to fires and cash holdings from 2013 to 2015

	Dependent variable: Bank deposits and cash / Total assets (cash)	
Linear Regression	**Coefficients**	
Neighbor	0.0014*	0.0015*
GROWP	3.37e-07	4.07e-07
SALES	0.0013*	0.0013*
ASSETS	-0.0243***	-0.02432***
BANKD	0.0182***	0.0177***
ZSCORE	0.0256***	0.0257***
LEV	-0.0000**	
LDEBT		0.0014
CFLOW	-0.1068***	0.0083***
LIQ	-0.4152***	0.0019***
RSPREAD	0.1685***	0.0075***

Source: Own elaboration. Note: Neighbor is a dummy variable of 1 if the location of the company headquarters is in the vicinity of a location whose burned area exceeds 10,000 hectares and equal to 0 if that location is in the rest of Portugal (excluding areas of disaster); GROWP, SALES, ASSETS, BANK, ZSCORE, LEV, LDEBT, CFLOW, LIQ, RSPREAD are control variables; ***, ** and * denote statistical significance at 1%, 5%, and 10%, respectively.

The results obtained are, in part, coincident with the study by Dessaint and Matray (2017). On the one hand, there is evidence that cash amounts are increased to provide greater protection against future events and that this change is due to the availability heuristic, where managers perceive risk differently from the actual risk. On the other hand, the timing of this increase is different. While in the article by Dessaint and Matray (2017) managers increase their companies' cash amounts after a particular hurricane occurs, in this study results seem to indicate that managers increase those amounts before a particular fire occurs. In other words, as there are fires in Portugal every year, managers try to anticipate these events by preventing the increase in cash.

It was previously seen that the average number of occurrences per year between January 1 and October 31, from 2007 to 2017, was almost 18,000 occurrences, where about 3,500 corresponded to forest fires. On the other hand, according to the National Oceanic & Atmospheric Administration (2017), the average US-named tropical storm is 11.7 per year, where only 6.3 become hurricanes and of these, only

1.7 touches the country ground. Thus, there is a disparity in the number of occurrences between the two events, which makes the seconds much less predictable than the first.

Thus, while it is possible to predict the occurrence of fires, as they occur every year in Portugal and often in repeated geographies, it is almost impossible to predict the occurrence of a hurricane in the United States of America, and therefore the cash increase timings are also different.

Kamiya and Yanase (2019) study the effects of direct and indirect loss experience of extreme catastrophes using Japanese earthquake examples. They find that both availability bias and representativeness help explain the effect of past loss experiences. Companies, like individuals, take decisions on behalf of others in many different contexts (Montinari and Rancan 2018). Many of the fires are large-scale man-made disasters (Gilbert et al. 2018) and apologies do not reduce the demand for compensation. It may even increase if the firm is a bad actor (Gilbert et al. 2018). Management policies implemented to minimize the negative impacts of forest fires require huge amounts of financial, human, organizational, and resource investment (Mavsar et al. 2013). Johansson and Lidskog (2020) point for a better-informed public administration, forest sector, and interrelated networks that take responsibility for their actions (human causes). Overall, ambiguity preferences will always play an important role in decision-making under uncertainty (Engle-Warnick and Laszlo 2017) and this should be accounted for by policymakers and managers in fire prevention and responses to deal with damages and risk at the cash prevention level.

CONCLUSION

Portugal has been, mainly in the last decade, harmed by the occurrence of fires in various parts of the country. Thus, there was a need to understand how these events impact companies. As such, studies by other authors and the consequences of other events in the countries studied were also addressed. For example, Froot (2001) analyzed the holdings made with insurers that are linked to losses associated with natural disasters such as hurricanes and earthquakes and how policyholders behave and protect themselves against such events. Gallagher (2014) used flood-related events, comparing residents in flooded areas with residents in non-flooded areas, to analyze the learning process used by economic agents to update their expectations regarding an uncertain and infrequent event.

In this study, the main objective was to understand the impact that fires can have on the cash amounts of Portuguese Small and Medium Enterprises (SMEs), using as the main basis the studies of Dessaint and Matray (2017) and García-Teruel and Martínez Solano (2008), having adapted the variables and methodologies used by these authors to the present study.

Thus, about this study and the impact of fires on the company's cash amounts, the study was carried out in the country context, firstly producing descriptive statistics for Portugal, where it was concluded that the companies would already be different before the sample period. Two reasons were highlighted for this: 1) that it was not possible to analyze the companies of this period, which means that they could already be under treatment and, besides, 2) the impact of the financial crisis that was already done, by itself, change the amounts in cash. Thus, we analyzed the trends in the evolution of companies' cash amounts regardless of their area, where it was possible to show that there is a downward trend of these amounts from 2010 to 2013 and subsequent increase. Also, and taking as an example the companies in the Tavira Municipality neighborhood, the same trend was observed, i.e. a decrease in cash amounts from 2010 to 2012 (this last year is filled with fires and very different from the rest) and increase thereafter. These two analyzes have served to show that the fact that the same trends occur in both situations does not imply that they need to have the same origin, which led to the conclusion that it was not possible to conclude the factor which causes these trends.

It was also found that the relationship of the Neighbor variable with the dependent variable is negative, which could indicate that companies located in the vicinity of the fires decrease their cash amounts, which would be contrary to expectable. However, as has been seen earlier that these amounts decrease regardless of the 'treatment' effect of fires (influenced, for example, by the financial crisis in Portugal), this is not a valid conclusion.

To complete this analysis and to eliminate the effect of the financial crisis, the years 2010 and 2012 were removed and, once again using lagged values, it was concluded that being in the neighborhood of fire affects the amounts in cash of companies and these increase them by 0.15%. These amounts change at a different timing than that demonstrated by Dessaint and Matray (2017), i.e. while these authors demonstrate that the cash amounts change after the event (in this case of a hurricane), this study shows that these amounts are changed before the (fire) event because all values are delayed by one year. This difference may be due to the nature and frequency of these events. That is, a fire is much more easily predicted than a hurricane, which makes managers prevent and increase these amounts even before they occur.

This study has some limitations. First of all, the SABI database has only annual information, which made the analysis performed also annual. However, it would be more interesting and better conclusions could be obtained with half-yearly information, as it would be easier to observe the evolution of cash amounts, semester to semester. Besides, a different definition for the "neighborhood zone" of fires could be considered. That is, instead of considering the municipalities on the borders of an affected municipality, it could have been considered zones from a certain distance (radius) from the affected zones. This leaves room for additional estimations and treatments of the data.

REFERENCES

Abdellaoui, M., Bleichrodt, H., & Kammoun, H. (2013). Do Financial Professionals Behave According to Prospect Theory? An Experimental Study. *Theory and Decision*, *74*(3), 411–429. doi:10.100711238-011-9282-3

Altman, E. (1968). Financial Ratios, Discriminant Analysis and the Prediction of the Corporate Bankruptcy. *The Journal of Finance*, *23*(4), 589–609. doi:10.1111/j.1540-6261.1968.tb00843.x

Baron, J. (2008). *Thinking and Deciding* (4th ed.). Cambridge University Press.

Bazerman, M., & Moore, D. (2009). *Judgment in Managerial Decision Making* (7th ed.). John Wiley & Sons, Inc.

Begley, J., Ming, T., & Watts, S. (1996). Bankruptcy Classification Errors in the 1980s: Empirical Analysis of Altman's and Ohlsons' Models. *Accounting Studies*, *1*(4), 267–284. doi:10.1007/BF00570833

Benartzi, S., & Thaler, R. (1995). Myopic Loss Aversion and the Equity Premium Puzzle. *The Quarterly Journal of Economics*, *110*(1), 73–92. doi:10.2307/2118511

Berejikian, J. D., & Early, B. R. (2013). Loss Aversion and Foreign Policy Resolve. *Political Psychology*, *34*(5), 649–671.

Bernile, G., Bhagwat, V., & Rau, P. R. (2017). What Doesn't Kill You Will Only Make You More Risk-Loving: Early-Life Disasters and CEO Behavior. *The Journal of Finance, 72*(1), 167–206. doi:10.1111/jofi.12432

Bernstein, P. L. (1997). *Desafio aos Deuses: A Fascinante História do Risco* (6th ed.). Gulf Professional Publishing.

Breiter, H., Aharon, I., Kahneman, D., Dale, A., & Shizgal, P. (2001). Functional Imaging of Neutral Responses to Expectancy and Experience of Monetary Gains and Losses. *Neuron, 30*(2), 619–639. doi:10.1016/S0896-6273(01)00303-8 PMID:11395019

Brown, J. R., Gustafson, M. T., & Ivanov, I. T. (2021). Weathering Cash Flow Shocks. *The Journal of Finance, 76*(4), 1731–1772. doi:10.1111/jofi.13024

Câmara Municipal de Lisboa. (2017). *1988 - Incêndio do Chiado*. Retrieved December 26, 2017, from http://www.cm-lisboa.pt/municipio/historia/historial-das-catastrofes-de-lisboa/1988-incendio-do-chiado

Europeia, C. (2003). Recomendação da Comissão Relativa à Definição de Micro, Pequenas e Médias empresas. *Jornal Oficial Da Comissão Europeia, 124*(36), 36–41.

Dessaint, O., & Matray, A. (2017). Do Managers Overreact to Salient Risks? Evidence from Hurricane Strikes. *Journal of Financial Economics, 126*(1), 97–121. doi:10.1016/j.jfineco.2017.07.002

Edwards, W. (1954). The Theory of Decision Making. *Psychological Bulletin, 51*(4), 380–417. doi:10.1037/h0053870 PMID:13177802

Engle-Warnick, J., & Laszlo, S. (2017). Learning-by-doing in an ambiguous environment. *Journal of Risk and Uncertainty, 55*(1), 71–94. doi:10.100711166-017-9264-0

Ferreira, M. A., & Vilela, A. S. (2004). Why Do Firms Hold Cash? Evidence from EMU Countries. *European Financial Management, 10*(2), 295–319. doi:10.1111/j.1354-7798.2004.00251.x

Froot, K. A. (2001). The Market for Catastrophe Risk: A Clinical Examination. *Journal of Financial Economics, 60*(2–3), 529–571. doi:10.1016/S0304-405X(01)00052-6

Froot, K., Scharfstein, D., & Stein, J. (1993). Risk Management: Coordinating Corporate Investment and Financing Policies. *The Journal of Finance, 48*(5), 1629–1658. doi:10.1111/j.1540-6261.1993.tb05123.x

Gächter, S., Johnson, E., & Herrmann, A. (2010). *Individual-level Loss Aversion in Riskless and Risky Choices*. Retrieved from https://www.econstor.eu/handle/10419/49656

Gallagher, J. (2014). Learning About an Infrequent Event: Evidence From Flood Insurance Take-Up in the United States. *Applied Economics, 6*(3), 206–233.

García-Teruel, P. J., & Martínez-Solano, P. (2008). On the Determinants of SME Cash Holdings: Evidence from Spain. *Journal of Business Finance & Accounting, 35*(1), 127–149. doi:10.1111/j.1468-5957.2007.02022.x

Gilbert, B., James, A., & Shogren, J. F. (2018). Corporate apology for environmental damage. *Journal of Risk and Uncertainty, 56*(1), 51–81. doi:10.100711166-018-9276-4

GillB. S. (2020). Flirting with Disasters: Do Firms Financially Plan Ahead for Disasters? Available at SSRN: https://ssrn.com/abstract=3525065 or doi:10.2139/ssrn.3525065

Guthrie, C. (2003). Prospect Theory, Risk Preference, and the Law. *Northwestern University Law Review*, *97*(3), 1115–1163.

Harris, C. (2017). *Climate Change Blamed as EU's Forest Fires More than Double*. Euronews. Retrieved from https://www.euronews.com/2017/10/16/how-europe-s-wildfires-have-more-than-trebled-in-2017

Hölmstrom, B., & Tirole, J. (1998). Private and Public Supply of Liquidity. *Journal of Political Economy*, *106*(1), 1–40. doi:10.1086/250001

Hsiao, C. (2005). Why Panel Data? *The Singapore Economic Review*, *50*(2), 143–154. doi:10.1142/S0217590805001937

Instituto da Conservação da Natureza e das Florestas. (2017a). *10.o Relatório Provisório de Incêndios Florestais*. Retrieved from http://www.icnf.pt/portal/florestas/dfci/Resource/doc/rel/2017/10-rel-prov-1jan-31out-2017.pdf

Instituto da Conservação da Natureza e das Florestas. (2017b). *Estatísticas*. Retrieved December 29, 2017, from http://www2.icnf.pt/portal/florestas/dfci/inc/estat-sgif

JavadiS.Al MasumA.MollagholamaliM.RaoR. P. (2020). *Climate Change and Corporate Cash Holdings: Global Evidence*. 2021 FMA Annual Meeting (Denver, Colorado, United States). https://ssrn.com/abstract=3717092 doi:10.2139/ssrn.3717092

Johansson, J., & Lidskog, R. (2020). Constructing and justifying risk and accountability after extreme events: Public administration and stakeholders' responses to a wildfire disaster. *Journal of Environmental Policy and Planning*, *22*(3), 353–365. doi:10.1080/1523908X.2020.1740656

Jones, S. (2017). Huge Forest Fires in Portugal Kill at Least 60. *The Guardian*. Retrieved from https://www.theguardian.com/world/2017/jun/18/portugal-more-than-20-people-killed-in-forest-fires

Kahneman, D. (2012). *Thinking, Fast and Slow*. Penguin Books.

Kahneman, D., Knetsch, J., & Thaler, R. (1991). Anomalies: The Endowment Effect, Loss Aversion, and the Status Quo Bias. *The Journal of Economic Perspectives*, *5*(1), 193–206. doi:10.1257/jep.5.1.193

Kahneman, D., & Tversky, A. (1979). Prospect Theory: An Analysis of Decision under Risk. *Econometrica*, *47*(2), 263–292. doi:10.2307/1914185

Kahneman, D., & Tversky, A. (1997). *Choices, Values and Frames*. Princeton University Press.

Kamiya, S., & Yanase, N. (2019). Learning from extreme catastrophes. *Journal of Risk and Uncertainty*, *59*(1), 85–124. doi:10.100711166-019-09310-8

Köbberling, V., & Wakker, P. (2005). An Index of Loss Aversion. *Journal of Economic Theory*, *122*(1), 119–131. doi:10.1016/j.jet.2004.03.009

Livet, P. (2009). Rational Choice, Neuroeconomy and Mixed Emotions. *Philosophical Transactions of the Royal Society Biological Science*, *365*(1538), 259–269. doi:10.1098/rstb.2009.0177 PMID:20026464

Markowitz, H. (1952). Portfolio Selection. *The Journal of Finance*, *7*(1), 77–91.

Marques, L. D. (2000). *Modelos Dinâmicos com Dados em Painel: Revisão de Literatura*. Universidade do Porto.

Mavsar, R., Cabán, A. G., & Varela, E. (2013). The state of development of fire management decision support systems in America and Europe. *Forest Policy and Economics*, *29*, 45–55. doi:10.1016/j.forpol.2012.11.009

Minder, R. (2017). Deadly Fires Sweep Portugal and Northern Spain. *The New York Times*. Retrieved from https://www.nytimes.com/2017/10/16/world/europe/portugal-spain-fires.html

Montinari, N., & Rancan, M. (2018). Risk taking on behalf of others: The role of social distance. *Journal of Risk and Uncertainty*, *57*(1), 81–109. doi:10.100711166-018-9286-2

National Oceanic & Atmospheric Administration. (2017). *Subject: E11) How many tropical cyclones have there been each year in the Atlantic basin? What years were the greatest and fewest seen?* Retrieved May 28, 2018, from https://www.aoml.noaa.gov/hrd/tcfaq/E11.html

Noth, F., & Rehbein, O. (2019). Badly hurt? Natural disasters and direct firm effects. *Finance Research Letters*, *28*, 254–258. doi:10.1016/j.frl.2018.05.009

Odean, T. (1998). Are Investors Reluctant to Realize Their Losses? *The Journal of Finance*, *53*(5), 1775–1798. doi:10.1111/0022-1082.00072

Pereira, P. (1993). *Incêndios em Edifícios na Cidade do Porto*. Universidade de Porto.

Primo, V. (2008). *Análise Estatística dos Incêndios em Edifícios no Porto*. LNEC-FCTUC.

Quiggin, J. (1982). A Theory of Anticipated Utility. *Journal of Economic Behavior & Organization*, *3*(4), 323–343. doi:10.1016/0167-2681(82)90008-7

Robbins, S. P. (2000). *Administração: Mudanças e Perspectivas*. Saraiva.

Rodrigues, F., & Russo, R. (2011). Heurísticas e Vieses. In *Tomada de decisão nas organizações* (pp. 79–108). Saraiva.

Scherr, F. C., & Hulburt, H. M. (2001). The Debt Maturiry Structure of Small Firms. *Financial Management*, *30*(1), 85–111. doi:10.2307/3666392

Simon, H. A. (1955). A Behavioral Model of Rational Choice. *The Quarterly Journal of Economics*, *69*(1), 99–118. doi:10.2307/1884852

Simon, H. A. (1960). *A Capacidade de Decisão e de Liderança*. Editora Fundo de Cultura.

Thaler, R. (1980). Toward a Positive Theory of Consumer Choice. *Journal of Economic Behavior & Organization*, *1*(1), 39–60. doi:10.1016/0167-2681(80)90051-7

Tom, S. M., Fox, C. R., Trepel, C., & Poldrack, R. A. (2007). The Neural Basis of Loss Aversion in Decision-making Under Risk. *Science*, *315*(5811), 515–518. doi:10.1126cience.1134239 PMID:17255512

Trejo-Pech, C., Gunderson, M., & Noguera, M. (2015). Corporate Cash Holdings and Economic Crises in Mexico. In A. Gevorkyan & O. Canuto (Eds.), *Financial Deepening and Post-Crisis Development in Emerging Markets.*, doi:10.1057/978-1-137-52246-7_6

Tversky, A., & Kahneman, D. (1974). Judgment Under Uncertainty: Heuristics and Biases. *Judgment Under Uncertainty, 185*(4157), 3–20.

Tversky, A., & Kahneman, D. (1986). Rational Choice and the Framing of Decisions. *The Journal of Business, 59*(4), 251–278. doi:10.1086/296365

Tversky, A., & Kahneman, D. (1991). Loss Aversion in Riskless Choice. A Reference-dependent Model. *The Quarterly Journal of Economics, 106*(4), 1039–1061. doi:10.2307/2937956

Tversky, A., & Kahneman, D. (1992). Advances in Prospect Theory: Cumulative Representation of Uncertainty. *Journal of Risk and Uncertainty, 5*(4), 297–323. doi:10.1007/BF00122574

U. S. Fire Administration. (2017a). *About the National Fire Incident Reporting System*. Retrieved December 26, 2017, from https://www.usfa.fema.gov/data/nfirs/about/index.html

U. S. Fire Administration. (2017b). *Fire in the United States 2006-2015*. Retrieved from https://www.usfa.fema.gov/downloads/pdf/publications/fius19th.pdf

Whitmarsh, L. (2008). Are Flood Victims More Concerned About Climate Change than Other People? The Role of Direct Experience in Risk Perception and Behavioural Response. *Journal of Risk Research, 11*(3), 351–374. doi:10.1080/13669870701552235

Yin, R. K. (2003). *Case Study Research. Design and Methods* (3rd ed.). SAGE Publications.

KEY TERMS AND DEFINITIONS

Bias: A disproportionate weight in favor of or against an idea or thing. Biases can be innate or learned. Can be closed-minded, prejudicial, or unfair. People may develop biases for or against an individual, a group, or a belief.

Cash Holdings: The money that a person or company keeps available to spend rather than invest. Low cash holdings take away the freedom of managers to react to the market. The assets that a person/company holds in ready cash, as opposed to property, shares, bonds, etc.

Debt: A debt is something, usually money, borrowed by one party from another. Debt is used by many corporations and individuals to make large purchases that they could not afford under normal circumstances.

Financial Crisis: A financial crisis is any of a broad variety of situations in which some financial assets suddenly lose a large part of their nominal value.

Financing: Financing is the process of providing funds for business activities, making purchases, or investing.

Heuristic: A mental shortcut that allows people to solve problems and make judgments quickly and efficiently. Heuristics are helpful in many situations, but they can also lead to cognitive biases.

Investment: An investment is essentially an asset that is created to allow money to grow.

Loss Aversion: An important concept associated with Prospect Theory and is encapsulated in the expression "losses loom larger than gains" (Kahneman & Tversky, 1979). It is thought that the pain of losing is psychologically about twice as powerful as the pleasure of gaining. People are more willing to take risks or behave dishonestly to avoid a loss than to make a gain. Loss aversion has been used to explain the endowment effect and sunk cost fallacy, and it may also play a role in the status quo bias.

Prospect Theory: A theory of behavioral economics and behavioral finance that was developed by Daniel Kahneman and Amos Tversky in 1979. It describes how individuals assess their loss and gain perspectives asymmetrically. Contrary to the expected utility theory (which models the decision that perfectly rational agents would make), prospect theory aims to describe the actual behavior of people.

Wildfire: The poor forest management and firefighting techniques make Portugal especially vulnerable to wildfires as climate change makes hotter, longer summers more likely.

Chapter 8
Risk of Business Bankruptcy:
The Application of DEA Method – Case Study of Slovak Businesses

Jarmila Horváthová
Faculty of Management and Business, University of Prešov, Slovakia

Martina Mokrišová
Faculty of Management and Business, University of Prešov, Slovakia

ABSTRACT

Recently, the demand of business owners to ensure the sustainability of their businesses has come to the fore. It results in a focus on identifying the risks of businesses' financial failure. Several prediction models can be applied in a given area. Which of these models is most suitable for Slovak companies? The aim of this chapter was to point out the possibility of applying the DEA method in measuring the financial health of companies and predicting the risk of their possible bankruptcy. The research was carried out on a sample of companies operating in the field of heat supply. The indicators were selected using related empirical studies, a univariate Logit model, and a correlation matrix. In this chapter, two main models were applied: the DEA model and the Logit model. The main conclusion of the paper is that the DEA method is a suitable alternative in assessing businesses' financial health.

INTRODUCTION

Diagnosing the financial health of companies, as well as predicting their financial failure, is currently one of the frequently discussed topics in the academic and business world of Slovakia. In order to maintain the prosperity and competitiveness of the company, it is very important to know what financial situation the company is in. In economic practice, it is not possible to make adequate managerial decisions without a detailed analysis of the company's financial health.

An important prerequisite for effective decision-making by business owners is a quality, comprehensive and timely diagnosis based on a detailed analysis of adverse events that threaten the company's activities.

DOI: 10.4018/978-1-7998-8609-9.ch008

Especially at the time of the COVID - 19 pandemic, it is very important to pay attention to the analysis of the financial health of companies. These analyzes are also necessary for strategic solutions at the country's macro level, as countries` governments need to know how companies respond to a pandemic. Based on it, it is possible to identify sectors of activity that are more vulnerable to the effects of the crisis, and the main financial management decisions which companies need to take in times of crisis (Achim et al. 2021).

In line with the increase in corporate bankruptcy risks, the aim of the chapter was to assess the financial health of companies using the DEA method and to compare its classification ability with the classification ability of Logit model.

FINANCIAL HEALTH OF THE COMPANY AND THE PROCESS OF ITS FAILURE

When focusing on health of the company, we must take into account all of its health issues. The company is perceived as "healthy" when it achieves a positive equity value, positive cash flow and positive economic result (Juárez, 2011).

In the early stages of a company's financial problems, the company fails to meet its liabilities, and this situation escalates into financial difficulties. These will subsequently result in the *failure* of the company, which means that the achieved rate of return on invested capital, taking into account the risk, is significantly lower than the rates achieved by others in similar positions (Klieštik et al., 2019). Karels and Prakash in 1987 reported several symptoms that are signs of failure, such as: negative net assets, no payments to creditors, collapse of corporate stock, inability to repay debt, bank overdrafts, non-payment of priority dividends, forced administration, etc. (Sanobar, 2012).

In 1932 FitzPatrick (Klieštik et al., 2019) defined 5 stages in the life of a company that lead to its failure. These are the following stages:

Stage 1 - Incubation: it is the period during which the unfavourable financial condition of the company develops and deepens.
Stage 2 - Financial Embarrassment: it is the period in which the first financial difficulties occur.
Stage 3 - Insolvency: (*Financial Insolvency*).
Stage 4 - Total Insolvency: liabilities exceed company's assets.
Stage 5 - Confirmed Insolvency: the status of insolvent business company is confirmed. At this stage, all legal instruments aimed at protecting creditors' rights are being implemented (Sanobar, 2012).

Bankruptcy is a forced state that follows after the company ran out of money and lost its ability to repay its liabilities or has too many debts. Bankruptcy can be defined as a situation where a company is unable to repay liabilities to its creditors, pay preference shares to shareholders, pay its suppliers or has overdrawn its accounts or the company has gone bankrupt under the relevant law Dimitras et al. (1996). Bankruptcy was also defined by the authors Ding, Song and Zen (2008), who state that bankruptcy is a situation where the company is unable to pay its liabilities, priority dividends and has overdrawn its accounts. In the vast majority of sources dealing with the issue, the authors define bankruptcy as the inability of the company to repay its liabilities, thus triggers bankruptcy processes (Pervan, Pervan and Vukoja, 2011). In 1993 Altman defined the concept of financial distress and pointed out that bankruptcy represents the legal end of financial distress (Ding, Song and Zen, 2008).

According to Achim et al. (2012), the risk of a company's bankruptcy is closely linked to economic and financial risks. While financial risk is determined by the level of indebtedness, economic risk depends on the ratio of fixed to variable costs. It can be said that, in general, knowing these risks allows us to quantify the risk of a company's bankruptcy. "Bankruptcy risk is a possibility of anticipated legal bankruptcy procedure, followed by unfavorable financial consequences such a loss resources or expecting income" (Rybak, 2006).

Diagnosis of Financial Health

The most common method of measuring and evaluating a company's financial health is the method of fundamental analysis, which evaluates the company from an economic point of view on the basis of a detailed study and analysis of financial statements (Fisher, 1992). According to many Slovak and foreign authors Ittner, Larcker and Randall (2003), Dixon, Nanni and Vollmann (1990), Synek et al. (2007), Petřík (2009), financial indicators are the most common indicators for measuring the financial health of companies. These traditional indicators are based mainly on profit maximization, which is the primary goal of the business. They map the main activities of the company in the areas of profitability, solvency, as well as the investment area, in order to increase value for investors.

In line with the emergence of new methods in measuring the financial health of companies, some companies shifted their attention to the application of newer and more modern methods of measuring the financial health of companies. These methods include:

- Evaluation using market characteristics, such as Economic Value Added (EVA), IN Economic Value Added (INEVA), Market Value Added (MVA), Return on Net Assets (RONA), Weighted Average Cost of Capital (WACC) or Free Cash Flow (FCF), Cash Value Added (CVA) and others.
- Evaluation using non-financial indicators. Comprehensive concept with the application of financial and non-financial measures is the Balanced Scorecard (BSC) introduced by Kaplan and Norton in 1996.
- Evaluation based exclusively on non-financial indicators, which includes various techniques for managing the organization, e.g. Capability Maturity Matrices (CMM), Effective Progress and Performance Measurement (EP^2M) and process performance management by Sink and Tuttle (1989). Modern management and performance measurement techniques also include Total Quality Management (TQM), Six Sigma, Benchmarking, Kaizen, process reengineering and others.

Prediction of Company's Bankruptcy and Historical Development of Bankruptcy Prediction Models

According to Aziz and Dar (2006), prediction of bankruptcy risk is of increasing importance to corporate governance. Many different models have been used to predict corporate bankruptcy. These methods all have their particular strengths and weaknesses, and choosing between them for empirical application is not straightforward. In 1932, Fitzpatrick was the first to deal with the prediction of bankruptcy when he compared the financial indicators of solvent and insolvent companies in his study (Klieštik et al., 2019). In the following years, Merwin (1942), Chudson (1945), Jackendoff (1962) and Beaver (1966) conducted research (Delina and Packová, 2013). Beaver pointed out that financial indicators can be useful in predicting the failure of companies (Šarlija and Jeger, 2011). At the same time, he confirmed that not all financial indicators are suitable to be used for this prediction. This fact was also confirmed in practice, in which the use of simple financial indicators was questioned due to the fact that they are frequently distorted because of managerial decisions. Therefore, Beaver suggested using a dichotomous classification test (Kidane, 2004). Using this test, it was possible to identify several financial indicators with the highest predictive power.

After one-dimensional discriminant analysis found its place in practice, methods of multidimensional discriminant analysis were introduced. In 1968, Altman developed a model of multidimensional discriminant analysis (MDA), known as the Z-score. Since Altman's (1968) study, the number as well as the complexity of these models have increased dramatically. It was used, among others, by Blum (1974), Deakin (1972), Elam (1975), Norton and Smith (1979), Wilcox (1973), Taffler (1983).

Academics in Slovakia also formulated models that meet the requirements placed upon these models. In 1999, Binkert (Klieštik et al., 2019) formulated the MDA model, the so-called Binkert's model. The sample under the model consisted of 160 companies (of which were 80 bankrupt and 80 non-bankrupt). It is also necessary to mention the model of Chrastinová (Ch-index) from 1998 (Klieštik et al., 2019), which was designed for agricultural enterprises (sample of 1,123 enterprises), as well as the model of Gurčík (2002), namely the G-index, the aim of which was to predict the financial situation of agricultural enterprises (a sample of 60 enterprises).

The use of multidimensional discriminant analysis requires that the following assumptions are met (Csikósová et al., 2019):

- Quantitative or binary characters;
- None of the characters may be a linear combination of another character or characters;
- It is not appropriate to use two or more strongly correlated characters at the same time;
- The covariance matrices for each group must be approximately identical;
- The characteristics describing each group should meet the requirement of a multidimensional normal distribution.

At the same time, it is preferable that the number of discriminatory variables is lower than the number of subjects in the analyzed sample (Stankovičová and Vojtková, 2007). Since the use of discriminant analysis has so many limitations, it is more appropriate to use logistic regression, which does not require meeting so many assumptions. This is also due to the fact, that financial ratios do not meet mentioned assumptions.

Logit Model

Based on the shortcomings of discriminant analysis, the next step in the theory of bankruptcy prediction was to develop methods and models that would be able to provide information on the probability of companies going bankrupt (Mihalovič, 2015). Models of multiple discriminant analysis have been replaced by less demanding techniques such as logistic regression (or just the "Logit model"), Probit analysis and linear probability models. Using these methods, conditional probability models were created (Vochozka et al., 2017).

Compared to methods based on multidimensional discriminant analysis, logistic regression has several advantages. Compared to discriminant analysis, it has a higher estimation accuracy and its application does not require compliance with assumptions that could limit its usability. In the case of discriminant analysis, the assumption that complicates the preparation of data for initial testing is also required. Other advantages of logistic regression include, e.g. unnecessary distribution of values of independent variables, unnecessary testing of the importance of individual variables before the analysis, as well as the unnecessary equality of variance-covariance matrices (Gundová, 2015). Logistic regression was firstly used by Martin (1977) to predict bankruptcy of banks and by Ohlson (1980) to predict bankruptcy of companies.

The logistic regression model is very similar to the linear regression model, except that the dependent variable in the Logit model is not continuous, but categorical or discrete. The dependent variable y_i can take only two values, namely $y_i = 1$ if the probability of bankruptcy occurs and $y_i = 0$ if the probability of bankruptcy does not occur. Furthermore, we can assume that the probability $y_i = 1$ is given by P_i and the probability $y_i = 0$ is given by $1 - P_i$.

The aim of logistic regression is to model the probability P_i in a way to ensure that bankruptcy will occur: $P_i = f(\alpha + \beta x_i)$, where x_i are selected financial indicators, α and β are estimated parameters (Gurný and Gurný, 2010). The maximum likelihood method is used to estimate the parameters of the Logit model. The aim of this method is to find the maximum of the likelihood function L or the function $-2\log L$. The estimate of the function L is obtained under the following formula (1) (Sláviček and Kuběnka, 2016):

$$-2\log L = -2\sum_{i=1}^{n} \log(p_i), \qquad (1)$$

where p_i are point estimates of the conditional probabilities of the modelled value for all combinations of explanatory variables obtained from available observations.

According to Hebák (2015) the Logit model is defined as follows (2) (In: Kováčová and Klieštik, 2017):

$$\log it = \ln\left(\frac{P_i}{1-P_i}\right) = f(\alpha + \beta x_i) \qquad (2)$$

Probability p_i (3) can be calculated with the use of the logistic function as follows:

$$P_i = \frac{e^{(\alpha+\beta x_i)}}{1+e^{(\alpha+\beta x_i)}} = \frac{1}{1+e^{-(\alpha+\beta x_i)}} \qquad (3)$$

This formula represents the logarithm of the odds ratio of both possible alternatives (p_1, p_0). The goal of the logistic regression is to calculate the Odds ratio ($\frac{P_i}{1-P_i}$). The logarithm in this formula represents the Logit transformation.

The essence of the Logit model solution is to divide companies into those facing bankruptcy and not facing bankruptcy on the basis of their Logit score and cut-off, which is usually 0.5. If $p_i = 0.5$, the probability of company's failure is equal to the probability that the company will not fail. The closer the value of p_i to 0, the lower the probability of failure of the company. The closer the value of p_i is to 1, the higher the probability of failure (Araghi and Makvandi, 2012).

The estimation accuracy of the Logit model can be assessed using the ROC curve. This curve shows the relationship between sensitivity and specificity. Sensitivity expresses the percentage of correctly classified bankrupt businesses and specificity expresses the percentage of correctly classified non-bankrupt businesses (Klepáč and Hampel, 2017). The area under the ROC curve (AUC) measures the overall estimation accuracy of the model. It can take any value from 0 to 1. The closer the AUC is to 1, the better the overall estimation accuracy (Park, Goo and Jo, 2004). According to Klepáč and Hampel (2017), the AUC usually takes a value between 0.5 and 1.

Methods of Mathematical Programming

Mathematical programming methods are an important group of methods that are used in predicting the risk of corporate bankruptcy. With regard to mathematical programming, the problem of linear programming stands out. The goal of linear programming is to find the optimal value so that all ratios are based on the optimal solution. When creating a model, it is necessary to pay close attention to the accuracy of determining individual limiting conditions. In the practical solution of a given task, it is necessary to proceed from its simplification. The most common algorithm for solving linear programming problems is the simplex method. Mangasarian (1965), Hand (1981) and Nath et al. (1992) were the first to apply linear programming to predict financial health (Dipak and Purnendu, 2007).

One of the methods which fits the issue of mathematical programming, and which we will describe in more detail, is the Data Envelopment Analysis (DEA) method (Horváthová and Mokrišová, 2018). Compared to statistical methods, DEA is a relatively new, non-parametric method, which represents one of many approaches to assessing the financial health of companies and the risk of their bankruptcy. Charnes, Cooper and Rhodes first used this method in 1978. It is based on the idea presented in the paper "Measuring efficiency of decision making units", published by Farrell in 1957, whose work was based on the work of Debreu (1951) and Koopmans (1951). Farrell (1957) proposed a new approach to measuring efficiency based on a convex efficient frontier and the use of functions to measure the distance between the observed enterprise and the projected point on the efficiency curve. In this way, he proposed a new measure of enterprise efficiency based on the calculation of two components of overall enterprise efficiency: technical and allocative efficiency. Farrell's approach was based on measuring the ability of the observed company to transform inputs into outputs, and is therefore called input-oriented. Charnes, Cooper, and Rhodes (1978) applied a multiplicative input/output model to measure business efficiency. The approach of these authors is described as a two-step calculation of efficiency. The first step is to identify the efficiency frontier. If the combination of inputs and outputs of the production unit lies on the frontier, it is efficient and financially healthy production unit. If the production unit is inefficient, it does not lie on the efficiency frontier. This unit need to reduce inputs or increase outputs. In the second step, the efficiency score for the analyzed companies and their distance from the efficiency frontier is calculated. DEA models can be divided into DEA CCR (Charnes, Cooper and Rhodes, 1978) and DEA BCC (Banker, Charnes and Cooper, 1984) in terms of whether each unit of input yields the same amount of output or a variable amount of output. The CCR and BCC models have been proposed in the literature in multiplier or envelopment (dual) form. From a practical point of view it is more appropriate to work with dual form of the models. (Jablonský, Dlouhý, 2015). The CCR and BCC model can be computationally oriented on inputs (input-oriented) or outputs (output-oriented) (Klieštik et al., 2019). Formulas for input-oriented and out-put-oriented dual models are stated in Table 1. Simak (1997) was the first who thought of using the DEA method to predict bankruptcy by comparing its results with the results of Altman's Z-score. In 2009, Premachandra, Bhabra and Sueyoshi used the additive DEA model and compared its results with the results of logistic regression. The research yielded a satisfactory level of correct prediction of bankruptcy.

Table 1. Formulas for DEA models in dual form

	Input-oriented models	
	CCR model	**BCC model**
To minimize Subject to	$\theta_q - \varepsilon \left(\sum_{i=1}^{m} s_i^- + \sum_{k=1}^{r} s_k^+ \right)$ $\sum_{j=1}^{n} x_{ij} \lambda_j + s_i^- = \theta_q x_{iq}, \quad i=1,2,...,m$ $\sum_{j=1}^{n} y_{kj} \lambda_j - s_k^+ = y_{kq}, \quad k=1,2,...,r$ $\lambda_j \geq 0, s_i^- \geq 0, s_k^+ \geq 0 \quad j=1,2,...,n$	$\theta_q - \varepsilon \left(\sum_{i=1}^{m} s_i^- + \sum_{k=1}^{r} s_k^+ \right)$ $\sum_{j=1}^{n} x_{ij} \lambda_j + s_i^- = \theta_q x_{iq}, \quad i=1,2,...,m$ $\sum_{j=1}^{n} y_{kj} \lambda_j - s_k^+ = y_{kq}, \quad k=1,2,...,r$ $\sum_{j=1}^{n} \lambda_j = 1, \quad j=1,2,...,n$ $s_i^- \geq 0, s_k^+ \geq 0$
	Output-oriented models	
	CCR model	**BCC model**
To maximize Subject to	$\phi_q + \varepsilon \left(\sum_{i=1}^{m} s_i^- + \sum_{k=1}^{r} s_k^+ \right)$ $\sum_{j=1}^{n} x_{ij} \lambda_j + s_i^- = x_{iq}, \quad i=1,2,...,m$ $\sum_{j=1}^{n} y_{kj} \lambda_j - s_k^+ = \phi_q y_{kq}, \quad k=1,2,...,r$ $\lambda_j \geq 0, s_i^- \geq 0, s_k^+ \geq 0, \quad j=1,2,...,n$	$\phi_q + \varepsilon \left(\sum_{i=1}^{m} s_i^- + \sum_{k=1}^{r} s_k^+ \right)$ $\sum_{j=1}^{n} x_{ij} \lambda_j + s_i^- = x_{iq}, \quad i=1,2,...,m$ $\sum_{j=1}^{n} y_{kj} \lambda_j - s_k^+ = \phi_q y_{kq}, \quad k=1,2,...,r$ $\sum_{j=1}^{n} \lambda_j = 1, \quad j=1,2,...,n$ $s_i^- \geq 0, s_k^+ \geq 0.$

Legend: θo and ϕo are the values of objective functions, ε is the non-Archimedean infinitesimal value, x_{ij} i = 1, 2, ..., m, j = 1, 2, ..., n is the value of i input for DMUi, y_{rj} r = 1, 2, ..., s, j = 1, 2, ..., n is the value of k output for DMUj, m and s are, respectively, the number of inputs and outputs, n is the number of enterprises, λ_j is convex coefficient, s_i^- and s_r^+ are input and output slacks.

Source: (Jablonský and Dlouhý, 2015)

In Slovakia, Roháčová and Kráľ applied the DEA method in 2015 in the field of agriculture and Mendelová and Bieliková applied this method in 2017 in bankruptcy prediction.

ANALYSIS OF BUSINESSES' FINANCIAL HEALTH APPLYING DEA MODELS

"Over the last few years, the demand of Slovak business owners and their managers for sustainability and growth solutions has been growing. The stakeholders are interested in the causes and symptoms of possible financial failure of companies. There are many prediction models that can be used to predict financial difficulties. Which of these models is most suitable for companies operating in Slovakia? Is the DEA a suitable method for measuring the financial health of companies?"

Table 2. Financial indicators used in the analysis of the financial health of companies

Indicator	Indicators' description	Method of calculation
CL	Current ratio	short term assets / short term liabilities
QR	Quick ratio	(current receivables + financial assets) / short term liabilities
NWC	Net working capital	short term assets − short term liabilities
ACP	Average collection period	current receivables / sales × 360
IT	Inventory turnover	inventory / sales × 360
CPP	Creditors payment period	current liabilities / sales × 360
APTR	Accounts payable turnover ratio	sales / short term liabilities
ROA	Return on assets	EBIT / assets × 100
ROE	Return on equity	EAT / equity × 100
ROS	Return on sales	EAT / sales × 100
ROC	Return on costs	EAT / costs × 100
ER	Equity ratio	equity / assets × 100
TDTA	Total debt to total assets	debt / assets × 100
EDR	Equity to debt ratio	equity / debt
DER	Debt to equity ratio	debt / equity
ICR	Interest coverage ratio	EBIT / interest expense
DSCR	Debt-service coverage ratio	interest expense / EBIT × 100
CR	Cost ratio	costs / revenues
NWCA	Net working capital to short-term assets	NWC / short term assets
NCFD	Netto cash flow to debt	NCF / debt
ROA_{EAT}	Return on assets with EAT	EAT / assets
LTLA	Long term liabilities to assets	long term liabilities / assets
STLA	Short term liabilities to assets	short term liabilities / assets

Legend: EAT – Earnings after Taxes, EBIT – Earning before Interest and Taxes, NWC – Net Working Capital, NCF – Netto Cash Flow.
Source: authors

With regard to the research problem and the research question, the main goal of the empirical study was formulated.

"To apply the DEA method to measure the financial health of companies and evaluate their estimation accuracy."

With regard to this problem, the following sub-goals were also set:

1. To analyze the financial health of companies.
2. To identify companies that are financially sound and those that are in financial distress with the use of DEA model.
3. To analyze the estimation accuracy of the DEA model.

To meet the sub-goal no. 1, 2, 3 financial indicators were selected from all areas of assessing the financial health of the company. Selected indicators are described in Table 2.

fulfill the sub-goal no. 2, the input parameters selection methods were applied, namely: one-dimensional logit model (it was described in section "Logit model"), correlation matrix and bibliography.

The correlation matrix was processed in the software Statistica. This matrix was used to assess the strength of relationships between a selected group of applied financial indicators. To analyze the financial health of companies, BCC and CCR DEA models were used. These models were described in section („Methods of mathematical programming"). DEA models were processed in software DEA Frontier provided by Joe Zhu. The Logit model was used to compare the estimation accuracy of DEA models (Logit model was described in section "Logit model").

Description of the Analyzed Industry

The input database of the empirical study was created using data from the balance sheets and profit and loss statements of companies operating in Slovakia in the field of heat supply. According to the branch classification of economic activities SK NACE Rev. 2, these companies belong to section D: "Electricity, gas, steam and air conditioning supply". The choice of the analyzed branch was conditioned by the fact that in this branch of the Slovak industry a larger number of companies go bankrupt every year compared to other industries. The analyzed industry is important from an economic as well as a social point of view, because it plays an important role in the daily life of citizens (Horváthová and Mokrišová, 2020). Companies operating in this sector are usually locally-based central heating system companies. In the analyzed sector, there are also companies that have a monopoly position within their geographical area.

Despite some similarities with other energy sectors, heat as a commodity cannot be traded between countries and due to significant heat losses during transmission and distribution it also cannot be traded between networks existing in different locations in Slovakia.

In total, there are around 590 companies operating in Slovakia in the selected sector, employing approximately 17,430 employees. Table 3 shows the volume of revenues for the entire industry of Slovakia, the volume of revenues for the analyzed branch and its share in the revenues of industry.

Table 3. Development of the share of revenues of the analyzed branch in the revenues of the Slovak industry

Year	Industry (mld. EUR)	Branch (mld. EUR)	Share (%)
2008	72.8	11.3	15.5
2009	57.5	10.7	18.7
2010	67.5	11.3	16.7
2011	77.05	13	16.8
2012	82.3	13.8	16.8
2013	82.3	12.6	15.3
2014	82.2	10.9	13.3
2015	87.1	11.2	12.9
2016	88.3	11.3	12.7
2017	93.0	12.3	13.2
2018	99.9	12.8	12.8
2019	100.2	12.5	12.5
2020	92	12.4	13.5

Source: authors based on data from Statistical Office of the Slovak Republic (SOSR, 2021)

Figure 1 shows the development of sales for own outputs and goods and development of production of the analyzed branch of industry in the years 2008 to 2018. The average value of production during the analyzed years reached the level of 10.64 mld. EUR.

Figure 1. Development of sales and production of the analyzed branch
Source: authors based on data from Statistical Office of the Slovak Republic (SOSR, 2021)

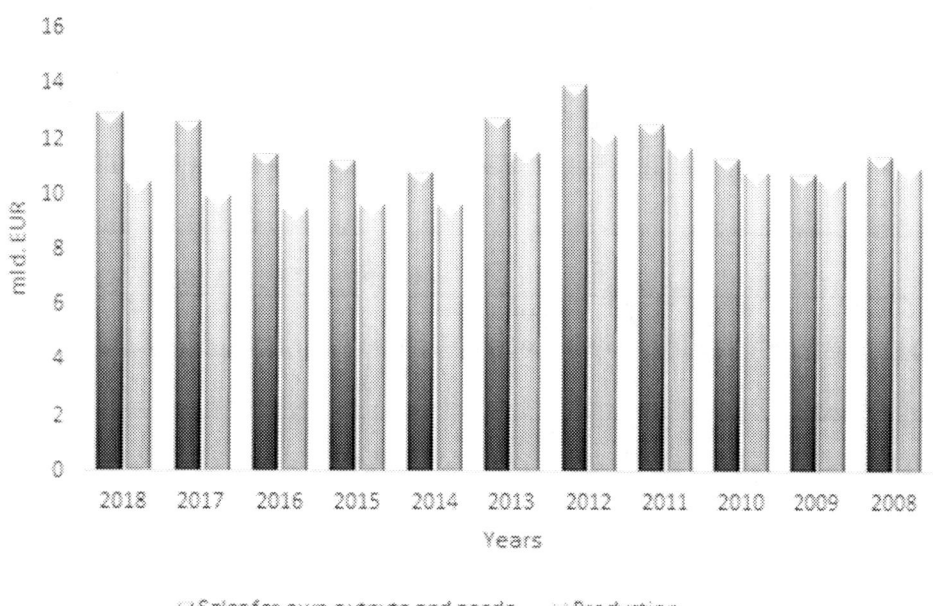

Figure 2 shows the development of costs, revenues and profit/loss of the analyzed branch of industry. The best results in the area of revenues were achieved in 2014 and the worst in 2009. The worst profit/loss result within the analyzed branch was achieved in 2018.

Figure 2. Development of revenues, costs and economic result of the selected branch of industry
Source: authors based on data from Statistical Office of the Slovak Republic (SOSR, 2021)

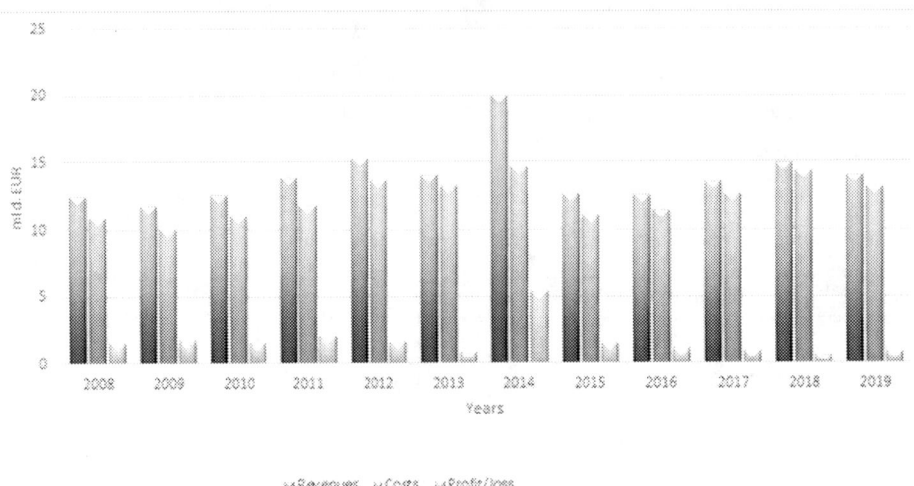

The pandemic of the new coronavirus in 2020 had, in addition to health consequences for the population, also significant effects on the economy of the world's countries. The economically most affected countries were those with a worse pandemic situation, mainly due to long-term anti-pandemic measures. The Slovak Republic is one of such countries. The development of the Slovak GDP indicates that the slowdown in the Slovak economy occurred in the first quarter of 2020, when economic performance did not reach the value of the first quarter of 2019. Behind this slowdown, the external environment and the adoption of the first measures in some economies can be seen. In terms of comparison between the individual quarters of 2019 and 2020, the most significant decline occurred in the 2nd quarter of 2020, when the value of the decline reached more than 9%. This decline was mainly due to anti-pandemic measures (SBA, 2021).

According to (Chang et al., 2020) the sectors which production has been affected by the pandemic may include international travel, hospitality and tourism industries. These sectors were also the most affected in Slovakia. However, the analyzed industry is not so affected, because heat is a commodity that is independent of the pandemic and it has even been sold more than in previous years (SBA, 2021, SOSR, 2021).

The fact that the pandemic did not have a significant impact on the analyzed industry can be seen in the development in 2021 when a significant increase in production and sales is being recorded in the given industry. The average production of the branch in 2021 is growing compared to previous years. In March 2021, compared to March 2020, the increase in production accounted to 22.2%, while in March 2020, a decrease of 10.5% was recorded compared to March 2019. In addition, at the beginning of 2021, there was a more significant increase in the branch's share in the industrial production, namely 1.64%. This increase in share is the most significant since 2013.

A sample was created for the implemented empirical study, which consisted of 292 companies operating in the branch of industry. The financial statements of these companies for 2016 (for which an analysis of the financial health of companies was carried out), were provided by the Slovak analytical agency CRIF - Slovak Credit Bureau, s.r.o. (CRIF, 2016).

Hypotheses

In accordance with the research problem and the goal of the empirical study, the following hypotheses were formulated:

Hypothesis 1: "It is assumed that the estimation accuracy of the DEA model for bankrupt businesses will not be lower than the estimation accuracy of the Logit model at a cut-off 0.5."

Hypothesis 2: "It is assumed that the DEA model and the Logit model will not have the same optimal estimation accuracy for bankrupt businesses."

These hypotheses were tested using the DEA CCR, DEA BCC and Logit models.

DEA Model Inputs

Following the results of the correlation matrix and the procedure according to Sperandei (2014), the indicators (Table 4) were selected. These served as inputs to the DEA model and the Logit model. This selection process followed one crucial requirement – it should include financial indicators from all areas of assessing the financial health of companies. The approach of Premachandra et al. (2009, 2011) was also implemented.

Table 4. Selected financial indicators for DEA models

Indicator	Orientation of DEA model
CR	Input
STLA	Input
LTLA	Input
ICR	Output
QR	Output
ROA_{EAT}	Output
NCFD	Output
NWCA	Output
APTR	Output

Source: authors

Results of the CCR DEA Model

Table 5 shows the companies that achieved a score of 1 under the CCR DEA model. Thus, in the case of these companies, it can be assumed that they are on financial health frontier. From a sample of 292 companies, 17 companies reached this value.

Table 5. Financially sound enterprises - CCR DEA model

			Input - oriented CCR DEA model				
No.	DMU	Score	Returns to scale	Benchmarks			
1	TP1	1,00000	Constant	1,000	TP1		
2	TP22	1,00000	Constant	1,000	TP22		
3	TP37	1,00000	Constant	1,000	TP37		
4	TP60	1,00000	Constant	1,000	TP60		
5	TP84	1,00000	Constant	1,000	TP84		
6	TP89	1,00000	Constant	1,000	TP89		
7	TP94	1,00000	Constant	1,000	TP94		
8	TP98	1,00000	Constant	1,000	TP98		
9	TP135	1,00000	Constant	1,000	TP135		
10	TP181	1,00000	Constant	1,000	TP181		
11	TP267	1,00000	Constant	1,000	TP267		
12	TP268	1,00000	Constant	1,000	TP268		
13	TP275	1,00000	Constant	1,000	TP275		
14	TP279	1,00000	Constant	1,000	TP279		
15	TP282	1,00000	Constant	1,000	TP282		
16	TP285	1,00000	Constant	0,135	TP275	0,865	TP282
17	TP341	1,00000	Constant	1,000	TP341		

Legend: DMU - Decision Making Unit.
Source: authors, processed in DEA Frontier (Zhu, 2019)

To confirm the financial health of the companies, slacks, i.e. distance from the financial health frontier were calculated. Only if the score is equal to 1 and the slacks of all indicators of the enterprise are equal to 0, it is possible to confirm that the company is financially sound and is located on financial health frontier. Of the companies identified in the first step, one company was confirmed as pseudo - efficient (TP285). This company scores 1, but the slacks of its indicators are not equal to 0.

Based on the achieved results, it can be stated that 16 companies are on financial health frontier and other companies are in a production possibility set. The results of the output-oriented CCR DEA model are identical to the results of the input-oriented CCR DEA model,

Results of the BCC DEA Model

Table 6 shows the results of the input-oriented BCC DEA model. The difference between the CCR model and the BCC model is in the addition of a constraint $\sum_{j=1}^{n} \lambda_j = 1$. The efficiency frontier given by the CCR model is in the form of a convex cone, while the efficiency frontier given by the BCC model represents the convex hull. It leads to a larger number of companies being on financial health frontier when using the BCC model. As the CCR DEA model is more suitable for companies that operate under optimal conditions, which is not the case of the analyzed sample of companies, it is more appropriate to apply the BCC DEA model to assess the financial health.

It is clear that the results of this model would yield a larger number of companies that are on financial health frontier. Thus, we talk about 27 companies. In order to confirm their financial health, it was necessary to calculate the slacks.

Table 6. Financially sound enterprises - BCC DEA model

			Input – oriented BCC DEA model				
No.	DMU	Score	Returns to scale		Benchmarks		
1	TP1	1,00000	Constant	1,000	TP1		
2	TP15	1,00000	Constant	1,000	TP15		
3	TP22	1,00000	Constant	1,000	TP22		
4	TP37	1,00000	Constant	1,000	TP37		
5	TP52	1,00000	Constant	1,000	TP52		
6	TP60	1,00000	Constant	1,000	TP60		
7	TP62	1,00000	Constant	1,000	TP62		
8	TP84	1,00000	Constant	1,000	TP84		
9	TP85	1,00000	Constant	1,000	TP85		
10	TP89	1,00000	Constant	1,000	TP89		
11	TP94	1,00000	Constant	1,000	TP94		
12	TP98	1,00000	Constant	1,000	TP98		
13	TP106	1,00000	Constant	1,000	TP106		
14	TP108	1,00000	Constant	1,000	TP108		
15	TP135	1,00000	Constant	1,000	TP135		
16	TP147	1,00000	Constant	1,000	TP147		
17	TP162	1,00000	Constant	1,000	TP162		
18	TP181	1,00000	Constant	1,000	TP181		
19	TP267	1,00000	Constant	1,000	TP267		
20	TP268	1,00000	Constant	1,000	TP268		
21	TP275	1,00000	Constant	1,000	TP275		
22	TP279	1,00000	Constant	1,000	TP279		
23	TP282	1,00000	Constant	1,000	TP282		
24	TP285	1,00000	Constant	0,134	TP275	0,866	TP282
25	TP296	1,00000	Constant	1,000	TP297		
26	TP297	1,00000	Constant	1,000	TP297		
27	TP341	1,00000	Constant	1,000	TP341		

Source: authors, processed in DEA Frontier (Zhu, 2019)

Companies' slacks in the BCC DEA model confirmed that TP285 is pseudo - efficient.

Based on the results, it can be stated that the BCC DEA model identified 26 companies that are financially sound and lie on the financial health frontier. These results were also confirmed by the BCC DEA output-oriented model. Figure 3 shows the limit of financial health of companies, which was constructed with the application of two variables, namely cost ratio (CR) and return on assets with EAT (ROA_{EAT}).

Figure 3. Financial health frontier for two indicators – BCC DEA model
Source: authors, processed in Statistica

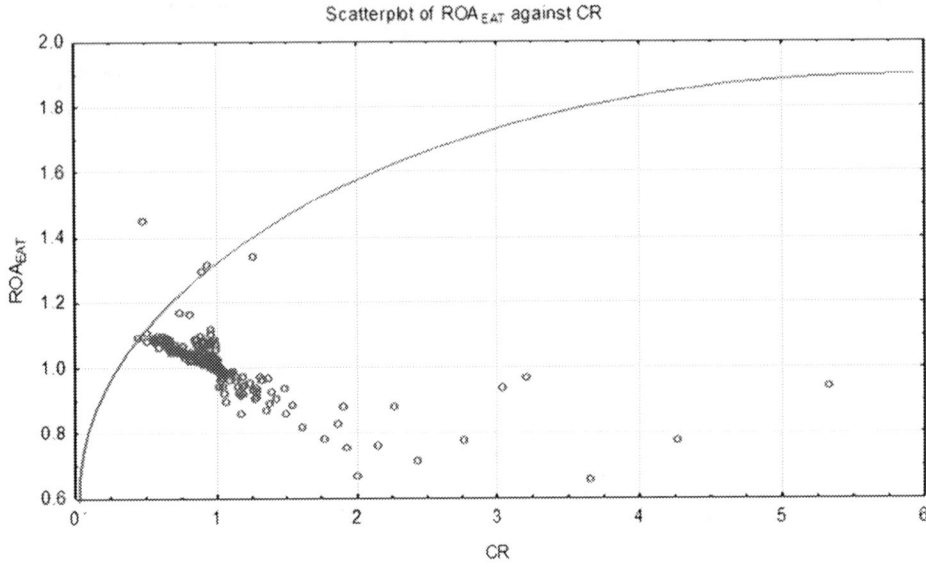

In the next part of the study, the analysis focused on the identification of companies that are in financial distress and are on financial distress frontier.

Results of DEA Models with Regard to Identification of Companies in Financial Distress

It follows from Table 7 that 6 companies are on financial distress frontier while the rest of the companies represent production possibility set. In the case of these companies, it can be stated that the distance of the values of the indicators from the financial distress frontier is equal to zero. These are companies that achieve a negative value of profitability, negative net working capital and negative value of interest coverage. On the input side, a high cost-ratio is recorded.

Table 7. Companies in financial distress - CCR DEA model

		Input - oriented CCR DEA model			
No.	DMU	Score	Returns to scale	Benchmarks	
1	TP74	1,00000	Constant	1,000	TP74
2	TP199	1,00000	Constant	1,000	TP199
3	TP209	1,00000	Constant	1,000	TP209
4	TP307	1,00000	Constant	1,000	TP307
5	TP320	1,00000	Constant	1,000	TP320
6	TP328	1,00000	Constant	1,000	TP328

Source: authors, processed in DEA Frontie (Zhu, 2019)

To compare the results, the BCC DEA model was also modelled as input-oriented with a focus on bankruptcy. The results of the model are shown in Table 8. In the BCC DEA model, 7 companies were identified that are expected to go bankrupt and are on financial distress frontier.

Table 8. Companies in financial distress - BCC DEA model

		Input - oriented BCC DEA model			
No.	DMU	Score	Returns to scale	Benchmarks	
1	TP74	1,00000	Constant	1,000	TP74
2	TP126	1,00000	Constant	1,000	TP126
3	TP199	1,00000	Constant	1,000	TP199
4	TP209	1,00000	Constant	1,000	TP209
5	TP307	1,00000	Constant	1,000	TP307
6	TP320	1,00000	Constant	1,000	TP320
7	TP328	1,00000	Constant	1,000	TP328

Source: authors, processed in DEA Frontier (Zhu, 2019)

Based on the comparison with the CCR DEA model, the input-oriented BCC DEA model confirmed that company TP126 is on financial distress frontier. The outputs of the software may be used to process the desired target values the companies in financial distress should strive to achieve to become financially sound again. For companies that are at the financial distress frontier, the target values of the analyzed financial indicators are given in Table 9.

Table 9. Target values for companies in financial distress - using the BCC DEA model

No	DMU	CR	LTLA	STLA	QR	ROA_{EAT}	NCFD	NWCA	APTR	ICR
1	TP74	0.5507	0.33640	0.09914	7.81415	0.07642	0.36650	0.86978	4.47171	13.494
2	TP126	0.4460	0.00000	0.26700	0.26700	0.09500	0.57900	-1.7220	0.81600	29.950
3	TP199	1.0343	0.21982	0.02060	10.84805	0.02736	0.38550	1.56302	7.88534	0.3841
4	TP209	0.6331	0.28120	0.05707	9.92490	0.06033	0.40963	1.48858	5.01662	7.4049
5	TP307	0.4460	0.00000	0.26700	0.26700	0.09500	0.57900	-1.7220	0.81600	29.950
6	TP320	0.6765	0.23541	0.03963	10.83594	0.05179	0.44334	1.74006	5.18155	4.5576
7	TP328	0.5781	0.25985	0.10151	7.82039	0.07080	0.41911	0.81735	4.22897	12.715

Source: authors, processed in DEA Frontier (Zhu, 2019)

Estimation Accuracy of the DEA Model

The estimation accuracy of the DEA model was compared at different cut-offs. Figure 4 shows the estimation accuracy of the DEA model for different cut off values.

Figure 4. Estimation accuracy of the DEA model at different cut-offs
Legend: B - percentage of bankrupt companies to the predicted number of companies that would go bankrupt, N - percentage of companies not facing bankruptcy to the predicted number of companies that would face bankruptcy.
Source: authors, processed in Statistica

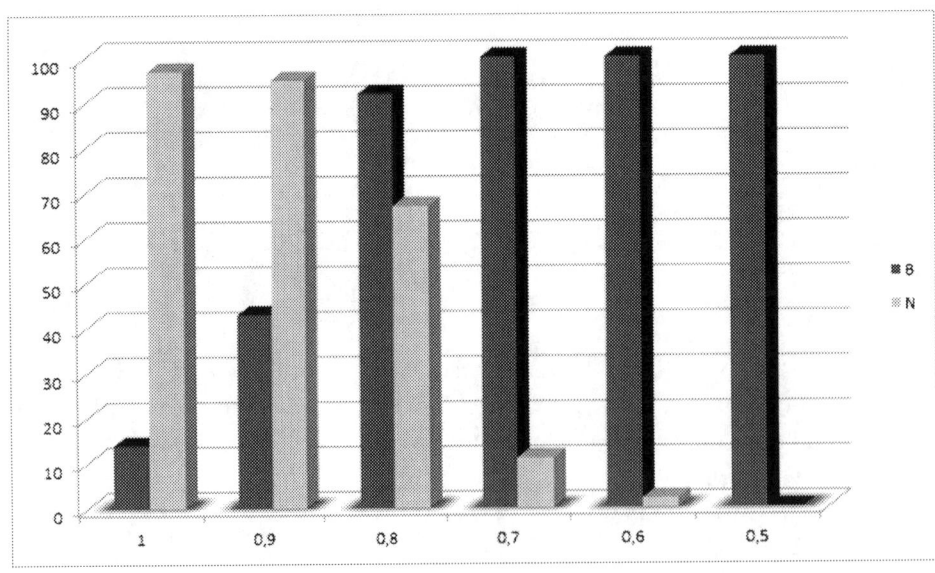

It is clear from Figure 4 that the highest estimation accuracy of the DEA model, in the case of bankrupt companies, is already at the cut-off 0.78 and remains at approximately the same level up to the cut-off 0.5, and for non-bankrupt companies it is at the cut-off 1. Based on the fact that bankrupt companies are those with a score of 1, the estimation accuracy of the CCR DEA model for bankrupt companies is only 14%. It should be pointed out that 14% of companies are located on financial distress frontier, but it can be assumed that there are more bankrupt companies than the number suggests. Based on this fact, it is necessary to lower the cut-off and find the optimal cut-off at which the highest possible number of bankrupt and non-bankrupt companies will be identified. This optimal limit is at the level of 0.83, at which the sum of sensitivity and specificity is the highest. This means that if the probability of bankruptcy is equal to or higher than 0.73, then the company has a high probability of going bankrupt.

The ROC curve was constructed to assess the estimation accuracy of the DEA model (Figure 5). This curve captures the relationship between sensitivity and specificity. The more convex the ROC curve and approaches the upper left corner, the better the discriminative ability of a particular model (Gajowniczek, Zabkowski and Szupiluk, 2014).

Figure 5. ROC curve for DEA model
Source: authors, processed in Statistica

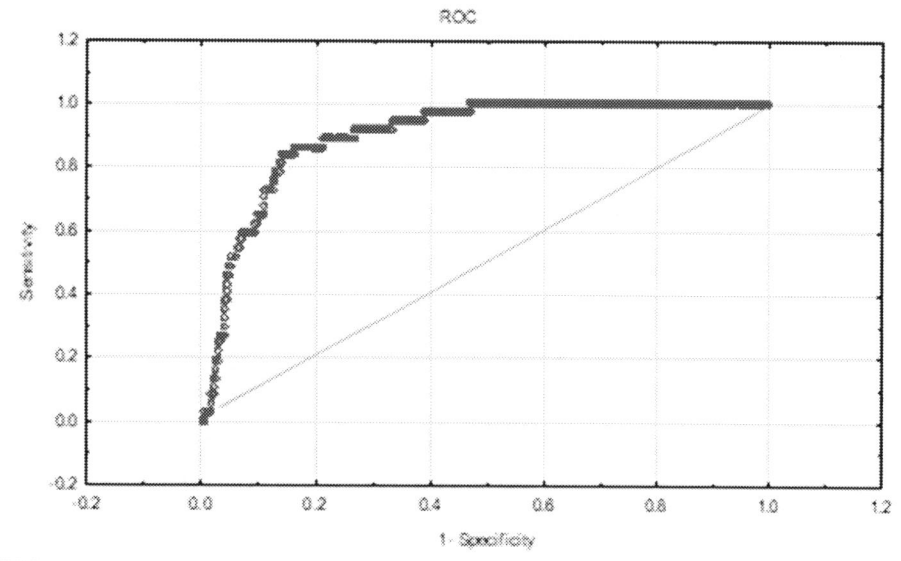

The area under the ROC curve (AUC) reaches a value of 0.85, which can be evaluated positively and it can be stated that the model has a very good estimation accuracy.

If we compare the results of this study with the results of some other authors, the model achieves approximately the same estimation accuracy. Mendelová, Bieliková (2017) achieved 24% accuracy with the DEA model in the identification of companies in financial distress and 96.7% accuracy in the classification of financially sound companies. In the case of some authors, the estimation accuracy of the DEA model was higher, in particular Premachandra et al. (2009) achieved 84.89% accuracy in predicting failing companies, Mendelová and Stachová (2016) 10-42.86% and Cielen et al. (2004) 74.4-75.7%.

However, these authors do not indicate a cut-off for the probability of bankruptcy. This low estimation accuracy of the DEA model in the area of bankruptcy prediction is due to the methodology of creating the financial distress frontier. Only a small number of companies fall within this limit - these are the companies that achieve extreme values in the analyzed indicators.

Results of the Logit Model

The Logit model was applied to compare the results resulting from the DEA model solution. The model used indicators that can be assumed to be significant in relation to the prediction of the company's bankruptcy. The output from the Statistics program is shown in Table 10.

Table 10. Results of the logit model

		Bankruptcy					
	Line	Estimate	Standard Error	Wald Stat.	Lower CL 95.0%	Upper CL 95.0%	P - value
Intercept	1	0.6281	2.54585	0.060861	-4.3617	5.61784	0.8051
QR	2	-5.2230	1.71419	9.283612	-8.5827	-1.86322	0.0023
CR	3	0.2547	0.97114	0.068765	-1.6487	2.15807	0.7931
NWCA	4	0.0971	0.07387	1.728180	-0.0477	0.24190	0.1886
NCFD	5	5.0325	3.86484	1.695550	-2.5424	12.60748	0.1928
APTR	6	0.1556	0.38050	0.167131	-0.5902	0.90133	0.6826
ROA_{EAT}	7	-30.9770	13.71868	5.098628	-57.865	-4.08885	0.0239
LTLA	8	-0.4473	1.62235	0.076004	-3.6270	2.73248	0.7827
STLA	9	-2.3728	2.54364	0.870169	-7.3582	2.61266	0.3509
ICR	10	-0.7785	0.26105	8.893215	-1.2901	-0.26684	0.0028

Source: authors, processed in Statistica

Based on Wald confidence intervals, it can be stated with 95% confidence that the values of the coefficients of the variables QR, ROA_{EAT}, ICR are within the specified range and none of the intervals contains the value 0, which exclude the variable from the model. This does not apply to other indicators which, based on the above results, can be considered statistically less significant in relation to the probability of bankruptcy. Nevertheless, they were left in the basic model. It follows from the above that the independent variables QR, ROA_{EAT}, ICR are significant for the model. Of these variables, the most important variable is ROA_{EAT}. The variables that were confirmed by the model as significant are among the symptoms of bankruptcy. Using the given indicators, it is possible to express the probability of whether the company is prosperous or not prosperous by the following formula (4):

$$p_i = \frac{1}{1+e^{-(0,6281-5,22x1+0,25x2+0,09x3+5,03x4+0,16x5-30,98x6-0,45x7-2,37x8-0,78x9)}} \qquad (4)$$

Based on the results shown in Table 11, the Logit model correctly classified companies in 284 cases (prosperous and those facing bankruptcy). This means that the model classified 253 companies as not facing bankruptcy, and these companies were indeed considered non-bankrupt on the basis of the established criteria. On the basis of the selected criteria the model also included 31 companies in the group of those facing bankruptcy and these companies were indeed facing financial difficulties. The model incorrectly classified 8 companies. The accuracy of the Logit model prediction is 99.22% for companies not facing bankruptcy and 83.78% for companies facing bankruptcy. The overall classification ability of the model is 97.26%.

Table 11. DEA classification table for the cut-off 0.5

	Classification of cases		
	Predicted: Yes	**Predicted: No**	**Percent correct**
Observed: Yes	31	6	83.78%
Observed: No	2	253	99.22%

Source: authors, processed in Statistica

The above Table 11 outlines the data at the most frequently applied cut-off value (0.5). To improve the estimation accuracy in the case of failing companies, it is necessary to choose the cut-off value 0.03. In this case, the estimation accuracy of companies facing bankruptcy would reach 100% and the estimation accuracy of companies not facing bankruptcy would reach 85%. The analysis of the estimation accuracy at different cut-off values is a suitable tool for comparing the achieved results of the Logit model and the DEA model. A comparison of the estimation accuracy of the Logit model at different cut-offs is shown in Figure 6.

Figure 6. Estimation accuracy of the Logit model
Source: authors, processed in MS Office
Legend: B – percentage of bankrupt companies to the predicted percentage of bankrupt companies, N - percentage of non-bankrupt companies to the predicted percentage of non-bankrupt companies

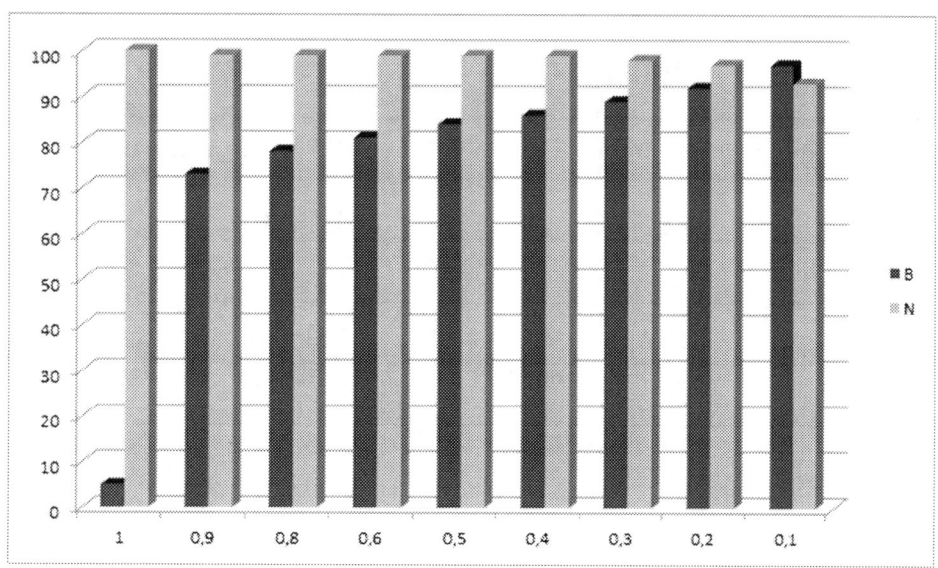

It is clear from Figure 6 that with the lowering of the cut-off in the Logit model, the estimation accuracy for failing companies increases. The optimal cut-off value is at the level of 0.1, at which the sum of sensitivity and specificity reaches the maximum value.

To assess the estimation accuracy of the model, an ROC curve was constructed (Figure 7). The area under the ROC curve (AUC) reached 0.9897. Based on this value, it can be stated that the Logit model has excellent estimation accuracy.

Figure 7. ROC curve for the Logit model
Source: authors, processed in Statistica

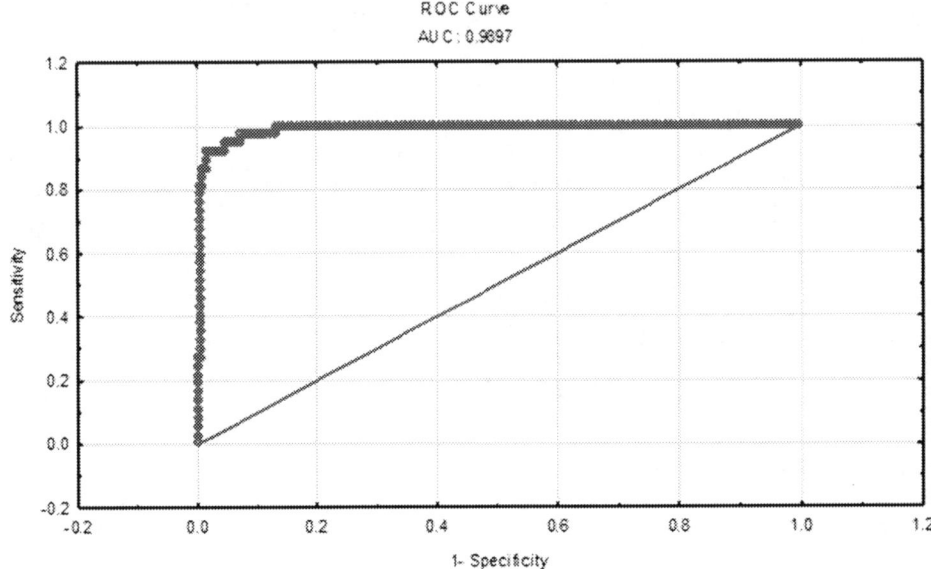

SOLUTION AND RECOMMENDATION

Comparison of the Results of the DEA Model and the Logit Model

From the results, it follows that the optimal cut-off value is different for each model. The results of the comparison of the estimation accuracy of models for failing companies are shown in Figure 8.

In the case of the cut-off value 1, the DEA model has a higher estimation accuracy. The estimation accuracy of the DEA model increases up to a cut-off 0.5. The estimation accuracy of the Logit model is also growing. At a cut off 0.9, the Logit model has a higher estimation accuracy of these models.

Figure 8. Estimation accuracy of Logit and DEA models at different cut-offs for bankrupt companies
Legend: BL - Bankruptcy Logit model, BD - Bankruptcy DEA model
Source: authors, processed in MS Office

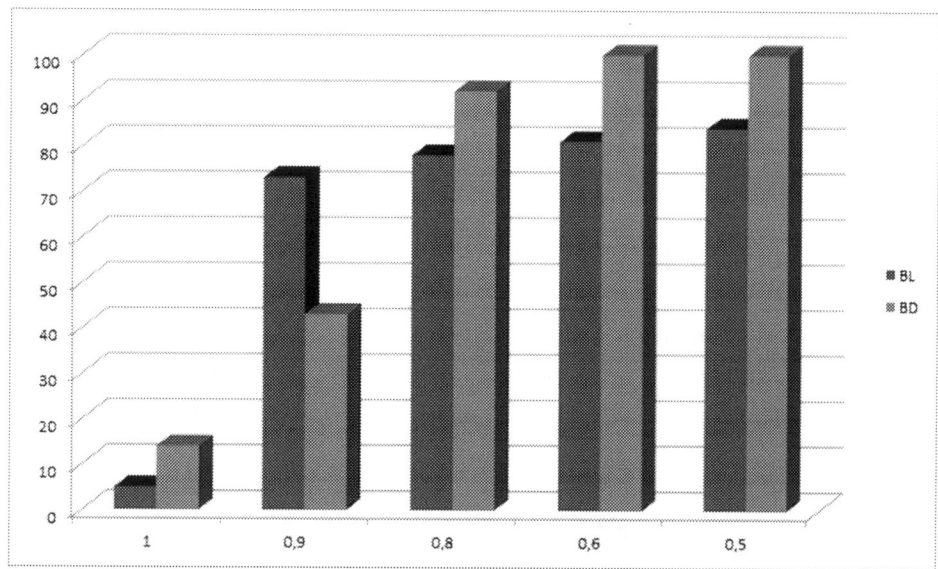

The different development of the estimation accuracy can be seen in Figure 9. This figure shows the estimation accuracy with regard to non-bankrupt companies. The estimation accuracy of the DEA model decreases significantly. At a cut-off 0.5, this accuracy is minimal. Conversely, the estimation accuracy of the Logit model is at approximately the same level at different cut-offs.

Figure 9. Estimation accuracy of Logit and DEA models at different cut-offs for non-bankrupt companies
Legend: NL - Non-Bankruptcy Logit model, ND - Non-Bankruptcy DEA model
Source: authors, processed in MS Office

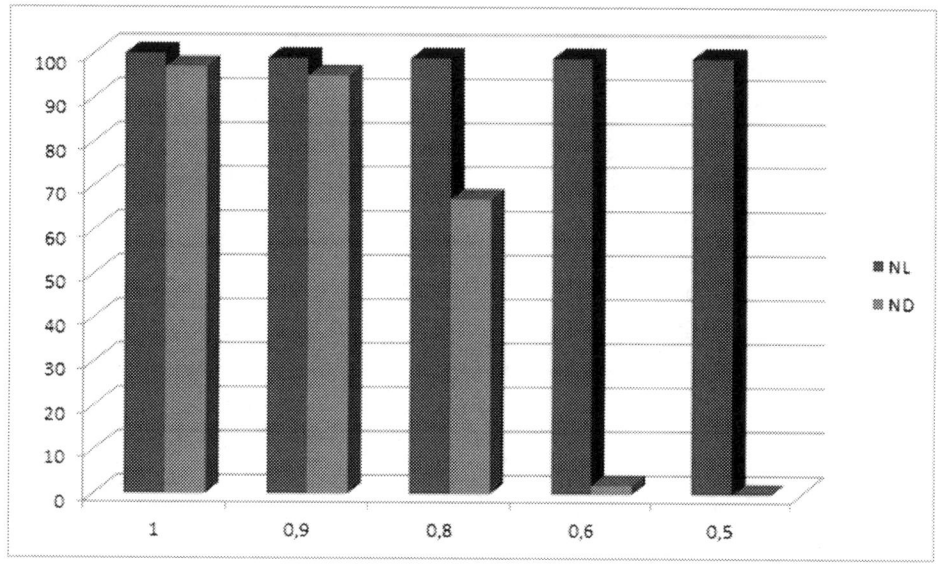

This comparison reveals the specifics of the application of DEA models, which are primarily aimed at defining companies that are on the financial health frontier or financial distress frontier and achieve cut-off equal to 1. These are companies with extreme indicators values.

Based on the comparison of the results of the applied models, it can be stated that Hypothesis 1 was confirmed. The DEA model does not have a lower estimation accuracy than the Logit model at the cut-off 0.5. Hypothesis 2 was also confirmed. The optimal estimation accuracy for bankrupt companies is different in both models, namely 0.83 in the case of the DEA model and 0.1 in the case of the Logit model. It is necessary to point out again the fact that when comparing the results, it is necessary to consider the applied indicators and the choice of the cut-off for the assessment of the estimation accuracy of the model.

To improve the estimation accuracy of the DEA model, a multi-step solution of the model with the gradual exclusion of companies with extreme values is necessary. Extreme values can be excluded also with the use of Kernel density. Another possibility of eliminating the problems arising from the application of the DEA model is to join the limit values of financial health and financial distress, and to combine the DEA method with other prediction techniques, such as logistic regression. The most advantageous thing is to create the prediction coefficient from the two DEA models described above, namely the model for financial health and the model for financial failure. When calculating this coefficient, the results of the models are assigned different weights of significance.

Another problem in solving DEA models is the negative values of indicators, which can be solved in several ways. Some software systems for solving DEA models give zero weight to negative inputs / outputs. Another frequently used option is to take negative outputs as inputs (thus minimize them) and to take the desired inputs as outputs (and thus maximize them). However, this procedure is not universally applicable. One of the simpler possibilities is the use of an additive model, in which positive and negative inputs and outputs are evaluated separately (Premachandra et al., 2009, Mendelová, Stachová, 2016). In the case of the application of DEA Frontier software (Zhu, 2019), it is necessary to follow the author's recommendations and remove negative values by adding a positive constant to the inputs and outputs of the DEA model.

FUTURE RESEARCH DIRECTIONS

DEA is a relatively new nonparametric method, which is one of the possible approaches to measuring the financial health of companies and predicting corporate bankruptcy. As already mentioned, it was originally intended to evaluate the efficiency of production units. In addition to identifying financially sound units, it can be used to identify the source of financial distress and determine how an entity can achieve financial soundness by reducing inputs or increasing outputs (depending on the orientation of the model). This finding creates preconditions for the application of this method in the area of predicting future success or failure of companies.

Since the DEA model brought several questions, these should be dealt with in further research. It is necessary to pay increased attention to the creation of the input database (without extreme values), as well as the selection of indicators as symptoms of corporate bankruptcy.

In terms of the challenges of the future direction of financial risk management, it is possible to point out possible extensions of DEA models. One of the extension options is to apply the Malmquist index. This index takes into account that inefficient companies can become more efficient over time by implementing various rationalization measures. On the contrary, companies in the category of efficient companies that underestimate the situation may find themselves among inefficient companies. However, we cannot quantify this important fact with basic DEA models. It is also possible to define a model of super-efficiency, which allows to distinguish efficient companies and create their order according to efficiency.

Also in line with future challenges, it is possible to apply a neural network when identifying businesses at risk of bankruptcy and compare its results with the results of the DEA model.

CONCLUSION

The DEA method is an important benchmarking tool for learning from the better players. It is a tool with significant potential in addressing financial health of companies.

Among the advantages of the DEA method, we can mention that DEA models focus either on inputs or outputs - on that basis DEA models are able to calculate the optimal values of inputs or outputs. DEA models focus on CCR models - with constant returns to scale or BCC - variable returns to scale. However, variable returns to scale are more appropriate as they respect the fact that business conditions are not optimal. Using the DEA method, it is possible to identify companies that have a 100% presumption of bankruptcy, that are in financial distress and lie on the financial distress frontier, and those with good financial health. DEA method allows us to assign a fictitious effective unit or reference unit to each inefficient unit, which is a model for this unit in setting its target values. DEA models eliminate subjectivity, they are not based on pre-entered data on bankruptcy assumptions and with the use of them, a large amount of data can be analyzed. A great advantage of DEA models is the ability to analyze financial and non-financial indicators, as well as environmental and social factors. With the application of these factors as inputs to the DEA model, it is possible to obtain a higher estimation accuracy than in the case of classical DEA models with the application of financial indicators. Another advantage of DEA models is that their reliability can be compared with the reliability of Logit models. While maintaining a unity of indicators, a high degree of comparability can be achieved.

The disadvantage of DEA models is that they are sensitive to extreme values. In addition, the financial health frontier and financial distress frontier are constructed from extreme values. As it is not possible for all financially healthy companies to form the financial health frontier, they can also be found in a production possibility set with companies in financial distress. For these reasons, the results of the DEA model need to be verified using another method, with logistic regression appearing to be the most appropriate

ACKNOWLEDGMENT

This research was supported by the Ministry of Education, Science, Research and Sport of the Slovak Republic [VEGA No. 1/0741/20].

REFERENCES

Achim, M. V., Mare, C., & Borlea, S. N. (2012). A statistical model of financial risk bankruptcy applied for Romanian manufacturing industry. *Procedia Economics and Finance*, *3*, 32–137. doi:10.1016/S2212-5671(12)00131-1

Achim, M. V., Safta, I. L., Vaidean, V. L., Mureşan, G. M., & Borlea, N. S. (2021). The impact of covid-19 on financial management: Evidence from Romania, Economic Research-. *Ekonomska Istrazivanja*, 1–26. Advance online publication. doi:10.1080/1331677X.2021.1922090

Altman, E. I. (1968). Financial Ratios, Discriminant Analysis and the Prediction of Corporate Bankruptcy. *The Journal of Finance*, *23*(4), 589–609. doi:10.1111/j.1540-6261.1968.tb00843.x

Araghi, K., & Makvandi, S. (2012). Evaluating Predictive power of Data Envelopment Analysis Technique Compared with Logit and Probit Models in Predicting Corporate Bankruptcy. *Australian Journal of Business and Management Research*, *2*(9), 38–46. doi:10.52283/NSWRCA.AJBMR.20120209A05

Aziz, M. A., & Dar, H. A. (2006). Predicting corporate bankruptcy: where we stand? *Corporate Governance*, *6*(1), 18-33. . doi:10.1108/14720700610649436

Banker, R. D., Charnes, A., & Cooper, W. W. (1984). Some Models for Estimating Technical Scale Inefficiencies in Data Envelopment Analysis. *Management Science*, *30*(9), 1078–1092. doi:10.1287/mnsc.30.9.1078

Beaver, W. H. (1966). Financial ratios as predictors of failure. *Journal of Accounting Research*, *4*, 71–111. doi:10.2307/2490171

Blum, M. (1974). Failing company discriminant analysis. *Journal of Accounting Research*, *12*(1), 1–25. doi:10.2307/2490525

Chang, C. L., McAleer, M., & Wong, W. K. (2020). Risk and Financial Management of COVID-19 in Business, Economics and Finance. *Journal of Risk and Financial Management*, *13*(5), 1–7. doi:10.3390/jrfm13050102

Charnes, A., Cooper, W. W., & Rhodes, E. (1978). Measuring the efficiency of decision making units. *European Journal of Operational Research*, *2*(6), 429–444. doi:10.1016/0377-2217(78)90138-8

Cielen, A., Peeters, L., & Vanhoof, K. (2004). Bankruptcy prediction using a data envelopment analysis. *European Journal of Operational Research*, *154*(2), 526–532. doi:10.1016/S0377-2217(03)00186-3

CRIF. (2016). Financial statements of businesses. Slovak Credit Bureau, s.r.o.

Csikósová, A., Janošková, M., & Čulková, K. (2019). Limitation of Financial Health Prediction in companies from Post-Communist Countries. *Journal of Risk and Financial Management*, *12*(1), 1–15. doi:10.3390/jrfm12010015

Deakin, E. B. (1972). A Discriminant Analysis of Predictors of Business Failure. *Journal of Accounting Research*, *10*(1), 167–179. doi:10.2307/2490225

Debreu, G. (1951). The coefficient of resource utilization. *Econometrica, 19*(3), 273–292. doi:10.2307/1906814

Delina, R., & Packová, M. (2013). Validácia predikčných bankrotových modelov v podmienkach SR [Prediction bankruptcy models validation in Slovak business environment]. *Ekonomie a Management, 16*(3), 101-112. http://www.ekonomie-management.cz/download/1404726193_54d6/2013_3+Validacia+predikcnych+bankrotivych+modelov+v+podmienkach+SR.pdf

Dimitras, A. I., Zanakis, S. H., & Zopounidis, C. (1996). A survey of business failures with an emphasis on prediction methods and industrial applications. *European Journal of Operational Research, 90*(6), 487–513. doi:10.1016/0377-2217(95)00070-4

Ding, Y. S., Song, X. P., & Zen, Y. M. (2008). Forecasting Financial Condition of Chinese Listed Companies Based on Support Vector Machine. *Expert Systems with Applications, 34*(4), 3081–3089. doi:10.1016/j.eswa.2007.06.037

Dipak, L., & Purnendu, M. (2007). *Handbook of Computational Intelligence in Manufacturing and Production Management*. Information Science Reference.

Dixon, J. R., Nanni, J., & Vollmann, T. E. (1990). *The New Performance Challenge: Measuring Operations for World-class Companies*. Dow Jones-Irwin.

Elam, R. (1975). The effect of lease data on the predictive ability of financial ratios. *The Accounting Review, 5*(1), 25–43. https://www.jstor.org/stable/244661

Farrell, M. J. (1957). The Measurement of Productive Efficiency. *Journal of the Royal Statistical Society. Series A (General), 120*(3), 253–290. doi:10.2307/2343100

Fisher, J. (1992). Use of Non-*Financial* Performance Measures. *Journal of Cost Management, 6*(1), 1–8.

Gajowniczek, K., Zabkowski, T., & Szupiluk, R. (2014). Estimating the ROC curve and its significance for classification model's assessment. *Quantitative Methods in Economics, 15*(2), 382-391. https://www.ceeol.com/search/article-detail?id=472340

Gundová, P. (2015). Verification of the selected prediction methods in Slovak companies. *Acta academica karviniensia, 14*(4), 26-38. http://aak.slu.cz/pdfs/aak/2014/04/03.pdf

Gurný, P., & Gurný, M. (2010). Logit vs Probit model při determinaci souhrnných ukazatelů výkonnosti bank [Logit vs Probit model in the determination of the aggregate performance indicators of banks]. In *Zborník z 5. medzinárodnej konferencie Řízení a modelování finančních rizik* [Proceedings of the 5th International Conference on Financial Risk Management and Modeling]. V3B-TU Ostrava, Ekonomická fakulta. https://adoc.pub/logit-vs-probit-model-pi-determinaci-souhrnnych-ukazatel-vyk.html

Hebák, J. (2015). *Statistické myšlení a nástroje analýzy dat* [Statistical thinking and data analysitools]. Informatorium.

Horváthová, J., & Mokrišová, M. (2018). Linear model as a tool in the process of improving financial health. In M. A Omazic, V. Roska, & A. Grobelna (Eds.), *Economic and Social Development: Conference Proceeding from 28th International Scientific Conference on Economic and Social Development* (pp. 425-444). Varazdin Development and Entrepreneurship Agency.

Horváthová, J., & Mokrišová, M. (2020). Comparison of the results of a data envelopment analysis model and logit model in assessing business financial health. *Information (Basel)*, *11*(3), 1–20. doi:10.3390/info11030160

Ittner, C., Larcker, D., & Randall, T. (2003). Performance implications of strategic performance measurement in financial services firms. *Accounting, Organizations and Society*, *28*(7/8), 715–741. doi:10.1016/S0361-3682(03)00033-3

Jablonský, J., & Dlouhý, M. (2015). *Modely hodnocení efektivnosti a alokace zdrojů* [Models of efficiency evaluation and resource allocation]. Professional Publishing.

Juárez, F. (2011). Applying the theory of chaos and a complex model of health to establish relations among financial indicators. *Procedia Computer Science*, *3*, 982–986. doi:10.1016/j.procs.2010.12.161

Kidane, H. W. (2004). *Predicting Financial Distress in IT and Services Companies in South Africa* [Master's thesis]. Faculty of Economics and Management Sciences. http://scholar.ufs.ac.za:8080/xmlui/handle/11660/1117

Klepáč, V., & Hampel, D. (2017). Predicting financial distress of agriculture companies in EU. *Agricultural Economics*, *63*(8), 347–355. doi:10.17221/374/2015-AGRICECON

Klieštik, T. (2019). *Predikcia finančného zdravia podnikov tranzitívnych ekonomík* [Prediction of financial health of businesses in transition economies]. EDIS.

Koopmans, T. C. (1951). Analysis of production as an efficient combination of activities. In T. C. Koopmans (Ed.), *Activity analysis of production and allocation, Proceeding of a Conference* (pp. 33-97), John Wiley and Sons Inc.

Kováčová, M., & Klieštik, T. (2017). Logit and Probit application for the prediction of bankruptcy in Slovak companies. *Equilibrium. Quarterly Journal of Economics and Economic Policy*, *12*(4), 775–791. doi:10.24136/eq.v12i4.40

Martin, D. (1977). Early warning of bank failure. A logit regession approach. *Journal of Banking & Finance*, *1*(3), 249–276. doi:10.1016/0378-4266(77)90022-X

Mendelová, V., & Bieliková, T. (2017). Diagnostikovanie finančného zdravia podnikov pomocou metódy DEA: Aplikácia na podniky v Slovenskej republike [Diagnosing the financial health of companies using the DEA method: application to companies in the Slovak Republic] [Political economy]. *Politicka Ekonomie*, *65*(1), 26–44. doi:10.18267/j.polek.1125

Mendelová, V., & Stachová, M. (2016). Comparing DEA and logistic regression in corporate financial distress prediction. In *Proceedings of International Scientific Conference FERNSTAT 2016* (pp. 95–104). Slovak Statistical and Demographic Society. http://fernstat.ssds.sk/proceedings/

Mihalovič, M. (2015). The Assessment of Corporate Financial Performance Via Discriminant Analysis. *Acta oeconomica Cassoviensia. Scientific Journal*, *8*(1), 57–69. doi:10.13140/RG.2.1.4153.7368

Norton, C. L., & Smith, R. E. (1979). A comparison of general price level and historical cost financial statements in the prediction of bankruptcy. *The Accounting Review*, *54*(1), 72–87. https://www.jstor.org/stable/246235

Ohlson, J. A. (1980). Financial Ratios and the Probabilistic Prediction of Bankruptcy. *Journal of Accounting Research, 18*(1), 109–131. doi:10.2307/2490395

Park, S. H., Goo, J. M., & Jo, Ch. (2004). Receiver Operating Characteristic (ROC) Curve: Practical Review for Radiologists. *Korean Journal of Radiology, 5*(1), 11–18. doi:10.3348/kjr.2004.5.1.11 PMID:15064554

Pervan, I., Pervan, M., & Vukoja, B. (2011). Prediction of company bankruptcy using statistical techniques. *Croatian Operational Research Review, 11*(2), 158-166. https://hrcak.srce.hr/96660

Petřík, T. (2009). *Ekonomické a finanční řízení firmy* [Economic and financial management of the company]. Grada Publishing.

Premachandra, I. M., Bhabra, G. S., & Sueyoshi, T. (2009). DEA as a tool for bankruptcy assessment: A comparative study with logistic regression technique. *European Journal of Operational Research, 193*(2), 412–424. doi:10.1016/j.ejor.2007.11.036

Premachandra, I. M., Chen, Y., & Watson, J. (2011). DEA as a Tool for Predicting Corporate Failure and Success: A Case of Bankruptcy Assessment. *Omega, 3*(6), 620–626. doi:10.1016/j.omega.2011.01.002

Roháčová, V., & Kráľ, P. (2015). *Corporate Failure Prediction Using DEA: An Application to Companies in the Slovak Republic* [Paper presentation]. 18th Applications of Mathematics and Statistics in Economics, International Scientific Conference. Jindřichův Hradec, Czech Republic. http://amse-conference.eu/history/amse2015/doc/Rohacova_Kral.pdf

Rybak, T. N. (2006). Analysis and estimate of the enterprises bankruptcy risk. In *Zborník z 3. Medzinárodní konference Řízení a modelování finančních rizik* [Proceedings of the 3rd International Conference on Financial Risk Management and Modeling] (pp. 315–320). VŠB TU Ostrava. https://scholar.google.com/scholar?cluster=6887450162738206801&hl=en&as_

SanobarA. (2012). Business Bankruptcy Prediction Models: A Significant Study of the Altman's Z-Score Model. https://ssrn.com/abstract=2128475

Šarlija, N., & Jeger, M. (2011). Comparing financial distress prediction models before and during recession. *Croatian Operational Research Review, 2*(1), 133–142. https://hrcak.srce.hr/96658

SBA. (2021). *Nepriaznivý vplyv pandémie koronavírusu na podnikovú ekonomiku SR* [Adverse impact of the coronavirus pandemic on the Slovak business economy]. Slovak Business Agency. http://monitoringmsp.sk/wp-content/uploads/2021/07/Nepriazniv%C3%BD-vplyv-pand%C3%A9mie-koronav%C3%ADrusu-na-podnikov%C3%BA-ekonomiku-SR.pdf

Simak, P. C. (1997). *DEA Based Analysis of Coporate Failure* [Master Thesis]. Faculty of Applied Sciences and Engineering, University of Toronto. https://tspace.library.utoronto.ca/bitstream/1807/11746/1/MQ29433.pdf

Sláviček, O., & Kuběnka, M. (2016). Bankruptcy prediction models based on the logistic regression for companies in the Czech Republic. In *Proceedings of the 8th International Scientific Conference Managing and Modelling of Financial Risks*. VŠB-TU of Ostrava, Faculty of Economics, Department of Finance. https://dk.upce.cz/handle/10195/67220

SOSR. (2021). *Statistical Office of the Slovak Republic: DATAcube*. https://slovak.statistics.sk/ wps/portal/ext/Databases/DATAcube_sk

Sperandei, S. (2014). Understanding logistic regression analysis. *Biochemia Medica, 24*(1), 12–18. doi:10.11613/BM.2014.003 PMID:24627710

Stankovičová, I., & Vojtková, M. (2007). *Viacrozmerné štatistické metódy s aplikáciami* [Multidimensional statistical methods with applications]. Iura Edition.

Synek, M. (2007). *Manažerská ekonomika* [Managerial economics] (4th ed.). Grada Publishing.

Taffler, R. J. (1983). The assessment of company solvency and performance using a statistical model. *Accounting and Business Research, 13*(52), 295–308. doi:10.1080/00014788.1983.9729767

Vochozka, M., Jelínek, J., Váchal, J., Straková, J., & Stehel, V. (2017). Využití neurónových sítí při komplexním hodnocení podniku (11th ed.). Praha: C.H.Beck.

Wilcox, J. W. (1973). A prediction of business failure using accounting data. *Journal of Accounting Research, Selected Studies, 11*, 163-179. . doi:10.2307/2490035

Zhu, J. (2019). *DEA Frontier software*. Foisie Business School, Worcester Polytechnic Institute.

ADDITIONAL READING

Charnes, A., Cooper, W. W., Golany, B., Seiford, L. M., & Stutz, J. (1985). Foundations of Data Envelopment Analysis for Pareto-Koopmans Efficient Empirical Production Functions. *Journal of Econometrics, 30*(12), 91–127. doi:10.1016/0304-4076(85)90133-2

Charnes, A., Cooper, W. W., & Rhodes, E. (1978). Measuring the efficiency of decision making units. *European Journal of Operational Research, 2*(6), 429–444. doi:10.1016/0377-2217(78)90138-8

Mendelová, V., & Stachová, M. (2016). Comparing DEA and logistic regression in corporate financial distress prediction. In *Proceedings of International Scientific Conference FERNSTAT 2016* (pp. 95–104). Slovak Statistical and Demographic Society. http://fernstat.ssds.sk/proceedings/

Premachandra, I. M., Bhabra, G. S., & Sueyoshi, T. (2009). DEA as a tool for bankruptcy assessment: A comparative study with logistic regression technique. *European Journal of Operational Research, 193*(2), 412–424. doi:10.1016/j.ejor.2007.11.036

Seiford, L. M., & Zhu, J. (1999). An Investigation of Returns to Scale in Data Envelopment Analysis. *Omega, 27*(1), 1–11. doi:10.1016/S0305-0483(98)00025-5

Zhu, J. (2015). DEA Based Benchmarking Models. In J. Zhu (Ed.), *Data Envelopment Analysis. International Series in Operations Research & Management Science* (Vol. 221). Springer. doi:10.1007/978-1-4899-7553-9_10

KEY TERMS AND DEFINITIONS

Bankruptcy: A situation where the company is unable to pay its liabilities, priority dividends, and its bill is overdrawn.

Cut-Off: A limit for distinguishing bankrupt from non-bankrupt businesses.

Risk: A characteristic of the activity that lies in the fact that the result of the activity is uncertain, and in case of failure, there are adverse consequences.

Sensitivity: Estimation accuracy for bankrupt businesses.

Specificity: Estimation accuracy for non-bankrupt businesses.

Symptom: A sign of company's financial failure.

Syndrome: A summary of related symptoms describing a particular situation that can lead to the bankruptcy.

Chapter 9
The Impact of Social Screening on the Performance of US and European Funds

Joana Pena
School of Economics and Management, University of Minho, Portugal

Maria Céu Cortez
NIPE, Portugal & School of Economics and Management, University of Minho, Portugal

ABSTRACT

This chapter investigates the relationship between the performance and the screening strategies of US and European socially responsible funds. For the full sample and, in particular, for US funds, the results show a curvilinear relationship between screening intensity and fund performance. Continental European funds exhibit a positive relationship between the number of screens and performance. Furthermore, for the full sample and US funds, screening on governance impacts performance positively. In turn, environment and products screens have a negative impact on US fund performance. Finally, funds certified with social labels tend to yield higher performance. Overall, the geographical differences in the impact of the screening process on SRI fund performance are consistent with the contextual nature of socially responsible investments.

INTRODUCTION

During the last decades, sustainable investments have experienced a substantial growth in financial markets.[1] The well-known corporate and environmental scandals of the beginning of the millennium and the events associated to the 2007-2008 international financial crisis have led to calls for reconsidering the role of finance in society, in particular the need to promote socially responsible corporate behavior and sustainable investments. Accompanying this trend, investors are increasingly willing to integrate non-financial criteria into their investment decisions to reflect their sensitivity to issues such as emissions control, global warming, human rights, labour relations and board diversity. Several recent papers

DOI: 10.4018/978-1-7998-8609-9.ch009

investigating the drivers of sustainable investments confirm that social preferences are more important than financial motives in the decision to invest in socially responsible investment (SRI) funds (e.g., Riedl & Smeets, 2017). This evidence is consistent with a segment of values driven investors that wish to incorporate their social and personal values into their investment decisions (Derwall et al., 2011), even if it comes at the cost of lower returns. Nevertheless, the mainstreaming of sustainable investments is anchored with an approach that accommodates investors who wish to integrate Environmental, Social, and Governance (ESG) issues into traditional asset management as a strategy to generate profitability (Derwall et al., 2011; Revelli, 2017). The increasing growth of socially responsible investing around the world has led to an intense debate on whether there is a financial premium or penalty for holding SRI funds, with empirical evidence showing that, in general, investors do not sacrifice performance compared to conventional funds (Revelli & Viviani, 2015). Additionally, from the investor's point of view, selecting companies with high levels of CSR can be viewed as a useful risk management tool, as there is evidence documenting the portfolio risk mitigating effects of ESG integration (e.g., Maxfield & Wang, 2020). As such, managing ESG risks plays an important role in the investment process, regardless of the motivations underlying SRI.

Despite the profusion of funds with sustainability features, there is still ambiguity on what makes a mutual fund socially responsible. The answer to this question is not straightforward, as there is no single and universal definition of what criteria a mutual fund should follow to be considered an ethical or socially responsible fund (Dunfee, 2003). SRI funds can use several social screening strategies. Negative screening strategies exclude stocks that are associated with products or activities considered socially unacceptable, while positive screening strategies involve selecting stocks of firms meeting superior standards on several dimensions of corporate social responsibility. To avoid possible diversification biases, such as the exclusion of entire industries, a popular screening strategy is the best-in-class strategy, which involves selecting the companies with best social practices in each sector. Besides using different screening strategies, SRI funds can also vary on the type of screens used (e.g., of the environmental or social type) and the number of screens used (i.e., screening intensity). Combining different screening strategies, types of screens, and the number of screens used by mutual funds may result in different understandings of the objectives the screening process encompasses and leads to considerable heterogeneity in the SRI fund landscape (Sandberg et al., 2009). Ultimately, the degree of heterogeneity in the criteria used by SRI funds reflects the wide diversity of investors' values. Despite the heterogeneity of SRI funds, many studies treat them as being homogenous. According to Galema et al. (2008) and Derwall et al. (2011), among others, one of the reasons why the empirical literature finds scarce significant relations between socially responsible investments and returns is the aggregation of different social dimensions that may have confounding effects in financial performance. We argue that the heterogeneity within the SRI fund industry in terms of the screening processes used should be considered when investigating the impact of social criteria on mutual fund performance.

In this context, the main objective of this paper is to investigate how the screening process used by mutual funds affects risk-adjusted performance, and also if the impact of the screening processes differs geographically. Thus, the research question addressed in this investigation is: Do different screening strategies, types of screens and number of screens affect SRI funds' financial performance and does this impact vary in different regions worldwide? This study comprises data from socially responsible mutual funds domiciled in European countries and in the US. The analysis of whether there are geographical differences in the impact of the screening process on SRI fund performance is relevant, considering the contextual nature of socially responsible investments, as well as regional and cultural idiosyncrasies in socially responsible investing (e.g., Louche & Lydenberg, 2006; Bengtsson, 2008; Neher & Hebb, 2016).

We contribute to the mutual fund literature in several ways. To the best of our knowledge, this is the first study to investigate geographical differences in the financial performance effects of the screening process in SRI funds. Although there are some papers in the SRI fund literature that explore the impact of screening, with the exception of Renneboog et al. (2008b), extant evidence is geographically limited. For example, Barnett and Salomon (2006) and Lee et al. (2010) focus on US funds, whereas Laurel (2011) analyzes European funds, and Capelle-Blancard and Monjon (2014) restrict their investigation to French funds. And although Renneboog et al. (2008b) evaluate SRI fund performance for different countries worldwide, the analysis of the relation between screening and performance is performed at the aggregate level and not by geographical region or country. Furthermore, previous studies include one or a just a few of the dimensions of the screening process such as screening intensity, type of screens or screening strategy (positive *versus* negative). Our research fills this gap in the literature by considering the multiple dimensions of the social screening process. Additionally, as far we are aware of, we are the first to include social labels as a potential determinant of the financial performance of SRI funds. Finally, we explore the impact of the screening process on SRI fund performance in different business cycles (expansion and recession periods).

For the global sample and for US funds, our analysis shows that screening intensity has a statistically significant impact on performance, specifically an inverted U-shaped effect: funds that screen more strictly have better risk-adjusted returns until a certain level of screening intensity; then, the returns start to decline. Continental European SRI funds exhibit a positive and linear relationship between screens and returns. We also find that the conclusions for the whole sample and US and continental European subsamples only stand in expansion periods.

Our findings also show that the type of screens used impact the performance of SRI funds. In particular, governance-oriented SRI funds are financially rewarded, considering the global sample and the US subsample. Besides that, environment- and products-oriented US SRI funds appear to have lower returns. In terms of social labels, we find weak evidence that US and European funds which are certified with such labels tend to have better performance, meaning that funds awarded for meeting high sustainability standards may benefit from improved financial performance.

Our results are relevant for several reasons. First, we extend the evidence on the effects of social screening on SRI fund performance to a broader setting (the US and Europe), which is an important issue considering the different cultural environments of these regions. Second, we document relevant results (in terms of screening intensity and qualitative differences in the screens) concerning the US, the biggest responsible investment player in the world, and continental Europe, whose SRI industry is growing at a fast pace. Finally, this study shows that the certification by social labels tends to enhance funds' financial performance when considering the whole sample. We consider this to be an important finding on the financial merits of social attributes.

The remainder of the paper is organized as follows. Section 2 surveys the empirical literature. Section 3 proposes a set of testable hypotheses and section 4 describes the data used in the study. The methodology is outlined in section 5. The empirical results are presented and discussed in section 6. Section 7 summarizes the main results and presents some concluding remarks.

BACKGROUND

Theoretically, two opposing views attempt to explain the financial effects of considering socially responsible criteria in the mutual fund selection process. The first viewpoint is motivated by modern portfolio theory (Markowitz, 1952) and claims that including socially responsible criteria in the portfolio selection process implies a financial penalty compared to conventional funds. Following portfolio theory, imposing any screens (of a social nature or not) will constrain the portfolio mean-variance optimization framework and limit the potential for diversification. Furthermore, the implementation of social screens will simply result in increased costs of obtaining and monitoring information (Barnett & Salomon, 2006). An additional reason in favour of the underperformance of SRI funds is based on the argument that stocks of companies in less socially desirable sectors (such as tobacco, weapons, gambling, alcohol) generate abnormal returns (e.g., Hong & Kacperzyck, 2009; Derwall et al., 2011). By shunning these stocks, SRI portfolios will not benefit from these abnormal returns.[2]

In contrast, another viewpoint, consistent with signaling theory (Spence, 1973) and stakeholder theory (Freeman, 1984), supports the outperformance of SRI funds. According to this line of reasoning, CSR practices may signal unobserved qualities to stakeholders (Su et al., 2016) and, therefore, social screens can be viewed as tools to identify better managed companies (Waddock & Graves, 1997). Furthermore, value-relevant information associated with CSR may not be fully incorporated into securities' prices due to errors-in-expectations, in which case portfolios formed on this information may generate abnormal returns (Derwall et al., 2011). As a consequence, the potential loss of efficiency as a result of the use of a restricted universe of securities can be more than offset by the inclusion of companies representing better investment opportunities (Barnett & Salomon, 2006).

On the empirical side, most studies find that the performance of SRI funds is not statistically different from the performance of conventional funds. Among others, Hamilton et al. (1993), Goldreyer et al. (1999), Statman (2000), Bello (2005), and Nofsinger and Varma (2014) find that US SRI fund performance is no better or worse than that of non-SRI funds and benchmark indexes[3]. In relation to the UK, Luther et al. (1992), and Mallin et al. (1995) find a weak outperformance of ethical funds compared to their conventional peers. Yet, Gregory et al. (1997) claim that this outperformance is a result of the small size effect and not the social characteristics of companies. In fact, when accounting for the small size factor, Gregory et al. (1997) and Gregory and Whittaker (2007) find no evidence of significant differences between the performance of UK SRI and conventional funds. Studies focusing on other individual markets, including Scholtens (2005) on Dutch funds, Bauer et al. (2006) and Ayadi et al. (2016) on Canadian funds, Bauer et al. (2007) on Australian funds, Fernandez-Isquierdo and Matallin-Saez (2008) on Spanish funds, and Leite et al. (2018) on Swedish funds, find similar results. Other studies, such as Schröder (2004), Bauer et al. (2005), Kreander et al. (2005) and Cortez et al. (2009, 2012) focus on multiple markets and also find that the performance of SRI funds is not statistically different from that of their conventional peers[4].

It is important to note, however, that these studies analyze SRI fund performance disregarding the fact that different funds might use different screening processes that may affect performance in different ways. Several papers move away from the simplistic analysis of SRI fund performance as a whole and focus on the question of *"when does it pay to be good"* (Capelle-Blancard & Monjon, 2014) by analyzing the effects of specific screening strategies on fund performance. Barnett and Salomon (2006) and Renneboog et al. (2008b) are two seminal studies that find that screening intensity and some dimensions of social responsibility are related to a higher SRI fund performance. Barnett and Salomon (2006) find a curvilinear relationship between screening intensity and financial performance for US funds. In particular, when the number of social screens used by SRI funds increases, financial returns decline at first, but then rebound as the number of screens reaches a maximum. The authors view these results as suggesting that the two long-competing viewpoints (modern portfolio and stakeholder theories) may be complementary, consistent with a trade-off between the effects of diversification and a selective choice of companies that engage in socially responsible practices. Additionally, Barnett and Salomon (2006) find that financial performance varies with the types of social screens used: community relations screening increases financial performance, whereas environmental and labour relations screening decrease financial performance. To determine if investors pay (or not) a price for ethics, Renneboog et al. (2008b) investigate the under- and outperformance hypotheses for US, UK and European and Asia-Pacific SRI funds. The authors find that fund returns decrease with screening intensity on social and corporate governance criteria, but not on ethical or environmental criteria. The number of ethical screens, "sin" screens, or environmental screens do not have significant impact on performance.

Lee et al. (2010), for US SRI funds, and Capelle-Blancard and Monjon (2014), for French SRI funds, observe that a high number of screens impacts performance negatively, while Humphrey and Lee (2011) find weak evidence that screening intensity increases risk-adjusted performance of Australian funds. Lee et al. (2010) also suggest that screened portfolios are able to obtain adequate levels of diversification (they find no relation between idiosyncratic risk and screening intensity), whilst Capelle-Blancard and Monjon (2014) highlight that only sectoral screens (such as avoiding "sin" stocks) decrease financial performance. Like Barnett and Salomon (2006), they also find that the initial negative effect is partly offset as the number of screens increases. Furthermore, Laurel (2011) finds that screening intensity has no effect on European SRI fund returns, but has a curvilinear effect on risk (inverted U-shaped effect). This means that the level of risk increases with the number of screens, but then decreases again with high screening intensity). In line with these studies, Renneboog et al. (2011) show that the flow-performance relationship for socially responsible investors depends on the types of screens used and on screening intensity.

A more recent generation of SRI fund studies address the performance of funds that focus on specific screens like green funds (Climent & Soriano, 2011; Muñoz et al., 2014; Silva & Cortez, 2016; Ibikunle & Steffen, 2017) or renewable energy funds (Reboredo et al., 2017) and Marti-Ballester, 2019a,b), with the evidence showing that, in general, they are neutral or underperformers regarding a benchmark or conventional funds. Moreover, several papers explore the impact of the screening features on SRI fund performance in different economic cycles (e.g., Nofsinger & Varma, 2014; Leite & Cortez, 2015; Henke, 2016) and support the resilience of SRI investments in times of crisis.[5]

Overall, the purpose of this investigation is to extend earlier research on the relationship between the financial performance of SRI funds and social screening by considering the multiple dimensions of the social screening process (i.e., screening strategies, types and number of screens), including social labels as a potential determinant of the financial performance of SRI funds, and exploiting the impact of the screening process on SRI fund performance in different business cycles. In this way, we intend to investigate and enlighten the impact of the heterogeneity in the SRI fund industry for a dataset of US and European funds, which represent the most developed SRI markets in the world.

RESEARCH HYPOTHESES

This paper investigates whether the funds' screening process, encompassing its screening strategy (positive *versus* negative), screening intensity (the number of screens employed) and the type of criteria used (i.e., Environmental, Social and Governance – ESG – screens) influence funds' financial performance. Accordingly, we develop a set of hypotheses on the relationship between portfolio financial performance and screening intensity as well as the type of social screens used.

As discussed in the previous section, the outperformance hypothesis (hypothesis 1a) stems directly from the loss of diversification argument put forward by modern portfolio theory and is further supported by the costs associated with screening and the opportunity costs that result from shunning stocks in sectors that yield abnormal returns. In contrast, the outperformance hypothesis (hypothesis 1b) is consistent with the argument that companies that integrate the interests of all stakeholders can reduce the potential costs associated to negative externalities and benefit from an improved financial performance. Thereby, we set up the following mutually exclusive hypotheses regarding screening intensity (i.e., the number of screens used by SRI funds):

Hypothesis 1a: A higher screening intensity reduces the performance of SRI funds (underperformance hypothesis).

Hypothesis 1b: A higher screening intensity enhances the performance of SRI funds (outperformance hypothesis).

Following Barnett and Salomon (2006), we also hypothesize a curvilinear relationship between screening intensity and financial performance (consistent with both modern portfolio theory and stakeholder theory). The intuition of this hypothesis is that the financial loss carried by a SRI fund when it imposes social restrictions is, after a certain level of screening intensity, offset by the financial benefits of including better-managed and more solid firms into the portfolio (Barnett and Salomon, 2006).

Hypothesis 2: The relationship between the intensity of social screening and financial performance for SRI funds is curvilinear.

We also integrate in the analysis the type of screens used, defined as the specific ESG factors the fund focuses on. Indeed, SRI funds may be oriented towards specific ESG criteria that affect performance differently. To account for different types of screens, Barnett and Salomon (2006) employ five dummies, namely for environment, labour relations, equal employment, community investment, and community relations screens. In turn, Renneboog et al. (2008b) define four types of screens, specifically "sin", ethical, environmental, and social and corporate governance, whereas Capelle-Blancard and Monjon (2014) and Nofsinger and Varma (2014) emphasize labour relations, community relations and environment. We follow the categorization employed by US SIF – The Forum for Sustainable and Responsible Investment[6] and consider screens on the following dimensions: environment, social, governance, products and shareholder engagement. Although this study is not restricted to American funds, the US SIF is a reference in the socially responsible investments research field, and establishes a relatively wide classification of screens (encompassing 16 positive and negative screens) that can also be applied to European funds[7]. Thus, we hypothesize that:

Hypothesis 3a: SRI funds that select firms based on environmental screening criteria obtain higher returns than those that do not screen on these criteria.

Hypothesis 3b: SRI funds that select firms based on social screening criteria obtain higher returns than those that do not screen on these criteria.

Hypothesis 3c: SRI funds that select firms based on governance screening criteria obtain higher returns than those that do not screen on these criteria.

Hypothesis 3d: SRI funds that select firms based on products screening criteria obtain higher returns than those that do not screen on these criteria.

Hypothesis 3e: SRI funds that select firms based on shareholder engagement screening criteria obtain higher returns than those that do not screen on these criteria.

Additionally, we will focus on the screening strategy and its signal: positive (seeking out stocks with good ESG performance) *versus* negative (weeding out poor ESG performing stocks) screening. There is evidence that positive screens have a positive impact on performance (Goldreyer et al., 1999) and that it significantly reduces risk (Humphrey & Lee, 2011), besides providing some protection in downturns (Nofsinger & Varma, 2014, Leite & Cortez, 2015). Therefore, concerning the impact of positive screening, we formulate the next hypothesis:

Hypothesis 4: A higher positive screening intensity increases the performance of SRI funds.

Finally, we will distinguish funds that have received at least one sustainability label. Social labels are certifications attributed to SRI funds with the purpose of providing investors with quality standards and more transparency on socially responsible investment products.[8] For the US market, we will identify the funds with the *Diamond Standard* label. For European funds, we will also distinguish the funds awarded with the following certifications: *Ethibel Pioneer, European SRI Transparency Code, Luxembourg Fund Labelling Agency* (LuxFLAG), *Novethic SRI Label, Novethic Green Fund Label, Austrian Eco Label,* and *United Nations Principles for Responsible Investment* (UNPRI). Although some of these labels result from private initiatives (e.g., the LuxFLAG), there are others that are launched and audited by governmental authorities (e.g., the *Novethic SRI Label* in France, or the *Austrian Eco Label*, created under the support of the Austrian Ministry of Agriculture and the Environment), reinforcing the idea that SRI labels may be effectively used to reassure investors about the sustainability features of the SRI funds in which they are investing. The evidence of Silva and Cortez (2016) suggests a tendency for green funds that are certified with a label to perform better than uncertified green funds. We assume that social labels are a guarantee of compliance with ESG principles awarded by associations recognized as experts, and not merely a marketing artefact. So, we postulate the following:

Hypothesis 5: SRI funds that operate under at least one social label obtain higher returns than those that do not.

The Impact of Social Screening on the Performance of US and European Funds

DATA AND METHODS

Sample Description

Although the US is oldest market for socially responsible investments, Europe is growing substantially in terms of assets and number of funds that integrate ESG criteria. France is the biggest European SRI retail market (37% of the total), while the UK comes in second place (12%). The four largest markets (France, UK, Switzerland and Netherlands) account for around 68% of European assets in the SRI segment, according to Vigeo Eiris.[9]

This study investigates US and European socially responsible mutual funds. With regard to European funds, we focus on the countries covered by the reports and surveys of Vigeo Eiris, namely Austria, Belgium, Denmark, France, Germany, Italy, Luxembourg, Netherlands, Norway, Sweden, Switzerland, and United Kingdom[10]. Our dataset includes SRI equity funds from these countries. To avoid data duplication, in the case of funds with different classes, only one class of each fund is considered. As first criterion, we select the oldest class; if the inception date is the same, we choose the class with higher assets under management. Finally, in order to be included in our sample, SRI funds must disclose at least one screen as part of their investment policies.

Our subsample of US funds consists of 80 SRI mutual funds over the period January 2000 to December 2014. The information on the funds is mainly extracted from two US SIF data sources: the Mutual Fund Performance Chart[11] on 31st December 2014 and the SRI Trends Reports[12]. The Mutual Fund Performance Chart provides information on the social screening processes of a set of surviving funds at the end of 2014. For the other funds of the sample, we manually collected the information on social screens through the funds prospectuses and websites, as well as from US Securities and Exchange Commission (SEC) files. Considering the problems that may arise due to survivorship bias (Brown et al., 1992), we included not only surviving funds but also funds that disappeared during the period under evaluation. Although we use the 2001 to 2012 US SIF SRI Trends Reports to identify funds that were liquidated or merged during the sample period, we cannot ensure we were able to identify all dead funds.

Information on the screening process used by funds is not available historically, so we assume that mutual funds' social objectives did not change over time. We recognize this is a strong assumption on the consistency of fund managers' policies, but given that the funds in the sample can be considered relatively young (with a mean age of 11 years), it is reasonable to assume that the screening processes did not change dramatically over time[13].

To identify SRI funds domiciled in Europe, we followed Renneboog et al. (2008b) and Nofsinger and Varma (2014) and first searched on Datastream for certain keywords that are common in SRI fund names, such as "Social", "Socially", "Ecology", "Environment", "Green", "Sustainability", "Sustainable", "Ethics", "Ethical", "Faith", "Religion", "Christian", "Islam", "Baptist", and "Lutheran". We then intersected the information obtained from Datastream with the funds' fact sheets available on the website yourSRI[14]. The fact sheets provide information about the investment objective, SRI classification (screens and social labels), and investment profile (investment category, regional focus, asset status, domicile, inception date, benchmarks), among other data, for SRI funds around the world. Although this procedure for identifying SRI funds has allowed us to detect dead funds, we acknowledge that our European SRI fund sample may not be survivorship bias free.

Since Luxembourg is chosen as domicile for many funds mainly because of its favourable tax laws[15], the geographic allocation of the funds is based on the countries of origin of the fund management companies, as in Renneboog et al. (2008b). Thereby, the resulting sample consists of 250 funds domiciled in 12 European countries, from January 2000 to December 2014. The majority of the funds are from Switzerland (26%), France (22%), and the United Kingdom (13%). Similar to US funds, we assume static screening strategies during the sample period (on average, our European funds live 9 years).

The final sample results in an unbalanced panel[16] of 330 US and European funds over the period 2000 to 2014[17].

Financial Performance

In line with previous studies (e.g. Barnett & Salomon, 2006; Renneboog et al., 2008b; Capelle-Blancard & Monjon, 2014), the dependent variable is the risk-adjusted performance, computed on the basis of the monthly returns of SRI funds denominated in US dollars. For both US and European funds, we use Datastream to collect each fund's end of month Return Index (from January 2000 through December 2014). Discrete returns are calculated on a monthly basis. A minimum of 36 months of return data across the sample period is required.

We use the Carhart (1997) four-factor model (as in Renneboog et al., 2008b, Lee et al., 2010, and Nofsinger & Varma, 2014, among others) to compute funds' risk-adjusted returns. Although a few papers apply the CAPM based single factor alpha (e.g., Barnett & Salomon, 2006; Renneboog et al., 2008b; Capelle-Blancard & Monjon, 2014), its limitations, namely the fact that it does not capture all relevant sources of systematic risk, motivates the use of multi-factor models. The Carhart (1997) model is one of the most commonly used models in the performance evaluation literature, and is represented as follows:

$$r_{it} - r_{f,t} = \alpha_i + \beta_{iMKT}\left(r_{mt} - r_{f,t}\right) + \beta_{iSMB}SMB_t + \beta_{iHML}HML_t + \beta_{iUMD}UMD_t + \varepsilon_{it}. \tag{1}$$

where r_{it} is the return of fund i in month t; $r_{f,t}$ is the risk-free rate in month t; r_{mt} is the market return in month t; SMB_t, HML_t, and UMD_t are the *Small Minus Big* (i.e. return spread between a small cap portfolio and a large cap portfolio at time t), *High Minus Low* (i.e. return difference between a value stock portfolio and a growth stock portfolio at time t), and *Momentum* (i.e. difference in return between a portfolio of past winners and a portfolio of past losers at time t) factors; α is the intercept; β_{MKT}, β_{SMB}, β_{HML}, β_{UMD} are the factor loadings on the four factors (market, size, book-to-market, and momentum); and ε_{it} stands for the error term.

The risk factors considered (market, size, book-to-market and momentum) and the risk-free rate are collected from the Professor Kenneth French Data Library. For domestic US funds, we employ the Fama/French 3 factors plus the momentum factor. Similarly, for European funds that invest only in Europe, we use the Fama/French European 3 factors plus the momentum factor. For funds investing internationally, we use the Kenneth French global factors. All the factors are in US dollars, and the risk-free rate is the US one-month Treasury-bill rate.

The procedure to estimate monthly risk-adjusted performance is based on Ferreira et al. (2013) and involves estimating regressions of 36 months on a rolling monthly basis. First, every month, we regress the previous 36 months of fund excess returns on the market excess returns and the size, value/growth and momentum factors, as in Carhart (1997). From each of these regressions, we obtain the monthly estimates from the beta coefficients. We then use these estimates along with the value of the respective factors to calculate the expected return of each fund in each month. Monthly alphas (i.e., the abnormal performance measure) are calculated by subtracting these values to the effective return of each fund. Since this process requires 36 months of prior information and the analysis begins in January 2000, we get the first performance estimates in January 2003. This performance measure is the dependent variable of our model.

Social Variables

Although the definition of the social variables differs among studies, generally they emerge in the form of two groups: by screening intensity and by type. Screening intensity is a quantitative variable constructed to measure the strength of the requirements imposed by fund managers to filter firms, the diversification of SRI funds and, to some extent, the quality of the process (Capelle-Blancard & Monjon, 2014). Differently, the second group of variables of interest is of a qualitative nature. Their aim is to emphasize the "best practices" among the SRI funds.

In this study, screening intensity is proxied by the number of screens applied by each fund. As mentioned previously, we will apply the US SIF's screening categorization to all (US and European) funds. The US SIF defines 16 types of screens that SRI funds may use to filter firms from their investment portfolios, namely climate/clean tech, pollution/toxics, environment/other, community development, diversity & equal employment opportunity policies, human rights, labour relations, Sudan, board issues, executive pay, alcohol, animal welfare, defense/weapons, gambling, tobacco and shareholder engagement. If a fund's screening intensity is given a value of 16, this indicates that the fund employs all 16 of the listed screens, whereas a value of 1 indicates that the fund uses only 1 of the 16 available screens.

The type of screen is measured using a dichotomous variable for each of the screening strategies employed by US SIF, namely environment (screens related to climate, clean technology, pollution, toxics and other environmental issues), social (screens associated with community development, diversity and equal employment, human rights, labour relations and Sudan), governance (screens that account for board and executive pay issues), products (screens that exclude companies involved in alcohol, animal welfare, defense/weapons, gambling and tobacco products) and shareholder engagement. For instance, in order to test hypothesis 3a, we will assign a value of 1 to the variable environment if a fund screened out firms based on at least one environmental factor, and zero otherwise.

Similarly, to assess hypothesis 4, we establish a variable for positive screening. Since most funds of our sample employ a combination of positive and negative screens, we compute this variable as the number of positive screens applied by the fund.

Finally, we will differentiate funds that have been awarded with at least one social label. The purpose of these labels is to provide investors with a quality standard (beyond the self-named label of SRI funds) by assuring the systematic integration of ESG criteria into mutual funds' management. We will use a dummy variable for funds that have been certified by sustainability labels.

Control Variables

Since the main goal of this paper is to determine how the screening process affects fund profitability, it is necessary to control for factors that could systematically affect SRI fund financial performance. We therefore include a variety of variables previously recognized as likely to influence the financial performance of mutual funds, namely funds' characteristics (age, size, and total expense ratio) and investment style (domestic or global funds).

To address the *"catching-up phase"* in SRI funds identified by Bauer et al. (2005)[18], and following Barnett and Salomon (2006), Humphrey and Lee (2011) and Nofsinger and Varma (2014), among others, we include the variable *Age*, defined as the number of months since the fund's inception. For surviving funds in December 2014, the variable is computed with reference to 31 December 2014; for missing funds, is calculated up to the liquidation or merger date.

In line with Barnett and Salomon (2006), Lee et al. (2010) and Capelle-Blancard and Monjon (2014), and in order to control for any potential fund size effect, we include the variable *Size*, measured by the fund total net assets (in million US dollars)[19]. Indro et al. (1999) and Chen et al. (2004) show that larger funds are subject to decreasing returns to scale. Ferreira et al. (2013) find a negative relation between fund size and performance only for US funds; for non-US funds, fund size is positively related to performance. Focusing on SRI funds, Gregory et al. (1997) find that fund size does not seem to affect performance results.

The *Total Expense Ratio* is a measure of the total costs associated with managing and operating an investment fund (management fees, trading fees, legal fees, auditor fees and other operational expenses)[20]. Empirical evidence on the impact of fees in performance is mixed. Chen et al. (2004) and Ferreira et al. (2013) do not find evidence of a relationship between fees and fund performance for US funds. Other authors find a negative relation between fees and fund performance (e.g., Carhart, 1997, and Gil-Bazo & Ruiz-Verdú, 2009, regarding US funds, and Dahlquist et al., 2000, and Otten & Bams, 2002, regarding European funds). Chang and Witte (2010) suggest that the costs of socially responsible investing are not homogeneous. Thus, the expense ratio may have impact on financial returns of SRI funds.

Table 1. Descriptive statistics and correlation matrix

	RAP	SI	ENV	SOC	GOV	PROD	SHENG	PSCR	LAB	L_AGE	L_SIZE	TER	GL
RAP	1.0000												
SI	-0.0406	1.0000											
ENV	0.0162	0.4842	1.0000										
SOC	-0.0319	0.6344	0.2472	1.0000									
GOV	-0.0327	0.6918	0.3007	0.2934	1.0000								
PROD	-0.0554	0.3883	-0.2952	0.2327	0.1489	1.0000							
SHENG	-0.0249	0.7050	0.3134	0.3220	0.7815	0.1562	1.0000						
PSCR	-0.0173	0.6377	0.5882	0.5574	0.3433	0.0614	0.3635	1.0000					
LAB	-0.0214	-0.0524	-0.0722	0.0806	-0.0279	0.0405	-0.0743	0.0413	1.0000				
L_AGE	0.0641	0.0389	-0.1141	0.0398	0.0523	0.1183	0.0374	-0.0064	0.0416	1.0000			
L_SIZE	-0.0458	0.0765	-0.0320	-0.0039	0.1553	0.0773	0.0607	0.0374	0.0252	0.4014	1.0000		
TER	0.0362	-0.0995	0.1664	-0.0452	-0.1630	-0.1261	-0.1270	0.0030	0.1137	-0.1673	-0.2199	1.0000	
GL	0.0656	-0.0826	0.1980	-0.1257	-0.1779	-0.1483	-0.1723	-0.0525	-0.0219	-0.2488	-0.1616	0.2662	1.0000
Mean	-0.0858	5.1005	0.5436	0.5179	0.1066	0.7627	0.1069	1.9333	0.6948	4.3665	3.7752	1.5450	0.5006
Std. Dev.	0.2174	4.1385	0.4981	0.4997	0.3086	0.4254	0.3090	2.2435	0.4605	0.9191	2.0690	0.6537	0.5000
Min	-7.4633	1	0	0	0	0	0	0	0	0	-9.2103	0	0
Max	10.1795	16	1	1	1	1	1	12	1	6.2226	11.1987	9.8	1
Skewness	1.8602	1.2492	-0.1752	-0.0715	2.5493	-1.2348	2.5439	1.8464	-0.8459	-0.7184	-0.3803	1.9378	-0.0024
Kurtosis	463.8212	3.7247	1.0307	1.0051	7.4990	2.5248	7.4716	7.0974	1.7157	3.4946	5.2032	25.5228	1.0000

Global and regional economic factors may also affect financial performance and thus funds with domestic holdings may perform differently from those with international holdings. To control for performance differentials across funds with domestic and international holdings, we follow several studies (e.g. Barnett & Salomon, 2006; Renneboog et al., 2008b; Capelle-Blancard & Monjon, 2014), and incorporate a dummy variable *Global*. For US (European) funds, this variable takes the value of 1 if the fund invests outside US (Europe), and zero otherwise.

Table 1 shows some descriptive statistics and the correlation matrix concerning the main variables of our study.

This table reports the pairwise correlations and the descriptive statistics (mean, standard deviation, minimum, maximum, skewness and kurtosis) of fund variables. The financial variable is the risk-adjusted performance (RAP), and the social variables include: screening intensity (SI), types of screening – environment (ENV), social (SOC), governance (GOV), products (PROD), and shareholder engagement (SHENG) –, positive screening intensity (PSCR), and labels (LAB). Control variables include: the logarithm of the variable Age, measured as the number of months since the fund's inception (L_AGE); the logarithm of the variable Size, measured by fund's total net assets in million US dollars (L_SIZE); Total Expense Ratio, in percentage (TER); and the geographic dummy (GL).

We observe that, on average, our sample of SRI funds displays negative risk-adjusted returns. Additionally, SRI funds apply, on average, five screens, with emphasis on products, environment and social concerns. Interestingly, there is a negative correlation between the two main variables of the model ($\rho_{SI,RAP}$ = -0.0406). With the exception of shareholder engagement and governance screens ($\rho_{SHENG,GOV}$ = 0.7815), and differently than expected, there is also a low correlation between many of the social screens[21]. Furthermore, there is a negative relation between the screens related with products and the environment ($\rho_{PROD,ENV}$ = -0.2952).

Relationship Between the Screening Process and Financial Performance

The monthly risk-adjusted performance of the SRI funds is the dependent variable, computed by estimating regression (1) on a rolling monthly basis, as described in sub-section 4.2. We then examine whether it is related to the to the screening process used, controlling for variables related to funds' characteristics and investment style, as described in the previous sections. In model (2), we postulate risk-adjusted performance as a linear function of social variables, to assess whether variables related to the screening process are positively or negatively related to fund financial performance, and estimate the following model:

$$RAP_{it} = \omega_0 + \omega_1 SI_i + \omega_2 ENV_i + \omega_3 SOC_i + \omega_4 GOV_i + \omega_5 PROD_i + \omega_6 SHENG_i \\ + \omega_7 PSCR_i + \omega_8 LAB_i + \omega_9 L\_AGE_{it} + \omega_{10} L\_SIZE_{it} + \omega_{11} TER_{it} + \omega_{12} GL_i + \mu_{it}. \quad (2)$$

Where RAP_{it} is the risk-adjusted performance of fund i in month t; SI_i is the screening intensity of fund i; ENV_i is a dummy variable equal to 1 if the fund i focuses on environmental issues, and 0 otherwise; SOC_i is a dummy variable equal to 1 if the fund i focuses on social issues, and 0 otherwise; GOV_i is a dummy variable equal to 1 if the fund i focuses on governance issues, and 0 otherwise; $PROD_i$ is a dummy variable equal to 1 if the fund i focuses on products' issues, and 0 otherwise; $SHENG_i$ is a dummy variable equal to 1 if the fund i focuses on shareholder engagement issues, and 0 otherwise; $PSCR_i$ is a dummy variable equal to 1 if the fund *i* employs a positive screening strategy, and 0 otherwise; LAB_i is a dummy variable equal to 1 if the fund *i* has received at least one social label, and 0 otherwise; L_AGE_{it} is the logarithm of the number of months since the fund's inception; L_SIZE_{it} is the logarithm of the fund size (total net assets in million US dollars); TER_{it} is the Total Expense Ratio of the fund *i*; GL_i is a dummy variable equal to 1 if the fund *i* invests outside US (US funds) or Europe (European funds), and 0 otherwise; and μ_{it} stands for the error term.

To capture a potential curvilinear relationship between social screening and financial performance, model (3) includes the square of the screening intensity $[(SI_i)^2]$.

$$RAP_{it} = \theta_0 + \theta_1 SI_i + \theta_2 SI_i^2 + \theta_3 ENV_i + \theta_4 SOC_i + \theta_5 GOV_i + \theta_6 PROD_i + \theta_7 SHENG_i \\ + \theta_8 PSCR_i + \theta_9 LAB_i + \theta_{10} L\_AGE_{it} + \theta_{11} L\_SIZE_{it} + \theta_{12} TER_{it} + \theta_{13} GL_i + \mu_{it}. \quad (3)$$

Fixed effects and random effects models are two common estimators for panel data. Given the structure of our main variables of interest (the social variables are constant over time) and fact that the fixed effects eliminates any time-invariant variables from the model, we consider that this estimator is not adequate. In turn, the random effects model assumes that all factors that affect the dependent variable, but have not been included as regressors, can be appropriately summarized by a random error term (Verbeek, 2012). We performed the Hausman test to compare both estimators (fixed and random effects), and we rejected the hypothesis that the preferred model is random effects. Since we have some time series variables (related to the social screening process) that have not changed during the sample period, the between effects model emerges as the most appropriate estimator. The between effects estimator performs an Ordinary Least Squares on a "collapsed" data set where all data are converted into individual specific averages, i.e., the between estimator effectively discards the time series information, and exploits the between dimension of the data (Verbeek, 2012). To capture the influence of aggregate trends, we include year dummies in the analysis.

EMPIRICAL RESULTS

Social Screening and SRI Fund Performance

The impact of the screening process in the risk-adjusted performance of SRI funds is assessed according to the models presented in the previous section. Model 2 estimates a potential linear association between risk-adjusted performance and social variables (screening intensity, types of screens, positive screening, and labels), while model 3 evaluates the possibility of a curvilinear effect.[22]

Although socially responsible investments are a global phenomenon, there is substantial heterogeneity in the development and adoption rates of this investment approach among countries and regions (Neher & Hebb, 2016). Given the geographic differences in socially responsible investing and the importance of the cultural and legislative contexts in which it has arisen, we will differentiate the analysis according to the following groups/individual countries: Global (all countries), US, continental Europe, and the UK.[23] The results are presented in table 2.

Table 2. Regression results – total screening intensity

	GLOBAL SAMPLE		CONTINENTAL EUROPEAN SUBSAMPLE		US SUBSAMPLE		UK SUBSAMPLE	
	Model (2)	Model (3)	Model (2)	Model (3)	Model (2)	Model (3)	Model (2)	Model (3)
Screening Intensity	-0.0001 (-0.07)	0.0028* (1.89)	0.0009** (2.26)	0.0011 (1.46)	-0.0015 (-0.83)	0.0131** (2.03)	-0.0160 (-1.55)	-0.0232 (-1.66)
Squared Screening Intensity		-0.0002** (-2.20)		-0.0000 (-0.26)		-0.0007** (-2.35)		0.0011 (0.78)
D_Environment	-0.0017 (-0.45)	-0.0032 (-0.86)	-0.0018 (-0.91)	-0.0018 (-0.92)	-0.0054 (-0.49)	-0.0315** (-2.06)	0.0055 (0.21)	0.0034 (0.13)
D_Social	0.0047 (1.47)	0.0024 (0.73)	-0.0004 (-0.27)	-0.0005 (-0.31)	0.0050 (0.55)	-0.0086 (-0.82)	0.0193 (0.73)	0.0273 (0.95)
D_Governance	0.0081 (1.28)	0.0132** (1.98)	0.0006 (0.14)	0.0005 (0.11)	0.0285** (2.40)	0.0289** (2.53)	(omitted)	(omitted)
D_Products	0.0018 (0.49)	-0.0005 (-0.14)	-0.0025 (-1.62)	-0.0025 (-1.62)	-0.0034 (-0.29)	-0.0302* (-1.89)	0.0928 (1.58)	0.0738 (1.14)
D_Shareholder Engagement	0.0046 (0.74)	0.0101 (1.53)	(omitted)	(omitted)	0.0013 (0.12)	0.0028 (0.27)	(omitted)	(omitted)
D_Positive Screening	-0.0010 (-1.28)	-0.0010 (-1.28)	-0.0010 (-1.22)	-0.0010 (-1.16)	-0.0012 (-0.92)	-0.0008 (-0.63)	0.0198 (1.09)	0.0061 (0.24)
D_Labels	0.0044* (1.84)	0.0043* (1.82)	0.0001 (0.06)	0.0001 (0.08)	0.0079 (1.06)	0.0073 (1.02)	0.0146 (0.51)	0.0244 (0.76)
Log Age	-0.0008 (-0.35)	-0.0007 (-0.32)	-0.0003 (-0.27)	-0.0003 (-0.27)	0.0030 (0.33)	0.0083 (0.92)	0.0046 (0.38)	0.0078 (0.60)
Log Size	0.0017*** (2.69)	0.0016** (2.46)	0.0008*** (2.86)	0.0008*** (2.80)	-0.0024 (-1.14)	-0.0027 (-1.33)	0.0100** (2.36)	0.0086* (1.85)
Total Expense Ratio	-0.0015 (-0.79)	-0.0017 (-0.91)	-0.0004 (-0.47)	-0.0004 (-0.49)	-0.0065 (-0.83)	-0.0046 (-0.60)	0.0239* (1.79)	0.0236 (1.74)
D_Global	-0.0001 (-0.04)	-0.0004 (-0.16)	-0.0001 (-0.09)	-0.0001 (-0.09)	-0.0097 (-1.10)	-0.0064 (-0.75)	0.0078 (0.44)	0.0028 (0.14)
Year dummies	Included		Included		Included		Included	
Nr. observations	30,921		19,047		8,649		3,225	
Nr. mutual funds	330		217		80		33	

This table reports the results from regressions of financial performance on a number of social and control variables. The dependent variable is the risk-adjusted performance (RAP) associated with SRI funds. Explanatory variables include Screening Intensity, defined as the number of screens used, and its square (Squared Screening Intensity), and the following dummy variables: Environment, Social, Governance, Products, Shareholder Engagement, which take a value of 1 if the fund focuses on environmental, social, governance, products, shareholder engagement, respectively, and 0 otherwise; Positive Screening, defined as the number of positive screens employed by the fund; Labels, a dummy variable equal to 1 if the fund has received at least one social label, and 0 otherwise. Control variables include: Size, measured by Log fund's total net assets (in millions of US dollars); Age, measured as the Log of the number of months since the fund's inception; Total Expense Ratio, a measure of the total costs associated with managing and operating an investment fund; Global, a dummy variable that takes the value of 1 if the fund invests internationally, and 0 otherwise. The sample includes 330 SRI equity mutual funds for the period 2003-2014. t-statistics are shown in parentheses. * p-value < 0.10; ** p-value < 0.05; *** p-value < 0.01

When we consider the whole sample, the results show a curvilinear relationship between financial performance and screening intensity, namely a positive sign for screening intensity and a negative sign for squared screening intensity (inverted U-shaped effect). This suggests that when a fund increases the number of screens, it is able to identify better managed companies, causing financial performance to increase. However, above a certain level of screening, given the narrowing of its investable universe, performance starts to decrease until the maximum screening intensity is achieved. Notwithstanding, *ceteris paribus*, financial performance is higher at the maximum screening intensity (16 screens) in comparison with the minimum level (1 screen). In terms of screening types, the results are mixed, and without statistical significance. The exception is the governance dimension: governance-screened funds exhibit a positive and statistically significant coefficient, suggesting that screening on this dimension impacts fund performance in a positive way. The results also show a positive and statistically significant (at the 10% level) coefficient of the dummy labels, thereby indicating a tendency for funds that are certified with a social label to perform better.

The results for continental Europe show a positive linear relationship between screening intensity and risk-adjusted returns at the 5% significance level. Nevertheless, there are no significant relationships with regards to particular types of screens, positive screening, or labels. Interestingly, the results for US funds show that several variables have a significant impact on the financial performance of SRI funds. We find evidence that the performance an US SRI fund investor can expect is dependent on the number and type of screens used by the funds. For a significance level of 5%, the findings in model 3 suggest there is a positive relationship between screening intensity and risk-adjusted returns, and a negative relationship between squared screening intensity and risk-adjusted returns. This means that the financial performance increases at first as the number of screens increases, but then declines continuously until it reaches the maximum screening intensity. Still, *ceteris paribus*, at the maximum of 16 screens, performance is superior to the level of funds with one screen. Therefore, unlike Barnett and Salomon (2006), who find that the risk-adjusted performance starts to decrease as the number of screens increases, and then recovers, we conclude for an inverted curvilinear (U-shaped) effect, as already observed for the overall sample. It is also evident that some screening strategies significantly influence the financial performance of US SRI funds. Similar to Barnett and Salomon (2006), funds that screen on environmental criteria have a relatively lower performance. Products-oriented screens also have a negative effect on performance, while screening on governance, in contrast with Renneboog et al. (2008b), generates a relatively stronger financial performance.

Regarding UK funds, there is a negative sign for the hypothesis of a linear relationship between financial performance and screening intensity, but without any of the coefficients being statistically significant. With respect to the square of the screening intensity, the coefficient is positive but not statistically significant. Both ESG-type and screening strategies exhibit positive signs and no significant coefficients.

In relation to the control variables, only Size and the Total Expense Ratio seem to affect financial performance. For the global sample, as well as for the continental European and UK subsamples, the Size variable exhibits a positive and statistically significant coefficient. This means that larger SRI funds may benefit from better financial returns. Concerning the Total Expense Ratio, UK funds show a positive sign (although only at the significance level of 10%) suggesting that the total costs incurred by a SRI fund do not detract risk-adjusted returns.

Furthermore, we explore whether the impact of screening strategies differs across different market states (expansion and recession periods). We start by identifying market states across the distinct geographies considered in our sample. For US funds, we use the National Bureau of Economic Research (NBER) business cycles. The NBER identifies a single recession period during our sample period (2003-2014), namely from December 2007 until June 2009. For the Euro Area funds, we use the cycles provided by the Centre for Economic Policy Research (CEPR). The CEPR distinguishes two recession periods for the Euro Area: January 2008 to April 2009, and July 2011 to March 2013. For UK, Swiss and Scandinavian funds, we use the business cycles of the Economic Cycle Research Institute (ECRI). The ECRI identifies one recession period for the UK – May 2008 to January 2010 – and two recession periods for Switzerland – January 2003 to March 2003, and May 2008 to May 2009. Finally, for Scandinavia, given the cultural homogeneity of the countries included, we employ the business cycles provided for Sweden: April 2008 to March 2009. The remaining periods are considered periods of expansion. We then estimate regressions for recession and expansion periods[24]. Table 3 presents the results.

This table reports the results from regressions of financial performance on a number of social and control variables. The dependent variable is the risk-adjusted performance (RAP) associated with SRI funds. Explanatory variables include Screening Intensity, defined as the number of screens used, and its square (Squared Screening Intensity), and the following dummy variables: Environment, Social, Governance, Products, Shareholder Engagement, which take a value of 1 if the fund focuses on environmental, social, governance, products, shareholder engagement, respectively, and 0 otherwise; Positive Screening is defined as the number of positive screens employed by the fund; Labels is a dummy variable equal to 1 if the fund has received at least one social label, and 0 otherwise. Control variables include: Size, measured by Log fund's total net assets (in millions of US dollars); Age, measured as the Log of the number of months since the fund's inception; Total Expense Ratio is a measure of the total costs associated with managing and operating an investment fund; Global is a dummy variable that takes the value of 1 if the fund invests internationally, and 0 otherwise. The sample includes 330 SRI equity mutual funds for the expansion and recession periods defined in section 5. t-statistics are shown in parentheses. * p-value < 0.10; ** p-value < 0.05; *** p-value < 0.01

Considering the whole sample, there are no significant relationships in periods of recession. However, the curvilinear relationship between screening intensity and financial performance, and the positive and significant coefficients previously obtained for the variables Governance, Labels and Size, hold in expansion periods. For continental European funds, some interesting results emerge in expansion periods. Both the positive relationship between screening intensity and financial performance and the positive impact of size on returns are preserved. In addition, the number of screens related to products and positive screens have a negative impact on performance, for a level of significance of 5% and 10%, respectively. This means that excluding "sin" stocks and incorporating positive screens damages the performance of continental European funds during "good times". Regarding US funds, all the previously identified relationships remain significant in periods of expansion. Aditionally, social screens and the Total Expense Ratio seem to detract funds' returns. In recession times, the Total Expense Ratio seems to have a positive effect on returns. Furthermore, in times of turmoil, investing outside the domestic market seems to penalize performance.

Table 3. Regression results – expansion and recession periods

	GLOBAL SAMPLE				CONTINENTAL EUROPEAN SUBSAMPLE				US SUBSAMPLE			
	Expansion Periods		Recession Periods		Expansion Periods		Recession Periods		Expansion Periods		Recession Periods	
	Model (2)	Model (3)	Model (2)	Model (3)	Model (2)	Model (3)	Model (2)	Model (3)	Model (2)	Model (3)	Model (2)	Model (3)
Screening Intensity	-0.0001	0.0028**	0.0005	-0.0031	0.0011***	0.0006	0.0028	0.0029	-0.0015	0.0152***	-0.0011	-0.0316
	(-0.18)	(1.99)	(0.17)	(-0.50)	(2.59)	(0.84)	(1.22)	(0.64)	(-1.06)	(3.16)	(-0.12)	(-0.91)
Squared Screening Intensity		-0.0002**		0.0003		0.0000		-0.0000		-0.0008***		0.0015
		(-2.36)		(0.64)		(0.71)		(-0.01)		(-3.61)		(0.91)
D_Environment	-0.0000	-0.0017	-0.0090	-0.0066	0.0005	0.0006	-0.0142	-0.0142	0.0003	-0.0290**	-0.0555	-0.0003
	(-0.01)	(-0.47)	(-0.61)	(-0.44)	(0.26)	(0.29)	(-1.29)	(-1.27)	(0.04)	(-2.54)	(-0.91)	(-0.00)
D_Social	0.0049	0.0024	0.0016	0.0044	0.0010	0.0012	-0.0036	-0.0037	0.0023	-0.0136*	0.0693	0.0954
	(1.60)	(0.74)	(0.12)	(0.33)	(0.58)	(0.72)	(-0.39)	(-0.38)	(0.32)	(-1.71)	(1.36)	(1.63)
D_Governance	0.0065	0.0120*	0.0031	-0.0034	-0.0007	-0.0004	-0.0126	-0.0126	0.0254***	0.0265***	0.0453	0.0305
	(1.10)	(1.90)	(0.11)	(-0.12)	(-0.14)	(-0.10)	(-0.50)	(-0.49)	(2.65)	(3.04)	(0.61)	(0.40)
D_Products	0.0004	-0.0020	0.0146	0.0181	-0.0031**	-0.0031**	-0.0057	-0.0057	-0.0080	-0.0397***	0.0503	0.1193
	(0.10)	(-0.56)	(0.95)	(1.11)	(-2.05)	(-2.02)	(-0.63)	(-0.63)	(-0.86)	(-3.26)	(0.73)	(1.16)
D_Shareholder Engagement	0.0038	0.0099	-0.0045	-0.0131	(omitted)	(omitted)	(omitted)	(omitted)	0.0002	0.0027	-0.0047	-0.0183
	(0.65)	(1.55)	(-0.16)	(-0.42)					(0.02)	(0.34)	(-0.08)	(-0.28)
D_Positive Screening	-0.0011	-0.0011	-0.0001	-0.0001	-0.0015*	-0.0016*	-0.0018	-0.0018	-0.0007	-0.0004	-0.0014	-0.0020
	(-1.41)	(-1.41)	(-0.03)	(-0.04)	(-1.79)	(-1.88)	(-0.38)	(-0.37)	(-0.68)	(-0.39)	(-0.24)	(-0.33)
D_Labels	0.0039*	0.0038	0.0137	0.0138	0.0000	-0.0000	0.0032	0.0033	0.0087	0.0086	-0.0463	-0.0494
	(1.68)	(1.63)	(1.30)	(1.30)	(0.04)	(-0.02)	(0.46)	(0.46)	(1.44)	(1.56)	(-1.13)	(-1.20)
Log Age	-0.0022	-0.0021	0.0012	0.0010	0.0003	0.0003	-0.0043	-0.0042	-0.0029	0.0021	0.0211	0.0199
	(-1.04)	(-1.02)	(0.18)	(0.15)	(0.26)	(0.27)	(-0.95)	(-0.94)	(-0.41)	(0.31)	(0.87)	(0.81)
Log Size	0.0020***	0.0019***	-0.0021	-0.0020	0.0005*	0.0006**	0.0014	0.0014	-0.0018	-0.0022	-0.0042	-0.0040
	(3.23)	(3.06)	(-0.78)	(-0.76)	(1.96)	(2.02)	(0.77)	(0.77)	(-1.05)	(-1.36)	(-0.41)	(-0.39)
Total Expense Ratio	-0.0026	-0.0028	0.0030	0.0034	-0.0003	-0.0002	-0.0049	-0.0049	-0.0129**	-0.0119**	0.0674*	0.0673*
	(-1.37)	(-1.46)	(0.47)	(0.53)	(-0.29)	(-0.23)	(-1.40)	(-1.39)	(-2.10)	(-2.13)	(1.80)	(1.80)
D_Global	0.0018	0.0016	-0.0084	-0.0081	-0.0004	-0.0004	-0.0005	-0.0005	-0.0018	0.0022	-0.1113**	-0.1085**
	(0.74)	(0.65)	(-0.82)	(-0.79)	(-0.33)	(-0.34)	(-0.08)	(-0.08)	(-0.25)	(0.33)	(-2.22)	(-2.16)
Year dummies	Included		Included		Included		Included		Included		Included	
Nr. Observations	24,872		6,049		14,621		4,426		7,507		1,142	
Nr. Mutual funds	330		264		217		173		80		67	

Robustness Tests

To ensure the robustness of our results, we performed several robustness tests[25]. First, like Barnett and Salomon (2006), we added each social variable in a different order and separately into the regressions. The results did not change substantially.

Second, we dropped those funds that reported extreme screening intensity values (fewer than 4 and greater than 12) to test for other influential points. Some results concerning the global sample and the US differ from those previously obtained. For the whole sample, we obtain a linear positive and statistically significant relationship between screening intensity and returns. Also, some social variables become significant, namely the dummies Products and Shareholder Engagement, and the positive screening intensity. Screening on shareholder engagement has a positive impact on performance, while screening on products has a negative effect. The number of positive screens also impacts performance negatively. Regarding US funds, some types of screens emerge as relevant: social-screened funds have lower returns, whilst shareholder engagement-screened funds benefit in terms of performance. Differently from the global sample, the number of positive screens has a positive impact on financial performance.

Third, like Barnett and Salomon (2006), we split the sample into low (1-4 screens), medium (5-12 screens), and high (13-16 screens) screening intensity subsets to decompose the screening patterns of the funds. The results remain unchanged except for the global sample, whose differences are observed at the medium level and explained in the previous paragraph.

Finally, to determine whether the funds' behaviour has changed over time, we split the sample into an early period from 2003 to 2008, and a later period from 2009 to 2014[26]. Concerning the whole sample, and the continental European and US subsamples, the results previously obtained for the relationship between screening and returns hold for the 2009 to 2014 subperiod. In addition, products screens seem to have a negative impact on the returns of continental European funds from 2009 to 2014. Regarding the control variables, age seems to erode the performance of continental European funds for the 2003-2008 subperiod, while there are mixed results for the global dummy: the variable is positive (negative) and statistically significant for the early (later) period. For the global sample, we also find that global funds have lower returns during 2009 to 2014.

CONCLUSION

This paper investigates the relationship between the risk-adjusted performance and the screening activities of a dataset of 330 US and European SRI mutual funds for the period 2003-2014. In particular, we extend previous academic research that investigates the heterogeneity within socially screened funds by exploring the impact of the number and type of the social screens on financial returns, the effects of using positive screening techniques and the potential of social labels to generate distinct patterns of risk-adjusted returns. In general, our results are consistent with the SRI fund literature in the sense that there does not seem to be a financial sacrifice for investors in highly screened funds.

Considering the global sample and the US subsample, we find an inverted U-shaped pattern between SRI fund financial performance and screening intensity. Although the shape of the curvilinear relationship is different from the one documented by Barnett and Salomon (2006), we interpret these findings as indicative that portfolio theory and stakeholder theory are actually complementary, instead of conflicting, in explaining the effects of social screening on mutual fund performance. The results are consistent with the existence of a trade-off between selectivity and diversification in the sense that when we intensify screening, we expect to form a portfolio composed of better firms (that comply with ESG standards), but we also significantly reduce the ability to fully diversify the portfolio. Initially, we are still able to create diversified portfolios; yet, from a certain level of screening, the adverse effects of excluding potentially profitable options from the portfolio become more evident. The results obtained for intermediate levels of screening (4 to 12 screens) support this conclusion: the relationship between selectivity and diversification is such that the global sample exhibits a positive relationship between the number of screens and returns. Notwithstanding, *ceteris paribus*, for both the global sample and the US, the risk-adjusted performance for the maximum screening intensity is higher than the one achieved for the minimum screening intensity.

Differently, for continental Europe, there is a linear positive relationship between screening intensity and financial performance. Although European countries have different histories, cultures and values, the exclusion of UK, whose socially responsible investing approach is more based on negative screening, may uncover a greater homogeneity in continental Europe which, according to Renneboog et al. (2008a), is more focused on "best-in-class" screening strategies.

When we incorporate qualitative differences on screening policies, we document some links between performance and particular screens. For the whole sample and US funds, we find that screening for governance criteria has a positive effect on performance. Corporate scandals such as Enron and WorldCom during the 2000's have placed the topic of corporate governance on investors' social agenda. The definition of stronger legal and regulatory frameworks, as well as more detailed guidelines and transparent procedures have strengthened this trend and its relevance for public opinion, thus favoring good governance practices. Additionally, we also show that US funds that exclude firms with excessive negative environmental impact, or that exclude entire sectors related to alcohol, gambling, or tobacco, among others, suffer a financial penalty. By its nature, most environmental factors are long-term or very long-term. Therefore, investments to mitigate environmental risks might negatively impact SRI fund performance in the short run. The conclusion regarding shunned stocks is in line with the empirical literature that finds that "sin" stocks have higher expected returns than otherwise comparable stocks (e.g., Hong & Karpercyzk, 2009; Statman & Glushkov, 2009; Derwall et al., 2011).

Concerning positive screening strategies, when we remove extreme points of screening intensity, it emerges as a relevant factor. Nevertheless, the results are mixed: US funds meeting superior ESG standards have higher financial performance but when we consider the whole sample of SRI funds, the financial performance is negatively affected by the number of positive screens. Interestingly, consistent with Silva and Cortez (2016), whose findings stress a tendency for certified green funds to perform better than uncertified green funds, our main results also indicate that funds that are certified with sustainability labels tend to have a better financial performance. Social labels are assigned by independent entities to reassure investors about the social and ethical standards of the fund in which they are investing, and they can play a critical role in providing more transparency to the SRI market, thereby allowing investors to make more informed investment decisions.

Furthermore, our evidence indicates that for the global sample, continental Europe and UK alone, larger funds have better financial performance. This result holds for expansion market cycles. So, consistent with Renneboog et al. (2008b), we argue that SRI funds are not subject to decreasing returns to scale. In relation to fees, Renneboog et al. (2008b) document that management fees significantly reduce the risk-adjusted returns of SRI funds. In general, we find that the Total Expense Ratio has a neutral effect on returns (with the exception of UK, where it emerges as a financial advantage). Yet, we corroborate their conclusions for US funds in expansion business cycles. In periods of turmoil, we also find that fees represent a financial advantage for US funds, whereas global US funds have lower returns.

Finally, we show that in periods of expansion US socially responsible investors pay a cost for incorporating additional social screens in their investment decisions. We show a similar effect of screens related to products, and positive screens, in continental Europe. Interestingly, when considering the global sample, and continental European and US subsamples, we observe that the results obtained for the whole period are driven by those obtained in expansion periods.

There are several reasons why we should expect discrepancies in the way responsible investment affects performance in different countries/regions. Sandberg et al. (2009) suggest three kind of explanations for the heterogeneity in SRI funds, namely: a) cultural and ideological differences between regions and countries; b) differences in values, norms and ideology between different actors involved in the SRI process (SRI stakeholders); and c) the market setting in which SRI actors operate. We illustrate this statement: the empirical evidence for the 13 countries in our sample is mixed, and the results are not geographically homogeneous. Each country/region has a unique social, political, legal, institutional context that determines the degree of development of the SRI market and, consequently, the outline of the relationship between social screening and financial returns.

Another relevant issue concerns the consequences of the global financial crisis of 2008 on socially responsible investments. This event might have changed investors' perceptions and awareness concerning SRI practices, but most studies on the relationship between screening and performance do not consider the post-crisis years. For example, Barnett and Salomon (2006) and Lee et al. (2010), that show a curvilinear (U-shaped) and negative relationship between screening and returns for US funds, respectively, look at periods prior to this event. Differently, we find an inverted U-shaped effect but considering the period from 2003 to 2014. The effects of the international financial crisis may contribute to explain the different results of this study.

It is also worth mentioning that the methodology used to assess fund performance and investment styles is crucial in analyzing how screening effects SRI fund performance. By way of example, Barnett and Salomon (2006) and Renneboog et al. (2008b) measure the risk-adjusted performance assuming that funds' systematic risk is constant over the entire period under analysis. In this paper, the risk-adjusted returns are computed on the basis of the Carhart (1997) four-factor model in 36 months rolling basis, thereby considering time-varying risk. Another limitation concerns the variation of screening strategies across time. Some papers consider that funds' social screening strategies are stable (e.g., Barnett & Salomon, 2006; Humphrey & Lee, 2011) but employ methodologies consistent with social variables that change over time. Given the data collected, we assume that the social screening variables are static, and so apply a between effects model, which is a more robust methodology to estimate the regressions on our panel data.

In light of the differences concerning the time periods under analysis, methodologies used for assessing risk-adjusted performance and geographic regions of focus analyzed, research on the relationship between the screening characteristics and the financial performance is still a work in progress. Yet, our paper contributes to the ongoing research providing relevant findings concerning the global sample, the world leader in terms of socially responsible finance and investing (US), as well as European SRI markets.

ACKNOWLEDGMENT

This paper was supported by National Funds of the FCT – Portuguese Foundation for Science and Technology within the project UIDB/03182/2020.

REFERENCES

Ayadi, M., Ben-Ameur, H., & Kryzanowski, L. (2016). Typical and Tail Performance of Canadian Equity SRI Mutual Funds. *Journal of Financial Services Research*, *50*(1), 57–94. doi:10.100710693-015-0215-0

Barnett, M., & Salomon, M. (2006). Beyond Dichotomy: The Curvilinear Relationship Between Social Responsibility and Financial Performance. *Strategic Management Journal*, *27*(11), 1101–1122. doi:10.1002mj.557

Bauer, R., Derwall, J., & Otten, R. (2007). The Ethical Mutual Fund Performance Debate: New Evidence from Canada. *Journal of Business Ethics*, *70*(2), 111–124. doi:10.100710551-006-9099-0

Bauer, R., Koedijk, K., & Otten, R. (2005). International Evidence on Ethical Mutual Fund Performance and Investment Style. *Journal of Banking & Finance*, *29*(7), 1751–1767. doi:10.1016/j.jbankfin.2004.06.035

Bauer, R., Otten, R., & Rad, A. (2006). Ethical Investing in Australia: Is There a Financial Penalty? *Pacific-Basin Finance Journal*, *14*(1), 33–48. doi:10.1016/j.pacfin.2004.12.004

Bello, Z. (2005). Socially Responsible Investing and Portfolio Diversification. *Journal of Financial Research*, *28*(1), 41–57. doi:10.1111/j.1475-6803.2005.00113.x

Bengtsson, E. (2008). A History of Scandinavian Socially Responsible Investing. *Journal of Business Ethics*, *82*(4), 969–983. doi:10.100710551-007-9606-y

Brown, S., Goetzmann, W., Ibbotson, R., & Ross, S. (1992). Survivorship Bias in Performance Studies. *Review of Financial Studies*, *5*(4), 553–580. doi:10.1093/rfs/5.4.553

Capelle-Blancard, G., & Monjon, S. (2014). The Performance of Socially Responsible Funds: Does the Screening Process Matter? *European Financial Management*, *20*(3), 494–520. doi:10.1111/j.1468-036X.2012.00643.x

Carhart, M. (1997). On Persistence in Mutual Fund Performance. *The Journal of Finance*, *52*(1), 57–82. doi:10.1111/j.1540-6261.1997.tb03808.x

Chang, E., & Witte, D. (2010). Performance Evaluation of US Socially Responsible Mutual Funds: Revisiting Doing Good and Doing Well. *American Journal of Business*, *25*(1), 9–21. doi:10.1108/19355181201000001

Chen, J., Hong, H., Huang, M., & Kubik, J. (2004). Does Fund Size Erode Mutual Fund Performance? The Role of Liquidity and Organization. *The American Economic Review*, *94*(5), 1276–1302. doi:10.1257/0002828043052277

Climent, F., & Soriano, P. (2011). Green and Good? The Investment Performance of US Environmental Mutual Funds. *Journal of Business Ethics*, *103*(2), 275–287. doi:10.100710551-011-0865-2

Cortez, M., Silva, F., & Areal, N. (2009). The Performance of European Socially Responsible Funds. *Journal of Business Ethics*, *87*(4), 573–588. doi:10.100710551-008-9959-x

Cortez, M., Silva, F., & Areal, N. (2012). Socially Responsible Investing in the Global Market: The Performance of US and European Funds. *International Journal of Finance & Economics*, *17*(3), 254–271. doi:10.1002/ijfe.454

Dahlquist, M., Engström, S., & Söderlind, P. (2000). Performance and Characteristics of Swedish Mutual Funds. *Journal of Financial and Quantitative Analysis*, *35*(3), 409–423. doi:10.2307/2676211

Derwall, J., Koedijk, K., & Horst, J. (2011). A Tale of Values-Driven and Profit-Seeking Social Investors. *Journal of Banking & Finance*, *35*(8), 2137–2147. doi:10.1016/j.jbankfin.2011.01.009

Dunfee, T. (2003). Social Investing: Mainstream or Backwater? *Journal of Business Ethics*, *43*(3), 247–252. doi:10.1023/A:1022914831479

Fernandez-Izquierdo, A., & Matallin-Saez, J. (2008). Performance of Ethical Mutual Funds in Spain: Sacrifice or Premium? *Journal of Business Ethics*, *81*(2), 247–260. doi:10.100710551-007-9492-3

Ferreira, M., Keswani, A., Miguel, A., & Ramos, S. (2013). The Determinants of Mutual Fund Performance: A Cross-Country Study. *Review of Finance*, *17*(2), 483–525. doi:10.1093/rof/rfs013

Ferriani, F., & Natoli, F. (2021). ESG risks in times of COVID-19. *Applied Economics Letters*, *28*(18), 1537–1541. doi:10.1080/13504851.2020.1830932

Freeman, R. (1984). *Strategic Management: A Stakeholder Approach*. Pitman.

Galema, R., Plantiga, A., & Scholtens, B. (2008). The Stocks at Stake: Return and Risk in Socially Responsible Investment. *Journal of Banking & Finance*, *32*(12), 2646–2654. doi:10.1016/j.jbankfin.2008.06.002

Gil-Bazo, J., & Ruiz-Verdú, P. (2009). Yet Another Puzzle? The Relation Between Price and Performance in the Mutual Fund Industry. *The Journal of Finance*, *64*(5), 2153–2183. doi:10.1111/j.1540-6261.2009.01497.x

Gil-Bazo, J., Ruiz-Verdú, P., & Santos, A. (2010). The Performance of Socially Responsible Mutual Funds: The Role of Fees and Management Companies. *Journal of Business Ethics*, *94*(2), 243–263. doi:10.100710551-009-0260-4

Global Sustainable Investment Alliance – GSIA. (2021). *Global Sustainable Investment Review 2020*. http://www.gsi-alliance.org/wp-content/uploads/2021/07/GSIR-2020.pdf

Goldreyer, E., Ahmed, P., & Diltz, J. (1999). The Performance of Socially Responsible Mutual Funds: Incorporating Sociopolitical Information in Portfolio Selection. *Managerial Finance*, *25*(1), 23–36. doi:10.1108/03074359910765830

Gregory, A., Matatko, J., & Luther, R. (1997). Ethical Unit Trust Financial Performance: Small Company Effects and Fund Size Effects. *Journal of Business Finance & Accounting*, *24*(5), 705–725. doi:10.1111/1468-5957.00130

Gregory, A., & Whittaker, J. (2007). Performance and Performance Persistence of "Ethical" Unit Trusts in the UK. *Journal of Business Finance & Accounting*, *34*(7-8), 1327–1344. doi:10.1111/j.1468-5957.2007.02006.x

Hamilton, S., Jo, H., & Statman, M. (1993). Doing Well While Doing Good? The Investment Performance of Socially Responsible Mutual Funds. *Financial Analysts Journal*, *49*(6), 62–66. doi:10.2469/faj.v49.n6.62

Henke, H. (2016). The Effect of Social Screening on Bond Mutual Fund Performance. *Journal of Banking & Finance*, *67*, 69–84. doi:10.1016/j.jbankfin.2016.01.010

Hong, H., & Kacperczyk, M. (2009). The Price of Sin: The Effects of Social Norms on Markets. *Journal of Financial Economics*, *93*(1), 15–36. doi:10.1016/j.jfineco.2008.09.001

Humphrey, J., & Lee, D. (2011). Australian Socially Responsible Funds: Performance, Risk and Screening Intensity. *Journal of Business Ethics*, *102*(4), 519–535. doi:10.100710551-011-0836-7

Ibikunle, G., & Steffen, T. (2017). European green mutual fund performance: A comparative analysis with their conventional and black peers. *Journal of Business Ethics*, *145*(2), 337–355. doi:10.100710551-015-2850-7

Indro, D., Jiang, C., Hu, M., & Lee, W. (1999). Mutual Fund Performance: Does Fund Size Matter? *Financial Analysts Journal*, *55*(3), 74–87. doi:10.2469/faj.v55.n3.2274

Kim, C. S. (2019). Can Socially Responsible Investments Be Compatible with Financial Performance? A Meta-analysis. *Asia-Pacific Journal of Financial Studies*, *48*(1), 30–64. doi:10.1111/ajfs.12244

Kreander, N., Gray, R., Power, D., & Sinclair, C. (2005). Evaluating the Performance of Ethical and Non-Ethical Funds: A Matched Pair Analysis. *Journal of Business Finance & Accounting*, *32*(7-8), 1465–1493. doi:10.1111/j.0306-686X.2005.00636.x

Laurel, D. (2011). *Socially Responsible Investments in Europe: The Effects of Screening on Risk and the Clusters in the Fund Space* [Working paper]. Politecnico di Milano.

Lee, D., Humphrey, J., Benson, K., & Ahn, J. (2010). Socially Responsible Investment Fund Performance: The Impact of Screening Activity. *Accounting and Finance*, *50*(2), 351–370. doi:10.1111/j.1467-629X.2009.00336.x

Leite, C., Cortez, M., Silva, F., & Adcock, C. (2018). The Performance of Socially Responsible Equity Mutual Funds: Evidence from Sweden. *Business Ethics (Oxford, England)*, *27*(2), 108–126. doi:10.1111/beer.12174

Leite, P., & Cortez, M. (2015). Performance of European Socially Responsible Funds During Market Crises: Evidence from France. *International Review of Financial Analysis*, *40*, 132–141. doi:10.1016/j.irfa.2015.05.012

Louche, C., & Lydenberg, S. (2006). *Socially Responsible Investment: Differences Between Europe and United States*. [Working paper]. Vlerick Leuven Gent Working Paper Series 22.

Luther, R., Matatko, J., & Corner, D. (1992). The Investment Performance of UK "Ethical" Unit Trusts. *Accounting, Auditing & Accountability Journal*, *5*(4), 57–70. doi:10.1108/09513579210019521

Mallin, C., Saadouni, B., & Briston, R. (1995). The Financial Performance of Ethical Investment Funds. *Journal of Business Finance & Accounting*, *22*(4), 483–496. doi:10.1111/j.1468-5957.1995.tb00373.x

Markowitz, H. (1952). Portfolio Selection. *The Journal of Finance*, *7*(1), 77–91.

Marti-Ballester, C. P. (2019a). The role of mutual funds in the sustainable energy sector. *Business Strategy and the Environment*, *28*(6), 1107–1120. doi:10.1002/bse.2305

Martí-Ballester, C. P. (2019b). Do European renewable energy mutual funds foster the transition to a low-carbon economy? *Renewable Energy, 143*, 1299–1309. doi:10.1016/j.renene.2019.05.095

Maxfield, S., & Wang, L. (2020). Does sustainable investing reduce portfolio risk? A multilevel analysis. *European Financial Management*, 1–22.

Merton, R. C. (1987). A simple model of capital market equilibrium with incomplete information. *The Journal of Finance, 42*(3), 483–510. doi:10.1111/j.1540-6261.1987.tb04565.x

Muñoz, F., Vargas, M., & Marco, I. (2014). Environmental mutual funds: Financial performance and managerial abilities. *Journal of Business Ethics, 124*(4), 551–569. doi:10.100710551-013-1893-x

Neher, A., & Hebb, T. (2016). The Responsible Investment Atlas – An Introduction. In *The Routledge Handbook of Responsible Investment*. Routledge.

Nofsinger, J., & Varma, A. (2014). Socially Responsible Funds and Market Crises. *Journal of Banking & Finance, 48*, 180–193. doi:10.1016/j.jbankfin.2013.12.016

Otten, R., & Bams, D. (2002). European Mutual Fund Performance. *European Financial Management, 8*(1), 75–101. doi:10.1111/1468-036X.00177

Pástor, Ľ., & Vorsatz, M. B. (2020). Mutual fund performance and flows during the COVID-19 crisis. *Review of Asset Pricing Studies, 10*(4), 791–833. doi:10.1093/rapstu/raaa015

Reboredo, J. C., Quintela, M., & Otero, L. A. (2017). Do investors pay a premium for going green? Evidence from alternative energy mutual funds. *Renewable & Sustainable Energy Reviews, 73*, 512–520. doi:10.1016/j.rser.2017.01.158

Renneboog, L., Horst, J., & Zhang, C. (2008a). Socially Responsible Investments: Institutional Aspects, Performance, and Investor Behaviour. *Journal of Banking & Finance, 32*(9), 1723–1742. doi:10.1016/j.jbankfin.2007.12.039

Renneboog, L., Horst, J., & Zhang, C. (2008b). The Price of Ethics and Stakeholder Governance: The Performance of Socially Responsible Mutual Funds. *Journal of Corporate Finance, 14*(3), 302–322. doi:10.1016/j.jcorpfin.2008.03.009

Renneboog, L., Horst, J., & Zhang, C. (2011). Is Ethical Money Financially Smart? Nonfinancial Attributes and Money Flows of Socially Responsible Investment Funds. *Journal of Financial Intermediation, 20*(4), 562–588. doi:10.1016/j.jfi.2010.12.003

Revelli, C. (2017). Socially responsible investing (SRI): From mainstream to margin? *Research in International Business and Finance, 39*, 711–717. doi:10.1016/j.ribaf.2015.11.003

Revelli, C., & Viviani, J. (2015). Financial Performance of Socially Responsible Investing (SRI): What Have We Learned? A Meta-Analysis. *Business Ethics (Oxford, England), 24*(2), 158–185. doi:10.1111/beer.12076

Riedl, A., & Smeets, P. (2017). Why do investors hold socially responsible mutual funds? *The Journal of Finance, 72*(6), 2505–2550. doi:10.1111/jofi.12547

Sandberg, J., Juravle, C., Hedesström, T., & Hamilton, I. (2009). The Heterogeneity of Socially Responsible Investment. *Journal of Business Ethics, 87*(4), 519–533. doi:10.100710551-008-9956-0

Scholtens, B. (2005). What Drives Socially Responsible Investment? The Case of the Netherlands. *Sustainable Development, 13*(2), 129–137. doi:10.1002d.252

Schröder, M. (2004). The Performance of Socially Responsible Investments: Investment Funds and Indices. *Financial Markets and Portfolio Management, 18*(2), 122–142. doi:10.100711408-004-0202-1

Silva, F., & Cortez, M. (2016). The Performance of US and European Green Funds in Different Market Conditions. *Journal of Cleaner Production, 135*, 558–566. doi:10.1016/j.jclepro.2016.06.112

Spence, M. (1973). Job market signaling. *The Quarterly Journal of Economics, 87*(3), 355–374. doi:10.2307/1882010

Statman, M. (2000). Socially Responsible Mutual Funds. *Financial Analysts Journal, 56*(3), 30–39. doi:10.2469/faj.v56.n3.2358

Statman, M., & Glushkov, D. (2009). The Wages of Social Responsibility. *Financial Analysts Journal, 65*(4), 33–46. doi:10.2469/faj.v65.n4.5

Su, W., Peng, M. W., Tan, W., & Cheung, Y. L. (2016). The signaling effect of corporate social responsibility in emerging economies. *Journal of Business Ethics, 134*(3), 479–491. doi:10.100710551-014-2404-4

Utz, S., & Wimmer, M. (2014). Are They Any Good at All? A Financial and Ethical Analysis of Socially Responsible Mutual Funds. *Journal of Asset Management, 15*(1), 72–82. doi:10.1057/jam.2014.8

Verbeek, M. (2012). *A Guide to Modern Econometrics*. John Wiley & Sons.

Waddock, S., & Graves, S. (1997). The Corporate Social Performance–Financial Performance Link. *Strategic Management Journal, 18*(4), 303–319. doi:10.1002/(SICI)1097-0266(199704)18:4<303::AID-SMJ869>3.0.CO;2-G

ENDNOTES

[1] Sustainable investment assets under management represented almost 40% of total global assets under management at the beginning of 2020 (GSIA, 2021).

[2] Following Merton's (1987) work on neglected and the concept of segmented markets, a high number of investors with tastes for sustainability investments would generate a price pressure that would lead these assets to be overpriced compared to shunned assets (Hong & Kacperzyck, 2009, Derwall et al., 2011).

[3] Although Nofsinger and Varma (2014) find comparable performance of SRI funds and a matched-sample of conventional funds for the overall period under evaluation, they further document that SRI funds outperform conventional funds in times of crisis.

[4] There are a few exceptions to this type of results. Gil-Bazo et al. (2010) show that US SRI funds outperform conventional funds. In contrast, Renneboog et al. (2008b) find that SRI funds in France,

Ireland, Sweden and Japan, perform worse than their conventional peers. For a more detailed discussion, see the meta-analysis of Revelli and Viviani (2015) and Kim (2019).

[5] The downside protection provided by SRI funds is also documented for the more recent crisis that emerged in the aftermath of the Covid-19 pandemic (Pástor & Vorsatz, 2020; and Ferriani & Natoli, 2021).

[6] The US SIF (www.ussif.org) is an organization that promotes the integration of socially responsible behaviour in the investment practices in the United States.

[7] It should be mentioned that the website yourSRI applies the classification of screens defined by US SIF.

[8] Considering concerns that the socially responsible denomination of mutual funds might be more of a marketing tool (Utz & Wimmer, 2014), the purpose of social labels is to ensure investors that the fund actually complies with the stated social screens.

[9] www.vigeo-eiris.com.

[10] We excluded Spain due to insufficient data.

[11] The US SIF Mutual Fund Performance Chart contains the SRI mutual funds offered by US SIF's institutional member firms.

[12] We exclude 5 categories from the US SIF listings, namely *Other pooled products*, *Annuity funds*, *Exchange-traded funds*, *Closed-end funds* and *Alternative investment funds*.

[13] Humphrey and Lee (2011) also mention this assumption, noting that none of the funds with completed survey information changed their screening practices over the sample period.

[14] yourSRI (www.yoursri.com) is a database for socially responsible products and services.

[15] Luxembourg is an important mutual fund hub due to factors such as tax incentives.

[16] Some of the Size and Total Expense Ratio data are missing.

[17] Fund lists are unreported for the sake of space, but are available upon request.

[18] Bauer et al. (2005) investigate the returns of ethical mutual funds (relative to those of their conventional counterparts) through time and document that ethical mutual funds went through a so-called catching-up phase, possible due to a learning effect.

[19] Monthly data on total net assets of US and European funds are a courtesy of Thomson Reuters.

[20] This monthly variable is obtained from Datastream for both US and European funds.

[21] Since high correlations between the variables may induce multicollinearity, this problem is somewhat mitigated.

[22] We also tested two simplified versions of these models - one with the risk-adjusted performance variable as a function of screening intensity and the control variables, and the other adding the squared screening intensity. The results are similar those obtained with models 2 and 3 and are available to readers upon request.

[23] Considering the differences between UK and other European financial markets, we analyze continental European and UK funds separately.

[24] We do not estimate these regressions for UK funds given the insufficient number of observations.

[25] The results, not reported for the sake of space, are available upon request.

[26] We do not perform this analysis on the UK subsample due to insufficient data.

Chapter 10
Stock Market Volatility:
A Pre– to Post–COVID–19 Analysis of Emerging Markets

Ezaz Ahmed
Columbia College, USA

Md. Mahadi Hasan
Anwer Khan Modern University, Bangladesh

Zakir Hossen Shaikh
https://orcid.org/0000-0003-4733-4166
Bahrain Training Institute, Bahrain

Mohammad Irfan
CMR Institute of Technology, India

ABSTRACT

Researchers examine stock volatility in emerging (E7) nations prior to and during COVID-19 announcements using multiple volatility estimations. The correlation coefficient matrix indicates that there is a strong positive correlation between the specified volatility estimators in the pre-COVID-19 and post-COVID-19 periods. Rogers-Satchell standard deviation has the first rank, and Garman-Klass has the last position in the pre-post-COVID-19 analysis volatility estimators. However, the authors discover a considerable influence of pre-post COVID-19 on the world's E7 countries. The findings' primary implication is that post-COVID-19 volatility is greater than pre-COVID-19 volatility. This means that investors' financial portfolios should be rebalanced to favor industries that are less impacted by COVID-19. Additionally, it serves as an early warning signal for investors and the government to take preventative measures in the event that it occurs again in the future.

DOI: 10.4018/978-1-7998-8609-9.ch010

INTRODUCTION

The World Health Organization (WHO) formally declared the coronavirus a Nobel illness and labeled its outbreak a global pandemic on March 11, 2020, the coronavirus's announcement date. Global c Coronavirus cases have surpassed, and the virus's spread continues. The entire world is afflicted by this disease; coronavirus cases have been reported in over 170 nations (WHO, 2020). The COVID-19 breakout has had a discernible effect on the global economy. Different countries used a variety of tactics to safeguard their people, resources, and economies. Certain countries implemented rigorous short-term quarantine regulations, adhered to them, and isolated all economy resources throughout the country. It noticed widespread long-term unemployment, industrial breakdown, corporate failure, aviation, and tourism stagnation around the world. The population undoubtedly had problems as a result of the coronavirus (Zhang, Hu, & Ji, 2020). The new regime's focus on intraday volatility contributes significantly to the significantly, and historical volatility is slowing in the covid19 event. Intraday volatility within pre- and post-trade has been shown to have trouble determining the order of stocks (El-Khatib & Samet, 2020; Mitchell & Catalano, 2021). Significantly impacted the behavior and performance of several algorithmic (algo) techniques, implying a rise in the volatility of the effect used to price-limit stocks. Prior to the crisis, data was less useful in anticipating algos' future decision-making performance. It is preferable to have a diversified portfolio and to weigh the distribution of obtained data in light of the new market conditions (Cree, 2020).

Yes, historical events have an effect on stock market volatility and liquidity, which the financial analyst must consider when making recommendations and suggestions to the client. Covid19 established that market friction occurs as a result of information flow in the market, causing prices to diverge greatly from their equilibrium value. The findings indicate that covid19 contributes to the industry's instability, particularly in the Meals, Games, and Mines sectors (Baek, Mohanty, & Glambosky, 2020). Second, Covid19's liquidity has deteriorated significantly in the market for ElcEq, Carry, and Other (Christensen, 2020). Due to Covid19, the financial industry has been disrupted, with India's stock market experiencing extreme volatility (Bora & Basistha, 2021). The study examined the period between September 2019 and July 2020. Comparative comparison of pre- and post-Covid19 results. The GARCH model was used to determine the Indian stock market's volatility. It established that pre-Covid19 returns were higher than post-Covid19 returns and indicated that BSE and NSE returns reached a nadir during the first lockdown period from March 24 to March 06, 2020. (Bora & Basistha, 2020).

Volatility is generally caused by new information entering the market, whether it is public, private, or semi-public private. It is derived by calculating the standard deviation of stock price changes from close to close of trading over a specified number of days, which is frequently 5, 10, 20, or 90 days. Indeed, historical price volatility is calculated as a standard deviation based on the daily returns on the stock price (Oyelami & Sambo, 2017). Volatility is a statistical term that refers to the measure of risk. It is used to determine the market risk associated with a single script or a portfolio of scripts. It could possibly have represented a different definition that finance refers to as a variable's standard deviation. Volatility is a critical factor in the stock market, as evidenced by historical statistics. This data was combined with a change in stock price, which reflected the difference between yesterday's and today's prices. The movement and pace of a stock price or future contract are quantified using the change rate. This change will be seen on a daily, weekly, quarterly, and annual basis. The more the volatility, the more stock price experience; it also determines the direction of a trend (John Summa, 2016).

Numerous research publications have been published estimating the stock market's volatility on a global scale. Volatility quantifies the risk associated with a certain script in the stock market, and it is also concerned with enhancing trading profits and mitigating investor risk. Historically, volatility has been associated with disorder and instability. Few things are stable enough to avoid volatility (Fontanills & Gentile, 2003). Volatility estimation is critical for portfolio efficient horizon pricing, portfolio analysis, portfolio creation, and risk management. Numerous writers have attempted to improve the classical standard deviation of daily basis return in order to evaluate the volatility of assets (Brandt & Kinlay, 2003). Parkinson (Parkinson, 1980), Garman and Klass (Garman & Klass, 1980), and Rogers and Satchell (Rogers & Satchell, 1994) produced their own volatility estimators, which make the information available to day traders. Volatility estimators, frequently referred to as "the investor's gauge of dread" by financial professionals, have evolved over time to become one of the modern financial market's highlights.

The purpose of this research is to assess the performance of six volatility estimators (Stdev, Close-to-close, Rogers & Satchell, Parkinson, Garman-Klass, and Yang-Zhang) that use the open, high, low, and close (OHLC) values of daily prices in emerging markets (E7). For this purpose, we collected data from the event window; an event referred to as the world health organization's (WHO) announcement date of COVID19; the researcher preferred to measure the event study on behalf of the pre-post event covid19, referred to as the event window. Numerous studies on volatility estimators have been published in order to determine the efficiency and accuracy of volatile data. Volatility estimators based on ranges, such as realized volatility, implied volatility, extreme value volatility, and historical volatility (Vipul & Jacob, 2007), expand on previously published approaches with dramatic increases. E7 addressed the eminent economists John Hawksworth and Gordon Cookson, as evidenced by the 2006 PwC report (Hawksworth & Cookson, 2008). The objective of forming this group is to determine the world's largest economy; it is also expected that the E7 would have larger economies than the G7 in 2030. (John Hawksworth, 2017). E7 has been calculated on the basis of purchasing power parity. In 2050, PwC predicted that the E7 will be 75% larger than the G7 in purchasing power parity (Thornton, 2006). According to the Future of the E7 Countries Economy in 2050, China has the greatest GDP per capita in the world at 70,710 USD. Turkey's economic growth will be the slowest. India ranked second in economic growth, with 37,668 USD; Brazil ranked third with 9,340 USD; and Mexico ranked fourth with 9,340 USD in the E7 countries' economy. Russia will be ranked fifth in the queue of 8,580 economic growth countries. Indonesia would be ranked sixth in the E7 countries' developing economies growth series. PwC Report (John Hawksworth, 2017). The purpose of this study is to ascertain the impact of pre-post covid19 volatility as measured by six volatility estimators in order to identify the relationship between all volatility estimators pre-post covid19.

Impact of Covid19 on Emerging Countries in the World

COVID19 is posing a threat to people and economy worldwide; the pandemic is still unfolding in each country. The global financial crisis had a significantly greater economic impact on the Covid19. Even conventional and orthodox policies are not immune to this pandemic risk. "Emerging markets are expected to confront an uphill battle," the IMF noted. Numerous shocks have wreaked havoc on emerging market economies. Domestic containment quantifies the effect of declining external demand (Mühleisen, Gudmundsson, & Ward, 2020).

China's stock market has seen the least value erosion compared to the MSCI emerging market index, the United States, Europe, and India, with India experiencing the most value loss. Even while China's stock market plummeted just 3-4 percent, emerging markets fell 13-16 percent, and Europe's stock market fell 19-20 percent, while the USA's stock market fell 14 percent. In fact, India's stock market plunged the most, by 26 percent (Sharma, 2020). The Indian stock market fell temporarily; each downturn allows investors with a long-term horizon to benefit from the market's excellent profits. Pre-post covid19 analysis revealed that the Sensex and Nifty had indicated a surge of 12,362 and 42,273 points, respectively, prior to covid19, when blue-chip businesses such as HDFC Bank, HDFC, TCS, Infosys, Reliance, Hindustan Unilever, ICICI Bank, and Kotak Bank were taken into account. In a comparison of pre- and post-COVID views of Indian stock markets, the Sensex and Nifty50 plummeted 38% and 27.3 percent, respectively, from the start of the year. India's stock market has mirrored the pandemic's effect on investors, both foreign and domestic (Ravi, 2020).

Coronavirus has a devastating effect on lives and businesses in Russia. It demonstrated the Russian economy's reliance on oil prices. Oil prices dropped drastically during the coronavirus outbreak, from roughly $60/barrel to around $15/barrel. Russian stock and currency markets decline in lockstep with the price of oil (Becker, 2020). Brazil's economies have experienced a severe decline in the consumer goods and services industries, but Euromonitor International continues to project growth in Brazil's economies through 2020. It is anticipated to have a short-term negative effect on sales in 2020. Sales concertation does not repeat in the same way as it did in Q1 and Q2 of 2020. It will rethink the consumption of Brazil's event (Euromonitor, 2020). Mexico's stock market has been recovering slowly in emerging markets as a result of trade. Mexican banks have likewise been slowly awakened in comparison to Brazil, Peru, and Chile, and have received scant assistance from industry (Perez-Gorozpe, 2020).

Indonesia's economy has slowed as a result of coronavirus infections in IHSG and the Rupiah. Organizations have also ceased production and overseas operations. Simultaneously, the company has begun allowing employees to work from home in order to protect their employees. Indonesia was afflicted by the COVID19 outbreak (PwC Indonesia, 2020). Turkey faced a headwind on the COVID19, because to the economy's slow recovery and lack of social progress. Turkey's government has aided businesses and households financially. The economic prognosis was more uncertain; it will depend on the country's exceptional predicament (The World Bank Group, 2020).

OBJECTIVES OF THE STUDY

The current study examined the volatility of the estimator's analysis of pre-post Covid19 in the world's developing economies (E7). The purpose of this study is to determine whether pre-post COVID19 improves volatility estimators. It accomplishes so by computing and comparing volatility performance before and after Covid19 utilizing volatility estimator's models on Standard Deviation (STDEV), Close to Close (CC), Rogers & Satchell (RS), Parkinson (PERK), Garman-Klass (GK), and Yang Zhang (YZ).

1. To analyze the impact of Covid19 on the estimation of the volatility of emerging countries in the world during the pre and post-announcement period.
2. To measure the volatility estimators of emerging countries during the pre and post the announcement of Covid19 in the world.

The study applied all six volatility estimators to emerging seven countries worldwide: China, India, Brazil, Mexico, Russia, Indonesia, and Turkey (Hawksworth & Cookson, 2008). As stated, these seven countries are most frequently referred to with the term "E7."

Literature Review

The literature review depends on the two parts' first background theory of concept and the second point-based on previous studies.

Background Theory

The study's standard stock price and logarithm follow the random walk of the stock price, which appears to be an outstanding approximation. The constant walk is characterized by diffusion. This operates similarly to the variance of return; hence, it becomes a key quantity when performing classical estimating to determine the stock price. It is demonstrated that the extreme values of high and low yield the most accurate approximation (Parkinson, 1980). Volatility is a term that refers to the increase in the value of a stock. These estimators made use of publicly available data such as open, close, high, low, and transaction value. These novel estimators deemed it to be more efficient than ordinary estimators (Garman & Klass, 1980). The volatility estimator is used in this study, which employs distinct period time series for the high, low, open, and close. This model considers three separate movements: the unbiased in the continuous limit, independent of drift, consistent in dealing with opening price surges, and consistent in dealing with all estimators' variances. From historical close-to-close volatility estimators to complete lifespan series, the accuracy has increased (Yang & Zhang, 2000).

Historically, volatility was quantified using the standard deviation and then expanded to range-based volatility using the Monte Carlo simulation. An alternative has emerged: the assessment of the stock price's volatility. Now, the term "efficiency" has been introduced to the volatility estimation process in order to improve the simple standard deviation. Except for high-frequency observations, Alizadeh-Brandt-Diebold volatility estimators gave a biased estimate of the true process of volatility. Their performance decreased in the presence of other departures (Brandt, & Kinlay, 2003). This study examined the expansion of realized volatility; it was motivated by a simple discrete-time series. Throughout the literature, continuous time series serve as the theoretical underpinning. Consideration of case studies with and without microstructure noise reveals several inconsistencies in estimating daily-realized volatility. Simple properties are examined in relation to the data's asymptotic properties. The multivariate model is ended and the covariance is realized; it is concentrated on predicting (Mcaleer & Medeiros, 2008). This study described how to calculate volatility using the open, low, high, and close of the stock price. Close to Close, Exponentially Weighted, Parkinson, Garman-Klass, Rogers-Satchell, and Yang and Zhang were all utilized in the survey (Bennett & Gil, 2012).

Previous Studies

The research employs the kernel function of spot volatility to assess the microstructure noise in the data. Itô semimartingale model established Central Limit Theorems for the estimation error at an optimal rate and investigated the issues of optimal bandwidth and kernel selection. Observed that the pre-averaging asymptotic variance. The possible implementation achieved optimal bandwidth, and Monte Carlo simulations confirm the suggested method's higher performance (Figueroa-López & Wu, 2020). This analysis is based on the indices of the G7 stock markets. To begin, the standard deviation was utilized to determine the effect of market volatility. Second, provide the daily case for the G7 countries' growth.

Third, using the GJR-GARCH model, determine the effect of Covid19. It discovered that all G7 indices will trade at a discount in March 2020. Additionally, it noted the low price in March 2020 in compared to the previous two decades of data. There is only one outlier in the Japan index (Nikkei 225), which had its smallest returns in October 2008. The regression analysis indicates that the G7 stock market has a strong positive reaction. Finally, GJR-GARCH had a strong favorable effect on the stock markets of all G7 countries; this shows that the Covid-19 boosted market volatility (Yousef, 2020). The study used more precise range-based volatility; Garman-Klass volatility was used to track the low and high stock price volatility. When data are normalized by their standard deviation, they approach a normal distribution. Although high-frequency data is recognized, low-frequency data is not, which is necessary for developing a more clear and precise calculation of volatility models (Molnar, 2012).

The paper mentioned the method for calculating the volatility risk premium and risk aversion on indices. The authors employed free realized and option-implied volatility metrics to do this. The Monte Carlo experiment established that process work on S&P 500 index option implied volatilities and high frequency was appraised on the basis of realized volatility. Short-term dependencies are used to estimate the volatility risk premium, which is then applied to macroeconomic variables. It established that the volatility risk premium accurately forecasts future stock market returns (Bollerslev, Gibson, & Zhou, 2011). Estimators of volatility used historical data on the open close low high (OHLC) value.

Another variance squared has been calculated, indicating that the standard deviation has been determined. This method was used to compare the volatility of the VIX in the United States and the VDAX in Germany. The empirical analysis discovered that both indices exhibit autocorrelation, cross-correlation functions of building blacks, and a potential for variance reduction in both series. The EWMA estimator style has a greater predictive capacity than the GARCH model of volatility (Jaresova, 2010). The overnight realized volatility that occurs 24 hours a day has been identified in this research. Numerous nighttime return procedures have been used, all of which have had an effect on the outcomes. For this study, the S&P 500 index was employed, with realized volatility calculated based on current literature. To begin, a statistical test of Patton's law, which calculates the weighted average of overnight returns and the sum of intraday squared returns, is the most accurate way to estimate realized volatility on overnight returns (Ahoniemi & Lanne, 2010).

The integrated variance of a general jump-diffusion model with volatility was computed in this article. The study took use of the link between speeds and calculated the Brownian motion's duration. The duration-based assessment of volatility revealed the robustness to jumps and microstructure noise (Andersen, Dobrev, & Schaumburg, 2008). The study analyzed market risk in portfolio trading as a result of stock price and interest rate change. The standard deviation quantifies risk exposure; another method quantifies risk exposure is through implied volatility, which forecasts future volatility. Data were critical to the standard point's efficiency, whereas time series served as the grease for a variety of difficulties (Soczo, 2003). This article examined the link between implied and realized volatility for the S&P 500 Index, using data from 1995 to 1999. Estimate realized volatility using standard deviation methods developed by Parkinson, Yang, and Zhang, as well as range estimators. For implied volatility, the Black-Scholes model was utilized to validate the option-pricing model. They discovered an improvement in implied volatility and discovered that volatility accurately forecasted the future. As a result, there is no discernible difference between realized and implied volatility; whereas, in the Black-Scholes and Heston models, there is (Shu & Zhang, 2003). This study includes an empirical examination of finance. The term "range-based multivariate volatility" refers to this approach of calculating volatility. The CARR model considers the superiority of range in forecasting volatility, whereas the GARCH model emphasizes elasticity volatility. Range-based volatility was quantified using the DCC model; high and low volatility were quantified using efficient estimators. The range-based volatility model has been used to estimate the sensitivity of data outliers. The discovery of the utility of quantile ranges as a substitute for standard ranges in determining the robustness of data (Chou, Chou, & Liu, 2002). This study explored the asymptotic analysis for rolling sample variance estimators on various sets of data with a different frequency, referred to as integrated volatility, which reflects the cumulative integral instantaneous volatility in the other data groups. Additionally, effective weighting strategies for integrated volatility estimators and Monte Carlo simulations were implemented (Andreou & Ghysels, 2002).

RESEARCH METHODOLOGY

This paper consists of the methodology section into three-parts. First, data used, second, research model, and third, the method used.

Data

The current study shows that the Covid19 pre-post analysis of the volatility of emerging stock markets globally and find the impact on the coronavirus on the individual country. Data collected from Google finance (https://in.finance.yahoo.com/).

Table 1. Emerging stock markets on Google finance

E7 Countries	Emerging Stock Markets	Yahoo Finance
China Stock Market	SSE Composite Index (000001.SS)	https://finance.yahoo.com/quote/000001.ss?ltr=1
Indian Stock Market	S&P BSE SENSEX (^BSESN)	https://in.finance.yahoo.com/quote/%5EBSESN/
Brazil Stock Market	IBOVESPA (^BVSP)	https://finance.yahoo.com/quote/%5EBVSP/
Mexico Stock Market	IPC MEXICO (^MXX)	https://finance.yahoo.com/quote/%5EMXX/
Russia Stock Market	MOEX Russia Index (IMOEX.ME)	https://finance.yahoo.com/quote/IMOEX.ME/
Indonesia Stock Market	Jakarta Composite Index (^JKSE)	https://finance.yahoo.com/quote/%5EJKSE/
Turkey Stock Market	MSCI Turkey (TUR)	https://finance.yahoo.com/quote/TUR/

The present study used the event window for the data collection, methodology, and data for finding out whether such an announcement of Covid19 on March 11, 2020. The pre-post data of all (Emerging Seven Countries) E7, which is 142 days plus and minus from the announcement date of covid19, find a significant impact on the emerging stock market performance.

Model Development

The data extracted of E7 countries of world from the premier source for global media property i.e. Yahoo! network special from the Yahoo! Finance. Volatility estimators can be measured with various methods ranging from the ordinary method standard deviation to a sophisticated estimator method. The present study used the well-known techniques of estimating emerging countries' volatility (E7) with particular reference to the pre and post. The Day 0, event window has been defined as the day on which the COVID19 announcement was made by the World Health Organization (WHO). The event window comprises 284 days, the Days -142 form announcement of COVID19, i.e., March 11, 2020, and Days +142. The pictorial representation of the event window, Figure 1 below.

Figure 1. Event study periods

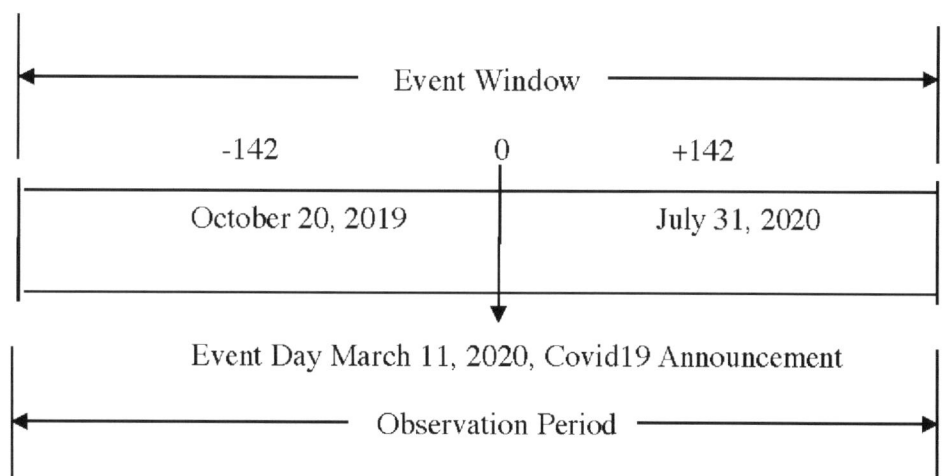

Solely this study used secondary data; the study sample consists of E7 emerging stock markets globally, i.e., China, India, Brazil, Russia, Mexico, Indonesia, and Turkey. The study aims to identify the impact of coronavirus on the volatility of emerging market stock prices.
For the accomplishment of the objectives of the study, the following null hypotheses are set:

H_{01} = There is no significant effect on the Volatility Estimator's of China before and after Coivd19.
H_{02} = There is no significant effect on the Volatility Estimator's of India before and after Coivd19.
H_{03} = There is no significant effect on the Volatility Estimator's of Brazil before and after Coivd19.
H_{04} = There is no significant effect on the Volatility Estimator's of Mexico before and after Coivd19.
H_{05} = There is no significant effect on the Volatility Estimator's of Russia before and after Coivd19.
H_{06} = There is no significant effect on the Volatility Estimator's of Indonesia before and after Coivd19.
H_{07} = There is no significant effect on the Volatility Estimator's of Turkey before and after Coivd19.

Method

As per the way path of the objective of the study based on the time-series data. There is a requirement of smooth showing the data to estimate emerging stock markets' volatility with various well-known methods (Bennett & Gil, 2012). There are several benchmark volatility estimators follows:

1. Standard Deviation (STDEV)

It measures the dispersion data relative to its mean after that calculated as the square root of variance. Which reflects the deviation from the mean? If the data set far from the mean, meaning that there is a higher deviation within the data set, the higher the standard deviation, the more spread out (Feller, 1951). In continuation of Michael (Parkinson, 1980) has given volatility definition in terms of the high and low prices of stocks as a deviation from the mean. The standard deviation formula has given: -

2. Close to Close (CC)

The Close-to-Close historical volatility estimator is a standard method of calculation of historical volatility. It is calculated by the through of logarithmic returns over a given period of observation. CC volatility reflects the historical price movements of the underlying stock. It is called the assets' actual volatility (Harbourfront Technologies, 2020).

$$Close\ to\ Close\ Volatility\ \sigma \sqrt{\frac{1}{N}\sum_{t=1}^{N} x_1^2}$$

3. Parkinson Volatility (PARK)

Parkinson volatility is the part of classic historical volatility that summarizes the price behavior of the stock. This volatility has been realized on the close-to-close prices. This volatility does not incorporate all the happenings during the day (Breaking Down Finance, 2020). Parkinson's volatility extended version of the standard calculation of volatility using the low and high-security matric price and summarized the data range. It will work more efficiently than the close-to-close volatility in the intraday (Parkinson, 1980).

$$Parkinson\ Volatility\ \sigma = \sqrt{\frac{1}{4\ln(2)}\sum_{t=1}^{N}\left[\ln\left(\frac{Ht}{L_t}\right)\right]^2}$$

4. Garman and Klass (GK)

Garman and Klass have viewed the volatility estimator using the open, close, low, and high price of the security. It has demonstrated a much high efficiency than the close-to-close volatility (Garman & Klass, 1980). The following formula is here:-

Garman and Klass Volatility $\sigma = \sqrt{\dfrac{z}{n}\sum\left[\dfrac{1}{2}(\log\dfrac{H_i}{L_i})^2 - (2\log 2 - 1)(\log\dfrac{C_i}{O_i})^2\right]}$

5. Yang Zhang (YZ)

Yang and Zhang have used volatility in the high jump opening in the stock price, which is constant, unbiased, and drift-independent. This is a unique feature of Yang and Zhang's stock price volatility (Yang & Zhang, 2000).

$$\sigma = \sqrt{\sigma_0^2 + k\sigma_c^2 + (1-k)\sigma_{rs}^2}$$

$$\sigma_0^2 = \frac{1}{N-1}\sum_{i=1}^{N}\left(\ln\frac{o_i}{c_{i-1}}\right)^2$$

$$\sigma_c^2 = \frac{1}{N-1}\sum_{i=1}^{N}\left(\ln\frac{c_i}{o_{i-1}}\right)^2$$

$$\sigma_{rs}^2 = \frac{1}{N-1}\sum_{i=1}^{N}\left\{\left(\ln\frac{h_i}{c_i}\right)\left(\ln\frac{h_i}{o_i}\right) + \left(\ln\frac{l_i}{c_i}\right)\left(\ln\frac{l_i}{o_i}\right)\right\}$$

$$k = \frac{0.34}{1.34 + \dfrac{N+1}{N-1}}$$

In 2000, Yang and Zhang created a volatility measure that handles both opening jumps and drifts. The sum of the overnight volatility (close-to-open volatility) and a weighted average of the Rogers-Satchell volatility and open-to-close volatility. The assumption of continuous prices does mean the measure tends slightly to underestimate the volatility.

6. Rogers-Satchell

Rogers-Satchell measures the volatility estimator of security price when the average return of a security is not equal to zero. Rogers-Satchell drift is also called Rogers-Satchell has used drift term, (which is mean return is not equal to zero). The results have given the better volatility estimation when showing the trending line of securities (Rogers & Satchell, 1994). The following formula has driven: -

$$Rogers-Satchell\ Volatility\ \sigma = \sqrt{\frac{1}{N-1}\sum_{i=1}^{N}\left\{\left(\ln\frac{h_i}{c_i}\right)\left(\ln\frac{h_i}{o_i}\right)+\left(\ln\frac{l_i}{c_i}\right)\left(\ln\frac{l_i}{o_i}\right)\right\}}$$

7. Paired T-test

The paired t-test was used to compare with the two groups of series. Another way, it is used where two values for the same sample (Shier, 2004). It provides a hypothesis test on a pair of random sample population means. The difference between the two means is approximately normally distributed (Kim, 2015). The paired t-statics is calculated:

$$Paired\ t-test = \frac{d}{\sqrt{S^2/n}}$$

RESULTS AND ANALYSIS

Results

Historical time series data analysis will carry the explained empirical finding, followed by the policy, implication, and amendments. This will also unlock new opportunities in a broad area of emerging stock in the world.

Table 2. Volatility estimators of Chinese stock market of pre-post COVID19

Volatility Estimators China	Pre	Post
STDEV	0.89%	1.25%
CC	1.31%	1.42%
PARK	0.79%	1.07%
GK	1.09%	1.48%
RS	0.72%	0.97%
YZ	1.30%	1.27%

Figure 2.

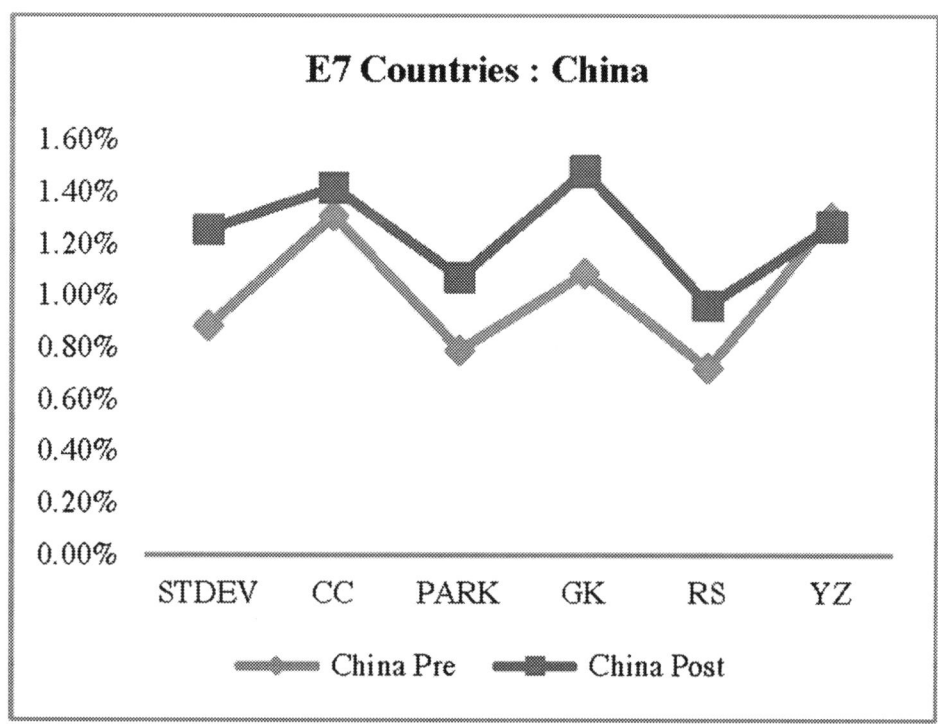

Table 2 explained the volatilities estimators of China stock market pre-post analysis. It was observed that the post-COVID19 China stock market was more volatile in comparison to the pre covid19. Garman and Klass volatility is highest, and Rogers -Satchell is lowest compared to all the volatility estimators in the post covid19. Close to close volatility is highest, and Rogers-Satchell is lowest in the pre COVID19 than all estimators of volatility, which means that Rogers-Satchell is less volatile in pre-post covid19 in comparison to all volatility estimators. RS has a perfect combination of all parameters of price moments in a market that is high of close & open and low of close & open.

Table 3. Volatility estimators of Chinese stock market of pre-post COVID19

Volatility Estimators India	Pre	Post
STDEV	0.81%	2.39%
CC	1.54%	2.97%
PARK	0.79%	2.24%
GK	1.05%	3.02%
RS	0.81%	2.13%
YZ	1.37%	2.82%

Figure 3.

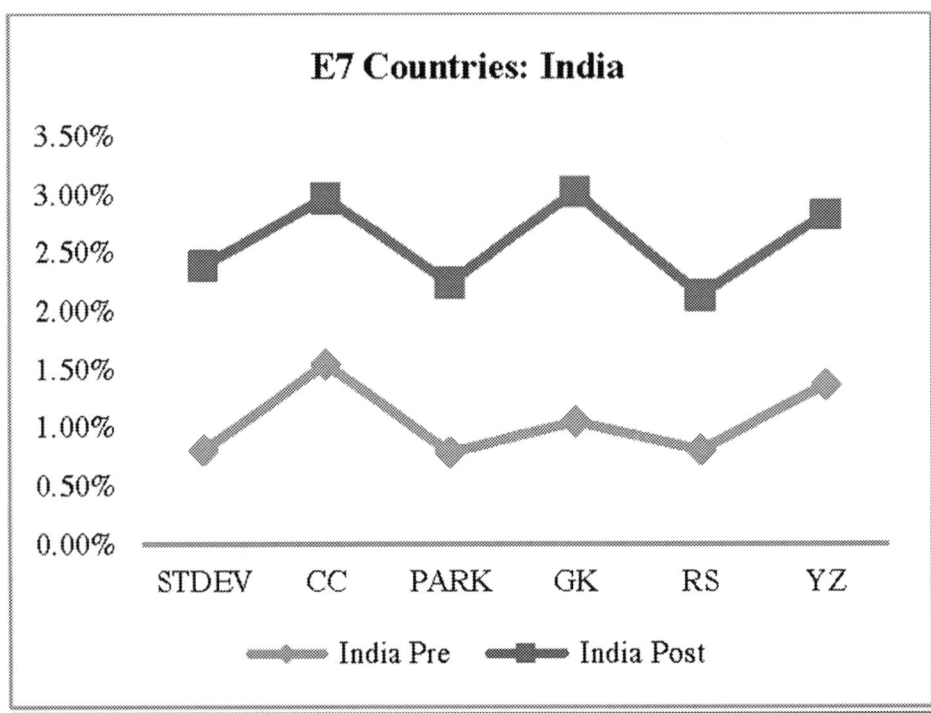

Table 3 interpreted the Indian stock market volatility estimators of pre-post covid19. It found that the post Covid19 Indian stock market was more volatile in comparison to the pre Covid19. Pre-Covid19 research found that Parkinson's volatility is less volatile in comparison to all volatility estimators. The close-to-close volatility was the highest performer in the pre covid19 scenario. Post-covid19 measurement identified the Garman-Klass volatility as an efficient measurement of volatility estimators; Rogers-Satchell has interpreted the low volatility in the post covid18 scenario. The central observation was post-COVID19 Indian stock market had fluctuated more in comparison to the pre-COVID19.

Table 4. Volatility estimators of Brazil stock market of pre-post COVID19

Volatility Estimators Brazil	Pre	Post
STDEV	1.97%	3.78%
CC	2.14%	3.77%
PARK	1.44%	3.33%
GK	2.09%	4.60%
RS	1.09%	2.98%
YZ	1.47%	3.11%

Figure 4.

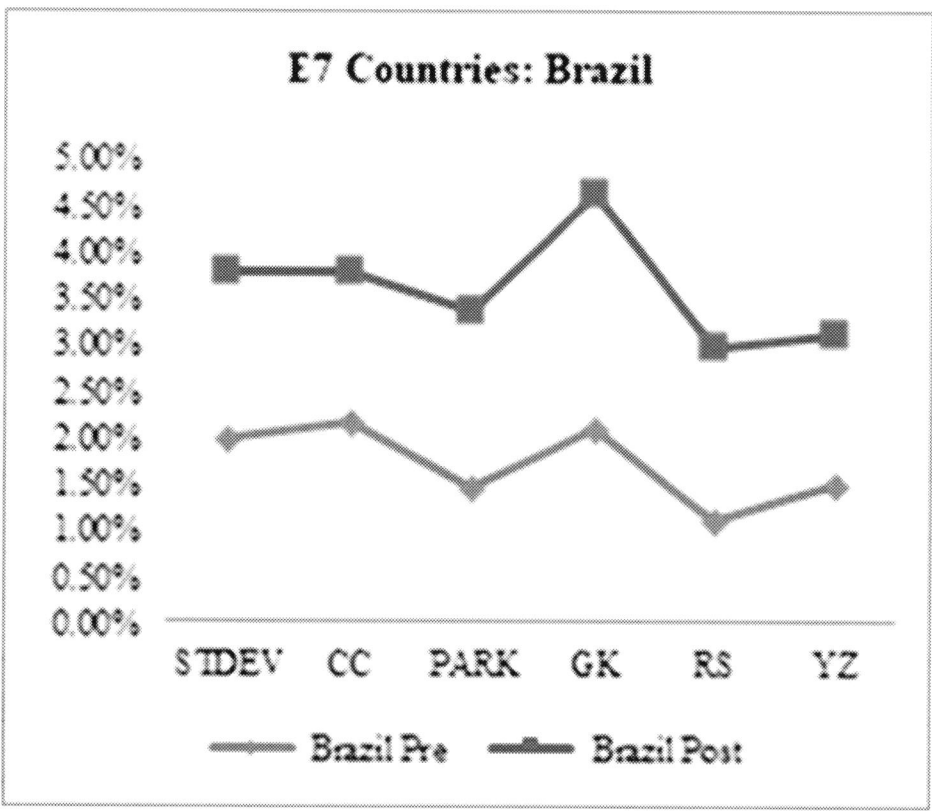

The Indian stock market volatility estimators of pre-post covid19 were interpreted in Table 3. It discovered that the Indian stock market was more volatile post-Covid19 than it was pre-Covid19. Parkinson's volatility is less volatile than other other volatility estimators, according to pre-Covid19 studies (Aslam, Ferreira, Mughal, & Bashir, 2021). In the pre-covid19 situation, close-to-close volatility was the best performer. The post-covid19 measurement established Garman-Klass volatility as an efficient measure of volatility estimators; Rogers-Satchell interpreted the post-covid19 scenario's low volatility. The noteworthy observation was that the Indian stock market has been more volatile post-covid19 than it was pre-covid19.

Table 5. Volatility estimators of Mexico stock market of pre-post COVID19

Volatility Estimators Mexico	Pre	Post
STDEV	0.95%	1.50%
CC	1.03%	1.93%
PARK	0.78%	1.55%
GK	1.08%	2.06%
RS	0.75%	1.67%
YZ	0.83%	1.81%

Figure 5.

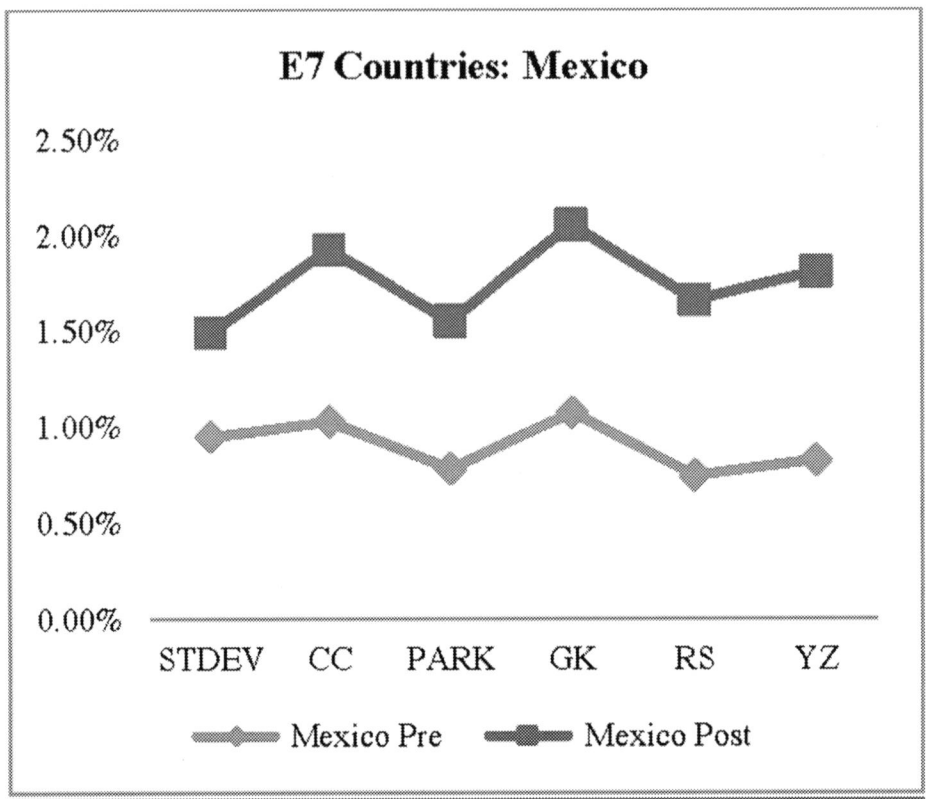

Table 5 summarized the Mexico stock market less volatile in Rogers-Satchell estimator of volatility in comparison all estimators in the pre-post data series. Garman-Klass was the highest volatile in the series of pre-post covid19 data in the volatility estimators.

Table 6. Volatility estimators of Russia stock market of pre-post COVID19

Volatility Estimators Russia		
Pre Post		
STDEV 0.69% 1.95%		
CC 1.38% 2.33%		
PARK 1.70% 2.09%		
GK 2.25% 2.74%		
RS 1.76% 2.15%		
YZ 2.12% 2.37%		

Figure 6.

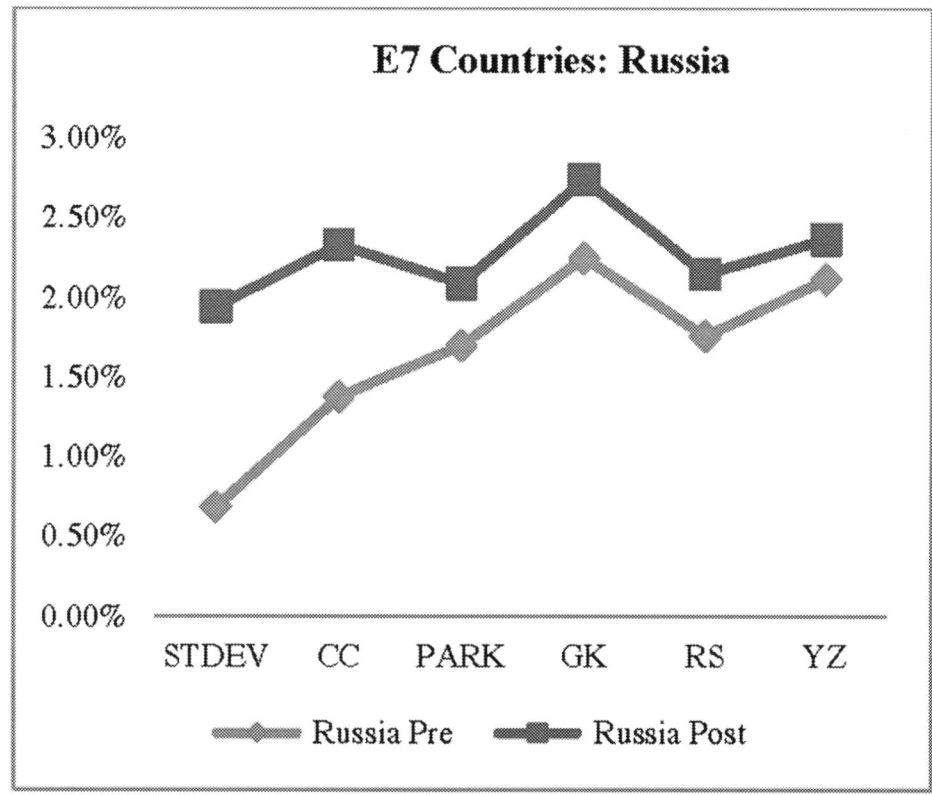

Table 6 estimated the volatility with different methods. STDEV is low volatile in the pre-post COVID19 volatility estimator's series, and Garman-Klass was the highest fluctuated volatility estimators in the pre-post covid19 data series.

Table 7. Volatility estimators of Indonesia stock market of pre-post COVID19

Volatility Estimators Indonesia	Pre	Post
STDEV	0.87%	2.10%
CC	0.87%	2.19%
PARK	0.64%	1.78%
GK	0.89%	2.46%
RS	0.60%	1.65%
YZ	1.67%	1.77%

Figure 7.

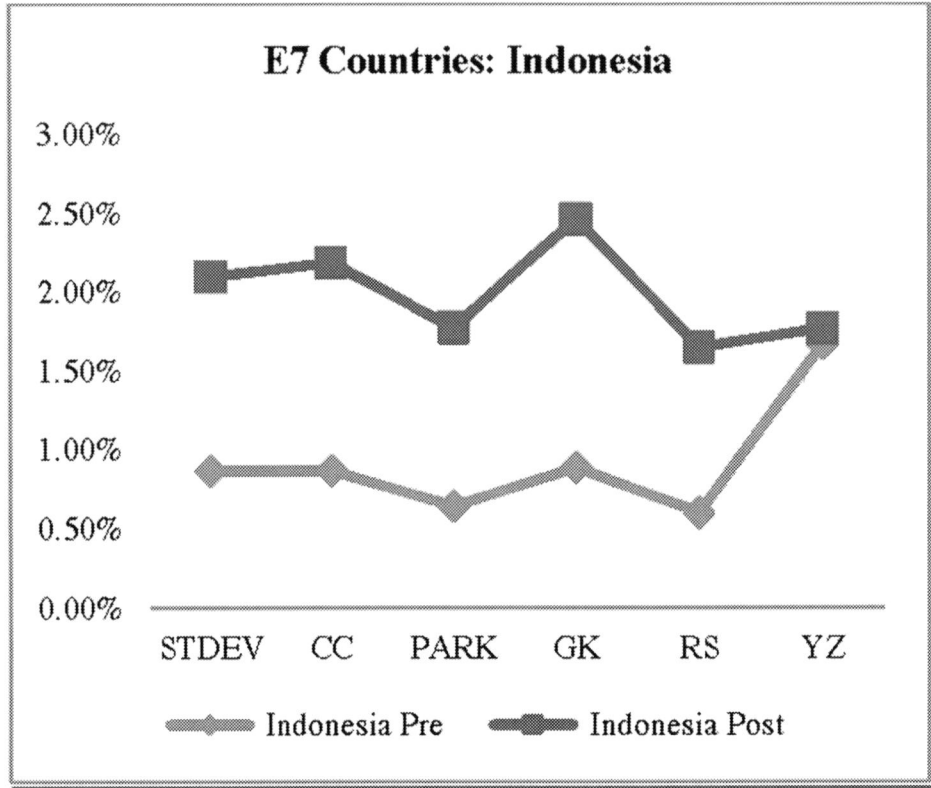

The performance of the Indonesia stock market in terms of fluctuation tabulated in table 7, the low volatility estimator was Rogers-Satchell in the data series of pre-post covid19. Yung-Zhang was the highest volatile estimator in pre-covid19 analysis, and the Garman-Klass volatility estimator was in the post-covid19 series.

Table 8. Volatility estimators of Turkey stock market of pre-post COVID19

Volatility Estimators Tukey	Pre	Post
STDEV	0.81%	1.37%
CC	1.54%	2.54%
PARK	0.79%	1.47%
GK	1.05%	1.93%
RS	0.81%	1.55%
YZ	1.37%	2.51%

Figure 8.

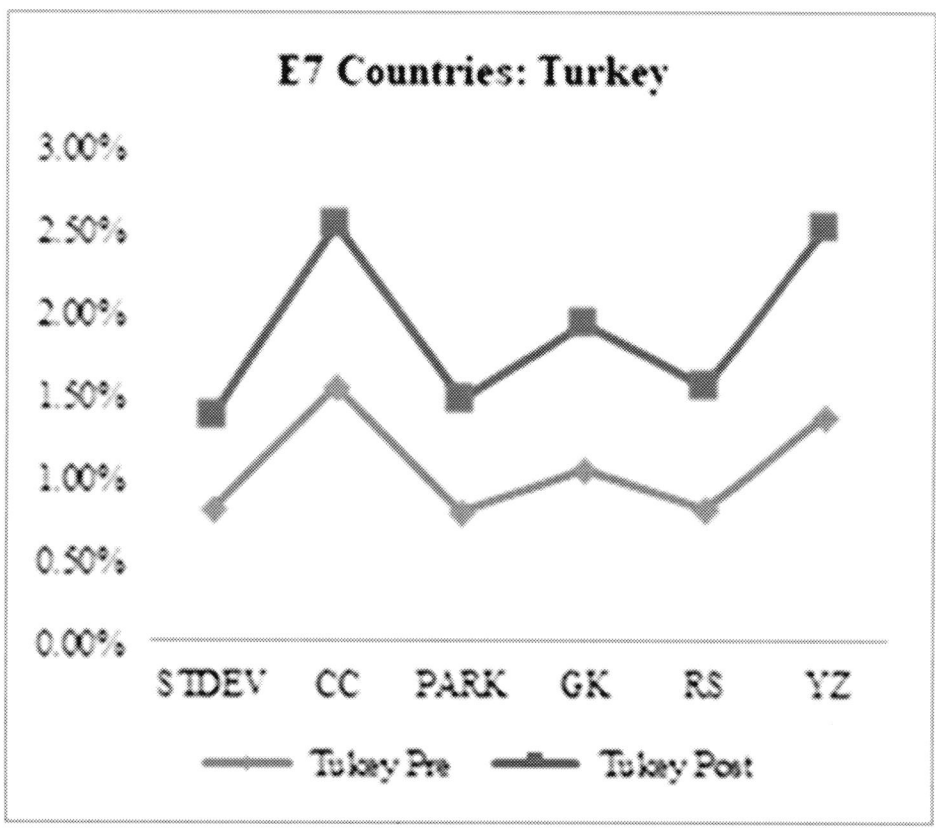

Table 8 shows that volatility estimators of the Turkey stock market, Parkinson Volatility, measure the low estimator in pre-post covid19 analysis. Close to close volatility was the highest volatility in the pre-post COVID19 study.

Table 9. Pre-COVID19 correlation of volatility of emerging countries (E7)

Estimator	STDEV	CC	PARK	GK	RS	YZ
STDEV	1					
CC	0.71	1				
PARK	0.35	0.54	1			
GK	0.44	0.58	0.99	1		
RS	0.02	0.33	0.94	0.90	1	
YZ	-0.16	-0.07	0.45	0.42	0.52	1

Table 9, the idea of using measuring the correlation between estimators is to determine the interrelationship of the various volatility estimators of pre-covid19. Here, moderate, low, and negative correlation applied to the estimators on pre-covid19 analysis.

Table 10. Post-COVID19 correlation of volatility of emerging countries (E7)

Estimator	STDEV	CC	PARK	GK	RS	YZ
STDEV	1					
CC	0.89	1				
PARK	0.98	0.93	1			
GK	0.99	0.92	0.98	1		
RS	0.92	0.92	0.98	0.97	1	
YZ	0.74	0.95	0.83	0.81	0.87	1

Table 10, Correlation coefficient shows a highly significant correlation between all the volatility estimators in post-covid19. Meaning that after covid19 highly positive correlation was found in the volatility estimators.

Table 11. Pre-COVID19 volatility estimators rank of emerging countries (E7)

E7 Countries	STDEV	CC	PARK	GK	RS	YZ	Rank in Ascending order
China	0.89%	1.31%	0.79%	1.09%	0.72%	1.30%	RS, PARK, STDEV, GK, YZ, CC
India	0.81%	1.54%	0.79%	1.05%	0.81%	1.37%	PARK, RS, STDEV, GK, YZ, CC
Brazil	1.97%	2.14%	1.44%	2.09%	1.09%	1.47%	RS, PARK, YZ, STDEV, GK, CC
Mexico	0.95%	1.03%	0.78%	1.08%	0.75%	0.83%	RS, PARK, YZ, STDEV, CC, GK
Russia	0.69%	1.38%	1.70%	2.25%	1.76%	2.12%	RS, PARK, YZ, STDEV, CC, GK
Indonesia	0.87%	0.87%	0.64%	0.89%	0.60%	2.00%	STDEV, CC, PARK, RS, YZ, GK
Turkey	0.81%	1.54%	0.79%	1.05%	0.81%	1.37%	RS, PARK, STDEV, CC, GK, YZ

The ranking of volatility estimators is requires treating differently in the forecasting of emerging stock market indices. To determine whether these changes affect the ranking of competing in volatility estimators. The order is using for determining high-frequency data; it referred to the scales using the valid latent target variable in all sample data.

The volatility estimation performance observed that the majority of Rogers-Satchell volatility has 1st rank in the ascending order of volatility estimators table 11, Parkinson, and standard, respectively. The majority of the 2nd position of volatility estimators was Parkinson, Rogers-Satchell, and close-to-close. The last place was Garman-Klass, Close-to-close, and Yung-Zhang.

Table 12. Post-COVID19 volatility estimators rank of emerging countries (E7)

E7 Countries	STDEV	CC	PARK	GK	RS	YZ	Rank in Ascending order
China	1.25%	1.42%	1.07%	1.48%	0.97%	1.27%	RS, PARK, STDEV, YZ, CC, GK
India	2.39%	2.97%	2.24%	3.02%	2.13%	2.82%	RS, PARK, STDEV, YZ, CC, GK
Brazil	3.78%	3.77%	3.33%	4.60%	2.98%	3.11%	RS, YZ, PARK, CC, STDEV, GK
Mexico	1.50%	1.93%	1.55%	2.06%	1.67%	1.81%	STDEV, PARK, RS, YZ, CC, GK
Russia	1.95%	2.33%	2.09%	2.74%	2.15%	2.37%	STDEV, PARK, RS, YZ, CC, GK
Indonesia	2.10%	2.19%	1.78%	2.46%	1.65%	1.77%	STDEV, PARK, RS, CC, YZ, GK
Turkey	1.37%	2.54%	1.47%	1.93%	1.55%	2.51%	RS, YZ, PARK, STDEV, CC, GK

Rank was the performance measurement of volatility among the estimators in table 12, which found Rogers-Satchell was the 1st rank, respectively Standard Deviation. The majority has supported to identify the last position out of all the volatility estimators was Garman-Klass.

Table 13. Pre-Post T-test of Volatility Estimators of Emerging Countries (E7)

	Emerging 7 Countries	Paired Differences					t - test	df	Sig. (2-tailed)
		Mean	Std. Devi.	Std. Error Mean	95% Confidence Interval of the Difference				
					Lower	Upper			
Pair 1	China Pre - China Post	-.0023	.0016	.0007	-.0040	-.0006	-3.41	5	.019
Pair 2	India Pre - India Post	-.0154	.0023	.0009	-.0178	-.0130	-16.46	5	.000
Pair 3	Brazil Pre - Brazil Post	-.0190	.0032	.0013	-.0224	-.0156	-14.31	5	.000
Pair 4	Mexico Pre - Mexico Post	-.0085	.0017	.0007	-.0102	-.0067	-12.39	5	.000
Pair 5	Russia Pre - Russia Post	-.0062	.0039	.0016	-.0104	-.0021	-3.86	5	.012
Pair 6	Indonesia Pre - Indonesia Post	-.0107	.0051	.0021	-.0160	-.0054	-5.17	5	.004
Pair 7	Turkey Pre - Turkey Post	-.0084	.0022	.0009	-.0106	-.0061	-9.48	5	.000

The paired T-test compares the two means that were of the same stock market table 13. Average difference of pre-post covid19 data of all the emerging stock markets. Standard has shown the difference score, standard deviation divided by the square root of the sample. The confidence interval of both upper and lower bound, a significant average difference between pre-post covid19 of emerging market stock prices. The other hand result shows that nearly all the volatility estimators show that post-covid19 is always higher than pre-covid19, and the statistical evidence shows a significant difference.

Analysis

The purpose of this study is to assess the volatility estimator in emerging stock markets in the pre-post period19. Volatility estimators were used to assess the effectiveness of the event window (-142 days, Event

Day (World Health Organization's announcement of COVID19, March 11, 2020, +142 days) pre-post covid19. Standard Deviation, Historical Close-to-Close, Parkinson, Garman-Klass, Rogers-Satchell, and Yang Zhang volatility estimators were used in the E7 countries (China, India, Brazil, Mexico, Russia, Indonesia, and Turkey) to identify efficient volatility estimators using daily open, high, low, and close (OHLC) prices in the emerging stock market of pre-post covid19. Garman-Klass and Close to close volatility estimators are the most volatile in pre-post covid19 of the Chinese stock market; Rogers- Satchell is the least volatile of all volatility estimators in pre-post covid19. It is the ideal mix of all the market's price characteristics. As a result, the high, open, low, and close were established. The Indian stock market is more volatile post-COVID19 than it was pre-COVID19. Parkinson volatility and Rogers-Satchell are less volatile in the pre-post COVID19 scenario, while near to close and Garman-Klass are the best performers (Bora & Basistha, 2020).

Brazil's stock market volatility was doubled from pre- to post-Covid19, according to all estimators. Rogers-Satchell volatility was low in pre-post covid19 data, close to zero, whereas Garman-Klass volatility was significant in pre-post covid19 data in the Brazilian stock market. Mexico's stock market is less volatile according to Rogers-Satchell, the volatility estimator, than it is according to the other estimators in the pre-post data series. In a series of pre-post covid19 evaluations, the Garman-Klass volatility estimator had the highest volatility. Russia's stock market estimated volatility, STDEV was the least volatile volatility estimator in pre-post covid19, and Garman-Klass was the most volatile volatility estimator in pre-post covid19. In the pre-post COVID19 data set for the Indonesian stock market, the low volatility estimator used was Rogers-Satchell. In pre-COVID19 analysis, Yung-Zhang was the most volatile estimator, while Garman-Klass was the most volatile estimator in the post-COVID19 series. The performance of Turkey's stock market volatility estimators, near to close volatility was the greatest in pre-post covid19 research. Parkinson Volatility is a metric used to characterize the low estimator in pre-post covid19 analysis. The correlation matrix demonstrates that the various volatility estimators of pre-covid19 are inextricably linked. On pre-covid19 analysis, it discovered a low, moderate, and negative correlation between all volatility estimators. Correlation coefficients following COVID19 exhibit a strong positive correlation as measured by volatility estimators. Rogers-Satchell and standard deviation are ranked first and second, respectively, in the ascending order of volatility estimators in pre-post COVID19; Garman-Klass is ranked third in pre-post COVID19. This article discovered that, upon rejection of the null hypothesis, there is a significant effect of pre-post COVID19 on the world's E7 countries (Yousef, 2020).

E7 Countries Stock Markets -Pre-Post Covid19 Analysis

The COVID19 pre- and post-event window, which reflected 142 days of data from the stock markets of the E7 countries. Each of the seven countries' stock markets reacted differently, as illustrated by a line diagram of China's stock market, where the coronavirus's tiny effect in the event window compared to the Indian stock market has a significant negative impact on covid19. In the initial 60 days following the coronavirus outbreak, the Brazilian stock market experienced a decline. Mexico's stock market is less volatile than Brazil's. Russia's stock market experiences a sharp decline in the first 45 days but then recovers to perform well. The coronavirus is wreaking havoc on the Jakarta stock market. It continues to fall for an extended period of time following two months of the covid19 announcement, which stabilized the market's position. Correctly, the Turkish stock market suffered a negative impact.

Table 14.

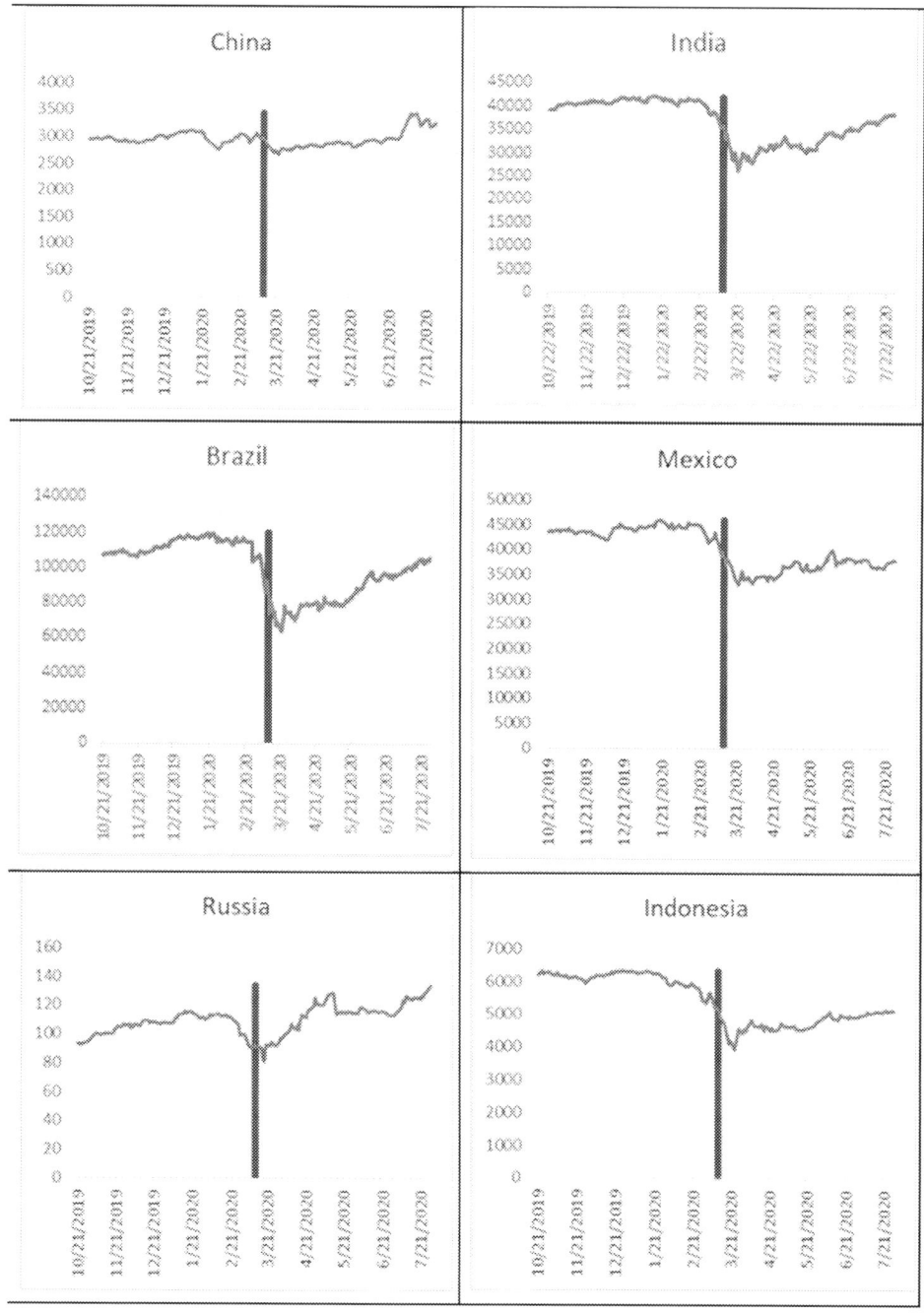

CONCLUSION AND RECOMMENDATION

We can conclude that the emerging stock market (E7), also known as One high low close (OHLC), employs a variety of volatility estimators to forecast the degree of efficiency in daily time series data.

However, to determine the pattern of up and down movements using the standard deviation and historical close-to-close volatility, which is the most frequently used technique of calculating volatility (Petnehazi & Gall, 2018). Another technique to measure volatility is to open with large jumps in the underlying stock market price. Which are the so-called close-to-close estimators of volatility? (Yang & Zhang, 2000). The statistical relevance of pre-post covid19 in developing market volatility is determined by historical volatility among the volatility estimators. It is demonstrated in pre-post COVID19 study that the Grauman-Klass volatility estimator is systemically more accurate than the remaining estimators (Stdev, Close to close, Parkinson, Rogers-Satchell, and Yung-Zhang) (Duque & Paxson, 1997). Previous volatility is more predictive of future value than implied volatility; a historical value reflected in implied volatility and open market information is critical to market efficiency (Shu & Zhang, 2003). If there is no technical error in the sample data, the correlation coefficient between financial markets will forecast the relationship (Soczo, 2003). According to Topcua and colleagues, the official response time of emerging stock markets and the magnitude of the government's stimulus package mitigated the effect of COVID19. Additionally, it noted that the Asian emerging market had the greatest impact, whereas emerging markets in Europe took a very little hit from COVID19 (Topcua & Gulalb, 2020). The study found that rising economies in the G7 countries had a negative effect on stock markets. According to all G7 stock markets, the covid19 had a greater impact on the FTSE MIB than on the Nikkei 500. All seven countries' financial markets are strained as a result of the coronavirus, with substantial external debt (Pata, 2020).

Recommendation

According to previous research, the standard deviation is assigned only to the stock market's best performing price moments. Statistically, the measure of volatility has defined the cross-checking of the various approaches for estimating volatility, which is critical for diagnostic analysis of research data. Which will substantiate the prediction of future volatility? (Oyelami & Sambo, 2017). This study established that Yang-Zhang and Rogers-Satchell models recently produced a volatility model that indicated the more efficient analysis in the world's emerging stock market. Finally, the findings indicate that the COVID-19 outbreak had a negative impact on emerging stock market indexes, increased volatility, and had a negative impact on the economy and financial system. This report presents unique data on the COVID19 pandemic's impact on emerging stock market indices. The coronavirus has claimed the lives of millions of people worldwide, posing extraordinary economic, employment, and financial market concerns. Emerging market risk significantly increases in reaction to the COVID19. Due to the pandemic, some countries reacted poorly. COVID19 overserved that the decline in GDP was a result of an extremely volatile market due to uncertainty. After assessing the nation's pandemic status, the respective government will alter the policy (Zhang, Hu, & Ji, 2020).

This study discovered that the stock markets in 64 nations reacted more pro-actively to the expected increase in the number of cases than to the change in the number of fatalities. It demonstrates that adverse market reaction was severe over the first 60 days following the implementation of COVID19. The finding indicates that the stock market reacts quickly to pandemics; however, this response differs according to the COVID19 outbreak's duration (Ashrafa, 2020). Capital market operators, research analysts, stockbrokers, professional brokers, and sub-brokers have limited knowledge of volatility estimators; this study will assist them in determining the open, high, low, and close (OHLC) for stock price analysis. As a result, a comprehension of the price stock's volatility becomes critical. As such, this article will demonstrate the volatility of indices, portfolios, and stock prices using a variety of volatility estimator methodologies, as investment decisions cannot be rendered useless.

REFERENCES

Ahoniemi, K., & Lanne, M. (2010). Realized volatility and overnight returns. *Bank of Finland Research Discussion Papers, 19*, 1–24.

Andersen, T. G., Dobrev, D., & Schaumburg, E. (2008). *Duration-Based Volatility Estimation.* Global COE Hi-Stat Discussion Paper Series, 08-034.

Andreou, E., & Ghysels, E. (2002). Rolling-Sample Volatility Estimators: Some New Theoretical, Simulation and Empirical Results. *Journal of Business & Economic Statistics, 20*(03), 363–376.

Ashrafa, B. N. (2020, December). Stock markets' reaction to COVID-19: Cases or fatalities? *Research in International Business and Finance, 54.* Advance online publication. doi:10.1016/j.ribaf.2020.101249

Aslam, F., Ferreira, P., Mughal, K. S., & Bashir, B. (2021). Intraday Volatility Spillovers among European Financial Markets during COVID-19. *International Journal of Financial Studies, 9*(1). Advance online publication. doi:10.3390/ijfs9010005

Baek, S., Mohanty, S. K., & Glambosky, M. (2020, November). COVID-19 and stock market volatility: An industry level analysis. *Elsevier Public Health Emergency Collection, 37*, 12–23. doi:10.1016/j.frl.2020.101748

Becker, T. (2020, April 15). *Russia Economic Update — Brace for the Covid-19 Impact!* Retrieved from https://freepolicybriefs.org/2020/04/15/russia-economic-covid-19-impact/

Bennett, C., & Gil, M. A. (2012, February 03). Measuring Historical Volatality. *Santander: Global Bank Marketing,* 1–13.

Bollerslev, T., Gibson, M., & Zhou, H. (2011). Dynamic Estimation of Volatility Risk Premia and Investor Risk Aversion from Option-Implied and Realized Volatilities. *Journal of Econometrics, 160*(1), 235–245.

Bora, D., & Basistha, D. (2020, August 14). The outbreak of COVID-19 pandemic and Its Impact on Stock Market, Research Square. doi:10.21203/rs.3.rs-57471/v1

Brandt, M. W., & Kinlay, J. (2003). Estimating Historical Volatility. *Journal of Business & Economic Statistics*, 146–153.

Breaking Down Finance. (2020, September 2). *Parkinson-Volatility.* Retrieved from https://breakingdownfinance.com/finance-topics/risk-management/parkinson-volatility/

Chou, R. Y., Chou, H., & Liu, N. (2002). Range Volatility Models and Their Applications in Finance. In *Quantitative Finance and Risk Management* (pp. 1273–1281). Springer.

Christensen, C. (2020). *The Relative Industry Specific Effects of COVID-19 on Market Volatility and Liquidity.* All Graduate Plan B and Other Reports. Retrieved from https://digitalcommons.usu.edu/gradreports/1470

Cree, A. (2020). *Intraday Volatility in the COVID Era: Why it Matters*. Retrieved from https://flextrade.com/intraday-volatility-in-the-covid-era-why-it-matters/

Duque, J., & Paxson, D. A. (1997). *Empirical Evidence On Volatility Estimators*. Academic Press.

El-KhatibR.SametA. (2020). The COVID-19 Impact: Evidence from Emerging Markets. https://ssrn.com/abstract=3685013

Euromonitor. (2020). *The Impact of Coronavirus in Brazil: Uneven Prospects Across Industries*. Retrieved from https://blog.euromonitor.com/the-impact-of-coronavirus-in-brazil-uneven-prospects-across-industries/

Feller, W. (1951). The Asymptotic Distribution of the Range of Sums of Independent Random Variables. *Annals of Mathematical Statistics, 22*, 427–432.

Figueroa-López, J. E., & Wu, B. (2020). Kernel Estimation of Spot Volatility with Microstructure Noise Using Pre-Averaging. Econometrics, 1-39.

Fontanills, G. A., & Gentile, T. (2003). *The Volatality Course Workbook*. John Wiley & Sons Inc.

Garman, M. B., & Klass, M. J. (1980). On the Estimation of Security Price Volatilities from Historical Data. *The Journal of Business, 53*(1), 67–78.

Gujarati, D. (2004). *Basic of Econometrics* (4th ed.). McGraw-Hill.

Hawksworth, J. (2017). *World 2050*. Price Water Coopers.

Hawksworth, J., & Cookson, G. (2008). *World 2050*. Price Waterhouse Coopers.

Jaresova, L. (2010). EWMA Historical Volatility Estimators. *Acta University Carolinae – Mathematica ET Physica, 51*(2), 17--28.

Khan, M. A., & Ahmad, E. (2019). Measurement of Investor Sentiment and Its Bi-Directional Contemporaneous and Lead–Lag Relationship with Returns: Evidence from Pakistan. *Sustainability*, 20.

Kim, T. K. (2015). T test as a parametric statistic. *Korean Journal of Anesthesiology, 68*(6), 540–546.

Mcaleer, M., & Medeiros, M. C. (2008). Realised Volatility: A Review. *Econometric Reviews, 27*(1-3), 10–45.

Medeiros, O. R., Van Doornik, B. F., & Oliveira, G. R. (2011). Modeling and forecasting a firm's financial statements with a VAR –VECM Model. *Brazilian Business Review, 8*(3), 20–39. doi:10.15728/bbr.2011.8.3.2

Mitchell, C., & Catalano, T. J. (2021, May 3). *Trading Strategies*. Retrieved from Rules for Picking Stocks When Intraday Trading: https://www.investopedia.com/day-trading/pick-stocks-intraday-trading/

Molnar, P. (2012, June). Properties of range-based volatility estimators. *International Review of Financial Analysis, 23*, 20–29.

Mühleisen, M., Gudmundsson, T., & Ward, H. P. (2020, August 6). *COVID-19 Response in Emerging Market Economies: Conventional Policies and Beyond*. Retrieved from https://blogs.imf.org/: https://blogs.imf.org/2020/08/06/covid-19-response-in-emerging-market-economies-conventional-policies-and-beyond/

Oyelami, B. O., & Sambo, E. E. (2017). Comparative Analysis of Some Volatility Estimators: An Application to Historical Data from the Nigerian Stock Exchange Market. *International Journal of Computational and Theoretical Statistics*, 13-35.

Parkinson, M. (1980). The Extreme Value Method for Estimating the Variance of the Rate of Return. *The Journal of Business*, 53(1), 61–65.

Pata, U. K. (2020, May). *Is the COVID-19 Pandemic a Financial Disaster for G7 Countries? Evidence from a Fourier Cointegration Test*. http://dx.doi.org/ doi:10.2139/ssrn.3603068

Perez-Gorozpe, J. M. (2020, May 26). *Mexican Toll Roads Remain Vulnerable Amid COVID-19; Recovery Could Come Quickly As Restrictions Ease*. Retrieved from https://www.spglobal.com/: https://www.spglobal.com/ratings/en/research/articles/200204-coronavirus-impact-key-takeaways-from-our-articles-11337257

Petnehazi, G., & Gall, J. (2018, March 19). Exploring the predictability of range-based volatility estimators using RNNs. *Intelligents Systems in Accounting Finance & Management*, 1-11. doi:arXiv:1803.07152v1

PwC Indonesia. (2020, APRIL 26). *COVID-19: Considering the potential business impacts for Indonesia*. Retrieved from https://www.pwc.com/id/en/covid-19-potential-business-impact-for-indonesia.html

Ravi, S. (2020, May 11). *Impact Of COVID 19 On The Indian Stock Markets*. Retrieved from http://www.businessworld.in/article/Impact-Of-COVID-19-On-The-Indian-Stock-Markets/11-05-2020-191755/

Rogers, L. G., & Satchell, S. (1994). Estimating the Volatility of Stock Prices: A Comparison of Methods That Use High and Low Prices. *Applied Financial Economics*, 4(3), 241–247.

Sharma, A. (2020, April 13). *Coronavirus impact: India worst hit stock market; China least-affected*. Retrieved from https://www.businesstoday.in/markets/stocks/coronavirus-impact-india-worst-hit-stock-market-china-least-affected/story/400890.html

Shier, R. (2004). *Statistics: Paired t-tests*. Mathematics Learning Support Centre. Retrieved from Paired t-tests: http://www.statstutor.ac.uk/resources/uploaded/paired-t-test.pdf

Shu, J., & Zhang, J. E. (2003, Jan). The Relationship Between Implied and Realized Volatility of S&P 500 Index. *Wilmott Magazine*, 1, 83-91.

Sims, C. A. (1980). Macroeconomics and Reality. *The Econometric Society*, 48(1), 1–48.

Soczo, C. (2003). 2003). Estimation of Future Volatality. *Periodica Polytechnica Ser. Soc. Man. SCI*, 11(02), 201–214.

Summa, J. (2016). *Option Volatility*. Investopedia. Retrieved from http://www.investopedia.com/university/optionvolatility/default.asp

Technologies, H. (2020, April 30). *Close-to-Close Historical Volatility Calculation*. Retrieved from http://tech.harbourfronts.com/trading/close-close-historical-volatility-calculation-volatility-analysis-python/

The World Bank Group. (2020, April 16). *The World Bank in Turkey*. Retrieved from https://www.worldbank.org/: https://www.worldbank.org/en/country/turkey/overview

Thornton, P. (2006, March 3). *New E7 nations will overtake G7 by 2050*. Retrieved from https://www.independent.co.uk/:https://www.independent.co.uk/news/business/news/new-e7-nations-will-overtake-g7-by-2050-6107791.html

Topcua, M., & Gulalb, O. S. (2020, July). The impact of COVID-19 on emerging stock markets. *Finance Research Letters*, 12–23. doi:10.1016/j.frl.2020.101691

Vipul, J. (2007, Nov). Forecasting performance of extreme-value volatility estimators. *The Journal of Future Markets, 27*(11), 1085-1105. doi:10.1002/fut.20283

WHO. (2020). *Coronavirus disease 2019 (COVID-19)*. World Health Organisation (WHO). Retrieved from https://www.who.int/docs/default-source/coronaviruse/situation-reports/20200327-sitrep-67-covid-19.pdf?sfvrsn=b65f68eb_4

Yang, D., & Zhang, Q. (2000). Drift-Independent Volatility Estimation Based on High, Low, Open, and Close Prices. *The Journal of Business, 73*(3), 477–491.

Yousef, I. (2020). Spillover of COVID-19: Impact on Stock Market Volatility. *International Journal of Psychosocial Rehabilitation, 24*(6), 18069–18081.

Zhang, D., Hu, M., & Ji, Q. (2020). Financial markets under the global pandemic of COVID-19. *Finance Research Letters*. Advance online publication. doi:10.1016/j.frl.2020.101528

Chapter 11
Environmental, Social, and Governance Assets:
Recent History of Green Bonds – Genesis and Current Perspectives

Helena I. B. Saraiva
https://orcid.org/0000-0003-1734-1250
Guarda's Polytechnic Institute, Portugal

Cristina Casalinho
Portuguese Treasury and Debt Management Agency, Portugal

ABSTRACT

This chapter presents a historical overview of the emergence and evolution of ESG assets and, in particular, analyses the main market trends that have been observed in recent years in relation to these assets. The authors intend to present a summary of the main moments and phases that these assets have gone through, from the moment of their appearance in 2007, the year in which the European Investment Bank carried out its Climate Awareness Bond as a test issuance. The movement associated with the issue of these assets is initiated by supranational entities with little homogeneity and no fixed conventions. To overcome this impasse, the green bond principles emerged and a process of defining the characteristics of these assets began, with a particular focus on transparency and the governance process. From this stage onwards, the market showed interest in these financial products and hence the emergence of a harmonising movement regarding green bond standards in which Europe seems to have taken a leading role.

INTRODUCTION

This chapter describes the process of appearance of the green bonds in Europe. Thus, the review of the phases and moments green bonds have gone through up to the present is related to the broader concept of ESG assets.

DOI: 10.4018/978-1-7998-8609-9.ch011

Our goal is to try to clarify how the financial reporting harmonization process can contribute to the development of markets based on ESG principles. Indeed, the way of reporting gives support and consistency to the reality of these assets and is the basis on which public trust and confidence is built. In this sense, the harmonisation process seems to be a key piece in the puzzle of the development of this market.

In this way, several reporting standardization initiatives have emerged in various regions and by various entities, including in the United States the Global Reporting Initiative (in its first years), the Shareholder Rights Directive II, the Securities and Exchange Commission and Sustainability Accounting Standards Board initiatives; in the Asia Pacific region, the regulations from Australia, Japan, China and Hong Kong, and in Europe that seems to be taking the lead in this field.

So, our aim in this chapter, is to present and analyse the specific case of the European process of harmonisation and standardisation, since is seems to be the most relevant and the most in-depth at the present time. We will follow a qualitative methodology, by reviewing the content of several official documents issued by the European Union and adopting the theoretical approach of institutional theory.

We will begin, after this introduction, by framing the ESG concept, in the Background section.

In the next section we will develop the focus of the chapter's theme, documenting the introduction of green bonds and the objectives that guided their emergence. Subsequently, we will move on to an analysis of the standardisation initiatives related to this type of assets and their issuance. Finally, we will focus on the harmonization process initiated by European authorities, under which the first proposals for EU green taxonomy and bond standard emerged, presented by the Technical Expert Group (TEG).

The European Green Bond initiative comprises a European Taxonomy, the European Green Bond Standard, the transparency, and disclosure aspects, and it aims to become a reference in carbon emission. In this section, the objectives defined by the European authorities with the aim of developing this market will also be presented, having in mind the content of the European Plan for Sustainable Finance, originally designated as Sustainable Finance Plan.

This plan involves several aspects, such as the establishment of the European Taxonomy in a clear and detailed way, the creation of a European Green Bond Standard and labels for financial products, the promotion of Investment in Sustainable Projects, the incorporation of sustainability in Risk Management, the introduction of a "green support factor" in the prudential rules of banks and insurers and the promotion of transparency and long-term vision, through the disclosure of sustainable information and the reinforcement of sustainable governance of entities.

An analysis of the market perspectives and recent trends will be conducted. At this point we observed that a marked initial trend generated on the supply side, was in a few years replaced by the pressure of demand in recent years.

The following section will address the development of the Solutions in practice and the Recommendations that are expected to be completed by the end of 2022, namely: the European Taxonomy, the European Green Bond Standard, Information Disclosure and Low Carbon Benchmarking.

The general goals of this chapter are to present a broad summary of the main legislative movements conducted in the EU regarding the reporting in the ESG asset market in Europe, identifying its most determinant moments, as well as the main evolution trends, both in terms of past and future. The subject of reporting in a form that ensures transparency and comparability is considered essential to support the functioning of the markets, as well as its further development and growth.

The chapter will conclude with the identification of future research opportunities regarding this subject and the Conclusions of the accomplished work.

BACKGROUND

When attempting to broadly frame the topic of ESG assets, we can view that the criteria for classifying them have been evolving through changes, adjustments, and improvements (Berg et al., 2020; Saraiva, 2020; Giese et al., 2019).

In a perspective of creating a normalisation or standardisation for a given sector, it is natural that these events occur (Saraiva & Carqueja, 2018), namely regarding the emergence of a set of standards that accommodate this reality, as well as the harmonisation process that usually takes place after this first phase.

On the other hand, the strong demand in recent times for funds that invest according to ESG principles makes the topic relevant, not only in economic and financial terms, but also academically. These funds attracted net flows of $71.1 billion globally between April and June 2020, despite the Covid-19 crisis, pushing assets under management to an all-time high of over $1 trillion. Already in previous periods, environmental indices appeared to be a good option in relation to international investment allocation and long-term investment diversification as an alternative to traditional indices (Gabriel, 2019).

Also, the growing interest shown by academic research runs in parallel with the massive increase in the importance of ESG data integration in the investment management industry (Berg et al., 2020; Hartzmark & Sussman, 2019; Giese et al., 2019).

It should also be considered that nowadays, an increasing number of organisations consider social and environmental factors when defining their strategy (de Sousa Gabriel et al., 2021), and when organisations do not consider the perspectives of different stakeholders, there are negative consequences for the competitiveness of companies in the medium and long term. In fact, the financial markets have been progressively incorporating new investment alternatives, according to this new management model and the value of the ESG market has been growing consistently in the last years, as can be found in figure 1. This trend also bodes well for the shift from the focus on value creation to purpose.

Figure 1. Quarterly global sustainable fund assets (USD Billion)
Source: Morningstar, 2021

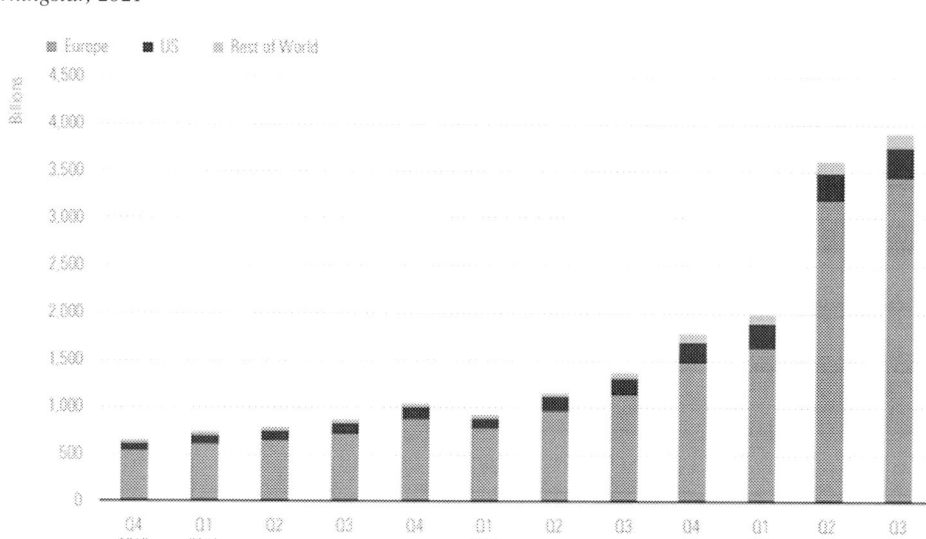

The concept of sustainable investment is broad and encompasses several more specific types of investment, such as the so-called impact investment, which combines financial investments with social objectives (labour and human rights, gender issues, amidst others); as well as green investment, which considers environmental objectives (environmental policies, external/internal management systems, climate change indicators, solid waste, water, and others), in addition to financial ones. This type of investment issues has attracted the attention not only of investors, but also of stock exchanges. As a result, many financial products associated with green investment have emerged, which also ends up contributing to the high growth of the respective levels of investments in ESG assets (de Sousa Gabriel & Rodeiro-Pazos, 2020; Giese et al., 2019; Gabriel & Pazos, 2018).

Despite much attention paid by researchers to ESG asset management and its financial benefits it should be noted that, while equally important, the issues of how to achieve consistency when integrating ESG criteria and which methodologies to use have not received the same level of attention. As a result, the integration of said criteria has been applied inconsistently and incompletely (Giese et al., 2019).

To combat such a predictable scenario, the United Nations presented in 2006, the United Nations-supported Principles for Responsible Investment (UNPRI), setting out six key themes for integrating environmental, social and governance factors into the management of financial assets. At that time, signatories to this document (UN, n/d.) were asked to incorporate ESG principles into their financial analysis and decision-making processes and to include these issues in their holding policies and practices. The PRI (Principles for Responsible Investment) initiative also provided guidance on how institutional investors could integrate ESG concepts into their asset management process.

Since 2006 there has been a strong evolution both in the number of signatories, the number of countries involved in this initiative, as well as in value, with the initiative representing some $59 trillion in assets in 2019 (UN, 2019).

By early 2020 the number of signatories holding assets of the PRI initiative reached the 500 mark, showing a remarkable increase, with an annual growth rate bove 20% (Saa, 2020), with a corresponding value of 90 trillion dollars, representing an impressive evolution in both perspectives, as it is illustrated in figure 2.

Figure 2. Number of signatories and AuM of PRI evolution
Source: PRI (https://www.unpri.org/pri/about-the-pri)

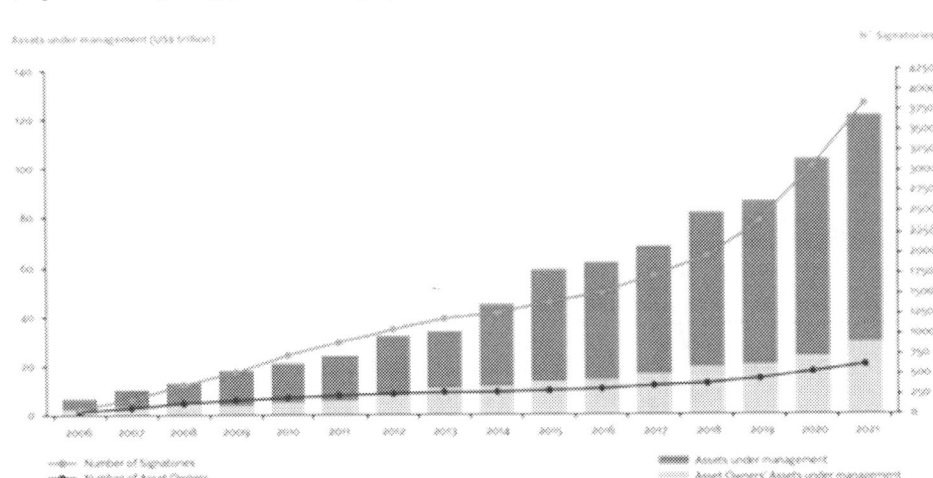

Other milestones in the evolution of sustainable investment were, in the early 1970s, the launch of the Pax World Fund, the first socially responsible mutual fund, in the United States; in the 1980s, divestment in South Africa, due to protests against apartheid; the launch in the early 1990s of the Domini 400 Social Index, one of the first social responsibility indices; towards the end of the same decade, the United Kingdom published the first Corporate Governance Code and the Dow Jones Sustainability Indexes were launched in the United States. In the early years of the 21st century, British multinational pharmaceutical company, GlaxoSmithKline, reduced the cost of drugs to treat Acquired Immune Deficiency Syndrome in developing countries due to pressure from activists and shareholders; after the launch of the PRI. In the middle of the first decade of this century, the World Bank issued the first green bond and, in the middle of 2010 decade, the United Nations formulated the Sustainable Development Goals (SDGs), which are now starting to become the benchmark from an investor perspective.

GREEN BONDS HARMONISATION PROCESS

The Emergence of Green Bonds

Broadly speaking, the asset class referred to as ESG includes green, sustainability, and social securities. Environmental, social and corporate governance investment focuses on companies that support environmental protection, social justice and ethical management practices. ESG investors value financial return; however, they do not only prioritise profits, but also want to support companies that fit their ethical benchmarks.

One of the classic ways of distinguishing ESG assets is the one based on the division of the three strands, although they can also be understood as a combination of them.

The systemic classification and definition of qualifying or eligible items is referred to as "taxonomy". In the case of classifying and defining green assets, it can be referred to by being aligned with climate issues or by green taxonomy or by the term sustainable finance, whether identifying assets that address climate change only, or broader environmental benefits, or alternatively social and environmental benefits or impacts (CBI, 2019).

As for green bonds, the history of this type of asset began in 2007 with issuances by the European Investment Bank (EIB or EIB) culminating recently with new categories, such as: transition bond and sustainability linked bonds (with returns indexed to the achievement of environmental or other targets defined by Key Performance Indicators (KPI).), and the proliferation of issuances by European sovereign entities. The market is thriving despite the non-existence of a standard, i.e. without a harmonised standard or normative.

The need for harmonisation and, even more so, standardisation leads to numerous market efforts of regulating green bonds. Several initiatives have emerged at different levels: regional, national and international, in order to lay down baseline standards to define the eligibility of assets within the intended category.

In 2010, the first Green Bond Standard was created by the CBI (Climate Bonds Initiative).

Among the the market driven initiatives, the Green Bond Principles by ICMA (International Capital Market Association) stands out. It was presented in a document called Green Bond Principles, initially in 2014 and then revised several times (in 2016, 2017, 2018 and the most current, in 2021), which contained guidelines on reporting and disclosure, aimed at market transparency.

The Principles (GBP) are a set of voluntary frameworks with a stated mission and vision to promote the role that global debt capital markets can play in financing progress towards environmental and social sustainability. They are thus a set of guidelines for the voluntary green bond issuance process to help identify the most common types of green projects and assets and to determine green project eligibility and reporting requirements.

The GBP have been planned to be comprehensive and provide issuers with guidance on the four main perspectives involved in issuing a green bond:

- the use of funds: how capital is applied to green projects with clear environmental objectives, and how the issuer can monitor and quantify the environmental benefits; the assessment of what is considered a green environmental project is carried out by the issuers themselves, although the types of projects that are financed in the market are disclosed;
- the appraisal and selection of projects: the assessment process should detail how to communicate to investors about the environmental objective, as well as defining the procedures to categorize and determine the eligibility criteria and how to manage the associated risks, and should be subject to an external screening process
- fund management: the way capital is allocated among projects, as well as its forms of internal monitoring and adjustment, also subject to external oversight;
- reporting: i.e. the disclosure of information on the allocated funds and the targeted environmental impacts of the projects, regularly updated, using qualitative and quantitative performance indicators.

As the adoption of these principles is voluntary, the recommendations obviously do not require the external screening mentioned above, but only point in that direction.

In a first stage, the market was dominated by supranational issuers or entities, of which the first example was the already mentioned EIB (European Investment Bank) issuance in 2007. EIB launched the first bond claiming the objective to promote climate protection. According to disclosure documentation issued by the institution:

"(...) the Bank promoting European objectives, owned by EU Member States (...), plans to issue a new euro bond combining innovative features focused on climate protection (...). This issue (...), is the first bond to be sold through public offering in all 27 EU Member States". Source: EIB (2007)

The same document also highlights the leading role assumed by the EU in the climate change topic, which was strengthened by the publication by the European Commission in January 2007 of the document called An Energy Policy for Europe and the Action Plan for the Energy Policy. A document adopted by the European Council in March 2007.

The EIB ESG issuance offered a pedagogical perspective or an example to be followed by other issuers.

The year immediately following, in 2008, it is the World Bank's turn to launch its first green bond, following EIB footsteps. According to Tu et al. (2020), and Febi et al. (2018), the green bond concept was introduced by the World Bank as a way to help countries around the world raise capital and finance projects designed to combat air pollution and global climate change.

Between 2008 and 2012 supranational entities continued to issue green bonds, although neither the definition nor the label conventions were established. In this regard, EIB and WB assumed a very relevant role in the development of this asset class, because outside the supra national and agency space, there was apparently no interest in the ESG topic as it was not clear to private issuers what were the benefits of the new instruments.

However, between 2013 and 2014, the launch of the GBP principles acted as a catalyst for the private sector' market. With these principles, guidelines emerged for defining the characteristics of a green bond, allowing issuers to rate it, taking into account aspects with a focus on transparency (by defining and using processes and reporting elements) and governance, namely on the areas of revenue management and impact assessment.

Thus, one can verify the relevant role that a standardisation initiative has assumed in the development of the economic, financial and social reality that it portrays. In the specific case now analysed, it is important to highlight that, contrary to what usually happens in the field of the uniformity of accounting practices, it starts from a more general scope (supranational) to a more specific scope (private entities), which, although they may be internationally oriented (the latter), are usually nationally based. Thus, in this more general context, the idea of the separation between standardisation and harmonisation regarding the evolution of accounting information (Guerreiro et al., 2015; Saraiva et al., 2015; Giner & Mora, 2001; Cañibano & Mora, 2000), does not seem to apply. In this specific situation, they do not seem to correspond to concepts that are different from each other, but rather that, starting from a harmonisation objective, an attempt is made to reach standardisation. In this case, the role of harmonisation seems to induce standardisation, as opposed to what is considered the normal route: from standardisation to formal or de jure harmonisation, to material or de facto harmonisation (Giner & Mora, 2001; Cañibano & Mora, 2000).

The need for harmonisation seems to be experienced essentially as a result of the globalisation of the economy and, by extension, of the functioning of capital markets - more specifically of investments in international stock exchanges. At this level, the baseline is precisely that of the global financial markets, with a process that would make financial, environmental, social and governance information of companies and organisations available, accessible and intelligible to any stakeholder. Beyond these aspects, the deeper goal is to go beyond the mere formal historical information, seeking, through the requirement of impact reports, to provide instruments for assessing the effectiveness of the efforts pursued, in an attempt to make entities accountable for the attainment of sustainability.

These developments pushed for strong growth in the following period, between 2015 and 2017, increasing interest, both from issuers and investors.

The appetite was sharpened thanks both to the Paris Climate Agreement and the attention the press started to dedicate to natural disasters, putting climate change themes in the spotlight. Abnormal climate events have apparently become more common and identifiable. Sovereign and corporate attention to this market raised, as knowledge regarding what a green product is and how it is defined increased. Investors can then escalate their interest, which in turn can encourage issuers to target these investors. These circumstances have resulted in increased investor diversification and generated record growth in 2014-2017 of over $150 billion, which persists, with a new all-time high anticipated in 2021.

Moving beyond the stage where it was necessary to understand the meaning of the green label, the market moved on to the concrete definition of what a green product actually is. This has meant formalising a reference to a taxonomy based on scientific research, such as the EU taxonomy, and increasing specialisation in order to avoid greenwashing or misdirected green capital.

Overall, there have been two opposing trends: the various global standards, that existed, have either converged to a scalable global product or continued to be regional with limited liquidity The market reaches its next inflection point, where stricter green standards consolidate product credibility but also lead to cost spirals and a reduced incentive to issue.

Such a fine line required a bottom-up approach, starting from the market, as with the ICMA initiative, and simultaneously a top-down regulatory standard to issue compliance with what could simply be the voluntary criteria, which if not met, could take credibility away from the market due to disengagement with the product. This top-down approach will then be examined in the next section.

The Harmonisation Process and the Standardisation Initiatives

In this context, the initiatives of the European Union (EU) have taken a leading role in the creation and development of legislation and regulations for sustainable finance in its area of influence.

In March 2018, it presented the Action Plan for Financing Sustainable Growth, corresponding to the objective of outlining a strategy to link financing with sustainability, in order to meet its commitment to limit warming to 1,50c°, as set out in the 2015 Paris Agreement. It also took on the creation of standards and ecolabels for green financial products, among other aspects.

In the same year, the expert group called TEG (Technical Expert Group on sustainable finance) was set up, which aimed to assist in the most critical areas of the Action Plan, namely:

- the creation of a uniform classification system for sustainable economic activities
- the definition of a European standard for green bonds: the EU Green Bond Standard, (EU-GBS);
- definition of benchmarks for low carbon investment strategies, becoming a reference in this area;
- definition of guidelines on transparency and reporting of climate-related information.

During 2020, the Taxonomy Regulation was approved, which defines a common language that allows the identification and classification of activities as green.

Currently developed and in voluntary application system, the proposal for Regulation on European Green Bonds was published in July 2021, i.e. the voluntary European Green Bond Standard, because the European Union understands that harmonisation is a fundamental piece in the puzzle of the development of this market and is taking the lead in this area.

In the wake of this apparently dominant position initially appears the European Plan for financing sustainable growth, issued by the European Commission. This plan was presented in March 2018 and revised in August 2020 and is based on three axes: redirecting capital to a more sustainable economy, incorporating sustainability into risk management and, finally, promoting transparency and long-term vision. More recently, in July 2021, the Commission updated and expanded its proposals through the publication of the Strategy for financing the transition to a sustainable economy, with the aim of making the EU a global leader in the definition of benchmarks and standards relating to sustainable financing.

In the scope of the first axis of this plan, the definition of the aforementioned European taxonomy for presenting concepts in a clear and detailed manner, as a means of classifying sustainable activities, and the creation of the European standard for green bonds and labels for financial products are presented as priorities. Other aspects are the incorporation of sustainability concerns in financial advice, fostering investment in sustainable projects and promoting the development of sustainable references.

In the second axis, the aspects of sustainability and its better integration in financial and credit analysis, the clarification of the obligations of asset managers and institutional investors regarding sustainability, as well as the introduction of a green support factor in the prudential rules of banks and insurers, are considered central.

As for the third axis, it is considered fundamental to strengthen the process of sustainable information disclosure, as well as to promote sustainable governance of the entities and fight the tendency to act essentially in the short term, in order to obtain quick results, verified in the capital markets.

However, to this short-term vision and to the urgency that is normally underlying the obtaining of quick results for evaluation purposes by financial markets, another type of urgency opposes: that which is required to address environmental issues. As highlighted in the Taxonomy Technical Report, issued by the TEG in March 2020:

since TEG's "(...) work began in June 2018, the urgency of the environmental challenges we face has increased" (TEG, 2020b).

On the other hand, other global institutional actors refer that this urgency about environmental and climate risks is assumed by many entities. According to WEF (World Economic Forum), for the first time in history, all the "major long-term risks by probability" are environmental, and climate change is ranked as the greatest global threat (WEF, 2020).

The Development of Initiatives Integrated in the Harmonisation Process

Taxonomy

Work on the development of the taxonomy began in 2018, when an early feedback report was produced in December of that year, and continued into 2019, during which a technical report emerged in June, both by TEG. This work culminated in March 2020 with the submission of the final taxonomy technical report. The final version benefited from input by the industry: market participants, business representatives, academia, environmental experts, civil society and public bodies.

Finally, in June 2020 the Taxonomy Regulation was adopted.

The definition of what should be considered a green project and the metrics and thresholds related to it are a major concern related to the objectives of the European taxonomy. The taxonomy gives issuers and investors greater clarity on the actual green credentials of green-labelled bonds by providing issuers and investors with a comprehensive list of mitigation and adaptation activities that qualify as environmentally sustainable for investment purposes. It also comprises a list of eligible activities, as well as a set of metrics and thresholds against which projects are assessed. For example, using GHG (Greenhouse Gas) emissions against a maximum threshold. The taxonomy also proposes an innovative principle: Do no significant harm (DNSH), with which it intends to favour or enable the eligibility of transition activities to be included in bonds classified as green. Thus, economic activities with a relevant contribution to meet climate change mitigation or adaptation objectives, as long as they do not produce significant damage with regard to the other three pre-defined objectives, are likely to be integrated in the set of activities fundable through green emissions. The five principles are: climate change mitigation, climate change adaptation, sustainable use of water and protection of marine resources, transition to the circular economy, waste prevention and recycling, pollution prevention and control, protection of healthy ecosystems.

The concern with market integrity has gained visibility, explaining the European Commission's efforts. In this regard, the decisions of the US Securities and Exchange Commission and the German financial markets regulator, BaFIn, to investigate alleged misclassification of ESG investment funds by a major German investment fund manager are relevant.

Despite the adoption of the Taxonomy Regulation in June 2020, in July 2021, as part of the strategy for financing the transition to a sustainable economy, the European Commission proposed to: study the possibility of extending the taxonomy framework to recognise activities with an intermediate level of environmental performance; develop a complementary Taxonomy Climate Delegated Regulation covering new sectors, including agriculture and certain energy activities (e.g. natural gas); and, adopt a delegated regulation incorporating the remaining environmental objectives (water resource, biodiversity, pollution prevention, circular economy) by the end of the second quarter of 2022.

EU Green Bond Standard – Green Normalisation

The green bond standard is a higher-level initiative than the taxonomy, setting criteria for issuers to launch an EU Green Bond.

This standard includes compliance with the EU taxonomy, while also requiring issuers to have second party reviews. Reporting of results is required annually and there are rules governing issuers' templates. The definition of green bond is part of the third building block of the European economic transition financing strategy, which refers to a set of investment tools, including indices, standards and labels. Complementary to this standard, the European Commission contemplates the possibility of creating other labels for bonds related to transition activities or linked to sustainability, labels for benchmarks, among others.

This final report, published in June 2019, highlights that one of the obstacles to the development of the green bond market is the lack of green projects and assets; in order to counter this situation, policy measures become necessary to increase investments in the real economy, as green assets and infrastructure are essential to achieve the defined objectives (TEG, 2019). The same report presents ten recommendations for the EU Commission to help establish and grow the EU green bond market, which cover aspects related to documentation, eligibility criteria, alignment with the taxonomy, verification by external entities, among others.

Thus, in 2019 the TEG publishes the EU GBS, recommending its voluntary application and not yet embodied in legislation. Then, in 2020 the User Guide is published, which provides guidance regarding the implementation of a market-based registration scheme for external entities performing verification. The proposed draft template links the use of EU Green Bond procedures to the EU Taxonomy Regulation, which establishes a classification system for environmentally sustainable economic activities. Green bonds constitute a limited but growing part of the total bond market with an issuance of approximately €257.7 billion in 2019 (with a growth of more than 50% over the previous year) and expected to continue its growth in subsequent periods.

Following the public consultation between twelve of June and two of October 2020, in July 2021, based on the outcome of the consultation, the Commission presented a legislative proposal regarding EU GBS. The proposed regulatory framework is based on four key requirements: alignment with the taxonomy; transparency (full transparency regarding resource allocation through the publication of detailed allocation reports); external audit requirement (all issuances will have to be audited by an external expert for validation of compliance with the regulation and alignment with the taxonomy); supervision of external experts by ESMA (European Securities Markets Authority). The aim is to create a gold standard for green issues, which will avoid the risk of misclassification of bonds, protecting the market and ensuring that genuine environmental projects obtain financing.

During the year 2021 the standard will be applied on a voluntary basis and from the beginning of January 2022, in explicit connection with the taxonomy, it will be of mandatory application.

Sustainable Finance Disclosure Regulation

The SFDR (Sustainable Finance Disclosure Regulation), is part of the EU action plan on sustainable finance, having entered into force in March 2021. The aim is to provide a standard and set of disclosures to facilitate comparisons between investments and better inform investors, as well as to channel investment into the area of sustainability. This regulation, alongside the Corporate Sustainability Reporting Directive (CSRD) and the sustainability preferences, respectively, proposed and adopted by the European Commission in April 2021, embody the second building block of the financing strategy for the transition to a sustainable economy. They represent a mandatory disclosure regime applicable to financial and non-financial companies, providing information for investors to make informed decisions on sustainable investment.

The disclosure rules are intended to encourage investors to consider the fundamentals of ESG assets and are designed to encourage them to disclose their commitment to them, making them more aware of the risks arising from ESG-related factors in the process. Disclosure is also intended to help prevent "greenwashing", i.e. the marketing of fake green products.

Investors must disclose the procedures they have in place to integrate ESG risks into their strategies, the potential impact on profitability arising from those risks, and also how ESG-friendly strategies are implemented.

The regulation introduces the following three types of sustainability disclosures: on the risk to investment posed by ESG-related factors (integration of sustainability risks); on the risk the investment poses to ESG elements (adverse sustainability impacts); on the source of the ESG criteria according to which the product is marketed (information related to product sustainability).

Depending on the rule, the disclosure will appear in one or more places, such as entities' websites, periodic reports relating to financial products, promotional material, pre-contractual documentation. Each disclosure rule has specific features, such as whether it is voluntary or mandatory and whether it is pre-contractual, presented on a website, or required in periodic reports.

The application of these rules varies between March 2021 and January 2023, depending on the specific situation that has to be disclosed.

EU Climate Benchmarks

The landmark EU climate regulation aims to reallocate capital for a climate resilient economy.

The new rules are designed to meet formal EU objectives, notably the commitment to the UN 2030 Agenda for Sustainable Development, linked to the Sustainable Development Goals (SDGs), along with the commitment to the Paris Agreement.

The new rules are part of a broader EU-led sustainable financing plan, which aims to develop policies conducive to a sustainable and climate-resilient economy by channelling investment towards sustainable efforts.

The regulation introduced two new low-carbon reference labels, CTBs (Climate Transition Benchmarks), or Benchmarks for Climate Transition, which can be seen as tools to track the transition to a low-carbon economy and PABs (Paris-aligned Benchmarks), EU-aligned Benchmarks relating to the Paris Agreement. These tools are at the forefront of this transition. The use of investment benchmarks allows fund or asset managers in this area to benchmark the performance of their financial products. The European Commission's proposal to create two benchmarks, one low carbon and one positive carbon impact, should provide clarity for investors regarding comparative performance.

The objectives of these benchmarks are as follows: to provide a meaningful level of comparability while allowing benchmark administrators flexibility in designing their framework; to provide investors with an appropriate tool according to their investment strategy; to increase transparency; to prevent greenwashing.

The CTB and PAB Regulations provide the minimum requirements for a benchmark to be labelled as a CTB or a PAB.

If the legislative text is taken into account, the Commission will review the minimum standards for benchmarks by 31 December 2022 to ensure consistency with the EU taxonomy.

Evolution Summary

According to what has already been referred to in this work, the summary of the main steps concerning the normative solution found by the EU, which underpins the development of a standardisation process on the ESG assets theme, is based on a notion of harmonisation of the information related to these assets.

This normative solution frames initiatives that have already occurred and others yet to occur in the near future. Currently, an initiative that will serve to systematically support the reporting and disclosure of information on green bonds is being developed. The main stages referring to definition of eligible activities, setting of standards and labels, and reporting and disclosure of information described in the previous sub-paragraphs and are pictured in figure 3.

Figure 3. Main milestones in the harmonisation process
Source: own

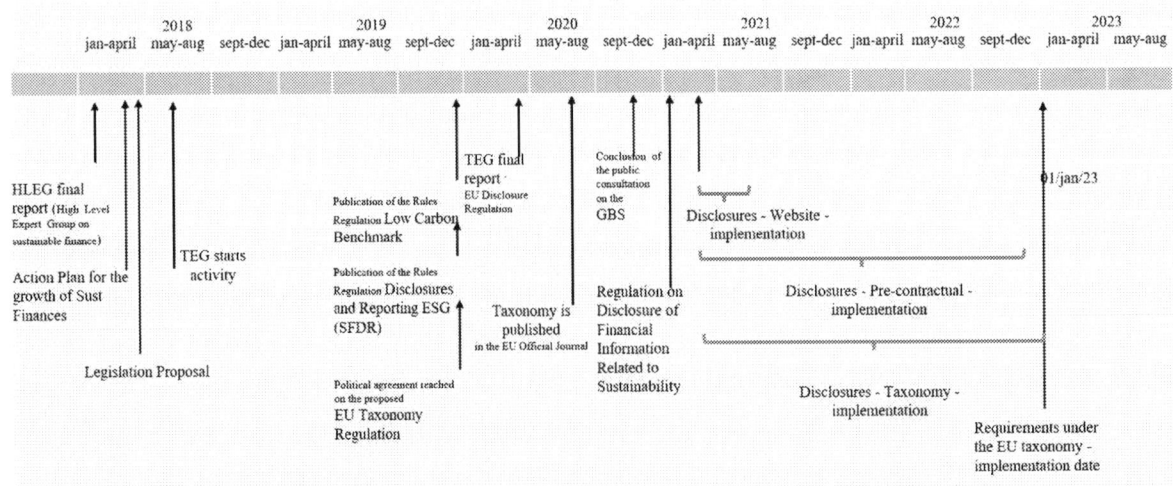

Environmental, Social, and Governance Assets

The specific harmonisation process and the underlying standardisation process will last around one five-year period, provided only the steps related to more specific initiatives in the scope of the standardisation phase that is intended to support harmonisation are considered.

In July 2021, the European Commission reaffirmed and detailed its strategy for financing the transition to a sustainable economy, relying on the development of new and ongoing initiatives. The European Commission wishes to play a key role in defining global standards for sustainable investment, promoting this market and mobilising public and private funds for the development of the necessary economic activities. Consequently, it aims to deepen the work done so far, which encompasses developing a more comprehensive taxonomy and promoting the financing of intermediary activities on the road to sustainability. With a view to strengthening economic and financial resilience to sustainability risks, it will also propose amendments to the Capital Requirements Regulation (CRR II), Capital Requirements Directive (CRD V) and Solvency II Directive to ensure the systematic integration of sustainability risks into the risk management systems of banks and insurers. It also intends by 2022 to assess the need to review investment funds' and investors' fiduciary duties to reflect the sustainability impact in the investment decision-making process. It will monitor the risks of green money laundering and assess the current set of supervisory and enforcement tools available to ensure that supervisory powers, capacities and obligations are fit for purpose.

The European Commission has taken a global lead in facilitating the establishment of an international architecture that includes robust international governance, a robust set of rules and a monitoring framework. Indeed, despite the successful proliferation of green, social or sustainable bond issues and growing demand for investment funds with an ESG dimension, the development of this market requires clear standards for issuers, for the investment decision process and robust rules on transparent reporting by investors and issuers, in a concomitant effort to prevent greenwashing.

DISCUSSION THROUGH THE LENS OF INSTITUTIONAL THEORY

According to Nee and Ingram (1998), the existence of institutions is important because they contribute to reduce uncertainty in human interactions and help solve the problem of coordination, especially in modern economies in which specialisation and the division of labour have given rise to the need to sustain complex exchanges over time and across space (Nee and Ingram, 1998, p.20-21).

Thus, the fact that the European Union is assuming a relevant role in the process of fostering accounting harmonisation can be explained by its intention to promote development and ensure a future with fewer risks for all its constituent countries, despite its expertise in this area of harmonisation is rather secondary. This appears to be of great importance in view of its main objective or mission.

On the other hand, it should be considered that currently there is not an international organisation that claims this specialisation and the corresponding task of division of labour. In this sense, the EU has assumed itself as the main standard-setting and harmonising organisation, and there is no other organisation with the same intent or purpose, as has happened with other accounting harmonisation processes, as Fritz and Lamlle (2003) point out in other convergence processes.

Thus, to date, the EU has taken on a mission that was not institutionally assigned to any other organisation.

In other words, despite the fact that it is not a traditional standard-setting entity, there currently seems to be a process of legitimisation favourable to the EU, opening up space for this entity to assume and implement the idea of specialisation and division of labour referred to by Nee and Ingram (1998).

SOLUTIONS IN PRACTICE AND RECOMMENDATIONS

The main concerns of capital market participants regarding the development of the environmental, social and governance market relate to the lack of common standards in structuring products and in understanding and gaining knowledge about these standards.

The absence of commonly accepted and understood rules and standards carries the risk that the products or their structure may not be adequate for the intended purpose. Taking as an example of these challenges, some recent situations in the capital market may be referred: that of banks, pressured by the double requirement of, on the one hand, having to finance sustainable activities and, on the other hand, having to count on capital financing instruments that allow the absorption of losses in insolvency risk. These entities face difficulties in structuring instruments with this double characteristic, being certain that yet other difficulties are added to these, given the obligations to allocate the funds obtained to green projects or portfolios, having also to ensure that the financing obtained through green instruments may be allocated to any sector in case of insolvency.

In the case of AT1 or Tier2 equity instruments, how to ensure that funds are allocated only to green projects, as they are leveraged instruments that leverage credit well beyond the amount issued (reference for reporting the allocation of funds). At the same time, European banks face increasing disclosure requirements. Indeed, asset managers are under pressure to disclose the alignment of their portfolios with the 2015 Paris Agreement targets while the EBA (European Banking Authority) designs a green asset ratio to measure the alignment of banks' assets with the Taxonomy Regulation. Even though the main issuers of green assets are sovereigns, the green asset ratio designed by the EBA, in a first version, does not include these financial instruments, shrinking the portfolio of potential investments available to banks.

Instruments aligned with ESG requirements remain relatively customised, creating difficulties in assessment and demands for greater transparency in fund allocation and impact reporting. Despite efforts to create generally applicable standards for structuring instruments with these characteristics and the emergence and consolidation of independent specialised entities for issuing programme analysis, fund allocation and impact reporting, some investors and issuers still shy away from the market due to the relative lack of standardisation. The establishment of common rules and standards, in which the European Commission has been striving, will be an important driver for its expansion.

Finally, fund allocation scrutiny, on both the issuer and investor side, has become more demanding. For example, in August 2021, the SEC in the US and BaFin in Germany opened investigation proceedings into DWS, a major financial asset manager, based on accusations of incorrect or inflated classification of ESG assets under management.

Similar accusations, including money laundering, have come to light following investigations by independent bodies. This phenomenon highlights both the increasing value attached to ESG-labelled assets and the relative difficulty of verifying the quality of ratings, imposing greater reporting and transparency obligations, which clearly benefit from a consolidated and global regulatory framework.

The solution, in practice, relies in those activities that are expected to be concluded by the end of 2022, namely as those regarding to the European Taxonomy, the European Green Bond Standard, the information Disclosure and the Low Carbon Benchmarking, that can bring clarity and some certainty to a market at an early stage of development.

FUTURE RESEARCH DIRECTIONS

The major effort to address the environmental challenge and restore social order carried out by the EU shows that it has clearly taken the lead with the development of ambitious policies, culminating in the elements of harmonisation and standardisation of information underpinning the reality of ESG assets and green bonds (Taxonomy, Green Deal, etc...). In this way, the EU is taking on, from the outset, the establishment of global standards to be implemented.

EU legislation thus seems to contribute to boost the fiduciary duties of institutional investors and asset managers, requiring them to act in the interest of their beneficiaries.

However, there are also other initiatives implemented in other regions, such as the US, the UK and major Asian economies, along with industry initiatives.

Policy and regulatory frameworks are changing to require the incorporation of ESG, in various geographies. Consequently, ESG regulations are becoming more of a focal point, with regulators coming up with new rules to govern the ESG space.

The limitations of the current work may be overcome in future analyses, namely regarding the degree and depth of use and application of the standards in the near future. Also, the fact that this text focuses on a subject that has a very generic and broad scope may be overcome in future works on more specific and partial aspects related to the subject.

Another difficulty relates to the fact that the standardisation process is not yet fully completed. It will also be important to monitor and analyse how the current standardisation and harmonisation initiatives will be transposed in terms of creation of a securities benchmark (establishing a benchmark in terms of legal and financial conditions and implications for the pricing model); how the sovereign and corporate debt markets will implement the regulatory framework, promoting its dissemination and stabilisation; or, how the efforts to establish a global standard will evolve versus the possibility of market fragmentation through the proliferation of national or regional models.

As for future research opportunities on the topic, they are vast, since this is an initial work on the subject, requiring, in several aspects, the deepening of the general framework identified.

The existence of other initiatives to attempt standardisation in other countries can and should also be analysed, as should the various pursued solutions be compared.

CONCLUSION

In the context of changing global dynamics, ESG factors have attracted much attention from investors and issuers. ESG investment has become part of the mainstream investment universe. With the development of ESG markets, there is considerable pressure from all stakeholders for greater transparency. Investors are engaging with companies on ESG issues, and companies are adapting their products and processes to ESG criteria.

There are also signs that the consideration of sustainability factors in capital allocation decisions may result in a better assessment of the risk and return profiles of financial products.

The incorporation of ESG assets and concepts has now become an investment norm. The concept of responsible investment is increasingly widely embraced. The PRI currently has over 2,500 signatories and the annual disclosure of these signatories demonstrates significant progress in implementing the Principles and shows that responsible investment criteria are increasingly being applied to investment in general. Incorporating ESG issues into investment analysis and decision making has become a centre piece of the investment process.

This exploratory work and review of the state of the art regarding the EU legislative initiative concludes that, as it is traditionally verified in the European space, also in this thematic we are witnessing a governmental and legislative based initiative to boost a standardisation and harmonisation process.

What is innovative in this case is that the harmonisation process induces a first line standardisation process. We intend with this last expression to highlight that, as a rule, there were no standards of a national nature prior to more general standards. What will be implemented next may be precisely what will shape the harmonisation process, when cascading the EU GBS to the national legislations of the countries integrating the European area. In this sense, this is an innovative process as far as accounting information is concerned.

In other financial and accounting harmonisation scenarios, the market induced harmonisation, building on standardisation previously developed in different countries or regions. In the current case, the prospect of the need for harmonisation has had an effect on standardisation processes and, even more so, on the evolution of markets.

On the other hand, it remains to be questioned whether time will effectively confirm the continued preponderance of the EU's role in this global harmonization process, or whether, from a certain point in time, an entity exclusively dedicated to this issue will stand out. If the emergence of a third entity, or set of entities, happens, this will be in line with what some authors of the new institutional theory advocate. The discovery of explanations in the way in which institutional structures respond to the conflict between government and economy, in order to privilege some interests while demobilising others. This process, thus, reveals an old tradition in political science, which attributes importance to formal political institutions, but developing a broader concept, in the sense of assessing *which institutions are important* and *how they are important* (Hall and Taylor, 1996, p.6).

REFERENCES

Berg, F., Fabisik, K., & Sautner, Z. (2020). *Rewriting History II: The (Un)Predictable Past of ESG Ratings.* European Corporate Governance Institute – Finance Working Paper 708/2020. doi:10.2139/ssrn.3722087

Cañibano, L., & Mora, A. (2000). Evaluating the statistical significance of de facto accounting harmonization: A study of European global players. *European Accounting Review, 9*(3), 349–369. doi:10.1080/09638180020017113

CBI - Climate Bonds Initiative. (2019). *Growing green bond markets: The development of taxonomies to identify green assets.* Available at: https://www.climatebonds.net/files/reports/policy_taxonomy_briefing_conference.pdf

de Sousa Gabriel, V. M., Miralles-Quirós, M. M., & Miralles-Quirós, J. L. (2021). Shades between Black and Green Investment: Balance or Imbalance? *Sustainability*, *13*(9), 5024. doi:10.3390u13095024

de Sousa Gabriel, V. M., & Rodeiro-Pazos, D. (2020). Environmental Investment Versus Traditional Investment: Alternative or Redundant Pathways? *Organization & Environment*, *33*(2), 245–261. doi:10.1177/1086026618783749

EIB - European Investment Bank. (2007). *EPOS II – The "Climate Awareness Bond" EIB promotes climate protection via pan-EU public offering*. Anúncio para fins publicitários. Available at: https://www.unicreditgroup.eu/content/dam/unicreditgroup/documents/inc/press-and-media/FOR_DISTRIBUTION_MAY_22_2007_EPOSeng.pdf, consulted at July 05, of 2021.

Febi, W., Schafer, D., Stephan, A., & Sun, C. (2018). The impact of liquidity risk on the yield spread of green bonds. *Finance Research Letters*, *27*, 53–59. doi:10.1016/j.frl.2018.02.025

Fritz, S., & Lammle, C. (2003). *The International Harmonization Process of accounting Standards*. Avdelning.

Gabriel, V. (2019). Environmentally sustainable investment: Dynamics between global thematic indices. *Cuadernos de Gestión*, *19*(1), 41–62. doi:10.5295/cdg.150545vg

Gabriel, V., & Pazos, D. (2018). Do Short- and Long-Term Environmental Investments Follow the Same Path? *Corporate Social Responsibility and Environmental Management*, *25*(1), 14–28. doi:10.1002/csr.1437

Giese, G., Lee, L., Melas, D., Nagy, Z., & Nishikawa, L. (2019, Spring). Performance and Risk Analysis of Index-Based ESG Portfolios. *The Journal of Index Investing*, *9*(4), 1–12. doi:10.3905/jii.2019.9.4.046

Giner, B., & Mora, A. (2001). The accounting harmonization process in Europe: Analysis of the relation between accounting research and the evolution of the economic reality. *Revista Española de Financiación y Contabilidad*, *30*(107), 103–128.

Guerreiro, M. S., Rodrigues, L. L., & Craig, R. (2015). Institutional Change of Accounting Systems: The Adoption of a Regime of Adapted International Financial Reporting Standards. European Accounting Review. *European Accounting Association*, *24*(2), 379–409. doi:10.1080/09638180.2014.887477

Hall, P. A., & Taylor, R. C. R. (1996). *Political Science and the Three New Institutionalisms*. Max-Planck-Institut für Gesellschaftsforschung, Discussion Paper 96/6.

Hartzmark, S. M., & Sussman, A. B. (2019). Do investors value sustainability? A natural experiment examining ranking and fund flows. *The Journal of Finance*, *74*(6), 2789–2837. doi:10.1111/jofi.12841

Morningstar. (2021). *Global Sustainable Fund Flows Report*. Available at: https://www.morningstar.com/content/dam/marketing/shared/pdfs/Research/Global-ESG-Q3-2021-Flows.pdf?utm_source=eloqua&utm_medium=email&utm_campaign=none&utm_content=27223

Nee, V., & Ingram, P. (1998). Embeddedness and Beyond: Instituitions, Exchange and Social Structure. In The New Institutionalism in Sociology. Russel Sage Foundation.

Regulation (EU) 2020/852 of the European Parliament and of the Council of 18 June 2020 on the establishment of a framework to facilitate sustainable investment and amending Regulation (EU) 2019/2088. PE/20/2020/INIT, OJ L 198, 22.6.2020, p. 13–43

Saa, L. (2020). *PRI welcomes 500th asset owner signatory*. PRI BLOG. Available at: https://www.unpri.org/pri-blog/pri-welcomes-500th-asset-owner-signatory/5367.article

Saraiva, H. (2020). The disclosure of non-financial information and the possibilities of contribution from management accounting. *Revista de la Asociación Española de Contabilidad y Administración, 131*, 61–62.

Saraiva, H. I. B., & Carqueja, H. O. (2018). Ensaio sobre o papel da organização das nações unidas no processo de harmonização contabilística - iniciativas durante o período 1953-2009. De Computis. *Revista Española de Historia de la Contabilidad, 15*(2), 108–132. doi:10.26784/issn.1886-1881.v15i2.336

TEG - EU Technical Expert Group on Sustainable Finance. (2019). *Financing a Sustainable European Economy – Report on EU Greenbond Standard - TEG Report Proposal for an EU Green Bond Standard.* Available at: https://ec.europa.eu/info/sites/info/files/business_economy_euro/banking_and_finance/documents/190618-sustainable-finance-teg-report-green-bond-standard_en.pdf

TEG - EU Technical Expert Group on Sustainable Finance. (2020a). *Financing a Sustainable European Economy – Technical Report - Taxonomy: Final report of the Technical Expert Group on Sustainable Finance.* Available at: https://ec.europa.eu/info/sites/info/files/business_economy_euro/banking_and_finance/documents/200302-sustainable-finance-teg-final-report-taxonomy-annexes_en.pdf

TEG - EU Technical Expert Group on Sustainable Finance. (2020b). *Taxonomy: Final report of the Technical Expert Group on Sustainable Finance.* Available at: https://ec.europa.eu/info/sites/default/files/business_economy_euro/banking_and_finance/documents/200309-sustainable-finance-teg-final-report-taxonomy_en.pdf

Tu, C. A., Rasoulinezhad, E., & Sarker, T. (2020). Investigating solutions for the development of a green bond market: Evidence from analytic hierarchy process. *Finance Research Letters, 34*, 101457. doi:10.1016/j.frl.2020.101457

WEF – Worl Economic Forum. (2020). *Global Risks Report 2020*. Insight Report in partnership with Marsh & McLennan and Zurich Insurance Group. Available at: https://www.weforum.org/reports/the-global-risks-report-2020

ADDITIONAL READING

Coqueret, G. (2021). Perspectives in ESG equity investing. Available at SSRN: https://ssrn.com/abstract=3715753 or http://dx.doi.org/ doi:10.2139/ssrn.3715753

Eccles, R. G., Lee, L.-E., & Stroehle, J. C. (2020). The Social Origins of ESG: An Analysis of Innovest and KLD. *Organization & Environment, 33*(4), 575–596. doi:10.1177/1086026619888994

Environmental, Social, and Governance Assets

EU Technical Expert Group (TEG) on Sustainable Finance. (2020). Financing a Sustainable European Economy –Taxonomy Report: Technical Annex - Updated methodology & Updated Technical Screening Criteria. March. Available at: https://ec.europa.eu/info/sites/info/files/business_economy_euro/banking_and_finance/documents/200309-sustainable-finance-teg-final-report-taxonomy_en.pdf (accessed on March 10, 2021).

EU Technical Expert Group (TEG) on Sustainable Finance. (2020). Financing a Sustainable European Economy – Usability Guide EU greenbond standard - usability guide teg proposal for an EU green bond standard. March. Available at: https://ec.europa.eu/info/sites/info/files/business_economy_euro/banking_and_finance/documents/190618-sustainable-finance-teg-report-green-bond-standard_en.pdf (accessed on March 10, 2021).

KEY TERMS AND DEFINITIONS

ESG Assets: Environmental, Social and Governance assets are nowadays considered by organisations, attaining to social and environmental factors when defining their strategy. On the other hand, financial markets have progressively incorporated new investment alternatives, in accordance with this new management model.

European Taxonomy: Defines what should be considered a green project and the metrics and thresholds related to it. The definition of the taxonomy gives issuers and investors greater clarity about the actual green credentials of green-labelled bonds by providing issuers and investors with a comprehensive list of mitigation and adaptation activities that qualify as environmentally sustainable for investment purposes, as well as a list of eligible activities, and a set of metrics and thresholds against which many can be judged, measured using GHG (Greenhouse Gas) emissions, according to a defined maximum threshold.

Green Bond Standard: Is a higher-level initiative than the taxonomy, setting criteria for issuers to issue an EU Green Bond. This standard includes adherence to the EU taxonomy, while also requiring issuers to have external entity reviews. Reporting of results is required annually and there are rules governing issuers' templates.

Green Bonds: The four main perspectives involved in issuing a green bond are the use of funds (how capital is applied to green projects with clear environmental objectives, and how the issuer can monitor and quantify the environmental benefits); the evaluation and selection of projects (communicate to investors about the environmental objective, defining the procedures to categorize and determine the eligibility criteria and to manage associated risks); the fund management; and reporting (disclosure of information on the funds applied and the desired environmental impacts of the projects).

Harmonisation Process: Harmonisation is the process of bringing international standards into some sort of agreement so that the financial statement from different countries are prepared according to a common set of principles of measurement and disclosure.

Chapter 12
Managing the Current Risks of Companies:
The Applicability of Tax Risk Management

Feride Bakar Türegün
https://orcid.org/0000-0002-2611-292X
Bursa Uludag University, Turkey

Adnan Gerçek
https://orcid.org/0000-0002-9495-2429
Bursa Uludag University, Turkey

ABSTRACT

The taxation power of governments affects companies' business activities. For this reason, the legal limit of tax law must be known by taxpayers. Uncertainty, frequent changes, and interpretation differences in the tax field and reporting reveal tax risks. Today, companies, especially large ones, accept tax risk as a part of the risk management process. Focusing on tax risk management, this chapter presents the discussions on various definitions of tax risk and on the tax risk categories, factors that affect tax risk. The applicability of tax risk management is evaluated from the following perspectives in the chapter: empirical analyses conducted in different countries, tax control framework, and tax risk management practice in various countries. As a result, tax risks are manageable with the support of cooperative compliance models of revenue administrations in countries, the necessity of corporate governance principles, the situation of legal regulations, and the increasing risk management experience of especially large companies.

INTRODUCTION

Recently, corporate governance and risk management issues were more emphasized with financial crises and corporate failures and frauds. Tax is also an important and manageable risk area in the financial indicators of companies. On the one hand, international accounting firms conducted studies about tax risk and its management, and then large companies were interested in the subject increasingly. On the other hand, tax administrations in many countries revised their audit selection strategies to collaborate with large taxpayers by "co-operative compliance" which involves understanding taxpayers and guiding them to the correct applications (OECD, 2013: 13). These two different approaches both conflicted and supported each other mutually.

In parallel with the growing importance of the subject, it should be discussed in detail. When examining previous studies on this topic, the study edited by Khwaja et al. (2011) observed that the issue was mainly discussed from the tax administrations' perspective. This study is critical because it deals with the experiences of different countries and guides the determination of the legal tax area in these countries. But tax risk must also be approached from the perspective of taxpayers. Therefore, some studies from this point Elgood et al. (2004), Henehan and Walsh (2008), and Bakker and Kloosterhof (2010) are important. In addition, researches have turned to empirical analysis of the in-depth interviews' results with tax managers over the past ten years. But these studies are insufficient to explain the applicability of tax risk management thoroughly as a new area and to discuss the current tax risks. The purpose of this study is to describe the types of tax risk, to determine the aims of tax risk management and its place in risk management, to examine the factors affecting tax risk and effects of the pandemic, to discuss the situation of tax risk management from different perspectives in various countries and finally to present applicability of a tax risk management for companies. The structure of the study is as follows. Primarily, the theoretical background and a description of "tax risk" and "tax risk management" will be explained due to archival research in the literature. Then, factors affecting the level of tax risk will be argued in detail, and tax risk management practices in various countries will be presented. The applicability of tax risk management will be discussed based on the theoretical and country practices in the final section.

THEORETICAL BACKGROUND OF TAX RISK MANAGEMENT

Risk, Risk Management and the Role of Tax Risk Management

The taxation power of governments affects companies' business activities. For this reason, the legal limit of tax law must be known by taxpayers. Risk is defined as "anything negative that can affect the organization's ability to achieve its objectives" (EC, 2006: 13). The concept of "risk" can be identified as the likelihood and magnitude of different outcomes than expected (Neubig & Sangha, 2004: 114). If there is a risk, people care about the outcomes, and they don't know what will happen. It seems that risk entails two essential components: exposure and uncertainty (Holton, 2004: 22). Because of these two factors, risk including in the tax area, must be managed. Risk management is defined as determining risk areas in an organization and replying to them appropriately (Merna & Al-Thani, 2008: 2).

With the effect of the financial crisis and the corporate failures and frauds, companies have become more interested in corporate governance with internal control and risk management than before (Daelen et al., 2010: 1). From the 1990s, focused on internal controls and risk and then faced the frauds, started corporate governance in tax authorities are very important to understand where is tax risk management in the corporate management process (Henehan & Walsh, 2008: 11-20). Managers, boards, shareholders and other stakeholders of companies interact in the corporate governance process in which companies' goals are determined, the steps to be followed to achieve them, and performance is monitored (OECD, 2015: 9). Companies that want to achieve their corporate governance goals also use risk management as a tool. Successfully applying risk management requires having the competence to analyze the risks faced or can be encountered by companies in different aspects (Merna & Al-Thani, 2008: 2). Therefore, recently, the enterprise risk management process covers risks in all areas of the organization (COSO, 2004), and tax risk management should be a part of it. If the risks faced by a unit in risk management are eliminated while other departments fail, it won't be easy to achieve the companies' objectives. As with other areas, the tax area should be controlled as part of risk management. Because some gray areas in countries' tax systems are accepted to be "barely legitimate tax avoidance" by the tax authorities, and companies are faced with being caused actions to have non-certain results (EC, 2006; Freedman, 2010: 112).

Companies aim to minimize tax costs in their tax strategy. They look for boundaries in the laws and use aggressive tax planning (Russo, 2010: 180). Companies, especially large ones, are in a gray area between tax evasion and tax avoidance due to their tax planning schemes (York, 2011: 40). A risk management approach strikes a balance between value-creating and risk-creating values. In tax risk management, this balance focuses on the realization of income and profit targets. Boundaries are set in the cycle of risk expectation, planning, foresight, and compliance. An unforeseen tax risk may create a domino effect by affecting other risks (Cosmei & Şerban, 2014: 1594).

Concepts of Tax Risk and Tax Risk Management

Like words that are uncertain and hard to define, there is no general definition of the term "tax risk", but there are some definitions. Wunder (2009) determined that tax risk is "the likelihood that tax outcome differs from what is expected, due to a variety of reasons". The main situations that cause these uncertainties are the judicial process, changes in the law or business assumptions, and increased intensity of audits, and uncertainty in the interpretation of the law, and any action is emanating from the tax function that subjects the company to adverse publicity. It is defined by Lavermicocca (2011) as "uncertain tax positions and vulnerabilities in tax financial controls and reporting" and described by Rensburg (2012) "uncertainty of how well interpretation of the tax laws is made, or it is the uncertainty of how well systems are implemented to mitigate those tax risks".

There may be different meanings of "tax risk" for companies, but this is important that how tax risk can be managed (Elgood et al., 2004: 3). Uncertainties in the tax area cause risks, and managing these risks is about managing tax uncertainties (Lavermicocca, 2011: 96). Tax risk management is defined by Henehan and Walsh (2008) as "a process by which a company attempts to ensure that the division of knowledge or the lack of knowledge within the company does not result in an adverse operational tax event for the firm", defined by Mik (2010) "has been an activity normally considered only by tax managers and CFOs" and described by Rensburg (2012) "a process of stepping from reactive tax monitoring and structuring to a more pro-active approach".

The following inferences can be made using the definitions: tax risk is defined as "uncertainties in tax and taxation" and tax risk management is explained as "a process conducted by managers to manage uncertainties in tax and taxation with the help of identification, comparison, analysis, and specialization".

Tax Risk Categories

According to Elgood et al. (2004), tax risk includes two main categories contain seven sub-categories: specific risk areas including transactional, operational, compliance and financial accounting risks and generic risk areas including portfolio, management and reputational risks. It is seen that this structure is used precisely in the studies after this classification. Tax risk areas and events can be seen in Table 1.

Table 1. Tax risk categories and typical events rise them

TYPE OF TAX RISK		TYPICAL EVENTS GIVING RISE TO TAX RISK
Specific Risk Areas	Transactional	Examples of situations that cause this risk: "Acquisitions, disposals, mergers, financing transactions, tax driven cross border transactions, internal reorganizations"
	Operational	Examples of situations that cause this risk: "New business ventures, new operating models, operating in new locations, new operating structures (e.g. JVs/partnerships), the impact of technological developments (e.g. internet trading)"
	Compliance	Examples of situations that cause this risk: "Lack proper management, weak accounting records or controls data integrity issues, insufficient resources, systems changes legislative changes, revenue investigations, specific local in country customs, approaches, and focuses in compliance"
	Financial accounting	Examples of situations that cause this risk: "Changes in legislation, changes in accounting systems, changes in accounting policies and GAAP"
Generic Risk Areas	Portfolio	Examples of situations that cause this risk: "A combination of any of these events"
	Management	Examples of situations that cause this risk: "Changes in personnel – both in tax and in the business, experienced tax people leaving – and information, being in their heads and not properly documented, new/inexperienced resources"
	Reputational	Examples of situations that cause this risk: "Revenue authority raid/investigation, press comment, court hearings/legal actions, political developments"

Source: Elgood et al., 2004: 35.

If the situation that arises in certain transactions of a company affects the tax area, such as one-off and non-routine transactions, this is transactional risk. Operational risk concerns the underlying risks of applying the tax laws, regulations and decisions to the routine everyday business operations. Compliance risk is about the risks associated with meeting an organization's tax compliance obligations and financial accounting risk concerns applying documents for internal controls and financial reporting (Elgood et al., 2004: 4-7). Portfolio risk is related to the overall aggregate level of risk when looking at transactional, operational, and compliance risks as a whole and considers the interaction of these three different specific risk areas; manage risk concerns expert personal and expertness in the risky area; reputational risk concerns the wider impact on the organization that might arise from an organization's actions if they become a matter of public knowledge (Elgood et al., 2004: 7-8).

Apart from this, tax risks can also be examined on the sectoral basis. On the other hand, there are many risk sectors to be identified in various countries such as construction, transport, restaurants, hairdressing, cleaning services, clothing and textiles, motor vehicle, art and antique dealers for Australia; construction, gambling, transport, car sales, diamond industry, dentists, e-commerce, heating oil for Belgium; construction, hospitality, agriculture, real estate agents, taxi firms, hairstylists for Canada; construction, restaurants, hairdressers, taxi firms, scrap metals, e-commerce, labor agents for Sweden; car sales, construction, health care, medical professions, restaurants, real estate agents for USA etc. (Loeprick & Engelschalk, 2011: 50).

Factors Affecting Tax Risk

Tax professionals work to reduce the compliance burden of taxpayers, minimizing the cost of taxation and decreasing the administrative burden of government (Henehan & Walsh, 2008: 8). In order to manage the emerging tax risks, first of all, it is necessary to determine the factors affecting the tax risks and make evaluations for them. The classification of factors influencing the level of risk must be made in the needs of sectors and companies. Therefore, factors affecting the level of tax risk also take into consideration the situation regarding taxes. Factors affecting the level of tax risk are examined in two main categories: internal and external factors. Internal factor includes; business structure and accounting system and external factor includes; administrative, legal, sectorial and other factors.

Figure 1. Factors affecting level of tax risk
Source: Authors' elaboration.

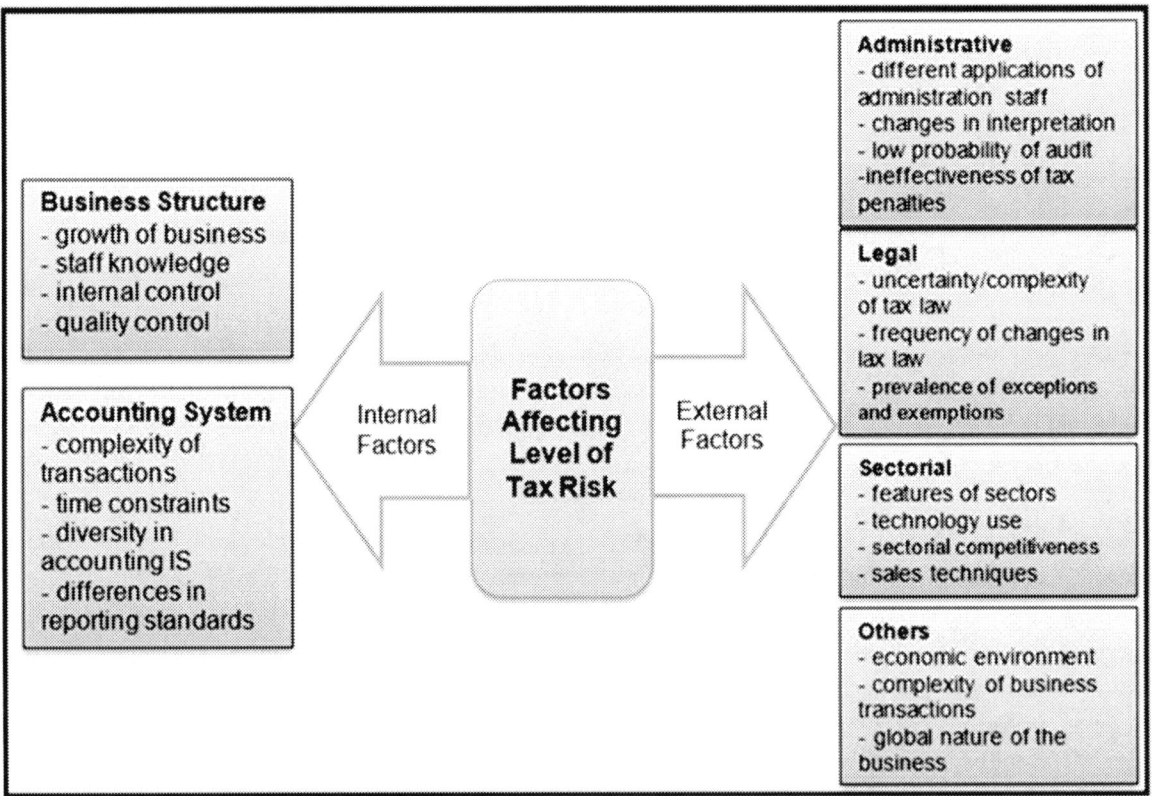

The first internal factor affecting the level of tax risk is business structure related to the growth of the business, staff knowledge, internal control and quality control system. The pressure of business growth affects the organization, especially the tax department, to accept new products or arrangements that limit the ability to manage tax risks (Lavermicocca, 2011: 105). Tax staffs in companies work to reduce the compliance burden of taxpayers, minimize the deadweight cost of taxation, and decrease government administrative burden (Henehan & Walsh, 2008: 8). Because of this, staff knowledge is essential to manage tax risk. Moreover, staffs informed concerning tax risks leaves the organization, there will be a gap in knowledge within the organization (Lavermicocca, 2011: 105). Companies should assess and seek to reduce tax risks to improve corporate governance standards and awareness of the consequences of significant transactions. For this reason, corporate governance, internal control and quality control standards of enterprises also play a role in determining the tax risk level (OECD, 2009: 9).

The second internal factor affecting the level of tax risk is the accounting system related to the complexity of transactions, time constraints, diversity in accounting information systems and differences in reporting standards. The preparation process of accounting and financial statements includes a complex structure that requires specialization. This process has become more complicated with growing transactions and improving technology. If a company consumes so much time on tax compliance issues, there is possible to increase tax risk. Accounting procedures must be performed in a predetermined time period. Time constraints affect the level of tax compliance to manage tax risks.

Moreover, accounting information systems have diversity affected suitability, presentation, comparability, verifiability, timeliness and understandability of financial knowledge. It is important to use a standard set all over the world to facilitate the comparison and auditing of financial information and at the same time to reduce the costs of preparing financial statements (Tarca, 2012: 1). Differences in reporting standards in various countries affect the level of the tax risks of investors. Especially new accounting and auditing standards are also more risk focused.

The first external factor affecting the level of tax risk is administrative related to different attitudes of tax administration employees, changes in administrative interpretation, the low probability of audit and ineffectiveness of tax penalties. If there is uncertainty in the interpretation of tax laws in some transactions and this situation results in different outcomes in the applications of the tax administration and the practices of tax office employees, tax risks will increase (OECD, 2009: 6). Where there is no certainty in the interpretation of tax legislation, it affects not only taxpayers but also tax administrations (Freedman, 2010: 113). In such a case, the tax administration may make different applications in the same situations and as a result, the trust in it may decrease. In contrast to developed countries, the taxation system in developing countries is based on audit distrust instead of declaration-trust. If taxpayers think that there is a low probability of audit for industry, business scale, period, etc., consistency of transactional reduce and tax risks increase in company. Inconsistencies occurring results of tax transactions should be identified and penalized. If there are some instruments for eradicating tax penalties in the taxation system, taxpayers don't consider the impact of tax risks. As a result of this, tax risks in companies increase.

The second external factor affecting tax risk is legal related to uncertainty/complexity of tax laws, frequency of changes in tax laws and prevalence of exceptions and exemptions. Especially uncertainty and complexity of the income tax law are important indicators contributing to the company's failure to comply with tax law (Lavermicocca, 2011: 104). The complexity of tax systems reduces the level of compliance, resulting in a tax gap and legal but undesirable tax avoidance (Kopczuk, 2006: 1). According to Paying Taxes Report (2020) is time to comply with taxes per year in some countries: Estonia has 50 hours, Switzerland has 63 hours, Finland has 90 hours, Australia has 105 hours, the UK has 114 hours, France has 139 hours, on the other hand, Turkey has 170 hours, the USA has 175 hours, Germany has 218, Portugal has 243 hours, Poland has 334 hours, Bulgaria has 441 hours and Brazil has 1501 hours. Companies, especially large ones, want to know with certainty which of their transactions will be considered risky by the tax administration and how they react (OECD, 2009: 8). The frequency of changes in tax laws is one of the factors affecting certainty. It affects tax risks if there is too much tax exemption in a tax system, implementations of these impress taxpayers' level of tax risks.

The third external factor affecting the level of tax risk is sectorial related to features of sectors, technology use, sectorial competitiveness and sales techniques. Features of sectors influence tax risks, and there are many risk sectors to be identified in various countries. Such as construction, transport, restaurants, hairdressing, cleaning services, clothing and textiles, motor vehicle, art and antique dealers for Australia; construction, gambling, transport, car sales, diamond industry, dentists, e-commerce, heating oil for Belgium; construction, hospitality, agriculture, real estate agents, taxi firms, hairstylists for Canada; construction, restaurants, hairdressers, taxi firms, scrap metals, e-commerce, labor agents for Sweden; car sales, construction, health care, medical professions, restaurants, real estate agents for US vs. are identified (Loeprick & Engelschalk, 2011: 50). The technology used by companies supports all business areas. New technology improves the ability to monitor risks, but its adaptation includes risks in some transactions. Competitiveness is both useful and harmful for sectors. This competition can lug the company into risky areas.

The last external factor affecting the level of tax risk is other factors related to the economic environment, the complexity of business transactions and the global nature of the business. The country's political, legal, and business systems in which the corporation carries on business have implications for managing tax risks. If the legal procedures are undeveloped and political systems are subject to corruption, managing tax risks is limited (Lavermicocca, 2011: 106). Nowadays, doing business has rendered risky by global transactions. Growing uncertainties, competition, changes of organizational and economical with globalization make doing business difficult. Besides, when a company is more global, compliance risk increases. For example, the effects of the OECD Base Erosion and Profit Shifting (BEPS) project and country-by-country (CbC) reporting standards have recently revealed new risk areas.

The Situation of New Tax Risks in the Pandemic (Covid-19) Period

The pandemic period that has emerged since 2019 has affected the tax area as other risk areas. Disruptions in the production, sales and management networks of the companies caused problems in the calculation of the tax and the payment phase. The most important public policy response in the process has been to enforce the temporary closure of non-essential business activity. Measures taken to remedy problems do not adequate for the lack of sales trading activity on business income and cash balances (Cowling et al., 2020: 593). SMEs have been affected more than large companies during the pandemic period. A weaker management and transaction process than large companies leave them exposed to risks. Some countries and supply networks were more affected by the pandemic period and the more companies depended on the countries affected by COVID-19, the more vulnerable they became. Many countries intensively adopted various measures such as tax stimuli, reliefs, deferral etc. (Cepel et al., 2020: 249; Eggers, 2020: 200). These stimulus measures will cause decreasing in tax revenues for the countries losing revenues due to the economic effects of the pandemic and will require tax increases in the following periods.

OECD (2021b) sets out the tax measures in response implemented in various countries. However, most of the tax changes were aimed at facilitating the transactions of taxpayers, adapting to these unexpected situations caused both transactional and compliance risks. Also, in the study of Tavares et al. (2021), the most important risk in legal risks was perceived as the result of changes in tax legislation during the pandemic. Legal risks include not only business and environmental issues but especially financial and tax issues. Most transactions in accounting have a certain deadline due to the legislation. During the pandemic, the accounting process, like all transactions, was interrupted. If businesses do not have a well-structured management process, this gap will create even more problems for them.

Since the terms of the period affect the economy and accordingly various regulations, tax risks will also change depending on the conditions. The conditions of the country where the business is established are also necessary. For example, during the pandemic period, some countries took stricter measures and more affected the transactions on a sectoral basis. Due to the pandemic, cross-border spillovers have disrupted financial and commodity markets, global trade, supply chains, travel, and tourism. The fall in activity has been concentrated in services sectors that are typically stable. For instance, tourism, an essential services sector globally, has fallen sharply due to travel restrictions and concerns (World Bank, 2020: 11). For this reason, it should be seen that sectoral risks also have arisen and environmental conditions affect them.

One of the most critical factors affecting the tax risks is the expert personnel. In the event that the loss of equipped personnel, switched to remote work or quit, the usual workflow was disrupted in the pandemic period. Remote working has also caused risks created by transaction security problems. In particular, many financial sector firms and officials started to work remotely, but they also needed to access potentially critical systems and data remotely. This situation revealed an unexpected security vulnerability. For example, according to EY (2021), the tax risks resulting from mobile workers have already been experienced by 45% of respondents of the survey. Companies must carry out or strengthen security controls to protect their data and prevent the risks that may arise (Adelmann & Gaidosch, 2020: 1).

Purposes and Process of Tax Risk Management

In recent years, there have been a few developments for risk management in taxation. One of the most important is ethics on tax matters and its increasing effect on companies. This situation is related to how companies contribute fairly share to the income of countries' governments that it does business with (Russo, 2010: 179).

Today, tax administrations and commercial organizations in various countries have begun to consider the tax risk management process as a separate element from general risk management (Wunder, 2009: 15). Governments and their tax authorities also use risk management in the tax audit process to determine which companies should be audited (Russo, 2010: 180). Tax authorities want to ensure that companies don't apply tax evasion or fraud or lack any internal control and the proper tax is not paid (Henehan & Walsh, 2008: 19).

Companies should manage tax risk to avoid risks, share, or reduce risks (Elgood et al., 2004: 39). Follows should be made by companies for reducing tax risk: reading business environment, tracking new domestic or global tax developments, comprehending global trends, identifying and taking measures for particular potential risk areas and planning how to resolve tax disputes (Owens et al., 2015: 2). Measures to prevent tax risks from arising in a company will also increase the tax compliance level of that company. Since increasing tax compliance of taxpayers is one of the main objectives of tax administrations, the management of companies' tax risks will directly concern them (Lavermicocca, 2011: 103).

Businesses can only overcome problems created by economic changes with a strong management and monitoring process. The pandemic has created unexpected effects on the economy. This process will make it easier to avoid tax risks by having the tax control framework process and using it effectively (EY, 2021: 9).

Companies aim to use tax risk management to avoid being a risky taxpayer for the administration, avoid tax penalties, provide effectiveness for tax planning, prevent reputation loss, get better decisions, reduce the impact of the deteriorating conditions, and ensure inferences to the administration. If a company aims to build effective risk management, it must focus on an integral approach to tax risk management. The process should start with the COSO model and then continue with identifying tax strategy, tax operations and risk, tax accounting and reporting, the statute of tax compliance, automation and technology integration, organization and resources, step by step (Hoyng et al., 2010: 30).

Adapting the COSO cube to tax risk management in Elgood et al. (2004), the process should follow these steps: determination of control environment, risk assessment, control activities, information and communication, monitoring like COSO process. In this process, if the company has been successful in internal audit and internal control processes, it will be easier to adapt to tax risk management. As an alternative to the COSO process, in some studies, applications such as tax risk map (Hoyng, 2010; Deloitte, 2015) and tax cube (Deloitte, 2012) are recommended to manage tax risk. But the most used and recommended way to manage tax risks is to create a tax control framework. The framework will be discussed in the next section, where the applicability of tax risk management is concerned.

APPLICABILITY OF TAX RISK MANAGEMENT IN COMPANIES

There are three ways to measure the applicability of tax risk management: first is by examining applied research and second is by analyzing the tax control framework process, and last is doing application process analysis in various countries. In this chapter, the applicability of tax risk management will be discussed from these aspects.

Literature Review

In the last two decades, there have been many studies that reveal the theoretical background of the subject. COSO (2004) is important in considering tax risk management as a separate structure. After a detailed research based on COSO (2004) by Elgood et al. (2004), corporate governance and tax risks issues were discussed in Neubig and Sangha (2004), focused on global tax risks in EY (2007), global developments were explained in Henehan and Walsh (2008). In the following period, country practices in tax risk management began to be discussed. For example, Erasmus (2009) and Mulligan and Oats (2009) described USA applications, in the book edited by Bakker and Kloosterhof (2010), both the theoretical aspect of the subject explained and the examples of Australia, Canada, China, France, Germany, Japan, Mexico, Netherlands, Singapore, South Africa, UK and USA examined in detail. In the same period, applied researches on businesses were started, and we will review these studies in Table 2 below.

At the same time, while risk analysis was examined from the private sector's perspective, OECD (2004) was examined risk analysis in auditing to improve tax compliance. After that, audit processes based on risk analysis and their interaction with cooperative compliance models were discussed in terms of tax administrations. In EC (2006) was researched tax administrations' risk management processes and tax risk areas. OECD (2008) drew attention to the relationship between tax authorities and large corporate taxpayers. In OECD (2009) was revealed a link between corporate governance and tax risk management. After that, tax administrations in countries have turned to cooperative compliance practices with large taxpayers. In the book edited by Khwaja et al. (2011), the audit application based on risk analysis of the UK, Turkey, Sweden, The Netherlands, Bulgaria, India, Ukraine and Kazakhstan were explicated. OECD (2013) is a report that explains cooperative compliance models, reveals their good aspects and recommends them, this approach continued in the following years (see. OECD, 2016; OECD, 2021a).

Managing the Current Risks of Companies

After this period, studies like Rensburg (2012), Segal and Maroun (2014), Cozmei and Şerban (2014), Owens et al. (2015) dealt with the theoretical structure of tax risk management and country comparisons. Deloitte (2012) developed a tax cube to manage tax risks. Recently, there has also been applied researches in the literature. Neuman et al. (2013) aimed that a structure was developed to predict more or less risky tax strategies with the help of statistical analysis. Guenther et al. (2013) estimated logit regression and found that tax policies only increased the firm's risk depending on the uncertainty regarding the tax payments. Hutchens and Rego (2015) analyzed whether higher levels of tax risk are associated with increased firm risk, as perceived by capital market participants with the help of regression. Quentin (2019) examined published tax policies including tax risks of 20 large European companies ranked by income and listed as headquartered in Europe in Fortune Magazine's "Fortune Global 500". Drake et al. (2019) found that tax risk perceptions influence investors' tax avoidance decisions. The study by Lin et al. (2019) revealed social responsibility allows better control of tax risk. Abernathy et al. (2021) examine the response to tax risk of external auditors using logistic regression.

When researches including questionnaires are examined, the conclusions in Table 2 have been reached.

Table 2. Studies that include questionnaires on tax risk management

KPMG (2007)	A survey was conducted among 546 board members, senior management, CFOs, tax executives, and finance and accounting professionals concerning tax risk management. %20 of the respondents explained that their organizations have a formal tax risk management strategy and 60% of them claimed that tax risk assessment and management had become more of a priority for their organization's leadership.
Wunder (2009)	A survey including 112 firms representing 27 different countries has been implemented in this study. It is made with the questions in accordance with the classification created by Elgood et al. (2004). The result shows differences in countries' tax risk profiles from least to most, and 43% of the respondents state a tax risk management policy to be documented in place and in process in the businesses they work.
Gmeiner (2009)	The study as a thesis includes a survey on 20 large companies in Austria, and tax risks are classified by giving points to its questions.
Freedman et al. (2009)	The survey presents the results on the opinion of tax directors by way of face-to-face interviews with representatives of 30 corporate groups in the UK. The questions focus on the workings of the Large Business Service (LBS), which administers the taxation of the largest UK businesses.
Mulligan & Oats (2009)	The study entails 20 in-depth interview sessions involving 26 in-house tax executives in total from fifteen USA companies. The interviewees identify specific technical-type areas of risk (for example, transfer pricing) and non-technical areas (for example, reputational risk) that need to be managed.
Erasmus (2010)	541 participants from 18 countries attend this study. It shows that 90% of companies mentioned that tax risk would be important for them soon. The most significant risk arises from the lack of skilled personnel.
Lavermicocca (2011)	This paper presents the results of in-depth interviews with 14 tax managers from large Australian corporations in which 19 open-ended questions were conducted. All participants declared that they have increasingly formalized tax risk management processes and stated that they applied tax risk management in order to present more explanatory documents about tax risks to the senior managers and to make more informed tax decisions, and thus they wanted to get rid of the surprises.
Walicka (2014)	It was conducted using 4 case studies approach and focus group interview method and indicated tax strategies were enabling limitation of tax risk for applying in family businesses.
Lavermicocca & Buchan (2015)	This article shows that the result of 123 participants from 14 large companies in Australia. This survey focuses on the results that relate specifically to an understanding of the role of reputational risk in tax decision making in a large company.
Oliveira Neto (2017)	An interview survey has been applied on 16 Brazilian enterprises to measure using their organizational information system to identify tax risks in this study. By analyzing the responses, it has been found that enterprises use some (internal or external) managerial information resources to identify tax risks.
Gerçek & Bakar Türegün (2018)	A survey is made in Turkey to identify risk areas based on questions that has been applied to 400 managers responsible for big companies' financial affairs. According to analysis results, companies doing tax planning, implementing enterprise risk management and having foreign subsidiaries have better tax related monitoring and reporting procedures. It has been determined that companies mostly have problems with management and reputational risk.
Brühne & Schanz (2019)	They conduct 33 expert interviews with 42 German tax risk experts. One important finding from research interviews is that firms engage in detached tax risk management practices.
Eberhartinger & Zieser (2021)	A survey has been conducted on 9 Austrian firms participating in horizontal monitoring and 31 large non-HM firms. Horizontal monitoring is a cooperative compliance model for large taxpayers that contributes to managing tax risk. The survey finds evidence that HM firms decreased tax risk and compliance costs depending on increased tax certainty.
KPMG (2021)	In repeated research for many years, rising significantly among CEO priorities: regulatory risk and tax risk tied for second place in 2021.
EY (2021)	The paper evaluated the results of repeated periodically Tax Risk and Controversy Survey conducted with 1.265 tax and finance leaders and found that 53% of respondents expect greater enforcement by budget pressure of the government, 35% of them expect higher levels of reputational risk in the next three years, 50% of them have tax control framework. Most businesses that adhered to the TCF process admitted that it was complex, but it significantly or entirely detected all tax disputes globally.

Source: Prepared by authors using relevant references.

When the literature is examined in this area including surveys or interviews, it is seen that tax risks are also addressed in the risk management process, with an increasing trend, especially in large companies. It is even noticed that they have adopted a separate documented tax risk management process. This is because tax is an essential part of financial indicators for companies, and the consequences of risks in the tax field can cause heavy penalties. Therefore, companies are increasingly adopting tax risk management practices, although not mandatory in countries.

Tax Control Framework (TCF)

TCF is a way to create effective, efficient and transparent tax functions. Companies must consider a tax control framework which is a system to identify, mitigate, control and report tax risks. TCF impacts tax risk management of legislative or regulatory changes and public opinions include rules, models, accounting standards, anti-avoidance mechanism, transfer pricing, commercial environment and common tax risk or nature of tax risk in taxation system (Hoyng et al., 2010: 19, 24).

The report by OECD (2016), TCF should be used as part of the internal control process of enterprises to ensure the accuracy of declarations and disclosures. At the same time, OECD's report contains recommendations as follows (OECD, 2016: 15): senior management and/or the board of an organization have a documented tax strategy; this strategy must be applied comprehensively; responsibility for the implementation should be clearly recognized; predetermined systems of rules and reporting must be used and should be reviewed periodically; the TCF must ensure the reliability of the organization's tax documentation and provide assurance that any risks associated with tax are controlled.

Tax risk management includes determining business risk related to taxpayers' tax position and determining how to manage these risks. The determination, application and maintenance of risk management and supporting systems generally are made in three phases. The first phase is finding measurements to identify critical risks of an organization. The second phase is applying a tax control framework to reduce these risks. And the last phase is maintenance, in which the organization controls its tax risks and updates the framework when necessary (Hoyng et al., 2010: 67-68).

Risk management by taxpayers using an internal control framework activates businesses to provide that their operating, financial and compliance objectives are met and ensure the proper management of risk. The framework's steps are risk assessment, control environment, control activities, information and communication, monitoring. Internal control framework needs specific tax requirement described as a "tax control framework" (OECD, 2013: 99). The tax control framework helps taxpayers for their tax results to be effective, efficient and transparent (Hoyng et al., 2010: 24). If a company aims to build effective risk management, it must focus on an integral approach to tax risk management. The process should start with the COSO model and then continue with identifying tax strategy, tax operations and risk, tax accounting and reporting, the statute of tax compliance, automation and technology integration, organization and resources, step by step (Hoyng et al., 2010: 30).

Tax Risk Management Practice in Various Countries

Tax risk management has been examined from two different aspects. The first one is discussed in terms of taxpayers who do not want to face tax penalties by acting in accordance with tax laws. When viewed from this perspective, international accounting firms conducted studies which continued periodically and then large companies were interested in the subject increasingly. Such as Quentin (2019) found that many companies today make determinations to include tax risk management when explaining their tax strategies. On the other hand, tax administrations in many countries revised their audit selection strategies to collaborate with large taxpayers by "co-operative compliance" which was reflected an increasing focus on the need to understand and influenced them (OECD, 2013: 13). Thus, these two different approaches both have conflicted and supported each other mutually. By addressing these two approaches, we will examine the developments in these four countries in this chapter: Australia, the USA, the UK and Turkey.

Today, separate tax offices for large taxpayers and cooperative compliance models are applied for these taxpayers who have more risk in many countries. Large taxpayer units, which were organized as a separate unit to better auditing companies that exceeded transactions of a specific size and carried out complex activities, then aimed to improve the service quality and finally moved towards creating cooperation-based compliance strategies between taxpayers and the tax administration. OECD (2013) revealed similar structures applied in the 24 countries examined are based on cooperation with the administration in managing tax risk. This number gradually increased in the following period. In the report of OECD (2021a), the number of planned and existing programs in countries increased to 36 of the 59 countries having advanced and emerging economies. These models are important to develop a better dialogue with large taxpayers, from which a significant portion of tax revenues are collected, to understand businesses by administrations, to improve tax compliance, to improve certainty, to obtain real-time information on commercial relations, to improve tax risk management and to increase the efficiency and effectiveness of the tax administration, to enhance confidence in the administration and the tax system. Tax administrations recommend the tax control framework to taxpayers involved in this application.

Australia is one of the first countries to use a tax risk management model, using risk analysis in audits and the compliance process through a tax compliance model (Freedman, 2010: 116). The revenue authority of Australia is the Australian Taxation Office (ATO) has an active role in promoting the significance of tax risk management and forcing organizations to consider their risk management policies (Henehan & Walsh, 2008: 19). In June 2003, ATO issued "Large Business and Tax Compliance" by the Commissioner of Taxation to start the process to increase managers' interest in tax governance (Wunder, 2009: 15). ATO has an active role in promoting the importance of tax risk management and forcing organizations to consider their risk management policies (Henehan & Walsh, 2008: 19). ATO has developed a range of products to assist taxpayers in managing their tax risks with greater certainty. These products are as follows: private binding rulings, class rulings, product rulings, annual compliance arrangements, advanced pricing agreements, forward compliance arrangements, GST annual compliance arrangements (Cox et al., 2010: 149). The specific compliance strategy includes risk categorization of the large business. ATO's compliance strategy for large enterprises does not only include auditing of the first 100 enterprises but also aims to provide certainty by identifying their tax risks and providing them with timely explanations. ATO developed some premium products such as Annual Compliance Arrangement (ACA), commenced in 2008 for an increasing relationship with the largest companies in the tax system. This arrangement is on a voluntary basis and is a cooperative arrangement between the ATO and large taxpayers on one or more tax issues. The arrangement is constructed on two basic situations: large taxpayers have a good tax governance process and the willingness to operate in an open and transparent relationship by making full and accurate disclosure of significant tax risks in a real time environment. ACA provides the following benefits for the taxpayers (OECD, 2013: 26): contact and dialogue; speedier resolution for technical issues; administrative solutions; concessional treatments of penalties and interest; a plan outlining agreed processes and timelines; extension for correcting goods and services tax mistakes; not being subject to post-lodgement risk reviews or audits for periods and income years covered by an ACA;

not needing to complete the Reportable Tax Position; not being subject to a pre-lodgment compliance review (PCR) (OECD, 2013: 37). Tax Transparency Code (the TTC) was endorsed as part of the 2016-17 Budget announcements as a new voluntary code on greater public disclosure of tax information by businesses, particularly large multinationals. According to the accepted "minimum standard" with the TTC, large companies must provide information on their 'tax policy' or 'tax strategy'. The information must include their acceptable level of tax risks and risk management. (Australia The Board of Taxation, 2019: 4, 8). Then existing programs were supported with new applications. After announcing the Justified Trust Program to be part of ACA and PCR, starting with the top 1.000 taxpayers in 2016, the ATO's Tax Risk Management and Governance Review Guide was published in 2017. The justified trust, which is a notion of OECD, guarantees taxpayers are paying the right amount of tax. The justified trust methodology of ATO expects companies to discover tax risk for further actions that having and using tax risk and governance frameworks adequately, eliminating flagged tax risks, ensuring the accuracy of new transactions and preventing transactional risks, harmonizing between tax and accounting results. Findings report of the Top 1.000 tax performance program supporting and facilitating the review process stated that 93% of companies have a tax control framework, 2% are working effectively in implementing them at an advanced stage, and only 5% have problems detected (ATO, 2020: 4-7).

The Taxpayer Compliance Measurement Program (TCMP), which has been implemented in the USA since 1964, went through a process with National Research Program – NRP, Discriminant Inventory Function System – DIF, Unreported Income Discriminant Index Formula UI-DIF (Torrey, 2008: 3-5), has reached an advanced level in the risk analysis of taxpayers today. With the Compliance Assurance Process – CAP that started with a pilot application in the USA in 2005 and became continuous in 2012, a cooperative compliance system was established for large taxpayers (OECD, 2013: 26). Companies that want to manage tax-related risk in the U.S. must first pay attention to taxes, expense taxes, withholding taxes, and other taxes levied on income at the federal, state, and sometimes local levels (Henehan & Walsh, 2008: 102). To measure and manage the tax risk of any taxpayer in the United States has become necessary with SOX 404 (Sarbanes-Oxley Act, 2002, Section 404) and FIN 48 (Financial Accounting Standards Board Interpretation No. 48). Both developments support a more transparent corporate governance (Erasmus, 2009: 1). FIN 48 This regulation is for transactions regulated as "uncertain tax position" or "unrecognized tax benefit" and is the set of measures that best detect aggressive tax transactions (Guenther et al., 2013: 3). Several policies have been established in the United States to identify and mitigate the tax risks faced by companies: disclosure policy, mandatory transactions policy, pre-filing agreement, limited issue focused examination, fast track settlement and accelerated issue resolution (Petolick, 2010: 458-460).

Risk analysis techniques in tax audit, which have been used in Her Majesty's Revenue and Customs (HMRC) since the 1980s, especially in the audit of direct taxes, emerged more systematically after the 2000s (Hainey, 2011: 65). The UK has also been developing an approach based on risk rating as part of their Review of Links with Large Business. The approach supports an improving relationship between HMRC and the taxpayer, based on trust and transparency. The aim of the approach covers the development of resource allocation and the promotion of companies according to their position to achieve the benefits of low risk rating, which may include changing their tax planning strategy (Freedman et al., 2009: 74). HMRC published Tax in the Boardroom in 2006 and developed risk assessment methodology. In 2007 HMRC introduced a formal co-operative compliance approach for large corporate taxpayers, based on a customer relationship management model and using the "Tax Compliance Risk Management" process framework (OECD, 2013: 24). In the UK, within the framework of the corporate governance regulation adopted in 2012, businesses should implement internal control and risk management as a requirement of the understanding of responsibility (UK Financial Reporting Council, 2012). The following practices are essential for taxpayers' tax risk management in the UK: tax compliance risk management (TCRM), penalty regime program, senior accounting officer, disclosure of tax avoidance schemes (DOTAS) (Segal & Maroun, 2014: 381-382). In 2016, a regulation related to tax strategy and sanctions for large businesses was made that included the disclosure of tax risk. The content of group tax strategies must set out the accepted level of tax risk and risk management, tax planning by UK legislation (UK Finance Act 2016 Schedule 19 Para 23).

In order to measure the compliance risks of taxpayers, the Turkish Revenue Administration (GİB), dependent on the Turkey Ministry of Treasury and Finance, carries out many projects such as VAT returns, forged document risk analysis and excise tax risk analysis (GİB, 2021). Another institution, the Turkish Tax Inspection Board (VDK), plans and executes tax audits by risk analysis. Directorate General of Risk Analysis at Turkey Ministry of Treasury and Finance was established as a separate unit in 2020. Risk management in the tax audit is carried out through many institutions in Turkey, but there isn't special cooperation with large companies like other international experiences. Risk management in Turkey is based on one-sided observation. This situation affects both efficiency of tax risk management in administration and the uncertainty tax positions of companies. Several policies have been established in Turkey to identify and mitigate the tax risks faced by companies. For companies listed on the stock exchange, there is an obligation to use international financial reporting standards and to adopt corporate governance principles. For companies above a certain size, there is an obligation to be subject to independent auditing. Companies' declarations and financial statements must be certified by sworn-in certified public accountants in some transactions, especially in VAT refunds. Current practices to prevent tax risks in legislation covering very few companies in Turkey are not sufficient to guide companies to implement tax risk management policies.

CONCLUSION

Tax risk is defined as uncertainties in tax and taxation procedures, and tax risk management is described as a process conducted by managers to manage uncertainties in tax and taxation with the aid of identify, comparison, analysis and specialization. National and international developments in the tax field have revealed tax as a more fragile area for companies.

Factors affecting the level of tax risk also take into consideration the situation regarding taxes. Factors affecting the level of tax risk are examined in two main categories: internal and external factors. Internal factors include; business structure and accounting system and external factors include; administrative, legal, sectorial and other factors. The conditions of the period and the situation of other risks affect the tax risk level. The Covid-19 pandemic has caused uncertainty in many areas. The measures taken in the countries have been to close the workplaces and switch to remote working. For this reason, the risks that emerged in the fields of production, sales and management affected many areas. In particular, businesses that do not perform internal control, internal audit and corporate risk management and have structural gaps in their management have suffered more from the process. It has been determined that these enterprises are mostly SMEs. Countries announced various fiscal measures packages, including tax. However, since it was unexpected to comply with them, transaction risks and legal risks emerged. It has been determined that the sectors are affected differently depending on the measures taken by the countries. For example, tourism and related investments and companies in this sector faced increasing risks. Risks arising from personnel in the tax field are quite common. The pandemic has caused specialist staff to quit their jobs, become sick and die. In addition to these extreme examples, the transition to remote work has created data security issues. Management and data security issues have revealed new tax risk areas.

One of the biggest risks for a manager is signing up for incomprehensible tax practices and transactions. The unexpected situations in the tax field can cause severe problems for the company. To avoid these situations, tax risks need to be managed, as in other areas. Companies adopting corporate governance principles use risk management to achieve their goals. For the success of risk management, it is necessary to evaluate the company as a whole. Companies that built internal control and internal audit and used the COSO model should use tax risk management with TCF to provide efficiency them. Therefore, companies should consider national or international compliance risks and risks of continuing activities or new investment risks. Companies should plan tax strategy by identifying tax risk, tax accounting and reporting.

The development of tax risk management in the literature started with the COSO (2004) enterprise risk management framework. Theoretical studies contributing to the literature like Elgood et al. (2004), Neubig and Sangha (2004), EY (2007), Henehan and Walsh (2008) have been replaced by applied research like Neuman et al. (2013), Guenther et al. (2013), Hutchens and Rego (2015), Drake et al. (2019) and Abernathy et al. (2021). In this study, we examined studies that included questionnaires and found that the tax risk management process is adopted with an increasing trend. Cooperative compliance models support this process. Recent developments like Justified Trust Program in Australia and large businesses: tax strategies and sanctions in the UK have led large companies to adopt more and more to the tax risk management process.

Tax administrations force taxpayers to improve their compliance in many ways. One way is to use information about each taxpayer to analyze and compare them to obtain results about risky situations. The administration can reach a lot of information to use against taxpayers. But, there must be some core principles of risk assessment by tax administration. These are trusted to taxpayers, equity and taxpayer service orientation (Awasthi, 2011: 120). Otherwise, taxpayers especially to be large company don't access information that is related to them easily. Tax administrations have press on taxpayers, especially in the tax audit process. There is a principle in the legal system called "equality of arms". This principle implies that "each party must be afforded a reasonable opportunity to present his case - including his evidence - under conditions that do not place him at a substantial disadvantage vis-à-vis his opponent" (Dombo Beheer B.V. vs. The Netherlands, 1993: 15, para. 33). The administration knows a lot of information about each taxpayer; analyzes and compares them to obtain results about risky situations. But it is difficult to identify risk areas for taxpayers. Additionally, in audits and evaluations that occurred without taxpayers' knowledge, if it has resulted for taxpayers, this is necessary to not hidden related information and documents from them.

In conclusion, tax risk management should be used for companies not to be risky taxpayers, avoid tax penalties, provide effectiveness for tax planning, prevent reputation loss, get better decisions, reduce the impact of the deteriorating conditions, and provide a cooperative relationship with the tax administration. In this process, the administration should support companies in tax risk management. Thus, both tax compliance increases and certainty in taxation are provided for taxpayers.

ACKNOWLEDGMENT

This study was prepared using Dr. Bakar Türegün's unpublished doctoral dissertation which named "Şirketlerde Vergi Riski Yönetimi: Türk Vergi Sistemi Açısından Bir Değerlendirme (Tax Risk Management in Companies: An Evaluation in terms of Turkish Tax System)" approved at Bursa Uludag University. The study was supported by the Scientific and Technological Research Council of Turkey (TUBITAK) – International Research Fellowship Programme for Ph.D. Students.

REFERENCES

Abernathy, J. L., Finley, A. R., Rapley, E. T., & Stekelberg, J. (2021). External Auditor Responses to Tax Risk. *Journal of Accounting, Auditing & Finance*, *36*(3), 489–516. doi:10.1177/0148558X19867821

Adelmann, F., & Gaidosch, T. (2020). *Cybersecurity of Remote Work During the Pandemic*. Special IMF Series on COVID-19. https://www.imf.org/~/media/Files/Publications/covid19-special-notes/en-special-series-on-covid-19-cybersecurity-of-remote-work-during-pandemic.ashx

ATO. (2020). *Top 1,000 (Income) Tax Performance Program Findings Report*. https://www.ato.gov.au/uploadedFiles/Content/SME/downloads/Top_1000_tax_%20performance_program_report_2020.pdf

Australia The Board of Taxation. (2019). *Post-Implementation Review of the Tax Transparency Code*. https://taxboard.gov.au/sites/taxboard.gov.au/files/migrated/2019/02/TTC-Consultation-Paper-final.pdf

Awasthi, R. (2011). Conclusion: Lessons for Reforms. In M. S. Khwaja, R. Awasthi, & J. Loeprick (Eds.), *Risk-Based Tax Audits: Approaches and Country Experiences* (pp. 119–126). The World Bank Publishing. doi:10.1596/9780821387542_CH15

Brühne, A. I., & Schanz, D. (2019). *Building Up a Protective Shield: The Role of Communication for Corporate Tax Risk Management*. Working Paper. https://papers.ssrn.com/sol3/papers.cfm?abstract_id=3254915

Cepel, M., Gavurova, B., Dvorsky, J., & Belas, J. (2020). The Impact of the COVID-19 Crisis on the Perception of Business Risk in the SME Segment. *Journal of International Students*, *13*(3), 248–263.

COSO. (2004). *Enterprise Risk Management – Integrated Framework*. COSO.

Cowling, M., Brown, R., & Rocha, A. (2020). Did You Save Some Cash for a Rainy COVID-19 Day? The Crisis and SMEs. *International Small Business Journal: Researching Entrepreneurship*, *38*(7), 593–604. doi:10.1177/0266242620945102

Cox, T., Morrin, D., & King, A. (2010). Australia. In A. Bakker & S. Kloosterhof (Eds.) Tax Risk Management: From Risk to Opportunity (pp. 135–160). IBFD.

Cozmei, C., & Şerban, E. C. (2014). Risk Management Triggers: From the Tax Risk Pitfalls to Organizational Risk. *Procedia Economics and Finance*, *15*, 1594–1602. doi:10.1016/S2212-5671(14)00630-3

Daelen, M., Elst, C. V., & Ven, A. (2010). Introducing Risk Management. In M. Daelen & C. Elst (Eds.), *Risk Management and Corporate Governance: Interconnections in Law, Accounting and Tax* (pp. 191–232). Edward Elgar Publishing. doi:10.4337/9781849807999.00008

Deloitte. (2012). *Global Tax Cube, Your First Step to Global Tax Risk Management.* http://www.deloitte.com/assets/DcomAustralia/Local%20Assets/Documents/Services/Tax%20services/Tax%20Management%20Consulting%201/Deloitte_Global_Tax_Cube_flyer.pdf

Deloitte. (2015). *Tax Risk Transformation Optimizing and enhancement of Tax Risk Management.* https://www2.deloitte.com/content/dam/Deloitte/nl/Documents/financial-services/deloitte-nl-fsi-tax-risk-transformation-optimizing-and-enhancement.pdf

Dombo Beheer, B. V. vs. The Netherlands, 27 October 1993, https://hudoc.echr.coe.int/app/conversion/pdf/?library=ECHR&id=001-57850&filename=001-57850.pdf

Drake, K. D., Lusch, S. J., & Stekelberg, J. (2019). Does Tax Risk Affect Investor Valuation of Tax Avoidance? *Journal of Accounting, Auditing & Finance, 34*(1), 151–176. doi:10.1177/0148558X17692674

Eberhartinger, E., & Zieser, M. (2021). The Effects of Cooperative Compliance on Firms' Tax Risk, Tax Risk Management and Compliance Costs, Schmalenbach. *Journal of Business Research, 73*, 125–178. PMID:34803211

Eggers, F. (2020). Masters of Disasters? Challenges and Opportunities for SMEs in Times of Crisis. *Journal of Business Research, 116*, 199–208. doi:10.1016/j.jbusres.2020.05.025 PMID:32501306

Elgood, T., Paroissien, I., & Quimby, L. (2004). *Tax Risk Management.* https://www.pwc.co.za/en/assets/pdf/tax-risk-management-guide.pdf

Erasmus, D. N. (2009). *Tax Risk Management under SOX 404 and FIN 48.* Thomas Jefferson School of Law Working Paper No. 1480978. https://papers.ssrn.com/sol3/papers.cfm?abstract_id=1480978.

Erasmus, D. N. (2010). *Special Report: Global Tax Audit and Controversy Risk Management.* Thomas Jefferson School of Law Research Paper No. 1575723. doi:10.2139/ssrn.1575723

European Commission (EC). (2006). *Risk Management Guide for Tax Administrations.* https://ec.europa.eu/taxation_customs/resources/documents/taxation/tax_cooperation/gen_overview/risk_management_guide_for_tax_administrations_en.pdf

EY. (2007). *Tax Risk: External Change, Internal Challenge Global Tax Risk Survey 2006.* https://www2.eycom.ch/publications/items/global_tax_risk_survey_2006/ey_global_tax_risk_survey_2006_e.pdf

EY. (2021). *How do You Adapt to the Changing Tax Risk Landscape?* https://assets.ey.com/content/dam/ey-sites/ey-com/en_gl/topics/tax/tax-pdfs/ey-the-tax-leader-imperative-how-do-you-adapt-to-the-changing-tax-risk-landscape.pdf?download

Freedman, J. (2010). Tax Risk Management and Corporate Taxpayers – International Tax Administration Developments. In A. Bakker & S. Kloosterhof (Eds.) Tax Risk Management: From Risk to Opportunity (pp. 111–134). IBFD.

Freedman, J., Loomer, G., & Vella, J. (2009). Corporate Tax Risk and Tax Avoidance: New Approaches. *British Tax Review*, *1*, 74–116.

Gerçek, A., & Bakar Türegün, F. (2018). Şirketlerde Vergi Riski Algısı ve Vergi Riski Yönetimi Üzerine Bir Araştırma. *Muhasebe ve Vergi Uygulamaları Dergisi*, *11*(3), 307–332. doi:10.29067/muvu.368807

GİB. (2021). *2020 Yılı Faaliyet Raporu*. https://www.gib.gov.tr/sites/default/files/fileadmin/faaliyetraporlari/2020/2020_faaliyet_raporu.pdf

Gmeiner, K. (2009). *Ausgestaltung Eines Tax Risk Management in Unternehmen*. Masterarbeit, Wirtschafts Universität.

Guenther, D. A., Masunaga, S. R., & Williams, B. M. (2013). *Tax Avoidance, Tax Aggressiveness, Tax Risk and Firm Risk*. Working Paper. https://business.illinois.edu/accountancy/wp-content/uploads/sites/12/2014/10/Tax-2013-Guenther.pdf

Hainey, M. (2011). Building and Integrating Databases for Risk Profiles in the United Kingdom. In M. S. Khwaja, R. Awasthi, & J. Loeprick (Eds.), *Risk-Based Tax Audits: Approaches and Country Experiences* (pp. 65–70). The World Bank Publishing. doi:10.1596/9780821387542_CH06

Henehan, P. J., & Walsh, A. (2008). *Global Tax Risk Management*. Bloomsbury Professional.

Holton, G. A. (2004). Defining Risk. *Financial Analysts Journal*, *60*(6), 19–25. doi:10.2469/faj.v60.n6.2669

Hoyng, R., Kloosterhof, S., & Macpherson, A. (2010). Tax Control Framework. In A. Bakker, S. Kloosterhof (Eds), Tax Risk Management From Risk to Opportunity (pp. 19–70). IBFD.

Hutchens, M., & Rego, S. O. (2015). *Does Greater Tax Risk Lead to Increased Firm Risk?* Working Paper. https://papers.ssrn.com/sol3/papers.cfm?abstract_id=2186564

Kopczuk, W. (2006). Tax Simplification and Tax Compliance: An Economic Perspective. In M. Sawicky (Ed.), *Bridging the Tax Gap. Addressing the Crisis in Tax Administration* (pp. 111–143). Economic Policy Institute.

KPMG. (2007). *Tax Governance Institute, Tax Risk Management eSurvey*. http://www.surveys.kpmg.com/aci/docs/surveys/Tax_Riskmanagement_esurvey.pdf

KPMG. (2021). *CEO Outlook Pulse Survey*. https://home.kpmg/xx/en/home/insights/2021/03/ceo-outlook-pulse.html.

Lavermicocca, C. (2011). Tax Risk Management Practices and Their Impact On Tax Compliance Behaviour – The Views of Tax Executives from Large Australian Companies. *eJournal of Tax Research*, *9*(1), 89-115.

Lavermicocca, C. & Buchan, J. (2015). Role of Reputational Risk in Tax Decision Making by Large Companies. *eJournal of Tax Research*, *13*(1), 5-50.

Lin, X., Liu, M., So, S., & Yuen, D. (2019). Corporate Social Responsibility, Firm Performance and Tax Risk. *Managerial Auditing Journal*, *34*(9), 1101–1130. doi:10.1108/MAJ-04-2018-1868

Loeprick, J., & Engelschalk, M. (2011). Simplified Risk Scoring for SMEs. In M. S. Khwaja, R. Awasthi, & J. Loeprick (Eds.), *Risk-Based Tax Audits: Approaches and Country Experiences* (pp. 45–54). The World Bank Publishing. doi:10.1596/9780821387542_CH04

Merna, T., & Al-Thani, F. (2008). *Corporate Risk Management* (Vol. 2). John Wiley & Sons.

Mik, B. (2010). Introduction to Tax Risk Management. In A. Bakker & S. Kloosterhof (Eds.) Tax Risk Management: From Risk to Opportunity (pp. 1–17). IBFD.

Mulligan, E., & Oats, L. (2009). Tax Risk Management: Evidence from The US. *British Tax Review*, 6(1), 680–703.

Neubig, T., & Sangha, B. (2004). Tax Risk and Strong Corporate Governance. *The Tax Executive*, (March-April), 114–119.

Neuman, S. S., Omer, T. C., & Schmidt, A. P. (2013). *Risk and Return: Does Tax Risk Reduce Firms' Effective Tax Rates?* https://pages.business.illinois.edu/accountancy/wp-content/uploads/sites/12/2014/10/Tax-2013-Consortium-Neuman.pdf

OECD. (2004). *Compliance Risk Management: Managing and Improving Tax Compliance*. https://www.oecd.org/tax/administration/33818656.pdf

OECD. (2008). *Study into the Role of Tax Intermediaries*. https://www.oecd.org/tax/administration/39882938.pdf

OECD. (2009). *General Administrative Principles: Corporate Governance and Tax Risk Management, Tax Guidance Series Forum on Tax Administration*. https://www.oecd.org/tax/administration/43239887.pdf

OECD. (2013). *Co-operative Compliance: A Framework: From Enhanced Relationship to Co-operative Compliance*. OECD Publishing. doi:10.1787/9789264200852-

OECD. (2015). *G20/OECD Principles of Corporate Governance*. OECD Publishing. doi:10.1787/9789264236882-

OECD. (2016). *Co-operative Tax Compliance: Building Better Tax Control Framework*. OECD Publishing. doi:10.1787/9789264253384-

OECD. (2021a). *Tax Administration 2021: Comparative Information on OECD and other Advanced and Emerging Economies*. OECD Publishing. doi:10.1787/cef472b9-

OECD. (2021b). Tax Policy Reforms 2021 Special Edition on Tax Policy during the COVID-19 Pandemic. OECD Publishing. doi:10.1787/427d2616-en

Oliveira Neto, A. M. (2017). *Governance and Risk Management in Taxation*. Springer. doi:10.1007/978-981-10-2297-5

Owens, J., Roy-Chowdhury, C., & Huibregtse, S. (2015). *Tax Risk and Tax Risk Management: How to Mitigate Tax Risk in a BEPS-driven Environment*. CFE Forum 2015, Tax Governance and Tax Risk Management in a post-BEPS World.

Petolick, G. (2010). United States. In A. Bakker & S. Kloosterhof (Eds.) Tax Risk Management: From Risk to Opportunity (pp. 431–468). IBFD.

PwC & World Bank. (2020). *Paying Taxes 2020*. https://www.pwc.com/gx/en/paying-taxes/pdf/pwc-paying-taxes-2020.pdf

Quentin, C. (2019). Acceptable Levels of Tax Risk as a Metric of Corporate Tax Responsibility: Theory, and a Survey of Practice. *Nordic Tax Journal, 1*(1), 1–15. doi:10.1515/ntaxj-2019-0001

Rensburg, J. (2012). *Tax Risk Management: A Framework for Implementation* (Master's thesis). University of Pretoria, South Africa.

Russo, R. (2010). Risk Management in Taxation. In M. Daelen & C. Elst (Eds.), *Risk Management and Corporate Governance: Interconnections in Law, Accounting and Tax* (pp. 163–190). Edward Elgar Publishing. doi:10.4337/9781849807999.00012

Segal, T., & Maroun, W. (2014). Tax Risk-Management Analysis: Comparison Between the United States of America, The United Kingdom and South Africa. *Journal of Economic and Financial Sciences, 7*(2), 375–392. doi:10.4102/jef.v7i2.146

Tarca, A. (2012). *The Case for Global Accounting Standards: Arguments and Evidence*. https://papers.ssrn.com/sol3/papers.cfm?abstract_id=2204889

Tavares, F., Santos, E. & Tavares, V. (2021). Risk Categorization in Portuguese Organizations in Times of the COVID-19 Pandemic – an Exploratory Statistical Analysis. *Journal of Entrepreneurship and Public Policy, 10*(3), 306-322. . doi:10.1108/JEPP-03-2021-0033

Torrey, A. (2008). *The Discriminant Analysis Used by the IRS to Predict Profitable Individual Tax Return Audits*. http://digitalcommons.bryant.edu/cgi/viewcontent.cgi?article=1000&context=honors_mathematics.

UK Finance Act 2016 Schedule 19, https://www.legislation.gov.uk/ukpga/2016/24/schedule/19/2016-09-15

UK Financial Reporting Council. (2012). https://www.frc.org.uk/getattachment/e322c20a-1181-4ac8-a3d3-1fcfbcea7914/UK-Corporate-Governance-Code-(September-2012).pdf

Walicka, M. (2014). Tax Risks Sources and Consequences as a part of Intercultural Management at Family Companies. *Journal of Intercultural Management, 6*(4), 191–201. doi:10.2478/joim-2014-0045

World Bank. (2020). *Global Economic Prospects, June 2020*. Washington, DC: World Bank. https://openknowledge.worldbank.org/handle/10986/33748

Wunder, H. F. (2009). Tax Risk Management and The Multinational Enterprise. *Journal of International Accounting, Auditing & Taxation, 18*(1), 14–28. doi:10.1016/j.intaccaudtax.2008.12.003

York, S. (2011). A Risk-Based Approach to Large Businesses. In M. S. Khwaja, R. Awasthi, & J. Loeprick (Eds.), *Risk-Based Tax Audits: Approaches and Country Experiences* (pp. 39–44). The World Bank Publishing. doi:10.1596/9780821387542_CH03

Chapter 13
Boosted Decision Trees for Credit Scoring

Luca Di Persio
University of Verona, Italy

Alberto Borelli
University of Verona, Italy

ABSTRACT

The chapter developed a tree-based method for credit scoring. It is useful because it helps lenders decide whether to grant or reject credit to their applicants. In particular, it proposes a credit scoring model based on boosted decision trees which is a technique consisting of an ensemble of several decision trees to form a single classifier. The analysis used three different publicly available datasets, and then the prediction accuracy of boosted decision trees is compared with the one of support vector machines method.

MACHINE LEARNING AND FINANCIAL RISK MANAGEMENT

During last decades we have witnessed to an impetuous growth of Machine Learning (ML) applications in almost all areas related to everything could have a relation with data, no matter about their proper organisation, source, deep, sampling frequency, even independently from the fact that they have been artificially generated or taken from real life scenario. From this point of view, one of the areas that have been received most attention has certainly been the one related to the modern theory of financial markets, particularly within the financial risk management (FRM) sector. The latter is mostly justified by the huge amount of organised data, as in the case of financial time series, that have been made available, often real time, by several both private and open access sources. Nevertheless, such a reason, being necessary, is far from being sufficient, since, as to efficiently deal with thousands of giga of heterogeneous data aiming at providing, e.g., accurate forecasting methods for risky quantities, we also need effective computational solutions. Toward this direction, classical approximation/calibration schemes, as in the case of Monte Carlo-based approaches, see, e.g., (Sandmann, G., Koopma, S.J., 1998), spectral and/or asymptotic solutions, see, e.g., (Albeverio, Cordoni, Di Persio, Pellegrini, 2019, Bonollo, Di Persio,

DOI: 10.4018/978-1-7998-8609-9.ch013

Pellegrini, 2015) and references therein, simply fail to produce results in reasonable amount of times, no matter about the use of personal computers or in-cloud solutions. From a theoretical point of view, an alternative has been given by schemes based on nested neural networks, ensemble of ML-methods, and possibly hybridized alternatives, e.g. mixing strong results belonging to the realm of S(P)Des with calibration procedures coming from the ML world. Nevertheless, such approaches started to be computationally walkable just during recent years, namely when proper algorithms have been developed, exploiting modern programming languages and shared programming platforms, together with a massive increasing of computational strength essentially realized by on-line calculus platforms, nowadays also reliable and secure, as in the case AWS, Azure, Kamatera, etc. As a result, aforementioned sophisticated, but classical, statistical-based models, have been progressively substituted by a massive use of ML-related solutions within everyday financial institutions' activities, spanning within different economics areas, such, e.g., management, banking, insurance, etc., where ML/NNs solutions are higher and higher implemented to derive financial predictions, risk modelling scenarios, optimal portfolio constructions, insurance strategies, etc.

The just depicted scenario traduces in a set of both theoretical and applied methodologies, applications, analytical solutions, numerical schemes, practical determinations, data collection and relative evaluations, which form a world simply too wide to be collapsed in just one chapter, or even in a series of books. Rather, we preferred to focus our attention on a specific class of NN-based approach to a specific financial tasks which is known as the credit scoring problem. As to better introduce both the methods used and the financial application considered, let us provide a brief overview about the financial risk management world. First of all, let us recall that financial risk sources are classically grouped into the following classes: adverse financial market movements, loan defaults, unexpected insurance claims, fraudulent activities, customers loss. According with such risk clusters, it is then possible to classify risk into different categories, i.e.: market risk, insurance or demographic risk, operating risk and credit risk .

Market risk refers to the uncertainties in the value of the company's underlying assets, liabilities, or income due to exposure to a highly dynamic financial market.

Insurance and Demographic risk is more specific to the insurance industry. Indeed, it refers to the variance in insurance claim experience due to unpredictable events (e.g. catastrophes, car accidents, etc.) as well as uncertainties involved with the demographic profile of its policyholders (e.g. mortality).

Operational risk refers to the risk of loss due to the unpredictability of business operation or loss of performance due to faulty or fraudulent business practices.

Finally, *Credit risk* refers to the uncertainty involving creditors' ability to perform their contractual obligation (loan defaults or bankruptcy). This is applicable for both retail lenders (lenders who provide loans to individuals or retail customers) and corporate lenders (lenders who provide loans to businesses).

For what concerns market risk, one of the principal tasks one has to consider when treating both its possible sources and related solution, is linked to the volatility measurement and associated forecasting. One of the possible models that can be effectively implemented to address such tasks is the Generalized Autoregressive Conditional Heteroskedasticity (GARCH) one, considering its output as one of the inputs for a Multi-Layered Perceptron model. Indeed, such a solution has shown to be able to provide accurate volatility prediction (Kristjanpoller, Fadic, & Minutolo, 2014), improving performances obtained implementing traditional methods like Exponentially Weighted Moving Average (EWMA), Autoregressive Conditional Heteroskedasticity (ARCH) or the classical GARCH. Experiments suggest also that Long Short-Term Memory (LSTM), which is a variant of Recurrent Neural Networks (RNN), can outperform the traditional GARCH model, while providing more robust forecasts (Liu, 2019).

Along the same line of applications, hybrid method as the one we have just recalled, can be applied to address portfolio optimization problems, when market risk refers to the process of allocating a set of financial contracts to maximise the expected return and minimize financial risk. For this purpose, Support Vector Machines (SVM) effectively help identifying the non-linear relationship between market variables (Lee, Cho, Kwon, & Sohn, 2018). Moreover, NNs-based methods, e.g., Convolutional Neural Networks (CNN), RNN and LSTM, are widely used to find the optimal portfolio (Jiang & Liang, Cryptocurrency Portfolio Management with Deep Reinforcement Learning, 2017), (Jiang, Xu, & Liang, A Deep Reinforcement Learning Framework for the Financial Portfolio Management Problem, 2017).

With respect to insurance and demographic risk management, then when the risk is the one of financial institution offering insurance services of different types, we must safeguard their operational activities, as well as investors' capitals, from running the peril of being overexposed, possibly limiting the probability for the insured investment to trespassing critical indebtedness. As to give an example, claim modelling help such insurance companies with the prediction of future costs regarding insurance claims made by policyholders. In this scenario, it has been shown that Boosted Trees (BT) architectures can outperform the traditional generalized linear models in forecasting claim frequency and severity (Guelman, 2012), (Wuthrich & Buser, 2020).

Concerning the operational risk, namely the consequence of fraudulent activities inside companies of the financial sector, it is worth stressing that this practice can be economically damaging for any type of business, therefore financial fraud detection systems using ML- based algorithms to recognize fraudulent activities have been widely implemented, particularly when huge quantities of data have to be taken into account, because of their speed of convergence in detecting anomalous behaviour that are classified into probability clusters identifying various confidence-like groups of malignant operational activities. In this scenario, different analysis have been conducted exploiting binary classification algorithm such as logistic regression, k-nearest neighbour, decision trees or SVM (Maniraj, Aditya, Shadab, & Swarna, Credit Card Fraud Detection using Machine Learning and Data Science, 2019), (Sharma & Panigrahi, 2013), (Sahin, Bulkan, & Duman, 2013).

Let us also remember that credit risk can be also related to the uncertainty of an individual borrower to recover the obligations of a loan or to corporations going bankrupt. Usually, credit scoring refers to the risk classification of a retail borrower and bankruptcy refers to institutional borrower. In both cases the situation is well described by a binary classification problem. The only difference regards predictors involved in it. In case of bankruptcy predictors are financial ratios derived from the company's balance sheets or income statements, while for credit scoring are used several financial and demographic information of the loan applicant. Models used for the credit risk evaluation can be divided into two main groups: *Supervised learning methods*, in fact many studies have shown that single classifiers like SVM, NN, Classification and Regression trees (CART), Gaussian Process-based classifiers and Deep belief networks (DBN) can be used and also improved through ensemble learning approaches (bagging, boosting, stacking) (Yu, Yue, Wang, & Lai, 2010), (West, 2000), (Khandani, Kim, & Lo, 2010), (Shian-Chang, 2011), (Luo, Wu, & Wu, 2016), (Ghodselahi, 2011), (Gang, Jinxing, M., & Hongbing, 2011); *Unsupervised learning methods*, in particular clustering methods, which help to identify groups of loan applicants with different characteristics.

INTRODUCTION TO CREDIT SCORING

Credit scoring is a technique which helps financial institutions to evaluate the probability for a credit applicant to default on the financial obligation and consequently decide if approve the credit or not. In particular, the accurate prediction on the creditworthiness allows the financial institutions to increase their volume of granted credit and in the meanwhile to minimize the losses. Moreover, the importance of these techniques is due to the fact that the large volume of loan portfolios also implies that modest improvements in scoring accuracy may result in significant savings for financial institutions (West, 2000).

The main aim of the credit scoring model is to classify the applicants into two classes; the first one is the "good credit" class which is composed by those applicants that will reimburse the financial obligation; the second one is the "bad credit" class which is composed by those applicants who have a high probability of defaulting the financial obligation. The classification is contingent on socio-demographic characteristics of the borrower (such as age, education level, occupation, and income), the repayment performance on previous loans and the type of loan.

Credit scoring models can be grouped within following categories: parametric, non-parametric and data mining models. Decision trees and support vector machines are both part of the class of non-parametric models. Moreover, it is possible to observe significant improvements in accuracies when aggregating scores predicted exploiting accurately tailored ensembles of individual classifiers.

Therefore we consider boosted decision trees rather than a single decision tree. Indeed, this technique consists in grouping the action of several decision trees as to form a single classifier by weighting majority vote of classifications predicted by each (tree) individual component of the ensemble itself. Finally, obtained performance is evaluated using three real world datasets taken from the UCI Irvine Machine Learning Repository (Lichman, s.d.), and then compared with those obtained by exploiting the support vector machines method.

BOOSTED DECISION TREES

Decision Trees

Let us suppose to have a dataset containing several credit applicants characterized by a number P of attributes that we denote with $X_1,...,X_P$. Moreover, assume that these applicants are divided into two classes: "good credit" and "bad credit". The latter implies, we are considering a binary classification problem in which the output variable Y can assume only two values.

Accordingly, the output space can be denoted as $\mathcal{Y} = \{c_1, c_2\}$ or $\mathcal{Y} = \{0,1\}$.

The aim of this classification task is to find a classifier φ able to separate the good credit applicants from the bad ones.

The algorithm starts from the root node, i.e. the one containing the learning set $\mathcal{L}$. and then it has to loop over all the possible splits to find the best one, which will be denoted by s^*, being the best of the best splits defined on each attribute X_j with $j \in \{1,...,P\}$. In other words, the algorithm run along the possible attributes to find the best splitting variable X_j and the correspondent best splitting threshold v_j.

The same procedure is then repeated on the correspondent child nodes until a stopping criterion, to be decided, is met.

If we denote with p the purity of a node, i.e. the fraction of good credit instances in it, then the Gini index of that node is given by $p(1-p)$.

Let us recall that the Gini index is a measure of the dispersion or diversity of the population in our dataset.

It then follows that minimizing such an index we obtain more homogeneous child nodes in the labels than the parent nodes. For this reason, at every node, we choose the splitting attribute and the splitting threshold that minimize the sum of the Gini indices of the corresponding child nodes. It is worth to note that, if at a given node it happens that the sum of the Gini indices of the child nodes is greater than the Gini index of the parent node, for any attribute and for any possible threshold, then the parent node cannot be split, since we would not have a positive impurity decrease Δ_i.

Figure 1. Example of decision tree for credit scoring

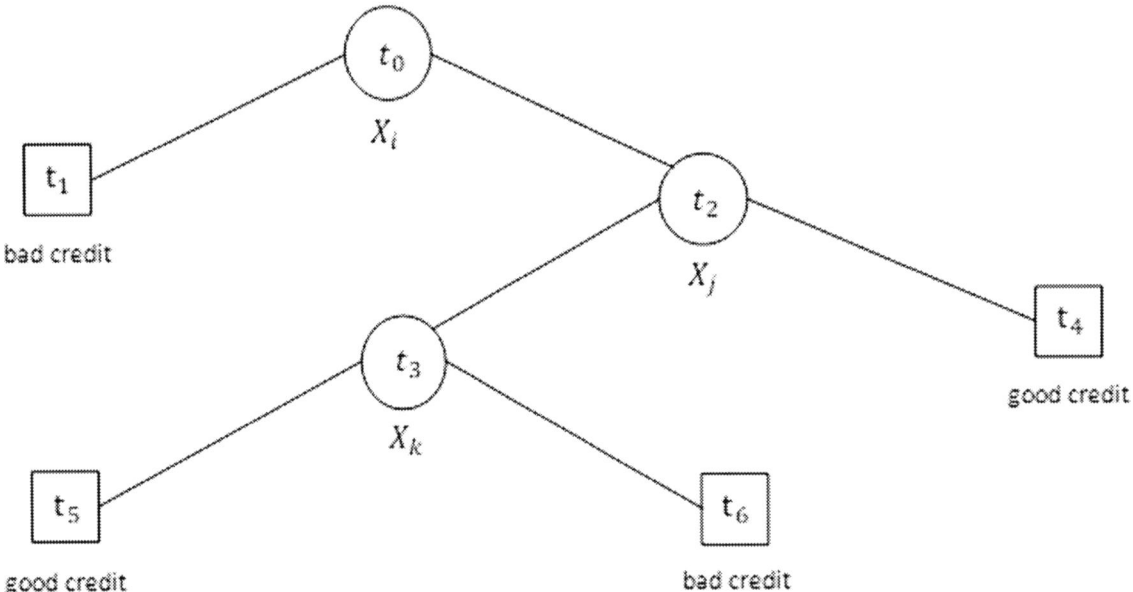

In the above Figure 1, terminal nodes (also called *leaves*) are depicted with rectangles, and they are classified according to the most prevalent class in them. Indeed, a leaf is labelled as "good credit" if the number of good credit applicants in there is greater than the number of the bad ones, and vice versa. Moreover, a good (bad) credit is correctly classified if it belongs to a good (bad) terminal node.

We have also to recall that a decision tree can be developed until terminal nodes contain only good credits or only bad credits, but, as we have already mentioned, this could cause the overfitting phenomena, then running the risk that the model captures spurious noise from the learning set. A possible solution to avoid overfitting consists in pruning the tree.

The latter means that, once the decision tree is fully developed, we remove all the nodes that are not statistically significant.

Boosted Decision Trees for Credit Scoring

Last, but not least, it is relevant to recall that decision trees show a defect, which is the instability that translates into small fluctuations in the input data that may cause huge variations in the classification provided by the model.

For instance, if there are two attributes giving rise to similar impurity decrease, a small fluctuation in one of them may cause the algorithm to split a given node using the other attribute, while without fluctuations the splitting attribute was the first one. Moreover, since the whole tree structure would be modified below this node, the fluctuation may produce a completely different classifier response.

To overcome this defect, we will take into consideration an ensemble of trees in such a way that we can classify the instances according to the majority vote of the classifications given by individual trees.

Boosting

Boosting is a procedure which aggregates many weak classifiers to get higher classification performance than the one obtained by its single components.

Moreover, this method improves the stability of the classifiers response with respect to fluctuations in the training sample.

Within the afore described financial scenario, the algorithm starts assigning to each credit applicant the same weight $\omega 0$.

Then, a classifier is built and the weight of each applicant is changed according to the result of that classifier. Hence a second classifier is built using new weights of the training sample. Such a scheme is repeated several times to obtain a final classification of a credit applicant which turns to be a weighted average of the individual classifications over all classifiers. It is worth mentioning that there exist several methods to update the weights and combine the classifiers. We adopted the AdaBoost one (Freund and Schapire, 1996). It consists in calculating the total misclassification error of the tree ϵk after the $k t^h$ decision tree is built. The error is computed as the sum of the weights of misclassified credits over the sum of the weights of all credits:

$$\epsilon_k = \frac{\sum_j \omega_j^{(k)}}{\sum_i \omega_i^{(k)}}$$

where j loops over misclassified instances and i loops over all the instances of the data sample. Then the weights of misclassified credit applicants are increased as follows:

$$\omega_j^{(k+1)} = \frac{(1-\epsilon_k)}{\epsilon_k} \omega_j^{(k)}$$

Furthermore, the new weights must be renormalized:

$$\omega_i^{(k+1)} \to \frac{\omega_i^{(k+1)}}{\sum_i \omega_i^{(k+1)}}$$

and the (k+1)th tree is constructed. Note that while the algorithm proceeds, the hard-to-classify instances become predominant. Finally, the score of each credit applicant *i* is a weighted sum of the classifications over the individual trees:

$$F_i = \sum_{k=1}^{N} \log\left(\frac{1-\epsilon_k}{\epsilon_k}\right) f_i^{(k)} \qquad (1)$$

where N is the number of trees used in the boosting algorithm, $f_i^{(k)} = +1$ if in the kth tree the applicant i is on a good credit leaf, while $f_i^{(k)} = -1$ on the contrary. By equation (1) we have that applicants classified as "good" will tend to have high positive scores, while applicants classified as "bad" will tend to have large negative scores. Moreover, trees with lower misclassification errors ϵk are given more weight when the final classification is computed.

SUPPORT VECTOR MACHINES

When data points from a learning set (e.g., credit card applicants from a real dataset) are linearly separable, there exist several hyperplanes (i.e. several linear models) that are in fact equivalent in class identification's task. In generalization however, these hyperplanes are usually not equivalent. The key idea of Support Vector Machines (SVM) models is that a good separation is intuitively achieved when the distance, also known as margin, to the nearest data points is as large as possible, since in general the larger the margin the lower the generalization error of the model.

From a formal point of view, let us define the learning set $\mathcal{L} = \{(x_i, y_i)\}_{i=1}^{N}$ with $x_i \in R^p$. In this case we assume, without loss of generality, that $y_i \in \{+1, -1\}$. In particular, we have that:

$y_i = +1$ if $x_i \in A$.

$y_i = -1$ if $x_i \in B$

where A and B are the two classes (e.g., good and bad credit applicants) we use to divide our data points. Then a typical SVM approach consists in finding a $(p-1)$ hyperplane which separates points with label +1 from points whose label is -1. Mathematically we want to learn the set of parameters $w \in R^p$ and b such that:

$x_i \in A$ if $w^T \psi(x_i) + b \geq 0$

$x_i \in B$ if $w^T \psi(x_i) + b < 0$

where:

$$D(x) = \sum_{j=1}^{p} \omega_j \psi_j(x) + b$$

is the so-called decision function. Note that such function is required to be linear in the parameters, but it is not necessarily linear w.r.t. x dependence. Defining the function D, we consider the ψ_j to be pre-defined functions of x while ωj and b are the adjustable parameters of the decision function itself.

In the dual space, the decision functions are of the form:

$$D(x) = \sum_{i=1}^{N} \alpha_i K(x_i, x) + b$$

where αi are the parameters to be adjusted, while K *is* a predefined kernel, for example a potential function or any radial basis function. Under certain conditions, symmetric kernels possess finite or infinite series expansions of the form:

$$K(x, x') = \sum_j \psi_j(x) \psi_j(x')$$

Provided that the expansion exists, then the two decision functions' equations are the dual representations of the same thing. Hence

$$\omega_j = \sum_{i=1}^{N} \alpha_i \psi_j(x_i)$$

are the direct parameters and αi are called dual parameters.

For example, if we take the *j*th component of x in place of $\psi_j(x)$ then, at the end of the learning task, we get the resulting hyperplane $H = \{x \mid w^{Tx} + b = 0\}$ which gives the decision boundary for the prediction of new data's class:

· Points on the positive side are classified with +1;
· Points on the negative side are classified with -1.

It is worth stressing that latter procedure has some drawbacks. Indeed, to be efficient, data must be linearly separable. Moreover, we may pick infinitely many hyperplanes satisfying our condition on the learning set. Nevertheless, such issues can be overcame working on the model conditions and applying some algebra as shown, e.g., in (Boser, Bernhard, & Guyon, 1996).

EMPIRICAL ANALYSIS

Figure 2. Age distribution of German applicants

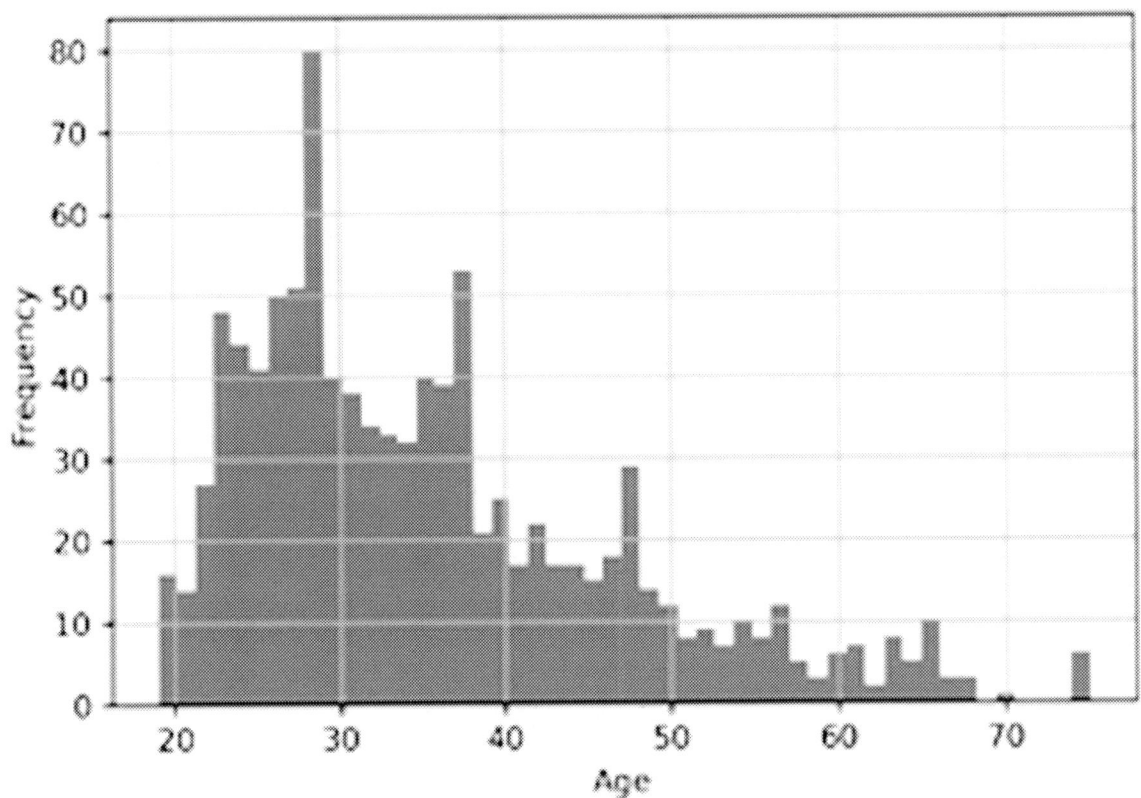

Dataset Description

In the following analysis, credit scoring models have been developed using three popular credit risk datasets taken from the UCI Irvine Machine Learning Repository (Lichman, s.d.). The first one is the German dataset, consisting of 1000 instances, where 700 instances correspond to creditworthy (good) applicants, while the remaining 300 are those (bad) applicants to whom credit should not be extended. Each applicant is described by 24 attributes concerning the status of existing accounts, credit history records, loan amount and purpose, employment status and an assortment of personal information such as age, sex and marital status.

The second dataset is the Australian one and it contains 690 instances divided in 307 creditworthy and 383 bad applicants. Each instance is described by 14 attributes. Six attributes are continuous while the remaining are categorical. To preserve the confidentiality of the data, the names and values of the attributes were replaced by meaningless identifiers. This dataset has the appealing feature of containing attributes that are continuous, nominal with small number of values and nominal with large number of values. A few instances had attributes with missing values. These were replaced by the mode and mean of the attribute for categorical and continuous variables, respectively.

Finally, the third dataset is the Japanese one which has been built in a similar way of the Australian one, containing 690 instances (307 good applicants, the remaining 383 considered to be bad ones) described by 15 attributes of which six are numerical and nine categorical.

Parameters Tuning

Usually in a classification problem, the available data sample is divided into a training set and a test set. This subdivision allows the model to learn population's features exploiting the training set, while its prediction performance is then evaluated using the test set. To allow the model to train on a large part of the dataset and then to evaluate the prediction accuracy on the complete dataset, we implemented a 10-fold cross validation. It consists in dividing the whole dataset into ten disjoint subsets of equal size and sequentially testing the prediction performance on each of these subsets, while the model is trained on the corresponding complementary set.

About the parameters optimal selection for each model, we implemented a grid-search approach. It implies that different parameter values have been considered and for each of them we computed the prediction accuracy in terms of the area under the Receiver Operating Characteristic (ROC) curve, see the next section for more details.

According to the boosted decision trees (BDT) method, the prediction has been optimized adjusting two parameters, namely: the number N of decision trees that are aggregated to form the final classifier, and the minimum number of credit applicants N_{min} that a tree node must contain to be split, observing that when the number of applicants in a node reaches this threshold value, the growth of the branch is terminated.

The support vector machines (SVM) method has been implemented using a Gaussian radial basis function, then performing the calibration according with two parameters: the *gamma parameter* γ, and the soft margin parameter C for the cost function. Accordingly, the tuning phase consists in finding the optimal pair (γ, C) in terms of prediction accuracy evaluated using the area under the ROC curve. In particular, γ is the inverse of the standard deviation of the Gaussian radial basis function, that can be seen as a similarity measure between two points. Thus, a small (large) value of gamma leads to a Gaussian function with large (small) variance, which intuitively means that two points can be considered similar even if they are far apart (only if they are close together). Instead, the selection of C is a trade-of between error penalty and stability.

Intuitively, C gives information on how aggressively you want the model to avoid misclassifying each sample. Therefore, large (small) values of C lead to the optimizer seeking a small-margin (large-margin) hyperplane if this results in more accurate classification (even if this leads to greater misclassification). When dealing with real data, the best pair (γ, C) has been achieved testing values for the two parameters taken from exponentially growing sequences. It is worth to note that both BDT and SVM methods have been implemented in Python, also exploiting the Scikit-learn library, and by using a personal computer equipped with an AMD Ryzen 5 processor with 8 GB of RAM, therefore exploiting a rather simple sw/hw solution.

Table 1. On the left, resp. right, the results for the BDT, resp. SVM, parameters tuning. Computational time for each procedure is reported in minutes and seconds, for each of the three datasets considered.

Datasete	N	N_{min}	Time	Dataset	γ	C	Time
German	500	5	18:57	German	2^{-17}	2^{13}	01:21
Australian	59	3	15:01	Australian	2^{-25}	2^{15}	00:27
Japanese	100	18	10:09	Japanese	2^{-19}	2^{13}	00:18

Results

The performance of the credit scoring model can be measured in terms of capability of distinguishing *good* from *bad* individuals within the credit population constituting the test set. In general, since a binary classifier divides all data instances as either positive or negative, then this classification produces four types of outcomes: two types of correct classification, true positives (TP) and true negatives (TN), and two types of incorrect classification, false positives (FP) and false negatives (FN); the last two are also known as Type I error and Type II error respectively. A 2x2 table formulated with these four outcomes is called confusion matrix. In Figure 3 are reported confusion matrices for the BDT and the SVM methods in all the three datasets.

The BTD algorithm assigns to each applicant a score according to the equation *1*. With that equation, good credit applicants will have high positive scores while bad credit applicants will get large negative scores. In this way, for those applicants with a score above a certain threshold, the credit can be granted; while, for those applicants whose score is below the same threshold, the credit must be rejected. In particular, once a cut-off is chosen, the model can commit two types of incorrect predictions: the model grants credit to applicants that will default on the financial obligation (Type I error) and the model rejects credit to those applicants that are creditworthy (Type II error). The cut-off value represents a compromise between a large efficiency for granting credit and a large rejection of bad credits. An excessively large efficiency for granting credit may result in severe economic losses due to delinquent costumers, while a credit policy that is too strict may result in opportunity costs that surpass the costs of default. The selected cut-off value will ultimately depend on the relative ratio of the misclassification costs associated to Type I and Type II errors. Moreover, it must be noted that in general misclassification errors related to bad applicants are financially more damaging than misclassification errors related to good applicants.

Since the cut-off value depends on the credit policy of the financial institution, to compare the performance of the BDT method with the one of the SVM method, a powerful solution is to use threshold-free measures such as ROC and PRC plots. These threshold-free measures require classifiers to produce *scores* to be used to divide the dataset into positively and negatively predicted classes, and not simply provide a static division.

Figure 3. Confusion matrices of different datasets for both BDT and SVM methods; the class of creditworthy applicants corresponds to 0 and the class of bad applicants corresponds to 1

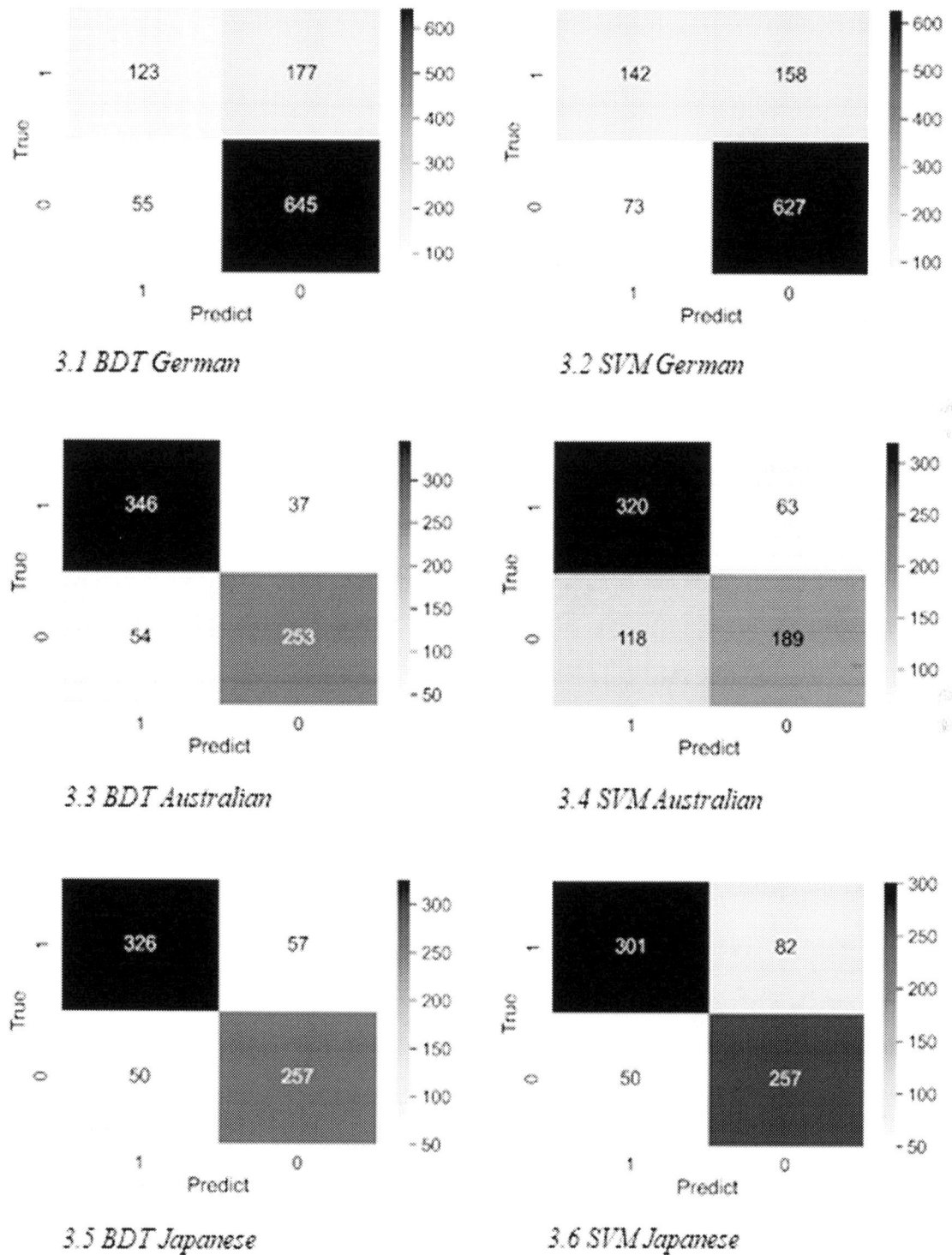

3.1 BDT German

3.2 SVM German

3.3 BDT Australian

3.4 SVM Australian

3.5 BDT Japanese

3.6 SVM Japanese

The ROC plot shows pairs of *specificity* and *sensitivity* values calculated at all possible threshold scores. In particular, the specificity value is given by:

$$SP = \frac{TN}{TN + FP}$$

being the proportion of bad credit that is correctly classified, while the sensitivity is computed as follows:

$$SN = \frac{TP}{TP + FN}$$

also called true positive rate (tpr), representing the proportion of good applicants that are correctly classified. Accordingly, the ROC curve can be seen as a plot of the true positive rate as function of the false positive rate (fpr) given by 1–SP. Figure 4 shows the ROC curve for the Australian credit dataset obtained by merging the 10 cross-validation test sets.

If a model could separate completely the two populations, it would give only correct predictions. In this case, the ROC curve would pass through the point (0,1) and the area under the ROC curve would be equal to 1. On the other hand, classifiers with random performance show a straight diagonal line from (0, 0) to (1, 1). A model that performs better than random guessing gives a concave ROC curve above this straight line.

Figure 4. ROC curve for both BDT and SVM methods applied to the Australian dataset

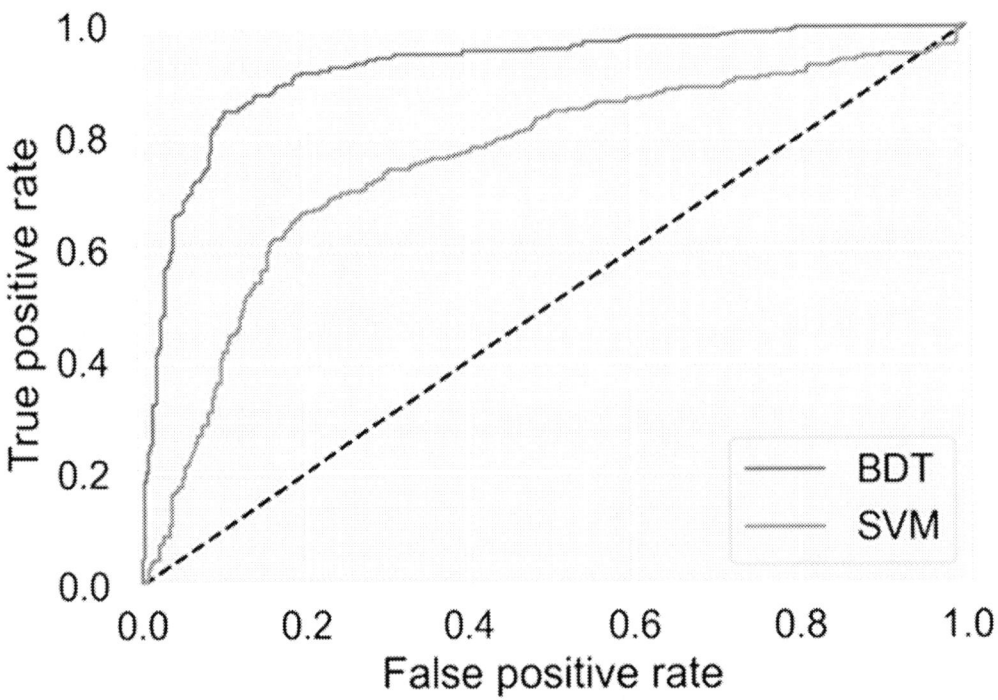

The higher is the model accuracy, the steeper will be the ROC curve. Therefore, the area under the ROC curve (AUC-ROC) is a measure of the accuracy generalization, which is independent of the cut-off value.

Table 2. Comparison of the area under the ROC curve for both BDT and SVM methods in all the datasets

Model	German	Australian	Japanese
SVM	0.8048	0.7538	0.8739
BDT	0.8018	0.9227	0.9032

In Table 2 we reported the values of the area under the ROC curve (calculated via Scikit-learn library), for both the BDT and the SVM methods. We note that for the German dataset the two methods reach almost the same performance, with a slight preference for the SVM. Concerning the Australian and the Japanese datasets, in both cases BDT performs better than SVM, nevertheless, see Figure 5.3, in the Japanese dataset case, one can notes that the SVM results are comparable to the one obtained by the BDT for false positive rates below 0.1 as well as for false positive rates above 0.5.

The visual interpretability of ROC plots in the context of imbalanced datasets can be deceptive with respect to conclusions about the reliability of classification performance, because of an intuitive but wrong interpretation of specificity. For this reason, in our analysis, we consider another measure for the performance's evaluation of both BDT and SVM. This alternative measure is the *positive predictive value* (PPV) and the related precision-recall curve, PRC. The latter can provide an accurate prediction of future classification performance since it evaluates the fraction of true positives among positive predictions. The PRC plot shows *precision* values for corresponding *recall* (equivalent to sensitivity) values, where the precision is given by:

$$\text{PREC} = \frac{\text{TP}}{\text{TP} + \text{FP}}$$

and it is equivalent to PPV. The precision is intuitively the ability of the classifier not to label as positive a sample that is negative. In Figure 6 we reported the PRC plot of both BDT and SVM methods about the Australian dataset; while, in Figure 5 we reported the plots for both the ROC and PRC curves about both the German and the Japanese datasets.

Figure 5. On the left plots of the ROC curves for both the German and the Japanese datasets; on the right the PRC plots for both German and Japanese datasets.

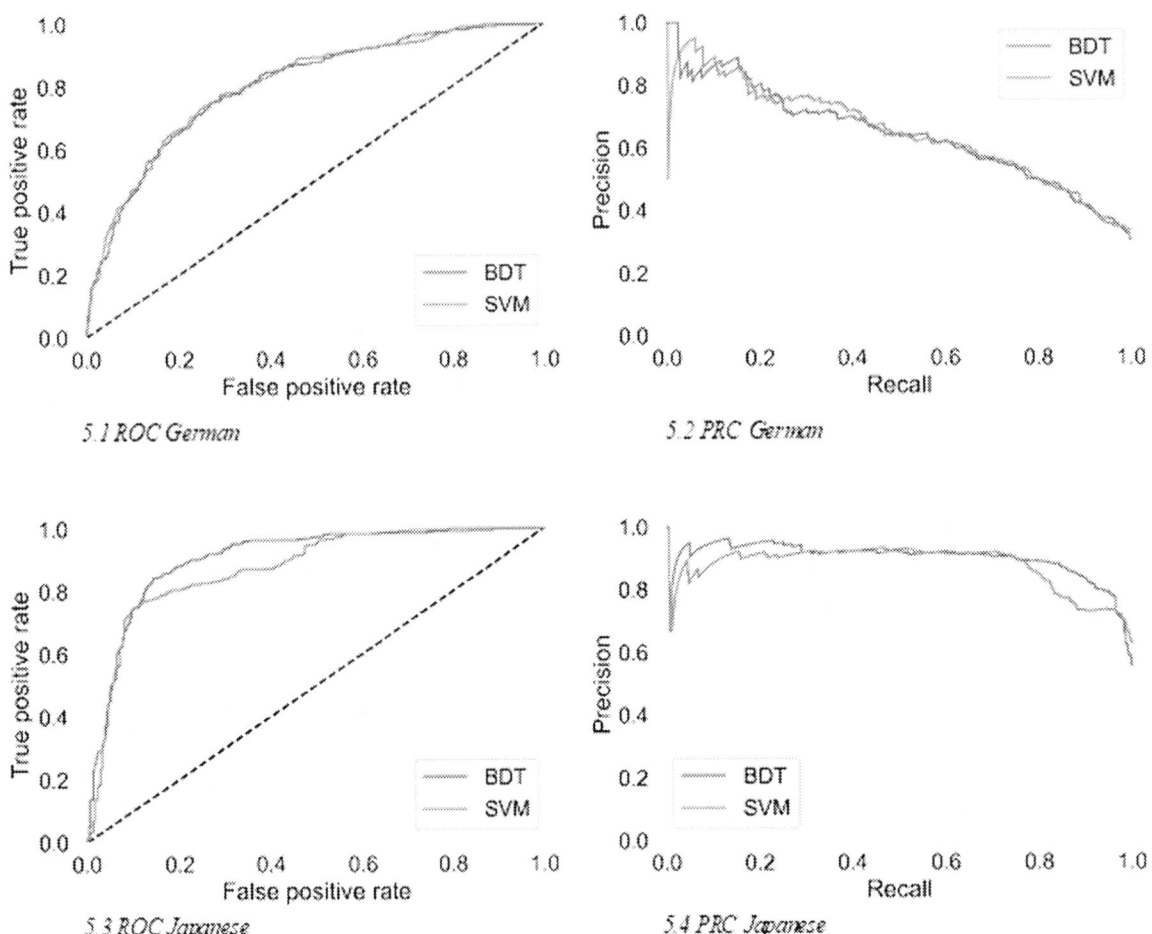

5.1 ROC German

5.2 PRC German

5.3 ROC Japanese

5.4 PRC Japanese

Similarly, to the ROC plot, the PRC plot provides a model-wide evaluation. Therefore, the AUC score of PRC is likewise effective in multiple-classifier comparisons. A high area under the curve represents both high recall and high precision, where high precision relates to a low false positive rate, and high recall relates to a low false negative rate.

Table 3. Comparison of the area under the PRC for both BDT and SVM methods in all the datasets

Model	German	Australian	Japanese
SVM	0.6467	0.6949	0.8727
BDT	0.6423	0.9029	0.8980

In Table 3 we reported the results for the computation of the area under the precision-recall curve. Let us note once again that BDT performs better than SVM for both the Australian and the Japanese datasets.

Instead, when dealing with the German dataset, we have that the score related to the SVM method is comparable, being slightly greater, to the BDT one. However, as already mentioned, the PRC criterion is useful in cases of imbalanced datasets. Summing up, we can conclude that both BDT and SVM methods do not reach good prediction accuracy in the case of German dataset, mainly because of its imbalance. Analogously, for the SVM performance when considering the Australian dataset, even if, in this case, it is worth considering that the dataset is not strongly imbalanced.

Figure 6. PRC plot for both BDT and SVM methods applied to the Australian dataset

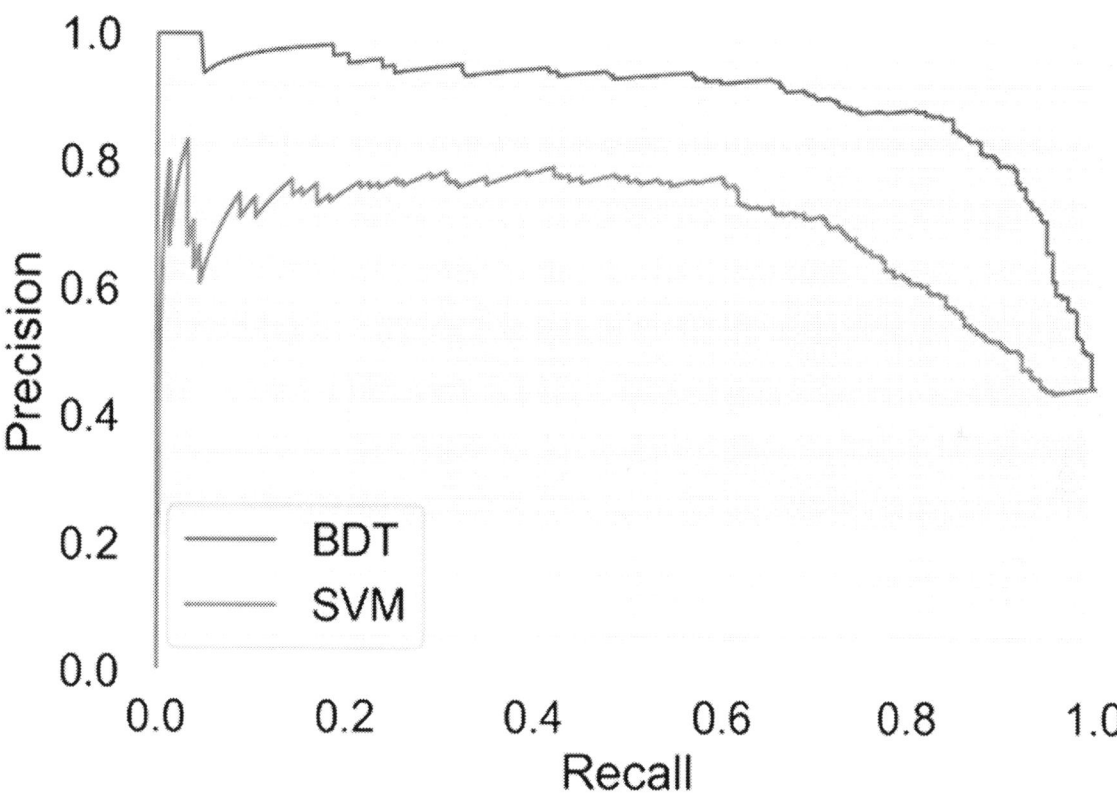

Comparison of the AUC-ROC Estimates

In this section we develop a comparison of the AUC-ROC scores reached by BDT and SVM, taking into consideration all the already considered three datasets. To test the statistical significance of the difference between the areas under the ROC curves obtained by the models under consideration, we considered a non-parametric model introduced by DeLong et al. (DeLong, DeLong, & Clarke-Pearson, 1988). The basic idea of this procedure relies on the fact that when calculated by the trapezoidal rule, the area falling under the points comprising an empirical ROC curve has been shown to be equal to the

Wilcoxon-Mann-Whitney U-statistic for comparing distributions of values from the two samples (see, e.g., Bamber, 1975). Therefore, the AUC-ROC can be interpreted as the probability that the score of a randomly selected good credit applicant is greater than or equal to the one of a randomly selected bad credit applicant.

Accordingly, let us denote by $X_i^{(g)}, i=1,\ldots,n_g$ the score of real good credit applicants and by $X_j^{(b)}, j=1,\ldots,n_b$, the estimated scores for real bad credit applicants, where n_g, resp. n_b, indicates the number of good, resp. bad, credit applicants belonging to the reference dataset. Thus, by the Wilcoxon-Mann-Whitney statistic, the area under the ROC curve can be estimated by:

$$\hat{\theta} = \frac{1}{n_g n_b}\sum_{j=1}^{n_b}\sum_{i=1}^{n_g} 1\left(X_i^{(g)} > X_j^{(b)}\right) + \frac{1}{2}1\left(X_i^{(g)} = X_j^{(b)}\right)$$

where the indicator function $1\left(X_i^{(g)} > X_j^{(b)}\right)$ equals 1 when $X_i^{(g)} > X_j^{(b)}$, while the indicator function $1\left(X_i^{(g)} = X_j^{(b)}\right)$ equals 1 when $X_i^{(g)} = X_j^{(b)}$. Moreover, to obtain an estimate of the variance of $\hat{\theta}$, the components of both the ith good credit and jth bad credit can be computed as follows:

$$v\left(X_i^{(g)}\right) = \frac{1}{n_b}\sum_{j=1}^{n_b} 1\left(X_i^{(g)} > X_j^{(b)}\right) + \frac{1}{2}1\left(X_i^{(g)} = X_j^{(b)}\right), \quad i=1,\ldots,n_g,$$

$$v\left(X_j^{(b)}\right) = \frac{1}{n_g}\sum_{i=1}^{n_g} 1\left(X_i^{(g)} > X_j^{(b)}\right) + \frac{1}{2}1\left(X_i^{(g)} = X_j^{(b)}\right), \quad j=1,\ldots,n_b.$$

So that the variance of $\hat{\theta}$ equals:

$$Var\left(\hat{\theta}\right) = \frac{1}{n_g(n_g-1)}\sum_{i=1}^{n_g}\left[v\left(X_i^{(g)}\right) - \hat{\theta}\right]^2 + \frac{1}{n_b(n_b-1)}\sum_{j=1}^{n_b}\left[v\left(X_j^{(b)}\right) - \hat{\theta}\right]^2.$$

Since we want to compare the AUC-ROC obtained by two alternative models, A and B, the covariance corresponding to $\hat{\theta}$ is:

$$Cov\left(\hat{\theta}_A, \hat{\theta}_B\right) = \frac{1}{n_g(n_g-1)}\sum_{i=1}^{n_g}\left[v_A\left(X_i^{(g)}\right) - \hat{\theta}_A\right]\left[v_B\left(X_i^{(g)}\right) - \hat{\theta}_B\right]$$
$$+ \frac{1}{n_b(n_b-1)}\sum_{j=1}^{n_b}\left[v_A\left(X_j^{(b)}\right) - \hat{\theta}_A\right]\left[v_B\left(X_j^{(b)}\right) - \hat{\theta}_B\right].$$

To test the null hypothesis $H_0 : \hat{\theta}_A = \hat{\theta}_B$ versus the alternative hypothesis $H_1 : \hat{\theta}_A \neq \hat{\theta}_B$, we used the following $\chi 2$ distributed test statistic with one degree of freedom:

$$T = \frac{\left(\widehat{\theta_A} - \widehat{\theta_B}\right)^2}{\widehat{Var\left(\theta_A - \theta_B\right)}}$$

where $\widehat{Var\left(\theta_A - \theta_B\right)} = \widehat{Var\left(\theta_A\right)} + \widehat{Var\left(\theta_B\right)} - 2\widehat{Cov\left(\theta_A, \theta_B\right)}$.

Table 4 reports the results of the previously described statistical test. As expected, there is strong evidence that performances of the BDT model concerning both the Australian and the Japanese datasets are better than the one provided by the SVM model. Indeed, we can reject the null hypothesis $\widehat{\theta_{BDT}} = \widehat{\theta_{SVM}}$ with a 95% significance level. Instead, for the German dataset, it is confirmed that the difference between the two methods is not particularly significant, since it is not possible to reject the null hypothesis.

Table 4. Statistical test for the significance in the difference between the area under the ROC curves estimated by the two different models

Test	German		Australian		Japanese	
	T	p-value	T	p-value	T	p-value
SVM-BDT	0.093	76.04%	79.935	<0.001%	7.476	0.63%

Importance of Attributes

Figure 7. Permutation feature importance of attributes in the BDT method for the German dataset

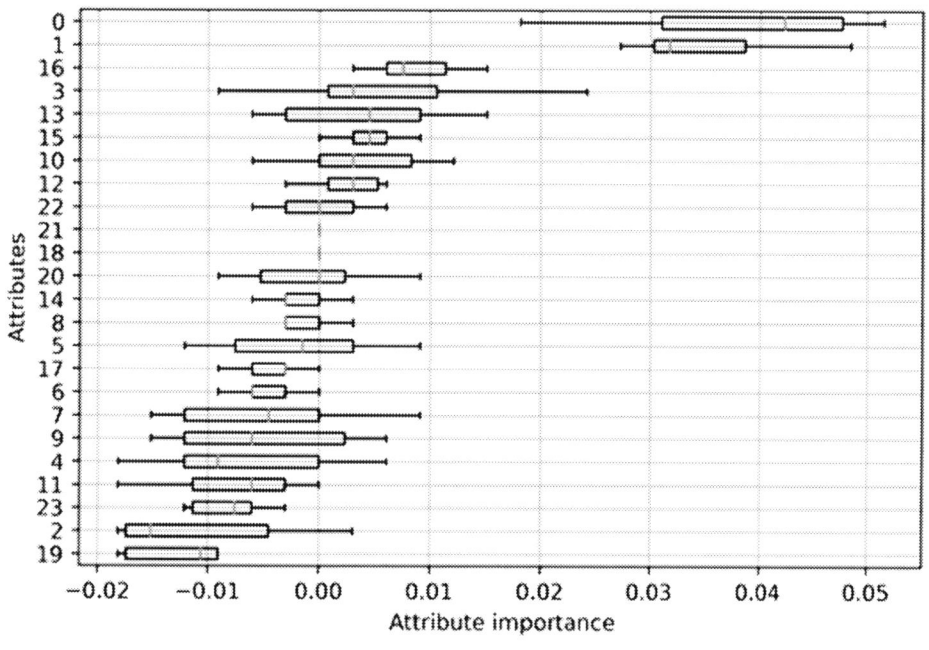

In what follows we provide an in-depth analysis of the role played by each attribute exploited by the BDT method. Impurity-based feature importance for decision trees tends to favour high cardinality features (typically numerical features) over low cardinality features, such as binary features or categorical variables with a small number of possible categories. For this reason, to measure the relevance of each feature, we implemented a permutation feature importance approach consisting in evaluating model score decrease when a single feature value is randomly shuffled. Such a procedure breaks the relationship between the feature and the target, and, accordingly, the drop in the model score indicates how much the model depends on the feature.

Figure 8. Permutation feature importance of attributes in the BDT method for both Australian and Japanese datasets

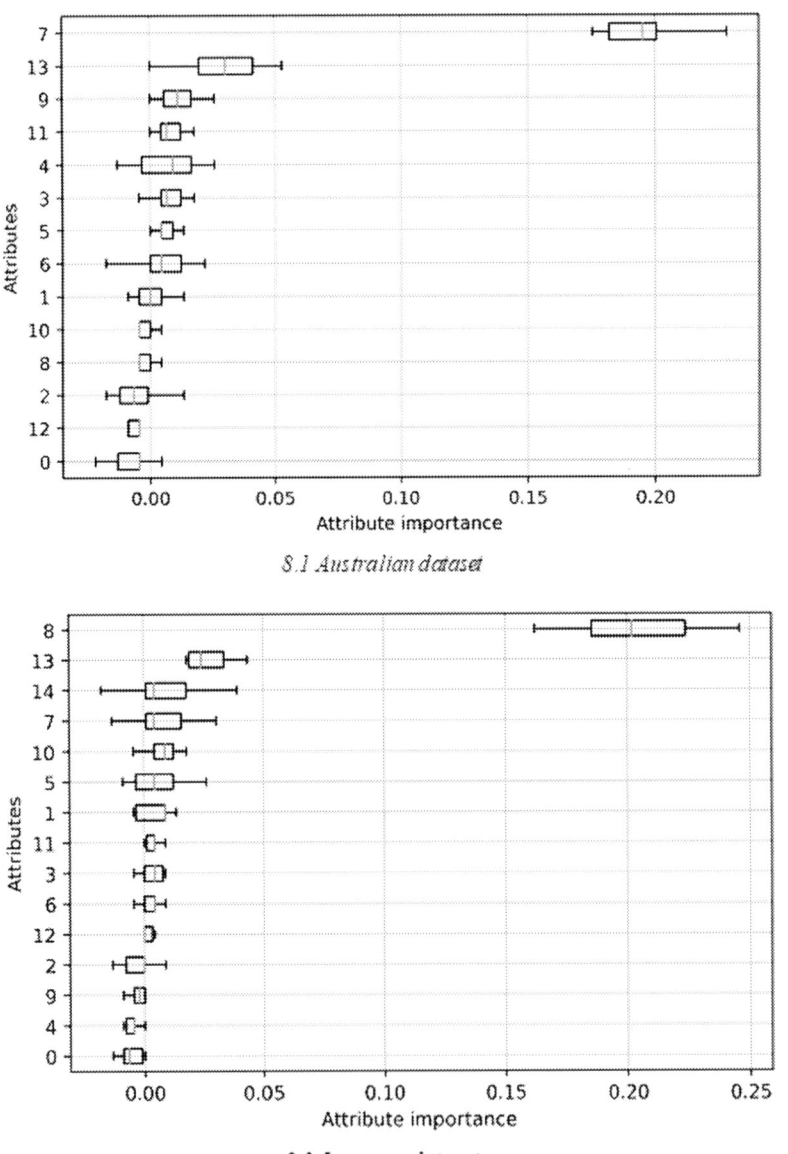

8.1 Australian dataset

8.2 Japanese dataset

In particular, the dataset is divided into a training set and a test set. Once the model has been fitted on the training set, the prediction score is computed on the test set. Then each feature is randomly shuffled K times, and, at each time, we compute the prediction score. The final step consists in evaluating the importance measure of each feature as the difference between the original score and the average of the K scores obtained performing the aforementioned permutations.

In Figure 7 we reported feature importance of the German credit dataset using $K=10$. We notice that the most important features are the first two concerning the status of existing accounts and the duration of the loan respectively.

Figure 8 shows feature importance of attributes for both Australian and Japanese credit datasets using $K=10$. In these cases, the nature of attributes is unknown due to the privacy protection. However, by Figure 8.1 is possible to observe that the most important features for the Australian dataset, are the eighth and the fourteenth.

Instead, by looking at Figure 8.2, we can note that the most important for the Japanese dataset are respectively the tenth and the fifteenth features.

CONCLUSION

Since one of the major drawbacks affecting decision trees-based methods is their instability when subjected to fluctuation in the input variables, in this chapter we have given an example about how to overcome such a defect by providing a credit scoring model, exploiting real-world data characterising consumer loans, by using boosted decision trees. In particular, we combined several decision trees to form a classifier which is then built based on a weighted majority vote of the classifications given by its individual components. The accuracy reached by our solution has been then compared with that of one of the best ML-model for analysing data, namely the support vector machine approach tuned to work on the real-world financial data we are interested in. In particular, we considered information of several credit applicants provided by various (German, Australian and Japanese) financial.

Performances have been evaluated by means of both ROC and precision-recall curve, mainly because of the imbalanced German dataset. Accordingly, we showed that boosted decision trees outperforms the support vector machines on two of the three credit card application datasets considered, namely the Australian and the Japanese one. Instead, concerning the German dataset, the two methods are comparable even if, in both cases, classification performances given by support vector machines are slightly higher than the ones provided by boosted decision trees.

Based on the obtained results, we concluded that boosted decision trees is really an effective technique in credit scoring applications. In particular, our study shows that it is not possible to derive a general rule able to a priori identify the best solution for a given (forecast) problem, the optimal solution being strongly dependent on the specific nature of the considered framework and associated datasets.

REFERENCES

Albeverio, S., Cordoni, F., Di Persio, L., & Pellegrini, G. (2019). Asymptotic expansion for some local volatility models arising in finance. *Decisions in Economics and Finance*.

Bastos, J. (2007). *Credit scoring with boosted decision trees*. Academic Press.

Bishop, C. M. (2006). *Pattern recognition and machine learning*. Springer.

Bonollo, M., Di Persio, L., & Pellegrini, G. (2015). Polynomial Chaos Expansion Approach to Interest Rate Models. *Journal of Probability and Statistics*.

Boser, I., Bernhard, V., & Guyon, V. (1996). A Training Algorithm for Optimal Margin Classifier. *Proceedings of the Fifth Annual ACM Workshop on Computational Learning Theory*.

Breiman, L., Friedman, J., Stone, C., & Olshen, R. (1984). *Classification and Regression Trees*. Taylor & Francis.

DeLong, E. R., DeLong, D. M., & Clarke-Pearson, D. L. (1988). Comparing the areas under two or more correlated receiver operating characteristic curves: A nonparametric approach. *Biometrics*, *44*(3), 837–845. doi:10.2307/2531595 PMID:3203132

Gang, W., Jinxing, H. M. J., & Hongbing, J. (2011). A comparative assessment of ensemble learning for credit scoring. *Expert Systems with Applications*, 223–230.

Ghodselahi, A. (2011). A Hybrid Support Vector Machine Ensemble Model for Credit Scoring. *International Journal of Computers and Applications*, 2220–2829.

Guelman, L. (2012). Gradient boosting trees for auto insurance loss cost modeling and prediction. *Expert Systems with Applications*, *39*(3), 3659–3667. doi:10.1016/j.eswa.2011.09.058

Jiang, Z., & Liang, J. (2017). Cryptocurrency Portfolio Management with Deep Reinforcement Learning. *Intelligent Systems Conference (IntelliSys)*. 10.1109/IntelliSys.2017.8324237

Jiang, Z., & Liang, J. (2017). *Cryptocurrency Portfolio Management with Deep Reinforcement Learning*. IntelliSys. doi:10.1109/IntelliSys.2017.8324237

Jiang, Z., Xu, D., & Liang, J. (2017). *A Deep Reinforcement Learning Framework for the Financial Portfolio Management Problem*. ArXiv.

Jiang, Z., Xu, D., & Liang, J. (2017). *A Deep Reinforcement Learning Framework for the Financial Portfolio Management Problem*. Academic Press.

Khandani, A., Kim, A., & Lo, A. (2010). Consumer Credit-Risk Models Via Machine-Learning Algorithms. *Journal of Banking & Finance*, *34*(11), 2767–2787. doi:10.1016/j.jbankfin.2010.06.001

Kristjanpoller, W., Fadic, A., & Minutolo, M. (2014). Volatility forecast using hybrid Neural Network models. *Expert Systems with Applications*, *41*(5), 2437–2442. doi:10.1016/j.eswa.2013.09.043

Lee, T., Cho, J., Kwon, D., & Sohn, S. (2018). Global stock market investment strategies based on financial network indicators using machine learning techniques. *Expert Systems with Applications*.

Lichman, M. (n.d.). *UCI machine learning repository*. Retrieved from http://archive.ics.uci.edu/ml/

Liu, Y. (2019). Novel volatility forecasting using deep learning-Long Short Term Memory Recurrent Neural Networks. *Expert Systems with Applications*, *132*, 99–109. doi:10.1016/j.eswa.2019.04.038

Luo, C., Wu, D., & Wu, D. (2016). A deep learning approach for credit scoring using credit default swaps. *Engineering Applications of Artificial Intelligence*.

Maniraj, S. P., Aditya, S., Shadab, A., & Swarna, S. (2019). Credit Card Fraud Detection using Machine Learning and Data Science. *International Journal of Engineering Research*.

Mashrur, A., Luo, W., Zaidi, N., & Robles-Kelly, A. (2020). Machine Learning for Financial Risk Management: A Survey. *IEEE Access: Practical Innovations, Open Solutions*, 8, 203203–203223. doi:10.1109/ACCESS.2020.3036322

Sahin, Y., Bulkan, S., & Duman, E. (2013). A cost-sensitive decision tree approach for fraud detection. *Expert Systems with Applications*, 5916–5923.

Saito, T., & Rehmsmeier, M. (2015). The precision-recall plot is more informative than the roc plot when evaluating binary classifiers on imbalanced datasets. *PLoS One*, *10*(3), e0118432. doi:10.1371/journal.pone.0118432 PMID:25738806

Sandman, G., & Koopman, S. J. (1998). Estimation of stochastic volatility models via Monte Carlo maximum likelihood. *Journal of Econometrics*.

Sharma, A., & Panigrahi, P. (2013). A Review of Financial Accounting Fraud Detection based on Data Mining Techniques. *International Journal of Computers and Applications*.

Shian-Chang, H. (2011). Using Gaussian process based kernel classifiers for credit rating forecasting. *Expert Systems with Applications*, 8607–8611.

West, D. (2000). Neural network credit scoring models. *Computers & Operations Research*, *27*(11-12), 1131–1152. doi:10.1016/S0305-0548(99)00149-5

Wuthrich, M. V., & Buser, C. (2020). *Data Analytics for Non-Life Insurance Pricing*. Swiss Finance Institute Research Paper, 16-68.

Yu, L., Yue, W., Wang, S., & Lai, K. K. (2010). Support vector machine based multiagent ensemble learning for credit risk evaluation. *Expert Systems with Applications*, *37*(2), 1351–1360. doi:10.1016/j.eswa.2009.06.083

ADDITIONAL READING

Bishop, C. M. (2006). *Pattern recognition and machine learning*. Springer.

Breiman, L., Friedman, J., Stone, C., & Olshen, R. (1984). *Classification and Regression Trees*. Taylor & Francis.

Saito, T., & Rehmsmeier, M. (2015). The precision-recall plot is more informative than the roc plot when evaluating binary classifiers on imbalanced datasets. *PLoS One*, *10*(3), e0118432. doi:10.1371/journal.pone.0118432 PMID:25738806

Yajing, Z., Chi, G., & Zhang, Z. (2018). Decision tree for credit scoring and discovery of significant features. *Filomat*, 1513-1521.

Yi, J. (2009). Credit scoring model based on the decision tree and the simulated annealing algorithm. *WRI World Congress on Computer Science and Information Engineering*, 18-22.

Zhang, D., Zhou, X., Leung, S., & Zheng, J. (2010). Vertical bagging decision trees model for credit scoring. *Expert Systems with Applications*, *37*(12), 7838–7843. doi:10.1016/j.eswa.2010.04.054

Chapter 14
The Role of Big Data Research Methodologies in Describing Investor Risk Attitudes and Predicting Stock Market Performance:
Deep Learning and Risk Tolerance

Wookjae Heo
Purdue University, USA

Eun Jin Kwak
https://orcid.org/0000-0002-4566-2492
University of Georgia, USA

John E. Grable
University of Georgia, USA

ABSTRACT

The purpose of this chapter is to compare the performance of a deep learning modeling technique to predict market performance compared to conventional prediction modeling techniques. A secondary purpose of this chapter is to describe the degree to which financial risk tolerance can be used to predict future stock market performance. Specifically, the models used in this chapter were developed to test whether aggregate investor financial risk tolerance is of value in establishing risk and return market expectations. Findings from this chapter's examples also provide insights into whether financial risk tolerance is more appropriately conceptualized as a predictor of market returns or as an outcome of returns.

DOI: 10.4018/978-1-7998-8609-9.ch014

INTRODUCTION

Portfolio theory assumes that in the aggregate, investors evaluate the return and risk characteristics of securities and the markets, form market expectations, select assets, and build portfolios that align with their expectations and willingness to take a risk (Merkle & Weber, 2014). In this regard, Merkle and Weber (2014) noted that investor beliefs are not useful predictors of short-term trading behavior, but over extended periods, changes in portfolio composition are systematically related to investor return and risk expectations. They concluded that risk-taking increases as return expectations increase and vice-a-versa.

From a practical standpoint, the conclusion of Merkle et al. (2014) helps explain a relatively common household-level risk-taking bias. Rather than hold stable portfolios, investors tend to switch between and among assets in a way that matches ever-changing expectations. Stated another way, portfolio risk appears to change in accordance with investor risk and return expectations. This implies that the willingness of investors to take financial risk might also exhibit a degree of elasticity.

This brings to mind the following question, which is the focus of this chapter: Does the collective willingness of investors to take a financial risk—as an indicator of market sentiment—help explain future market returns? The underlying argument supporting why this might be the case was presented by Keynes (1936). Keynes argued that 'animal spirits' help explain why even when individual security values vary, market averages move in general unison, particularly in times of economic stress. In essence, animal spirits is a term used to describe investor confidence, which is thought to be driven by risk and return expectations. There is an argument to be made that the inverse could also be true. It is possible that rather than being explained by the collective risk attitude of investors, financial risk tolerance—the willingness of investors to invest in assets where future returns are unknown and potentially negative (Nobre & Grable, 2015)—varies with market returns.

The purpose of this chapter is to describe, in non-technical language, how an Artificial Intelligence Deep Learning big data research methodological approach can be used to predict future stock market performance using investor risk tolerance as an indicator of market expectations (i.e., sentiment). The chapter focuses on comparing the prediction reliability of a traditional regression model against a deep learning estimation model. The tests described in this chapter are intended to provide readers with information about whether aggregate investor financial risk tolerance is of value in explaining future market performance or whether financial risk tolerance is more appropriately used as an outcome measure associated with market conditions. This chapter advances the risk-tolerance, investment management, and personal finance methodological literature by showing how a deep learning prediction model can provide a much more robust indication of future market returns. The deep learning prediction model that is described in this chapter provides researchers, educators, policymakers, and financial services professionals insights into the kinds of variables that are important when predicting stock prices.

BACKGROUND

Investor expectations regarding future market gains and losses drive investment flows. Investments in the markets can thus be seen as being influenced by the degree to which investors proactively participate in the market. The more participation, as evidenced by consistent buying of securities, the higher the value of a given market index. The opposite is true as well. As investor participation in a market wanes, so does the value of the market index.

When establishing expectations, investors can generally be classified into two broad groups. The first group consists of those who follow a fundamental asset valuation process. These investors seek out information about the intrinsic value of investments and make buy and sell decisions based on their estimation of the relative value of an asset or market. The second group consists of technicians. These investors care less about the fundamental value of an investment, asset, or market. Instead, technicians hope to identify trading opportunities based on an analysis of security and market factors. The investment marketplace is where the prediction estimates of these two types of investors converge. Fluctuations in the price of a market index can be seen as the aggregate willingness of investors to participate in the market. When viewed this way, market volatility can be seen to be associated with the willingness to take risks among investors (Kamstra, Kramer, Levi, & Wermers, 2017; Michaelides & Zhang, 2017).

While it is possible to use the value of a given market index as an indicator of investor risk tolerance, in the aggregate and by investor, this approach can lead to biased estimates. Guillemette and Finke (2014) and Rabbani, Grable, Heo, Nobre, and Kuzniak (2017) reported that while market returns and investors' willingness to take risk are correlated, market returns vary to a much greater extent than risk preferences. This is one reason much of the personal finance literature suggests that investor risk tolerance be measured using a standard test or scale (e.g., Anderson, Dreber, & Vestman, 2015; Grable & Lytton, 1999; Ryack, Kraten, & Sheikh, 2016). In fact, nearly all financial advisors do use some type of revealed preference or propensity measure to evaluate their clients' willingness to take a financial risk (Brayman, Finke, Bessner, Grable, Griffin, & Clement, 2015: Hubble, Grable, & Dannhauser, 2020). Scores from such tests and scales are presumably used to guide the development of portfolios that match a client's willingness to take a risk in alignment with a general forecast of market risk and return expectations.

As noted by Merkle and Weber (2014), investor beliefs appear to be systematically related to investor risk and return expectations. In other words, investor sentiment is thought to drive not only market returns but also how investor portfolios are managed. Financial risk tolerance can be thought of as a measurable indicator of sentiment. Theoretically, investor sentiment should then be a useful predictor of future market returns. It is interesting to note, however, that the literature is relatively silent on this possibility. One reason is that the causal effect from aggregate investor sentiment (i.e., financial risk tolerance) to market returns is still being debated. Rather than be a predictor of market returns, sentiment may instead be an outcome associated with experienced returns and volatility. Endogeneity issues make the decomposition of the effect difficult to conceptualize and test.

The primary outcome of the work presented in this chapter is to examine both directional possibilities empirically and to build a robust model of market prediction using factors associated with investor sentiment, specifically focusing on financial risk tolerance. To do this, models were developed and tested, with several control variables used to account for individual investor differences related to financial risk tolerance. The following investor characteristics, each of which is known to be related to the degree to which an investor is willing to engage in risky behavior, as well as actual risk-taking behavior, were controlled in the models: gender (i.e., with males thought to be more risk tolerant), marital status (i.e., with singles assumed to be more risk tolerant), education (i.e., with those reporting greater attained education thought to be more risk tolerant), age (i.e., with younger individuals assumed to be more willing to take a risk), financial resources (e.g., cash, equities, bonds, etc.), household income (i.e., with high income assumed to be associated with increased risk tolerance), and being responsible for household investment decisions (see Furnham, von Stumm, & Fenton-O'Creevy, 2015; Grable, Lyons, & Heo, 2019; Hallahan, Faff, & McKenzie, 2004; Hirschl, Altobelli, & Rank, 2003; Jones, 2015; Yao & Hanna, 2004; Zumbrun, 2014). When coupled with a measure of an investor's risk attitude, these individual difference characteristics were utilized as indicators of stock market participation. This collection of variables were then incorporated into models that utilized a deep learning evaluation analytical technique.

THEORETICAL FOUNDATIONS

This chapter provides a practical example of how a big data analytical procedure can be used to model complex systems and decision-making quandaries in the domains of investing and personal finance. In the context of this chapter, big data refers to any large amount of data in the "networked, digitized, sensor-laden, information-driven world" (Chang & Grady, 2019, p. iii).[1] The discussion that follows illustrates how data from a large number of investors can be organized and analyzed in a way that provides useful insights into the direction of a market (in this chapter, the market is represented by the U.S. S&P 500 stock index). In order to make the methodological illustration accessible to a wide variety of readers, the model used in the chapter is limited in the number of framework variables.

In accordance with Breiman (2001), Ho (1998), and Liaw and Wiender (2002), a two-step approach to the development of the tested deep learning algorithm was used. Specifically, the prediction of price changes in the S&P 500 index was made in two stages. The first stage featured a selection algorithm, whereas the second stage applied a prediction algorithm. Formula 1 and Formula 2 describe the two-step approach employed in the analysis:

$$Y_{t+1} = f_{rf}\left[\sum x_{it}\right] \tag{1}$$

$$Y_{t+1} = f_{brnn}\left[\sum x_{jt}\right] \tag{2}$$

where, Y_{t+1} = stock market performance next period (t+1); f_{rt} = a function of Random Forest; x_{it} = all predictors in the current period (t); f_{brnn} = a function of Bayesian Regulated Neural Network; and x_{jt} = all predictors in the current period (t) after being selected by random forest.

Random Forest is an ensemble method that combines machine learning algorithms with decision tree methods (Kursa & Rudnicki, 2010). Specifically, a machine (i.e., a computing system) estimates multiple decision trees using inputs from a dataset. Multiple decision trees then produce the average predicted value with a certain range of standard deviation. The algorithms will produce a set of predictors to maximize the prediction level. For the analyses described in this chapter, a Random Forest Boruta was utilized. The following eight-step procedure was used (Kursa & Rudnicki, 2010): (a) duplicate (e.g., copy and paste) variables in the dataset multiple times; (b) shuffle the duplicated variables; (c) execute Random Forest using the duplicated dataset; (d) use the duplicated dataset of a specific variable and estimate multiple z-scores of the specific variable; (e) if the z-score from one of the copied variables is higher than the z-score of the original variable, then the variable is defined as unimportant; (f) if the z-score from one of the copied variables is lower than the z-score of the original variable, then the variable is defined as important; (g) after determining the importance of a specific variable, the copied variable is removed; and (h) repeat steps (a) through (g) until the importance of all variables is determined.

Following Random Forest Boruta established standards and procedures to select important variables, the next step involved a prediction estimation. Specifically, a Bayesian Regularized Neural Network (BRNN) was utilized as a type of Artificial Neural Network (ANN) (Sariev & Germano, 2020). Conceptually, ANN embodies hidden layers when estimating a model. The hidden layers connect all predictors to each other as well as connect the predictors to the targeted output(s), which can be a single layer to multiple layers. When a set of predictors are connected to the targeted output(s) through hidden layers, the weights of each predictor are functioned. The weights employed in this analysis were conceptually similar to the coefficients that might be used in a linear estimation. However, ANN weights use shared-covariance (Minai, 1997) among predictors and output(s) whereas the coefficients in a linear estimation use only unique-covariance. This makes ANN a powerful predicting tool that specifically patterns a dataset (Herbrich, Keilbach, Graepel, Bollmann-Sdorra, & Obermayer, 1999; Kovalerchuk & Vityaev, 2000).

BRNN is a specific application of ANN that is based on Bayes's theorem, which states that predictions can be reversely produced by conditional probability (Burden & Winkler, 2008). BRNN is an advanced version of ANN, which is a type of feed-forward neural network (Sariev & Germano, 2020). The feed-forward neural network assumes that the learning process looks forward using a repeated process. There are four advantages associated with using BRNN (Burden & Winkler, 2008). First, BRNN is not easy to overtrain. Because of the feed-forward method, the algorithms stop when overtraining occurs. Second, BRNN is hard to overfit. Third, compared to ANN, which is sensitive to the architecture of networks (e.g., number of hidden layers), BRNN is relatively insensitive to the architecture of networks (e.g., number of neurons). Finally, BRNN remains valid when cross-validation is not possible because of a small dataset.

To summarize, the goal of this chapter is to illustrate the ANN algorithm development process by focusing on the role of hidden layers (i.e., neurons) between predictors and the outcome variable when making forecasts (Kim, Jung, Kim, & Park, 1996). The chapter shows how a BRNN can serve as a cross-validation algorithm based on ANN.[2] Figure 1 illustrates the analytical process described in the chapter. As explained above, the upper box of Figure 1 shows the two-step learning algorithms (i.e., Random Forest Boruta and BRNN). Figure 1 also shows the two conventional prediction methods that were used to compare the forecast performance of the deep learning algorithms: (1) a forward stepwise variable selection regression methodology and (2) a backward stepwise variable selection regression.[3] Similar to Formula 1 and Formula 2, Formula 3 and Formula 4 indicate how the two-steps in the conventional prediction models functioned in this analysis:

$$Y_{t+1} = f_{sw}\left[\sum x_{it}\right] \quad (3)$$

$$Y_{t+1} = f_{ts}\left[\sum x_{kt}\right] \quad (4)$$

where, f_{sw} = a function of the stepwise regression; f_{ts} = a function of the time-series regression; and x_{kt} = all predictors in the current period (t) after being selected by the stepwise regression.

Figure 1. Analytic algorithm methodology: deep learning prediction and regression prediction algorithms

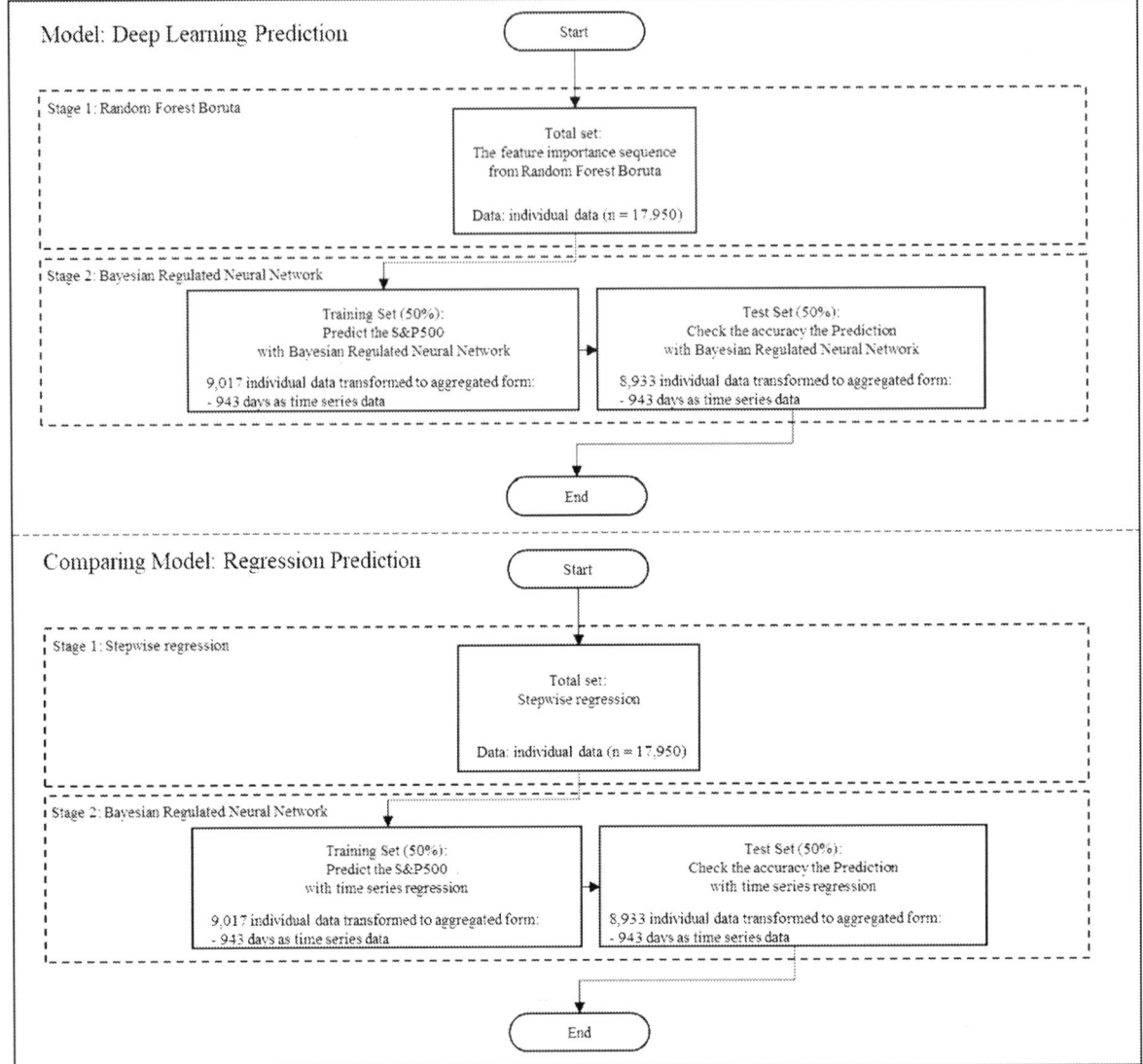

SOURCE OF DATA, VARIABLES, AND PROCEDURES

Data

Data used in the analyses described in this chapter were collected through a proprietary multiyear data gathering university online survey platform.[4] Data for this chapter's examples were collected over the period February 2015 to August 2017. The sample included 179,449 survey respondents. Given the possibility that a small variance in response data could be magnified by the use of such a large sample (Lanz, 2012), a random selection of 10% of the sample was used in the analyses ($n = 17{,}950$).

Variables

The following individual difference investor characteristics were assessed in the survey: education level, age, the proportion of assets held by respondents, marital status, household income, whether a respondent made their own investment decisions, gender, and financial risk tolerance. Education level was measured as an ordinal variable (1 = Some high school or less; 2 = High school graduate; 3 = Some college/trade/vocational training; 4 = Associate degree; 5 = Bachelor's degree; and 6 = Graduate or professional degree). Age was measured on an ordinal scale (1 = Under 25; 2 = 25-34; 3 = 35-44; 4 = 45-54; 5 = 55-64; 6 = 65-74; and 7 = 75 and over). The proportion of assets held by respondents was measured using a set of ratio variables based on ownership of equities, cash, bonds, and other assets. Marital status was measured as a nominal variable as married, living with another, never married, shared housing arrangement, widowed, and separated; this variable was transformed into six binary variables for use in the analyses. Household income was measured on an ordinal scale (1 = Less than $25,000; 2 = $25,000 - $49,999; 3 = $50,000-$74,999; 4 = $75,000-$99,999; and 5 = $100,000 or greater). Whether a respondent made their own investment decisions was coded as a binary variable (0 = did not make decisions alone and 1 = make decisions alone). Gender was coded dichotomously (i.e., 1 = male and 2 = female). Financial risk tolerance was measured using a propensity measure developed by Grable and Lytton (1999). The scale has been shown to be empirically reliable and valid (Chung & Au, 2020; Grable, Lyons, & Heo, 2019; Kuzniak, Rabbani, Heo, Ruiz-Menjivar, & Grable, 2015; Nguyen, Gallery, & Newton, 2019). Each respondent's data file was linked with the following market data by date: U.S. T-bill rate, the risk premium, and following month S&P 500 market value.

Deep Learning Algorithms

The primary goal of the model development and testing procedures described in this chapter was to predict the future value (price) of the S&P 500. As shown in Figure 1, the algorithms used to predict the stock price of the S&P 500 index comprised two stages. The first stage was a feature selection algorithm, whereas the second stage was a prediction algorithm.

The first stage of the analysis used a Random Forest Boruta. As described previously, the Random Forest technique represents a type of machine learning data classification modeling process (Breiman, 2001). The technique is based on ensemble learning. The ensemble learning procedure attempts to merge two or more algorithms into one algorithm. In the case of a Random Forest, decision trees, mean predictions, and bagging samples are merged into a single algorithm (Ho, 1998; Liaw & Wiener, 2002). Kursa and Rudnicki (2008) improved the Random Forest algorithm by empowering the feature selection performance, which is now known as the Boruta algorithm. In the context of this chapter, the Boruta algorithm used monthly S&P 500 data as the outcome variable with 17,950 predictors that represented the individual difference characteristics, the T-bill rate, and the market risk premium. The resulting algorithm was then used to identify the most important variables when predicting future values of the S&P 500.

At the second stage of the analysis, another deep learning algorithm was utilized to predict values of the S&P 500: A Bayesian Regularized Neural Network (BRNN). BRNN is a type of Artificial Neural Network (ANN) (Sariev & Germano, 2020). The ANN algorithm assumes that there are certain numbers of hidden layers between predictors and an outcome variable (Kim et al., 1996). These hidden layers are referred to as neurons in the case of BRNN. The number of hidden layers is determined by a multiple learning computation method designed to find the best prediction or classification model. In this chapter's examples, all predictors were linked to all hidden layers and all hidden layers were used to predict the outcomes. By linking all predictors, hidden layers, and the outcome, the ANN algorithm can identify the most valuable variables for use as prediction factors.[5] The BRNN employed an advanced algorithm based on ANN (i.e., a type of feed-forward neural network) (Sariev & Germano, 2020). The feed-forward neural network assumes that the learning process looks forward using a repeated process.[6] The BRNN was based on a Gauss-Newton approximation that utilized a Bayesian estimation and regularization approach (Mackay, 1992). Because of this regularization, the BRNN is generally thought to outperform traditional prediction models (Sariev & Germano, 2020).

Given the two-stage approach employed in the analysis (i.e., a learning process at stage one and a testing process at stage two), the dataset was randomly divided into two sets: (a) a training dataset with 50% of the sample ($n = 9,017$ based on 943 days of analysis) and (b) a test dataset with 50% of the sample ($n = 8,933$ based on 943 days of analysis).[7] The training dataset was used to identify the best-performing prediction model utilizing the selected features. The test dataset was used to check whether the prediction model exhibited a robust prediction rate. The following procedure was used to check prediction accuracy: (a) we determined the best prediction model using the training dataset; (b) we used the model with the test dataset; and (c) we compared the predicted S&P 500 value with the actual S&P 500 value in the test dataset. In order to facilitate the analysis, data were transformed to a time-series format with 943 days from February 2015 to July 2017. Likewise, the dataset used for training ($n = 9,017$) was transformed to a time-series dataset with 943 days, whereas the test dataset ($n = 8,933$) was also transformed to time-series data.

Traditional Prediction Models

Two conventional prediction methods were used to compare the forecast performance of the deep learning algorithms. The first traditional prediction model was based on a forward stepwise variable selection regression methodology. The second traditional prediction model was a backward stepwise variable selection regression. Significant variables from the regressions were then used in the second stage for prediction. The choice to use a stepwise procedure to identify variables was made to align with the first stage of analysis with the Boruta algorithm technique. At the second stage, a time-series regression model was utilized to predict the future value of the S&P 500. Similar to the deep learning procedure, the sample was split into approximately equal halves. The first half was used to build the model, whereas the second half was used to test the model.

Evaluation Procedures

Given the purpose of this chapter—to compare the performance of the deep learning modeling technique to a conventional prediction modeling procedure—and because the model outputs were different, it was not possible to compare levels of explained variance directly. As such, the models were compared using the root mean of squared error (RMSE) and the mean of absolute error (MAE). RMSE and MAE are typically used by researchers as criteria for evaluating forecasting models (Hyndman & Koehler, 2006; Wooldridge, 2013). Generally, for interpretation purposes, a higher RMSE means a model has lower accuracy, whereas a higher MAE denotes less than optimal accuracy.

ANALYTIC RESULTS

Stage 1. Feature Selection: Random Forest Boruta vs. Stepwise Regression

As shown in Table 1 and Figure 2, the following 14 variables were selected as important predictors of the future value of the S&P 500 using the Random Forest Boruta procedure: T-bill rate, the risk premium, education, age, equity holdings, cash holdings, other asset holdings, bond holdings, married status, living with other status, household income, making investment decisions alone, financial risk tolerance, and gender.

Table 1. Variables predicting the future value of the S&P 500 using the Forest Boruta Method

	Importance				Decision
	Mean	Median	Min.	Max.	
T-bill Rate	41.81	41.73	39.00	45.81	Confirmed
Risk Premium	36.74	36.86	33.95	39.55	Confirmed
Education	12.82	12.89	8.68	16.27	Confirmed
Age	11.35	11.39	7.68	14.17	Confirmed
Equities	10.58	10.81	5.60	14.81	Confirmed
Cash	9.94	9.97	5.81	14.12	Confirmed
Other Assets	9.57	9.81	5.26	12.27	Confirmed
Bonds	8.79	9.30	3.85	11.99	Confirmed
Married	8.37	8.23	6.02	11.29	Confirmed
Living with Other	7.83	7.83	5.35	10.05	Confirmed
Household Income	6.15	5.95	4.13	8.59	Confirmed
Make Decisions Alone	4.34	4.34	1.86	6.55	Confirmed
Financial Risk Tolerance	3.70	3.74	1.37	6.46	Confirmed
Gender	2.40	2.54	-0.52	4.56	Confirmed
Separated Marital Status	0.58	0.54	-1.10	2.58	Rejected
Never Married	0.25	0.67	-1.37	1.66	Rejected
Shared Housing Arrangement	-0.10	-0.07	-1.92	1.73	Rejected
Widowed	-1.29	-0.86	-3.24	0.30	Rejected

Figure 2. Importance of variables using the Forest Boruta Method

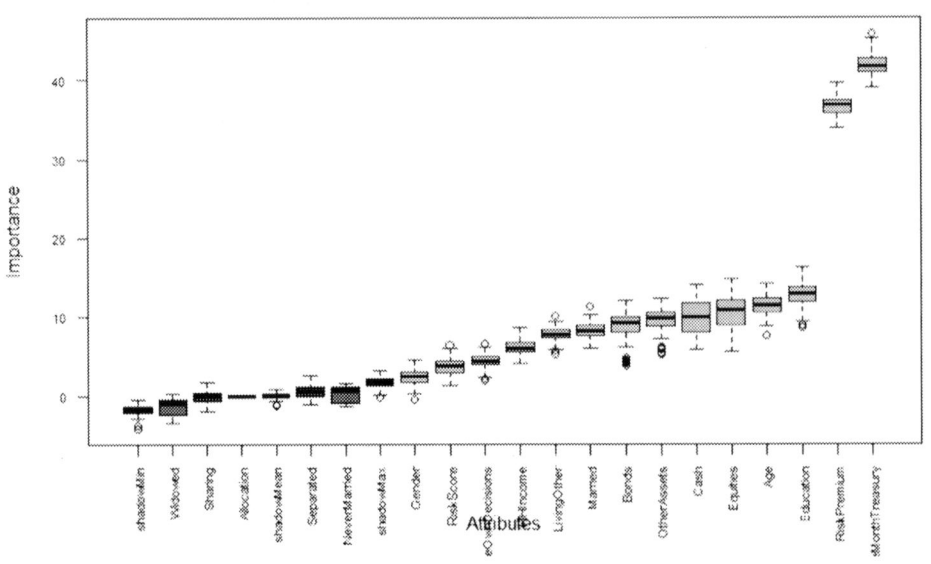

Table 2. Variables predicting S&P 500 values using stepwise regression procedures

	Forward Stepwise		Backward Stepwise	
	b	SE	b	SE
T-bill Rate	121.25***	2.40	121.40***	2.39
Risk Premium	3802.15***	20.35	3801.55***	20.33
Age	-1.78***	.41	-1.63***	.28
Make Decisions Alone	-1.89**	.72	-1.96**	.71
Separated Marital Status	3.64	3.90	4.78*	2.21
Shared housing arrangement	4.91	5.26		
Household Income	.33	.25		
Equities	-.04	.03		
Gender	.69	.73		
Financial Risk Tolerance	.06	.07		
Education	.19	.26		
Cash	-0.2	.02		
Other Assets	-.02	.03		
Never Married	-.91	3.54		
Married	-1.44	3.27		
Live with Sig. Other	-1.46	3.37		
Intercept	-14217.82	87.07	-14214.68***	86.83
R^2	.91		.91	
F	11868.95***		37983.72***	

Notes. * $p < .05$; ** $p < .01$; *** $p < .001$.

As shown in Table 2, the list of variables identified as being significant in the stepwise regressions was smaller than the corresponding list of variables identified using the Random Forest Boruta approach. The following variables were significant using the forward stepwise estimation procedure: T-bill rate, the risk premium, age, and making investment decisions alone. The following variables were significant in the backward stepwise model: T-bill rate, the risk premium, age, making investment decisions alone, and separated marital status. The other individual difference characteristics were eliminated from the final models. Of particular relevance, financial risk tolerance was not significant in either regression model.

Stage 2. Predicting S&P 500 Values: BRNN vs. Time-Series Regressions

The BRNN algorithm was executed by resampling 50 times as a way to check the cross-validation of the model. Cross-validation means that random samples from the original dataset were conducted 50 unique times. As a result, the BRNN model with 50 repeats produced the average value of errors (i.e., RMSE and MAE). The error standard deviations are shown in Table 3. Table 3 shows that the 10 neurons model (a hidden layer from a BRNN model is known as a neuron) was the optimal BRNN model. This means that when the number of neurons (i.e., hidden layers) reached 10, the prediction rate of the model (i.e., RMSE and MAE) was maximized (RMSE = 13.57; MAE = 9.48) and the R^2 was similarly maximized (.99).

Table 3. BRNN model fit based on number of model neurons

Number of Neurons	RMSE	RMSE SD	MAE	MAE SD	R^2	R^2 SD
2	44.70	8.94	33.24	6.20	.92	.03
3	37.80	10.79	28.15	7.67	.96	.04
4	26.37	11.44	20.36	7.99	.97	.04
5	19.44	5.46	14.63	3.66	.98	.01
7	15.22	3.73	11.04	2.69	.99	.01
8	14.97	6.36	10.37	4.44	.99	.01
10	**13.57**	**6.41**	**9.48**	**4.52**	**.99**	**.01**
16	21.90	12.86	14.41	7.60	.98	.03
20	23.34	12.10	16.27	7.95	.97	.03

Table 4 provides information about the best-fit model using the BRNN algorithm. The risk premium, which represents the historical returns on equity investments less the risk-free rate, and the T-bill rate were the best predictors of future S&P 500 values. It is important to note that the risk premium and the T-bill rate are highly correlated with the S&P 500. As such, it was not surprising that these variables would emerge as significant predictors of the future value of the S&P 500. The third most important predictor was financial risk tolerance (importance = .93).[8] The 'other assets' ratio was also important in predicting the value of the S&P 500 (importance = .90). Age was the next important variable in the prediction of the S&P 500 (importance = .83). Financial risk tolerance and the 'other assets' variable were approximately four times as important in describing the performance of the S&P 500 as compared to household income and education. Financial risk tolerance was twenty times more important than making investment decisions in a household variable.

Table 4. Overall importance of predictors based on the BRNN model (n = 943 days)

Predictors	Importance
Risk Premium	100.00
T-bill Rate	84.02
Financial Risk Tolerance	.93
Other Assets	.90
Age	.83
Bonds	.77
Cash	.56
Household income	.27
Education	.24
Equities	.22
Married	.17
Make Decisions Alone	.04
Gender	.01
Live with Sig. Other	.00

Table 5 shows the comparison results based on the two time-series regressions. The first time-series regression used the same predictors associated with the BRNN model. The second time-series regression included the variables from the backward stepwise regression (Table 2). When using the BRNN predictors, four variables were found to be significantly associated with future S&P 500 values: T-bill rate ($b = 135.00, p < .001$), the risk premium ($b = 3626.48, p < .001$), age ($b = -10.34, p < .01$), and make decisions alone ($b = -19.96, p < .01$). When using the variable list from the backward stepwise regression, the same four variables were significant but the coefficients were different: T-bill rate ($b = 136.63, p < .001$), risk premium ($b = 3621.35, p < .001$), age ($b = -7.27, p < .001$), and make decisions alone ($b = -18.86, p < .01$). Two variables (i.e., T-bill rate and the risk premium) were the most important predictors of future S&P 500 values. Financial risk tolerance was not significant in either regression model.

Table 5. Significant variables using a time-series regression (training dataset) (n = 943 days)

	Same list with BRNN		Stepwise Variables	
	b	SE	b	SE
T-bill Rate	135.00***	10.86	136.63***	10.79
Risk Premium	3626.48***	92.41	3621.35***	91.94
Education	-.59	2.17		
Age	-10.34**	3.23	-7.27***	2.07
Make Decisions Alone	-19.96**	7.14	-18.86**	6.81
Separated Marital Status			27.60	18.07
Equities	-.18	.22		
Cash	-.31	.19		
Other Assets	-.17	.31		
Married	-2.50	11.36		
Live with Sig. Other	13.44	11.30		
Household Income	.53	2.43		
Financial Risk Tolerance	.03	.71		
Gender	5.58	7.28		
Intercept	-13427.20***	396.05		
R^2	.91			
F	673.20***			

Notes. * p < .05; ** p < .01; *** p < .001. Coefficient for bonds was omitted because of multicollinearity.

Table 6 compares the prediction accuracy of the BRNN algorithm and the time-series regressions. In terms of the BRNN algorithm, the RMSE and MAE were significantly more robust than the RMSE and MAE scores for the time-series regressions. Generally, when making a comparison, if one RMSE is lower than 70% of the value of the other RMSE, then the lower RMSE can be considered significantly accurate (Nau, 2020). Using the same variable list, the RMSE of the BRNN algorithm was at the 30.10% level (= 14.36/47.70) compared to the RMSE of the time-series regression. Using the stepwise selection variable list, the RMSE of the BRNN algorithm was at the 30.36% level (= 14.36/47.30) compared to the RMSE of the time-series regression. Regardless of the variable list, the BRNN algorithm exhibited a much more robust degree of accuracy.

The MAE can also be used to check the mean difference between models. A *t* test is typically used when making comparisons. The BRNN algorithm and the time-series regression, using the same list of variables, were significantly different ($t = -22.94, p < .001$). Similarly, the BRNN algorithm and the time-series regression, using the variables from the stepwise selection list, were significantly different ($t = -22.58, p < .001$). This can be interpreted to mean that the BRNN algorithm offered a much higher level of prediction accuracy compared to either of the time-series regression models.

Table 6. Prediction accuracy comparison between BRNN algorithm and time-Series regressions

BRNN		Time-Series Regression			
		Regression using BRNN		Stepwise List Variables	
RMSE	MAE	RMSE	MAE	RMSE	MAE
14.36	10.01	47.70	35.19	47.30	34.75

There is an important caveat associated with these findings. The results from this chapter's examples do not indicate that the regression results were not useful. As shown in Figures 3 and 4, the regression models exhibited a similar prediction trend when compared to the BRNN algorithm results. This implies that each model was able to predict future S&P 500 values with reasonable accuracy. However, the accuracy of the prediction was superior using the BRNN algorithm.

Figure 4. Comparison of actual monthly S&P 500 values and predicted S&P 500 value using time series regressions

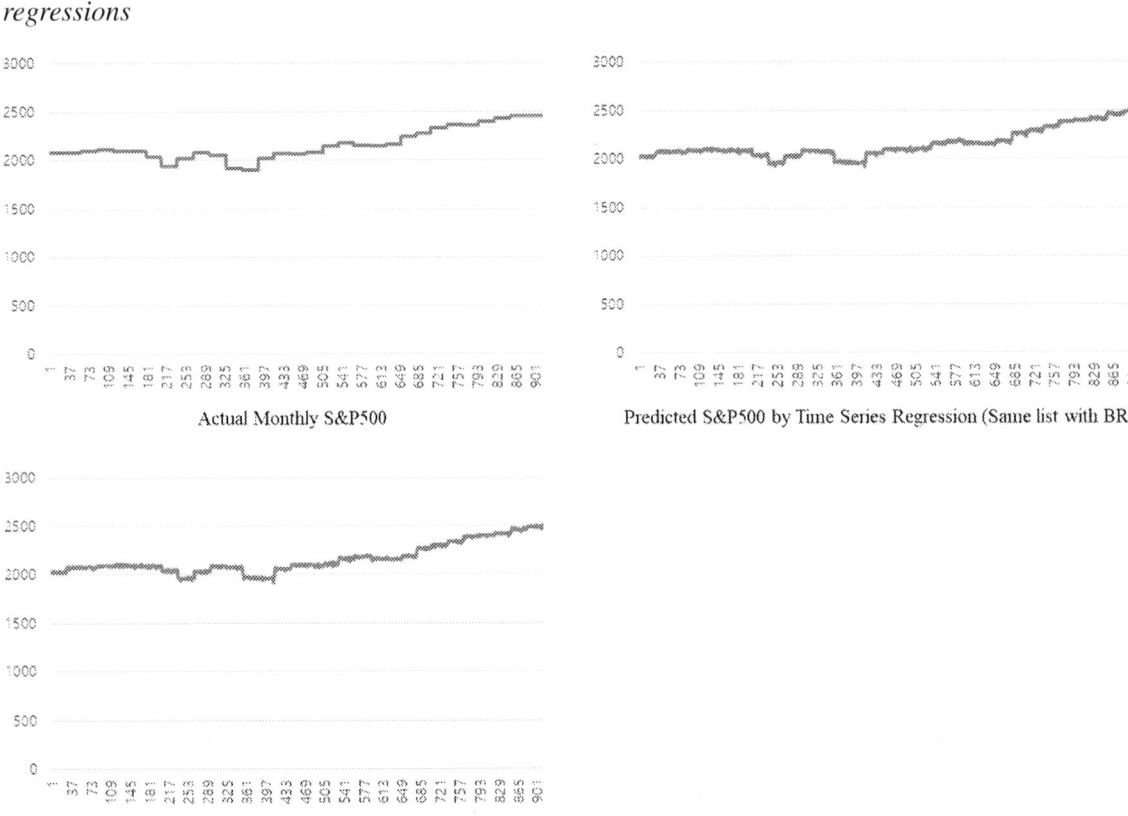

Figure 3. Comparison of actual monthly S&P 500 values and predicted S&P 500 value using the BRNN algorithm

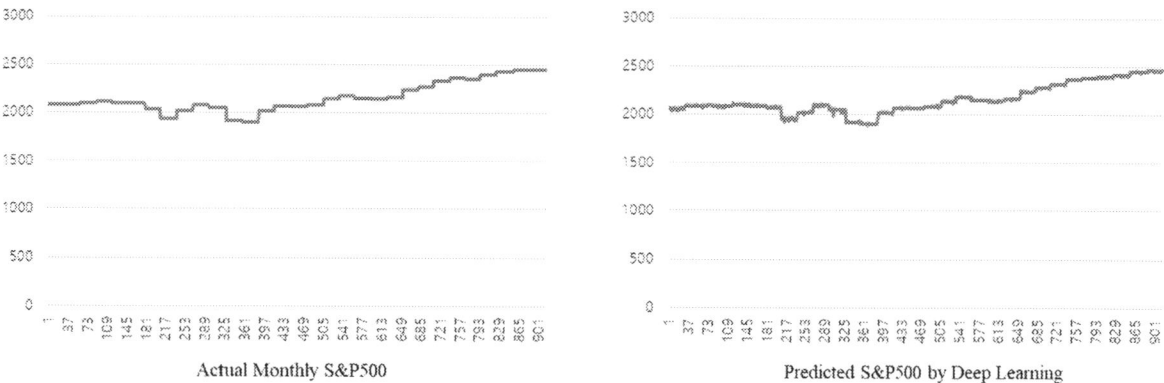

Interpreting the Role of Financial Risk Tolerance as a Predictor

The test results reported above suggest that financial risk tolerance is an important predictor when viewed from a deep learning prediction model perspective. This implies that financial risk tolerance, as an indicator of investor sentiment, can be thought of as an input or factor describing future market valuation. Some have argued, however, that even if this is a valid conclusion, financial risk tolerance is more likely to be an outcome of changes in market values. The thought is that market results shape investor risk tolerance. If this endogeneity issue is valid, this has important implications for not only the prediction of future market returns but also for the way financial risk tolerance is conceptualized in the development and management of investment portfolios. Currently, an investor's willingness to take financial risk is considered to be a primary input into the portfolio selection process. If it is determined that financial risk tolerance is essentially an outcome measure of market volatility, then its role in investment selection may currently be over-weighted. To test for the possibility, each of the models discussed above was estimated again using financial risk tolerance as the outcome variable and the S&P 500 as a predictor variable.

Tables 7 and 8 summarize the key findings from the re-analyses. Using the Random Forest Boruta procedure (Table 7), it was determined that the S&P was associated with financial risk tolerance; however,

Table 7. Variables predicting financial risk tolerance values using the Forest Boruta Method

	Importance				Decision
	Mean	**Median**	**Min.**	**Max.**	
Cash	37.3715	37.50542	32.40727	41.68611	Confirmed
Bonds	24.56854	24.53655	19.61261	31.97587	Confirmed
Equities	54.91358	54.80697	52.46071	56.89576	Confirmed
Other Assets	25.81419	25.74184	22.13093	28.94005	Confirmed
Gender	59.15808	59.19646	56.62418	61.59233	Confirmed
Age	31.34429	31.22362	28.57635	34.74511	Confirmed
Education	31.49349	31.33565	29.96181	34.07539	Confirmed
Household Income	17.40715	17.38953	15.32851	20.05793	Confirmed
Make Decisions Alone	7.233663	7.436102	4.864883	8.998851	Confirmed
S&P 500	17.82544	17.85841	16.12368	20.09838	Confirmed
T-bill Rate	14.80074	14.91828	11.97083	16.83333	Confirmed
Risk Premium	17.79008	17.95905	15.19401	21.12095	Confirmed
Married	19.36301	19.19253	17.44909	22.14589	Confirmed
Never Married	5.724484	6.031873	2.790941	6.956838	Confirmed
Living with Other	15.68971	15.60947	13.96326	17.57726	Confirmed
Separated	4.765856	4.44822	3.268644	7.334982	Confirmed
Shared Housing Arrangement	3.677368	3.755112	1.64854	5.602032	Confirmed
Widowed	-0.37839	0.257173	-3.0535	1.681675	Rejected

the overall importance of the variable in the tested model (not shown) was very low. Variables such as the percent of equities held in portfolios and gender were more significant by large margins.

Table 8 shows the results from the stepwise regression analyses with financial risk tolerance as the outcome variable. The S&P 500 variable was not statistically significant in either model (nor was the variable significant in the testing models).

The RMSE and MAE scores across the training and testing models ranged from 1.50 to 2.08, which suggests that none of the re-estimated models were particularly useful in predicting the financial risk tolerance of survey respondents. When viewed holistically, these findings suggest that financial risk

Table 8. Variables predicting financial risk tolerance values using stepwise regression procedures

	Forward Stepwise		Backward Stepwise	
	b	SE	b	SE
T-bill Rate			-.26	.27
Risk Premium			-1.77	3.65
Age	-.34***	.04	-.34***	.04
Make Decisions Alone			.14	.08
Separated			-.37	.41
Shared Living Arrangement	1.22**	.03	.96	.55
Household Income	.22***	.03	.22***	.03
Equities	.05***	.00	.05***	0.0
Gender	-1.96***	.07	-1.95***	.07
S&P 500			.00	.00
Education	.25***	.03	.25***	.03
Cash	.01***	.00	.01**	.00
Other Assets	.04***	.00	.04***	.00
Never Married			-.25	.37
Married	-.72***	.14	-.95**	.34
Living with Other	-.83***	.15	-1.09**	.35
Intercept	28.35***	.29	34.80*	14.34
R^2	.12		.12	
F	248.23***		155.50***	

tolerance, as a measure of investor sentiment, is more effective as a model input rather than serving as a model outcome.

DISCUSSION

Findings from tests of the models presented in this chapter suggest that deep machine learning (i.e., BRNN) and traditional regression modeling provide insights into the role investor risk attitudes, as indicators of investor sentiment (Merkle & Weber, 2014), play in explaining future market performance. It was determined that, in terms of offering the best prediction, a deep machine learning algorithm surpasses traditional modeling techniques. While not a significant predictor in the regression models, the level of financial risk tolerance exhibited among investors was found to be an important determinant of future market performance in the deep machine learning models. Technically, the shared-covariance among other predictors and financial risk tolerance was ignored in the stepwise and time-series regressions. However, the shared-covariance was important within the deep machine learning algorithms. This suggests that the dynamic of financial risk tolerance is not observable using conventional methods but is evident when viewed from a deep machine learning perspective. Consequently, results provide insights into the question of whether investor risk tolerance should be viewed primarily as an input to or an outcome of market valuation. Based on the results from the analyses presented in this chapter, risk tolerance appears to be a better descriptor (and predictor) of market performance than as an outcome of market performance.[9]

The primary takeaway from this chapter is principally methodological and theoretical. Researchers, policymakers, and financial services professionals who are interested in making forecasts of future market performance, regardless of the set of variables used in a model, should consider the advantages offered by deep machine learning techniques. The models described in this chapter indicate that machine learning allows for more nuanced explanations of variable interactions and effects (Samek, Wiegand, & Muller, 2017).[10] Financial risk tolerance provides a useful insight in this regard. Whereas financial risk tolerance was not found to be significantly related to future values of the S&P 500 in the traditional regression estimations, this variable was highly important when viewed from a multi-layer perspective. The deep machine learning that occurs in an algorithm allows for hidden interrelationships to emerge. Traditional modeling techniques are unable to uncover these types of variable relationships.

There is a downside associated with the use of deep machine learning algorithms. Unlike a traditional regression technique, current models do not provide an easily identified model that can be used to make estimates. The algorithms primarily provide information about what variables are most important when making a prediction. It is up to a researcher, policymaker, or financial services professional to use this information when building models to explain or describe future market conditions (or any other outcome variable). In this regard, the use of a traditional regression model can be a useful tool when used in conjunction with a deep machine learning algorithm output. Whereas the algorithm output will indicate the most important predictors, the direction of the coefficients from a regression model can be used to provide insights into the likely association each variable has with the outcome. In this chapter's examples, it was shown that the T-bill rate, the risk premium, financial risk tolerance, and the percent of portfolios held in other assets by investors were important predictors of future market performance. The regression models showed that the relationships were positive in regard to the T-bill rate, the risk premium, and financial risk tolerance but negative for the other assets variable. This means, broadly speaking, that a positive increase in T-bill rates, coupled with an increase in the risk premium and aggregate investor risk tolerance, along with a reduction of portfolio assets held in other assets (e.g., gold, silver, real estate), should correspond with an increase in market values the following month. Of course, this is a very rudimentary approach to forecasting. Future studies are needed to identify more precise prediction models, but as this chapter's examples illustrate, it is possible to link outcomes from a deep machine learning model to the realities faced by end-users.

CONCLUSION

The purpose of this chapter was to describe how an Artificial Intelligence Deep Learning big data research methodology can be used to predict future stock market performance. Using investor risk tolerance as an indicator of market expectations (i.e., sentiment), the chapter focused on comparing the prediction robustness of a traditional regression model against a deep learning estimation model. It was concluded that a deep machine learning approach, like the one presented in this chapter, offers more nuanced insights into variable relationships than traditional prediction approaches. This chapter adds to the risk-tolerance, investment management, and personal finance literature by illustrating how big data statistical analysis approaches can expand the description and interpretation of complex systems and markets.

The Role of Big Data Research Methodologies

As with all research that uses artificial neural network and deep machine learning techniques, results from the examples described in this chapter should be considered exploratory. While the sample used in this chapter's examples was large, the sample was not intended to be representative of the U.S. population or a particular subset of the population. Instead, the sample was meant to be representative of investors and consumers who have access to the internet and an interest in obtaining personal finance information from university websites. It is possible that had another sample been used, the results might have changed. Future research is needed to determine the robustness of the models and findings presented in this chapter.

REFERENCES

Agostinelli, C. (2010). Robust stepwise regression. *Journal of Applied Statistics*, *29*(6), 825–840. doi:10.1080/02664760220136168

Anderson, A., Dreber, A., & Vestman, R. (2015). Risk taking, behavioral biases and genes: Results from 149 active investors. *Journal of Behavioral and Experimental Finance*, *6*, 93–100. doi:10.1016/j.jbef.2015.04.002

Beer, D. (2016). How should we do the history of Big Data? *Big Data & Society*, *3*(1), 1–10. doi:10.1177/2053951716646135

Bell, J. (2015). *Machine Learning*. Wiley.

Bonini, S., & Caivano, G. (2018). Probability of default modeling: A machine learning approach. In M. Corazza, M. Durbàn, A. Grané, C. Perna, & M. Sibillo (Ed.), *Proceedings of the Mathematical and Statistical Methods for Actuarial Sciences and Finance* (173–177). Cham: Springer. 10.1007/978-3-319-89824-7_32

Brayman, S., Finke, M., Bessner, E., Grable, J., Griffin, P., & Clement, R. (2015). *Current Practices for Risk Profiling in Canada and Review of Global Best Practices. Research Report prepared for the Investor Advisory Panel of the Ontario Securities Commission.* https://www.osc.gov.on.ca/documents/en/Investors/iap_20151112_risk-profiling-report.pdf

Breiman, L. (2001). Random Forests. *Machine Learning*, *45*(1), 5–32. doi:10.1023/A:1010933404324

Burden, F., & Winkler, D. (2008). Bayesian Regularization of Neural Networks. In D. J. Livingstone (Ed.), *Artificial Neural Networks. Methods in Molecular Biology™* (Vol. 458). Humana Press. doi:10.1007/978-1-60327-101-1_3

Chang, W., & Grady, N. (2019), NIST Big Data Interoperability Framework: Volume 1, Definitions, Special Publication (NIST SP). National Institute of Standards and Technology. doi:10.6028/NIST.SP.1500-1r2

Chung, W. K., & Au, W. T. (2020). Risk tolerance profiling measure: Testing its reliability and validities. *Financial Counseling and Planning*, *32*(2), 311–325.

Furnham, A., von Stumm, S., & Fenton-O'Creevy, M. (2015). Sex differences in money pathology in the general population. *Social Indicators Research*, *123*(3), 701–711. doi:10.100711205-014-0756-x PMID:26316675

Grable, J. E., Lyons, A. C., & Heo, W. (2019). A test of traditional and psychometric relative risk tolerance measures on household financial risk taking. *Finance Research Letters*, *30*, 8–13. doi:10.1016/j.frl.2019.03.012

Grable, J. E., & Lytton, R. H. (1999). Financial risk tolerance revisited: The development of a risk assessment instrument. *Financial Services Review*, *8*(3), 163–181. doi:10.1016/S1057-0810(99)00041-4

Guillemette, M. A., & Finke, M. (2014). Do large swings in equity values change risk tolerance? *Journal of Financial Planning*, *27*(6), 44–50.

Gutmann, M. P., Merchant, E. K., & Roberts, E. (2018). "Big data" in economic history. *The Journal of Economic History*, *78*(1), 268–299. doi:10.1017/S0022050718000177 PMID:29713093

Hallahan, T. A., Faff, R. W., & McKenzie, M. D. (2004). An empirical investigation of personal financial tolerance. *Financial Services Review*, *13*, 57–58.

Heaton, J. B., Polson, N. G., & Witte, J. H. (2016). *Deep learning in finance*. arXiv/1602.06561.

Herbrich, R., Keilbach, M., Graepel, T., Bollmann-Sdorra, P., & Obermayer, K. (1999). Neural networks in economics. In T. Brenner (Ed.), *Computational techniques for modeling learning in economics* (pp. 169–196). Kluwer Academic Publishers. doi:10.1007/978-1-4615-5029-7_7

Hirschl, T. A., Altobelli, J., & Rank, M. R. (2003). Does marriage increase the odds of affluence: Exploring the life course probabilities. *Journal of Marriage and Family*, *65*(4), 927–938. doi:10.1111/j.1741-3737.2003.00927.x

Ho, T. K. (1998). The random subspace method for constructing decision forests. *IEEE Transactions on Pattern Analysis and Machine Intelligence*, *20*(8), 832–844. doi:10.1109/34.709601

Horrigan, M. W. (2013, January). Big data: A perspective from the BLS. *Amstat News*, 25-27.

Hubble, A., Grable, J. E., & Dannhauser, B. (2020). *Investment Risk Profiling: A Guide for Financial Advisors*. CFA Research Reports. https://www.cfainstitute.org/en/research/industry-research/investment-risk-profiling

Hyndman, R. J., & Koehler, A. B. (2006). Another look at measures of forecast accuracy. *International Journal of Forecasting*, *22*(4), 679–688. doi:10.1016/j.ijforecast.2006.03.001

Jones, C. I. (2015). Pareto and Piketty: The macroeconomics of top income and wealth inequality. *The Journal of Economic Perspectives*, *29*(1), 29–46. doi:10.1257/jep.29.1.29

Kamstra, M. J., Kramer, L. A., Levi, M. D., & Wermers, R. (2017). Seasonal asset allocation: Evidence from mutual fund flows. *Journal of Financial and Quantitative Analysis*, *52*(1), 71–109. doi:10.1017/S002210901600082X

Keynes, J. M. (1936). *The General Theory of Employment, Interest and Money*. Macmillan.

Kim, H., Jung, S., Kim, T., & Park, K. (1996). Fast learning method for back-propagation neural network by evolutionary adaptation of learning rates. *Neurocomputing*, *11*(1), 101–106. doi:10.1016/0925-2312(96)00009-4

Kovalerchuk, B., & Vityaev, E. (2000). *Data mining in finance: Advances in relational and hybrid methods*. Kluwer Academic Publishers.

Kursa, M. B., & Rudnicki, W. R. (2010). Feature selection with the Boruta package. *Journal of Statistical Software, 36*(11), 1–13. doi:10.18637/jss.v036.i11

Kuzniak, S., Rabbani, A., Heo, W., Ruiz-Menjivar, J., & Grable, J. E. (2015). The Grable and Lytton risk tolerance scale: A15-year retrospective. *Financial Services Review, 24*, 177–192.

Lanz, B. (2012). The large sample size fallacy. *Scandinavian Journal of Caring Sciences, 27*(2), 487–492. doi:10.1111/j.1471-6712.2012.01052.x PMID:22862286

Liaw, A., & Wiener, M. (2002). Classification and regression by random forest. *R News, 2*(3), 18–22.

MacKay, D. (1992). Bayesian interpolation. *Neural Computation, 4*(3), 415–447. doi:10.1162/neco.1992.4.3.415

Merkle, C., & Weber, M. (2014). Do investors put their money where their mouth is? Stock market expectations and investing behavior. *Journal of Banking & Finance, 46*, 372–386. doi:10.1016/j.jbankfin.2014.03.042

Michaelides, A., & Zhang, Y. (2017). Stock market mean reversion and portfolio choice over the life cycle. *Journal of Financial and Quantitative Analysis, 52*(3), 1183–1209. doi:10.1017/S0022109017000357

Minai, A. A. (1997). Covariance learning of correlated patterns in competitive networks. *Neural Computation, 9*(3), 667–681. doi:10.1162/neco.1997.9.3.667 PMID:9097478

Nau, R. (2020). *What's the bottom line? How to compare models.* https://people.duke.edu/~rnau/compare.htm

Nguyen, L., Gallery, G., & Newton, C. (2019). The joint influence of financial risk perception and risk tolerance on individual investment decision-making. *Accounting and Finance, 59*(S1), 747–771. doi:10.1111/acfi.12295

Nobre, L. H. N., & Grable, J. E. (2015). The role of risk profiles and risk tolerance in shaping client investment decisions. *Journal of Financial Service Professionals, 69*(3), 18–21.

Rabbani, A. G., Grable, J. E., Heo, W., Nobre, L., & Kuzniak, S. (2017). Stock market volatility and changes in financial risk tolerance during the great recession. *Financial Counseling and Planning, 28*(1), 140–154. doi:10.1891/1052-3073.28.1.140

Rodriguez, R. N. (2012, June). Big data and better data. *Amstat News*, 3-4.

Ryack, K. N., Kraten, M., & Sheikh, A. (2016). Incorporating financial risk tolerance research into the financial planning process. *Journal of Financial Planning, 29*(10), 51–61.

Samek, W., Wiegand, T., & Muller, K. (2017). *Explainable artificial intelligence; Understanding, visualizing and interpreting deep learning models.* Retrieved from https://arxiv.org/pdf/1708.08296.pdf

Sariev, E., & Germano, G. (2020). Bayesian regularized artificial neural networks for the estimation of the probability of default. *Quantitative Finance, 20*(2), 311–328. doi:10.1080/14697688.2019.1633014

Wooldridge, J. M. (2013). *Introductory Econometrics: A Modern Approach* (5th ed.). South-Western.

Yao, R., & Curl, A. L. (2010). Do market returns influence risk tolerance? Evidence from panel data. *Journal of Family and Economic Issues, 32*(3), 532–544. doi:10.100710834-010-9223-2

Yao, R., & Hanna, S. D. (2004). The effect of gender and marital status on financial risk tolerance. *Consumer Interest Annual, 50*, 123–124.

Zumbrun, J. (2014, October 27). *Who owns stocks? It's not just the rich*. The Wall Street Journal, Real Time Economics Blog. Retrieved from http://blogs.wsj.com/economics/2014/10/27/who-owns-stocksits-not-just-the-rich/

KEY TERMS AND DEFINITIONS

Artificial Neural Network (ANN): A basic technique in machine learning used to find a pattern or trend in a large dataset. All input data are assumed to be connected through hidden layers(s), which is similar to the concept of biological neurons.

Bayesian Regularized Neural Network (BRNN): An advanced algorithm based on ANN, which is a feed-forward learning process using neurons. Neurons connect all input predictors to find a pattern and trend.

Big Data: A large amount of data that can be utilized to find patterns related to a given outcome or output.

Deep Learning: A subset of machine learning, this is an advanced type of machine learning. The technique outperforms other prediction methodologies because deep learning utilizes unsupervised data forms.

Financial Risk Tolerance: The maximized degree of a person's willingness to invest in a financial market or a particular investment in which the outcome is both unknown and potentially negative.

Machine Learning: A data analysis technique where a machine, with data, repeats a certain calculation to find a pattern or trend. Machine learning includes various algorithms to find patterns.

Random Forest: An ensemble technique used to combine classification and regression into one model.

S&P 500: A representative market index of large publicly traded companies in the United States.

ENDNOTES

[1] Rodriguez (2012) defined big data as information generated on a massive scale by countless online interactions among people, transactions between people and systems, and sensor-enabled machinery. Horrigan (2013) argued that big data is characterized by the creation of databases from electronic sources whose primary purpose is something other than statistical inference. It is important to note, as pointed out by Beer (2016) and Guttmann, Merchant, and Roberts (2018), that a key purpose related to the analysis of big data is to guide governance and provide insights into best practices.

[2] As conceptualized in this chapter, the BRNN was based on a Gauss-Newton approximation that utilized a Bayesian estimation and regularization approach (Mackay, 1992).

3   Stepwise regression is a well-known technique using algorithms to select a subset of significant variables when classification and prediction is the goal (Agostinelli, 2010). The stepwise regression was employed in this analysis to evaluate the effectiveness of the Random Forest Boruta variable selection technique. As shown in Formula 4, the selected predictors were utilized within a time-series regression to predict stock market performance using a conventional linear estimation technique.

4   The authors wish to thank Dr. Barbara O'Neill for her assistance in collecting the data used in this chapter.

5   The ANN modeling technique is known to be efficient when used to predict financial outcomes (e.g., Bell, 2015; Heaton, Polson, & Witte, 2016; Bonini & Caivano, 2018).

6   Some other algorithms, such as a Recurrent Neural Network (RNN), repeat the learning process by using a backward-looking process. For instance, the RNN process repeats the analysis process by going between predictors and hidden layers until reaching a better prediction (Sariev & Germano, 2020).

7   When predicting the next month's S&P 500 value, the BRNN algorithm was run on a reduced sample size of 17,764 respondents because data from the previous month (i.e., August 2017) were omitted.

8   In the context of deep learning methodologies, importance refers to the number of times a variable is found to be a significant predictor of an outcome across the multiple interactions or cycles of calculations. In this chapter, the risk premium was observed to be significantly related to S&P values 100% of the time across the thousands of estimations, whereas gender was significant only 1% of the time.

9   It is important to note that the results presented in this chapter do not indicate a cause-and-effect association between financial risk tolerance and stock market performance. The findings simply indicate that financial risk tolerance appears to be a better predictor of future stock market valuation than as an outcome variable. Additional research is needed to test for endogeneity effects related to risk tolerance and market expectations.

10 Deep learning algorithms employ multiple repeated calculations, with each new calculation improving the overall prediction rate. However, to maximize the prediction rate, deep learning algorithms sacrifice the explanatory power of each factor.

Chapter 15
Determining Consumer Purchase Intention Toward Counterfeit Luxury Goods Based on the Perceived Risk Theory

Cláudio Félix Canguende-Valentim
https://orcid.org/0000-0002-4798-2588
University of Aveiro, Portugal

ABSTRACT

This study aims to understand the impact of financial, psychological, and social risk dimensions on attitude and intention to purchase counterfeit luxury goods. Data were collected through a questionnaire conducted with 116 Angolan consumers and were treated with structural equation modeling. The results revealed that only financial risk and social risk were influential in attitude toward counterfeit luxury goods. Attitude had a significant influence on the intention to purchase counterfeit luxury goods. The research contributes to the literature because there has been no previous study in an African country that seeks to understand the purchase intention of counterfeit luxury goods according to risk perception theory. On the other hand, this study is one of the few to report that social risk perception positively impacts attitudes towards counterfeit luxury goods.

INTRODUCTION

Counterfeiting is increasing faster than ever before and is becoming an impossible global economic problem (Bian, Wang, Smith, & Yannopoulou, 2016).

The issue of counterfeiting remains a major concern for global trade in many countries (Ting et al., 2016). Counterfeits have a detrimental effect on the luxury market. Counterfeit products are on the market where there is consumer demand (Ting et al., 2016). The purchase of counterfeit luxury leads the consumer to benefit from the attributes of luxury goods through low cost. The attributes of luxury

DOI: 10.4018/978-1-7998-8609-9.ch015

goods are beauty, rarity, quality, premium price, and also the existence of an inspiring brand endorsing the product (Godey et al., 2013).

Counterfeit luxury goods refer to products with a trademark identical to a registered trademark, thus violating the trademark owner's rights (Bian & Moutinho 2009). Counterfeit luxury goods, such as clothing, shoes and handbags, are made in varying quality, with the greatest effort being made to imitate fashionable details (Norashikin, 2009); however, they are usually sold at drastically reduced prices with compromised quality (Koay, 2018).

By buying counterfeits at low prices, pretending to use the originals, consumers seek to associate themselves with the image created by luxury brands, benefiting from their aura of prestige and refusing to pay the prices demanded by the originals (Perez et al., 2010). While luxury fakes may not deliver the same level of excellence intangible attributes like the originals, they preserve the brand image that the originals convey (Pueschel et al., 2017).

Three main themes describe the internal benefits that consumers derive from buying and consuming counterfeit luxury goods: first, being efficient by optimizing their resources; second, having fun by experiencing adventure, pleasure and risk; and third, fooling others hoping not to get caught (Perez et al., 2010).

In an effort to understand consumer consumption of counterfeit products, most existing studies use the theory of planned behavior (Chiu & Leng, 2016; Ting et al., 2016). Traditionally, research has focused on ethical consumption (Manchiraju & Sadachar, 2014, Wilcox et al., 2009), the sociocultural characteristics of the consumer that facilitate counterfeiting (Bian & Veloutsou, 2007) and the financial motives driving non-misleading counterfeit luxury consumption, where consumers knowingly and willingly buy counterfeit products (Grossman & Shapiro, 1988; Staake et al., 2009; Koay, 2018).

The purchase of counterfeit products is considered a risky action, given the possibility of consumers putting themselves exposed to various types of risk (Matos et al., 2007; Yeap & Ramayah 2006).

In the consumer research literature, perceived risk refers to individuals' perceived uncertainties regarding adverse outcomes related to a purchase decision (Dowling & Staelin, 1994; Forsythe & Shi, 2003; Chen & Chang, 2012).

However, to date, there have been a minimal number of studies investigating the impacts of various dimensions of risk on consumers' purchase intention towards counterfeit luxury goods (Koay, 2018). In addition, existing research has explored the effect of risk perceptions, focused primarily on overall perceived risk (Matos et al., 2007; Tang et al., 2019). This method may not be suitable because the risks are different and their effects on consumers may vary (Peng, 2020), given that perceived risk is a multidimensional construct (Lin & Liu, 2010; Koay, 2018).

Several studies have shown evidence that risk dimensions are relevant to risk factors in the context of luxury counterfeiting (Vida, 2007; Phau, Teah & Lee, 2009; Ting et al., 2016; Pueschel et al., 2017; Koay, 2018; Peng, 2020). Perceived risk influences consumer attitudes towards counterfeit luxury goods (Matos et al., 2007; Ting et al., 2016; Pueschel et al., 2017).

Previous marketing literature has recognized that perceived risk influences purchase decisions, with consumers seeking to reduce uncertainty and unintended consequences during purchase decisions (Matos et al., 2007).

The theory of perceived risk is valuable, being that it provides explanations of consumers' intention to purchase counterfeit luxury goods (Koay, 2018). Risk dimensions predict overall risk perception and increase understanding of consumer behaviour (Featherman & Pavlou, 2003).

Therefore, this study is an attempt to understand consumers' willingness to buy non-misleading luxury counterfeit products, which means that consumers are fully aware of the fact that the products are not genuine.

Non-misleading counterfeit products are cases where the consumer knowingly buys a counterfeit product (Heike, 2010).

The choice of the non-misleading counterfeiting context is important, because these circumstances allow the investigation of true consumer perceptions (Bian & Moutinho, 2009).

Buying luxury brands is particularly growing when it comes to non-misleading buying behavior (Hanzaee & Taghipourian, 2012).

On the other hand, most scholars who explore counterfeiting from a consumer perspective base their research on data collected in the Western world (Eisend & Schuchert-Güler, 2006), although more recent research also considers Asian countries (for example, Pueschel et al., 2017; Chen et al., 2014; Phau & Teah, 2009). There is still a strong need to understand the factors that explain purchasing behavior towards counterfeit luxury goods in the context of emerging economies. Furthermore, it has been suggested that consumer behavior towards the purchase of counterfeit products differs between countries (Chiu & Leng, 2016).

Thus, the present study will consider luxury goods in general and seeks to understand the impact of financial, psychological and social risk dimensions on attitude and purchase intention towards counterfeit luxury goods. Consumer attitude, has been extensively investigated as an antecedent of consumer behaviour (Ajzen, 1991, Riqueme et al., 2008; Kassim, 2017). This study will be applied to Angolan consumers. This is a study conducted in an African country.

Few studies in Africa have sought to understand the buying behavior towards counterfeit luxury goods, with the exception of Cant et al. (2014) and Kutu (2015) studies in South Africa.

However, there has been no previous study in an African country that seeks to understand the purchase intention of counterfeit luxury goods according to risk perception theory. This study aims to fill this gap in the existing literature. Therefore, it is important to develop an in-depth understanding of the risk perceived by luxury consumers (Chang & Ko, 2017). Considering the scarce nature of studies on counterfeiting, an exploration of the impact of different dimensions of consumers' perceived risks on attitude and purchase intentions towards luxury counterfeiting in Angola made the current study necessary due to the relatively recent trends of using Africa as a transit route (Meissner, 2010) and also as the destination of counterfeits (Haman, 2010).

The research findings of this study are useful in understanding the impacts of various dimensions of perceived risk on consumers' attitude and intention to buy counterfeit luxury goods. Subsequently, the results can serve as a reference for companies in formulating marketing strategies and for governments in combating counterfeiting issues.

The following sections of this book chapter will discuss the relevant theories and literature on consumers' intention to purchase counterfeit luxury goods. Next, each proposed hypothesis will be presented. Subsequently, the methodology, data analysis, and discussion of the findings will be discussed. Finally, the theoretical and practical implications, as well as recommendations for future study will be presented.

LITERATURE REVIEW

The Counterfeit Markets

Counterfeiting is a global phenomenon, but its magnitude varies between countries (Eisend et al., 2017). Counterfeiting has been a cause for great concern over the years and is a trade that continues to thrive (Cant et al., 2014). However, it is important to recognize that the profits generated by the counterfeit trade come at the expense of the economic loss of the original manufacturers (Koay, 2018) and relies on consumer cooperation.

Genuine luxury brands are financially unaffordable for many consumers in developing countries, so these consumers have lower income levels (Eisend et al., 2017).

Efforts to convince consumers not to buy counterfeit products may be ineffective unless the specific needs of those belonging to diverse populations and markets are fully understood and addressed (Eisend et al., 2017). Given the increasingly sophisticated machinery used to produce counterfeit products, consumers are often unable to recognize the differences between a genuine and a counterfeit product due to the nearly identical appearance and only a slight difference in quality (Koay, 2018).

The production of counterfeit products is not only limited to everyday products including personal care products, health supplements, and food but is also found in luxury products with symbolic value (Koay, 2018).

Counterfeits of luxury products are commonly defined as reproduction or a replicated version of the original product, usually of a well-known trademark (Thi et al., 2017).

Global markets for counterfeit luxury goods exceeded $600 billion per year, which represented about 5-7% of the annual value of world trade (Zampetakis, 2014).

Several researchers seek to understand the motivations for purchasing counterfeit luxury goods (Geiger- Oneto et al., 2013; Huyen et al., 2016; Ting et al., 2016; Eisend et al., 2017; Thi et al., 2017; Wang et al., 2019). On the other hand, a growing number of research seeks to understand the motivations for purchasing counterfeit luxury goods, taking into consideration, among other variables, the perceived risk (Riquelme et al., 2008; Pueschel et al. 2017; Koay, 2018).

Despite these abundant studies, many researchers agree that the reasons for consumers' intention to buy counterfeit products are still not fully covered (Li et al., 2018; Qin et al., 2018).

The Counterfeit Market in Africa

Africa has always been seen only as a destination for counterfeit products and therefore, anti-counterfeiting strategies have been prioritized towards Europe, America, and Asia (Haman, 2010).

Few studies in Africa have sought to study the purchase intentions of counterfeit products (Cant et al., 2014; Kutu, 2015; Ansah, 2017; Souiden et al., 2018).

In a study in Tunisia investigating the effect of individuals' ethics, religiosity, and attitudes toward counterfeits on counterfeit product purchase intentions, the results indicated that religiosity, ethics, and attitudes influence the intention to purchase counterfeits (Souiden et al., 2018).

In another study that compared the influence of price and country of origin effects on consumer attitude and purchase intention of counterfeit consumer products in the Kumasi metropolis of Ghana, the results indicated that the country of origin effect influences consumer attitude and purchase intention more than the price of counterfeit products (Ansah, 2017). The results also showed a significant association between the level of education and the counterfeit products purchased by the consumer.

Regarding counterfeit luxury goods, in a study that sought to describe the buying behaviour towards counterfeit luxury fashion brand products in South African consumers, one of the key findings of the research is that South African consumers have a relatively low buying behaviour and demand for counterfeit luxury fashion brand products (Cant et al., 2014).

In their study, Kutu (2015) described South African consumers' intention to buy authentic luxury fashion brands compared to counterfeit products. The results of the study indicated that consumers in Johannesburg have a high intention to buy fake luxury fashion products.

Social group behavior related to counterfeit products differs between developing and developed countries and therefore plays a different role in building consumer identity through counterfeit brands (Eisend et al., 2017).

There has been no previous study in an African country that seeks to understand the intention to purchase counterfeit luxury goods by taking into consideration the dimensions of perceived risk. This study, however, will be applied in Angola. Angola is a country located in Sub-Saharan Africa. However, it is important to develop a deep understanding of luxury consumers' perceived risk, and the dominant risk components and their relative importance may vary across research contexts (Liao et al., 2010).

In the following, we will present risk perception theory.

Perception Risk Theory

Perceived risk refers to individuals' perceived uncertainties regarding adverse outcomes related to a purchase decision (Dowling & Staelin, 1994; Forsythe & Shi, 2003; Chen & Chang, 2012).

According to Bauer (1960), consumer behavior involves risk because his purchasing actions will produce consequences that he cannot anticipate with anything approaching certainty, and some of which, at least, are likely to be unpleasant.

Also, according to the theory of perceived risk, consumers are more often motivated to avoid errors than to maximize utility in purchasing (Mitchell, 1999). The risk that consumers perceive can strongly influence their behavior (Chiu & Won, 2015). Therefore, the more risk they perceive, the less likely they are to buy (Lim, 2003). Risk is seen as a significant concern during purchase decisions, indicating that consumers are looking for ways to decrease ambiguity and unfavorable outcomes of purchase decisions (Bian & Moutinho, 2009).

People differ in their risk assessments of the same object, depending on individual and situational factors (Pueschel et al., 2017). In general, people tend to avoid mistakes rather than maximize utility when engaging in risky decision-making (Liao et al., 2010).

Several studies have shown evidence that risk dimensions are the relevant risk factors in the context of counterfeiting (Koay, 2018).

In a study that considers perceived risk as a salient belief that influences attitude and intention to use pirated software, the results indicated that perceived process risk has an impact on the intention to use pirated software, and perceived psychological risk is a strong predictor of attitude toward using pirated software (Liao et al., 2010).

In another study that investigated consumer intention to dine in luxury restaurants when new green practices are implemented, considering trust and perceived risks, the results showed that perceived risks (functional, physical, financial, hedonic and self-image) significantly affected consumers' consumption intention (Peng, 2020).

A study aimed to assess the relationship between various dimensions of perceived risk and consumer resistance to the generic drug indicated that only performance-technology risk and physical risk are positively related to consumer resistance to the generic drug (Abzakh et al., 2013). On the other hand, the study also states that financial risk, performance-infrastructure risk, time risk, social risk, and psychological risk have no significant relationships with consumer resistance to generic drugs.

Therefore, according to the previous studies, perceived risk was a strong factor in influencing consumer attitudes toward counterfeit luxury goods (Ting et al., 2016).

Several studies have shown evidence that risk dimensions are relevant risk factors in the context of luxury counterfeiting (Ting et al., 2016; Koay, 2018). The intention to purchase counterfeit luxury goods is negative influenced by dimensions of perceived risk: functional, physical, hedonic, self-image (Peng, 2020), moral (Pueschel et al., 2017), financial (Cordell et al., 1996; Bamossy & Scammon, 1985; Peng, 2020), psychological (Liao et al., 2010; Martin et al., 2015; Quintal et al., 2016 e Pueschel etal., 2017), social (Vida, 2007; Phau, Teah & Lee, 2009; Koay, 2018) and performance (Koay, 2018).

As mentioned earlier, only the dimensions of financial risk, psychological risk and social risk are of interest to this study.

Perceived Financial Risk

Financial risk refers to the potential monetary loss arising from the need to repair, replace, or refund a purchase (Horton, 1976). Pueschel et al., (2017), the perceived financial risk refers to disappointment about value for money, waste or loss in case of product malfunction.

By buying counterfeit luxury goods, consumers take advantage of cost savings while risking compromised quality (Ang et al., 2001; Wang et al., 2005).

Consumers may perceive more financial risk in buying a counterfeit luxury brand rather than an original luxury brand because of the large performance doubt and as a result, they may lose money (financial risk) in buying a defective or unreliable product (Cordell et al., 1996; Bamossy & Scammon, 1985).

In the context of this research, consumers may face financial risks related to the intention to purchase counterfeit luxury goods if they do not meet the requirement as expected. Thus, the higher the perceived financial risk, the less likely consumers are to buy counterfeit luxury goods. Therefore, we formulate the following hypothesis:

Hypothesis 1: Perceived financial risk will negatively affect the intention to purchase counterfeit luxury goods.

Perceived Psychological Risk

Perceived psychological risk refers to the likely anxiety or regret of a post-purchase reaction (Quintal et al., 2016).

Perceived psychological risk includes concerns about a consumer's self-concept, such as the fear of not making the right product choice, or the possibility of an individual suffering mental stress from using counterfeit luxury goods (Liao et al., 2010; Pueschel et al., 2017).

Through their experiences in buying and consuming counterfeit luxury goods, consumers build a self-concept, viewing themselves as astute consumers who optimize their economic resources, and as pleasure-loving people who know how to enjoy themselves (Perez et al., 2010).

Psychological risk negatively predicts purchase intentions (Mortimer et al., 2020), it has been amply demonstrated in several studies that psychological risk represents a barrier to purchase intentions, and that the higher the perceived psychological risk, the lower the purchase intentions (Martin et al., 2015; Quintal et al., 2016).

In this research, consumers may face some psychological risks related to the purchase intention of counterfeit luxury goods. Therefore, we formulate the following hypothesis:

Hypothesis 2: Perceived psychological risk will negatively affect the intention to purchase counterfeit luxury goods.

Perceived Social Risk

Social risk is understood as the probability of a product or service affecting the way others think about an individual (Riquelme et al., 2008). It is possible that consumers' purchasing behavior will not be accepted by other members of society (Lim, 2003).

Individuals obtain real and symbolic benefits from their purchase and consumption, projecting a desired social image and contributing to the construction of their identity (Perez et al., 2010). Identities are formed not only by the meaning provided by brands and products, but also by social interactions (Eisend et al., 2017).

Perceived social risk confronts consumers with negative reactions or thoughts of other people, having the probability that the use of counterfeit luxury goods will affect the way others think about the individual (Fraedrich & Ferrell, 1992; Pueschel et al., 2017).

Social risk is significantly related to the intention to purchase counterfeit luxury goods, consistent with previous studies (Phau, Teah & Lee, 2009; Koay, 2018). Perceived social risk not only has a direct negative impact on the intention to purchase counterfeit luxury goods, but can also indirectly influence intention through partial mediation of attitudes (Wu & Zhao, 2021). In this sense, consumers are less likely to buy counterfeit luxury goods if they think it is embarrassing and shameful if others find out the truth (Herstein et al., 2015; Koay, 2018). When consumers buy counterfeit luxury goods, they are affected by the social group they belong to and the social group they wish to join (Wu & Zhao, 2021). Thus, if the consumer's social group aspires to disapprove of such consumption, the perceived social risk involved in buying counterfeit products decreases the consumer's intention to buy counterfeit products (Miyazaki et al., 2009). Your need for social approval for owning a counterfeit increases social risk (Davidson et al., 2019) and the risk of being ostracized (Tang et al., 2019).

In the context of this research, the possibility exists that consumers who make use of counterfeit luxury goods are not accepted by members of their society. Therefore, we formulate the following hypothesis:

Hypothesis 3: Perceived social risk will negatively affect the intention to purchase counterfeit luxury goods.

Attitude towards Counterfeit Luxury Goods

Attitude, defined as a learned predisposition to respond to an object in a consistently favorable or unfavorable way, is significant as a predictor of consumer behavior, and highly correlated with one's intentions (Ajzen, 1991).

According to the theory of planned behavior, attitude is the most influential factor in predicting intentional behavior (Riquelme et al., 2008). If consumers perceive that their personality is demonstrated through luxury products, they will have favorable attitudes toward the products (Ting et al., 2016).

Consumer attitudes towards counterfeits of luxury brands play an important role in influencing consumer purchase intention (Phau, 2009).

Kassim (2017) found that status consumption and value consciousness did not effect consumer attitudes toward such products, but there was a significant positive moderating effect of value consciousness on the consumption of products to gain social status and also on attitude toward the products.

In a study that examined consumers' attitudes towards buying counterfeit luxury goods in two cities in two different countries (Saudi Arabia and Malaysia), it was found that quality, price, popularity and status signaling represents the main motivating factors for their choices of counterfeit luxury goods brands among consumer groups in the two countries (Kassim et al., 2021).

In a survey aimed at understanding the factors that influence attitudes towards counterfeits and the intention to buy these illegal products in a Muslim country, the results indicated that value awareness, performance risk, norms (subjective and descriptive) and ethical awareness influence attitude (Riquelme et al., 2008).

In their study, Ting et al. (2016) adapted the Theory of Reasoned Action (TRA) to examine how social and personality factors influence consumer attitudes toward counterfeit luxury goods and how consumer attitudes mediate these two sets of variables in consumer purchase intention. According to the author, the result of the study demonstrated that perceived risk was a strong factor in influencing consumer attitudes towards counterfeit luxury goods, followed by value awareness and status consumption.

In another study that looked at the factors driving the market for counterfeit goods in the UK, the results showed that consumers have a negative attitude towards counterfeit luxury goods, so the attitude and acceptance of counterfeiting are not very prevalent in the market (Huyen et al., 2016).

In the study by Matos et al. (2007), aiming to propose and test a model integrating the main predictors of consumers' attitudes and behavioral intentions towards counterfeits, the results indicate that attitudes towards counterfeits are more influenced by perceived risk if consumers have purchased a counterfeit product before.

Another study that examine how social and personality factors influence Chinese consumers' attitudes towards counterfeit luxury brands indicated that attitude towards counterfeit luxury brands influences purchase intention (Phau, 2009).

In the study by Pueschel et al. (2017) investigating the consumption of counterfeit luxury goods in Gulf Cooperation Council (GCC) countries, the results showed that although consumers purchase counterfeit luxury goods, perceived performance, psychosocial and moral risks may prevent them from engaging in such consumption.

Eisend's (2017) meta-analysis summarizes the influence of consumer demographics and psychographics on attitudes, intentions, and behaviors toward branded counterfeit luxury goods among developed and developing countries. Their results indicated that risk propensity and reduced integrity are stronger determinants of counterfeit purchases in developed countries and are related to brand signals that refer to identities that consumers try to avoid. The author also mentions that in developing countries, consumers are more influenced by psychographics, such as status-seeking, which is related to the positive signals of the brand to the consumer's identity.

In another study conducted in Singapore, Phau et al. (2009) stated that consumers are more willing to buy counterfeit luxury products if their attitudes towards buying the products are positive. Thus, in this study, we are interested in determining the perception of risk in consumer attitudes towards the purchase intention of counterfeit luxury goods among Angolan consumers.

Consumers who perceive greater risk in purchasing counterfeit goods will have unfavorable attitudes toward counterfeit luxury goods (Ting et al., 2016).

Perceived risk has a negative relationship with consumer attitudes toward counterfeit luxury goods, which is consistent with previous studies (Matos et al., 2007; Ting et al., 2016). Consumers may consider counterfeit luxury goods unsafe because they come with no guarantees or they may worry about being convicted by third parties or even arrested and charged by law enforcement authorities (Ting et al., 2016).

Therefore, from the literature review, it was found that there are many and varied reasons that influence consumer attitudes toward counterfeit luxury goods in various countries.

However, in this study, we examine the relationship between perceived financial risk, psychological risk, and social risk in consumers' attitudes toward counterfeit luxury goods. Therefore, we formulate the following hypotheses:

Hypothesis 4: Perceived financial risk has a negative effect in influencing consumer attitudes toward counterfeit luxury goods.

Hypothesis 5: Perceived psychological risk has a negative effect in influencing consumer attitudes toward counterfeit luxury goods.

Hypothesis 6: Perceived social risk has a negative effect in influencing consumer attitudes toward counterfeit luxury goods.

Purchase Intentions towards Counterfeit Luxury Goods

Recently, a growing body of research has investigated the factors influencing purchase intentions toward counterfeit luxury goods (Matos et al., 2007; Phau et al., 2009; Koay, 2018).

Several studies have highlighted consumers' significant predictors of purchase intention toward counterfeit luxury goods. In Koay's (2018) study, among the significant predictors of consumers' purchase intention toward counterfeit luxury goods include denial of responsibility, victim denial, performance risk, and social risk.

According to Matos et al. (2007), consumers' intentions to purchase counterfeit luxury goods depend on several factors, including their perceptions of risk, their attitudes towards counterfeit luxury goods, whether they have purchased counterfeit luxury goods before, as well as on their personal gratification and their subjective norm, integrity, price-quality inference.

In another study that compared attitudes towards buying counterfeit luxury goods among consumers in Singapore and Taiwan, Chiu & Leng (2016) found that consumer intention to buy counterfeit luxury goods in both countries, can be predicted based on certain factors including consumer attitude, subjective norm, and brand awareness.

In another study examining some antecedents of intention and behavior towards the purchase of counterfeit luxury goods among young consumers in Vietnam, their results indicate that materialism (the centrality component) has a positive impact on attitude towards the purchase of counterfeit luxury goods (Thi et al., 2017). The study further states that attitude and subjective norm toward counterfeit luxury goods is positively related to purchase intention, while perceived behavioral control has no direct impact on purchase intention.

The positive relationship between attitude and intention to purchase counterfeit products has been established from the literature (Chiu & Leng, 2016; Phau et al., 2009).

If the consumer's attitude towards buying counterfeit luxury goods is favorable, he is more likely to buy counterfeit luxury goods (Thi et al., 2017). Therefore, we formulate the following hypothesis:

Hypothesis 7: Attitude positively influences the purchase intention of counterfeit luxury goods.

The conceptual model of the study is the one proposed in figure 1, derived from the above hypotheses.

Figure 1. The conceptual model

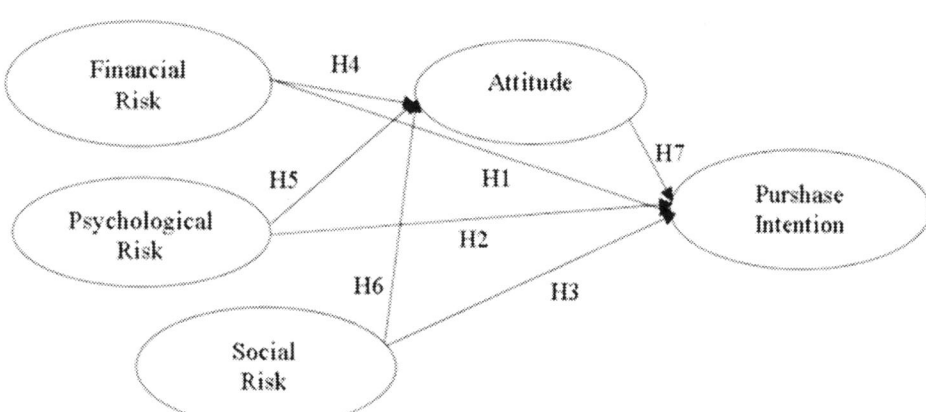

METHODOLOGY

Participants and Data Collection

Angola was selected as the study context to empirically investigate the purchase intention of counterfeit luxury goods based on perceived risk theory, considering financial, psychological and social dimensions, and consumer attitude. A convenience sampling method was adopted and the questionnaire was distributed online. Data were collected from May 12 to June 18, 2021, in the Northern and Southern regions of Angola. To ensure that only individuals knowledgeable about luxury brands could be part of the data set, as suggested in previous studies (Christodoulides et al., 2008; Shukla, 2010; Jain & Mishra, 2017), a screening question was asked of the participants, whereby we asked respondents to indicate ("yes" or "no") whether they could identify the difference between counterfeit and genuine products, as suggested (Kassim et al., 2021).

Similar to Matos et al. (2007), no particular counterfeit product was specified in this study. The questions considered the term "counterfeit goods" in general because the goal at this point was to assess consumers' attitudes towards counterfeit luxury goods in general (Matos et al., 2007).

A total of 123 questionnaires were answered, of which 116 were valid and included for analysis. The sample size of this study is within the minimum requirement of 100 elements established by Hair et al.

(2010) for structural equations. Of the respondents, 62,9% (n = 73) were male and 37,1% (n = 43) were female. The age distribution of the respondents was classified into two ranges: 52,6% (n=61) of the sample were between the ages of 18-35 years, and the remainder, 47,4% (n=55), were over the age of 35 years. 20,7% (n=24) had secondary education; 50,9% (n=59) of the sample were college graduates and 28,4% (n=33) were post-graduates; 62,9% (n=73) were from Southern Angola and 37,1% (n=43) were from Northern Angola.

Instrument Development

The questionnaire was developed based on standard item scales in English and later translated into Portuguese because the respondents were Angolan, so they were more proficient in Portuguese. From the existing literature, established and validated scales were used to measure financial risk, psychological risk, social risk, attitude, and purchase intention. The scales were adopted from several studies conducted in the area related to the behavior of the luxury counterfeit consumer.

For perceived financial risk (FR), we adopted three items from Chang & Ko (2017), namely: "that I really would not get my money's worth from it"; "that it would be a bad way to spend my money on it"; "that the financial investment in it would not be wise".

For perceived social risk (SR), four items from Koay (2018) were adopted, namely: "I would feel very embarrassed if people discovered that I carry a counterfeit luxury product"; "If I bought a counterfeit product, I would feel guilty"; "Friends, relatives or associates will lose their respect to me because they will regard me as unethical"; "I avoid carrying counterfeit products in the important social events".

For perceived psychological risk (PR), we adopted three items from Koay (2018), namely: "Purchasing counterfeit luxury goods makes me feel psychologically uncomfortable"; "Purchasing counterfeit luxury goods gives me a feeling of unwanted anxiety"; "Purchasing counterfeit luxury goods causes me to experience unnecessary tension".

For the attitude (ATT) toward counterfeiting, we adopted five items from Ting et al. (2016), namely: "Considering price, I prefer counterfeit luxury goods"; "I like shopping for counterfeit of luxury goods"; "Buying counterfeit luxury goods generally benefits the consumer"; "There i's nothing wrong with purchasing counterfeit luxury goods"; "Generally speaking, buying counterfeit luxury goods is a better choice".

For the purchase intention (PI) toward counterfeiting, we adopted five items from Matos et al. (2007), namely: "I intend to purchase counterfeit products"; "I think about a counterfeited product as a choice when buying something"; "I recommend to friends and relatives that they buy a counterfeited product"; "I say favorable things about counterfeited products".

All items were measured on a five-point Likert scale, where "1" denoted "strongly disagree" and "5" denoted "strongly agree."

Data Analysis

To achieve the objective of this study and test hypotheses, the statistical package programs SPSS 23.0 and AMOS 23.0 were used. With SPSS 23.0, descriptive analysis was adopted to know the demographic characteristics of the sample, on the other hand, scale reliability tests were conducted by exploratory factor analysis. With AMOS 23.0 the data analysis was performed, following the two-step approach. The parameters were estimated using the maximum likelihood method. First, the reliability and validity of the measures were tested using confirmatory factor analysis (CFA). Second, structural equation modeling (SEM) was used to test the hypotheses in the proposed conceptual model. The ability to analyse observed and latent variables distinguishes SEM from more standard statistical techniques, such as analysis of variance (ANOVA) and multiple regression, which analyse only observed variables (Kline, 2016). The most important strength of SEM is that the relationships among numerous latent constructs can be examined in a way that reduces the error in the model (Hair, Hult, Ringle & Sarstedt, 2014). The criticisms that have been made of SEM cluster around two main topics: sample quality/quantity and causal interpretation (Hox & Becher, 1998).

RESULTS

Scale Evaluation

To evaluate the scales used in this study, we first conducted Exploratory Factor Analysis (PCA using Varimax rotation with an eigenvalue criterion greater than 1,0).

The results of the Exploratory Factor Analysis showed good convergent and discriminant validity of the constructs in our study (i.e., the number of factors emerged as expected and items loaded high on the assigned factor while loading low on the others) according to table 1. The factor loadings of the construct indicators were all greater than 0,50.

Convergent Validity

Convergent validity is the degree to which multiple items measuring the same concept agree. Convergent validity depends on the internal consistency that multiple measures converge on a reliable basis (Babin & Zikmund, 2016). According to Hair et al. (2010), establishing convergent validity requires the main loadings, namely composite reliability (CR) and average variance extracted (AVE). The composite reliability (CR) values ranged from 0,878 (for perceived social risk) to 0,940 (for purchase intention), and the AVE values were all greater than 0,5 meet the criteria suggested by Hair et al. (2010), ranging from 0,643 (for perceived social risk) to 0,802 (for perceived social risk), as shown in Table 1.

Discriminant Validity

Discriminant validity represents how unique or distinct a measure is. A scale should not correlate very highly with a measure of a different construct (Babin & Zikmund, 2016). The study used the Fornell & Larcker (1981) assessment. As recommended by Fornell & Larcker (1981), The correlation coefficients (from − 0,024 to 0,773) were far less than the AVE square roots for the individual variables (ranging from 0,801 to 0,895), supporting the good discriminant validity of the constructs in this study.

To assess internal reliability, the study employed composite reliability (CR) values (Hair et al., 2014) and Cronbach's alpha (Fornell & Larcker, 1981).

The results presented in Table 1 show that the composite reliability (CR) values ranged from 0,878 (for perceived social risk) to 0,940 (for purchase intention), exceeding the criterion (0,70) suggested by (Hair et al., 2014; Fornell & Larcker, 1981). All Cronbach's alpha values for all scales in this study ranged from 0,861 (for perceived social risk) to 0,967 (for purchase intention). These results showed a good level of reliability, with the coefficient alphas exceeding the minimum recommended level of 0,70 (Fornell & Larcker, 1981). Therefore, we can conclude that the measures are reliable.

Table 1. Statistics precision

Code	Constructs and the scale items	Factor loadings	CA[a]	CR[b]	AVE[c]
	Perceived Financial Risk		0,953	0,924	0,802
FR1	that I really would not get my money's worth from it	0,902			
FR2	that it would be a bad way to spend my money on it	0,921			
FR3	that the financial investment in it would not be wise	0,911			
	Perceived Psychological risk		0,909	0,899	0,749
PR1	Purchasing counterfeit luxury goods makes me feel psychologically uncomfortable	0,857			
PR2	Purchasing counterfeit luxury goods gives me a feeling of unwanted anxiety	0,875			
PR3	Purchasing counterfeit luxury goods causes me to experience unnecessary tension	0,812			
	Perceived social risk		0,861	0,878	0,643
PR1	I would feel very embarrassed if people discovered that I carry a counterfeit luxury product	0,729			
PR2	If I bought a counterfeit product, I would feel guilty	0,659			
PR3	Friends, relatives or associates will lose their respect to me because they will regard me as unethical	0,803			
PR4	I avoid carrying counterfeit products in the important social events	0,705			
	Attitude		0,937	0,914	0,681
ATT1	Considering price, I prefer counterfeit luxury goods	0,668			
ATT2	I like shopping for counterfeit of luxury goods	0,818			
ATT3	Buying counterfeit luxury goods generally benefits the consumer	0,675			
ATT4	There i's nothing wrong with purchasing counterfeit luxury goods	0,701			
ATT5	Generally speaking, buying counterfeit luxury goods is a better choice	0,778			
	Purchase Intention		0,967	0,940	0,798
PI1	I intend to purchase counterfeit products	0,846			
PI2	I think about a counterfeited product as a choice when buying something	0,804			
PI3	I recommend to friends and relatives that they buy a counterfeited product	0,820			
PI4	I say favorable things about counterfeited products	0,819			

CA[a] = Cronbach's alpha
CR[b] = Composite Reliability
AVE[c] = Average Variance Extracted

Determining Consumer Purchase Intention

These results demonstrated a good level of reliability, with the coefficient alphas exceeding the minimum recommended level of 0,70 (Fornell & Larcker, 1981). Table 1 presents the results of the EFA and Cronbach's alpha tests.

Table 2. Model fit índices (CFA)

Fit index	Recommended Values*	Observed Values
CFI	> 0,90	0,982
CMIN/DF	<3	1,292
TLI	> 0,90	0,978
RMSEA	<0,080	0,050

*Source: Hu & Bentler, 1999; Hair et al., 2010; Kline 2016

Figure 2. Proposed research model
(FR = Perceived Financial Risk; PR = Perceived Psychological Risk; SR = Perceived Social Risk; ATT = Attitude; PI = Purchase Intention)

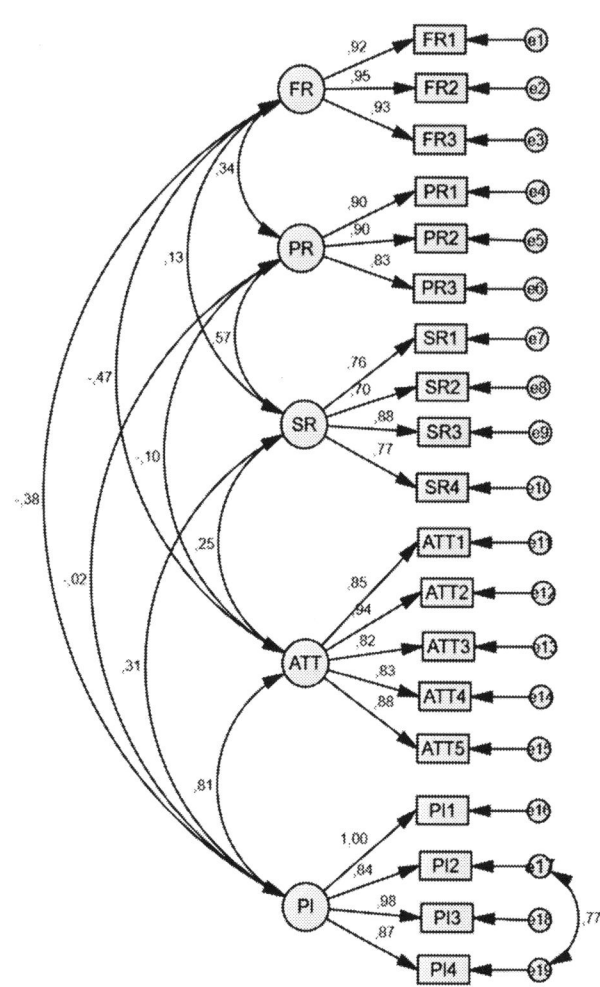

Confirmatory factor analysis. We performed confirmatory factor analysis (CFA) to analyze the complete measurement model before analyzing the structural model, as shown in figure 2. An acceptable measurement model is required before going to the second stage, which involves testing hypotheses about the structural model (Kline, 2016). The confirmatory factor analysis (CFA) was used to validate the measurement model, which consists of five constructs, measured by 19 observed items. Since the main interest of using SEM in this study was to see how well the hypothesized model fits or adequately describes the data, several steps were taken to detect sources of the misfit.

CFA results showed that the measures produced an adequate level of model fit, $\chi 2 = 182{,}15$, df = 141, p = 0,01, normalized $\chi 2$ (CMIN/DF) = 1,292, confirmatory fit index (CFI) = 0,982, Tucker-Lewis index (TLI) = 0,978, root mean square error of approximation (RMSEA) = 0,050. The overall summary of the fit statistics for the proposed model is shown in Table 2.

The Structural Equation Model and Hypothesis Testing

The structural model was tested after the overall measurement model was deemed acceptable.

The structural model was built to examine the hypothesized relationships between the constructs. Structural equation analysis was applied to estimate the path coefficients for each proposed relationship in the structural model, as shown in figure 3. The SEM results, however, had the same level of fit against the measurement model. The conceptual model showed an adequate level of fit, $\chi 2 = 182{,}15$, p = 0,01, df = 141, CMIN/DF = 1,292, CFI = 0,982, TLI = 0,978, RMSEA = 0,050. The overall summary of the fit statistics for the structural model is shown in Table 3.

Table 3. Model fit índices (SEM)

Fit index	Recommended Values*	Observed Values
CFI	> 0,90	0,982
CMIN/DF	<3	1,292
TLI	> 0,90	0,978
RMSEA	<0,080	0,050

*Source: Hu & Bentler, 1999; Hair et al., 2010; Kline, 2016

Figure 3. SEM on proposed model
(FR = Perceived Financial Risk; PR = Perceived Psychological Risk; SR = Perceived Social Risk; ATT = Attitude; PI = Purchase Intention)

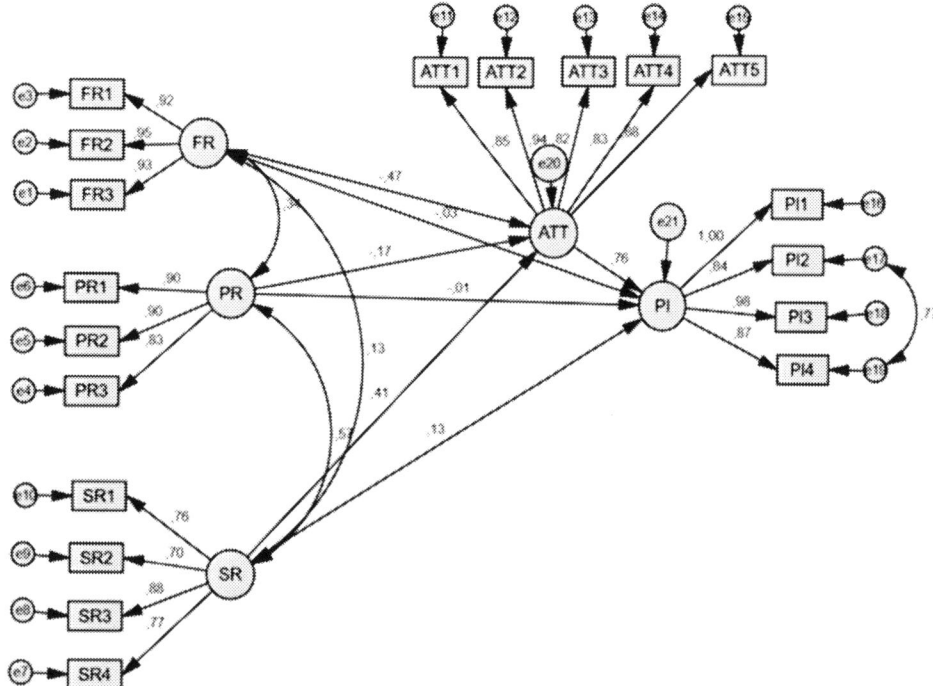

The paths of perceived financial risk, psychological risk, and social risk, in relation to purchase intention, were not significant and therefore hypotheses 1, 2, and 3 were not supported.

The paths of perceived financial risk in relation to attitude were statistically significant ($p < 0,001$), supporting hypothesis 4.

The path of perceived psychological risk in relation to attitude was not significant and therefore hypothesis 5 was not supported.

The results also provided support for the path of social risk perception in relation to attitude, which was significantly positive ($p < 0,001$), contrary to our expectation, with the relationship being in the opposite direction.

Finally, the results provided support for the attitude path toward intention to purchase counterfeit luxury goods, so hypothesis 7 was supported. The results of the hypothesis tests are summarized in Table 4.

Table 4. Estimates of structural equation coefficients

Hypothesis	Structural path	Standardized estimate	P - value	Empirical result
H1	Financial Risk - Purchase intention	- 0,030	0,703	Not supported
H2	Psychological Risk - Purchase intention	-0,020	0,857	Not supported
H3	Social Risk - Purchase intention	0,200	0,133	Not supported
H4	Financial Risk - Attitude	-0,424	0,001	Supported
H5	Psychological Risk - Attitude	-0,194	0,142	Not supported
H6	Social Risk - Attitude	0,526	0,001	Supported
H7	Attitude – Purchase intention	0,918	0,001	Supported

DISCUSSION AND IMPLICATIONS

Discussion

This research focuses on examining the impact of perceived risk on attitude and intention to purchase counterfeit luxury goods, among consumers in Angola, an emerging economy in Africa. The study was based on the theory of perceived risk, adding attitude, a very important variable in the study of consumer behavior. Seven hypotheses were developed and tested, two of which were supported by the data. Specifically, the findings share some similarities compared to the findings of previous studies on the significant impact of perceived financial risk on attitude towards counterfeit luxury goods, the findings share some similarities compared to the findings of previous studies on the significant impact of perceived financial risk on attitude towards counterfeit luxury goods. Furthermore, financial risk had no significant relationship with purchase intention. However, perceived financial risk significantly influences on attitude toward use, but no significant impact on intention to purchase counterfeit luxury goods.

On the other hand, the psychological risk was not significantly related to attitude towards counterfeit luxury goods, as well as to the intention to buy counterfeits. The insignificant relationship between psychological risk and purchase intention, suggests that although consumers may experience mental stress when purchasing counterfeit luxury goods, the perceived psychological risk is not sufficient to influence their intention to purchase counterfeit luxury goods (Koay, 2018).

Social risk in relation to attitude was significantly positive ($p < 0,001$), contrary to our expectation that the relationship was in the opposite direction. This result was in contrast to the findings of previous studies (Wu & Zhao, 2021), with literature suggesting that perceived social risk has a significant negative impact on attitude. Thus, the social risk may no longer be a concern in the attitude to use counterfeit luxury goods. According to Cant et al. (2014), many consumers around the world and perhaps more in emerging economies do not mind buying counterfeit products, especially those consumers who want to be fashionable but cannot afford them.

Hypotheses 1, 2, and 3 investigate whether perceived risk predicts consumer purchase behavior of counterfeit luxury goods. None of the risk dimensions (financial risk, social risk, psychological risk) influenced purchase intention. This result was similar to that found in the Engizek & Sekerkaya's (2015) study, which explored the effects of non-price sources of motivation on consumers' voluntary purchase intention of counterfeit luxury brands. This shows that consumers do not really understand the adverse effects and risks involved in buying counterfeit products (Engizek & Sekerkaya, 2015).

On the other hand, social risk had no significant relationship with the intention to purchase counterfeit luxury goods. The opposite result has been verified in several studies (Wu & Zhao, 2021). Previous literature suggests that consumer perception of social risks is higher, the willingness to buy counterfeit luxury goods is weaker.

Attitude had a significant impact on the purchase intention of counterfeit luxury goods. This result is consistent with the studies of Wu & Zhao (2021), who explore the impact of value awareness, social risk perception, and face awareness on the purchase intention of counterfeit luxury.

THEORETICAL IMPLICATIONS

This study enriches the understanding of the role of perceived risk in attitude and purchase intention towards counterfeit luxury goods. The theory of perceived risk is valuable and complementary, and thus provides alternative explanations of purchase intention for counterfeit luxury goods (Koay, 2018). Our results indicate that not all components of perceived risk proposed in the study significantly influence decisions to buy counterfeit luxury goods. Only financial risk and social risk were considered influential in the attitude towards counterfeit luxury goods. Angolans associate consumption of counterfeit luxury goods mainly with financial and social risks. This indicates that not all dimensions of perceived risk contribute to the formation of overall risk in an analogous way in this context.

Attitude had a significant influence on the intention to buy counterfeit luxury goods.

Furthermore, the dominant risk components and their relative importance may vary between research contexts (Liao et al., 2010).

On the other hand, the results of this research also contribute to the literature on the consumption intention of counterfeit luxury goods, and this study is one of the few to report that the perception of social risk shows a positive relationship in the attitude towards counterfeit luxury goods.

Given the results presented, there is room for new thoughts and propositions regarding the aborted theme. However, it is necessary to consider some limitations of the study. The sample size was the main limitation of this research. Another limitation of this study was that it focused on only three dimensions of perceived risk. Future research should further examine in a cross-cultural study, the impact of the dimensions of perceived risk on the intention to purchase luxury counterfeit, in a larger sample compared to that of this study.

PRACTICAL IMPLICATIONS

An individual's attitude towards the intention to purchase counterfeit luxury goods is clearly a precursor to their intention to use counterfeit luxury goods. Therefore, promoting favorable attitudes against luxury goods piracy could be useful in combating and deterring the use of counterfeit luxury goods, and improving and enhancing anti-counterfeiting education would be fundamental and necessary to achieve this goal. Although very little of the resource allocation has been directed to Africa to combat the counterfeiting dilemma (Cant et al., 2014), the government and original manufacturers should find ways to inform the public that supporting counterfeit luxury goods has detrimental effects on government and original manufacturers' revenue because they receive less tax and sales revenue through campaigns or advertisements. (Koay, 2018). On the other hand, it is recommended that government authorities share information with neighboring African countries about counterfeiting activities to create awareness and also that government authorities collaborate with other African countries to try to limit the spread (Cant et al., 2014). The fact that attitude is the strongest predictor of purchase intention makes it even more important to determine the factors that predict attitude (Liao et al., 2010). If we can change someone's attitude towards the use of counterfeit luxury goods, it should be possible to decrease the use of counterfeit luxury goods.

Perceived risk actually plays a role in the purchase decisions of counterfeit luxury goods. Of the three identified risk components, the social risk is the dominant risk component that influences attitude toward the intention to purchase counterfeit luxury goods.

REFERENCES

Abzakh, A. A., Ling, K. C., & Alkilani, K. (2013). The Impact of Perceived Risks on the Consumer Resistance towards Generic Drugs in the Malaysia Pharmaceutical Industry. *International Journal of Business and Management*, *8*(3), 42–50. doi:10.5539/ijbm.v8n3p42

Ajzen, I. (1991). The theory of planned behavior. *Organizational Behavior and Human Decision Processes*, *50*(2), 179–211. doi:10.1016/0749-5978(91)90020-T

Ang, S. H., Cheng, P. S., Lim, E. A. C., & Tambyah, S. K. (2001). Spot the difference: Consumer responses towards counterfeits. *Journal of Consumer Marketing*, *18*(3), 219–235. doi:10.1108/07363760110392967

Ansah, M. O. (2017). A Comparison of Price Effect and Country of Origin Effect on Consumer A Comparison of Price Effect and Country of Origin Effect on Consumer Counterfeit Products Purchase. *Journal of Social Sciences*, *13*(November), 216–228. Advance online publication. doi:10.3844/jssp.2017.216.228

Babin, J., & Zikmund, W. (2016). Exploring marketing Research (11th ed.). Cengage Learning.

Bamossy, G., & Scammon, D. L. (1985). Product counterfeiting: Consumers and manufacturers beware. *Advances in Consumer Research. Association for Consumer Research (U. S.)*, *12*(1), 334–339.

Bauer, R. A. (1960). Consumer behavior as risk taking. In *Proceedings of the 43rd National Conference of the American Marketing Assocation*. American Marketing Association.

Bian, X., & Moutinho, L. (2009). An investigation of determinants of counterfeit purchase consideration. *Journal of Business Research*, *62*(3), 368–378. doi:10.1016/j.jbusres.2008.05.012

Bian, X., & Veloutsou, C. (2007). Consumers' attitudes regarding non-deceptive counterfeit brands in the UK and China. *Journal of Brand Management*, *14*(3), 211–222. doi:10.1057/palgrave.bm.2550046

Cant, M. C., Wiid, J. A., & Manley, L. L. (2014). Counterfeit luxury fashion brands: Consumer purchase behaviour. *Corporate Ownership & Control*, *11*(3), 175–183. doi:10.22495/cocv11i3c1p4

Chang, Y., & Ko, Y. (2017). International Journal of Hospitality Management Consumers' perceived post purchase risk in luxury services. *International Journal of Hospitality Management*, *61*, 94–106. doi:10.1016/j.ijhm.2016.09.005

Chen, Y., & Chang, C. (2012). Enhance green purchase intentions: The roles of green perceived value, green perceived risks, and green trust. *Management Decision*, *50*(3), 502–520. doi:10.1108/00251741211216250

Chen, Y.-Q., Zhu, H., Le, M., & Wu, Y.-Z. (2014). The effect of face consciousness on consumption of counterfeit luxury goods. *Social Behavior and Personality*, *42*(6), 1007–1014. doi:10.2224bp.2014.42.6.1007

Chiu, W., Lee, K.-Y., & Won, D. (2014). Chiu, Weisheng, & Won, D. (2015). Consumer behavior toward counterfeit sporting goods. *Social Behavior and Personality*, *42*(May), 615–624. Advance online publication. doi:10.2224bp.2014.42.4.615

Chiu, W., & Leng, H. (2016). Consumers' Intention to Purchase Counterfeit Sporting Goods in Singapore and Taiwan. *Asia Pacific Journal of Marketing and Logistics*, *28*(1), 23–36. doi:10.1108/APJML-02-2015-0031

Christodoulides, G., Michaelidou, N., & Li, C. H. (2008). Measuring perceived brand luxury: An evaluation of the BLI scale. *Journal of Brand Management*, *16*(5), 395–405.

Cordell, V., Wongtada, N., & Kieschnick, L. Jr. (1996). Counterfeit purchase intentions: Role of lawfulness attitudes and product traits as determinants. *Journal of Business Research*, *35*(1), 41–53. doi:10.1016/0148-2963(95)00009-7

Davidson, A., Vinhal, M., & Michel, N. (2019). Shame on You: When Materialism Leads to Purchase Intentions Toward Counterfeit Products. *Journal of Business Ethics*, *155*(2), 479–494. doi:10.100710551-017-3479-5

De Matos, C. A., Alberto, C., & Rossi, V. (2007). Consumer attitudes toward counterfeits: A review and extension. *Journal of Consumer Marketing*, *24*(1), 1, 36–47. doi:10.1108/07363760710720975

Dowling, G. R., & Staelin, R. (1994). A model of perceived risk and intended riskhandling activity. *The Journal of Consumer Research*, *21*(1), 119–134. doi:10.1086/209386

Eisend, M., Hartmann, P., & Apaolaza, V. (2017). Who Buys Counterfeit Luxury Brands? *Journal of International Marketing*, *25*(4), 89–111. doi:10.1509/jim.16.0133

Eisend, M., & Schuchert-Güler, P. (2006). Explaining Counterfeit Purchases: A Review and Preview Explaining Counterfeit Purchases: A Review and Preview. *Academy of Marketing Science*, *12*, 1–25.

Engizek, N., & Sekerkaya, A. (2015). Is the price only motivation source to purchase counterfeit luxury products? *Journal of Academic Research in Economics*, *7*(1), 89–119.

Featherman, M. S., & Pavlou, P. A. (2003). Predicting e-services adoption: A perceived risk facets perspective. *International Journal of Human-Computer Studies*, *59*(4), 451–474. doi:10.1016/S1071-5819(03)00111-3

Fornell, C., & Larcker, D. (1981). Evaluating structural equation models with unobservable variables and measurement error. *JMR, Journal of Marketing Research*, *18*(1), 39–50. doi:10.1177/002224378101800104

Forsythe, S., & Shi, B. (2003). Consumer patronage and risk perceptions in Internet shopping. *Journal of Business Research*, *56*(11), 867–875. doi:10.1016/S0148-2963(01)00273-9

Fraedrich, J. P., & Ferrell, O. C. (1992). The impact of perceived risk and moral philosophy type on ethical decision making in business organizations. *Journal of Business Research*, *24*(4), 283–295. doi:10.1016/0148-2963(92)90035-A

Geiger-Oneto, S., Gelb, B. D., Walker, D., & Hess, J. D. (2013). Buying status" by choosing or rejecting luxury brands and their counterfeits. *Journal of the Academy of Marketing Science*, *41*(3), 357–372. doi:10.100711747-012-0314-5

Godey, B., Pederzoli, D., Aziendali, S., Wiedmann, K., & Hennigs, N. (2013). A cross-cultural exploratory content analysis of the perception of luxury from six countries. *Journal of Product and Brand Management*, *3*(3), 229–237. doi:10.1108/JPBM-02-2013-0254

Grossman, G. M., & Shapiro, C. (1988). Foreign counterfeiting of status goods. *The Quarterly Journal of Economics*, *103*(1), 79–100. doi:10.2307/1882643

Hair, J. F., Black, W. C., Babin, B. J., & Anderson, R. E. (2010). *Multivariate data analysis: A global perspective* (7th ed.). Prentice-Hall.

Hair, J. F., Hult, G. T. M., Ringle, C. M., & Sarstedt, M. (2014). *A Primer on Partial Least Squares Structural Equation Modeling (PLS-SEM)*. Sage.

Haman, M. (2010). Africa rising to the anti-counterfeit challenge. *Journal of Intellectual Property Law & Practice*, *5*(5), 344–349.

Hanzaee, K. H., & Taghipourian, M. J. (2012). Attitudes toward counterfeit products and generation differentia. *Research Journal of Applied Sciences, Engineering and Technology*, *4*(9), 1147–1154.

Heike, S. (2010). Effects of counterfeits on the image of luxury brands: An empirical study from the consumer perspective. *Journal of Brand Management*, *18*(2), 159–173. doi:10.1057/bm.2010.28

Herstein, R., Drori, N., Berger, R., & Barnes, B. R. (2015). Anticounterfeiting strategies and their influence on attitudes of different counterfeit consumer types. *Psychology and Marketing*, *32*(8), 842–859. doi:10.1002/mar.20822

Horton, R. L. (1976). The structure of perceived risk: Some further progress. *Journal of the Academy of Marketing Science*, *4*(4), 694–706. doi:10.1007/BF02729830

Hox, J. J., & Bechger, T. M. (1998). An introduction to structural equation modeling. *Family Science Review*, *11*, 354–373.

Hu, L.-T., & Bentler, P. M. (1999). Cutoff criteria for fit indexes in covariance structure analysis: Conventional criteria versus new alternatives. *Structural Equation Modeling*, *6*(1), 1–55. doi:10.1080/10705519909540118

Huyen, T., Pham, M., & Nasir, M. A. (2016). Conspicuous consumption, luxury products and counterfeit market in the UK. *The European Journal of Applied Economics*, *13*(1), 72–83. doi:10.5937/ejae13-10012

Jain, S., Khan, M. N., & Mishra, S. (2017). Understanding consumer behavior regarding luxury fashion goods in India based on the theory of planned behavior. *Journal of Asia Business Studies*, *11*(1), 4–21. doi:10.1108/JABS-08-2015-0118

Kassim, N. M. (2017). What leads Saudi Arabian consumers to purchase counterfeit luxury products. *Journal for Global Business Advancement*, *10*(2), 125–139. doi:10.1504/JGBA.2017.083411

Kassim, N. M., Zain, M., Bogari, N., & Khurram, S. (2021). Why do consumers buy counterfeit luxury products? A tale of two major cities in two different countries. *Asia Pacific Journal of Marketing and Logistics*, *33*(2), 418–448. doi:10.1108/APJML-06-2019-0361

Kline, R. B. (2016). Principles and practices of structural equation modelling (4th ed.). In Methodology in the Social Sciences.

Koay, K. Y. (2018). Understanding consumers' purchase intention towards counterfeit luxury goods An integrated model of neutralisation techniques and perceived risk theory. *Asia Pacific Journal of Marketing and Logistics*, *30*(2), 495–516. doi:10.1108/APJML-05-2017-0100

Kutu, K. (2015). Luxury Fashion Brands: An observation into Johannesburg consumers preferred counterfeit branded products. Vega School of Brand Leadership.

Li, E. P. H., Lam, M., & Liu, W. S. (2018). Consuming counterfeit: A study of consumer moralism in China. *International Journal of Consumer Studies*, *42*(3), 367–377. doi:10.1111/ijcs.12428

Liao, C., Lin, H., & Liu, Y. (2010). *Predicting the Use of Pirated Software: A Contingency Model Integrating Perceived Risk with the Theory of Planned Behavior Chechen Liao*. doi:10.1007/s10551-009-0081-5

Lim, N. (2003). Consumers' perceived risk: Sources versus consequences. *Electronic Commerce Research and Applications*, *2*(3), 216–228. doi:10.1016/S1567-4223(03)00025-5

Manchiraju, S., & Sadachar, A. (2014). Personal values and ethical fashion consumption. *Journal of Fashion Marketing and Management*, *18*(3), 357–374. doi:10.1108/JFMM-02-2013-0013

Martin, J., Mortimer, G., & Andrews, L. (2015). Re-examining online customer experience to include purchase frequency and perceived risk. *Journal of Retailing and Consumer Services*, *25*, 81–95. doi:10.1016/j.jretconser.2015.03.008

Meissner, R. (2010). *The trade in counterfeit goods: What is it, why is it a problem and what is its impact on Africa?* https://www.polity.org.za/article/the-trade-in-counterfeit-goods-what-is-it-why-is-it-a-problem-and-what-is-its-impact-on-africa-2010-08-04

Mitchell, V. (1999). Consumer perceived risk: Conceptualisations and models. *European Journal of Marketing*, *33*(1), 163–195. doi:10.1108/03090569910249229

Miyazaki, A., Rodriguez, A. A., & Langenderfer, J. (2009). Price, scarcity, and consumer willingness to purchase pirated media products. *Journal of Public Policy & Marketing*, *28*(1), 71–84. doi:10.1509/jppm.28.1.71

Mortimer, G., Fazal-e-hasan, S. M., Grimmer, M., & Grimmer, L. (2020). Explaining the impact of consumer religiosity, perceived risk and moral potency on purchase intentions. *Journal of Retailing and Consumer Services*, *55*(November), 102115. doi:10.1016/j.jretconser.2020.102115

Norashikin, N. (2009). *A study on consumers' attitude towards counterfeit products in Malaysia* (Unpublished master's thesis). Graduate School of Business Faculty of Business and Accountancy University of Malaya.

Peng, N. (2020). Luxury restaurants' risks when implementing new environmentally friendly programs – evidence from luxury restaurants in Taiwan. *International Journal of Contemporary Hospitality Management, 32*(7), 2409–2427. doi:10.1108/IJCHM-11-2019-0933

Perez, E., Castan, R., & Quintanilla, C. (2010). Constructing identity through the consumption of counterfeit luxury goods. *Qualitative Market Research: AnInternational Journal, 13*(3), 219–235. doi:10.1108/13522751011053608

Phau, I., & Teah, M. (2009). Devil wears (counterfeit) Prada: A study of antecedents and outcomes of attitudes towards counterfeits of luxury brands. *Journal of Consumer Marketing, 26*(1), 15–27. doi:10.1108/07363760910927019

Phau, I., Teah, M., & Lee, A. (2009). Targeting buyers of counterfeits of luxury brands: A study on attitudes of Singaporean consumers. *Journal of Targeting, Measurement and Analysis for Marketing, 17*(1), 3-15.

Phau, J., & Teah, M. (2009). Devil wears (counterfeit) Prada: A study of antecedents and outcomes of attitudes towards counterfeits of luxury brands. *Journal of Consumer Marketing, 26*(1), 15–27. doi:10.1108/07363760910927019

Pueschel, J., Chamaret, C., & Parguel, B. (2017). *Coping with copies: The influence of risk perceptions in luxury counterfeit consumption in GCC countries.* doi:10.1016/j.jbusres.2016.11.008

Qin, Y., Hui Shi, L., Song, L., Stöttinger, B., & Tan, K. (2018). Integrating consumers' motives with suppliers' solutions to combat Shanzhai: A phenomenon beyond counterfeit. *Business Horizons, 61*(2), 229–237. doi:10.1016/j.bushor.2017.11.009

Quintal, V., Phau, I., Sims, D., & Cheah, I. (2016). Factors in fl uencing generation Y's purchase intentions of prototypical versus me-too brands. *Journal of Retailing and Consumer Services, 30*, 175–183. doi:10.1016/j.jretconser.2016.01.019

Riquelme, H. E., Mahdi, E., Abbas, S., & Rios, R. E. (2008). Intention to purchase fake products in an Islamic country. *Education, Business and Society, 5*(1), 6–22. doi:10.1108/17537981211225835

Shukla, P. (2010). Status consumption in cross-national context: Socio-psychological, brand and situational antecedents. *International Marketing Review, 27*(1), 108–129. doi:10.1108/02651331011020429

Souiden, N., Ladhari, R., & Amri, A. Z. (2018). Is buying counterfeit sinful? Investigation of consumers' attitudes and purchase intentions of counterfeit products in a Muslim country. *International Journal of Consumer Studies, 42*(November), 687–703. doi:10.1111/ijcs.12466

Staake, T., Thiesse, F., & Fleisch, E. (2009). The emergence of counterfeit trade: A literature review. *European Journal of Marketing, 43*(3/4), 320–349. doi:10.1108/03090560910935451

Tang, F., Tian, V.-I., & Zaichkowsky, J. (2019). Understanding Motivations to Purchase Counterfeit Items in China Understanding counterfeit consumption. *Asia Pacific Journal of Marketing and Logistics*, (March). Advance online publication. doi:10.1007/978-3-319-10963-3

Thi, N., Mai, T., & Linh, N. H. (2017). Antecedents of the intention and behavior toward purchase of counterfeit luxury goods in an emerging economy: A study of young vietnamese consumers. *Organizations and Markets in Emerging Economies*, 8(2), 207–225. doi:10.15388/omee.2017.8.2.14189

Ting, M., Goh, Y., & Mohd, S. (2016). Determining consumer purchase intentions toward counterfeit luxury goods in Malaysia. *Asia Pacific Management Review*, 21(4), 219–230. doi:10.1016/j.apmrv.2016.07.003

Wang, F., Zhang, H., Zang, H., & Ouyang, M. (2005). Purchasing pirated software: An initial examination of Chinese consumers. *Journal of Consumer Marketing*, 22(6), 340–351. doi:10.1108/07363760510623939

Wang, Y., Stoner, J. L., & John, D. R. (2019). Counterfeit luxury consumption in a social context: The effects on females' moral disengagement and behaviour. *Journal of Consumer Psychology*, 29(2), 207–225. doi:10.1002/jcpy.1071

Wilcox, K., Kim, H. M., & Sen, S. (2009). Why do consumers buy counterfeit luxury, brands? *Journal of Marketing Research*, 46(2), 247-259.

Wu, Q., & Zhao, S. (2021). Determinants of Consumers' Willingness to Buy Counterfeit Luxury Products: An Empirical Test of Linear and Inverted U-Shaped Relationship. *Sustainability*, 13(3), 1194. doi:10.3390u13031194

Yeap, A. L., & Ramayah, T. (2006). Unraveling perceptions on counterfeit goods: Insights from the Malaysian mindset. *Delhi Business Review*, 7(1), 47-58.

Zampetakis, L. A. (2014). The emotional dimension of the consumption of luxury counterfeit goods: An empirical taxonomy. *Marketing Intelligence & Planning*, 32(1), 21–40. doi:10.1108/MIP-10-2012-0102

Chapter 16
Insider Transactions and Performance:
The Portuguese Case

Maria Elisabete Neves
https://orcid.org/0000-0002-6250-1113
Coimbra Business School Research Centre, ISCAC, Polytechnic of Coimbra, Coimbra, Portugal & CETRAD, University of Trás-os-Montes and Alto Douro, Portugal

Germano Maurício
Coimbra Business School, ISCAC, Instituto Politécnico de Coimbra, Portugal

Lucas Rodrigues
Coimbra Business School, ISCAC, Instituto Politécnico de Coimbra, Portugal

ABSTRACT

This study investigates the relevance of stock buy/sell transactions by insiders in Portuguese companies' performance. To achieve this aim, the sample covers the period from 2013 to 2017. The data from buy/sell transactions by insiders were collected in the internal transaction reports delivered by the companies to the Portuguese Securities Market Commission for the same time interval. The results, using panel data methodology, suggest a negative relationship between the long/short positions and the companies' performance, although the volume traded is not significant. Therefore, the increased control of Portuguese companies by their managers signals the existence of conflicts of interest of the managers, whether due to financial reasons or to strengthen their continuity in the position. As far as the authors are aware, this is the first time that a study has been carried out using insider transactions for Portuguese companies and their influence on corporate performance.

DOI: 10.4018/978-1-7998-8609-9.ch016

INTRODUCTION

The abuse of privileged information is an almost unexplored topic in Portugal and this was the main motivation for carrying out this work. Portuguese law prohibits the improper transmission and use of this information to improve investor confidence in the functioning of the market. However, these situations still prevail, and we feel an increased motivation to work on this topic in a country where the market benchmark consists of only 18 companies, with very little liquidity and little international recognition.

We all know the power of information in terms of its influence on the economic performance of companies. Fama (1970) suggests that the efficient market theory is closely related to information and the market price, and it proposes that the market as a whole is efficient concerning information, that is, the prices of assets reflect the information available.

Thus, investors who are theoretically rational and have access to all existing information, will not be able to obtain abnormal returns above the market average. For example, Clarke, Dunbar & Kahle (2001) argue that insiders exploit windows of opportunity by attempting to issue overvalued equity and by canceling the issue when the market reaction to the announcement eliminates the overvaluation. In another point of view Collin-Dufresne and Fos (2015) also studied the problem of insider trading and concluded that when informed traders can select when and how to trade, standard adverse selection measures may fail to capture the presence of informed trading and consequently change prices and performance.

However, there is no consensus in the literature among the authors regarding the impact of the use of information, as well as insider information, on corporate performance.

This article tends to contribute to recent studies in the literature, which seek to define factors that may be significant in the performance of companies, among them, the use of privileged information for stock purchase/sale operations, insider trading, by their managers. Such performance was evaluated based on the accounting indicator Return On Assets, ROA, given some financial indicators, such as liquidity, level of financial leverage, operating expenses, and company size. For example, exploring the fact that insiders trade for a variety of reasons, Cohen, Malloy, & Pomorski (2012) show that routine trading is predictable and identifiable, with inside information but that may not be informative about the future of companies. This may imply that the effects are current and that our measure of performance may be adequate.

Portugal is an embryonic market, not very liquid, where the benchmark consists of only 18 companies. This is an underexplored market, namely in these issues of risk and performance inherent to the misuse of private information.

Given this scenario, in addition to investigating the effect of corporate performance metrics, this work also aims to research the impact of transactions carried out by insiders and their respective volumes on the performance of non-financial companies listed on the PSI-20 index during the years of 2013 to 2017. The results obtained after estimating the model with panel data show that insiders can have a negative impact on corporate performance, through their share purchase/sale transactions, however, the volume of shares traded was not shown significant.

This study is organized as follows: Section 2 presents the literature review, with some of the indicators that are most used to determine the companies performance. In addition to formulating the hypotheses, this section also presents other variables, since we believe that these variables complement our investigation. Section 3 presents the research design, database, and sample construction, as well as the estimation method used. Section 4 sets out the results and respective analyzes, finally, the conclusions of the authors, limitations of the study, and points for future studies are covered in section 5.

BACKGROUND

The present study can be divided into two main matrices to determine whether insider transactions are relevant in the performance of PSI companies - 20. On the one hand, Insider Information (Pettit & Venkatesh, 1995; Claessens, Djankov, Fan, & Lang 2002 Kamardin, 2014 or Ahern, 2017) and on the other hand Corporate Performance (Modigliani and Miller 1958; Deloof, 2001; Aktan, Turen, Tvaronavičienė, Celik, & Alsadeh 2018; Ibhagui, & Olokoyo, 2018).

Some articles, use market variables, namely stock returns to measure performance. However, we think that the introduction of an internal variable to management could reveal the direct "manipulation" of the insider's actions in the organization. There are even authors who empirically show that sales increase before the issue of bonds due to the manager's private information (eg, Kahle, 2000).

Prior research provides evidence that insiders time their trades strategically around voluntary disclosures of information to maximize their wealth (Noe, 1999 or Cheng & Lo, 2006). Therefore, in our opinion, since ROA is a management variable and recognition of the manager (Vieira et al), it can be understood as a way that the manager finds to prove his value to the general public.

Cheung, & Wei, (2006) also measured the asset's pricing power, when the insider has private information, through three variables, including two for management and one for the market, with ROA being one of those used. The authors found that insider ownership is significantly positively associated with corporate performance.

In addition, earnings volatility can also be a consequence of insider trading, and this volatility is calculated based on the ROA (Kusnadi, 2015).

In fact, several variables can be used for the construction of the model, but there is no consensus in the scientific world to determine which is the best; Vieira, Neves, and Dias (2019) or Cancela, Neves, Rodrigues, and Dias, 2020). If, on the one hand, accounting measures are subject to manipulation and may underestimate the values of assets (Rhoades, Rechner, & Sundaramurthy 2001), on the other, market measures reflect risk-adjusted performance, but are often subject to influences beyond the control of managers, Zahra and Pearce (1989). Thus, although these authors disagree with the use of accounting measures such as ROA, several other studies use the indicator as a metric to evaluate performance, such as Finkelstein and Boyd (1998); or recently Vieira et al, (2019), Cancela et al., (2020); Neves and Branco (2020), or Neves, Henriques, and Vilas (2019).

Given the above arguments, we are aware that we may suffer criticism because of the measure chosen, however, it is important to note that it is widely used in the scientific community.

Corporate Performance Factors

Size

The influence of a company's size on its performance has been the subject of several studies in the literature and is considered one of the fundamental metrics in the estimation of organizational performance. Some authors point out, a positive relationship based on the concept that large companies have accessibility to diversify their portfolio and investment opportunities in larger-scale businesses. Large firms can generate asset gains and borrow debts at more favorable rates than small firms (Ibhagui, & Olokoyo 2018). Also, for Yang and Chen (2009); Pantea, Gligor, and Anis (2014), or Neves, Serrasqueiro, and

Hermano (2020); the company size positively influences the performance of organizations, using ROA and ROE as measures of performance evaluation.

On the other hand, there are studies, which show a negative relationship between companies companies' size and performance. For example, Drew, Naughton, and Madhu (2007) or Aktan et al (2018) suggest that initial companies have a greater capacity to generate profits than large companies. Also, Vintila and Nenu (2015) show a negative relationship between size and corporate performance, using the stock returns as a measure of performance evaluation.

Hatem (2014) has obtained a positive relationship between the size and performance of Swedish companies and a negative relationship between Swiss and Italian companies, using the accounting metric ROA as a measure of performance.

Regarding the Portuguese market, the previous literature also presents discordant results, Serrasqueiro (2008) found a positive relationship between the size of the company (small and medium) and its performance. However, Vieira, Neves, and Dias (2019) show that the size of the company is not significant in determining corporate performance.

From the non-consensual results present in the literature, we formulate the following hypothesis

H1: The company size has a significant impact on corporate performance.

Leverage

From the model proposed by Modigliani and Miller (1958), who argues that the value of the company is independent of its form of financing, that there are many scientific studies on the influence of the capital structure on business performance. For example, Serrasqueiro (2009), for a sample of Portuguese companies, finds a negative relationship between total debt and performance. The author justifies this result with the argument that companies with a higher level of indebtedness are exposed to periodic charge payments, which make it impossible for funds to be channeled to non-profit projects. Also for the Portuguese market, Vieira, Neves, and Dias (2019) in their study on the determining factors for business performance, obtained a negative relationship with corporate indebtedness using TobinsQ as a measure of performance evaluation.

On the other hand, several studies demonstrate a positive relationship between performance and the company's leverage level, such as the study by Margaritis, and Psillaki (2010) or by Akhtar et al (2012), which states that more financial leverage can translate into greater sustainable growth and to that extent in more performance.

According to the literature, we formulate the following hypothesis.

H2: The company's leverage has a significant impact on corporate performance.

Operating Expenses

A company's operating expenses can affect its performance levels. For example, Doyran (2013) found a significant relationship in increasing the company's profitability by reducing operating expenses, suggesting that a higher level of business efficiency benefits its performance.

So far, the existing literature has gaps concerning the definition of the factors that are decisive in the performance of Portuguese companies, and for this reason, we believe that the analysis of the metric of operational expenses will contribute to the literature and provide more details of the profile of Portuguese companies, even because at a time of great social concerns, the interest in safeguarding a better quality life for employees, will be important.

In fact, some arguments justify the outsourcing of some operational activities exactly to make the management of operational expenses more efficient (Jiang, Frazier & Prater, 2006). At a time when the concern should be social well-being, the appropriate training to think about a sustainable future, are companies and their managers aware that better wages and better social conditions can promote performance? Based on these assumptions, we formulate the following hypothesis:

H3: The company's operating expenses have a significant impact on corporate performance.

Sales Growth

Usually, sales growth is seen as having a positive impact on corporate performance, mainly due to the additional income that the company generates (Lazăr, 2016).

Some authors who demonstrate this positive relationship are, for example, Asimakopoulos, Samitas, and Papadogonas (2009); Nunes, Serrasqueiro, and Sequeira (2009); Yazdanfar (2013); Alarussi and Alhaderi (2018), among others.

Based on this assumption, we put our following hypothesis:

H3: Sales growth has a significant impact on corporate performance.

Liquidity

Liquidity reflects the company's ability and speed to transform its assets into cash. This is an important indicator of business financial balance because it demonstrates the company's ability in the short term to honor its financial commitments as they fall due. In the real world, unforeseen events happen and generate costs that could be avoided if companies had liquid resources (Deloof, 2001). Enqvist, Graham, and Nikkinen (2014) demonstrate that liquidity management in times of crisis positively affects the company's performance.

It is evident that liquidity plays an important role in the company's growth, however, the results regarding the sign of the relationship do not follow only one direction. Deloof (2003) and Palazzo (2012), conclude that there is a positive relationship between reserves and cash return. Safdar et al. (2016) show a positive relationship between liquidity and ROA using companies from the Pakistani sugar industry.

On the other hand, Wang (2002) or Pasiouras, and Kosmidou (2007), find a negative relationship between profitability and liquidity. Also, Veira et al. (2019) demonstrate in their study that liquidity negatively affects the performance of Portuguese non-financial companies in the period from 2010 to 2015, indicating a possible increase in the agency problem between the shareholder and manager, signaled by Fama and Jensen (1983). Observing the arguments presented, we formulate the following hypothesis.

H5: Liquidity has a significant impact on the company's profitability

Insider Trading

Insider trading, despite being a subject of several scientific studies, continues to generate debates regarding its participation in the company's performance. Insider trades convey informational value, which depends on the traits of the insider (e.g., their position within the firm) and firm characteristics. Since information plays a key role in insider trading it is important to study their impact on firms' performance. Pettit and Venkatesh (1995), Kamardin (2014), or Ahern (2017) find a positive relationship between decision making by insiders and the company's performance, observing an alignment of interests between insiders and the shareholders (alignment effect). Akbas et al. (2016) point out that sophisticated institutions perform better when trading stocks of companies with large networks of advisers, and Ahern (2017) finds that investors with access to valuable executive tips through strong social connections obtain abnormal returns. Goergen, Renneboog and Zhao, (2019) found that directors with top chains and top positions in their networks are considered to have more information because their stock purchases generate significantly higher abnormal returns.

Based on previous literature, we formulate the next two hypotheses:

H6: Insiders have a significant impact on the company's profitability.
H7: The volume of transactions carried out by insiders has a significant impact on corporate performance.

Empirical Research

The sample was constructed using 13 non-financial companies listed on Euronext Lisbon and that made up the PSI-20 index for at least three years during the period from 2013 to 2017. Naturally, this small number of companies is related to the fact that this fraudulent behavior is punishable, including imprisonment, provided for in the Portuguese Securities Code, article 378, n° 1 and n°2. In the 2018 annual report of the Securities Market Commission, 63 investors investigated on suspicion of market abuse can be identified, and of these, 6 used improperly inside information, and 7 were even communicated to the public prosecutors.

Financial companies were excluded from the model, because they have certain specifications, and therefore should be studied separately (Cancela, Neves, Rodrigues & Dias, 2020).

To study the hypotheses formulated in the previous section, we used the SABI database to obtain the Corporate Performance variables, and to build the Insiders Information variables we used the reports made available by the companies and delivered to the CMVM.

Estimation Method

To investigate the impact of insider transactions on the company's performance, we used the panel data methodology. This method has a notable characteristic that it can be estimated even in the absence of some observations. Hsiao (2007) also highlights the greater control over endogeneity and collinearity, allowing a greater number of degrees of freedom and greater efficiency in estimating variables. The model also allows the suppression of the heterogeneity that could influence the results (Neves 2018 or Neves, Serrasqueiro, Dias & Hermano). Specifically, the following model is estimated.

$$ROA_{it} = \alpha_0 + \alpha_1 Size_{it} + \alpha_2 Leverage_{it} + \alpha_3 OpExp_{it}$$
$$+ \alpha_4 SGrowth_{it} + \alpha_5 Liq_{it} + \alpha_6 TIns_{it} + \alpha_7 Insider_{it} + \varepsilon_{it} \quad (1)$$

The analysis carried out using panel data is extremely important for the present study, since it allows us to control individual heterogeneity, and this fact is relevant because the dependent variable is driven by human decisions and in certain circumstances can be closely related to the specificity of each company (Vieira, Neves & Dias 2019).

We estimated equation 1 by the ordinary least squares (OLS), random effects (ER), or fixed effects (FE) model. To choose the most appropriate model, the pool or not to pool tests, the Breusch-Pagan test, and the Hausman test were performed, after the completion of all tests, it was concluded that the fixed effects model was the most suitable for analysis.

Variables

Table 1 shows the variables used in the previous model.

Table 1. Variables

Variable	Proxy
ROA	*Dependent Variable*
	EBIT/ Total Assets
	Independent Variables
Size	Total Asset Logarithm
Leverage	Total Liabilities / Total Assets
Operating Expenses	the logarithm of Operating Expenses
Sales Growth	Rate of growth in Sales
Liquidity	Current ratio
TInsider	Insider Transactions / Total Transaction Volume
Insider	Dummy variable that assumes 1 if the insider made a transaction and 0 otherwise

It should be noted that the ROA variable was selected insofar as it is an imminently imminent management variable, it will be more directly related to possible abuses by the manager.

Results

In this section, we will discuss the results according to the literature review and the formulated hypotheses. First, the main descriptive statistics of the variables used in this article are presented.

Table 2. Descriptive statistics

	Mean	Standard Deviation	Minimum	Maximum
ROA	0,05407	0,03635	-0,05273	0,14079
Size	15,33203	1,10430	12,46007	17,60160
SGrowth	0,71982	0,66308	0,03036	2,86268
OpExp	13,79712	2,06445	8,47637	16,68650
TIns	0,01426	0,02312	0,00000	0,10229
Liq	1,36874	1,40928	0,33558	7,64363
Leverage	0,62633	0,23100	0,00590	1,01979

We observe that all variables present a positive mean and the transactions carried out by insiders represent on average about 1.42% of the volume traded, and with maximum participation of 10% traded in a given asset. This fact gives the information that the participation of insiders in the Portuguese stock exchange in most companies is not very marked, although in isolated cases, it may represent a significant portion of the shares traded on the stock exchange, concerning the standard deviation, the variable shows level, that is, the variable has the least dispersion around the average. The correlation index between the variables covered in the study is shown in table 3. It is possible to notice the negative relationship between the company size and ROA, however, this relationship was not significant after estimating the model.

Table 3. Correlation matrix

	ROA	Size	SGrowth	OpExp	TIns	Liq	Leverage	Insider
ROA	1,00000							
Size	-0,10383	1,00000						
SGrowth	0,38408	-0,01016	1,00000					
OpExp	0,47002	0,50755	0,63867	1,00000				
TIns	0,12012	-0,11298	-0,25121	0,00256	1,00000			
Liq	-0,51557	-0,25974	-0,11178	-0,47904	-0,20859	1,00000		
Leverage	0,19925	0,09510	-0,51872	0,01011	0,20678	-0,59134	1,00000	
Insider	-0,18875	0,04935	-0,12111	-0,10101	0,09855	-0,02223	0,31381	1,00000

Table 4 presents the results of the model, where the main objective is to analyze the relevance of insider transactions and their respective volumes in corporate performance.

Table 4. Results of model 1

Variables	ROA-Dependent variable	
	Coefficient	P - Value
Const	1,08094	0,15780
Size	−0,03041	0,54430
SGrowth	0,09499	0,0783 *
OpExp	−0,02478	0,0089 ***
TIns	−0,00753	0,96500
Liq	0,03112	0,01 **
Leverage	−0,37279	0,0027 ***
Insider	−0,04157	0,0802*
R^2	0,89275	-
Test F	8,78617	0.0000

This table presents the results of the variables of the fixed-effects model. All variables are defined in table 1. ***, **, and * indicate the significance of 1%, 5%, and 10%, respectively.

Insiders own firm-specific information and exploit information asymmetries (Ting, 2013).

The results show, unlike most of the literature presented, that insider transactions do not have a positive impact on corporate performance. The existence of transactions by insiders causes a decrease in profitability, suggesting that the signal that the manager wants to send to the market is contrary to the company's valuation. Insiders, possessing superior private information, act as opposites (Piotroski and Roulstone, 2005). As we described, the volume of transactions is not significant in the sample analyzed, suggesting that regardless of the number of transactions, the influence of the insider on corporate performance is always the same, and in this case, negative. No relationship is detected between abnormal returns and volume also in Nanda, and Barai (2021).

Our evidence is consistent with the results of Claessens et al. (2002), or Hachana, and Hajri (2008) who show that insider transactions have the ability to can negatively influence the company's profitability, which is justified due to one of the conflicts arising from the agency's theory, the manager's entrenchment, which validates our hypothesis 6. This effect is negative because insiders tend to make decisions based on personal objectives, neglecting the shareholders' objectives and company value, namely in countries like Portugal, with little liquidity in the market, weak legal protection for investors, and, huge asymmetric information problems.

Regarding the specific characteristics of the company, which the manager dominates, the variables of leverage and operating expenses, present a negative and significant relationship with companies companies' performance. As for Leverage, this result indicates that indebtedness exposes companies to periodic charge payments, which makes it impossible to use more resources for profitable projects. This result is also consistent with the agency theory of Jensen and Meckling (1976), that debt generates conflicts of interest between managers and creditors and which have a negative impact on the company's value. Such results validate our hypothesis 2.

On the negative relationship between operating expenses and the level of performance of the companies, this result points out that poor operational management and inefficiency in the company's core business process results in lower levels of performance, such response is in line with those obtained by Doyran (2013) and allows corroborating hypothesis 3.

Concerning the sales growth, we obtain a positive and significant relationship suggesting that a possible increase in the productivity of the company's operational activity increases the corporate profitability. This result allows us to corroborate our hypotheses hypothesis 4, following for Alarussi and Alhaderi (2018).

Another interesting point is about the current ratio. In fact, the positive relationship of liquidity in the corporate performance stands out, which indicates that managers rely on the efficient management of working capital needs for the company's profitability, which is consistent with the results of Deloof (2001) allowing to corroborate hypothesis 5.

CONCLUSION

In order to show whether insiders can influence the performance of Portuguese companies, this study used a sample of 13 non-financial companies that remained listed on the PSI-20 for at least 3 years between 2013-2017. Using ROA as a performance measure, highly influenced by management decisions, the results show that buy/sell transactions by company managers have the ability to can negatively influence the performance of their respective companies, and regardless of the number of transactions, the influence of the insider on corporate performance is always the same. Thus, the results suggest that the existence of transactions by those who are better informed about the company's position may lead to results contrary to what the other stakeholders want. He can adopt decisions that benefit his own interests, either for his financial return, or to strengthen his perpetuity in corporate control. It should be noted that given the small number of companies in the sample, separating into buying or selling inside transactions would be difficult for the model and eventually lead to inconclusive results. Nanda and Barai (2021) also show that insider trades affect prices and return and that results are identical for both buy and sell transactions.

The existence of financial positions by insiders, regardless of the volume traded, is enough for this to affect business performance. Stakeholders, generally aware of the profitability variable, perceive that the influence of insiders will be in the sense of expropriating some interested parties to the detriment of their acquaintances and friends.

Another important point is the analysis of the role of operating expenses in business performance, with which we can conclude that the level of operational efficiency appears to be vital for the performance of Portuguese companies. Is it at the expense of social responsibility? Or is it management efficiency?

The results obtained also suggest that the performance of companies in the Portuguese market has obedience about the capital structure and financial efficiency, indicating that companies that have a low debt level and with capital invested efficiently in assets with liquidity tend to have more returns.

The results emphasized that in a small country like Portugal, regardless of the volume transacted, it is enough that there are managers who improperly use private information for this to affect the companies' results and the consequent performance.

Our work can be useful to several stakeholders: firstly to regulators, who must continue to seek reinforcement of legislation in order to eliminate the abuse of private information, with recourse to more effective punishments; to the manager himself who understands the scrutiny that the general public can make to his management decisions; to potential investors as they become aware of the existence of this problem and its dimension in the market and finally to civil society, attentive to the capital market, which realizes the existence of these cases of private information and the impact they can have on the results of companies, regardless of the volume of transactions carried out by managers, can insist on greater effective penalties for fraudulent management.

The main limitations of the study are the small number of companies analyzed and the possible transactions carried out by insiders who were not informed at the securities market Commission. For future studies, other market performance metrics can be analyzed, such as Tobin's, the share price, among others. We also believe that characteristics of managers can be considered, such as time in office, holding shares with voting rights and remuneration compensation, in different macroeconomic environments, and with different cultural and institutional aspects. It could also be interesting separating into buying or selling inside transactions.

In addition, with more data, it will be possible to use dynamic measures combined with other research methodologies such as GMM and DEA.

ACKNOWLEDGMENT

This work is supported by national funds, through the FCT – Portuguese Foundation for Science and Technology under the project UIDB/04011/2020.

REFERENCES

Abad, C., Thore, S. A., & Laffarga, J. (2004). Fundamental analysis of stocks by two-stage DEA. *Managerial and Decision Economics*, *25*(5), 231–241. doi:10.1002/mde.1145

Ahern, K. R. (2017). Information networks: Evidence from illegal insider trading tips. *Journal of Financial Economics*, *125*(1), 26–47. doi:10.1016/j.jfineco.2017.03.009

Akbas, F., Meschke, F., & Wintoki, M. B. (2016). Director networks and informed traders. *Journal of Accounting and Economics*, *62*(1), 1–23. doi:10.1016/j.jacceco.2016.03.003

Akhtar, S., Javed, B., Maryam, A., & Sadia, H. (2012). Relationship between financial leverage and financial performance: Evidence from fuel & energy sector of Pakistan. *European Journal of Business and Management*, *4*(11), 7–17.

Aktan, B., Turen, S., Tvaronavičienė, M., Celik, S., & Alsadeh, H. A. (2018). Corporate governance and performance of the financial firms in Bahrain. *Polish Journal of Management Studies*, *17*(1), 39–58. doi:10.17512/pjms.2018.17.1.04

Alarussi, A. S., & Alhaderi, S. M. (2018). Factors affecting profitability in Malaysia. *Journal of Economic Studies (Glasgow, Scotland)*, *45*(3), 442–458. doi:10.1108/JES-05-2017-0124

Asimakopoulos, I., Samitas, A., & Papadogonas, T. (2009). Firm-specific and Economy Wide Determinants of Firm Profitability: Greek Evidence using Panel Data. *Managerial Finance*, *35*(11), 930–939. doi:10.1108/03074350910993818

Aysen Doyran, M. (2013). Net interest margins and firm performance in developing countries. *Management Research Review*, *36*(7), 720–742. doi:10.1108/MRR-05-2012-0100

Cancela, B., Neves, M. E., Rodrigues, L. L., & Dias, A. (2020). The influence of Corporate Governance on Corporate Sustainability: New evidence using panel data in the Iberian macroeconomic environment. *International Journal of Accounting and Information Management*, *28*(4), 785–806. doi:10.1108/IJAIM-05-2020-0068

Cheng, Q., & Lo, K. (2006). Insider trading and voluntary disclosures. *Journal of Accounting Research*, *44*(5), 815–848. doi:10.1111/j.1475-679X.2006.00222.x

Cheung, W. A., & Wei, K. J. (2006). Insider ownership and corporate performance: Evidence from the adjustment cost approach. *Journal of Corporate Finance*, *12*(5), 906–925. doi:10.1016/j.jcorpfin.2006.02.002

Claessens, S., Djankov, S., Fan, J. P., & Lang, L. H. (2002). Disentangling the incentive and entrenchment effects of large shareholdings. *The Journal of Finance*, *57*(6), 2741–2771. doi:10.1111/1540-6261.00511

Clarke, J., Dunbar, C., & Kahle, K. M. (2001). Long-run performance and insider trading in completed and canceled seasoned equity offerings. *Journal of Financial and Quantitative Analysis*, *36*(4), 415–430. doi:10.2307/2676218

Cohen, L., Malloy, C., & Pomorski, L. (2012). Decoding inside information. *The Journal of Finance*, *67*(3), 1009–1043. doi:10.1111/j.1540-6261.2012.01740.x

Collin-Dufresne, P., & Fos, V. (2015). Do prices reveal the presence of informed trading? *The Journal of Finance*, *70*(4), 1555–1582. doi:10.1111/jofi.12260

Deloof, M. (2001). Belgian intragroup relations and the determinants of corporate liquid reserves. *European Financial Management*, *7*(3), 375–392. doi:10.1111/1468-036X.00161

Deloof, M. (2003). Does working capital management affect profitability of Belgian firms? *Journal of Business Finance & Accounting*, *30*(3-4), 573–588. doi:10.1111/1468-5957.00008

Drew, M., Naughton, T., & Madhu, V. (2003). Firm-size, book-to-market equity and security returns: Evidence from the Shanghai stock exchange. *Australian Journal of Management*, *28*(2), 119–140.

Enqvist, J., Graham, M., & Nikkinen, J. (2014). The impact of working capital management on firm profitability in different business cycles: Evidence from Finland. *Research in International Business and Finance*, *32*, 36–49. doi:10.1016/j.ribaf.2014.03.005

Fama, E. F., & Jensen, M. C. (1983). Agency problems and residual claims. *The Journal of Law & Economics*, *26*(2), 327–349. doi:10.1086/467038

Finkelstein, S., & Boyd, B. (1998). How much does the CEO matter? The role of managerial discretion in the setting of CEO compensation. *Academy of Management Journal*, *41*, 179–200.

Goergen, M., Renneboog, L., & Zhao, Y. (2019). Insider trading and networked directors. *Journal of Corporate Finance*, *56*, 152–175. doi:10.1016/j.jcorpfin.2019.02.001

Hachana, R., & Hajri, J.(2008). Management Entrenchment and performance: case of Tunisian firms. *Corporate Ownership & control*, *5*(3), 418-427.

Hatem, B. S. (2014). Determinants of firm performance: A comparison of European countries. *International Journal of Economics and Finance, 6*(10), 243–249. doi:10.5539/ijef.v6n10p243

Hsiao, C. (2007). Panel data analysis—Advantages and challenges. *Test, 16*(1), 1–22. doi:10.100711749-007-0046-x

Ibhagui, O. W., & Olokoyo, F. O. (2018). Leverage and firm performance: New evidence on the role of firm size. *The North American Journal of Economics and Finance, 45*, 57–82. doi:10.1016/j.najef.2018.02.002

Jensen, M. C., & Meckling, W. H. (1976). Theory of the firm: Managerial behavior, agency costs and ownership structure. *Journal of Financial Economics, 3*(4), 305–360. doi:10.1016/0304-405X(76)90026-X

Ji, S., Mauer, D. C., & Zhang, Y. (2019). Managerial entrenchment and capital structure: The effect of diversification. *Journal of Corporate Finance, 65*, 101505. doi:10.1016/j.jcorpfin.2019.101505

Jiang, B., Frazier, G. V., & Prater, E. L. (2006). Outsourcing effects on firms' operational performance: An empirical study. *International Journal of Operations & Production Management, 26*(12), 1280–1300. doi:10.1108/01443570610710551

Kahle, K. M. (2000). Insider trading and the long-run performance of new security issues. *Journal of Corporate Finance, 6*(1), 25–53. doi:10.1016/S0929-1199(99)00015-2

Kamardin, H. (2014). *Managerial ownership and firm performance: the influence of family directors and non-family directors. In Ethics, Governance and Corporate Crime: Challenges and Consequences (Developments in Corporate Governance and Responsibility)* (Vol. 6). Emerald Group Publishing.

Kusnadi, Y. (2015). Insider trading restrictions and corporate risk-taking. *Pacific-Basin Finance Journal, 35*, 125–142. doi:10.1016/j.pacfin.2014.11.004

Malkiel, B. G., & Fama, E. F. (1970). Efficient Capital Markets: A review of theory and empirical work. *The Journal of Finance, 25*(2), 383–417. doi:10.1111/j.1540-6261.1970.tb00518.x

Margaritis, D., & Psillaki, M. (2010). Capital structure, equity ownership and firm performance. *Journal of Banking & Finance, 34*(3), 621–632. doi:10.1016/j.jbankfin.2009.08.023

Modigliani, F., & Miller, M. H. (1958). The cost of capital, corporation finance and the theory of investment. *The American Economic Review, 48*(3), 261–297.

Nanda, S. K., & Barai, P. (2021). Effect of insider trading on stock characteristics. *Asian Journal of Accounting Research, 6*(2), 210-227.

Neves, M., & Branco, J. (2020). Determinants of R&D on European high technology industry: Panel data evidence. *Management Research, 18*(3), 285–305. doi:10.1108/MRJIAM-11-2019-0969

Neves, M. E., Henriques, C., & Vilas, J. (2019). Financial performance assessment of electricity companies: Evidence from Portugal. *Operations Research*, 1–49.

Neves, M. E. D. (2018). Payout and firm's catering. *International Journal of Managerial Finance, 14*(1), 2–22. doi:10.1108/IJMF-03-2017-0055

Noe, C. (1999). Voluntary Disclosures and Insider Transactions. *Journal of Accounting and Economics, 27*(3), 305–326. doi:10.1016/S0165-4101(99)00014-2

Nunes, P. J. M., Serrasqueiro, Z., & Sequeira, T. N. (2009). Profitability in Portuguese Service Industries: A Panel Data Approach. *Service Industries Journal*, *29*(5), 693–707. doi:10.1080/02642060902720188

Palazzo, B. (2012). Cash holdings, risk, and expected returns. *Journal of Financial Economics*, *164*(1), 162-185.

Pantea, M., Gligor, D., & Anis, C. (2014). Economic determinants of Romanian firm's financial performance. *Procedia: Social and Behavioral Sciences*, *124*, 272–281. doi:10.1016/j.sbspro.2014.02.486

Pasiouras, F., & Kosmidou, K. (2007). Factors influencing the profitability of domestic and foreign commercial banks in the European Union. *Research in International Business and Finance*, *21*(2), 222–237. doi:10.1016/j.ribaf.2006.03.007

Pettit, R. R., & Venkatesh, P. C. (1995). Insider trading and long-run return performance. *Financial Management*, *24*(2), 88–103. doi:10.2307/3665537

Rhoades, D.L., Rechner, P.L., & Sundaramurthy, C. (2001). A meta-analysis of board leadership structure and financial performance: are 'two heads better than one'? *Corporate Governance: An International Review*, *9*(4), 311-319.

Safdar, M.Z., Awan, M.Z., Ahmed, Z., Qureshi, M.I., & Hasnain, T. (2016). What does matter? Liquidity or profitability: a case of sugar industry in Pakistan. *International Journal of Economics and Financial Issues*, *6*(2), 144-152.

Serrasqueiro, Z. (2009). Growth and profitability in Portuguese companies: A dynamic panel data approach. *Economic Interferences*, *11*(26), 265–279.

Stulz, R. (1988). Managerial control of voting rights. *Journal of Financial Economics*, *20*, 25–54. doi:10.1016/0304-405X(88)90039-6

Ting, H. I. (2013). The influence of insiders and institutional investors on firm performance. *Review of Pacific Basin Financial Markets and Policies*, *16*(04), 1350027. doi:10.1142/S0219091513500276

Vieira, E. S., Neves, M. E., & Dias, A. G. (2019). Determinants of Portuguese firms' financial performance: Panel data evidence. *International Journal of Productivity and Performance Management*, *68*(7), 1323–1342. doi:10.1108/IJPPM-06-2018-0210

Vintila, G., & Nenu, E. A. (2015). An analysis of determinants of corporate financial performance: Evidence from the Bucharest stock exchange-listed companies. *International Journal of Economics and Financial Issues*, *5*(3), 732–739.

Wang. (2002). Liquidity management, operating performance, and corporate value: evidence from Japan and Taiwan. *Journal of Multinational Financial Management*, *12*, 159–169.

Yang, C. H., & Chen, K. H. (2009). Are Small Firms less Efficient? *Small Business Economics*, *32*(4), 375-395.

Yazdanfar, D. (2013). Profitability determinants among micro-firms: Evidence from Swedish data. *International Journal of Managerial Finance*, *9*(2), 150–160. doi:10.1108/17439131311307565

Zahra, S. A., & Pearce, J. A. II. (1989). Boards of directors and corporate financial performance: A review and integrative model. *Journal of Management*, *15*(2), 291–334. doi:10.1177/014920638901500208

Chapter 17
Does Technical Analysis Win?
Evidence From the Period Between Donald Trump's Campaign and the First Date for Brexit

Maria Neves
https://orcid.org/0000-0002-6250-1113
Coimbra Business School Research Centre, ISCAC, Polytechnic of Coimbra, Coimbra, Portugal & CETRAD, University of Trás-os-Montes and Alto Douro, Portugal

Joana Leite
Coimbra Business School Research Centre, ISCAC, Polytechnic of Coimbra, Coimbra, Portugal

Renato Neves
Coimbra Business School Research Centre, ISCAC, Polytechnic of Coimbra, Coimbra, Portugal

ABSTRACT

The main goal of this chapter is to analyze the performance of four investment strategies within a recent period of international political uncertainties. RSI and MACD supported three competing investment strategies, which were compared to the conservative Buy and Hold strategy. Euro Stoxx 50 Index was selected through the Markowitz Theory, and the DAX index was established as a benchmark. The period considered was between the start of Donald Trump's official campaign to the US elections and the first date set for Brexit. Two subsequent additional studies were performed to evaluate their profitability. The entry and exit points were determined by international economic reports. Alternative time lengths for the RSI window were considered. The results suggest that, when the market is bear or undefined, the investor should have a strategy supported on technical analysis and he should consider more than one indicator to increase the information that is taken from the market. The passive Buy and Hold strategy should be considered when the market is considered a bull market.

DOI: 10.4018/978-1-7998-8609-9.ch017

INTRODUCTION

Nowadays, investing in more traditional financial products in Europe such as term deposits, capitalization insurance, retirement savings plans, and savings bonds produce average returns of around 0.005%. A net return below inflation is considered a product with negative profitability. Thus, the search for alternative investments includes the stock market. Within this context, this paper aims to study the Technical Analysis (TA) through Technical Indicators (TI) used by traders to support their decisions, comparing them with the conservative Buy and Hold (B&H) stance.

Investment strategies performance analysis depends on empirical studies, which need to be reviewed, updated, refined, and expanded. The recent wave of global political turmoil has affected the financial markets. Brexit and Donald Trump's victory in the US election are some of the most influential and internationally impacting events in recent memory. In both cases, the political analysis, polls, and international markets' expectations were contradicted by the popular vote (BBC, 2016). Therefore, it is relevant to analyze if and how an investor can make a profit in this context, as these episodes will continue to affect the financial markets.

Numerous studies are examining the profitability of various TI, including the Relative Strength Index (RSI) and the Moving Average Convergence Divergence (MACD). However, there is a lack of research when it comes to assessing the effectiveness of these two indicators together as a tool of TA.

The main goal of this paper is to contribute to the practitioner and academic literature, regarding the use of TI to provide practical intuition for trading individual stocks within a period of international political uncertainties. It is an amazing yet repeatable period, so this work can be interesting not only for fund managers and potential investors but also for the general public.

Our examination provides traders with a more practical trading exercise, based on some trading rules, which help traders in making investment decisions and showing the importance of creating a diversified portfolio. It also extends the literature dealing with the predictability of the market.

To achieve this aim, Section 2 will focus on reviewing the literature, framing the definitions of TA – including TI and B&H – followed by a review of strategies. This also includes a brief explanation of bull and bear markets. Section 3 presents the methods used, samples, and periods. Section 4 materializes the results obtained with each strategy, produced using Python. Section 5 features conclusions, limitations, and future lines of research.

BACKGROUND

Trading Strategies

Many people believe that investing in the stock market is a matter of luck, giving it a casino-like appeal. As attractive as an asset may seem, the decision should never be made without having a good knowledge of where to invest. Although it is impossible to predict the market, an investor can use important mechanisms to aid in their decision-making. Some of them use TA, and others use the more traditional Fundamental Analysis (FA). Some buy financial assets and let them value over time (i.e., use the B&H strategy). The first step is to understand how these strategies work.

Technical Analysis (TA)

The origin of TA is the editorials of Henry Charles Dow in the Wall Street Journal, which later formed Dow Theory established on its the well-known six principles (Murphy, 1999).

According to several authors such as Murphy (1999) and Lohpetch e Corne (2010), TA is the study of market movements, using graphs to predict future trends. According to Brock, Lakonishok, and LeBaron (1992), TA is the general term for the abundance of existing trading techniques. Technical analysts attempt to forecast prices by studying past trends and other securities-related statistics, believing that changes in supply and demand can be determined by a market's asset chart. According to technical analyst Pring (2002), the approach to investing is essentially a reflection of the idea that prices move in trends determined by investors' ever-changing attitudes toward a variety of economic, monetary, political, and psychological forces. The "art" of TA is to identify a trend reversal at a relatively early stage and follow it until the evidence shows or proves that the trend has reversed. For investors, Park and Irwin (2007) and Chong and Ng (2008), TA is a forecasting method that studies historical price patterns or trends or any indicative signs of future movements. Lohpetch and Corne (2010) and Bodas Sagi, Soltero, Hidalgo, Fernandez and Fernandez (2012) consider that, for AT to be successful, the investor must use TI such as RSI, moving averages, MACD, among others. These TI are configured according to a set of parameters that work in a series of discrete-time frames. There is a wide range of TI – some simple, others more mathematically complex. These analysis tools are used to obtain relevant information to help investors make decisions during market uncertainty. Chong, Ng, and Liew (2014) claim technical analysts believe that historical market performance is an indication of future trends, and an analyst can develop profitable trading rules using historical prices, as well as charts and related statistics. According to Murphy (1999) of the six principles presented by Dow, three play a key role in TA. The first, "Market Action Discounts Everything", means that all factors affecting price, such as fundamental, political, psychological, are already immediately discounted by the market and reflected in the current price of the asset. The second, "Prices Move in Trends", means that once a trend has been established the future price movement is more likely to head in the direction of the trend, rather than in the opposite direction. The third, "History Repeats Itself", means that past events tend to reoccur. For Murphy (1999) the belief that history repeats itself is the pillar of TA.

Fundamental Analysis (FA)

FA studies the entire economy of a country taking into account market indicators and real company data. Also, instead of its financial reports, it tries to ascertain the real value of the company, i.e. the fair price of a stock.

Murphy (1999) states that while TA focuses on studying market behavior, FA focuses on the economic forces of supply and demand that cause prices to fluctuate. FA examines all relevant factors affecting market price to determine the intrinsic value of the asset. Abad, Thore, and Laffarga (2004) confirmed that FA determines the "fundamental" value of an action by analyzing available information, emphasizing accounting, and price information. FA is predictive, examining financial reports that generate a market value forecast. According to Bartram and Grinblatt (2018), FA is based on the notion that stocks have an intrinsic fair value and investors can derive abnormal profits from stock-specific signals indicating fair value deviations. Abnormal profits arise from convergence to fair value.

Buy and Hold (B&H)

One of the most common investment strategies for trading is called B&H. This consists of buying stocks and holding them for a certain period, as long-term financial markets tend to have a good rate of return – even considering the volatility characteristics of short-term periods. Investors holding long-term stakes are less involved in trading, so transaction costs are kept to a minimum. This in turn increases the overall net return on the portfolio. According to Lohpetch and Corne (2010) and Cohen and Cabiri (2015), the B&H strategy is to buy shares at the beginning of a trading period and sell at the end; therefore, it is considered a good strategy in growing markets.

Technical Indicators (TI)

TI is one of the main tools used for TA. They help identify trends and prevailing sentiments and are also used to determine turning points, entry points, and exit points for the current portfolio. There is a variety of TI for the analysis and interpretation of market graphs such as MACD, RSI, and the Larry Williams rule (Ni & Yin, 2009). Although some indicators can be more complex than others, there is no degree of efficiency. These indicators are classified into trend, strength, cyclical, and momentum indicators. Trend indicators are depicted as continuous lines on a stock chart. They are often used in pairs of two or more indicators with distinct periods (Lento, Gradojevic, & Wright, 2007). Strength indicators showcase strength by comparing the upward or downward movements of successive closing prices. To measure market strength, these indicators are mainly based on an existing volume (Macedo, Godinho, & Alves, 2017). Cyclical indicators describe price fluctuations to determine active cycles and when they occur (Colby, 2002). Momentum indicators determine the vitality of a trend over time. Momentum identifies the strength or speed of price changes (Lento, 2007).

RSI Indicator

The Relative Strength Index (RSI)[1] describes the speed at which the asset price varies over time. It was developed by Wilder (1978) to measure the strength of an asset concerning itself. The indicator aims to compare the magnitude of recent gains or losses on a scale of 0 to 100, determining overbought or oversold situations. When the indicator is above 70 points, it signals the asset is overvalued, i.e. the market value is higher than its core value. This shows that from that moment there may be a decrease in the asset's price (the asset is considered overbought). At such times there is an opportunity to sell. On the other hand, when the indicator is below 30 points, it means the asset is cheap, which could lead buyers to acquire the asset at that time (the asset is considered oversold). The default time interval for RSI calculation is 14 days according to its author. This means the indicator will return 14 time periods based on the graph in use. The RSI formula is as follows:

$$RSI = 100 - 100 / (1 + RS) \qquad (1)$$

where,

$$RS = (Average\ Gain) / (Average\ Loss) \qquad (2)$$

$$\text{Average Gain}_{(t)} = [\text{Average Gain}_{(t-1)} \times 13 + \text{Current Gain}_{(t)}]/14 \qquad (3)$$

$$\text{Average Loss}_{(t)} = [\text{Average Loss}_{(t-1)} \times 13 + \text{Current Loss}_{(t)}]/14 \qquad (4)$$

Using Wilder's formula (1978) for calculating average gain and loss, positive or negative changes in asset prices are used, respectively. That is, to calculate the average gain on the first day, add the positive changes in the first 14 days and divide by 14. The average loss on the first day is calculated the same way, but by using the negative price changes. The calculations for the second and subsequent days are based on data from the previous day and the variation of the day itself as described in the previous equations. This procedure serves as a smoothing factor in RSI calculation, which becomes more accurate as further calculations are made.

Graphically, the RSI indicator has the following configuration, as shown in Figure 1[2].

Figure 1. RSI indicator
Source: Adapted from Investing.com

MACD Indicator

The Moving Average Convergence/Divergence indicator (MACD) was created by Gerald Appel in the late 1970s and is one of the most used TA indicators. According to Cohen and Cabiri (2015), its goal is to identify developing trends – convergence and divergence of moving averages – representing the difference between long- and short-term exponential moving averages (EMAs). The result is a line that fluctuates above or below zero without any upper or lower limit. The asset is deemed expensive compared to its recent or overbought developments when the MACD and signal lines are far above zero. Otherwise, the asset is considered undervalued or oversold. Long- and short-term EMAs have default values of 26 and 12 days, respectively (Murphy, 1999). The indicator consists of two lines: the MACD line, which represents the difference between the two EMAs mentioned above, and the signal line. The latter is an exponential moving average – usually nine days – on the MACD line. Using visuals, the MACD and signal lines are graphically illustrated with one line each. Given their fluctuating nature, the values obtained by the two lines are displayed around their center axis – also called zero lines. The MACD is also made up of a histogram developed by Thomas Aspray (Ozturk, Toroslu, & Fidan, 2016) which measures the difference between MACD and signal.

The MACD formula is as follows:

$$MACD_{(t)} = EMA[12]_{(t)} - EMA[26]_{(t)} \tag{5}$$

where,

$$EMA[N]_{(t)} = CA_{(t)} \times k + EMA_{(t-1)} \times (1 - k) \tag{6}$$

$$Sign[9]_{(t)} = MACD_{(t)} \times k + EMA_{(t-1)} \times (1 - k) \tag{7}$$

$$k = 2 / (1 + n) \tag{8}$$

The first EMA value is an average of n days, where n is the number of days, and CA is the asset's value on day t.

The MACD indicator is displayed in Figure 2[3].

Figure 2. MACD indicator
Source: Adapted from Investing.com

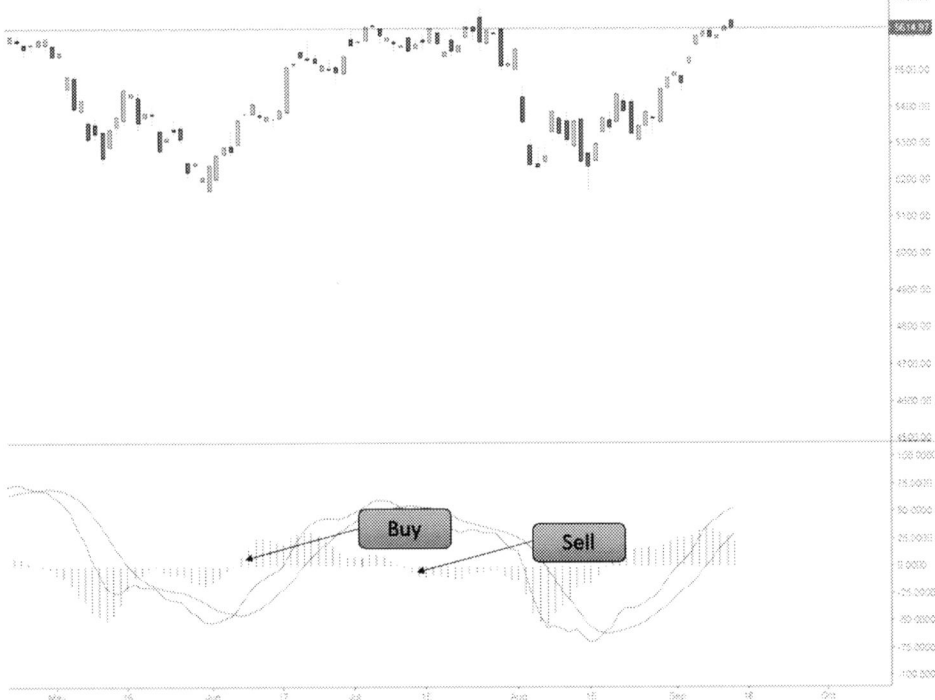

Empirical Research

TA and FA Studies

In addressing the financial market, there are two methods to consider: TA and FA. Both have the same underlying basis: markets do not instantly reflect all information and it is thus possible to buy or sell assets that will increase or decrease in price.

As previously mentioned, the TA follows price fluctuations and uses this knowledge to predict future prices. FA, on the other hand, looks at the economic factors of an asset. These two can be used individually or together, although there is some contention between their supporters. Several studies contributed to this debate, such as Allen and Taylor (1990), De Long, Shleifer, Summers, and Waldmann, (1990), Lui and Mole (1998), Oberlechner (2001), Bettman, Sault and Schultz (2009).

From many traders' experience, Schwager (1984) has empirically shown that FA does not work and concludes that the data used is incorrect or incomplete. According to Fama (1995), FA is valuable only when analysts have new information that has not been fully considered in price formation or have new insights into the effects of generally available information that is not implicit in current prices. In case the analyst has no better insights or new information, he should opt for some random selection procedure rather than FA. Similarly, Menkhoff (2010) concluded that TA should be used to detriment of FA. For Edwards, Magee, and Bassetti (2018), FA's main problem is that its indicators are taken from the market itself. This creates a causality between external events and market movements.

On the other hand, Nazário, Silva, Sobreiro, and Kimura (2017) and Neves and Costa (2017) state that FA should support TA. These mixed investor strategies lead to better portfolio performance. Eiamkanitchat, Moontuy, and Ramingwong (2017) sought to investigate TA and FA as two complementary tools. The goal was to create a system that could indicate a set of 5,000 investors whether they should buy or sell their shares within two months. Using the Thai stock exchange, those with the highest profits in ten years were selected. By applying these fundamental criteria, it was possible to form a basis of analysis composed of 300 companies. TI, EMA, MACD, RSI and SO (Stochastic Oscillator) were used in all cases. The results show that the application of this mixed system gave investors an average profit of 19.05%, exceeding the average return of the Thai market by 12.31%. Thus, the importance of FA cannot be ignored.

TA and B&H Studies

Since the work of Fama e Blume (1966), several researchers have focused on TA at the time of investing, studying whether it provides significant financial signals and can outperform the B&H strategy. Authors such as Brock, Lakonishok and LeBaron (1992), Bessembinder and Chan (1995), Mills (1997), Kwon and Kish (2002), Hsu and Kuan (2005), Jothimani, Shankar and Yadav (2015), Metghalchi, Chen and Hayes (2015), made it famous by proving that TA produces higher returns than B&H. On the other hand, people such as Hudson, Dempsey, and Keasey (1996), Chong, Ng, and Liew (2014), proved that TA is not superior to B&H or when considering transaction costs.

To analyze profitability evidence based on TA, Park and Irwin (2007) categorize studies into two groups: early (1960-1987) and modern (1988-2004). The results of early studies led to the conclusion that returns on the stock market using TI are very limited, while currency and futures market studies provide considerable profits. Modern studies improve limitations and increase the number of trading systems under scrutiny. The results of modern studies led to the conclusion that technical trading rules yielded economic profits in the US stock market only until the late 1980s.

Lukac, Brorsen, and Irwin (1988) analyzed twelve TI futures between 1978 to 1984. The results show that of the twelve indicators, seven produced significant returns greater than zero. However, considering transaction costs and comparing them with the B&H strategy, the number decreased to four. In the UK market, Dryden (1970) noted that even after costs, trading rules outperform the B&H strategy. Gunasekarage and Power (2001) analyzed TI performance using four emerging South Asian markets from January 1990 to March 2000 and concluded that stock returns in those markets were predictable. These findings indicated that TI generated higher returns than the B&H strategy in three of the four markets. Jasic and Wood (2004) analyzed the daily returns of the US, Germany, Japan, and UK stock indexes between 1965 and 1999 and concluded that applying a simple trading strategy yielded higher profits than the B&H strategy, assuming transaction costs of 0.5%. Fifield, Power, and Donald Sinclair (2005) analyzed eleven European country stock indices from January 1991 to December 2000. Using TI, the filtering rule, and the oscillator of moving average (OsMA), they concluded that the first indicator generated large profits, outperforming the B&H strategy – even taking transaction costs into account. Meanwhile, OsMA's profitability varies dramatically from market to market. Finally, they claim that European equity markets exhibited very different characteristics, while the emerging markets studied depicted some predictability in their returns. McKenzie (2007) analyzed seventeen emerging markets from 1986 to 2003 against a US benchmark applying some TI and concluded that no rule systematically generated higher returns than the B&H. Metghalchi, Chang, and Marcucci (2008) tested three moving average trading rules in the Swedish stock market between 1986 and 2004. They concluded that, generally, trading rules outperform the B&H strategy, after taking transaction costs and data snooping bias into account.

To assess the performance of TI, RSI, and MACD, Chong, Ng, and Liew (2014) analyzed a day-to-day database created by Milan Comit General, S & P / TSX Composite, DAX, Dow Jones Industrials and Nikkei 225, from January 1976 to December 2002. They concluded that RSI(21,50)[4] and MACD(16,26)[5], generated significant abnormal returns in the Italian and Canadian stock markets. However, none of the rules beat the B&H strategy in Japan. Cohen and Cabiri (2015) compared four indicators with the B&H strategy for four world indices in a sample from 2007 to 2012. They concluded that RSI was the best indicator, outperforming B&H in three of the four indices. Results also prove that when the market is in recession, RSI and MACD generate better gains than B&H, however, when the market is up, B&H outperforms.

Chang, Jong, and Wang (2017) evaluated the profitability of TA compared to the B&H strategy. Using variable-length moving averages (VMA) on stock listed on the Taiwan stock exchange, they computed the excess returns of technical trading relative to B&H on stocks. To control the firm size and trading volume, they grouped the sample by firm size and volume. They concluded that the VMA strategy performed better than the B&H strategy.

Jiang, Tong, and Song (2019) examined the predictiveness of TA in the Chinese aggregate stock market. Using five TI and investigate more than 28 thousand trading rules, they conclude that data snooping bias has a large impact on the identification of profitable rules, however, among these identified rules, the top-performing ones could achieve economically large profits.

Gerritsen, Bouri, Ramezanifar, and Roubaud (2020) examined whether TI can outperform a B&H strategy in the bitcoin market, applying TI such as RSI, MACD, among five others. They evaluated their performance with three strategies based on the Sharpe ratio. In the first, they take the trading signal literally. In the second, they acknowledge that taking short positions in Bitcoin is in reality not possible across many exchanges. In the third, a strategy where an investor has by default a long position in bitcoin is applied.

Their results showed that for MACD rules, it significantly outperforms only in strategy 2, however, the RSI not only underperforms the B&H but also, in some instances, even yield negative Sharpe ratios.

Yamani (2020) examined the profitability of three technical trading rules before, and after the 2007-2008 global financial crisis in the foreign exchange market. His conclusion shows that traders could beat the market during the crisis by using simple technical rules.

Bull Market and Bear Market

Any financial market in the world is like a heartbeat that is volatile depending on various circumstances. In this case, one must know how to distinguish the difference between bull and bear markets. For Chauvet and Potter (2000) in stock market terminology, a bull market corresponds to generally increasing market price periods, while a bear market corresponds to generally decreasing price periods.

The bull market is a financial market where prices are rising or expected to rise, the economy is growing, and GDP and job creation are on the up. This type of market is characterized by optimism, investor confidence, and expectations that good results will continue.

On the opposite end, a bear market is marked by falling prices, pessimism, and economic recession. Investors focus on short selling. Short selling is the sale of securities before the investor has acquired them to gain capital from asset devaluation. Traders use short selling as speculation and portfolio investors or managers use short selling as a hedge against the risk of falling markets. In bear market periods, many investors, anticipating subsequent valuations, take advantage of buying assets at more affordable prices.

Based on Bry and Boschan's (1971) approach, referenced by Yu, Chen, Xu, and Fu (2017) the stock market is classified as a bull market or bear market if certain criteria are met. At the end of each month, if the closing value compared to the previous five months and the subsequent five months is the highest (or lowest), there is a change in market trend. This method can generate continuous maximums (or minimums), but only the highest (or lowest) is considered a turning point. Finally, the period between the highs and lows is defined as a bear market; the opposite is considered a bull market. The duration of each period should be five months and this criterion is disregarded if there is a sharp increase (or fall) in asset value.

Methodological Framework

Goal and Data Overview

This section depicts the guidelines used to conduct an empirical investigation to achieve the main goal. In what follows, we will do an overview of the approach to sample selection and periods analyzed. We then move on to general assumptions common to all strategies. This section concludes with a detailed description of the strategies adopted and their implementation.

The main goal of this investigation is to find out if RSI and/or MACD can outperform the market with different assets and in recent times. These were chosen as they are two of the most used indicators in the financial market and they belong to different analysis categories, which may lead to different market analysis (Chong & Ng, 2008; Cohen & Cabiri, 2015; Eiamkanitchat, Moontuy, & Ramingwong, 2017; Kamble, 2017).

To this end, the first step is to define a sample, namely a set of stocks that would be used in the study. The Euro Stoxx 50 was chosen because it is Europe's leading blue-chip index for the Euro Zone. This index currently consists of 50 companies from 11 countries. Then, it was defined that the method of selection would follow Markowitz's theory, (1952). In other words, the efficient frontier of the Euro Stoxx 50's companies was analyzed, and the best were selected to maximize returns and minimize risk. This approach considered daily historical data from April 20, 2011, to June 15, 2015. Companies are listed in Table 1, which also shows their country of origin and corresponding relative value.

Table 1. Set of actions understudy, country and relative weights

Company Name	Country	Relative Value
Anheuser Busch Inbev SA NV	Belgium	34.57%
ASML Holding NV	Netherlands	29.44%
Koninklijke Ahold Delhaize NV	Netherlands	21.59%
Safran SA	France	8.82%
Airbus Group SE	France	5.58%

Anheuser Bush Inbev (ABI) is a multinational engaged in the production, distribution, and sale of beer, spirits, and soft drinks. It was founded in 2004 through the merger of a Belgian and a Brazilian company. Headquartered in Leuven, Belgium, it has offices in London, Mexico City, Johannesburg, Sao Paulo, among others. ABI is the global leader for beer, controlling 21.2% of the market, dominating Central Europe and Brazil. It owns over 200 brands, including Budweiser, Corona, and Stella Artois (Anheuser-Busch InBev, 2019).

Dutch-based ASML Holding NV (ASML) is the world's largest supplier of photolithography systems for the semiconductor industry. The company develops, produces, markets sells, and maintains semiconductor equipment systems. Its focus is in the Netherlands, the US, and Asia (HL, 2019).

Koninklijke Ahold Delhaize NV (AD) is one of the world's largest retail groups, a leader in supermarkets and e-commerce. At the forefront of sustainable retailing, AD's international headquarters is in Zaandam, Netherlands. It operates in Europe, the US, and Indonesia. It owns brands such as Food Lion, MAXI, Pingo Doce, Super Indo, among others (Ahold Delhaize, 2019).

Founded in 2005 via a merger between an aircraft and rocket engine manufacturer, a group of aerospace component manufacturers and a security company, Safran SA (SAF) is an international high-tech group operating in the propulsion equipment, space, and defense sectors. Headquartered in Paris, it is a leader in its main markets. SAF conducts research and development programs to meet rapidly changing market requirements (Safran, 2019).

Based in Toulouse, France, the Airbus Group SE (AIR) is a European leader in space development and a global leader in the manufacturing of civil helicopters. The Airbus Group was founded in 2000 and currently manufactures military aircraft and equipment, as well as satellites, and defense and telecommunications systems. It operates in over 170 locations around the world. Most of the company's orders are cross-border (Airbus, 2019).

In the sample selection stage, it was necessary to establish a benchmark. The choice fell towards the German stock index: the DAX. DAX is Germany's most important stock market index, containing the 30 largest companies in the country. It is considered one of the largest indices in the world and harbors some of the largest transaction volumes in Europe.

In the second phase, four strategies were applied to the previously selected stocks. These were analyzed collectively and compared to the benchmark, the DAX. Daily historical data considered spans from June 16, 2015, to March 29, 2019. The former marked Donald Trump's official campaign for the US presidency. The latter was the initial date for Brexit. These dates were selected to see how the market reacts to these two distinct global events but worldwide impact. The results are displayed in Table 2.

Table 2. Periods understudy

	Period	Start	End
1st Period	Full Sample	June 16, 2015	March 29, 2019
2nd Period	Between the official start of Trump's campaign and the US elections	June 16, 2015	October 8, 2016
3rd Period	Between Trump's election and Brexit's[6] formal start	October 8, 2016	March 29, 2017
4th Period	Between the formal start of Brexit and the first date set for Brexit	March 29, 2017	March 29, 2019
5th Period	Between Trump's election and the first Brexit date	October 8, 2016	March 29, 2019

Figure 3 shows the price of the Euro Stoxx 50, highlighting the five periods under consideration. It also indicates how it goes from a bear market in the second period, a bull market in the third, and in the fourth period, it goes back to a bear market being that the last few months demonstrate a bull market state.

Figure 3. Euro Stoxx rates for the periods' understudy
Source: Adapted from Investing.com

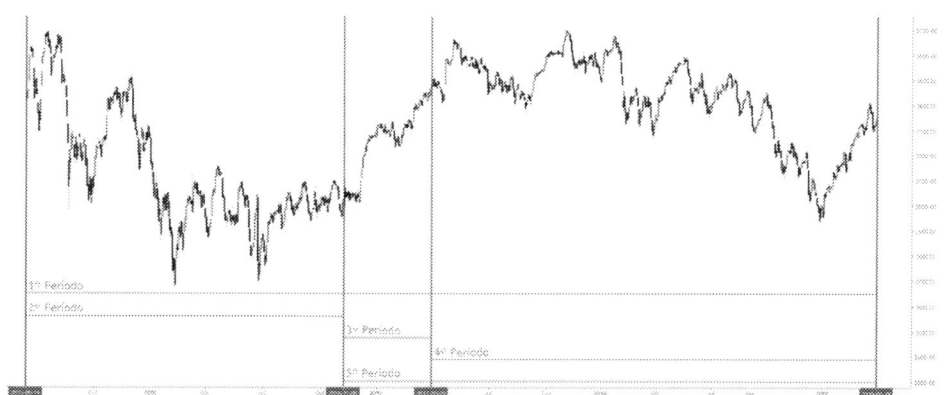

Premise

To analyze the profitability of each asset for each adopted strategy, it is necessary to establish a common base. For this purpose, the following premises were defined:

1. The initial investment sum is € 100,000. It will be considered that a particular investor has this available capital by inheritance.
2. For the sake of simplicity, transactions will be based on daily closing prices.
3. When investing, the maximum number of shares available per asset will always be bought.
4. The investor will not undertake short selling; a long position must first be verified before a short one can exist.
5. The investor will begin without stocks, acquiring them at the first buy signal issued by each respective strategy. On the last day, if the investor holds assets, they will be sold at the price set for that day.
6. A brokerage commission of 0.12%[7] for each transaction will be charged.
7. Taxation on capital gains will not be considered, nor dividends.

Strategies

Among the existing indicators to study market behavior, RSI and MACD were used to verify profitability when compared to the B&H strategy. These were assessed separately as well as together. The two were chosen as they combine the strength of movement with market fluctuations.

Strategy Nº1 – RSI

According to Wong, Manzur, and Chew (2013) and Chong and Ng (2008), o RSI would generate a buy order when the $RSI_{(t)}$ value was greater than 50 and a sell order when it was less than 50. However, in this study, buy and sell orders are based on Wilder (1978) or as shown in the works of Murphy (1999), Pring (2002), Rosillo, De la Fuente, and Brugos (2013) and Cohen and Cabiri (2015). When the $RSI_{(t)}$ value is greater than 30 and the $RSI_{(t-1)}$ value is less than or equal to 30, a buy order is generated. When the $RSI_{(t)}$ value is greater than 70 and the $RSI_{(t-1)}$ value is less than or equal to 70, a sale order is created.

Strategy Nº2 – MACD

In Chong and Ng (2008), a buy signal occurs when $MACD_{(t)}$ is greater than 0, and $MACD_{(t-1)}$ value is less than or equal to 0. A sell signal occurs when the opposite takes place. In this study, buy and sell orders are based on Murphy (1999) and Cohen and Cabiri (2015). Buy and sell signals occur when the two lines – MACD and signal – intersect. When the $MACD_{(t)}$ line crosses the signal line upwards, a purchase order is placed. When it crosses the signal line downwards a sell order is placed.

Strategy Nº3 – RSI & MACD

According to Wilder (1978), no tool will produce 100% correct answers. A successful trader uses various types of indicators in their decisions. From this perspective, the third strategy was developed to reconcile the two indicators to determine if a combination provides better results.

The investor will enter the market if one of the indicators provides a buy signal and the second indicator gives its buy signal within ten days. This means the second indicator confirms the trend of the first, and the investor will move forward with confidence. On the other hand, if a sell signal appears, the investor will wait up to ten days for the second indicator to confirm and issue its signal. This is used to ascertain whether the market is experiencing a changing trend.

To summarize, a buy order is generated when indicators emit their buy signal individually within ten days, i.e. a buy order is generated when $RSI_{(t)}$ is greater than 30, the value of the $RSI_{(t-1)}$ is less than or equal to 30, and when the $MACD_{(t)}$ crosses the signaling line upwards. A sell order is created when the indicators give their sell signal within ten days, i.e. when the $RSI_{(t)}$ value is greater than 70, $RSI_{(t-1)}$ is less than or equal to 70, and the $MACD_{(t)}$ line crosses the downward signaling line.

Strategy Nº4 – B&H

The last investment strategy is B&H and consist of only two transactions per asset: a long position (asset purchase) taking place on the first day of the period under consideration, and a short position (asset sale) on the final day

RESULTS

In this section, the results produced are analyzed, while trying to answer the questions above – namely, whether TI is used individually or together can deliver superior profitability to B&H.

Considering the first results, two additional studies were developed. A new period was considered based on international news affecting the economy. The aim is to determine the performance of each strategy and to see if it is possible to add returns using news at the time of investing. The second study changes the default time interval of the RSI strategy, exploring a possible performance improvement by changing indicator timeframes.

First Period

The first period encompasses the entire sample period (June 15, 2015, to March 29, 2019), with 972 days of transactions. It has two long bear market phases interspersed by two shorter bull ones. Table 3 shows the results of the four strategies under analysis applied to the set of stocks, as well as the benchmark. Figure 4 highlights the profit/loss line in Table 3.

Table 3. Technical indicators versus B&H for 1st period

	1st Strategy - RSI		2nd Strategy - MACD		3rd Strategy - RSI & MACD		4th Strategy - Buy and hold	
	RSI - Set of Stocks	RSI - Benchmark	MACD - Set of Stocks	MACD - Benchmark	RSI & MACD - Set of Stocks	RSI & MACD - Benchmark	B&H - Set of Stocks	B&H - Benchmark
Initial Balance	100,000.00 €	100,000.00 €	100,000.00 €	100,000.00 €	100,000.00 €	100,000.00 €	100,000.00 €	100,000.00 €
					1st Period			
Number of Transactions	16	4	206	44	14	4	5	1
(%) Won Transactions	63%	75%	33%	25%	71%	75%	80%	100%
Final Balance	108,963.79 €	115,866.48 €	92,499.20 €	66,996.42 €	118,674.58 €	112,279.94 €	131,491.54 €	104,094.51 €
Profit / Loss	8,963.79 €	15,866.48 €	- 7,500.80 €	- 33,003.58 €	18,674.58 €	12,279.94 €	31,491.54 €	4,094.51 €
(%) Profit / Loss	8.96%	15.87%	-7.50%	-33.00%	18.67%	12.28%	31.49%	4.09%

Figure 4. Profit / loss percentage for 1st period

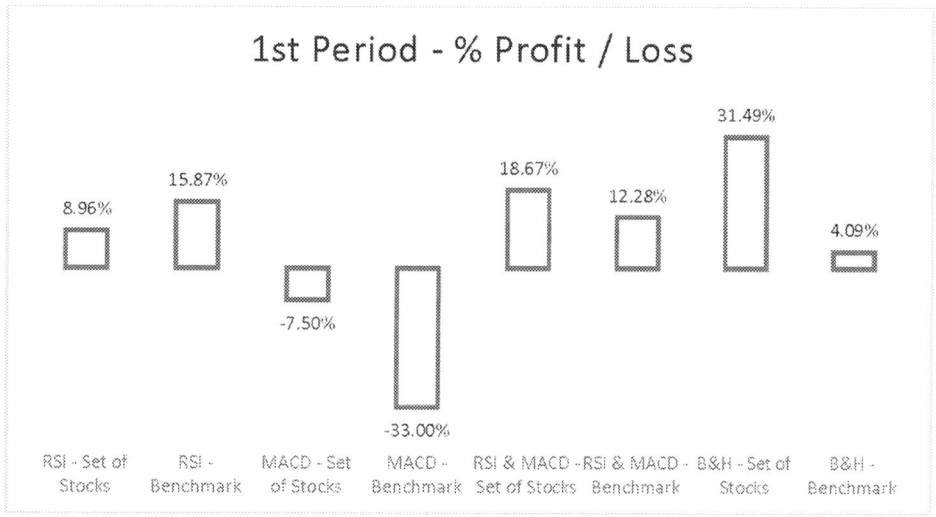

For the set of stocks, the best performing strategy was B&H. Performance stood at 31.49%, which resulted in a gain of € 31,491.54. The worst performance was MACD with a loss of 7.50%, leaving investors with only € 92,499.20 in their portfolio.

Regarding the benchmark, the best strategy was RSI with a 15.87% profit, offering a € 15,866.48 return. However, if the investor had opted for MACD it would have suffered a 33% loss, which would lead to a final balance of € 66,996.42. This indicator issued 44 orders, 75% of which lead to monetary losses.

Comparing the set of stocks with the benchmark, strategy by strategy, it appears that the former outperformed the latter in three of the four strategies (namely, MACD, RSI & MACD, and B&H). The benchmark only surpassed the stocks using RSI.

It is worth noting that the RSI & MACD strategy achieved profits of over 10% on the stock and benchmark, with the percentage of successful transactions sitting above 70%. Also, profits achieved with B&H sat at over 30% for the set of stocks, although the benchmark did not follow the trend, gaining only 4.09%. MACD was the only strategy to underperform, never surpassing a third of successful transactions.

Second Period

The second period under analysis marks the first bear market phase, and its great volatility should be noted. It begins on June 16, 2015, the day Donald Trump made his campaign for US President official, and ends on November 8, 2016, with his election, accounting for 362 days of transactions. Like in the previous section, Table 4 presents the overall results for this period, with Figure 5 focusing on the profit/loss percentage.

Table 4. Technical indicators vs. B&H for 2nd period

	1st Strategy - RSI		2nd Strategy - MACD		3rd Strategy - RSI & MACD		4th Strategy - Buy and hold	
	RSI - Set of Stocks	RSI - Benchmark	MACD - Set of Stocks	MACD - Benchmark	RSI & MACD - Set of Stocks	RSI & MACD - Benchmark	B&H - Set of Stocks	B&H - Benchmark
Initial Balance	100,000.00 €	100,000.00 €	100,000.00 €	100,000.00 €	100,000.00 €	100,000.00 €	100,000.00 €	100,000.00 €
				2nd Period				
Number of Transactions	7	2	80	16	6	2	5	1
(%) Won Transactions	57%	100%	25%	19%	50%	100%	40%	0%
Final Balance	114,239.57 €	115,814.43 €	89,671.86 €	80,454.49 €	114,636.00 €	113,938.07 €	99,730.13 €	94,712.31 €
Profit / Loss	14,239.57 €	15,814.43 €	- 10,328.14 €	- 19,545.51 €	14,636.00 €	13,938.07 €	- 269.87 €	- 5,287.69 €
(%) Profit / Loss	14.24%	15.81%	-10.33%	-19.55%	14.64%	13.94%	-0.27%	-5.29%

Figure 5. Profit / loss percentage for 2nd period

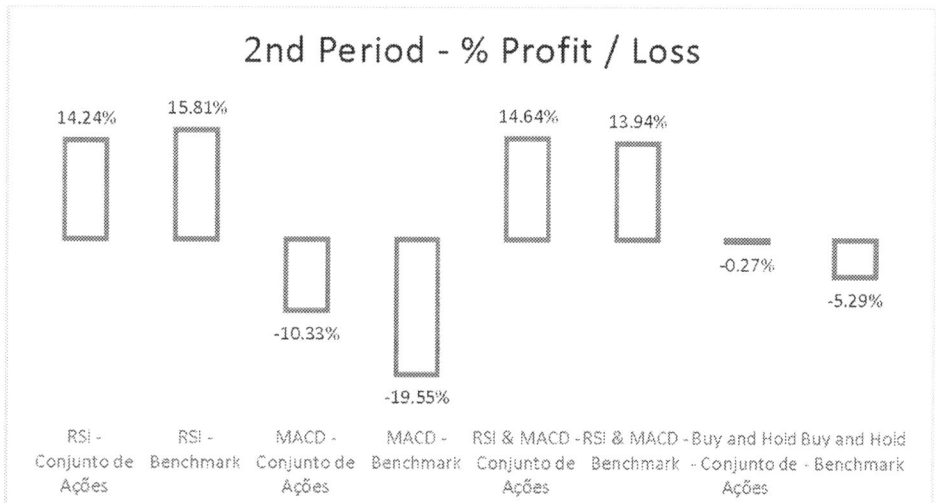

The strategy that obtained the best result for the set of stocks was RSI & MACD, followed very closely by RSI, with a performance of 14.64%, which translates into an increase of € 14,636.00 in the investor portfolio. On the other hand, MACD was the worst-performing strategy with a loss of 10.33%, resulting from 80 operations in which only 25% produced gains for the investor.

The best performing strategy for the benchmark was RSI, boasting a 15.81% return – although it only issued two buy and sell signals. These translated 100% into profit, garnering a final balance of € 115,814.43. It should also be noted that the worst-performing strategy for the benchmark was MACD with a loss of 19.55%, generating 16 buy signals – 81% of which resulted in losses.

Comparing strategies, we observe that stocks exceeded the benchmark with MACD, RSI & MACD, and B&H. RSI joins RSI & MACD as a strategy capable of generating profits of over 10% on both stock and benchmark. These also are the only strategies that have a 50% or higher number of successful transactions. MACD is once again the worst. As expected, the loss in performance of the B&H strategy is noticeable.

Third Period

Some 101 transactions were made during the third period, which runs from November 8, 2016, to March 29, 2017, between the US elections and the start of Brexit. The global economy experienced a positive moment during this time, a bull market – the first of the sample. Figure 6 highlights the profit/loss line shown in Table 5.

Table 5. Technical indicators vs. B&H for 3rd period

	1st Strategy - RSI		2nd Strategy - MACD		3rd Strategy - RSI & MACD		4th Strategy - Buy and hold	
	RSI - Set of Stocks	RSI - Benchmark	MACD - Set of Stocks	MACD - Benchmark	RSI & MACD - Set of Stocks	RSI & MACD - Benchmark	B&H - Set of Stocks	B&H - Benchmark
Initial Balance	100,000.00 €	100,000.00 €	100,000.00 €	100,000.00 €	100,000.00 €	100,000.00 €	100,000.00 €	100,000.00 €
	3rd Period							
Number of Transactions	3	0	18	5	3	0	5	1
(%) Won Transactions	100%		50%	40%	100%		60%	100%
Final Balance	103,830.09 €	100,000.00 €	102,761.74 €	103,517.37 €	103,417.39 €	100,000.00 €	111,228.64 €	115,241.12 €
Profit / Loss	3,830.09 €	- €	2,761.74 €	3,517.37 €	3,417.39 €	- €	11,228.64 €	15,241.12 €
(%) Profit / Loss	3.83%	0.00%	2.76%	3.52%	3.42%	0.00%	11.23%	15.24%

Figure 6. Profit / loss percentage for 3rd period

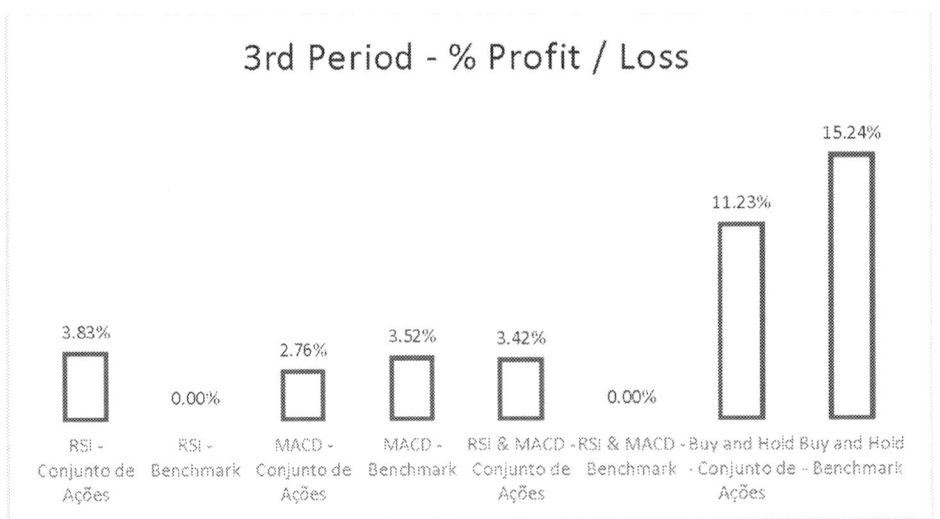

The strategy with the best results was B&H, with a performance of 11.23%, which translates into a final balance of € 11,228.64. However, if the investor had opted for MACD, they would have obtained the worst result for the set of stocks (2.76%). Although this strategy was deemed the worst in this category, investors would have still made a profit of € 102,761.74.

With regards to the benchmark, the strategy with the highest profit was B&H (15.24%). If the investor opted for this and entered the market on November 8, 2016, relinquishing their stake on March 29, 2017, he/she would have profited € 15,241.12. RSI and RSI & MACD did not carry out transactions.

Comparing the stocks and benchmark, both obtained the best performance in two of the four strategies. Stocks outperformed the benchmark with RSI and RSI & MACD, while MACD and B&H helped the benchmark outperform the stocks.

Does Technical Analysis Win?

It is worth noting that none of the four strategies had a negative result, and the passive strategy yielded returns of over 10% in both stocks and benchmark.

Fourth Period

The fourth period, from March 29, 2017 to March 29, 2019, sits between the official beginning of Brexit and its stipulated date. Around 511 days of transactions were studied. At the time, the market was in a bear state. In the last months, it underwent a bull phase. Table 6 shows the results of each strategy and the profit/loss percentage is detailed in Figure 7.

Table 6. Technical indicators versus B&H for 4th period

	1st Strategy - RSI		2nd Strategy - MACD		3rd Strategy - RSI & MACD		4th Strategy - Buy and hold	
	RSI - Set of Stocks	RSI - Benchmark	MACD - Set of Stocks	MACD - Benchmark	RSI & MACD - Set of Stocks	RSI & MACD - Benchmark	B&H - Set of Stocks	B&H - Benchmark
Initial Balance	100,000.00 €	100,000.00 €	100,000.00 €	100,000.00 €	100,000.00 €	100,000.00 €	100,000.00 €	100,000.00 €
				4th Period				
Number of Transactions	8	2	102	21	7	2	5	1
(%) Won Transactions	50%	50%	44%	48%	57%	50%	80%	0%
Final Balance	95,567.30 €	99,931.92 €	101,607.44 €	82,212.27 €	100,990.69 €	98,526.10 €	115,166.90 €	94,356.52 €
Profit / Loss	- 4,432.70 €	- 68.08 €	1,607.44 €	- 17,787.73 €	990.69 €	- 1,473.90 €	15,166.90 €	- 5,643.48 €
(%) Profit / Loss	-4.43%	-0.07%	1.61%	-17.79%	0.99%	-1.47%	15.17%	-5.64%

Figure 7. Profit / loss percentage for 4th period

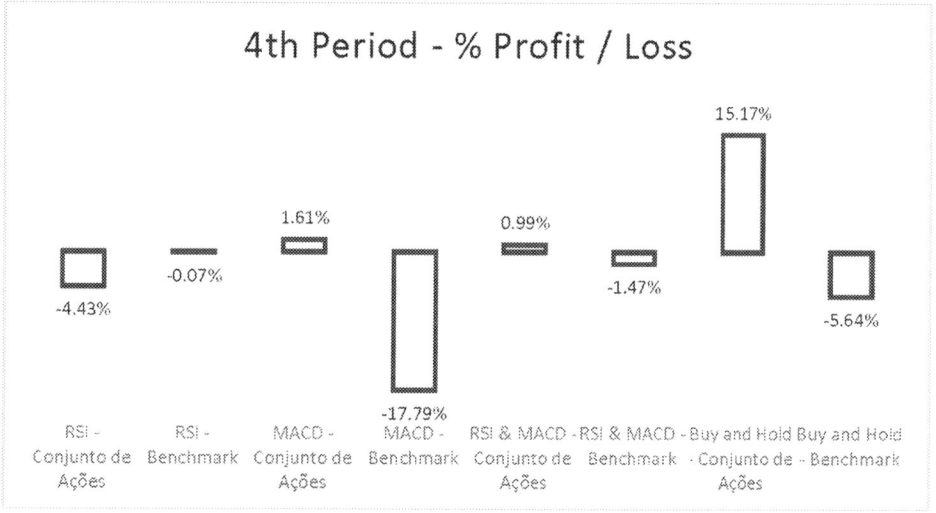

371

The best performing strategy for stocks was B&H, with a performance of 15.17%. Had investors used this, they would have made a profit of € 115,166.90. The worst performing strategy was RSI, with a loss of 4.43%, or € 4,432.70.

Regarding the benchmark, none of the strategies obtained positive returns. The one that presented the smallest losses was RSI (0.07%). The worst performing was MACD with a loss of 17.79%. If the investors chose this strategy, they would have a final balance of € 82,212.27.

Comparing stocks with a benchmark, we see the former yielded better returns than the latter in three of the four strategies: MACD, RSI & MACD, and B&H. These results are identical to those of the first and second periods.

Overall, investors would have taken losses in five of the eight cases presented, making this period the worst to invest.

Fifth Period

The fifth period runs from November 8, 2016, to March 29, 2019. This sample sits between the US election and the first Brexit date. During this period, 611 days of transactions were analyzed and contain the 3rd and 4th periods. Figure 8 details the gains/losses from Table 7.

Table 7. Technical indicators versus B&H for 5th period

	1st Strategy - RSI		2nd Strategy - MACD		3rd Strategy - RSI & MACD		4th Strategy - Buy and hold	
	RSI - Set of Stocks	RSI - Benchmark	MACD - Set of Stocks	MACD - Benchmark	RSI & MACD - Set of Stocks	RSI & MACD - Benchmark	B&H - Set of Stocks	B&H - Benchmark
Initial Balance	100,000.00 €	100,000.00 €	100,000.00 €	100,000.00 €	100,000.00 €	100,000.00 €	100,000.00 €	100,000.00 €
				5th Period				
Number of Transactions	10	2	123	27	9	2	5	1
(%) Won Transactions	60%	50%	42%	41%	67%	50%	80%	100%
Final Balance	98,330.48 €	99,931.92 €	104,307.51 €	83,987.71 €	104,629.00 €	98,526.10 €	131,985.92 €	109,155.79 €
Profit / Loss	- 1,669.52 €	- 68.08 €	4,307.51 €	- 16,012.29 €	4,629.00 €	- 1,473.90 €	31,985.92 €	9,155.79 €
(%) Profit / Loss	-1.67%	-0.07%	4.31%	-16.01%	4.63%	-1.47%	31.99%	9.16%

Does Technical Analysis Win?

Figure 8. Profit / loss percentage for 5th period

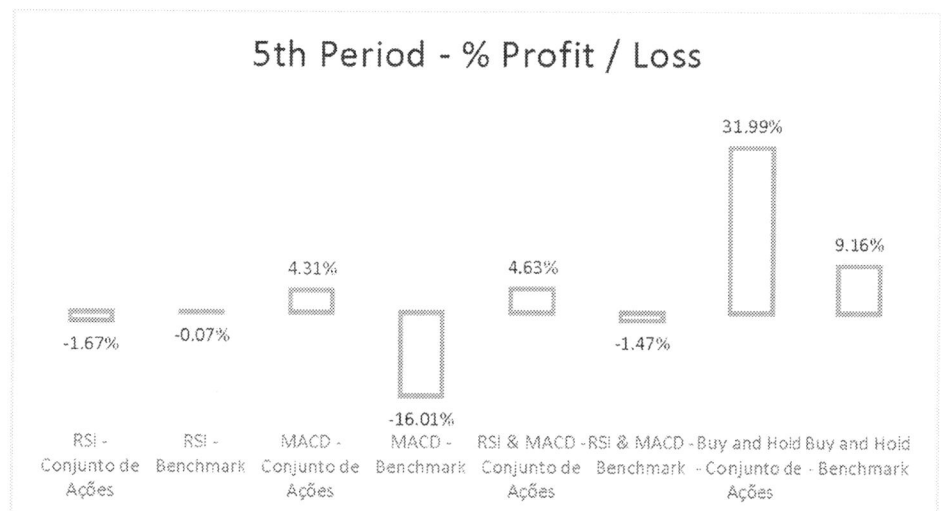

Looking at stocks, we see that B&H presented the best performance, with 31.99%. If investors had chosen this strategy, they would have profited € 31,985.92. The strategy with the highest losses was RSI, presenting a negative return of 1.67% (a loss of € 1,669.52).

With the benchmark, we see B&H standing out once more, with profits of 9.16%. It is also verified that the strategy that presented the worst result in this period was MACD with an investor loss of 16.01%. This strategy issued 27 buy signals with only 41% of these generating gains.

Comparing stocks and benchmarks, the former outperformed the latter using MACD, RSI & MACD, and B&H. These results are similar to the first, second, and fourth periods. RSI posted negative results for both.

Discussion of Overall Results for the Periods Considered

Considering all strategies under review, as seen in Table 8, B&H obtained the best returns for a set of stocks. Only in one of the five periods did it not provide a return on investment. The worst performing strategy was MACD, which failed to achieve profitability results over 5% across the spectrum.

When it comes to the benchmark, the strategy with the best returns was RSI. Profits were over 15% in the first and second periods, although they did not record any transactions during the third. MACD was the worst one. This strategy only has a positive net effect in the third period, being unable to exceed 5% profitability.

Comparing both, RSI had a better benchmark performance. However, MACD, RSI & MACD, and B&H showed better stock returns.

RSI achieved satisfactory performance in the first period. Stocks made profits of 8.96% and the benchmark sits at 15.87%. The fourth period recorded the worst average transactions with 50%. RSI has been deemed a reliable indicator. However, as time goes on, it generates many consecutive buys or sells signals. Besides, this indicator does not provide many entry and exit moments, meaning investors do not take advantage of market fluctuations.

MACD proved to be a very sensitive indicator, as it generated a large number of signals – 642 buy and sell orders. Nonetheless, it could not secure a percentage of successful transactions greater than 50%. This strategy obtained the worst result in the study, dropping 33% in the benchmark and 7.50% in stocks during the first period. Of the five periods under review, only in the third did MACD achieve a positive return on the benchmark. The indicator gave many to buy or sell signals, though, meaning it predicted a possible trend reversal. However, this inversion occurred very rarely. Thus, we can conclude that this strategy provides many false entries, causing investors to enter the market prematurely, making investments expensive.

Figure 9. Profit / Loss percentage for all periods

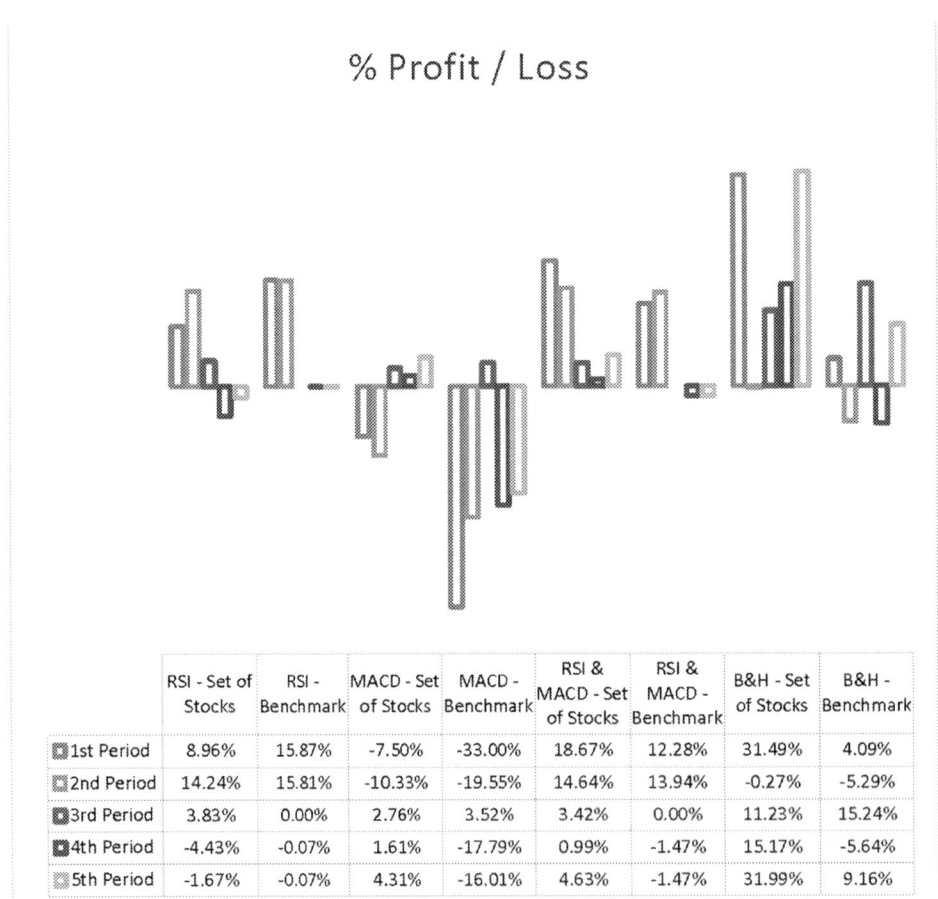

	RSI - Set of Stocks	RSI - Benchmark	MACD - Set of Stocks	MACD - Benchmark	RSI & MACD - Set of Stocks	RSI & MACD - Benchmark	B&H - Set of Stocks	B&H - Benchmark
1st Period	8.96%	15.87%	-7.50%	-33.00%	18.67%	12.28%	31.49%	4.09%
2nd Period	14.24%	15.81%	-10.33%	-19.55%	14.64%	13.94%	-0.27%	-5.29%
3rd Period	3.83%	0.00%	2.76%	3.52%	3.42%	0.00%	11.23%	15.24%
4th Period	-4.43%	-0.07%	1.61%	-17.79%	0.99%	-1.47%	15.17%	-5.64%
5th Period	-1.67%	-0.07%	4.31%	-16.01%	4.63%	-1.47%	31.99%	9.16%

RSI & MACD recorded the highest number of successful transactions, giving it the best positive result ratio. It stands out for its consistency, reliability, and safety. If investors opted for this strategy, they would not suffer losses in any of the periods under study for stocks. It stands out as a useful tool for investors.

The beginning of Donald Trump's election campaign was a period of great volatility and uncertainty. During this period, the strategy that best met expectations was RSI & MACD, followed by RSI. B&H failed to add positive investment returns.

As soon as Donald Trump was elected US President there was a short-term bullish reaction in the third period. The strategy that best-met expectations was B&H.

It should be noted that during Brexit, the market experienced a bear state, always trying to react in the short term. Nevertheless, the B&H strategy achieved the best performance compared to TA.

Overall, when the market is indeterminate and volatile, RSI gets better results compared to B&H. This happens as RSI obtains more buy and sell signals when the market is volatile. On the other hand, when the market is in a bull phase, B&H outperforms TA indicators.

Additional Strategies

In this subchapter, we will analyze two supplementary strategies. The goal is to understand if investors can obtain higher profits following other premises.

Afterward, these strategies will be scrutinized under certain periods, chosen for news articles with an international impact on the economy.

Finally, we will look at how RSI acts at different intervals while trying to understand if it is possible to obtain higher returns when this time frame changes.

The Importance of International News

If untrained investors want to put their capital on the stock exchange, they wonder what the ideal time is. With that in mind, the goal is to analyze the profitability of an investment using international news to determine entry and exit points, and not FA or TA.

On January 22, 2018, the International Monetary Fund (IMF) released a world economic outlook report for 2018 and 2019. "Global economic activity continues to firm up. ... Global growth forecasts for 2018 and 2019 have been revised upwards by 0.2 percentage points to 3.9%. The review reflects the increased global growth momentum and the expected impact of recently approved changes in US tax policy." (Internacional Monetary Fund, 2018).

By analyzing this report, the positive sentiment of an investor is strengthened, and they want to enter the financial market due to the IMF's short/medium-term projections. In the period under review, the investor will enter the market on January 23, 2018, and with no exit date.

Not setting an exit date, the investor watches their movements and news about the economy to find the best time to leave. In this particular case, on December 31, 2018, CNN released the following news: "2018 was the worst for stocks in ten years"[8]. Reading this article, the investor decides to leave the market for fear this wave continues.

Between January 23, 2018, and January 2, 2019, 241 days of transactions were studied. Table 9 shows the results of strategies under scrutiny and the profit/loss percentage is detailed in Figure 9.

Table 9. Technical indicators versus B&H for the period between January 23, 2018, and January 2, 2019

	1st Strategy - RSI		2nd Strategy - MACD		3rd Strategy - RSI & MACD		4th Strategy - Buy and hold	
	RSI - Set of Stocks	RSI - Benchmark	MACD - Set of Stocks	MACD - Benchmark	RSI & MACD - Set of Stocks	RSI & MACD - Benchmark	B&H - Set of Stocks	B&H - Benchmark
Initial Balance	100,000.00 €	100,000.00 €	100,000.00 €	100,000.00 €	100,000.00 €	100,000.00 €	100,000.00 €	100,000.00 €
	23/01/2018 to 02/01/2019							
Number of Transactions	6	2	48	9	5	2	5	1
(%) Won Transactions	33%	50%	31%	22%	60%	50%	40%	0%
Final Balance	88,392.48 €	91,987.50 €	89,894.47 €	83,569.97 €	91,769.89 €	90,968.38 €	86,068.61 €	78,941.36 €
Profit / Loss	- 11,607.52 €	- 8,012.50 €	- 10,105.53 €	- 16,430.03 €	- 8,230.11 €	- 9,031.62 €	- 13,931.39 €	- 21,058.64 €
(%) Profit / Loss	-11.61%	-8.01%	-10.11%	-16.43%	-8.23%	-9.03%	-13.93%	-21.06%

Figure 10. Profit / loss percentage for the period between January 23, 2018 and January 2, 2019

We verify that none of the above strategies obtained positive returns.

The strategy with the highest stock loss was B&H with 13.93%. It also achieved the worst benchmark results with a negative return of 21.06%. The strategy with the least negative impact for the stock was RSI & MACD, with -8.23%. As for the benchmark, RSI garnered the least negative result.

In a falling market, it is natural for B&H to deliver negative results. However, other TA strategies failed to achieve positive results. Despite this, it should be noted that MACD & RSI have a successful transaction volume of over 50%. These numbers reflect confidence in the use of this indicator.

That said, the economy is indeed decisive, and it is not possible to just consider past returns. In this period, international events indicated that it would be a great year for the economy. That was not the case. As such, investors must be aware of events that happen in all economies.

RSI for Different Time Frames

Based on the analysis, results and conclusions obtained previously, and to find a strategy that allows the investor to increase his performance in the financial market, the first strategy - RSI will be analyzed for the first period under study at different time intervals. Oscillator sensitivity depends on the number of lookback periods. Under shorter periods, RSI is more sensitive than RSI with a longer time frame, meaning it will produce more overbought or oversold readings.

This analysis aims to show whether a more sensitive RSI is more useful and performs better than a less sensitive and more conservative one.

The formula used is equation (1), while also maintaining (2), with formulas (3) and (4) extended to accommodate other lookback periods, namely:

$$\text{Average Gain}_{(t)} = [\text{Average Gain}_{(t-1)} \times (D - 1) + \text{Current Gain}_{(t)}] / D \tag{9}$$

$$\text{Average Loss}_{(t)} = [\text{Average Loss}_{(t-1)} \times (D - 1) + \text{Current Loss}_{(t)}] / D \tag{10}$$

D is the time interval under consideration. Some five periods will be studied, namely 5, 9, 14, 21, and 25 days. For this purpose, an additional Python code has been created. Results for the five RSIs are viewable in Table 10 for the stocks and the benchmark.

As expected, the RSI with the shortest time interval (RSI 5) provided the highest number of transactions. AIR and SAF shares had the highest return, exceeding 45% each, contrarily, ABI suffered a 38.64% loss with 22 transactions.

RSI 25, the one with the longest interval, only got four transactions in total. No transactions were registered for three of the five shares. For the ones that did, AD obtained 8.19% profitability and DAX got 13%. ABI netted a negative result of 1.55%.

Analyzing the performance of the different RSI, and comparing the set of stocks against the benchmark, the latter outperformed the former in four of the five indicators.

The RSI with the highest profitability in an individual analysis was RSI 5, with a benchmark performance of 23.32%. Those investing exclusively in DAX using only this indicator would make profits of € 23,323.63. It issued 52 buy signals over the period, with only 42% of these resulting in gains for the investor. With regards to stock, the most profitable RSI was RSI 9 with a performance of 17.33%. It accounted for 73% of successful transactions from a universe of 45 transactions.

Overall, RSI 14 was the best option for investing during the period, as it was the most constant, achieving a return of 8.96% and 15.87% for stocks and benchmark, respectively.

By shortening the RSI timeframe, the indicator becomes much more sensitive and the difference in the number of signals generated is evident. However, this can lead to increased false flags, which could result in transactions with a loss. If the interval increases, the smoothing effect increases as well. When a signal is issued, it will have a higher reliability level than a shorter RSI. Even so, as it issues a very small number of signals, it often causes the investor to be "trapped" inside or out of the market, failing to capitalize on its fluctuation.

Table 10. Detailed result of the set of stocks versus benchmark based on RSI 5, 9, 14, 21 and 25

	Stocks					Set of Stocks	Benchmark
	AIR	SAF	AD	ASML	ABI		DAX
Size	5.58%	8.82%	21.59%	29.44%	34.57%	100.00%	100.00%
Initial Balance	5,580.00 €	8,820.00 €	21,590.00 €	29,440.00 €	34,570.00 €	100,000.00 €	100,000.00 €
RSI 25							
Number of Transactions	0	0	1	0	2	3	1
(%) Won Transactions	0%	0%	100%	0%	50%	67%	100%
Final Balance	5,580.00 €	8,820.00 €	23,358.24 €	29,440.00 €	34,033.19 €	101,231.43 €	112,997.24 €
Profit / Loss	- €	- €	1,768.24 €	- €	- 536.81 €	1,231.43 €	12,997.24 €
(%) Profit / Loss	0.00%	0.00%	8.19%	0.00%	-1.55%	1.23%	13.00%
RSI 21							
Number of Transactions	0	1	2	1	2	6	2
(%) Won Transactions	0%	100%	100%	100%	50%	83%	100%
Final Balance	5,580.00 €	11,245.21 €	26,386.93 €	31,397.40 €	30,802.84 €	105,412.38 €	112,974.14 €
Profit / Loss	- €	2,425.21 €	4,796.93 €	1,957.40 €	- 3,767.16 €	5,412.38 €	12,974.14 €
(%) Profit / Loss	0.00%	27.50%	22.22%	6.65%	-10.90%	5.41%	12.97%
RSI 14							
Number of Transactions	3	3	3	2	5	16	4
(%) Won Transactions	33%	100%	67%	100%	40%	63%	75%
Final Balance	5,947.66 €	11,135.63 €	22,417.09 €	36,630.74 €	32,832.67 €	108,963.79 €	115,866.48 €
Profit / Loss	367.66 €	2,315.63 €	827.09 €	7,190.74 €	1,737.33 €	8,963.79 €	15,866.48 €
(%) Profit / Loss	6.59%	26.25%	3.83%	24.43%	-5.03%	8.96%	15.87%
RSI 9							
Number of Transactions	6	9	11	9	10	45	7
(%) Won Transactions	67%	89%	73%	78%	60%	73%	57%
Final Balance	6,271.77 €	13,638.87 €	26,889.29 €	34,270.86 €	36,260.27 €	117,331.06 €	104,669.59 €
Profit / Loss	691.77 €	4,818.87 €	5,299.29 €	4,830.86 €	1,690.27 €	17,331.06 €	4,669.59 €
(%) Profit / Loss	12.40%	54.64%	24.55%	16.41%	4.89%	17.33%	4.67%
RSI 5							
Number of Transactions	30	29	25	21	22	127	52
(%) Won Transactions	87%	93%	68%	67%	55%	76%	42%
Final Balance	8,130.05 €	16,333.97 €	23,093.51 €	32,362.30 €	21,211.68 €	101,131.51 €	123,323.63 €
Profit / Loss	2,550.05 €	7,513.97 €	1,503.51 €	2,922.30 €	- 13,358.32 €	1,131.51 €	23,323.63 €
(%) Profit / Loss	45.70%	85.19%	6.96%	9.93%	-38.64%	1.13%	23.32%

CONCLUSION

The use of TI to increase return on investment in financial markets has been one of the most exciting questions in financial literature, but also one whose answers are less unanimous.

This paper aimed to analyze the two most used indicators in TA and to understand if these, individually or together, can overcome the B&H strategy in different periods. To this end, four codes were created in Python to execute the scenarios. Stocks of the Euro Stoxx 50 index were selected through the Markowitz theory, so investors could have a diversified portfolio and also compare stocks to a benchmark.

The results of this work suggest that for a diversified portfolio, in bull market periods, B&H yields perform better than a TA strategy. When the market is in a bear stage, RSI & MACD is the best strategy. When the market is in recession, TI generally yields better results than the passive strategy. When it is bullish, B&H outperforms indicators. TI strategies have proven to be more profitable for the benchmark. In this case, when investors prefer indices, our study points to RSI as preferable. This is explained by indices containing more volatile assets that improve the performance of indicators such as RSI. Finally, the empirical evidence from this research suggests that it is preferable to invest using a diversified equity portfolio than to invest in a benchmark.

This investigation also examined whether a strategy consisting of RSI and MACD indicators would have better results used alone or in combination. The outcome shows that using a combination of these indicators garners a higher return than using them individually.

As for the indicator with the highest reliability, the one that got the most successful transactions was RSI & MACD. These two indicators work well together because they belong to different categories, which gives rise to different market analysis. This research supports current literature suggesting that it is important to pay attention to more than one TA indicator from different categories, improving investor confidence.

The period was chosen to study how the market reacts to international events with worldwide impact. We concluded that it is necessary to pay attention to the point when investors enter the market. To generate returns for the portfolio, one must analyze where the market is and adapt strategies accordingly. To be successful, investors need to be aware of international events affecting the economy, as globalization now plays a key role in how markets operate.

In conclusion, the B&H strategy still has much to offer, although it can be considered high-risk. If investors enter the market during a bear period, the passive strategy may bring significant monetary losses to the portfolio. On the other hand, if they opt for TA or to reduce the risk of investing in a bear market, it was proved that several indicators should be considered together, instead of individually. By doing this, more information can be withdrawn from the market to substantiate decisions. Prior research shows that investors choose TI over B&H, although they may lose potential profits from the B&H strategy in a possible bull market. If the market is in a bear state, TI such as RSI or RSI & MACD halts losses early on, preventing them from expanding, boosting gains.

To address some of the limitations of this paper, future lines of research should address dividend taxes and capital gains, as well as the possibility of using intraday TI and graphic standards. Another suggestion is to study MACD by changing the values of moving lines and/or other markets to refine this strategy. A different approach would be to refine RSI & MACD to explore a possible performance improvement of these two indicators to obtain results when used together. Finally, it would be of value to expand the period of this study, given the postponement of Brexit, and analyze how the market and TA indicators react to this.

ACKNOWLEDGMENT

This work is supported by national funds, through the FCT – Portuguese Foundation for Science and Technology under the project UIDB/04011/2020.

REFERENCES

Abad, C., Thore, S. A., & Laffarga, J. (2004). Fundamental analysis of stocks by two-stage DEA. *Managerial and Decision Economics*, *25*(5), 231–241. doi:10.1002/mde.1145

Ahold Delhaize. (2019). *Ahold Delhaize*. Retrieved from Ahold Delhaize: https://www.aholddelhaize.com/en/home/

Allen, H., & Taylor, M. P. (1990). Charts, noise and fundamentals in the London foreign exchange market. *Economic Journal (London)*, *100*(400), 49–59. doi:10.2307/2234183

Bartram, S. M., & Grinblatt, M. (2018). Agnostic fundamental analysis works. *Journal of Financial Economics*, *128*(1), 125–147. doi:10.1016/j.jfineco.2016.11.008

BBC. (2016, November 10). *Trump e Brexit: 5 fatores em comum*. Retrieved from BBC News: https://www.bbc.com/portuguese/internacional-37934191

Bessembinder, H., & Chan, K. (1995). The profitability of technical trading rules in the Asian stock markets. *Pacific-Basin Finance Journal*, *3*(2-3), 257–284. doi:10.1016/0927-538X(95)00002-3

Bettman, J. L., Sault, S. J., & Schultz, E. L. (2009). Fundamental and technical analysis substitutes or complements. *Accounting and Finance*, *49*(1), 21–36. doi:10.1111/j.1467-629X.2008.00277.x

Bodas Sagi, D. J., Soltero, F. J., Hidalgo, J. I., Fernandez, P., & Fernandez, F. (2012). A technique for the otimization of the parameters of technical indicators with Multi-Objective Evolutionary Algorithms. *2012 IEEE Congress on Evolutionary Computation*, 1-8.

Brock, W., Lakonishok, J., & LeBaron, B. (1992). Simple technical trading rules and the stochastic properties of stock returns. *The Journal of Finance*, *47*(5), 1731–1764. doi:10.1111/j.1540-6261.1992.tb04681.x

Chang, Y. H., Jong, C. C., & Wang, S. C. (2017). Size, trading volume, and the profitability of technical trading. *International Journal of Managerial Finance*, 1-38.

Chauvet, M., & Potter, S. (2000). Coincident and leading indicators of the stock market. *Journal of Empirical Finance*, *71*(1), 87–111. doi:10.1016/S0927-5398(99)00015-8

Chong, T. T., & Ng, W. K. (2008). Technical analysis and the London stock exchange: Testing the MACD and RSI rules using the FT30. *Applied Economics Letters*, *15*(14), 1111–1114. doi:10.1080/13504850600993598

Chong, T. T., Ng, W. K., & Liew, V. K. (2014). Revisiting the Performance of MACD and RSI Oscillators. *Journal of Risk and Financial Management*, *7*(1), 1-12.

Cohen, G., & Cabiri, E. (2015). Can technical oscillators outperform the buy and hold strategy? *Applied Economics*, *47*(30), 3189–3197. doi:10.1080/00036846.2015.1013609

Colby, R. W. (2002). *The Encyclopedia of Technical Market Indicators*. McGraw-Hill.

De Long, J. B., Shleifer, A., Summers, L. H., & Waldmann, R. J. (1990). Noise Trader Risk in Financial Markets. *Journal of Political Economy*, *98*(4), 703–738. doi:10.1086/261703

Dryden, M. M. (1970). Filter tests of UK share prices. *Applied Economics*, *1*(4), 261–275. doi:10.1080/00036847000000002

Edwards, R. D., Magee, J., & Bassetti, W. C. (2018). *Technical analysis of stock trends*. CRC press. doi:10.4324/9781315115719

Eiamkanitchat, N., Moontuy, T., & Ramingwong, S. (2017). Fundamental analysis and technical analysis integrated system for stock filtration. *Cluster Computing*, *20*(19), 889–894. doi:10.100710586-016-0694-2

Fama, E. F. (1995). Random walks in stock market prices. *Financial Analysts Journal*, *51*(1), 75–80. doi:10.2469/faj.v51.n1.1861

Fama, E. F., & Blume, M. E. (1966). Filter rules and stock-market trading. *The Journal of Business*, *39*(1), 226–241. doi:10.1086/294849

Fifield, S. G., Power, D. M., & Donald Sinclair, C. (2005). An analysis of trading strategies in eleven European stock markets. *European Journal of Finance*, *11*(6), 531–548. doi:10.1080/1351847042000304099

Gerritsen, D. F., Bouri, E., Ramezanifar, E., & Roubaud, D. (2020). The profitability of technical trading rules in the Bitcoin market. *Finance Research Letters*, *34*, 1–10. doi:10.1016/j.frl.2019.08.011

Gunasekarage, A., & Power, D. M. (2001). The profitability of moving average trading rules in South Asian stock markets. *Emerging Markets Review*, *2*(1), 17–33. doi:10.1016/S1566-0141(00)00017-0

HL. (2019, September 12). *ASML Holding NV (ASML)*. Retrieved from Hargreaves Lansdown: https://www.hl.co.uk/shares/shares-search-results/a/asml-holding-nv-eur0.09/company-information

Hsu, P. H., & Kuan, C. M. (2005). Reexamining the profitability of technical analysis with data snooping checks. *Journal of Financial Econometrics*, *3*(4), 606–628. doi:10.1093/jjfinec/nbi026

Hudson, R., Dempsey, M., & Keasey, K. (1996). A note on the weak form efficiency of capital markets: The application of simple technical trading rules to UK stock prices-1935 to 1994. *Journal of Banking & Finance*, *20*(6), 1121–1132. doi:10.1016/0378-4266(95)00043-7

Internacional Monetary Fund. (2018). *Brighter Prospects*. Optimistic Markets, Challenges Ahead.

Isidore, C. (2018, December 31). *2018 was the worst for stocks in 10 years*. Retrieved from CNN Business: https://edition.cnn.com/2018/12/31/investing/dow-stock-market-today/index.html

Jasic, T., & Wood, D. (2004). The profitability of daily stock market indices trades based on neural network predictions: Case study for the S&P 500, the DAX, the TOPIX and the FTSE in the period 1965–1999. *Applied Financial Economics*, *14*(4), 285–297. doi:10.1080/0960310042000201228

Jiang, F., Tong, G., & Song, G. (2019). Technical analysis profitability without data snooping bias: Evidence from Chinese stock market. *International Review of Finance*, *19*(1), 191–206. doi:10.1111/irfi.12161

Jothimani, D., Shankar, R., & Yadav, S. S. (2015). Discrete Wavelet Transform-Based Prediction of Stock Index: A Study on National Stock Exchange Fifty Index. *Journal of Financial Management and Analysis*, *28*(2), 35–49.

Kwon, K. Y., & Kish, R. J. (2002). Technical trading strategies and return predictability: NYSE. *Applied Financial Economics, 12*(9), 639–653. doi:10.1080/09603100010016139

Lento, C. (2007). Tests of technical trading rules in the Asian-Pacific equity markets: A bootstrap approach. *Academy of Financial and Accounting Studies Journal, 11*(2), 51-73.

Lento, C., Gradojevic, N., & Wright, C. S. (2007). Investment information content in Bollinger Bands? *Applied Financial Economics Letters, 3*(4), 263–267. doi:10.1080/17446540701206576

Lohpetch, D., & Corne, D. (2010). Outperforming Buy-and-Hold with Evolved Technical Trading Rules: Daily, Weekly and Monthly Trading. Applications of Evolutionary Computation, 171-181.

Lui, Y. H., & Mole, D. (1998). The use of fundamental and technical analyses by foreign exchange dealers: Hong Kong evidence. *Journal of International Money and Finance, 17*(3), 535–545. doi:10.1016/S0261-5606(98)00011-4

Lukac, L. P., Brorsen, B. W., & Irwin, S. H. (1988). A test of futures market disequilibrium using twelve different technical trading systems. *Applied Economics, 20*(5), 623–639. doi:10.1080/00036848800000113

Macedo, L. L., Godinho, P., & Alves, M. J. (2017). Mean-semivariance portfolio optimization with multiobjective evolutionary algorithms and technical analysis rules. *Expert Systems with Applications, 79*, 33–43. doi:10.1016/j.eswa.2017.02.033

Markowitz, H. (1952). Portfolio selection. *The Journal of Finance, 7*(1), 77–91.

McKenzie, M. D. (2007). Technical trading rules in emerging markets and the 1997 Asian currency crises. *Emerging Markets Finance & Trade, 43*(4), 46–73. doi:10.2753/REE1540-496X430403

Menkhoff, L. (2010). The use of technical analysis by fund managers: International evidence. *Journal of Banking & Finance, 34*(11), 2573–2586. doi:10.1016/j.jbankfin.2010.04.014

Metghalchi, M., Chang, Y. H., & Marcucci, J. (2008). Is the Swedish stock market efficient? Evidence from some simple trading rules. *International Review of Financial Analysis, 17*(3), 475–490. doi:10.1016/j.irfa.2007.05.001

Metghalchi, M., Chen, C. P., & Hayes, L. A. (2015). History of share prices and market efficiency of the Madrid general stock index. *International Review of Financial Analysis, 40*, 178–184. doi:10.1016/j.irfa.2015.05.016

Mills, T. C. (1997). Technical analysis and the London Stock Exchange: Testing trading rules using the FT30. *Journal of Financial Economics, 2*(4), 319–331.

Murphy, J. J. (1999). *Technical Analysis of the Financial Markets: A comprehensive guide to trading methods and applications*. New York Institute of Finance.

Nazário, R. T., Silva, J. L., Sobreiro, V. A., & Kimura, H. (2017). A literature review of technical analysis on stock markets. *The Quarterly Review of Economics and Finance, 66*, 115–126. doi:10.1016/j.qref.2017.01.014

Neves, E. D., & Costa, N. A. (2017). Investimento racional no PSI20. *European Journal of Applied Business and Management, 3*(2), 69–91.

Ni, H., & Yin, H. (2009). Exchange rate prediction using hybrid neural networks and trading indicators. *Neurocomputing, 72*(13), 2815–2823. doi:10.1016/j.neucom.2008.09.023

Oberlechner, T. (2001). Importance of technical and fundamental analysis in the European foreign exchange market. *International Journal of Finance & Economics, 6*(1), 81–93. doi:10.1002/ijfe.145

Ozturk, M., Toroslu, I. H., & Fidan, G. (2016). Heuristic based trading system on Forex data using technical indicator rules. *Applied Soft Computing, 43*, 170–186. doi:10.1016/j.asoc.2016.01.048

Park, C. H., & Irwin, S. H. (2007). What do we know about the profitability of technical analysis? *Journal of Economic Surveys, 21*(4), 786–826. doi:10.1111/j.1467-6419.2007.00519.x

Pring, M. J. (2002). Technical analysis explained: The successful investor's guide to spotting investment trends and turning points. McGraw-Hill.

Rosillo, R., De la Fuente, D., & Brugos, J. A. (2013). Technical analysis and the Spanish stock exchange: Testing the RSI, MACD, momentum and stochastic rules using Spanish market companies. *Applied Economics, 45*(12), 1451–1550. doi:10.1080/00036846.2011.631894

Safran. (2019). *Safran Group*. Retrieved from Safran: https://www.safran-group.com/group-0#1

Schwager, J. D. (1984). A complete guide to the futures markets: fundamental analysis, technical analysis, trading, spreads, and options. John Wiley & Sons.

Wilder, W. (1978). *New Concepts in Technical Trading Systems*. Trend Research.

Wong, W. K., Manzur, M., & Chew, B. K. (2013). How rewarding is technical analysis? Evidence from Singapore stock market. *Applied Financial Economics, 13*(7), 543–551. doi:10.1080/0960310022000020906

Yamani, E. (2020). Can technical trading beat the foreign exchange market in times of crisis? *Global Finance Journal, 100550*, 1–17.

Yu, X., Chen, Z., Xu, W., & Fu, J. (2017). Forecasting bull and bear markets: Evidence from China. *Emerging Markets Finance & Trade, 53*(8), 1720–1733. doi:10.1080/1540496X.2016.1184141

ENDNOTES

[1] Not to be confused with Relative Strength, which compares the performance between assets.
[2] https://www.investing.com/indices/eu-stoxx50-chart, consulted on September 14, 2019.
[3] https://www.investing.com/indices/eu-stoxx50-chart, consulted on September 14, 2019.
[4] The buy signal is triggered when RSI crosses the centre line from below, while the sell signal is obtained when RSI crosses the centre line from above. This trading rule is denoted as RSI(N,50). he number of days to consider when calculating the indicator is 21.
[5] MACD is calculated with a 16-day and a 26-day EMA.
[6] This date was chosen because Prime Minister Theresa May invoked Article 50 of the Treaty of Lisbon, initiating the UK's formal withdrawal from the European Union.
[7] This value was chosen by analysing banks and brokerage firms operating in Portugal. It is an average of commissions charged in the country for the markets in question.
[8] (Isidore, 2018), consulted on September 10, 2019.

Chapter 18
Hedging Effectiveness of the VIX ETPs:
An Analysis of the Time-Varying Performance of the VXX

Özcan Ceylan
https://orcid.org/0000-0003-2924-2903
Özyeğin University, Turkey

ABSTRACT

This study introduces basic concepts about hedging and provides an overview of common hedging practices. This theoretical introduction is followed by an empirical application in which the hedging effectiveness of the VIX ETPs is evaluated. The iPath Series B S&P 500 VIX Short Term Futures ETN (VXX) and the SPDR S&P 500 Trust ETF (SPY) are taken for the empirical application. Dynamic conditional correlations between the VXX and SPY are obtained from DCC-GARCH framework. Based on the estimated conditional volatilities of the SPY and the hedged portfolio, a hedging effectiveness index is constructed. Results show that the hedging effectiveness of the VXX increases in turbulent periods such as the last three months of 2018 marked by the plummeting oil prices, increasing uncertainties about the Brexit deal, and rising federal funds rates and the month of March 2020 when the COVID-19 pandemic became a global concern.

INTRODUCTION

Investors need to secure their holdings against adverse price movements in financial markets. Hedging is a common practice followed by informed investors to reduce their exposure to risk. Options and futures are widely used to hedge against the variability in their underlying asset returns. Futures have very high positive correlation with underlying assets. In this case, hedging strategy consists of taking opposite positions, i.e., going long in futures and short in the underlying or vice versa. This strategy may provide a nearly perfect hedge, but that does not come without a cost: the hedged portfolio would

DOI: 10.4018/978-1-7998-8609-9.ch018

generate considerably lower returns. It may be desirable for investors to set a lower target hedging level to earn higher portfolio returns. Alternatively, commodities like gold and silver are also used for hedging and diversifying equity portfolios provided that these commodities are weakly correlated with equities.

Since the Long Term Capital Management hedge fund collapse in 1998, financial instabilities have become a growing concern for investors as the financial markets have frequently gone through several crises. The global financial crisis in 2008 (GFC) and the recent global pandemic of Covid-19 have been the most devastating ones, and compared to the GFC the latter had more severe impacts on the financial markets (Sharif et al., 2020). In March 2020, large and sudden drops in the U.S. stock and futures markets triggered circuit breaker mechanism four times in ten days, while trading was never halted during the GFC (Zhang et al., 2020). Although during both crises the volatility spiked to similar extremely high levels, the crisis evolved much faster in 2020 (Löwen et al., 2021). This fact is also reflected by significantly higher volatility of volatility levels observed during the Covid-19 pandemic (Brenner and Izhakian, 2021). In such turbulent periods, investors need to reconsider the effectiveness of hedging instruments. It is now well known that correlations between different asset classes tend to increase during financial crises. During the GFC, significant increases in correlations between stocks, bonds and commodities cast doubt on standard risk management practices (Szado, 2009). In high volatility periods, spot-futures relationship may also be weakened leading to a deterioration in hedging effectiveness of futures (Ait-Sahalia and Xiu, 2016).

Baur and Lucey (2010) distinguished diversifier, hedge, and safe haven properties of assets. A diversifier has a weakly positive correlation with other assets. To be classified as a hedge, an asset should be uncorrelated or negatively correlated with a portfolio on average. Given that the correlations between assets are time-varying, a hedge may also have positive correlations with other assets during a subperiod of an investment horizon. Thus, a hedge is not necessarily effective during periods of market stress. A safe haven is an asset that has negative correlations with a portfolio in times of market turmoil. During financial crises, investors realize that a hedging instrument should have safe haven properties to offset extreme losses in their portfolios (Hasan et al., 2021). Gold, for instance, is conventionally considered a safe heaven. Areal et al. (2015) and Beckmann et al. (2015) showed that gold was an effective hedge for equities during the GFC. On the other hand, Lucey and Li (2015) found that gold acts as safe haven against U.S. equity with a significant lag after the GFC, in the last quarter of 2009. Moreover, important proportions of funds need to be allocated to gold to construct optimally hedged portfolios of stocks (Shrydeh et al., 2019). Several studies argued that gold is likely to lose its safe haven property in the post-GFC period (Baur and Glover, 2012; Bekiros et al., 2017; Klein, 2017). Safe haven property of gold remained disputable also in the Covid-19 period. While Ji et. al. (2020) and Salisu et al. (2021) asserted that gold is a safe haven in that period, Cheema et al. (2020) and Akhtaruzzaman et al. (2021) showed that it has lost this property by March 2020. Tanin et. al. (2021) found that when the Covid-19 pandemics unfolded, sharp increases in volatilities considerably repressed gold prices inhibiting its appeal as a safe haven in the short run. Several unconventional assets such as green bonds (Haq et al., 2021) and soybean futures (Ji et al., 2020) are also proposed as alternative hedges for the Covid-19 era. Cryptocurrencies were considered a valuable hedge against stock markets due to their low correlation with traditional assets classes in the pre-Covid 19 period (Baur et al., 2018). Chemkha et al. (2021) found that this property does not hold anymore during the Covid-19 pandemic. Conlon and McGee (2020) found that Bitcoin is not a safe haven against the S&P500, as both decrease in value during the bear market in 2020. Thus, in this highly instable and fragile conjuncture, finding an efficient hedge with safe haven property remains a crucial question that still needs a prompt answer.

During the last decades, volatility indexes have increasingly attracted attention in the practitioner and academic literature. The VIX, the first variance index developed by CBOE, has led to various alternative financial derivatives that can be conveniently used for hedging. The VIX index is constructed based on the S&P 500 index (SPX) options. As a measure of implied volatility, the VIX provides information not only on the expected market volatility but also on investor sentiment. The VIX exhibits strong negative correlation with the SPX and that negative correlation becomes even stronger during market turmoil. Hood and Malik (2013) suggested that the VIX is a safe haven and a better hedge than gold for the U.S. stock market. However, the VIX itself is not a tradable asset. Instead, investors trade the VIX options and futures for hedging and speculation. More recently, the VIX exchange traded products (ETPs) are introduced as new financial instruments that replicate the futures indices on the VIX. The VIX ETPs have gained fast increasing popularity among investors.

Surprisingly, there is a limited amount of research conducted on the behavior of VIX-related instruments in the Covid-19 period. Ahmed et al. (2021) showed that the Covid-19 pandemics has strengthened the spillover effect of the U.S. stocks on the VIX. Although, as stated before, the VIX is not a tradable asset, this finding has important implications on the hedging ability of VIX related instruments. Shahzad et al. (2021) found that the VIX futures are effective hedges for several countries during the Covid-19 outbreak. Tarchella and Dhaoui (2021) argue that VIX has important diversification benefits for Shanghai stock market in this period. To the best of my knowledge, there is no work that studies the hedging effectiveness of VIX-related financial instruments during the Covid-19 pandemics. The present book chapter addresses this significant gap in the literature.

This study introduces basic concepts about hedging and provides an overview of common hedging practices with a focus on volatility hedging. This theoretical introduction is followed by an empirical application in which the hedging effectiveness of the VIX ETPs is evaluated. The iPath Series B S&P 500 VIX Short Term Futures ETN (VXX), one of the most liquid volatility ETPs, and the SPDR S&P 500 Trust ETF (SPY), one of the most popular exchange traded funds that tracks the SPX are taken for the empirical application. Daily data cover the last three years from March 2018 through March 2021. Dynamic conditional correlations between VXX and SPY are obtained from DCC-GARCH framework proposed by Engle (2002). The estimated conditional correlations are negative throughout the sample signaling that the VXX may be an efficient hedge and a safe haven against the SPY. The corresponding optimal hedge ratios are computed as in Baillie and Myers (1991) and Kroner and Sultan (1993). Based on the estimated conditional volatilities of the SPY and the hedged portfolio, a hedging effectiveness index is constructed following Ku et al. (2007) and Chang et al. (2011). Results show that the hedging effectiveness of the VXX increases in turbulent periods such as the last three months of 2018 marked by the plummeting oil prices, increasing uncertainties about the Brexit deal, and rising federal funds rates; and the month of March 2020 when the Covid-19 pandemic became a global concern.

The remainder of the chapter is organized as follows: First, basic characteristics of conventional hedging instruments and common hedging strategies involving these financial derivatives are summarized. This part also includes an overview of more recent financial instruments that are mainly used for hedging volatility risk. The empirical application part that evaluates the effectiveness of these volatility hedging instruments presents the data, explains the empirical methodology, and discusses the results.

HEDGING STRATEGIES AND INSTRUMENTS

Investors may undertake various hedging strategies to manage price and volatility risks associated with their assets. Derivatives are often used for hedging purposes. The most popular derivatives are Options, Forwards, Futures and Swaps. These are financial contracts with a value that varies conditionally on the changes in the underlying reference prices. The underlying may be an asset like commodities, precious metals, stocks and bonds, or merely a measure such as stock market indexes, interest rates and exchange rates. In this study, only two of these basic derivatives, options and futures will be covered in order to explain several hedging practices commonly employed by investors. Then, new generation hedging instruments that are primarily designed for volatility hedging, volatility options, volatility futures, and volatility ETPs will be presented.

Hedging Using Options

Options are derivative instruments where the holder has the right, but not the obligation to buy or sell the underlying. The date and the price at which the transaction may be exercised are specified in the option contract. This specified date is known as the expiration date, and the exercise price is called the strike price. American options may be exercised at any time till it matures, while the holder of a European option would have to wait until the expiration date. As American options offer more flexibility for their holders, investors have to pay a higher premium to buy this type of options.

A call (put) option provides its holder the right to buy (sell) the underlying at the specified strike price. A call (put) option is in-the-money when the strike price is lower (higher) than the underlying price. Exercising an option would only be beneficial when it is in-the-money. Following a very straightforward hedging strategy, an investor who has a long (short) position in the underlying may buy a put (call) option. The investor would exercise the put (call) option if the price of the underlying goes below (above) the strike price to limit the loss.

More complex hedging strategies may also be undertaken by using a combination of call and put options. A straddle consists of a long position in one call and one put options with the same strike price and expiration date. The options should be at-the-money, meaning that the strike price of the options should be the same as or very close to the price of the underlying security. The straddle strategy would be appropriate when the investor expects a significant move in the underlying price but is not sure about the direction of the move. Straddles provide the investor with a protection or even a profit opportunity in volatile periods such as the ones that are often observed around earnings announcements. If the underlying price ends up being close to the strike price by the expiration date, the straddle leads to a loss due to premiums paid to buy the options. If the underlying price moves up (down) significantly, the gains from exercising the call (put) option would be enough to offset the trading costs and result in profits for the investor. A strangle is a slightly different version of a straddle. Here again, the investor buys one call and one put with the same expiration date, but with different strike prices. In a strangle, both the call and put options are out-of-the-money (the strike price of the call (put) option is higher (lower) than the current price of the underlying security). Thus, the investor pays a lower premium to buy these options. However, there has to be a bigger rise (fall) in the underlying price for the call (put) option to be exercised and hence for the strangle to generate profits.

Alternative strategies using different combinations of options may also be appropriate if the investor has an expectation about the direction of the change in the underlying price. A strip is constructed buying one at-the-money call option and two at-the-money put options. The strip generates profits when the underlying price moves significantly in either direction, but the payoff would be even higher when the price of the underlying security moves downwards. As opposed to a strip, a strap strategy would be followed when the investor expects that a significant upward move in the underlying price is more likely. To construct a strap, the investor buys one at-the-money put option and two at-the-money call options. The value of the strap increases much more in case of a sharp rise in the underlying price.

Hedging Using Futures

Futures contracts are standardized agreements to buy or sell an underlying asset at a predetermined price on a specified period in the future. This predetermined price is called the futures price; the specified trading period is called the delivery period; and the price of the underlying asset is called the spot price. An investor who agrees to buy (sell) the underlying asset is said to have a long (short) position in futures. By the delivery period, the investor with the short position must provide the underlying asset to the investor with the long position.

Theoretically, the futures price should be equal to the spot price by the delivery period. However, futures are generally used for hedging, and investors usually close out their positions by taking an offsetting position prior to the delivery period. This may result in a difference between the spot price and the futures price. This difference is called the basis. Occasionally, the asset to be hedged may be different from the underlying asset. That will be the case in the empirical application where the theoretical investor's positon in a stock market index tracking ETF is hedged by using an ETN which is assumed to track volatility index futures. Such cases where the underlying asset and the asset to be hedged are not the same are called cross hedging. Obviously, cross hedging is also a source of basis risk. If there were no basis, the hedging strategy with futures would be straightforward: a long (short) position in futures and a short (long) position in the underlying would lead to a perfect hedge that completely eliminates the risk. In a perfect hedge, the hedging ratio, the ratio of the size of the futures position to the size of the positon in the underlying would be 1. However, when there is a basis risk this hedge ratio would no longer be effective. In that case, the investor should find the optimal hedge ratio that would minimize her overall exposure to risk.

Johnson (1960) and Stein (1961) are the first to propose an approach to compute the optimal hedge ratio in the presence of basis risk. The optimal hedge ratio is defined as the one that minimizes the variance of the hedged portfolio. Assuming a long position in the underlying, and a short position in the futures, the return on the optimally hedged portfolio, R_H is given as follows:

$$R_H = R_U - hR_F$$

where R_U is the return on the underlying, R_F is the return on the futures, and h is the optimal hedge ratio. The variance of the hedged portfolio, σ_H^2 would then be:

$$\sigma_H^2 = \sigma_U^2 + h^2 \sigma_F^2 - 2h\sigma_U \sigma_F \rho_{UF}$$

where σ_U^2 is the variance of the spot returns, σ_F^2 is the variance of the futures returns, and ρU_F is the correlation coefficient between the spot and futures returns. The optimal hedge ratio is the one that minimizes the variance of the hedged portfolio. Thus, the optimal hedge ratio may be derived as follows:

$$h = \rho_{UF} \frac{\sigma_U}{\sigma_F}.$$

From this expression, it may easily be discerned that the optimal hedge ratio may be estimated by regressing spot returns against futures returns. Ederington (1979) and Hill and Schneeweis (1981) use ordinary least squares (OLS) regression to estimate the optimal hedge ratio. The problem with this method is that it assumes that variances of return series are constant over time (Park and Bera (1987)). Since Mandelbrot (1963) time-varying volatilities and volatility clustering have been well-known stylized facts concerning financial security returns. These stylized facts are handled by rapidly proliferated conditional heteroscedastic models that were first developed by Engle (1982) and Bollerslev (1986). Following these lines, Baillie and Myers (1991), and Kroner and Sultan (1991; 1993) propose time-varying optimal hedge ratios accounting for the dynamic nature of the joint distribution of spot and futures returns.

Different versions of GARCH models are employed to estimate conditional variances that are used to compute time-varying hedge ratios. Park and Switzer (1995) and Lien et al. (2002) estimated dynamic hedge ratios using Constant Conditional Correlation (CCC) GARCH model developed by Bollerslev (1990). Tse and Tsui (2002) revealed evidence that correlations between financial securities' returns are also time-varying even after taking heteroscedasticity into account. Dynamic Conditional Correlations (DCC) GARCH model developed by Engle (2002) incorporates this feature. Chang et al. (2011) and Sadorsky (2014) compared different GARCH-based dynamic hedging strategies and concluded that DCC-GARCH specification leads to better hedging performance. In this study, the DCC-GARCH model will be adopted to estimate the optimal hedging ratios, thus, this model will be presented in detail in the empirical application.

Volatility Hedging Instruments

The above cited standard financial derivatives are mainly designed for hedging price risk. It is well known that financial asset returns are negatively skewed and leptokurtic. The reason behind these statistical properties is that financial markets often go through uncertain and distressed periods including globally devastating events such as the Long Term Capital Management collapse, the East Asian financial crisis, Lehman Brothers bankruptcy, the European sovereign debt crisis and the Covid-19 pandemic. These periods are marked by excessively low returns and sharp rises in volatility. These catastrophic events raised the need for new hedging instruments that are sensitive to changes in volatility.

Theoretical infrastructure of volatility derivatives is started to be established by late 1980s. Brenner and Galai (1989) proposed to develop a volatility index and designing options and futures written on this index. Whaley (1993) developed the first Market Volatility Index (the VIX) for the Chicago Board of Options Exchange (CBOE) based on the implied volatilities of at-the-money options on the S&P 100 Index. Brenner and Galai (1993) and Grünbichler & Longstaff (1996) developed the first valuation models for volatility options and futures. In 2003, CBOE renewed the VIX methodology. The new VIX is based on the SPX and on a wider range of strike prices: the new values are computed by using a weighted average of out-of-the-money put and call prices. As such, the VIX has become a better representation of the market's expectation of volatility.

Volatility derivatives such as volatility swaps have already been traded over the counter since the mid-1990s, but volatility trading had drastic changes by the mid-2000s. In 2004, CBOE introduced the VIX futures to be traded on its newly founded futures exchange. The following year, Eurex introduced the volatility futures written on the VSTOXX, the VDAX, and the VSMI in the European markets. These volatility futures have reached very high levels of trading volumes. Upon this success of the volatility futures, CBOE launched the VIX options in 2006. In 2014, CBOE renewed again the VIX methodology by including the SPX weekly options in the computation of the VIX. In this way, it has been possible for the expectation horizon of the VIX index to match exactly 30 days.

The settlement values for VIX derivatives are computed through a Special Opening Quotation (SOQ) of the VIX. The SOQ for the VIX options is calculated on the morning of their expiration date. The SOQ for the VIX options is calculated from the sequence of opening prices of the SPX options on the settlement date, and these settlement values are periodically published by the CBOE under the VRO ticker. A VIX call (put) is in-the-money when the option's strike price is lower (higher) than the VRO quotation on the expiration date. An investor with a long position in the SPX may hedge its exposure to volatility risk by buying VIX calls. Compared to SPX put options, VIX calls may be better hedging instruments against large downward moves in the SPX as there is a strong negative correlation between the VIX and SPX. Likewise, a long position in the SPX may be hedged by taking a long position in VIX futures.

An alternative group of financial instruments that may be used for hedging include the ETPs. ETPs track the performance of the underlying asset or index. This may be done by either investing in derivatives or by directly holding the underlying itself. ETPs provide investors with an easier access to different indexes or financial instruments at a lower cost. ETPs include exchange traded funds (ETFs), exchange traded vehicles (ETVs), and exchange traded notes (ETNs). Index-tracking ETFs aim to replicate the performance of the underlying by directly holding the index components with their appropriate weights. It may be too costly for the fund to rebalance these weights frequently. This may prevent an ETF from perfectly mimicking the underlying index and thus leads to a tracking error. ETNs do not have any tracking error as they simply do not track the underlying asset or index. ETNs just pay its holders the exact amount of return generated by the underlying. On the other hand, ETNs are riskier than the ETFs in terms of liquidity: trading volumes of ETNs are generally much lower compared to those of ETFs, and bid-ask spreads may be very wide for ETNs. A more important problem with the ETNs concerns the credit risk. ETNs are unsecured debt instruments that are issued by large banks and financial institutions. In case of a bankruptcy, ETN holders may lose all of their investments while ETF holders continue to own the underlying assets.

Volatility-related ETNs provide exposure to market volatility. The first volatility ETNs were introduced by Barclays Bank in 2009. These ETNs were linked to the U.S. market volatility measured by the VIX. VIX ETNs have been very popular especially among retail investors who usually do not have enough capacity to trade volatility derivatives. This rising popularity led to introduction of many other volatility ETNs major financial markets. Volatility ETNs do not replicate the volatility index itself. They rather track the performance of the relevant index of futures written on the corresponding volatility index. Standard volatility ETNs are appropriate instruments for hedging volatility. They track the underlying volatility futures returns directly and proportionately. Non-standard volatility ETNs include inverse and leveraged ETNs that are traded mainly for speculation. Returns on an inverse ETN move in the opposite direction of the underlying futures returns. Leveraged volatility ETNs provide amplified exposure to market volatility through generating magnified returns based on the underlying.

EMPIRICAL APPLICATION

For the empirical application, an investor with a long position in the SPY will be assumed to hedge her exposure by taking a long position in the VXX. The optimal hedge ratios will be updated daily so as to have the minimum portfolio variance. A hedging effectiveness index will then be constructed to analyze the variations in the hedging performance for the hedged portfolio. Optimal hedge ratios and the corresponding hedging performance vary because of the time-varying variance-covariance matrix of the SPY and VXX. In the empirical application this time-varying variance-covariance structure is assessed through DCC-GARCH framework. This framework will be presented in detail after describing the data used for the empirical application.

Data

The empirical study is based on daily returns of the SPY and VXX for a period of three years spanning from March 2018 through March 2021. Data is downloaded from Yahoo Finance. SPY is the first U.S. listed ETF introduced in 1993. It is one of the most liquid ETFs in the world and tracks the S&P 500 index. Similarly, the VXX is the first and the most heavily traded volatility ETN. It is introduced in 2009.

Figure 1 shows the time series-plots of the VXX and SPY for the sample period. It may be remarked that large drops in the SPY coincide with sharp increases in the VXX and that upward trends in the SPY correspond to downward trends in the VXX. There is a strong negative correlation between these two series with an unconditional correlation coefficient of -0.76.

Figure 1. Time-series plots of the VXX (solid line, left axis) and the SPY (dotted line, right axis).

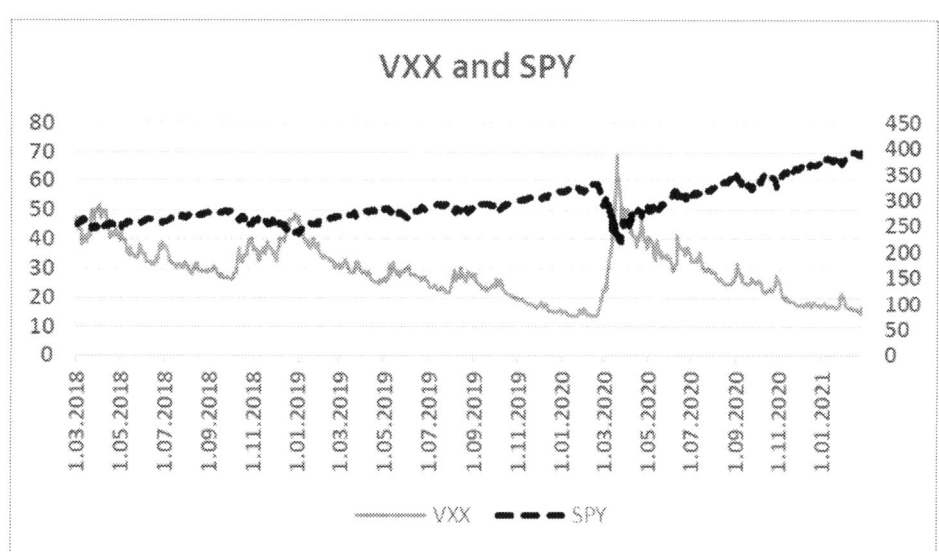

Descriptive statistics for the VXX and SPY are provided in Table 1 below. ΔVXX and ΔSPY stand for the percentage log-returns of the VXX and SPY respectively. From the table, it may be seen that the VXX returns are more volatile. As expected, the VXX is much more sensitive to events that lead to market distress. In line with the stylized facts about the financial return distributions, ΔSPY has a left skew and an excess kurtosis. Not surprisingly, ΔVXX has a right skew: returns from the VXX increases as the market volatility rises.

Table 1. Descriptive statistics for the VXX, the SPY, and their percentage log-returns.

	Min	Q1	Median	Q3	Max	Mean	Standard Deviation	Skewness	Excess Kurtosis
VXX	13.29	22.59	28.64	35.12	69.00	29.10	9.37	0.47	0.13
SPY	220.15	264.81	282.86	317.67	392.64	293.63	37.47	0.84	-0.07
ΔVXX	-16.91	-2.85	-0.81	1.53	31.52	-0.14	4.76	1.60	6.05
ΔSPY	-11.59	-0.38	0.11	0.68	8.67	0.05	1.44	-1.00	14.61

Empirical Methodology

As mentioned earlier, this study uses DCC-GARCH model to estimate conditional volatilities and conditional correlations. These are estimated through a two-step process. First, the GARCH parameters are estimated, and then conditional correlations are measured through decomposing the conditional covariance matrix obtained from this multivariate GARCH model.

In this empirical study, there are two return series to be modeled. Thus, in the conditional mean equation of the bivariate GARCH model, the vector containing the bivariate asset return series (Y_t) should be modeled first. A very general representation for the conditional mean equation may be given as follows:

$$Y_t \mid \Gamma_{t-1} = \epsilon_t \sim MD(0, H_t)$$

where ϵ_t is a vector of innovations following a multivariate density function MD with mean zero and a dynamic conditional covariance matrix, H_t. Γ_t denotes the information set to time t. Y_t should be modeled based on Γ_{t-1} for the innovations to have no serial correlation. For instance, autoregressive and moving average components may be added into the conditional mean equation.

In the DCC-GARCH framework, the conditional covariance matrix of returns is decomposed into the product of dynamic conditional standard deviations and dynamic conditional correlations:

$$H_t = D_t R_t D_t$$

where R_t is the time-varying correlation matrix and D_t is a diagonal matrix of conditional standard deviations, $\sigma_{1,t}, \sigma_{2,t}$. each following a univariate GARCH(r,s) process:

$$\sigma_t^2 = \omega + \sum_{k=1}^{r} \alpha_k \epsilon_{t-k}^2 + \sum_{l=1}^{s} \beta_l \sigma_{t-l}^2$$

where ω is the constant, α and β are the ARCH and GARCH coefficients, respectively.

In the Constant Conditional Correlation (CCC) GARCH Model of Bollerslev (1990), the variance-covariance matrix above was assumed to be time-invariant. Engle (2002) used a GARCH-type specification to model the variations in conditional correlations. For a DCC(m,n) model, the evolution of conditional correlations is specified as follows:

$$Q_t = (1 - \sum_{i=1}^{m} \tau_i - \sum_{j=1}^{n} \zeta_j) R + \sum_{i=1}^{m} \tau_i \eta_{t-1} \eta_{t-1}^T + \sum_{j=1}^{n} \zeta_j Q_{t-1}$$

where R is the unconditional covariance matrix of the standardized residuals (which is equivalent of the unconditional correlation matrix of returns), η is the vector of standardized residuals, τ and ζ are non-negative parameters of interest that determine the variations in conditional correlations. The corresponding dynamic conditional correlation matrix is then computed through the following standardization:

$$R_t = diag\{Q_t\}^{-0.5} Q_t diag\{Q_t\}^{-0.5}$$

The optimal hedge ratio should be redefined accordingly by using the conditional correlations and volatilities estimated by the empirical model. An important point to note here is that, in this empirical study, as there is a negative correlation between the hedged asset and the hedging instrument, the investor would take a long position in both. Thus, the formula for variance of the hedged portfolio, σ_H^2, should be modified as follows:

$$\sigma_H^2 = Var(r_{SPY} + h r_{VXX}) = \sigma_{SPY}^2 + h^2 \sigma_{VXX}^2 + 2h \sigma_{SPY} \sigma_{VXX} \rho_{VXX-SPY}.$$

where r_{SPY} and r_{VXX} are the returns on the hedged asset and hedging instrument, and ρV_{XX-SPY} is the correlation coefficient between these returns. Time-varying version of the corresponding optimal hedge ratio would then be:

$$h_t = -\rho_{VXX-SPY,t} \frac{\sigma_{SPY,t}}{\sigma_{VXX,t}}$$

The objective of the empirical study is to measure the hedging performance of the VXX. The most commonly used criterion for evaluating the performance of a hedging instrument is the hedging effectiveness measure developed by Ederington (1979). Hedging effectiveness (*HE*) measure is simply the percentage reduction in the variance of the hedged portfolio compared to the variance of the unhedged portfolio.

$$HE = \frac{\sigma^2_{unhedged} - \sigma^2_{hedged}}{\sigma^2_{unhedged}}$$

Ku et al. (2007) and Chang et al. (2011) employed conditional versions of this hedging effectiveness measure. Along the same lines, this study computes the time-varying hedging effectiveness measure as follows:

$$HE_t = \frac{\sigma^2_{SPY,t} - \sigma^2_{H,t}}{\sigma^2_{SPY,t}}$$

Empirical Results

Before carrying out the DCC-GARCH estimation, several preliminary tests are performed on the log-returns data. Data series are first tested for unit-root and stationarity. For both data series, Augmented Dickey-Fuller test results reject the null hypothesis of presence of a unit-root with p-values lower than 0.01. As a cross-check, Kwiatkowski-Phillips-Schmidt-Shin (KPSS) test is also performed on the data. KPSS test results do not reject the null hypothesis of stationarity at any reasonable significance level. Some multivariate ARCH tests (LM test, Rank-based test, Robust test) are also conducted on the log-returns data to check for conditional heteroscedasticity. They all reject the null hypothesis of homoscedasticity at the 1% significance level.

DCC-GARCH estimation results are presented in Table 2. A DCC(1,1)-GARCH(1,1) model is specified based on the BIC and statistical significance of model coefficients. As the return series exhibit heavy tails, the DCC model, where the residuals are assumed to follow a multivariate Laplace distribution, gives the best results. The standardized residuals and the squared standardized residuals of the estimated model are checked for heteroscedasticity by using Hosking's multivariate portmanteau test. Results show that the conditional mean and variance equations are appropriately specified as the null hypothesis of presence of any heteroscedasticity problem is strongly rejected.

Table 2. DCC estimation results

Parameter	Estimate	Standard Error	t-value	Pr(>|t|)
μV_{XX}	-0.3420	0.1384	-2.4704	0.013495
ωV_{XX}	3.2768	0.8891	3.6855	0.000228
αV_{XX}	0.2613	0.0792	3.2981	0.000973
βV_{XX}	0.6148	0.0595	10.3249	0.000000
μS_{PY}	0.1185	0.0274	4.3173	0.000016
$AR(1)_{SPY}$	-0.1001	0.0425	-2.3565	0.018448
ωS_{PY}	0.0464	0.0171	2.7090	0.006748
αS_{PY}	0.2695	0.0630	4.2748	0.000019
βS_{PY}	0.7295	0.0413	17.6677	0.000000
τ	0.0754	0.0186	4.0434	0.000053
ζ	0.8188	0.0411	19.9068	0.000000
Log-likelihood	-2726.43			

All parameters are strongly significant. τ and ζ are the DCC parameters that govern the variations in conditional correlations. Conditional correlations between the log returns of VXX and SPY are depicted in Figure 2. Conditional correlations have a mean of -0.81 which is fairly close to the level of the unconditional correlation. Conditional correlations vary within a range between -0.95 and -0.39.

Figure 2. Estimated dynamic conditional correlations between the VXX and the SPY.

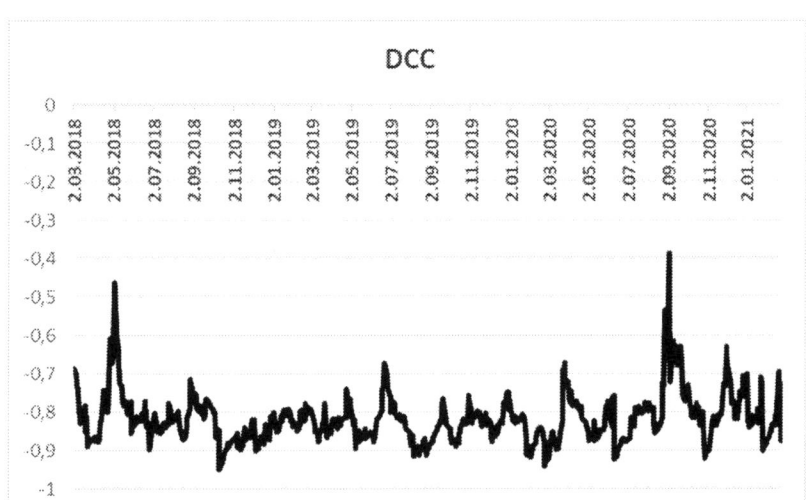

Based on the estimated conditional correlations and conditional volatilities of the VXX and SPY, time-varying optimal hedge ratios are computed. Figure 3 shows how the optimal hedge ratios vary through the estimation period. The average hedge ratio is 0.2 and the ratios range from 0.07 to 0.6. It is worth to note that the weight of the VXX in the hedged portfolio increases generally in periods of high market volatility.

Figure 3. Time-varying optimal hedge ratios

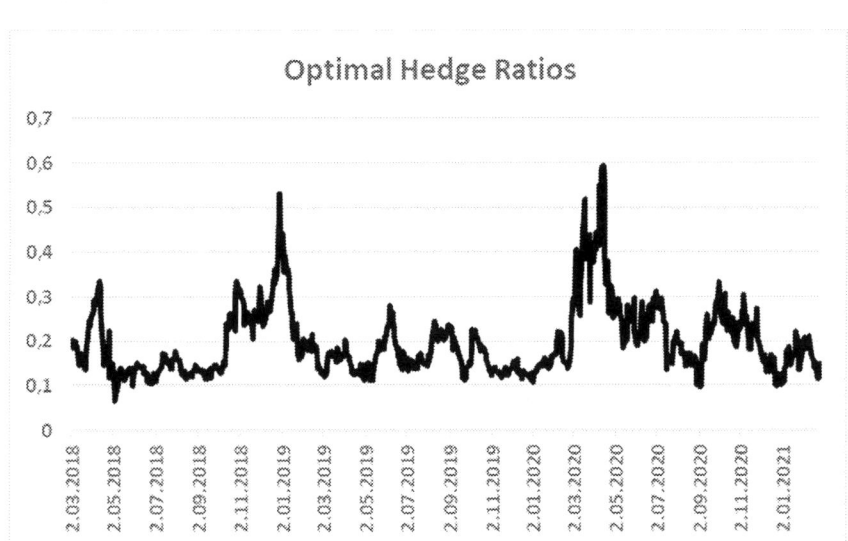

By using the optimal hedge ratios, conditional variances are computed for the hedged portfolio. Finally, the hedging effectiveness index is constructed through comparing the variances of the hedged portfolio and SPY. The hedging effectiveness index of the VXX is depicted in Figure 4. The average hedging effectiveness is 0.67, and its standard deviation is 0.105. In spite of this low standard deviation, the range is relatively wide: hedging effectiveness levels range between 0.12 and 0.91. Apparently, this is due to large and sudden drops in hedging effectiveness that occurred in the beginning of May 2018 and the beginning of September 2020. From Figure 2, it may be seen that these dates also correspond to sharp rises in the estimated conditional correlations between the VXX and SPY. Apart from these short-lived drops in the hedging effectiveness, the VXX performed fairly well, and its hedging effectiveness increased especially in turbulent periods. The first significant increase in the hedging effectiveness had been on March 23, 2018, the day after the U.S. imposed very heavy tariffs on Chinese goods and thus triggered fears of a trade war. On that date the hedging effectiveness had increased to 0.8 and remained above 0.76 through the following two weeks. The VXX had proved its worth in the last three months of 2018. This was a period with high uncertainties marked by the plummeting oil prices, increasing uncertainties about the Brexit deal, and rising federal funds rates. The average hedging effectiveness in this period had been 0.76. The hedging effectiveness had reached its maximum within that period, on October 11, 2018 and remained very high till mid-November with an average of 0.8. The average hedging effectiveness index had seen the same level in August 2019. This month had started with the U.S. President Trump's announcement on placing extra tariffs on Chinese goods. Combined with negative developments in the bond market that were pointing toward a recession, the escalating political tensions in U.S.-China trade relations had led to a highly volatile month for the U.S. financial markets. 2020 had been a very tough year for the financial markets. The damage due to the Covid-19 pandemic was comparable to that of the global financial crisis in 2008. It has been revealed that in such periods investors become more sensitive to bad news and that this attitude magnifies the instability in the financial markets (Ceylan, 2014). Accordingly, in this long period of increased uncertainty, the hedging effectiveness had risen to high levels more frequently. The hedging effectiveness index had risen to 0.9 on February 25, 2020. From that date through mid-March the average value of the index had been 0.81. The index had seen above the 0.85 level in mid-June and at the end of October 2020.

Figure 4. Hedging effectiveness of the VXX

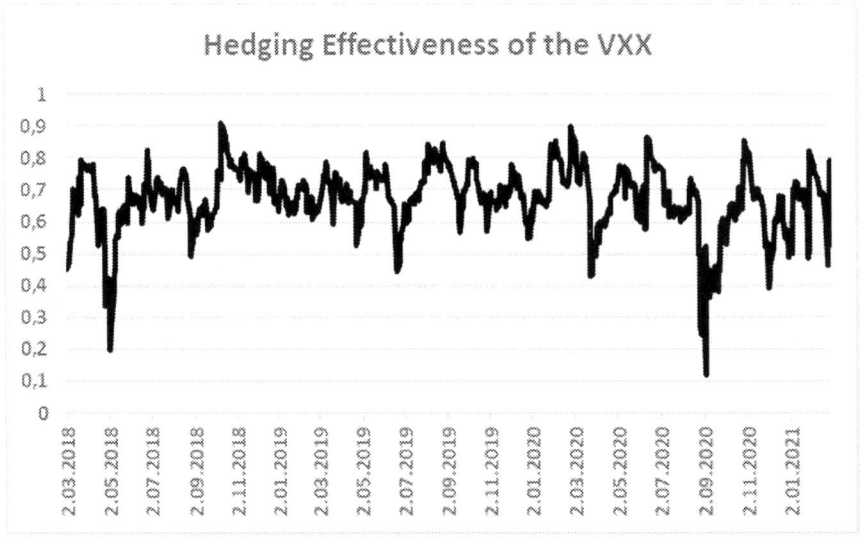

CONCLUSION

This chapter investigated the time-varying hedging effectiveness of the VXX from March 2018 through March 2021. A DCC-GARCH model is used to estimate conditional correlations between the VXX and SPY. Conditional correlations are found to be negative throughout the estimation period signaling that the VXX may be an effective hedge with a strong safe haven property against the U.S. equities. Based on these conditional correlations, optimal hedge ratios are computed, and a hedging effectiveness index is constructed for the VXX. Results show that the average hedging effectiveness of the VXX is 0.7. The hedging effectiveness increases above the level of 0.8 in turbulent periods such as the last three months of 2018 marked by the plummeting oil prices, increasing uncertainties about the Brexit deal, and rising federal funds rates; and the month of August 2019 when the escalating trade war between the U.S. and China had become a major concern. Increases in the hedging effectiveness are observed more frequently after February 2020 as the financial markets have become more vulnerable due to the Covid-19 pandemic.

Unlike the conventional hedging instruments such as options and futures, volatility hedging instruments are especially sensitive to changes in volatility. Thus, the hedging effectiveness of the VXX would be lower in relatively calm periods with low levels of volatility. On the other hand, an investor should keep in mind that major events that trigger an increase in volatilities such as bankruptcies or wars are highly unpredictable, and that hedging is all about buying protection against the unexpected. The onset of Covid-19 pandemic was also very unpredictable and the crisis unfolded much faster than any other financial crisis. Moreover, this unprecedented impact of pandemics rendered the financial markets highly fragile and sensitive to bad news. This "new normal" is likely to persist for a while, and in this period the unexpected should always be expected. In such circumstances, the VIX ETPs should be considered effective hedges and safe havens that would shelter investors from downside risks.

REFERENCES

Ahmad, W., Hernandez, J. A., Saini, S., & Mishra, R. K. (2021). The US equity sectors, implied volatilities, and COVID-19: What does the spillover analysis reveal? *Resources Policy, 72*, 102102.

Ait-Sahalia, Y., & Xiu, D. (2016). Increased correlation among asset classes: Are volatility or jumps to blame, or both? *Journal of Econometrics, 194*(2), 205–219.

Akhtaruzzaman, M., Boubaker, S., Lucey, B. M., & Sensoy, A. (2021). Is gold a hedge or a safe-haven asset in the COVID-19 crisis? *Economic Modelling, 102*, 105588.

Areal, N., Oliveira, B., & Sampaio, R. (2015). When times get tough, gold is golden. *European Journal of Finance, 21*(6), 507–526.

Baillie, R. T., & Myers, R. J. (1991). Bivariate GARCH estimation of the optimal commodity futures hedge. *Journal of Applied Econometrics, 6*(2), 109–124. doi:10.1002/jae.3950060202

Baur, D. G., & Glover, K. (2012). The destruction of a safe haven asset? *Applied Finance Letters, 1*(1), 8–15.

Baur, D. G., Hong, K., & Lee, A. D. (2018). Bitcoin: Medium of exchange or speculative assets? *Journal of International Financial Markets, Institutions and Money, 54*, 177–189.

Baur, D. G., & Lucey, B. M. (2010). Is gold a hedge or safe haven? An analysis of stocks, bonds, and gold. *Financial Review*, *45*(2), 217–229.

Beckmann, J., Berger, T., & Czudaj, R. (2015). Does gold act as a hedge or a safe haven for stocks? A smooth transition approach. *Economic Modelling*, *48*, 16–24.

Bekiros, S., Boubaker, S., Nguyen, D. K., & Uddin, G. S. (2017). Black swan events and safe havens: The role of gold in globally integrated emerging markets. *Journal of International Money and Finance*, *73*, 317–334.

Bollerslev, T. (1986). Generalized autoregressive conditional heteroscedasticity. *Journal of Econometrics*, *31*(3), 307–327. doi:10.1016/0304-4076(86)90063-1

Bollerslev, T. (1990). Modelling the coherence in short-run nominal exchange rates: A multivariate generalized ARCH model. *The Review of Economics and Statistics*, *72*(3), 498–505. doi:10.2307/2109358

Brenner, M., & Galai, D. (1989). New financial instruments for hedging changes in volatility. *Financial Analysts Journal*, *45*(4), 61–65. doi:10.2469/faj.v45.n4.61

Brenner, M., & Izhakian, Y. (2021). Risk and ambiguity in turbulent times. *The Quarterly Journal of Finance*. Advance online publication. doi:10.1142/S2010139222400018

Ceylan, Ö. (2014). Time-varying volatility asymmetry: A Conditioned HAR-RV (CJ) EGARCH-M Model. *The Journal of Risk*, *17*(2), 21–49. doi:10.21314/JOR.2014.295

Chang, C.-L., McAleer, M., & Tansuchat, R. (2011). Crude oil hedging strategies using dynamic multivariate GARCH. *Energy Economics*, *33*(5), 912–923. doi:10.1016/j.eneco.2011.01.009

Cheema, M. A., Faff, R. W., & Szulczuk, K. (2020). The 2008 global financial crisis and COVID-19 pandemic: How safe are the safe haven assets? *Covid Economics*, *34*, 88–115.

Chemkha, R., BenSaïda, A., Ghorbel, A., & Tayachi, T. (2021). Hedge and safe haven properties during COVID-19: Evidence from Bitcoin and gold. *The Quarterly Review of Economics and Finance*, *82*, 71–85.

Conlon, T., & McGee, R. (2020). Safe haven or risky hazard? Bitcoin during the Covid-19 bear market. *Finance Research Letters*, *35*, 101607.

Ederington, L. H. (1979). The hedging performance of the new futures markets. *The Journal of Finance*, *34*(1), 157–170. doi:10.1111/j.1540-6261.1979.tb02077.x

Engle, R. (2002). Dynamic conditional correlation. *Journal of Business & Economic Statistics*, *20*(3), 339–350. doi:10.1198/073500102288618487

Engle, R. F. (1982). Autoregressive conditional heteroscedasticity with estimates of the variance of United Kingdom Inflation. *Econometrica*, *50*(4), 987–1007. doi:10.2307/1912773

Haq, I. U., Chupradit, S., & Huo, C. (2021). Do green bonds act as a hedge or a safe haven against economic policy uncertainty? Evidence from the USA and China. *International Journal of Financial Studies*, *9*, 40. doi:10.3390/ijfs9030040

Hasan, M. B., Hassan, M. K., Rashid, M. M., & Alhenawi, Y. (2021). Are safe haven assets really safe during the 2008 global financial crisis and COVID-19 pandemic? *Global Finance Journal, 50*. Advance online publication. doi:10.1016/j.gfj.2021.100668

Hill, J., & Schneeweis, T. (1981). A note on the hedging effectiveness of foreign currency futures. *Journal of Futures Markets, 1*(4), 659–664. doi:10.1002/fut.3990010408

Hood, M., & Malik, F. (2013). Is gold the best hedge and a safe haven under changing stock market volatility? *Review of Financial Economics, 22*(2), 47–52.

Ji, Q., Zhang, D., & Zhao, Y. (2020). Searching for safe-haven assets during the COVID-19 pandemic. *International Review of Financial Analysis, 71*, 101526.

Johnson, L. L. (1960). The theory of hedging and speculation in commodity futures. *The Review of Economic Studies, 27*(3), 139–151. doi:10.2307/2296076

Klein, T. (2017). Dynamic correlation of precious metals and flight-to-quality in developed markets. *Finance Research Letters, 23*, 283–290.

Kroner, F. K., & Sultan, J. (1993). Time-varying distributions and dynamic hedging with foreign currency futures. *Journal of Financial and Quantitative Analysis, 28*(4), 535–551. doi:10.2307/2331164

Kroner, K. F., & Sultan, J. (1991). Exchange rate volatility and time-varying hedge ratios. In Pacific-Basin Capital Markets Research. Elsevier.

Ku, Y. H., Chen, H. C., & Chen, K. H. (2007). On the application of the dynamic conditional correlation model in estimating optimal time-varying hedge ratios. *Applied Economics Letters, 14*(7), 503–509. doi:10.1080/13504850500447331

Lien, D., Tse, Y. K., & Tsui, A. K. C. (2002). Evaluating the hedging performance of the constant-correlation GARCH model. *Applied Financial Economics, 12*(11), 791–798. doi:10.1080/09603100110046045

Löwen, C., Kchouri, B., & Lehnert, T. (2021). Is this time really different? Flight-to-safety and the COVID-19 crisis. *PLoS One, 16*(5), e0251752.

Lucey, B. M., & Li, S. (2015). What precious metals act as safe havens, and when? Some US evidence. *Applied Economics Letters, 22*(1), 35–45.

Mandelbrot, B. (1963). The variation of certain speculative prices. *The Journal of Business, 4*(4), 394–419. doi:10.1086/294632

Park, H. Y., & Bera, A. K. (1987). Interest rate volatility, basis, and heteroscedasticity in hedging mortgages. *Real Estate Economics, 15*(2), 79–97. doi:10.1111/1540-6229.00420

Park, T. H., & Switzer, L. N. (1995). Bivariate GARCH estimation of the optimal hedge ratios for stock index futures: A note. *Journal of Futures Markets, 15*(1), 61–67. doi:10.1002/fut.3990150106

Sadorsky, P. (2014). Modeling volatility and correlations between emerging market stock prices and the prices of copper, oil and wheat. *Energy Economics, 43*, 72–81. doi:10.1016/j.eneco.2014.02.014

Salisu, A. A., Raheem, I., & Vo, X. V. (2021). Assessing the safe haven property of the gold market during COVID-19 pandemic. *International Review of Financial Analysis*, *74*, 101666.

Shahzad, S. J. H., Bouri, E., Ur Rehman, M., & Roubaud, D. (2021). The hedge asset for BRICS stock markets: Bitcoin, gold or VIX. *World Economy*. Advance online publication. doi:10.1111/twec.13138

Sharif, A., Aloui, C., & Yarovaya, L. (2020). COVID-19 pandemic, oil prices, stock market, geopolitical risk and policy uncertainty nexus in the US economy: Fresh evidence from the wavelet-based approach. *International Review of Financial Analysis*, *70*, 1–9.

Shrydeh, N., Shahateet, M., Mohammad, S., & Sumadi, M. (2019). The hedging effectiveness of gold against US stocks in a post-financial crisis era. *Cogent Economics & Finance*, *7*(1). Advance online publication. doi:10.1080/23322039.2019.1698268

Stein, J. L. (1961). The simultaneous determination of spot and futures prices. *The American Economic Review*, *51*(5), 1012–1025.

Szado, E. (2009). VIX futures and options: A case study of portfolio diversification during the 2008 financial crisis. *Journal of Alternative Investments*, *12*(2), 68–85.

Tanin, T. I., Sarker, A., Hammoudeh, S., & Shahbaz, M. (2021). Do volatility indices diminish gold's appeal as a safe haven to investors before and during the COVID-19 pandemic? *Journal of Economic Behavior & Organization*, *191*, 214–235.

Tarchella, S., & Dhaoui, A. (2021). Chinese jigsaw: Solving the equity market response to the COVID-19 crisis: Do alternative asset provide effective hedging performance? *Research in International Business and Finance*, *58*, 101499.

Tse, Y. K., & Tsui, A. K. C. (2002). A multivariate GARCH model with time-varying correlations. *Journal of Business & Economic Statistics*, *20*(3), 351–362. doi:10.1198/073500102288618496

Whaley, R. E. (1993). Derivatives on market volatility: Hedging tools long overdue. *Journal of Derivatives*, *1*(1), 71–84. doi:10.3905/jod.1993.407868

Zhang, D., Hu, M., & Ji, Q. (2020). Financial markets under the global pandemic of COVID-19. *Finance Research Letters*, *36*. Advance online publication. doi:10.1016/j.frl.2020.101528

ADDITIONAL READING

Alexander, C., Kapraun, J., & Korovilas, D. (2015). Trading and investing in volatility products. *Financial Markets, Institutions and Instruments*, *24*(4), 313–347. doi:10.1111/fmii.12032

Carr, P., & Lee, R. (2009). Volatility derivatives. *Annual Review of Financial Economics*, *1*(1), 319–339. doi:10.1146/annurev.financial.050808.114304

Christensen, K., Christiansen, C., & Posselt, A. M. (2020). The economic value of VIX ETPs. *Journal of Empirical Finance*, *58*, 121–138. doi:10.1016/j.jempfin.2020.05.009

Hull, J. C. (2012). *Options, futures and other derivatives* (8th ed.). Prentice-Hall.

Lin, Y.-N., & Lin, A. Y. (2016). Using VIX futures to hedge forward implied volatility risk. *International Review of Economics & Finance, 43*, 88–106. doi:10.1016/j.iref.2015.10.033

Sinclair, E. (2013). *Volatility trading* (2nd ed.). Wiley.

KEY TERMS AND DEFINITIONS

Cross Hedging: A hedging strategy that is adopted when a derivative for the asset to be hedged does not exist. It involves using an asset that is highly correlated with the asset to be hedged, to cover potential losses from one asset with gains from the other one.

Exchange Traded Fund: A marketable security that tracks the value of another security, an index, or an industry.

Exchange Traded Note: An unsecured debt obligation that is issued by large banks and financial institutions. It tracks the performance of an index or a benchmark and pays its holders the amount of returns equal to those that are generated by what it tracks.

Financial Derivative: A financial contract with a value that varies conditionally on the changes in the underlying reference prices.

Optimal Hedge Ratio: The ratio of the value of a hedging instrument to that of the asset to be hedged, needed to minimize the variance of the overall position.

Price Risk: The potential for the decline in the value of an asset, a portfolio, or a financial instrument.

Volatility Risk: The potential for a sharp decline in the value of an asset, a portfolio or a financial instrument as a result of changes in volatility of returns on the investment itself, or on a related entity such as the market or the underlying.

Compilation of References

Abad, C., Thore, S. A., & Laffarga, J. (2004). Fundamental analysis of stocks by two-stage DEA. *Managerial and Decision Economics*, *25*(5), 231–241. doi:10.1002/mde.1145

Abbasi, K., Alam, A., & Bhuiyan, M. B. U. (2020). Audit committees, female directors and the types of female and male financial experts: Further evidence. *Journal of Business Research*, *114*(February), 186–197. doi:10.1016/j.jbusres.2020.04.013

Abdellaoui, M., Bleichrodt, H., & Kammoun, H. (2013). Do Financial Professionals Behave According to Prospect Theory? An Experimental Study. *Theory and Decision*, *74*(3), 411–429. doi:10.100711238-011-9282-3

Abdullah, M., Shukor, Z. A., Mohamed, Z. M., & Ahmad, A. (2015). Risk management disclosure: A study on the effect of voluntary risk management disclosure toward firm value. *Journal of Applied Accounting Research*, *16*(3), 400–432. doi:10.1108/JAAR-10-2014-0106

Abdullah, M., Shukor, Z. A., & Rahmat, M. M. (2017). The Influences of Risk Management Committee and Audit Committee towards Voluntary Risk Management Disclosure. *Jurnal Pengurusan*, *50*, 83–95. doi:10.17576/pengurusan-2017-50-08

Abdullah, S. (2012). Risk Management via Takaful from a Perspective of Maqasid of Shariah. *Procedia: Social and Behavioral Sciences*, *65*(3), 535–541. doi:10.1016/j.sbspro.2012.11.161

Abernathy, J. L., Finley, A. R., Rapley, E. T., & Stekelberg, J. (2021). External Auditor Responses to Tax Risk. *Journal of Accounting, Auditing & Finance*, *36*(3), 489–516. doi:10.1177/0148558X19867821

Abraham, S., & Cox, P. (2007). Analysing the determinants of narrative risk information in UK FTSE 100 annual reports. *The British Accounting Review*, *39*(3), 227–248. doi:10.1016/j.bar.2007.06.002

Abzakh, A. A., Ling, K. C., & Alkilani, K. (2013). The Impact of Perceived Risks on the Consumer Resistance towards Generic Drugs in the Malaysia Pharmaceutical Industry. *International Journal of Business and Management*, *8*(3), 42–50. doi:10.5539/ijbm.v8n3p42

Achim, M. V., Mare, C., & Borlea, S. N. (2012). A statistical model of financial risk bankruptcy applied for Romanian manufacturing industry. *Procedia Economics and Finance*, *3*, 32–137. doi:10.1016/S2212-5671(12)00131-1

Achim, M. V., Safta, I. L., Vaidean, V. L., Mureşan, G. M., & Borlea, N. S. (2021). The impact of covid-19 on financial management: Evidence from Romania, Economic Research-. *Ekonomska Istrazivanja*, 1–26. Advance online publication. doi:10.1080/1331677X.2021.1922090

Adams, M., & Jiang, W. (2016). Do outside directors influence the financial performance of risk-trading firms? Evidence from the United Kingdom (UK) insurance industry. *Journal of Banking & Finance*, *64*, 36–51. doi:10.1016/j.jbankfin.2015.11.018

Compilation of References

Adams, M., & Jiang, W. (2020). Do Financial Experts on the Board Matter? An Empirical Test From the United Kingdom's Non-Life Insurance Industry. *Journal of Accounting, Auditing & Finance, 35*(1), 168–195. doi:10.1177/0148558X17705201

Adams, R. B., & Ferreira, D. (2007). A theory of friendly boards. *The Journal of Finance, 62*(1), 217–250. doi:10.1111/j.1540-6261.2007.01206.x

Adelmann, F., & Gaidosch, T. (2020). *Cybersecurity of Remote Work During the Pandemic*. Special IMF Series on COVID-19. https://www.imf.org/~/media/Files/Publications/covid19-special-notes/en-special-series-on-covid-19-cybersecurity-of-remote-work-during-pandemic.ashx

Adhikari, B. K., & O'Leary, V. E. (2011). Gender Differences in Risk Aversion: A Developing Nation's Case. *Journal of Personal Finance, 10*(2), 122–147.

Aebi, V., Sabato, G., & Schmid, M. (2012). Risk management, corporate governance, and bank performance in the financial crisis. *Journal of Banking & Finance, 36*(12), 3213–3226. doi:10.1016/j.jbankfin.2011.10.020

Aganin, A., & Volpin, P. (2002). The History of Corporate Ownership in Italy. In A History of Corporate Governance Around the World. The University of Chicago Press.

Agoraki, M. E. K., Delis, M. D., & Pasiouras, F. (2011). Regulations, competition and bank risk-taking in transition countries. *Journal of Financial Stability, 7*(1), 38–48. doi:10.1016/j.jfs.2009.08.002

Agostinelli, C. (2010). Robust stepwise regression. *Journal of Applied Statistics, 29*(6), 825–840. doi:10.1080/02664760220136168

Ahern, K. R. (2017). Information networks: Evidence from illegal insider trading tips. *Journal of Financial Economics, 125*(1), 26–47. doi:10.1016/j.jfineco.2017.03.009

Ahern, K. R., & Dittmar, A. K. (2012). The changing of the boards: The impact on firm valuation of mandated female board representation. *The Quarterly Journal of Economics, 127*(1), 137–197. doi:10.1093/qje/qjr049

Ahmad, W., Hernandez, J. A., Saini, S., & Mishra, R. K. (2021). The US equity sectors, implied volatilities, and COVID-19: What does the spillover analysis reveal? *Resources Policy, 72*, 102102.

Ahmed, A., & Ali, S. (2017). Boardroom gender diversity and stock liquidity: Evidence from Australia. *Journal of Contemporary Accounting & Economics, 13*(2), 148–165. doi:10.1016/j.jcae.2017.06.001

Ahold Delhaize. (2019). *Ahold Delhaize*. Retrieved from Ahold Delhaize: https://www.aholddelhaize.com/en/home/

Ahoniemi, K., & Lanne, M. (2010). Realized volatility and overnight returns. *Bank of Finland Research Discussion Papers, 19*, 1–24.

Ait-Sahalia, Y., & Xiu, D. (2016). Increased correlation among asset classes: Are volatility or jumps to blame, or both? *Journal of Econometrics, 194*(2), 205–219.

Ajzen, I. (1991). The theory of planned behavior. *Organizational Behavior and Human Decision Processes, 50*(2), 179–211. doi:10.1016/0749-5978(91)90020-T

Akbas, F., Meschke, F., & Wintoki, M. B. (2016). Director networks and informed traders. *Journal of Accounting and Economics, 62*(1), 1–23. doi:10.1016/j.jacceco.2016.03.003

Akhtar, S., Javed, B., Maryam, A., & Sadia, H. (2012). Relationship between financial leverage and financial performance: Evidence from fuel & energy sector of Pakistan. *European Journal of Business and Management, 4*(11), 7–17.

Akhtaruzzaman, M., Boubaker, S., Lucey, B. M., & Sensoy, A. (2021). Is gold a hedge or a safe-haven asset in the COVID-19 crisis? *Economic Modelling*, *102*, 105588.

Aktan, B., Turen, S., Tvaronavičienė, M., Celik, S., & Alsadeh, H. A. (2018). Corporate governance and performance of the financial firms in Bahrain. *Polish Journal of Management Studies*, *17*(1), 39–58. doi:10.17512/pjms.2018.17.1.04

Al-Ajmi, J. Y. (2008). Risk Tolerance of Individual Investors in an Emerging Market. *International Research Journal of Finance and Economics*, *17*, 15–26.

Alarussi, A. S., & Alhaderi, S. M. (2018). Factors affecting profitability in Malaysia. *Journal of Economic Studies (Glasgow, Scotland)*, *45*(3), 442–458. doi:10.1108/JES-05-2017-0124

Albaity, M., Mallek, R. S., & Noman, A. H. M. (2019). Competition and bank stability in the MENA region: The moderating effect of Islamic versus conventional banks. *Emerging Markets Review*, *38*(January), 310–325. doi:10.1016/j.ememar.2019.01.003

Albeverio, S., Cordoni, F., Di Persio, L., & Pellegrini, G. (2019). Asymptotic expansion for some local volatility models arising in finance. *Decisions in Economics and Finance*.

Alderson, M., & Betker, B. (1999). Assessing Post-Bankruptcy Performance: An Analysis of Reorganized Firms' Cash Flows. *Financial Management*, *28*(2), 68–82. doi:10.2307/3666196

Aldhamari, R., Nor, M. N. M., Boudiab, M., & Mas'ud, A. (2020). The impact of political connection and risk committee on corporate financial performance : Evidence from financial firms in Malaysia. *Corporate Governance*, *20*(7), 1281–1305. doi:10.1108/CG-04-2020-0122

Ali, M. M., & Nasir, N. M. (2018). Corporate governance and financial distress: Malaysian perspective. *Asian Journal of Accounting Perspectives*, *11*(1), 108–128. doi:10.22452/AJAP.vol11no1.5

Ali, M., Sohail, A., Khan, L., & Puah, C. H. (2019). Exploring the role of risk and corruption on bank stability: Evidence from Pakistan. *Journal of Money Laundering Control*, *22*(2), 270–288. doi:10.1108/JMLC-03-2018-0019

Aljughaiman, A. A., & Salama, A. (2019). Do banks effectively manage their risks? The role of risk governance in the MENA region. *Journal of Accounting and Public Policy*, *38*(5), 106680. doi:10.1016/j.jaccpubpol.2019.106680

Allen, H., & Taylor, M. P. (1990). Charts, noise and fundamentals in the London foreign exchange market. *Economic Journal (London)*, *100*(400), 49–59. doi:10.2307/2234183

Alnabsha, A., Abdou, H. A., Ntim, C. G., & Elamer, A. A. (2018). Corporate boards, ownership structures and corporate disclosures: Evidence from a developing country. *Journal of Applied Accounting Research*, *19*(1), 20–41. doi:10.1108/JAAR-01-2016-0001

Al-Tamimi, H. A. (2012). The effects of corporate governance on performance and financial distress. *Journal of Financial Regulation Compliance*, *20*(2), 169–181. doi:10.1108/13581981211218315

Altman, E. I. (1968). Financial ratios, discriminant analysis and the prediction of corporate bankruptcy. *The Journal of Finance*, *23*(4), 589–609. doi:10.1111/j.1540-6261.1968.tb00843.x

Aluchna, M. (2016). Applying Corporate Governance in Europe. In Global Perspectives on Corporate Governance and CSR. Routledge.

Ames, D. A., Hines, C. S., & Sankara, J. (2018). Board risk committees: Insurer financial strength ratings and performance. *Journal of Accounting and Public Policy*, *37*(2), 130–145. doi:10.1016/j.jaccpubpol.2018.02.003

Compilation of References

Amihud, Y., & Mendelson, H. (1988). Liquidity and asset prices: Financial management implications. *Financial Management*, *17*(1), 5–15. doi:10.2307/3665910

Amihud, Y., Mendelson, H., & Pedersen, L. H. (2006). *Liquidity and asset prices*. Now Publishers Inc.

Anarfo, E. B., Abor, J. Y., & osei, K. A. (2019, July). Financial regulation and financial inclusion in Sub-Saharan Africa: Does financial stability play a moderating role? *Research in International Business and Finance*, *51*, 101070. doi:10.1016/j.ribaf.2019.101070

Anarfo, E. B., Abor, J. Y., Osei, K. A., & Gyeke-Dako, A. (2019a). Financial inclusion and financial sector development in Sub-Saharan Africa: A panel VAR approach. *International Journal of Managerial Finance*, *15*(4), 444–463. doi:10.1108/IJMF-07-2018-0205

Anarfo, E. B., Abor, J. Y., Osei, K. A., & Gyeke-Dako, A. (2019b). Monetary Policy and Financial Inclusion in Sub-Sahara Africa: A Panel VAR Approach. *Journal of African Business*, *20*(4), 549–572. doi:10.1080/15228916.2019.1580998

Andersen, T. G., Dobrev, D., & Schaumburg, E. (2008). *Duration-Based Volatility Estimation*. Global COE Hi-Stat Discussion Paper Series, 08-034.

Anderson, A., Dreber, A., & Vestman, R. (2015). Risk taking, behavioral biases and genes: Results from 149 active investors. *Journal of Behavioral and Experimental Finance*, *6*, 93–100. doi:10.1016/j.jbef.2015.04.002

Andreou, E., & Ghysels, E. (2002). Rolling-Sample Volatility Estimators: Some New Theoretical, Simulation and Empirical Results. *Journal of Business & Economic Statistics*, *20*(03), 363–376.

Ang, S. H., Cheng, P. S., Lim, E. A. C., & Tambyah, S. K. (2001). Spot the difference: Consumer responses towards counterfeits. *Journal of Consumer Marketing*, *18*(3), 219–235. doi:10.1108/07363760110392967

Ansah, M. O. (2017). A Comparison of Price Effect and Country of Origin Effect on Consumer A Comparison of Price Effect and Country of Origin Effect on Consumer Counterfeit Products Purchase. *Journal of Social Sciences*, *13*(November), 216–228. Advance online publication. doi:10.3844/jssp.2017.216.228

Apergis, N. (2019). Financial Experts on the Board: Does It Matter for the Profitability and Risk of the U.K. Banking Industry? *Journal of Financial Research*, *42*(2), 243–270. doi:10.1111/jfir.12168

Araghi, K., & Makvandi, S. (2012). Evaluating Predictive power of Data Envelopment Analysis Technique Compared with Logit and Probit Models in Predicting Corporate Bankruptcy. *Australian Journal of Business and Management Research*, *2*(9), 38–46. doi:10.52283/NSWRCA.AJBMR.20120209A05

Arano, K., Parker, C., & Terry, R. (2010). Gender-based risk aversion and retirement asset allocation. *Economic Inquiry*, *48*(1), 147–155. doi:10.1111/j.1465-7295.2008.00201.x

Arayssi, M., Dah, M., & Jizi, M. (2016). Women on boards, sustainability reporting and firm performance. *Sustainability Accounting. Management and Policy Journal*, *7*(3), 376–401.

Areal, N., Oliveira, B., & Sampaio, R. (2015). When times get tough, gold is golden. *European Journal of Finance*, *21*(6), 507–526.

Arellano, C. (2008). Default Risk and Income Fluctuations in Emerging Economies. *American Economic Review*, *98*(3), 690–712. doi:10.1257/aer.98.3.690

Arntz, M., Ben Yahmed, S., & Berlingieri, F. (2020). Working from home and COVID-19: The chances and risks for gender gaps. *Inter Economics*, *55*(6), 381–386. doi:10.100710272-020-0938-5 PMID:33281218

Ashrafa, B. N. (2020, December). Stock markets' reaction to COVID-19: Cases or fatalities? *Research in International Business and Finance, 54*. Advance online publication. doi:10.1016/j.ribaf.2020.101249

Asimakopoulos, I., Samitas, A., & Papadogonas, T. (2009). Firm-specific and Economy Wide Determinants of Firm Profitability: Greek Evidence using Panel Data. *Managerial Finance, 35*(11), 930–939. doi:10.1108/03074350910993818

Aslam, F., Ferreira, P., Mughal, K. S., & Bashir, B. (2021). Intraday Volatility Spillovers among European Financial Markets during COVID-19. *International Journal of Financial Studies, 9*(1). Advance online publication. doi:10.3390/ijfs9010005

Asravor, R. K. (2020). Moonlighting to survive in a pandemic: Multiple motives and gender differences in ghana. *International Journal of Development Issues, 20*(2), 243–257. doi:10.1108/IJDI-08-2020-0180

Atkinson, S., Samantha, B., & Frye, M. (2003). Do female fund managers manage differently? *Journal of Financial Research, 26*(1), 1–18. doi:10.1111/1475-6803.00041

ATO. (2020). *Top 1,000 (Income) Tax Performance Program Findings Report*. https://www.ato.gov.au/uploadedFiles/Content/SME/downloads/Top_1000_tax_%20performance_program_report_2020.pdf

Audia, P., & Greve, H. (2006). Less Likely to Fail: Low Performance, Firm Size, and Factory Expansion in the Shipbuilding Industry. *Management Science, 52*(1), 83–94. doi:10.1287/mnsc.1050.0446

Australia The Board of Taxation. (2019). *Post-Implementation Review of the Tax Transparency Code*. https://taxboard.gov.au/sites/taxboard.gov.au/files/migrated/2019/02/TTC-Consultation-Paper-final.pdf

Awan, T., Shah, S. Z. A., Khan, M. Y., & Javeed, A. (2020). Impact of corporate governance, financial and regulatory factors on firms' acquisition ability. *Corporate Governance: The International Journal of Business in Society, 20*(3), 461–484. doi:10.1108/CG-07-2019-0214

Awasthi, R. (2011). Conclusion: Lessons for Reforms. In M. S. Khwaja, R. Awasthi, & J. Loeprick (Eds.), *Risk-Based Tax Audits: Approaches and Country Experiences* (pp. 119–126). The World Bank Publishing. doi:10.1596/9780821387542_CH15

Ayadi, M., Ben-Ameur, H., & Kryzanowski, L. (2016). Typical and Tail Performance of Canadian Equity SRI Mutual Funds. *Journal of Financial Services Research, 50*(1), 57–94. doi:10.100710693-015-0215-0

Ayesha, S., Fatima, S. A., & Krishnadas, L. (2020). Impact of loan portfolio diversification on central bank performance and risk mitigation. *International Journal of Management, 11*(5), 644–661. doi:10.34218/IJM.11.5.2020.058

Aysen Doyran, M. (2013). Net interest margins and firm performance in developing countries. *Management Research Review, 36*(7), 720–742. doi:10.1108/MRR-05-2012-0100

Aziz, M. A., & Dar, H. A. (2006). Predicting corporate bankruptcy: where we stand? *Corporate Governance, 6*(1), 18-33. . doi:10.1108/14720700610649436

Babin, J., & Zikmund, W. (2016). Exploring marketing Research (11th ed.). Cengage Learning.

Baek, S., Mohanty, S. K., & Glambosky, M. (2020, November). COVID-19 and stock market volatility: An industry level analysis. *Elsevier Public Health Emergency Collection, 37*, 12–23. doi:10.1016/j.frl.2020.101748

Bae, S. Y., & Chang, P. (2021). The effect of coronavirus disease-19 (COVID-19) risk perception on behavioural intention towards 'untact' tourism in south korea during the first wave of the pandemic (march 2020). *Current Issues in Tourism, 24*(7), 1017–1035. doi:10.1080/13683500.2020.1798895

Compilation of References

Bai, J., Malesky, E., Jayachandran, S., & Olken, A. B. (2013). Does economic growth reduce corruption? Theory and evidence. In The Bureau of economic research (No. 19483). doi:10.3386/w19483

Bailey, C. (2019). The Relationship Between Chief Risk Officer Expertise, ERM Quality, and Firm Performance. *Journal of Accounting, Auditing & Finance*, •••, 1–25. doi:10.1177/0148558X19850424

Baillie, R. T., & Myers, R. J. (1991). Bivariate GARCH estimation of the optimal commodity futures hedge. *Journal of Applied Econometrics*, *6*(2), 109–124. doi:10.1002/jae.3950060202

Bajtelsmit, V., Bernasek, A., & Jianakopolos, N. A. (1996). Gender effects in pension investment allocation decisions. Center for Pension and Retirement Research, 145–156.

Bajtelsmit, V., & Bernasek, A. (1996). Why do women invest differently than men? *Financial Counseling and Planning*, *7*, 1–10.

Baker, H. K., Pandey, N., Kumar, S., & Haldar, A. (2020). A bibliometric analysis of board diversity: Current status, development, and future research directions. *Journal of Business Research*, *108*, 232–246. doi:10.1016/j.jbusres.2019.11.025

Bamossy, G., & Scammon, D. L. (1985). Product counterfeiting: Consumers and manufacturers beware. *Advances in Consumer Research. Association for Consumer Research (U. S.)*, *12*(1), 334–339.

Banker, R. D., Charnes, A., & Cooper, W. W. (1984). Some Models for Estimating Technical Scale Inefficiencies in Data Envelopment Analysis. *Management Science*, *30*(9), 1078–1092. doi:10.1287/mnsc.30.9.1078

Barako, D. G., & Brown, A. M. (2008). Corporate social reporting and board representation: Evidence from the Kenyan banking sector. *The Journal of Management and Governance*, *12*(4), 309–324. doi:10.100710997-008-9053-x

Barber, B., & Odean, T. (2001). Boys will be boys: Gender, overconfidence and common stock investment. *The Quarterly Journal of Economics*, *116*(1), 261–292. doi:10.1162/003355301556400

Barinov, A. (2014). Turnover: Liquidity or Uncertainty? *Management Science*, *60*(10), 2478–2495. doi:10.1287/mnsc.2014.1913

Barke, R., Jenkins-Smith, H., & Slovic, P. (1997). Risk Perceptions of Men and Women Scientists. *Social Science Quarterly*, *78*, 167–176.

Barnett, M., & Salomon, M. (2006). Beyond Dichotomy: The Curvilinear Relationship Between Social Responsibility and Financial Performance. *Strategic Management Journal*, *27*(11), 1101–1122. doi:10.1002mj.557

Barone, A. (2021). *Bank*. Investopedia. Retrieved from https://www.investopedia.com/terms/b/bank.asp

Baron, J. (2008). *Thinking and Deciding* (4th ed.). Cambridge University Press.

Barsky, R. B., Juster, T., Kimball, M. S., & Shapiro, M. D. (1997). Preference parameters and behavioral heterogeneity. *The Quarterly Journal of Economics*, *112*(2), 537–579. doi:10.1162/003355397555280

Bart, C., & McQueen, G. (2013). Why women make better directors. *International Journal of Business Governance and Ethics*, *8*(1), 93–99. doi:10.1504/IJBGE.2013.052743

Bartram, S. M., & Grinblatt, M. (2018). Agnostic fundamental analysis works. *Journal of Financial Economics*, *128*(1), 125–147. doi:10.1016/j.jfineco.2016.11.008

Bastos, J. (2007). *Credit scoring with boosted decision trees*. Academic Press.

Battaglia, F., & Gallo, A. (2015). Risk governance and Asian bank performance : An empirical investigation over the financial crisis. *Emerging Markets Review*, *25*, 53–68. doi:10.1016/j.ememar.2015.04.004

Baudier, P., Kondrateva, G., Ammi, C., Chang, V., & Schiavone, F. (2021). Patients' perceptions of teleconsultation during COVID-19: A cross-national study. *Technological Forecasting and Social Change*, *163*, 120510. Advance online publication. doi:10.1016/j.techfore.2020.120510 PMID:33318716

Bauer, R. A. (1960). Consumer behavior as risk taking. In *Proceedings of the 43rd National Conference of the American Marketing Assocation*. American Marketing Association.

Bauer, R., Derwall, J., & Otten, R. (2007). The Ethical Mutual Fund Performance Debate: New Evidence from Canada. *Journal of Business Ethics*, *70*(2), 111–124. doi:10.100710551-006-9099-0

Bauer, R., Koedijk, K., & Otten, R. (2005). International Evidence on Ethical Mutual Fund Performance and Investment Style. *Journal of Banking & Finance*, *29*(7), 1751–1767. doi:10.1016/j.jbankfin.2004.06.035

Bauer, R., Otten, R., & Rad, A. (2006). Ethical Investing in Australia: Is There a Financial Penalty? *Pacific-Basin Finance Journal*, *14*(1), 33–48. doi:10.1016/j.pacfin.2004.12.004

Baur, D. G., & Glover, K. (2012). The destruction of a safe haven asset? *Applied Finance Letters*, *1*(1), 8–15.

Baur, D. G., Hong, K., & Lee, A. D. (2018). Bitcoin: Medium of exchange or speculative assets? *Journal of International Financial Markets, Institutions and Money*, *54*, 177–189.

Baur, D. G., & Lucey, B. M. (2010). Is gold a hedge or safe haven? An analysis of stocks, bonds, and gold. *Financial Review*, *45*(2), 217–229.

Bazerman, M., & Moore, D. (2009). *Judgment in Managerial Decision Making* (7th ed.). John Wiley & Sons, Inc.

BBC. (2016, November 10). *Trump e Brexit: 5 fatores em comum*. Retrieved from BBC News: https://www.bbc.com/portuguese/internacional-37934191

Beaver, W. H. (1966). Financial ratios as predictors of failure. *Journal of Accounting Research*, *4*, 71–111. doi:10.2307/2490171

Becker, T. (2020, April 15). *Russia Economic Update — Brace for the Covid-19 Impact!* Retrieved from https://freepolicybriefs.org/2020/04/15/russia-economic-covid-19-impact/

Beck, K. (2019). A Note on Teaching Liquidity Risk. *Journal of Financial Education*, *45*(1), 94–100. Retrieved June 17, 2021, from https://www.jstor.org/stable/26918028

Beckmann, J., Berger, T., & Czudaj, R. (2015). Does gold act as a hedge or a safe haven for stocks? A smooth transition approach. *Economic Modelling*, *48*, 16–24.

Beer, D. (2016). How should we do the history of Big Data? *Big Data & Society*, *3*(1), 1–10. doi:10.1177/2053951716646135

Begley, J., Ming, T., & Watts, S. (1996). Bankruptcy Classification Errors in the 1980s: Empirical Analysis of Altman's and Ohlsons' Models. *Accounting Studies*, *1*(4), 267–284. doi:10.1007/BF00570833

Bekiros, S., Boubaker, S., Nguyen, D. K., & Uddin, G. S. (2017). Black swan events and safe havens: The role of gold in globally integrated emerging markets. *Journal of International Money and Finance*, *73*, 317–334.

Bell, J. (2015). *Machine Learning*. Wiley.

Bello, Z. (2005). Socially Responsible Investing and Portfolio Diversification. *Journal of Financial Research*, *28*(1), 41–57. doi:10.1111/j.1475-6803.2005.00113.x

Bell, T. R. (2021). SportsCenter: A case study of media framing U.S. sport as the COVID-19 epicenter. *International Journal of Sport Communication*, *14*(2), 298–317. doi:10.1123/ijsc.2020-0258

Ben Moussa, F. (2019). The Influence of Internal Corporate Governance on Bank Credit Risk: An Empirical Analysis for Tunisia. *Global Business Review*, *20*(3), 640–667. doi:10.1177/0972150919837078

Benartzi, S., & Thaler, R. (1995). Myopic Loss Aversion and the Equity Premium Puzzle. *The Quarterly Journal of Economics*, *110*(1), 73–92. doi:10.2307/2118511

Bengtsson, E. (2008). A History of Scandinavian Socially Responsible Investing. *Journal of Business Ethics*, *82*(4), 969–983. doi:10.100710551-007-9606-y

Benlemlih, M., & Girerd-Potin, I. (2017). Corporate social responsibility and firm financial risk reduction: On the moderating role of the legal environment. *Journal of Business Finance & Accounting*, *44*(7-8), 1137–1166. doi:10.1111/jbfa.12251

Bennett, C., & Gil, M. A. (2012, February 03). Measuring Historical Volatality. *Santander: Global Bank Marketing*, 1–13.

Berejikian, J. D., & Early, B. R. (2013). Loss Aversion and Foreign Policy Resolve. *Political Psychology*, *34*(5), 649–671.

Berg, F., Fabisik, K., & Sautner, Z. (2020). *Rewriting History II: The (Un)Predictable Past of ESG Ratings*. European Corporate Governance Institute – Finance Working Paper 708/2020. doi:10.2139/ssrn.3722087

Berger, A. N., El Ghoul, S., Guedhami, O., & Roman, R. A. (2017). Internationalization and bank risk. *Management Science*, *63*(7), 2283–2301. doi:10.1287/mnsc.2016.2422

Berger, A. N., Kick, T., & Schaeck, K. (2014). Executive board composition and bank risk taking. *Journal of Corporate Finance*, *28*, 48–65. doi:10.1016/j.jcorpfin.2013.11.006

Berman, S., Wicks, A., Kotha, S., & Jones, T. (1999). Does Stakeholder Orientation Matter? The Relationship between Stakeholder Management Models and Firm Financial Performance. *Academy of Management Journal*, *42*(5), 488–506. Retrieved April 3, 2021, from https://www.jstor.org/stable/256972

Bernile, G., Bhagwat, V., & Rau, P. R. (2017). What Doesn't Kill You Will Only Make You More Risk-Loving: Early-Life Disasters and CEO Behavior. *The Journal of Finance*, *72*(1), 167–206. doi:10.1111/jofi.12432

Bernile, G., Bhagwat, V., & Yonker, S. (2018). Board diversity, firm risk, and corporate policies. *Journal of Financial Economics*, *127*(3), 588–612. doi:10.1016/j.jfineco.2017.12.009

Bernstein, P. L. (1997). *Desafio aos Deuses: A Fascinante História do Risco* (6th ed.). Gulf Professional Publishing.

Bessembinder, H., & Chan, K. (1995). The profitability of technical trading rules in the Asian stock markets. *Pacific-Basin Finance Journal*, *3*(2-3), 257–284. doi:10.1016/0927-538X(95)00002-3

Bettman, J. L., Sault, S. J., & Schultz, E. L. (2009). Fundamental and technical analysis substitutes or complements. *Accounting and Finance*, *49*(1), 21–36. doi:10.1111/j.1467-629X.2008.00277.x

Beyer, S., & Bowden, E. (1997). Gender Differences in Self-perceptions: Convergent Evidence from Three Measures of Accuracy and Bias. *Personality and Social Psychology Bulletin*, *23*(2), 157–172. doi:10.1177/0146167297232005

Bhagat, S., Bolton, B., & Lu, J. (2015). Size, leverage, and risk-taking of financial institutions. *Journal of Banking & Finance*, *59*, 520–537. doi:10.1016/j.jbankfin.2015.06.018

Bhuiyan, B. U., Cheema, M. A., & Man, Y. (2021). Risk committee, corporate risk-taking and firm value. *Managerial Finance*, *47*(3), 285–309. doi:10.1108/MF-07-2019-0322

Bian, X., & Moutinho, L. (2009). An investigation of determinants of counterfeit purchase consideration. *Journal of Business Research*, *62*(3), 368–378. doi:10.1016/j.jbusres.2008.05.012

Bian, X., & Veloutsou, C. (2007). Consumers' attitudes regarding non-deceptive counterfeit brands in the UK and China. *Journal of Brand Management*, *14*(3), 211–222. doi:10.1057/palgrave.bm.2550046

Bilal, C., Chen, S., & Komal, B. (2016, November). Audit committee financial expertise and earnings quality: A meta-analysis. *Journal of Business Research*, *84*, 253–270. doi:10.1016/j.jbusres.2017.11.048

Bishop, C. M. (2006). *Pattern recognition and machine learning*. Springer.

Bley, J., Saad, M., & Samet, A. (2019). Auditor choice and bank risk taking. *International Review of Financial Analysis*, *61*(December), 37–52. doi:10.1016/j.irfa.2018.11.003

Blum, M. (1974). Failing company discriminant analysis. *Journal of Accounting Research*, *12*(1), 1–25. doi:10.2307/2490525

Bodas Sagi, D. J., Soltero, F. J., Hidalgo, J. I., Fernandez, P., & Fernandez, F. (2012). A technique for the otimization of the parameters of technical indicators with Multi-Objective Evolutionary Algorithms. *2012 IEEE Congress on Evolutionary Computation*, 1-8.

Boholm, A. (1998). Comparative studies of risk perception: A review of 20 years of research. *Journal of Risk Research*, *1*(2), 135–163. doi:10.1080/136698798377231

Bollerslev, T. (1986). Generalized autoregressive conditional heteroscedasticity. *Journal of Econometrics*, *31*(3), 307–327. doi:10.1016/0304-4076(86)90063-1

Bollerslev, T. (1990). Modelling the coherence in short-run nominal exchange rates: A multivariate generalized ARCH model. *The Review of Economics and Statistics*, *72*(3), 498–505. doi:10.2307/2109358

Bollerslev, T., Gibson, M., & Zhou, H. (2011). Dynamic Estimation of Volatility Risk Premia and Investor Risk Aversion from Option-Implied and Realized Volatilities. *Journal of Econometrics*, *160*(1), 235–245.

Bonini, S., & Caivano, G. (2018). Probability of default modeling: A machine learning approach. In M. Corazza, M. Durbàn, A. Grané, C. Perna, & M. Sibillo (Ed.), *Proceedings of the Mathematical and Statistical Methods for Actuarial Sciences and Finance* (173–177). Cham: Springer. 10.1007/978-3-319-89824-7_32

Bonollo, M., Di Persio, L., & Pellegrini, G. (2015). Polynomial Chaos Expansion Approach to Interest Rate Models. *Journal of Probability and Statistics*.

Booth, A., Cardona-Sosa, L., & Nolen, P. (2014). Gender differences in risk aversion: Do single-sex environments affect their development? *Journal of Economic Behavior & Organization*, *99*, 126–154. doi:10.1016/j.jebo.2013.12.017

Bora, D., & Basistha, D. (2020, August 14). The outbreak of COVID-19 pandemic and Its Impact on Stock Market, Research Square. doi:10.21203/rs.3.rs-57471/v1

Boser, I., Bernhard, V., & Guyon, V. (1996). A Training Algorithm for Optimal Margin Classifier. *Proceedings of the Fifth Annual ACM Workshop on Computational Learning Theory*.

Boulu-Reshef, B., Comeig, I., Donze, R., & Weiss, G. D. (2016). Risk aversion in prediction markets: A framed-field experiment. *Journal of Business Research*, *69*(11), 5071–5075. doi:10.1016/j.jbusres.2016.04.082

Brandt, M. W., & Kinlay, J. (2003). Estimating Historical Volatility. *Journal of Business & Economic Statistics*, 146–153.

Brayman, S., Finke, M., Bessner, E., Grable, J., Griffin, P., & Clement, R. (2015). *Current Practices for Risk Profiling in Canada and Review of Global Best Practices. Research Report prepared for the Investor Advisory Panel of the Ontario Securities Commission.* https://www.osc.gov.on.ca/documents/en/Investors/iap_20151112_risk-profiling-report.pdf

Breaking Down Finance. (2020, September 2). *Parkinson-Volatility*. Retrieved from https://breakingdownfinance.com/finance-topics/risk-management/parkinson-volatility/

Breiman, L. (2001). Random Forests. *Machine Learning*, *45*(1), 5–32. doi:10.1023/A:1010933404324

Breiman, L., Friedman, J., Stone, C., & Olshen, R. (1984). *Classification and Regression Trees*. Taylor & Francis.

Breiter, H., Aharon, I., Kahneman, D., Dale, A., & Shizgal, P. (2001). Functional Imaging of Neutral Responses to Expectancy and Experience of Monetary Gains and Losses. *Neuron*, *30*(2), 619–639. doi:10.1016/S0896-6273(01)00303-8 PMID:11395019

Breitung, J. (2000). The Local Power of Some Unit Root Tests for Panel Data. In B. Baltagi (Ed.), Nonstationary Panels, Panel Cointegration, and Dynamic Panels Advances in Econometrics. JAI. doi:10.1016/S0731-9053(00)15006-6

Breitung, J., & Pesaran, M. (2005). *Unitroots and Cointegration in Panels* (No. 1565). https://www.ifo.de/DocDL/cesifo1_wp1565.pdf

Brenner, M., & Galai, D. (1989). New financial instruments for hedging changes in volatility. *Financial Analysts Journal*, *45*(4), 61–65. doi:10.2469/faj.v45.n4.61

Brenner, M., & Izhakian, Y. (2021). Risk and ambiguity in turbulent times. *The Quarterly Journal of Finance*. Advance online publication. doi:10.1142/S2010139222400018

Brock, W., Lakonishok, J., & LeBaron, B. (1992). Simple technical trading rules and the stochastic properties of stock returns. *The Journal of Finance*, *47*(5), 1731–1764. doi:10.1111/j.1540-6261.1992.tb04681.x

Brogaard, J., Li, D., & Xia, Y. (2017). Stock liquidity and default risk. *Journal of Financial Economics*, *124*(3), 486–502. doi:10.1016/j.jfineco.2017.03.003

Bromiley, P. (1991). Testing a Causal Model of Corporate Risk Taking and Performance. *Academy of Management Journal*, *34*(1), 37–59. Retrieved April 3, 2021, from https://www.jstor.org/stable/256301

Brown, J. R., Gustafson, M. T., & Ivanov, I. T. (2021). Weathering Cash Flow Shocks. *The Journal of Finance*, *76*(4), 1731–1772. doi:10.1111/jofi.13024

Brown, R., Coventry, L., & Pepper, G. (2021). Information seeking, personal experiences, and their association with COVID-19 risk perceptions: Demographic and occupational inequalities. *Journal of Risk Research*, *24*(3-4), 506–520. doi:10.1080/13669877.2021.1908403

Brown, S., Goetzmann, W., Ibbotson, R., & Ross, S. (1992). Survivorship Bias in Performance Studies. *Review of Financial Studies*, *5*(4), 553–580. doi:10.1093/rfs/5.4.553

Brühne, A. I., & Schanz, D. (2019). *Building Up a Protective Shield: The Role of Communication for Corporate Tax Risk Management*. Working Paper. https://papers.ssrn.com/sol3/papers.cfm?abstract_id=3254915

Brunnermeier, M., Gorton, G., & Krishnamurthy, A. (2012). Risk Topography. *NBER Macroeconomics Annual*, *26*(1), 149–176. doi:10.1086/663991

Bufarwa, I. M., Elamer, A. A., Ntim, C. G., & AlHares, A. (2020). Gender diversity, corporate governance and financial risk disclosure in the UK. *International Journal of Law and Management*, *62*(6), 521–538. doi:10.1108/IJLMA-10-2018-0245

Burden, F., & Winkler, D. (2008). Bayesian Regularization of Neural Networks. In D. J. Livingstone (Ed.), *Artificial Neural Networks. Methods in Molecular Biology™* (Vol. 458). Humana Press. doi:10.1007/978-1-60327-101-1_3

Busru, S. A., Shanmugasundaram, G., & Bhat, S. A. (2020). Corporate Governance an Imperative for Stakeholders Protection : Evidence from Risk Management of Indian Listed Firms. *Business Perspectives and Research*, *8*(2), 89–116. doi:10.1177/2278533719886995

Buss, D. (1999). *Evolutionary Psychology*. Allyn and Bacon.

Byrd, K., Her, E., Fan, A., Almanza, B., Liu, Y., & Leitch, S. (2021). Restaurants and COVID-19: What are consumers' risk perceptions about restaurant food and its packaging during the pandemic? *International Journal of Hospitality Management*, *94*, 102821. Advance online publication. doi:10.1016/j.ijhm.2020.102821 PMID:34866742

Byrnes, J. P., Miller, D. C., & Schafer, W. D. (1999). Gender differences in risk taking: A meta-analysis. *Psychological Bulletin*, *125*(3), 367–383. doi:10.1037/0033-2909.125.3.367

Cagle, J. A. B., & Baucus, M. M. (2006). Case Studies of Ethics Scandals: Effects on Ethical Perceptions of Finance Students. *Journal of Business Ethics*, *64*(3), 213–229. doi:10.100710551-005-8503-5

Cakici, N., & Zaremba, A. (2021). Liquidity and the cross-section of international stock returns. *Journal of Banking & Finance*, *127*, 106123. doi:10.1016/j.jbankfin.2021.106123

Câmara Municipal de Lisboa. (2017). *1988 - Incêndio do Chiado*. Retrieved December 26, 2017, from http://www.cm-lisboa.pt/municipio/historia/historial-das-catastrofes-de-lisboa/1988-incendio-do-chiado

Cancela, B., Neves, M. E., Rodrigues, L. L., & Dias, A. (2020). The influence of Corporate Governance on Corporate Sustainability: New evidence using panel data in the Iberian macroeconomic environment. *International Journal of Accounting and Information Management*, *28*(4), 785–806. doi:10.1108/IJAIM-05-2020-0068

Cañibano, L., & Mora, A. (2000). Evaluating the statistical significance of de facto accounting harmonization: A study of European global players. *European Accounting Review*, *9*(3), 349–369. doi:10.1080/09638180020017113

Cantillon, S., Moore, E., & Teasdale, N. (2021). COVID-19 and the pivotal role of grandparents: Childcare and income support in the UK and south africa. *Feminist Economics*, *27*(1-2), 188–202. doi:10.1080/13545701.2020.1860246

Cant, M. C., Wiid, J. A., & Manley, L. L. (2014). Counterfeit luxury fashion brands: Consumer purchase behaviour. *Corporate Ownership & Control*, *11*(3), 175–183. doi:10.22495/cocv11i3c1p4

Capelle-Blancard, G., & Monjon, S. (2014). The Performance of Socially Responsible Funds: Does the Screening Process Matter? *European Financial Management*, *20*(3), 494–520. doi:10.1111/j.1468-036X.2012.00643.x

Carhart, M. (1997). On Persistence in Mutual Fund Performance. *The Journal of Finance*, *52*(1), 57–82. doi:10.1111/j.1540-6261.1997.tb03808.x

Cassell, C. A., Giroux, G. A., Myers, L. A., & Omer, T. C. (2012). The effect of corporate governance on auditor-client realignments. *Auditing*, *31*(2), 167–188. doi:10.2308/ajpt-10240

Castillo, M. E., & Cross, P. J. (2008). Of mice and men: Within gender variation in strategic behavior. *Games and Economic Behavior*, *64*(2), 421–432. doi:10.1016/j.geb.2008.01.009

CBI - Climate Bonds Initiative. (2019). *Growing green bond markets: The development of taxonomies to identify green assets*. Available at: https://www.climatebonds.net/files/reports/policy_taxonomy_briefing_conference.pdf

CEDESA. (2021). Combate à corrupção em Angola: Radiografia para investidores. *Dinheiro Vivo*. https://www.dinheirovivo.pt/opiniao/combate-a-corrupcao-em-angola-radiografia-para-investidores-13714984.html

Cepel, M., Gavurova, B., Dvorsky, J., & Belas, J. (2020). The Impact of the COVID-19 Crisis on the Perception of Business Risk in the SME Segment. *Journal of International Students*, *13*(3), 248–263.

Compilation of References

Ceylan, Ö. (2014). Time-varying volatility asymmetry: A Conditioned HAR-RV (CJ) EGARCH-M Model. *The Journal of Risk*, *17*(2), 21–49. doi:10.21314/JOR.2014.295

Chandra, R., & Walton, M. (2020). Big potential, big risks? Indian capitalism, economic reform and populism in the BJP era. *India Review*, *19*(2), 176–205. doi:10.1080/14736489.2020.1744997

Chang, W., & Grady, N. (2019), NIST Big Data Interoperability Framework: Volume 1, Definitions, Special Publication (NIST SP). National Institute of Standards and Technology. doi:10.6028/NIST.SP.1500-1r2

Chang, Y. H., Jong, C. C., & Wang, S. C. (2017). Size, trading volume, and the profitability of technical trading. *International Journal of Managerial Finance*, 1-38.

Chang, C. L., McAleer, M., & Wong, W. K. (2020). Risk and Financial Management of COVID-19 in Business, Economics and Finance. *Journal of Risk and Financial Management*, *13*(5), 1–7. doi:10.3390/jrfm13050102

Chang, C.-L., McAleer, M., & Tansuchat, R. (2011). Crude oil hedging strategies using dynamic multivariate GARCH. *Energy Economics*, *33*(5), 912–923. doi:10.1016/j.eneco.2011.01.009

Chang, Ch., Yu, Sh., & Hung, Ch. (2015). Firm risk and performance: The role of corporate governance. *Review of Managerial Science*, *9*(1), 141–173. doi:10.100711846-014-0132-x

Chang, E., & Witte, D. (2010). Performance Evaluation of US Socially Responsible Mutual Funds: Revisiting Doing Good and Doing Well. *American Journal of Business*, *25*(1), 9–21. doi:10.1108/19355181201000001

Chang, X., Chen, Y., & Zolotoy, L. (2017). Stock liquidity and stock price crash risk. *Journal of Financial and Quantitative Analysis*, *52*(4), 1605–1637. doi:10.1017/S0022109017000473

Chang, Y., & Ko, Y. (2017). International Journal of Hospitality Management Consumers' perceived post purchase risk in luxury services. *International Journal of Hospitality Management*, *61*, 94–106. doi:10.1016/j.ijhm.2016.09.005

Charitou, A., Lambertides, N., & Theodoulou, G. (2011). Dividend Increases and Initiations and Default Risk in Equity Returns. *Journal of Financial and Quantitative Analysis*, *46*(5), 1521–1543. doi:10.1017/S0022109011000305

Charnes, A., Cooper, W. W., & Rhodes, E. (1978). Measuring the efficiency of decision making units. *European Journal of Operational Research*, *2*(6), 429–444. doi:10.1016/0377-2217(78)90138-8

Chaulk, B., Johnson, P. J., & Bulcroft, R. (2003). Effects of Marriage and Children on Financial Risk Tolerance: A Synthesis of Family Development and Prospect Theory. *Journal of Family and Economic Issues*, *24*(3), 257–279. doi:10.1023/A:1025495221519

Chauvet, M., & Potter, S. (2000). Coincident and leading indicators of the stock market. *Journal of Empirical Finance*, *71*(1), 87–111. doi:10.1016/S0927-5398(99)00015-8

Chavarín, R. (2020). Risk governance, banks affiliated to business groups, and foreign ownership. In Risk Management (Vol. 22, Issue 1). Palgrave Macmillan UK. doi:10.105741283-019-00049-9

Chava, S., & Purnanandam, A. (2010). Is Default Risk Negatively Related to Stock Returns? *Review of Financial Studies*, *23*(6), 2523–2559. doi:10.1093/rfs/hhp107

Cheema, M. A., Faff, R. W., & Szulczuk, K. (2020). The 2008 global financial crisis and COVID-19 pandemic: How safe are the safe haven assets? *Covid Economics*, *34*, 88–115.

Chemkha, R., BenSaïda, A., Ghorbel, A., & Tayachi, T. (2021). Hedge and safe haven properties during COVID-19: Evidence from Bitcoin and gold. *The Quarterly Review of Economics and Finance*, *82*, 71–85.

Chen, C., & Lee, H. (2013). Default Risk, Liquidity Risk, and Equity Returns: Evidence from the Taiwan Market. *Emerging Markets Finance & Trade*, *49*(1), 101–129. doi:10.2753/REE1540-496X490106

Cheng, Q., & Lo, K. (2006). Insider trading and voluntary disclosures. *Journal of Accounting Research*, *44*(5), 815–848. doi:10.1111/j.1475-679X.2006.00222.x

Chen, J., Cheng, C., Ku, C. Y., & Liao, W. (2021). Are Banks Improving Risk Governance After the Financial Crisis? *Journal of Accounting, Auditing & Finance*, *36*(3), 540–556. doi:10.1177/0148558X19870099

Chen, J., Hong, H., Huang, M., & Kubik, J. (2004). Does Fund Size Erode Mutual Fund Performance? The Role of Liquidity and Organization. *The American Economic Review*, *94*(5), 1276–1302. doi:10.1257/0002828043052277

Chen, Y., & Chang, C. (2012). Enhance green purchase intentions: The roles of green perceived value, green perceived risks, and green trust. *Management Decision*, *50*(3), 502–520. doi:10.1108/00251741211216250

Chen, Y.-Q., Zhu, H., Le, M., & Wu, Y.-Z. (2014). The effect of face consciousness on consumption of counterfeit luxury goods. *Social Behavior and Personality*, *42*(6), 1007–1014. doi:10.2224bp.2014.42.6.1007

Cheung, W. A., & Wei, K. J. (2006). Insider ownership and corporate performance: Evidence from the adjustment cost approach. *Journal of Corporate Finance*, *12*(5), 906–925. doi:10.1016/j.jcorpfin.2006.02.002

Chiu, W., Lee, K.-Y., & Won, D. (2014). Chiu, Weisheng, & Won, D. (2015). Consumer behavior toward counterfeit sporting goods. *Social Behavior and Personality*, *42*(May), 615–624. Advance online publication. doi:10.2224bp.2014.42.4.615

Chiu, W., & Leng, H. (2016). Consumers' Intention to Purchase Counterfeit Sporting Goods in Singapore and Taiwan. *Asia Pacific Journal of Marketing and Logistics*, *28*(1), 23–36. doi:10.1108/APJML-02-2015-0031

Cho, E., Okafor, C., Ujah, N., & Zhang, L. (2021). Executives' gender-diversity, education, and firm's bankruptcy risk: Evidence from China. *Journal of Behavioral and Experimental Finance*, *30*, 100500. doi:10.1016/j.jbef.2021.100500

Cho, J., & Lee, J. (2006). An integrated model of risk and risk-reducing strategies. *Journal of Business Research*, *59*(1), 112–120. doi:10.1016/j.jbusres.2005.03.006

Chong, T. T., Ng, W. K., & Liew, V. K. (2014). Revisiting the Performance of MACD and RSI Oscillators. *Journal of Risk and Financial Management*, *7*(1), 1-12.

Chong, L.-L., Ong, H.-B., & Tan, S.-H. (2018). Corporate risk-taking and performance in Malaysia: The effect of board composition, political connections and sustainability practices. *Corporate Governance*, *18*(4), 635–654.

Chong, T. T., & Ng, W. K. (2008). Technical analysis and the London stock exchange: Testing the MACD and RSI rules using the FT30. *Applied Economics Letters*, *15*(14), 1111–1114. doi:10.1080/13504850600993598

Chou, R. Y., Chou, H., & Liu, N. (2002). Range Volatility Models and Their Applications in Finance. In *Quantitative Finance and Risk Management* (pp. 1273–1281). Springer.

Christensen, C. (2020). *The Relative Industry Specific Effects of COVID-19 on Market Volatility and Liquidity.* All Graduate Plan B and Other Reports. Retrieved from https://digitalcommons.usu.edu/gradreports/1470

Christodoulides, G., Michaelidou, N., & Li, C. H. (2008). Measuring perceived brand luxury: An evaluation of the BLI scale. *Journal of Brand Management*, *16*(5), 395–405.

Chuang, Y., & Chung-En Liu, J. (2020). Who wears a mask? gender differences in risk behaviors in the covid-19 early days in taiwan. *Economic Bulletin*, *40*(4), 2619–2627. www.scopus.com

Chung, W. K., & Au, W. T. (2020). Risk tolerance profiling measure: Testing its reliability and validities. *Financial Counseling and Planning*, *32*(2), 311–325.

Churchill, B. (2021). COVID-19 and the immediate impact on young people and employment in australia: A gendered analysis. *Gender, Work and Organization*, *28*(2), 783–794. doi:10.1111/gwao.12563 PMID:33230375

Cielen, A., Peeters, L., & Vanhoof, K. (2004). Bankruptcy prediction using a data envelopment analysis. *European Journal of Operational Research*, *154*(2), 526–532. doi:10.1016/S0377-2217(03)00186-3

Claessens, S., Djankov, S., Fan, J. P., & Lang, L. H. (2002). Disentangling the incentive and entrenchment effects of large shareholdings. *The Journal of Finance*, *57*(6), 2741–2771. doi:10.1111/1540-6261.00511

Clarke, J., Dunbar, C., & Kahle, K. M. (2001). Long-run performance and insider trading in completed and canceled seasoned equity offerings. *Journal of Financial and Quantitative Analysis*, *36*(4), 415–430. doi:10.2307/2676218

Climent, F., & Soriano, P. (2011). Green and Good? The Investment Performance of US Environmental Mutual Funds. *Journal of Business Ethics*, *103*(2), 275–287. doi:10.100710551-011-0865-2

Coates, J. M., & Herbert, J. (2008). Endogenous steroids and financial risk taking on a London trading floor. *Proceedings of the National Academy of Sciences of the United States of America*, *105*(16), 6167–6172. doi:10.1073/pnas.0704025105 PMID:18413617

Cohen, G., & Cabiri, E. (2015). Can technical oscillators outperform the buy and hold strategy? *Applied Economics*, *47*(30), 3189–3197. doi:10.1080/00036846.2015.1013609

Cohen, L., Malloy, C., & Pomorski, L. (2012). Decoding inside information. *The Journal of Finance*, *67*(3), 1009–1043. doi:10.1111/j.1540-6261.2012.01740.x

Colby, R. W. (2002). *The Encyclopedia of Technical Market Indicators*. McGraw-Hill.

Collin-Dufresne, P., & Fos, V. (2015). Do prices reveal the presence of informed trading? *The Journal of Finance*, *70*(4), 1555–1582. doi:10.1111/jofi.12260

Conlon, T., & McGee, R. (2020). Safe haven or risky hazard? Bitcoin during the Covid-19 bear market. *Finance Research Letters*, *35*, 101607.

Cordell, V., Wongtada, N., & Kieschnick, L. Jr. (1996). Counterfeit purchase intentions: Role of lawfulness attitudes and product traits as determinants. *Journal of Business Research*, *35*(1), 41–53. doi:10.1016/0148-2963(95)00009-7

Corman, J. (2001). Gender comparisons in strategic decision-making: An entrepreneurial analyses of the entrepreneurial strategy mix. *Journal of Small Business Management*, *39*(2), 165–173. doi:10.1111/1540-627X.00015

Cortez, M., Silva, F., & Areal, N. (2009). The Performance of European Socially Responsible Funds. *Journal of Business Ethics*, *87*(4), 573–588. doi:10.100710551-008-9959-x

Cortez, M., Silva, F., & Areal, N. (2012). Socially Responsible Investing in the Global Market: The Performance of US and European Funds. *International Journal of Finance & Economics*, *17*(3), 254–271. doi:10.1002/ijfe.454

COSO. (2004). *Enterprise Risk Management – Integrated Framework*. COSO.

COSO. (2010). *Board Risk Oversight-A progress report*. https://www.coso.org/pages/erm.aspx

Cowling, M., Brown, R., & Rocha, A. (2020). Did You Save Some Cash for a Rainy COVID-19 Day? The Crisis and SMEs. *International Small Business Journal: Researching Entrepreneurship*, *38*(7), 593–604. doi:10.1177/0266242620945102

Cox, T., Morrin, D., & King, A. (2010). Australia. In A. Bakker & S. Kloosterhof (Eds.) Tax Risk Management: From Risk to Opportunity (pp. 135–160). IBFD.

Cozmei, C., & Şerban, E. C. (2014). Risk Management Triggers: From the Tax Risk Pitfalls to Organizational Risk. *Procedia Economics and Finance*, *15*, 1594–1602. doi:10.1016/S2212-5671(14)00630-3

Craig, L., & Churchill, B. (2021). Working and caring at home: Gender differences in the effects of covid-19 on paid and unpaid labor in australia. *Feminist Economics*, *27*(1-2), 310–326. doi:10.1080/13545701.2020.1831039

Cree, A. (2020). *Intraday Volatility in the COVID Era: Why it Matters*. Retrieved from https://flextrade.com/intraday-volatility-in-the-covid-era-why-it-matters/

CRIF. (2016). Financial statements of businesses. Slovak Credit Bureau, s.r.o.

Croson, R., & Gneezy, U. (2009). Gender differences in preferences. *Journal of Economic Literature*, *47*(2), 1–27. doi:10.1257/jel.47.2.448

Csikósová, A., Janošková, M., & Čulková, K. (2019). Limitation of Financial Health Prediction in companies from Post-Communist Countries. *Journal of Risk and Financial Management*, *12*(1), 1–15. doi:10.3390/jrfm12010015

Custódio, C., & Metzger, D. (2014). Financial expert CEOs: CEO's work experience and firm's financial policies. *Journal of Financial Economics*, *114*(1), 125–154. doi:10.1016/j.jfineco.2014.06.002

da Silva, C. R. M., Aquino, C. V. M. G., Oliveira, L. V. C., Beserra, E. P., & Romero, C. B. A. (2021). Trust in government and social isolation during the covid-19 pandemic: Evidence from brazil. *International Journal of Public Administration*, *44*(11-12), 974–983. doi:10.1080/01900692.2021.1920611

Daelen, M., Elst, C. V., & Ven, A. (2010). Introducing Risk Management. In M. Daelen & C. Elst (Eds.), *Risk Management and Corporate Governance: Interconnections in Law, Accounting and Tax* (pp. 191–232). Edward Elgar Publishing. doi:10.4337/9781849807999.00008

Dahlquist, M., Engström, S., & Söderlind, P. (2000). Performance and Characteristics of Swedish Mutual Funds. *Journal of Financial and Quantitative Analysis*, *35*(3), 409–423. doi:10.2307/2676211

Dang, T. L., & Nguyen, Th. M. H. (2020). Liquidity risk and stock performance during the financial crisis. *Research in International Business and Finance*, *52*, 101165. doi:10.1016/j.ribaf.2019.101165

Davidson, A., Vinhal, M., & Michel, N. (2019). Shame on You: When Materialism Leads to Purchase Intentions Toward Counterfeit Products. *Journal of Business Ethics*, *155*(2), 479–494. doi:10.100710551-017-3479-5

Davydenko, S., Strebulaev, I., & Zhao, X. (2012). A Market-Based Study of the Cost of Default. *Review of Financial Studies*, *25*(10), 2959–2999. doi:10.1093/rfs/hhs091

De Long, J. B., Shleifer, A., Summers, L. H., & Waldmann, R. J. (1990). Noise Trader Risk in Financial Markets. *Journal of Political Economy*, *98*(4), 703–738. doi:10.1086/261703

De Matos, C. A., Alberto, C., & Rossi, V. (2007). Consumer attitudes toward counterfeits: A review and extension. *Journal of Consumer Marketing*, *24*(1), 1, 36–47. doi:10.1108/07363760710720975

de Sousa Gabriel, V. M., Miralles-Quirós, M. M., & Miralles-Quirós, J. L. (2021). Shades between Black and Green Investment: Balance or Imbalance? *Sustainability*, *13*(9), 5024. doi:10.3390u13095024

de Sousa Gabriel, V. M., & Rodeiro-Pazos, D. (2020). Environmental Investment Versus Traditional Investment: Alternative or Redundant Pathways? *Organization & Environment*, *33*(2), 245–261. doi:10.1177/1086026618783749

Deakin, E. B. (1972). A Discriminant Analysis of Predictors of Business Failure. *Journal of Accounting Research*, *10*(1), 167–179. doi:10.2307/2490225

Deaux, K., & Ennsuiller, T. (1994). Explanations of Successful Performance on Sex Linked Traits: What is Skill for the Male is Luck for the Female. *Journal of Personality and Social Psychology*, *29*(1), 80–85. doi:10.1037/h0035733

Debreu, G. (1951). The coefficient of resource utilization. *Econometrica*, *19*(3), 273–292. doi:10.2307/1906814

Defond, M. L., Hann, R. N., Xuesong, H. U., & Engel, E. (2005). Does the market value financial expertise on audit committees of boards of directors? *Journal of Accounting Research*, *43*(2), 153–193. doi:10.1111/j.1475-679x.2005.00166.x

Delina, R., & Packová, M. (2013). Validácia predikčných bankrotových modelov v podmienkach SR [Prediction bankruptcy models validation in Slovak business environment]. *Ekonomie a Management*, *16*(3), 101-112. http://www.ekonomie-management.cz/download/1404726193_54d6/2013_3+Validacia+predikcnych+bankrotivych+modelov+v+podmienkach+SR.pdf

Deloitte. (2012). *Global Tax Cube, Your First Step to Global Tax Risk Management*. http://www.deloitte.com/assets/DcomAustralia/Local%20Assets/Documents/Services/Tax%20services/Tax%20Management%20Consulting%201/Deloitte_Global_Tax_Cube_flyer.pdf

Deloitte. (2015). *Tax Risk Transformation Optimizing and enhancement of Tax Risk Management*. https://www2.deloitte.com/content/dam/Deloitte/nl/Documents/financial-services/deloitte-nl-fsi-tax-risk-transformation-optimizing-and-enhancement.pdf

DeLong, E. R., DeLong, D. M., & Clarke-Pearson, D. L. (1988). Comparing the areas under two or more correlated receiver operating characteristic curves: A nonparametric approach. *Biometrics*, *44*(3), 837–845. doi:10.2307/2531595 PMID:3203132

Deloof, M. (2001). Belgian intragroup relations and the determinants of corporate liquid reserves. *European Financial Management*, *7*(3), 375–392. doi:10.1111/1468-036X.00161

Deloof, M. (2003). Does working capital management affect profitability of Belgian firms? *Journal of Business Finance & Accounting*, *30*(3-4), 573–588. doi:10.1111/1468-5957.00008

Demers, E., Hendrikse, J., Joos, P., & Lev, B. (2021). ESG did not immunize stocks during the COVID-19 crisis, but investments in intangible assets did. *Journal of Business Finance & Accounting*, *48*(3-4), 433–462. doi:10.1111/jbfa.12523 PMID:34230747

Demey, D., Berrington, A., Evandrou, M., & Falkingham, J. (2013). Pathways into living alone in mid-life: Diversity and policy implications. *Advances in Life Course Research*, *18*(3), 161–174. doi:10.1016/j.alcr.2013.02.001 PMID:24796556

Derwall, J., Koedijk, K., & Horst, J. (2011). A Tale of Values-Driven and Profit-Seeking Social Investors. *Journal of Banking & Finance*, *35*(8), 2137–2147. doi:10.1016/j.jbankfin.2011.01.009

Deshmukh, S., Gamble, K., & Howe, K. (2015). Short Selling and Firm Operating Performance. *Financial Management*, *44*(1), 217–236. doi:10.1111/fima.12081

Dessaint, O., & Matray, A. (2017). Do Managers Overreact to Salient Risks? Evidence from Hurricane Strikes. *Journal of Financial Economics*, *126*(1), 97–121. doi:10.1016/j.jfineco.2017.07.002

Dhamija, A., Yadav, S. S., & Jain, P. (2014). The impact of corporate governance on the financial performance: A study of nifty companies. *International Research Journal of Finance and Economics*, *121*, 60–75.

Dichev, I. (1998). Is the Risk of Bankruptcy a Systematic Risk? *Journal of Finance*, *53*(3), 1131–1147. doi:10.1111/0022-1082.00046

Dimitras, A. I., Zanakis, S. H., & Zopounidis, C. (1996). A survey of business failures with an emphasis on prediction methods and industrial applications. *European Journal of Operational Research*, *90*(6), 487–513. doi:10.1016/0377-2217(95)00070-4

Ding, Y. S., Song, X. P., & Zen, Y. M. (2008). Forecasting Financial Condition of Chinese Listed Companies Based on Support Vector Machine. *Expert Systems with Applications*, *34*(4), 3081–3089. doi:10.1016/j.eswa.2007.06.037

Dipak, L., & Purnendu, M. (2007). *Handbook of Computational Intelligence in Manufacturing and Production Management*. Information Science Reference.

Dixon, J. R., Nanni, J., & Vollmann, T. E. (1990). *The New Performance Challenge: Measuring Operations for World-class Companies*. Dow Jones-Irwin.

Dombo Beheer, B. V. vs. The Netherlands, 27 October 1993, https://hudoc.echr.coe.int/app/conversion/pdf/?library=ECHR&id=001-57850&filename=001-57850.pdf

Donthu, N., Kumar, S., Mukherjee, D., Pandey, N., & Lim, W. M. (2021). How to conduct a bibliometric analysis: An overview and guidelines. *Journal of Business Research*, *133*, 285–296. doi:10.1016/j.jbusres.2021.04.070

Dou, W. W., Ji, Y., Reibstein, D., & Wu, W. (2021). Inalienable customer capital, corporate liquidity, and stock returns. *Journal of Finance*, *76*(1), 211–265. doi:10.1111/jofi.12960

Dowling, R., & Staelin, R. (1994). A model of perceived risk and intended risk-handling activity. *The Journal of Consumer Research*, *21*(1), 119–125. doi:10.1086/209386

Drake, K. D., Lusch, S. J., & Stekelberg, J. (2019). Does Tax Risk Affect Investor Valuation of Tax Avoidance? *Journal of Accounting, Auditing & Finance*, *34*(1), 151–176. doi:10.1177/0148558X17692674

Drew, M., Naughton, T., & Madhu, V. (2003). Firm-size, book-to-market equity and security returns: Evidence from the Shanghai stock exchange. *Australian Journal of Management*, *28*(2), 119–140.

Driessen, J. (2005). Is Default Event Risk Priced in Corporate Bonds? *Review of Financial Studies*, *18*(1), 165–195. doi:10.1093/rfs/hhi009

Dryden, M. M. (1970). Filter tests of UK share prices. *Applied Economics*, *1*(4), 261–275. doi:10.1080/00036847000000002

Dunfee, T. (2003). Social Investing: Mainstream or Backwater? *Journal of Business Ethics*, *43*(3), 247–252. doi:10.1023/A:1022914831479

Dupire, M., & Slagmulder, R. (2019). Risk governance of financial institutions : The effect of ownership structure and board independence. *Finance Research Letters*, *28*, 227–237. doi:10.1016/j.frl.2018.05.001

Duque, J., & Paxson, D. A. (1997). *Empirical Evidence On Volatility Estimators*. Academic Press.

Eberhartinger, E., & Zieser, M. (2021). The Effects of Cooperative Compliance on Firms' Tax Risk, Tax Risk Management and Compliance Costs, Schmalenbach. *Journal of Business Research*, *73*, 125–178. PMID:34803211

Eckel, C. C., & Grossman, P. J. (2008). Forecasting risk attitudes: An experimental study using actual and forecast gamble choices. *Journal of Economic Behavior & Organization*, *68*(1), 1–17. doi:10.1016/j.jebo.2008.04.006

Ederington, L. H. (1979). The hedging performance of the new futures markets. *The Journal of Finance*, *34*(1), 157–170. doi:10.1111/j.1540-6261.1979.tb02077.x

Education, C. F. I. (n.d.). *Credit Risk*. Retrieved from https://corporatefinanceinstitute.com/resources/knowledge/finance/credit-risk/

Edwards, R. D., Magee, J., & Bassetti, W. C. (2018). *Technical analysis of stock trends*. CRC press. doi:10.4324/9781315115719

Edwards, W. (1954). The Theory of Decision Making. *Psychological Bulletin*, *51*(4), 380–417. doi:10.1037/h0053870 PMID:13177802

Eggers, F. (2020). Masters of Disasters? Challenges and Opportunities for SMEs in Times of Crisis. *Journal of Business Research*, *116*, 199–208. doi:10.1016/j.jbusres.2020.05.025 PMID:32501306

Eiamkanitchat, N., Moontuy, T., & Ramingwong, S. (2017). Fundamental analysis and technical analysis integrated system for stock filtration. *Cluster Computing*, *20*(19), 889–894. doi:10.100710586-016-0694-2

EIB - European Investment Bank. (2007). *EPOS II – The "Climate Awareness Bond" EIB promotes climate protection via pan-EU public offering*. Anúncio para fins publicitários. Available at: https://www.unicreditgroup.eu/content/dam/unicreditgroup/documents/inc/press-and-media/FOR_DISTRIBUTION_MAY_22_2007_EPOSeng.pdf, consulted at July 05, of 2021.

Eisend, M., Hartmann, P., & Apaolaza, V. (2017). Who Buys Counterfeit Luxury Brands? *Journal of International Marketing*, *25*(4), 89–111. doi:10.1509/jim.16.0133

Eisend, M., & Schuchert-Güler, P. (2006). Explaining Counterfeit Purchases: A Review and Preview Explaining Counterfeit Purchases: A Review and Preview. *Academy of Marketing Science*, *12*, 1–25.

Elamer, A. A., & Benyazid, I. (2018). The impact of risk committee on financial performance of UK financial institutions. *International Journal of Accounting and Finance*, *8*(2), 161–180. doi:10.1504/IJAF.2018.093290

Elam, R. (1975). The effect of lease data on the predictive ability of financial ratios. *The Accounting Review*, *5*(1), 25–43. https://www.jstor.org/stable/244661

Elgood, T., Paroissien, I., & Quimby, L. (2004). *Tax Risk Management*. https://www.pwc.co.za/en/assets/pdf/tax-risk-management-guide.pdf

Eling, M., & Marek, S. D. (2013). Corporate governance and risk taking: Evidence from the U.K. and German insurance markets. *The Journal of Risk and Insurance*, *81*(3), 653–682. doi:10.1111/j.1539-6975.2012.01510.x

El-KhatibR.SametA. (2020). The COVID-19 Impact: Evidence from Emerging Markets. https://ssrn.com/abstract=3685013

Elsherif, M. (2019). *The Relationship Between Financial Inclusion and Monetary Policy Transmission: the Case of Egypt*. doi:10.20472/IAC.2019.045.014

Elzahar, H., & Hussainey, K. (2012). Determinants of narrative risk disclosures in UK interim reports. *The Journal of Risk Finance*, *13*(2), 133–147. doi:10.1108/15265941211203189

Embrey, L., & Fox, J. (1997). Gender differences in the investment decision-making process. *Financial Counseling and Planning*, *8*(2), 33–40.

Engizek, N., & Sekerkaya, A. (2015). Is the price only motivation source to purchase counterfeit luxury products? *Journal of Academic Research in Economics*, *7*(1), 89–119.

Engle, R. (2002). Dynamic conditional correlation. *Journal of Business & Economic Statistics*, *20*(3), 339–350. doi:10.1198/073500102288618487

Engle, R. F. (1982). Autoregressive conditional heteroscedasticity with estimates of the variance of United Kingdom Inflation. *Econometrica*, *50*(4), 987–1007. doi:10.2307/1912773

Engle-Warnick, J., & Laszlo, S. (2017). Learning-by-doing in an ambiguous environment. *Journal of Risk and Uncertainty*, *55*(1), 71–94. doi:10.100711166-017-9264-0

Enqvist, J., Graham, M., & Nikkinen, J. (2014). The impact of working capital management on firm profitability in different business cycles: Evidence from Finland. *Research in International Business and Finance*, *32*, 36–49. doi:10.1016/j.ribaf.2014.03.005

Erasmus, D. N. (2009). *Tax Risk Management under SOX 404 and FIN 48*. Thomas Jefferson School of Law Working Paper No. 1480978. https://papers.ssrn.com/sol3/papers.cfm?abstract_id=1480978.

Erasmus, D. N. (2010). *Special Report: Global Tax Audit and Controversy Risk Management*. Thomas Jefferson School of Law Research Paper No. 1575723. doi:10.2139/ssrn.1575723

Eriksson, K., & Simpson, B. (2010). Emotional reactions to losing explain gender differences in entering a risky lottery. *Judgment and Decision Making*, *5*(3), 159–163.

Erin, O., Adebola, D. K., & Abdurafiu, O. N. (2020). Risk governance and cybercrime : The hierarchical regression approach. *Future Business Journal*, *6*(1), 1–15. doi:10.118643093-020-00020-1

Erin, O., Asiriuwa, O., Olojede, P., Ajetunmobi, O., & Usman, T. (2018). Does Risk Governance Impact Bank Performance? Evidence from the Nigerian Banking Sector. *Academy of Accounting and Financial Studies Journal*, *22*(4), 1–15.

Ettredge, M., Johnstone, K., Stone, M., & Wang, Q. (2011). The effects of firm size, corporate governance quality, and bad news on disclosure compliance. *Review of Accounting Studies*, *16*(4), 866–889. doi:10.100711142-011-9153-8

Euromonitor. (2020). *The Impact of Coronavirus in Brazil: Uneven Prospects Across Industries*. Retrieved from https://blog.euromonitor.com/the-impact-of-coronavirus-in-brazil-uneven-prospects-across-industries/

European Commission (EC). (2006). *Risk Management Guide for Tax Administrations*. https://ec.europa.eu/taxation_customs/resources/documents/taxation/tax_cooperation/gen_overview/risk_management_guide_for_tax_administrations_en.pdf

Europeia, C. (2003). Recomendação da Comissão Relativa à Definição de Micro, Pequenas e Médias empresas. *Jornal Oficial Da Comissão Europeia*, *124*(36), 36–41.

EY. (2007). *Tax Risk: External Change, Internal Challenge Global Tax Risk Survey 2006*. https://www2.eycom.ch/publications/items/global_tax_risk_survey_2006/ey_global_tax_risk_survey_2006_e.pdf

EY. (2021). *How do You Adapt to the Changing Tax Risk Landscape?* https://assets.ey.com/content/dam/ey-sites/ey-com/en_gl/topics/tax/tax-pdfs/ey-the-tax-leader-imperative-how-do-you-adapt-to-the-changing-tax-risk-landscape.pdf?download

Faccio, M., Marchica, M. T., & Mura, R. (2016). CEO gender, corporate risk-taking, and the efficiency of capital allocation. *Journal of Corporate Finance*, *39*, 193–209. doi:10.1016/j.jcorpfin.2016.02.008

Faff, R., Mulino, D., & Chai, D. (2008). On the linkage between financial risk tolerance and risk aversion. *Journal of Financial Research*, *31*(1), 1–23. doi:10.1111/j.1475-6803.2008.00229.x

Fama, E. F. (1995). Random walks in stock market prices. *Financial Analysts Journal*, *51*(1), 75–80. doi:10.2469/faj.v51.n1.1861

Compilation of References

Fama, E. F., & Blume, M. E. (1966). Filter rules and stock-market trading. *The Journal of Business*, *39*(1), 226–241. doi:10.1086/294849

Fama, E. F., & Jensen, M. C. (1983). Agency problems and residual claims. *The Journal of Law & Economics*, *26*(2), 327–349. doi:10.1086/467038

Fang, V. W., Tian, X., & Tice, S. (2014). Does Stock Liquidity Enhance or Impede Firm Innovation? *Journal of Finance*, *69*(5), 2085-2125. . doi:10.1111/jofi.12187

Fang, V. W., Noe, T. H., & Tice, S. (2009). Stock market liquidity and firm value. *Journal of Financial Economics*, *94*(1), 150–169. doi:10.1016/j.jfineco.2008.08.007

Farhan, M., Zaman, M., & Buckby, S. (2020). Enterprise risk management and firm performance : Role of the risk committee. *Journal of Contemporary Accounting & Economics*, *16*(1), 100178. doi:10.1016/j.jcae.2019.100178

Farrell, M. J. (1957). The Measurement of Productive Efficiency. *Journal of the Royal Statistical Society. Series A (General)*, *120*(3), 253–290. doi:10.2307/2343100

Fassas, A., Bellos, S., & Kladakis, G. (2021). *Corporate liquidity, supply chain and cost issues awareness within the covid-19 context: Evidence from US management reports' textual analysis*. Corporate Governance. doi:10.1108/CG-09-2020-0399

Featherman, M. S., & Pavlou, P. A. (2003). Predicting e-services adoption: A perceived risk facets perspective. *International Journal of Human-Computer Studies*, *59*(4), 451–474. doi:10.1016/S1071-5819(03)00111-3

Febi, W., Schafer, D., Stephan, A., & Sun, C. (2018). The impact of liquidity risk on the yield spread of green bonds. *Finance Research Letters*, *27*, 53–59. doi:10.1016/j.frl.2018.02.025

Feller, W. (1951). The Asymptotic Distribution of the Range of Sums of Independent Random Variables. *Annals of Mathematical Statistics*, *22*, 427–432.

Fernandez-Izquierdo, A., & Matallin-Saez, J. (2008). Performance of Ethical Mutual Funds in Spain: Sacrifice or Premium? *Journal of Business Ethics*, *81*(2), 247–260. doi:10.100710551-007-9492-3

Ferreira, M. A., & Vilela, A. S. (2004). Why Do Firms Hold Cash? Evidence from EMU Countries. *European Financial Management*, *10*(2), 295–319. doi:10.1111/j.1354-7798.2004.00251.x

Ferreira, M., Keswani, A., Miguel, A., & Ramos, S. (2013). The Determinants of Mutual Fund Performance: A Cross-Country Study. *Review of Finance*, *17*(2), 483–525. doi:10.1093/rof/rfs013

Ferriani, F., & Natoli, F. (2021). ESG risks in times of COVID-19. *Applied Economics Letters*, *28*(18), 1537–1541. doi:10.1080/13504851.2020.1830932

Fichtner, J., Heemskerk, E. M., & Garcia-Bernardo, J. (2017). Hidden power of the Big Three? Passive index funds, re-concentration of corporate ownership, and new financial risk. *Business and Politics*, *19*(2), 298–326. doi:10.1017/bap.2017.6

Fifield, S. G., Power, D. M., & Donald Sinclair, C. (2005). An analysis of trading strategies in eleven European stock markets. *European Journal of Finance*, *11*(6), 531–548. doi:10.1080/1351847042000304099

Figueroa-López, J. E., & Wu, B. (2020). Kernel Estimation of Spot Volatility with Microstructure Noise Using Pre-Averaging. Econometrics, 1-39.

Filippin, A., & Crosetto, P. (2016). A reconsideration of gender differences in risk attitudes. *Management Science*, *62*(11), 3138–3160. doi:10.1287/mnsc.2015.2294

Finkelstein, S., & Boyd, B. (1998). How much does the CEO matter? The role of managerial discretion in the setting of CEO compensation. *Academy of Management Journal*, *41*, 179–200.

Finke, M. S., & Huston, S. J. (2003). The Brighter Side of Financial Risk: Financial Risk Tolerance and Wealth. *Journal of Family and Economic Issues*, *24*(3), 233–256. doi:10.1023/A:1025443204681

Finucane, M. L., Slovic, P., Mertz, C. K., Flynn, J., & Satterfield, T. A. (2000). Gender, race, and perceived risk: The 'white male' effect. *Health Risk & Society*, *2*(2), 159–172. doi:10.1080/713670162

Fisher, J. (1992). Use of Non-*Financial* Performance Measures. *Journal of Cost Management*, *6*(1), 1–8.

Fisher, P. J., & Yao, R. (2017). Gender Differences in financial risk tolerance. *Journal of Economic Psychology*, *61*, 191–202. doi:10.1016/j.joep.2017.03.006

Florio, C., & Leoni, G. (2017). Enterprise risk management and firm performance: The Italian case. *British Accounting Review*, *49*(1), 56–74. doi:10.1016/j.bar.2016.08.003

Fontanills, G. A., & Gentile, T. (2003). *The Volatality Course Workbook*. John Wiley & Sons Inc.

Fornell, C., & Larcker, D. (1981). Evaluating structural equation models with unobservable variables and measurement error. *JMR, Journal of Marketing Research*, *18*(1), 39–50. doi:10.1177/002224378101800104

Forsythe, S., & Shi, B. (2003). Consumer patronage and risk perceptions in Internet shopping. *Journal of Business Research*, *56*(11), 867–875. doi:10.1016/S0148-2963(01)00273-9

Fortier, N. (2020). Covid-19, gender inequality, and the responsibility of the state. *International Journal of Wellbeing*, *10*(3), 77–93. doi:10.5502/ijw.v10i3.1305

Fraedrich, J. P., & Ferrell, O. C. (1992). The impact of perceived risk and moral philosophy type on ethical decision making in business organizations. *Journal of Business Research*, *24*(4), 283–295. doi:10.1016/0148-2963(92)90035-A

Francoeur, C., Labelle, R., & Sinclair-Desgagné, B. (2008). Gender diversity in corporate governance and top management. *Journal of Business Ethics*, *81*(1), 83–95. doi:10.100710551-007-9482-5

Franzoni, F., Nowak, E., & Phalippou, L. (2012). Private Equity Performance and Liquidity Risk. *Journal of Finance*, *67*(6), 2341–2373. doi:10.1111/j.1540-6261.2012.01788.x

Freedman, J. (2010). Tax Risk Management and Corporate Taxpayers – International Tax Administration Developments. In A. Bakker & S. Kloosterhof (Eds.) Tax Risk Management: From Risk to Opportunity (pp. 111–134). IBFD.

Freedman, J., Loomer, G., & Vella, J. (2009). Corporate Tax Risk and Tax Avoidance: New Approaches. *British Tax Review*, *1*, 74–116.

Freeman, R. (1984). *Strategic Management: A Stakeholder Approach*. Pitman.

Friehs, C. G., & Craig, C. L. (2008). Assessing the Effectiveness of Online Library Instruction with Finance Students. *Journal of Web Librarianship*, *2*(4), 493–509. doi:10.1080/19322900802484438

Fritz, S., & Lammle, C. (2003). *The International Harmonization Process of accounting Standards*. Avdelning.

Froot, K. A. (2001). The Market for Catastrophe Risk: A Clinical Examination. *Journal of Financial Economics*, *60*(2–3), 529–571. doi:10.1016/S0304-405X(01)00052-6

Froot, K., Scharfstein, D., & Stein, J. (1993). Risk Management: Coordinating Corporate Investment and Financing Policies. *The Journal of Finance*, *48*(5), 1629–1658. doi:10.1111/j.1540-6261.1993.tb05123.x

Furnham, A., von Stumm, S., & Fenton-O'Creevy, M. (2015). Sex differences in money pathology in the general population. *Social Indicators Research*, *123*(3), 701–711. doi:10.100711205-014-0756-x PMID:26316675

Gabriel, V. (2019). Environmentally sustainable investment: Dynamics between global thematic indices. *Cuadernos de Gestión*, *19*(1), 41–62. doi:10.5295/cdg.150545vg

Gabriel, V., & Pazos, D. (2018). Do Short- and Long-Term Environmental Investments Follow the Same Path? *Corporate Social Responsibility and Environmental Management*, *25*(1), 14–28. doi:10.1002/csr.1437

Gächter, S., Johnson, E., & Herrmann, A. (2010). *Individual-level Loss Aversion in Riskless and Risky Choices*. Retrieved from https://www.econstor.eu/handle/10419/49656

Gajowniczek, K., Zabkowski, T., & Szupiluk, R. (2014). Estimating the ROC curve and its significance for classification model's assessment. *Quantitative Methods in Economics*, *15*(2), 382-391. https://www.ceeol.com/search/article-detail?id=472340

Galema, R., Plantiga, A., & Scholtens, B. (2008). The Stocks at Stake: Return and Risk in Socially Responsible Investment. *Journal of Banking & Finance*, *32*(12), 2646–2654. doi:10.1016/j.jbankfin.2008.06.002

Gallagher, J. (2014). Learning About an Infrequent Event: Evidence From Flood Insurance Take-Up in the United States. *Applied Economics*, *6*(3), 206–233.

Gang, W., Jinxing, H. M. J., & Hongbing, J. (2011). A comparative assessment of ensemble learning for credit scoring. *Expert Systems with Applications*, 223–230.

Garbarino, E., & Strahilevitz, M. (2004). Gender differences in the perceived risk of buying online and the effects of receiving a site recommendation. *Journal of Business Research*, *57*(7), 768–775. doi:10.1016/S0148-2963(02)00363-6

García-Teruel, P. J., & Martínez-Solano, P. (2008). On the Determinants of SME Cash Holdings: Evidence from Spain. *Journal of Business Finance & Accounting*, *35*(1), 127–149. doi:10.1111/j.1468-5957.2007.02022.x

Garikipati, S., & Kambhampati, U. (2021). Leading the fight against the pandemic: Does gender really matter? *Feminist Economics*, *27*(1-2), 401–418. doi:10.1080/13545701.2021.1874614

Garman, M. B., & Klass, M. J. (1980). On the Estimation of Security Price Volatilities from Historical Data. *The Journal of Business*, *53*(1), 67–78.

Gavazza, A. (2010). Asset liquidity and financial contracts: Evidence from aircraft leases. *Journal of Financial Economics*, *95*(1), 62–84. doi:10.1016/j.jfineco.2009.01.004

Geiger-Oneto, S., Gelb, B. D., Walker, D., & Hess, J. D. (2013). Buying status" by choosing or rejecting luxury brands and their counterfeits. *Journal of the Academy of Marketing Science*, *41*(3), 357–372. doi:10.100711747-012-0314-5

Gerçek, A., & Bakar Türegün, F. (2018). Şirketlerde Vergi Riski Algısı ve Vergi Riski Yönetimi Üzerine Bir Araştırma. *Muhasebe ve Vergi Uygulamaları Dergisi*, *11*(3), 307–332. doi:10.29067/muvu.368807

Geromichalos, A., Jung, K. M., Lee, S., & Carlos, D. (2021). A model of endogenous direct and indirect asset liquidity. *European Economic Review*, *132*, 103627. doi:10.1016/j.euroecorev.2020.103627

Geromichalos, A., & Simonovska, I. (2014). Asset liquidity and international portfolio choice. *Journal of Economic Theory*, *151*, 342–380. doi:10.1016/j.jet.2014.01.004

Gerritsen, D. F., Bouri, E., Ramezanifar, E., & Roubaud, D. (2020). The profitability of technical trading rules in the Bitcoin market. *Finance Research Letters*, *34*, 1–10. doi:10.1016/j.frl.2019.08.011

Ghodselahi, A. (2011). A Hybrid Support Vector Machine Ensemble Model for Credit Scoring. *International Journal of Computers and Applications*, 2220–2829.

GİB. (2021). *2020 Yılı Faaliyet Raporu*. https://www.gib.gov.tr/sites/default/files/fileadmin/faaliyetraporlari/2020/2020_faaliyet_raporu.pdf

Gibson, R., Michayluk, D., & Van de Venter, G. (2013). Financial risk tolerance: An analysis of unexplored factors. *Financial Services Review*, 22(1), 23–50.

Giese, G., Lee, L., Melas, D., Nagy, Z., & Nishikawa, L. (2019, Spring). Performance and Risk Analysis of Index-Based ESG Portfolios. *The Journal of Index Investing*, 9(4), 1–12. doi:10.3905/jii.2019.9.4.046

Gil-Bazo, J., & Ruiz-Verdú, P. (2009). Yet Another Puzzle? The Relation Between Price and Performance in the Mutual Fund Industry. *The Journal of Finance*, 64(5), 2153–2183. doi:10.1111/j.1540-6261.2009.01497.x

Gil-Bazo, J., Ruiz-Verdú, P., & Santos, A. (2010). The Performance of Socially Responsible Mutual Funds: The Role of Fees and Management Companies. *Journal of Business Ethics*, 94(2), 243–263. doi:10.100710551-009-0260-4

Gilbert, B., James, A., & Shogren, J. F. (2018). Corporate apology for environmental damage. *Journal of Risk and Uncertainty*, 56(1), 51–81. doi:10.100711166-018-9276-4

GillB. S. (2020). Flirting with Disasters: Do Firms Financially Plan Ahead for Disasters? Available at SSRN: https://ssrn.com/abstract=3525065 or doi:10.2139/ssrn.3525065

Gilliam, J., Chatterjee, S., & Grable, J. (2010). Measuring the perception of financial risk tolerance: A tale of two measures. *Financial Counseling and Planning*, 21, 30–43.

Giner, B., & Mora, A. (2001). The accounting harmonization process in Europe: Analysis of the relation between accounting research and the evolution of the economic reality. *Revista Española de Financiación y Contabilidad*, 30(107), 103–128.

Girling, P. (2013). *Operational risk management: a complete guide to a successful operational risk framework*. Wiley. doi:10.1002/9781118755754

Global Sustainable Investment Alliance – GSIA. (2021). *Global Sustainable Investment Review 2020*. http://www.gsi-alliance.org/wp-content/uploads/2021/07/GSIR-2020.pdf

Gmeiner, K. (2009). *Ausgestaltung Eines Tax Risk Management in Unternehmen*. Masterarbeit, Wirtschafts Universität.

Godey, B., Pederzoli, D., Aziendali, S., Wiedmann, K., & Hennigs, N. (2013). A cross-cultural exploratory content analysis of the perception of luxury from six countries. *Journal of Product and Brand Management*, 3(3), 229–237. doi:10.1108/JPBM-02-2013-0254

Goergen, M., Renneboog, L., & Zhao, Y. (2019). Insider trading and networked directors. *Journal of Corporate Finance*, 56, 152–175. doi:10.1016/j.jcorpfin.2019.02.001

Goldreyer, E., Ahmed, P., & Diltz, J. (1999). The Performance of Socially Responsible Mutual Funds: Incorporating Sociopolitical Information in Portfolio Selection. *Managerial Finance*, 25(1), 23–36. doi:10.1108/03074359910765830

Gontarek, W., & Belghitar, Y. (2018). Risk governance : Examining its impact upon bank performance and risk-taking. *Financial Markets, Institutions and Instruments*, 27(5), 187–224. doi:10.1111/fmii.12103

González, L. O., Santomil, P. D., & Herrera, A. T. (2020). The effect of Enterprise Risk Management on the risk and the performance of Spanish listed companies. *European Research on Management and Business Economics*, 26(3), 111–120. doi:10.1016/j.iedeen.2020.08.002

Gopalan, R., Kadan, O., & Pevzner, M. (2012). Asset Liquidity and Stock Liquidity. *Journal of Financial and Quantitative Analysis*, *47*(2), 333–364. doi:10.1017/S0022109012000130

Gordon, L. A., Loeb, M. P., & Tseng, Ch. (2009). Enterprise risk management and firm performance: A contingency perspective. *Journal of Accounting and Public Policy*, *28*(4), 301–327. doi:10.1016/j.jaccpubpol.2009.06.006

Gounopoulos, D., & Pham, H. (2018). Financial Expert CEOs and Earnings Management Around Initial Public Offerings. *The International Journal of Accounting*, *53*(2), 102–117. doi:10.1016/j.intacc.2018.04.002

Goyal, V., & Wang, W. (2013). Debt Maturity and Asymmetric Information: Evidence from Default Risk Changes. *Journal of Financial and Quantitative Analysis*, *48*(3), 789–817. doi:10.1017/S0022109013000240

Gozgor, G. (2018). Determinants of the domestic credits in developing economies: The role of political risks. *Research in International Business and Finance*, *46*(May), 430–443. doi:10.1016/j.ribaf.2018.05.002

Grable, J. (2000). Financial Risk Tolerance and Additional Factors that Affect Risk Taking in Everyday Money Matters. *Journal of Business and Psychology*, *14*(4), 25–63. doi:10.1023/A:1022994314982

Grable, J. E., Lyons, A. C., & Heo, W. (2019). A test of traditional and psychometric relative risk tolerance measures on household financial risk taking. *Finance Research Letters*, *30*, 8–13. doi:10.1016/j.frl.2019.03.012

Grable, J., & Joo, S. (1999). Factors related to risk tolerance: A further examination. *Consumer Interests Annual*, *45*, 53–58.

Grable, J., & Joo, S. (2004). Environmental and Biopsychosocial Factors Associated with Financial Risk Tolerance. *Financial Counseling and Planning*, *15*(1), 73–82.

Grable, J., & Lytton, R. H. (1998). Investor Risk Tolerance: Testing the Efficacy of Demographics as Differentiating and Classifying Factors. *Financial Counseling and Planning*, *9*(1), 61–73.

Grable, J., & Lytton, R. H. (1999). Financial risk revisited: The development of a risk assessment instrument. *Financial Services Review*, *8*(3), 163–181. doi:10.1016/S1057-0810(99)00041-4

Grable, J., & Lytton, R. H. (2001). Investor risk tolerance: Testing the efficacy of demographics as differentiating and classifying factors. *Financial Counseling and Planning*, *9*, 61–74.

Grable, J., & Lytton, R. H. (2003). The Development of a Risk Assessment Instrument: A Follow-Up Study. *Financial Services Review*, *12*, 257–274.

Grable, J., McGill, S., & Britt, S. (2009). Risk tolerance estimation bias: The age effect. *Journal of Business & Economics Research*, *7*(7), 1–12.

Greene, W. H. (2018). *Econometric Analysis* (8th ed.). Stern School of Business.

Gregory, A., Matatko, J., & Luther, R. (1997). Ethical Unit Trust Financial Performance: Small Company Effects and Fund Size Effects. *Journal of Business Finance & Accounting*, *24*(5), 705–725. doi:10.1111/1468-5957.00130

Gregory, A., & Whittaker, J. (2007). Performance and Performance Persistence of "Ethical" Unit Trusts in the UK. *Journal of Business Finance & Accounting*, *34*(7-8), 1327–1344. doi:10.1111/j.1468-5957.2007.02006.x

Grossman, G. M., & Shapiro, C. (1988). Foreign counterfeiting of status goods. *The Quarterly Journal of Economics*, *103*(1), 79–100. doi:10.2307/1882643

Guelman, L. (2012). Gradient boosting trees for auto insurance loss cost modeling and prediction. *Expert Systems with Applications*, *39*(3), 3659–3667. doi:10.1016/j.eswa.2011.09.058

Guenther, D. A., Masunaga, S. R., & Williams, B. M. (2013). *Tax Avoidance, Tax Aggressiveness, Tax Risk and Firm Risk.* Working Paper. https://business.illinois.edu/accountancy/wp-content/uploads/sites/12/2014/10/Tax-2013-Guenther.pdf

Guerreiro, M. S., Rodrigues, L. L., & Craig, R. (2015). Institutional Change of Accounting Systems: The Adoption of a Regime of Adapted International Financial Reporting Standards. European Accounting Review. *European Accounting Association*, *24*(2), 379–409. doi:10.1080/09638180.2014.887477

Guillemette, M. A., & Finke, M. (2014). Do large swings in equity values change risk tolerance? *Journal of Financial Planning*, *27*(6), 44–50.

Gujarati, D. (2004). *Basic of Econometrics* (4th ed.). McGraw-Hill.

Gu, L., Wang, Y., Yao, W., & Zhang, Y. (2018). Stock liquidity and corporate diversification: Evidence from China's split share structure reform. *Journal of Empirical Finance*, *49*, 57–80. doi:10.1016/j.jempfin.2018.09.002

Gunasekarage, A., & Power, D. M. (2001). The profitability of moving average trading rules in South Asian stock markets. *Emerging Markets Review*, *2*(1), 17–33. doi:10.1016/S1566-0141(00)00017-0

Gundová, P. (2015). Verification of the selected prediction methods in Slovak companies. *Acta academica karviniensia*, *14*(4), 26-38. http://aak.slu.cz/pdfs/aak/2014/04/03.pdf

Gurný, P., & Gurný, M. (2010). Logit vs Probit model při determinaci souhrnných ukazatelů výkonnosti bank [Logit vs Probit model in the determination of the aggregate performance indicators of banks]. In *Zborník z 5. medzinárodnej konferencie Řízení a modelování finančních rizik* [Proceedings of the 5th International Conference on Financial Risk Management and Modeling]. V3B-TU Ostrava, Ekonomická fakulta. https://adoc.pub/logit-vs-probit-model-pi-determinaci-souhrnnych-ukazatel-vyk.html

Guthrie, C. (2003). Prospect Theory, Risk Preference, and the Law. *Northwestern University Law Review*, *97*(3), 1115–1163.

Gutmann, M. P., Merchant, E. K., & Roberts, E. (2018). "Big data" in economic history. *The Journal of Economic History*, *78*(1), 268–299. doi:10.1017/S0022050718000177 PMID:29713093

Hachana, R., & Hajri, J.(2008). Management Entrenchment and performance: case of Tunisian firms. *Corporate Ownership & control*, *5*(3), 418-427.

Hainey, M. (2011). Building and Integrating Databases for Risk Profiles in the United Kingdom. In M. S. Khwaja, R. Awasthi, & J. Loeprick (Eds.), *Risk-Based Tax Audits: Approaches and Country Experiences* (pp. 65–70). The World Bank Publishing. doi:10.1596/9780821387542_CH06

Hair, J. F., Black, W. C., Babin, B. J., & Anderson, R. E. (2010). *Multivariate data analysis: A global perspective* (7th ed.). Prentice-Hall.

Hair, J. F., Hult, G. T. M., Ringle, C. M., & Sarstedt, M. (2014). *A Primer on Partial Least Squares Structural Equation Modeling (PLS-SEM)*. Sage.

Haliassos, M., & Bertaut, C. C. (1995). Why Do So Few Hold Stocks? *Economic Journal (London)*, *105*(432), 1110–1129. doi:10.2307/2235407

Hall, P. A., & Taylor, R. C. R. (1996). *Political Science and the Three New Institutionalisms*. Max-Planck-Institut für Gesellschaftsforschung, Discussion Paper 96/6.

Hallahan, T. A., Faff, R. W., & McKenzie, M. D. (2003). An Exploratory Investigation of the Relation between Risk Tolerance Scores and Demographic Characteristics. *Journal of Multinational Financial Management*, *13*(4-5), 483–502. doi:10.1016/S1042-444X(03)00022-7

Hallahan, T. A., Faff, R. W., & McKenzie, M. D. (2004). An empirical investigation of personal financial risk tolerance. *Financial Services Review*, *13*, 57–78.

Hallahan, T. A., Faff, R. W., & McKenzie, M. D. (2004). An empirical investigation of personal financial tolerance. *Financial Services Review*, *13*, 57–58.

Haman, M. (2010). Africa rising to the anti-counterfeit challenge. *Journal of Intellectual Property Law & Practice*, *5*(5), 344–349.

Hamilton, S., Jo, H., & Statman, M. (1993). Doing Well While Doing Good? The Investment Performance of Socially Responsible Mutual Funds. *Financial Analysts Journal*, *49*(6), 62–66. doi:10.2469/faj.v49.n6.62

Handriania, E., & Ghozalib, I. (2021). Corporate governance on financial distress: Evidence from Indonesia. *Management Science Letters*, *11*, 1833–1844. doi:10.5267/j.msl.2021.1.020

Han, K., Mittal, V., & Zhang, Y. (2017). Relative Strategic Emphasis and Firm-Idiosyncratic Risk: The Moderating Role of Relative Performance and Demand Instability. *Journal of Marketing*, *81*(4), 25–44. doi:10.1509/jm.15.0509

Hanna, S. D., Gutter, M., & Fan, J. (1998). A theory-based measure of risk tolerance. *Proceedings of the Academy of Financial Services*, 10–11.

Hansson, S. O. (1989). Dimensions of risk. *Risk Analysis*, *9*(1), 107–112. doi:10.1111/j.1539-6924.1989.tb01225.x

Hanzaee, K. H., & Taghipourian, M. J. (2012). Attitudes toward counterfeit products and generation differentia. *Research Journal of Applied Sciences, Engineering and Technology*, *4*(9), 1147–1154.

Haq, I. U., Chupradit, S., & Huo, C. (2021). Do green bonds act as a hedge or a safe haven against economic policy uncertainty? Evidence from the USA and China. *International Journal of Financial Studies*, *9*, 40. doi:10.3390/ijfs9030040

Haque, F. (2017). The effects of board characteristics and sustainable compensation policy on carbon performance of UK firms. *The British Accounting Review*, *49*(3), 347–364. doi:10.1016/j.bar.2017.01.001

Harrant, V., & Vaillant, N. G. (2008). Are women less risk averse than men? *Evolution and Human Behavior*, *29*(6), 396–401. doi:10.1016/j.evolhumbehav.2008.05.003

Harris, C. (2017). *Climate Change Blamed as EU's Forest Fires More than Double*. Euronews. Retrieved from https://www.euronews.com/2017/10/16/how-europe-s-wildfires-have-more-than-trebled-in-2017

Harris, C., Jenkins, M., & Glaser, D. (2006). Gender differences in risk assessment. *Judgment and Decision Making*, *1*(1), 48–63.

Hartzmark, S. M., & Sussman, A. B. (2019). Do investors value sustainability? A natural experiment examining ranking and fund flows. *The Journal of Finance*, *74*(6), 2789–2837. doi:10.1111/jofi.12841

Hasan, M. B., Hassan, M. K., Rashid, M. M., & Alhenawi, Y. (2021). Are safe haven assets really safe during the 2008 global financial crisis and COVID-19 pandemic? *Global Finance Journal*, *50*. Advance online publication. doi:10.1016/j.gfj.2021.100668

Hatem, B. S. (2014). Determinants of firm performance: A comparison of European countries. *International Journal of Economics and Finance*, *6*(10), 243–249. doi:10.5539/ijef.v6n10p243

Hawksworth, J. (2017). *World 2050*. Price Water Coopers.

Hawksworth, J., & Cookson, G. (2008). *World 2050*. Price Waterhouse Coopers.

Hawley, C. B., & Fujii, E. T. (1993). An empirical analysis of preferences for financial risk: Further evidence on the Friedman-Savage model. *Journal of Post Keynesian Economics*, *16*(2), 197–204. doi:10.1080/01603477.1993.11489978

Heaton, J. B., Polson, N. G., & Witte, J. H. (2016). *Deep learning in finance*. arXiv/1602.06561.

Hebák, J. (2015). *Statistické myšlení a nástroje analýzy dat* [Statistical thinking and data analysitools]. Informatorium.

Heike, S. (2010). Effects of counterfeits on the image of luxury brands: An empirical study from the consumer perspective. *Journal of Brand Management*, *18*(2), 159–173. doi:10.1057/bm.2010.28

Henehan, P. J., & Walsh, A. (2008). *Global Tax Risk Management*. Bloomsbury Professional.

Henke, H. (2016). The Effect of Social Screening on Bond Mutual Fund Performance. *Journal of Banking & Finance*, *67*, 69–84. doi:10.1016/j.jbankfin.2016.01.010

Herbrich, R., Keilbach, M., Graepel, T., Bollmann-Sdorra, P., & Obermayer, K. (1999). Neural networks in economics. In T. Brenner (Ed.), *Computational techniques for modeling learning in economics* (pp. 169–196). Kluwer Academic Publishers. doi:10.1007/978-1-4615-5029-7_7

Herranz, N., Krasa, S., & Villamil, A. (2015). Entrepreneurs, Risk Aversion, and Dynamic Firms. *Journal of Political Economy*, *123*(5), 1133–1176. doi:10.1086/682678

Herrenbrueck, L., & Geromichalos, A. (2017). A tractable model of indirect asset liquidity. *Journal of Economic Theory*, *168*, 252–260. doi:10.1016/j.jet.2016.12.009

Herstein, R., Drori, N., Berger, R., & Barnes, B. R. (2015). Anticounterfeiting strategies and their influence on attitudes of different counterfeit consumer types. *Psychology and Marketing*, *32*(8), 842–859. doi:10.1002/mar.20822

Hewa Wellalage, N., Locke, S., & Samujh, H. (2020). Firm bribery and credit access: Evidence from Indian SMEs. *Small Business Economics*, *55*(1), 283–304. doi:10.100711187-019-00161-w

He, X., Inman, J. J., & Mittal, V. (2007). Gender jeopardy in financial risk taking. *JMR, Journal of Marketing Research*, *44*, 414–424.

He, Z., & Xiong, W. (2012). Rollover Risk and Credit Risk. *Journal of Finance*, *67*(2), 391–429. doi:10.1111/j.1540-6261.2012.01721.x

Hill, J., & Schneeweis, T. (1981). A note on the hedging effectiveness of foreign currency futures. *Journal of Futures Markets*, *1*(4), 659–664. doi:10.1002/fut.3990010408

Hinz, R. P., McCarthy, D. D., & Turner, J. A. (1997). Are women more conservative investors? Gender differences in participant-directed pension investments. In M. S. Gordon, O. S. Mitchell, & M. M. Twinney (Eds.), *Positioning pensions for the twenty-first century* (pp. 91–103). University of Pennsylvania Press.

Hirsch, J. E. (2005). An index to quantify an individual's scientific research output. *Proceedings of the National Academy of Sciences of the United States of America*, *102*(46), 16569–16572. doi:10.1073/pnas.0507655102 PMID:16275915

Hirschl, T. A., Altobelli, J., & Rank, M. R. (2003). Does marriage increase the odds of affluence: Exploring the life course probabilities. *Journal of Marriage and Family*, *65*(4), 927–938. doi:10.1111/j.1741-3737.2003.00927.x

HL. (2019, September 12). *ASML Holding NV (ASML)*. Retrieved from Hargreaves Lansdown: https://www.hl.co.uk/shares/shares-search-results/a/asml-holding-nv-eur0.09/company-information

Compilation of References

Hock-Doepgen, M., Clauss, T., Kraus, S., & Cheng, C.-F. (2021). Knowledge management capabilities and organizational risk-taking for business model innovation in SMEs. *Journal of Business Research*, *130*, 683–697. doi:10.1016/j.jbusres.2019.12.001

Högfeldt, P. (2003). The History and Politics of Corporate Ownership in Sweden. In History of Corporate Governance around the World. The University of Chicago Press.

Hölmstrom, B., & Tirole, J. (1998). Private and Public Supply of Liquidity. *Journal of Political Economy*, *106*(1), 1–40. doi:10.1086/250001

Holmström, B., & Tirole, J. (2000). Liquidity and Risk Management. *Journal of Money, Credit and Banking*, *32*(3), 295–319. doi:10.2307/2601167

Holton, G. A. (2004). Defining Risk. *Financial Analysts Journal*, *60*(6), 19–25. doi:10.2469/faj.v60.n6.2669

Hong, H., & Kacperczyk, M. (2009). The Price of Sin: The Effects of Social Norms on Markets. *Journal of Financial Economics*, *93*(1), 15–36. doi:10.1016/j.jfineco.2008.09.001

Hood, M., & Malik, F. (2013). Is gold the best hedge and a safe haven under changing stock market volatility? *Review of Financial Economics*, *22*(2), 47–52.

Hoque, M. Z., Islam, M. R., & Azam, M. N. (2013). Board Committee Meetings and Firm Financial Performance : An Investigation of Australian Companies. *International Review of Finance*, *13*(4), 503–528. doi:10.1111/irfi.12009

Horrigan, M. W. (2013, January). Big data: A perspective from the BLS. *Amstat News*, 25-27.

Horton, M. (2021). *The Difference Between Profitability and Profit*. Investopedia. Retrieved from https://www.investopedia.com/ask/answers/012715/what-difference-between-profitability-and-profit.asp

Horton, R. L. (1976). The structure of perceived risk: Some further progress. *Journal of the Academy of Marketing Science*, *4*(4), 694–706. doi:10.1007/BF02729830

Horváthová, J., & Mokrišová, M. (2018). Linear model as a tool in the process of improving financial health. In M. A Omazic, V. Roska, & A. Grobelna (Eds.), *Economic and Social Development: Conference Proceeding from 28th International Scientific Conference on Economic and Social Development* (pp. 425-444). Varazdin Development and Entrepreneurship Agency.

Horváthová, J., & Mokrišová, M. (2020). Comparison of the results of a data envelopment analysis model and logit model in assessing business financial health. *Information (Basel)*, *11*(3), 1–20. doi:10.3390/info11030160

Ho, S. S. M., Li, A. Y., Tam, K., & Zhang, F. (2015). CEO Gender, Ethical Leadership, and Accounting Conservatism. *Journal of Business Ethics*, *127*(2), 351–370. doi:10.100710551-013-2044-0

Ho, T. K. (1998). The random subspace method for constructing decision forests. *IEEE Transactions on Pattern Analysis and Machine Intelligence*, *20*(8), 832–844. doi:10.1109/34.709601

Hox, J. J., & Bechger, T. M. (1998). An introduction to structural equation modeling. *Family Science Review*, *11*, 354–373.

Hoyng, R., Kloosterhof, S., & Macpherson, A. (2010). Tax Control Framework. In A. Bakker, S. Kloosterhof (Eds), Tax Risk Management From Risk to Opportunity (pp. 19–70). IBFD.

Hsiao, C. (2005). Why Panel Data? *The Singapore Economic Review*, *50*(2), 143–154. doi:10.1142/S0217590805001937

Hsiao, C. (2007). Panel data analysis—Advantages and challenges. *Test*, *16*(1), 1–22. doi:10.100711749-007-0046-x

Hsu, P. H., & Kuan, C. M. (2005). Reexamining the profitability of technical analysis with data snooping checks. *Journal of Financial Econometrics*, *3*(4), 606–628. doi:10.1093/jjfinec/nbi026

Hsu, P. H., Moore, J. A., & Neubaum, D. O. (2018). Tax avoidance, financial experts on the audit committee, and business strategy. *Journal of Business Finance & Accounting*, *45*(9–10), 1293–1321. doi:10.1111/jbfa.12352

Huang, H. H., Kerstein, J., & Wang, Ch. (2018). The impact of climate risk on firm performance and financing choices: An international comparison. *Journal of International Business Studies*, *49*(5), 633–656. doi:10.105741267-017-0125-5

Huang, H., & Zhang, W. (2020). Financial expertise and corporate tax avoidance. *Asia-Pacific Journal of Accounting & Economics*, *27*(3), 312–326. doi:10.1080/16081625.2019.1566008

Huang, J., & Kisgen, D. J. (2013). Gender and Corporate Finance: Are Male Executives Overconfident Relative to Female Executives? *Journal of Financial Economics*, *108*(3), 822–839. doi:10.1016/j.jfineco.2012.12.005

Hubble, A., Grable, J. E., & Dannhauser, B. (2020). *Investment Risk Profiling: A Guide for Financial Advisors*. CFA Research Reports. https://www.cfainstitute.org/en/research/industry-research/investment-risk-profiling

Hudson, R., Dempsey, M., & Keasey, K. (1996). A note on the weak form efficiency of capital markets: The application of simple technical trading rules to UK stock prices-1935 to 1994. *Journal of Banking & Finance*, *20*(6), 1121–1132. doi:10.1016/0378-4266(95)00043-7

Hu, L.-T., & Bentler, P. M. (1999). Cutoff criteria for fit indexes in covariance structure analysis: Conventional criteria versus new alternatives. *Structural Equation Modeling*, *6*(1), 1–55. doi:10.1080/10705519909540118

Humphrey, J., & Lee, D. (2011). Australian Socially Responsible Funds: Performance, Risk and Screening Intensity. *Journal of Business Ethics*, *102*(4), 519–535. doi:10.100710551-011-0836-7

Hurley, D., & Choudhary, A. (2020). Role of gender and corporate risk taking. *Corporate Governance*, *20*(3), 383–399. doi:10.1108/CG-10-2018-0313

Huse, M., & Solberg, A. G. (2006). Gender-related boardroom dynamics: How scandinavian women make and can make contributions on corporate boards. *Women in Management Review*, *21*(1), 113–130. doi:10.1108/09649420610650693

Hutchens, M., & Rego, S. O. (2015). *Does Greater Tax Risk Lead to Increased Firm Risk?* Working Paper. https://papers.ssrn.com/sol3/papers.cfm?abstract_id=2186564

Hutchinson, M., Mack, J., & Plastow, K. (2015). Who selects the 'right' directors? An examination of the association between board selection, gender diversity and outcomes. *Accounting and Finance*, *55*(4), 1071–1103. doi:10.1111/acfi.12082

Huyen, T., Pham, M., & Nasir, M. A. (2016). Conspicuous consumption, luxury products and counterfeit market in the UK. *The European Journal of Applied Economics*, *13*(1), 72–83. doi:10.5937/ejae13-10012

Hyndman, R. J., & Koehler, A. B. (2006). Another look at measures of forecast accuracy. *International Journal of Forecasting*, *22*(4), 679–688. doi:10.1016/j.ijforecast.2006.03.001

Ibhagui, O. W., & Olokoyo, F. O. (2018). Leverage and firm performance: New evidence on the role of firm size. *The North American Journal of Economics and Finance*, *45*, 57–82. doi:10.1016/j.najef.2018.02.002

Ibikunle, G., & Steffen, T. (2017). European green mutual fund performance: A comparative analysis with their conventional and black peers. *Journal of Business Ethics*, *145*(2), 337–355. doi:10.100710551-015-2850-7

Indro, D., Jiang, C., Hu, M., & Lee, W. (1999). Mutual Fund Performance: Does Fund Size Matter? *Financial Analysts Journal*, *55*(3), 74–87. doi:10.2469/faj.v55.n3.2274

Instituto da Conservação da Natureza e das Florestas. (2017a). *10.o Relatório Provisório de Incêndios Florestais*. Retrieved from http://www.icnf.pt/portal/florestas/dfci/Resource/doc/rel/2017/10-rel-prov-1jan-31out-2017.pdf

Instituto da Conservação da Natureza e das Florestas. (2017b). *Estatísticas*. Retrieved December 29, 2017, from http://www2.icnf.pt/portal/florestas/dfci/inc/estat-sgif

Internacional Monetary Fund. (2018). *Brighter Prospects*. Optimistic Markets, Challenges Ahead.

Iselin, M. (2020). Estimating the potential impact of requiring a stand-alone board-level risk committee. *Journal of Accounting and Public Policy*, *39*(5), 106709. doi:10.1016/j.jaccpubpol.2019.106709

Isidore, C. (2018, December 31). *2018 was the worst for stocks in 10 years*. Retrieved from CNN Business: https://edition.cnn.com/2018/12/31/investing/dow-stock-market-today/index.html

Ittner, C., Larcker, D., & Randall, T. (2003). Performance implications of strategic performance measurement in financial services firms. *Accounting, Organizations and Society*, *28*(7/8), 715–741. doi:10.1016/S0361-3682(03)00033-3

Jablonský, J., & Dlouhý, M. (2015). *Modely hodnocení efektivnosti a alokace zdrojů* [Models of efficiency evaluation and resource allocation]. Professional Publishing.

Jacobs, B. W., & Singhal, V. R. (2017). The effect of the Rana Plaza disaster on shareholder wealth of retailers: Implications for sourcing strategies and supply chain governance. *Journal of Operations Management*, *49-51*(1), 52–66. doi:10.1016/j.jom.2017.01.002

Jain, S., Khan, M. N., & Mishra, S. (2017). Understanding consumer behavior regarding luxury fashion goods in India based on the theory of planned behavior. *Journal of Asia Business Studies*, *11*(1), 4–21. doi:10.1108/JABS-08-2015-0118

Jalles, J. T. (2016). *A new theory of innovation and growth: The role of banking intermediation and corruption*. doi:10.1108/SEF-01-2016-0017

Jane Lenard, M., Yu, B., Anne York, E., & Wu, S. (2014). Impact of board gender diversity on firm risk. *Managerial Finance*, *40*(8), 787–803. doi:10.1108/MF-06-2013-0164

Jaresova, L. (2010). EWMA Historical Volatility Estimators. *Acta University Carolinae – Mathematica ET Physica*, *51*(2), 17--28.

Jasic, T., & Wood, D. (2004). The profitability of daily stock market indices trades based on neural network predictions: Case study for the S&P 500, the DAX, the TOPIX and the FTSE in the period 1965–1999. *Applied Financial Economics*, *14*(4), 285–297. doi:10.1080/0960310042000201228

JavadiS.Al MasumA.MollagholamaliM.RaoR. P. (2020). *Climate Change and Corporate Cash Holdings: Global Evidence*. 2021 FMA Annual Meeting (Denver, Colorado, United States). https://ssrn.com/abstract=3717092 doi:10.2139/ssrn.3717092

Jebran, K., & Chen, S. (2021). Can we learn lessons from the past? COVID‐19 crisis and corporate governance responses. *International Journal of Finance & Economics*, ijfe.2428. Advance online publication. doi:10.1002/ijfe.2428

Jenkins, H., Alshareef, E., & Mohamad, A. (2021). The impact of corruption on commercial banks' credit risk: Evidence from a panel quantile regression. *International Journal of Finance and Economics*, 1–12. doi:10.1002/ijfe.2481

Jensen, M. C., & Meckling, W. H. (1976). Theory of the firm: Managerial behavior, agency costs and ownership structure. *Journal of Financial Economics*, *3*(4), 305–360. doi:10.1016/0304-405X(76)90026-X

Jeong, S., & Harrison, D. A. (2017). Glass breaking, strategy making, and value creating: Meta analytic outcomes of women as CEOs and TMT members. *Academy of Management Journal*, *60*(4), 1219–1252. doi:10.5465/amj.2014.0716

Jia, J. (2019). Does risk management committee gender diversity matter? A financial distress perspective. *Managerial Auditing Journal*, *34*(8), 1050–1072. doi:10.1108/MAJ-05-2018-1874

Jia, J., & Bradbury, M. E. (2020). Complying with best practice risk management committee guidance and performance. *Journal of Contemporary Accounting & Economics*, *16*(3), 100225. doi:10.1016/j.jcae.2020.100225

Jia, J., & Bradbury, M. E. (2021). Risk management committees and firm performance. *Australian Journal of Management*, *46*(3), 369–388. doi:10.1177/0312896220959124

Jia, J., Li, Z., & Munro, L. (2019). Risk management committee and risk management disclosure : Evidence from Australia. *Pacific Accounting Review*, *31*(3), 438–461. doi:10.1108/PAR-11-2018-0097

Jianakoplos, N. A., & Bernasek, A. (1998). Are women more risk averse? *Economic Inquiry*, *36*(4), 620–630. doi:10.1111/j.1465-7295.1998.tb01740.x

Jianakoplos, N. A., & Bernasek, A. (2006). Financial Risk Taking by Age and Birth Cohort. *Southern Economic Journal*, *72*(4), 981–1001.

Jiang, Z., Xu, D., & Liang, J. (2017). *A Deep Reinforcement Learning Framework for the Financial Portfolio Management Problem*. Academic Press.

Jiang, B., Frazier, G. V., & Prater, E. L. (2006). Outsourcing effects on firms' operational performance: An empirical study. *International Journal of Operations & Production Management*, *26*(12), 1280–1300. doi:10.1108/01443570610710551

Jiang, F., Ma, Y., & Shi, B. (2017). Stock liquidity and dividend payouts. *Journal of Corporate Finance*, *42*, 295–314. doi:10.1016/j.jcorpfin.2016.12.005

Jiang, F., Tong, G., & Song, G. (2019). Technical analysis profitability without data snooping bias: Evidence from Chinese stock market. *International Review of Finance*, *19*(1), 191–206. doi:10.1111/irfi.12161

Jiang, Z., & Liang, J. (2017). Cryptocurrency Portfolio Management with Deep Reinforcement Learning. *Intelligent Systems Conference (IntelliSys)*. 10.1109/IntelliSys.2017.8324237

Jiang, Z., Xu, D., & Liang, J. (2017). *A Deep Reinforcement Learning Framework for the Financial Portfolio Management Problem*. ArXiv.

Ji, Q., Zhang, D., & Zhao, Y. (2020). Searching for safe-haven assets during the COVID-19 pandemic. *International Review of Financial Analysis*, *71*, 101526.

Ji, S., Mauer, D. C., & Zhang, Y. (2019). Managerial entrenchment and capital structure: The effect of diversification. *Journal of Corporate Finance*, *65*, 101505. doi:10.1016/j.jcorpfin.2019.101505

Johansson, J., & Lidskog, R. (2020). Constructing and justifying risk and accountability after extreme events: Public administration and stakeholders' responses to a wildfire disaster. *Journal of Environmental Policy and Planning*, *22*(3), 353–365. doi:10.1080/1523908X.2020.1740656

Johnson, J. E. V., & Powell, P. L. (1993). Decision making, risk and gender: Are managers different? *British Journal of Management*, *5*(2), 123–138. doi:10.1111/j.1467-8551.1994.tb00073.x

Johnson, L. L. (1960). The theory of hedging and speculation in commodity futures. *The Review of Economic Studies*, *27*(3), 139–151. doi:10.2307/2296076

JokhadzeV.SchmidtW. M. (2018). Measuring model risk in financial risk management and pricing. SSRN. doi:10.2139/ssrn.3113139

Jokhadze, V., & Schmidt, W. M. (2020). Measuring model risk in financial risk management and pricing. *International Journal of Theoretical and Applied Finance*, *23*(02), 2050012. Advance online publication. doi:10.1142/S0219024920500120

Jones, S. (2017). Huge Forest Fires in Portugal Kill at Least 60. *The Guardian*. Retrieved from https://www.theguardian.com/world/2017/jun/18/portugal-more-than-20-people-killed-in-forest-fires

Jones, C. I. (2015). Pareto and Piketty: The macroeconomics of top income and wealth inequality. *The Journal of Economic Perspectives*, *29*(1), 29–46. doi:10.1257/jep.29.1.29

Jothimani, D., Shankar, R., & Yadav, S. S. (2015). Discrete Wavelet Transform-Based Prediction of Stock Index: A Study on National Stock Exchange Fifty Index. *Journal of Financial Management and Analysis*, *28*(2), 35–49.

Juárez, F. (2011). Applying the theory of chaos and a complex model of health to establish relations among financial indicators. *Procedia Computer Science*, *3*, 982–986. doi:10.1016/j.procs.2010.12.161

Julizaerma, M. K., & Sori, Z. M. (2012). Gender diversity in the boardroom and firm performance of Malaysian public listed companies. *Procedia: Social and Behavioral Sciences*, *65*(1), 1077–1085. doi:10.1016/j.sbspro.2012.11.374

Kahle, K. M. (2000). Insider trading and the long-run performance of new security issues. *Journal of Corporate Finance*, *6*(1), 25–53. doi:10.1016/S0929-1199(99)00015-2

Kahneman, D. (2012). *Thinking, Fast and Slow*. Penguin Books.

Kahneman, D., Knetsch, J., & Thaler, R. (1991). Anomalies: The Endowment Effect, Loss Aversion, and the Status Quo Bias. *The Journal of Economic Perspectives*, *5*(1), 193–206. doi:10.1257/jep.5.1.193

Kahneman, D., & Tversky, A. (1979). Prospect Theory: An Analysis of Decision under Risk. *Econometrica*, *47*(2), 263–292. doi:10.2307/1914185

Kahneman, D., & Tversky, A. (1997). *Choices, Values and Frames*. Princeton University Press.

Kakanda, M. M., Salim, B., & Chandren, S. A. (2018). Risk Management Committee Characteristics and Market Performance: Empirical Evidence from Listed Review financial service firms in Nigeria. *International Journal of Management and Applied Science*, *4*(2), 6–10. http://www.iraj.in/journal/journal_file/journal_pdf/14-440-15230079706-10.pdf

Kamardin, H. (2014). *Managerial ownership and firm performance: the influence of family directors and non-family directors. In Ethics, Governance and Corporate Crime: Challenges and Consequences (Developments in Corporate Governance and Responsibility)* (Vol. 6). Emerald Group Publishing.

Kamiya, S., & Yanase, N. (2019). Learning from extreme catastrophes. *Journal of Risk and Uncertainty*, *59*(1), 85–124. doi:10.100711166-019-09310-8

Kamran, H. W., Arshad, S. B. B. M., & Omran, A. (2019). Country governance, market concentration and financial market dynamics for banks stability in Pakistan. *Research in World Economy*, *10*(2), 136–146. doi:10.5430/rwe.v10n2p136

Kamstra, M. J., Kramer, L. A., Levi, M. D., & Wermers, R. (2017). Seasonal asset allocation: Evidence from mutual fund flows. *Journal of Financial and Quantitative Analysis*, *52*(1), 71–109. doi:10.1017/S002210901600082X

Kassim, N. M. (2017). What leads Saudi Arabian consumers to purchase counterfeit luxury products. *Journal for Global Business Advancement*, *10*(2), 125–139. doi:10.1504/JGBA.2017.083411

Kassim, N. M., Zain, M., Bogari, N., & Khurram, S. (2021). Why do consumers buy counterfeit luxury products? A tale of two major cities in two different countries. *Asia Pacific Journal of Marketing and Logistics*, *33*(2), 418–448. doi:10.1108/APJML-06-2019-0361

Kelley, E., & Tetlock, P. (2017). Retail Short Selling and Stock Prices. *Review of Financial Studies*, *30*(3), 801–834. doi:10.1093/rfs/hhw089

Keynes, J. M. (1936). *The General Theory of Employment, Interest and Money*. Macmillan.

Khandani, A., Kim, A., & Lo, A. (2010). Consumer Credit-Risk Models Via Machine-Learning Algorithms. *Journal of Banking & Finance*, *34*(11), 2767–2787. doi:10.1016/j.jbankfin.2010.06.001

Khan, M. A., & Ahmad, E. (2019). Measurement of Investor Sentiment and Its Bi-Directional Contemporaneous and Lead–Lag Relationship with Returns: Evidence from Pakistan. *Sustainability*, 20.

Kidane, H. W. (2004). *Predicting Financial Distress in IT and Services Companies in South Africa* [Master's thesis]. Faculty of Economics and Management Sciences. http://scholar.ufs.ac.za:8080/xmlui/handle/11660/1117

Kim, C. S. (2019). Can Socially Responsible Investments Be Compatible with Financial Performance? A Meta-analysis. *Asia-Pacific Journal of Financial Studies*, *48*(1), 30–64. doi:10.1111/ajfs.12244

Kim, H., Jung, S., Kim, T., & Park, K. (1996). Fast learning method for back-propagation neural network by evolutionary adaptation of learning rates. *Neurocomputing*, *11*(1), 101–106. doi:10.1016/0925-2312(96)00009-4

Kim, K., Patro, S., & Pereira, R. (2017). Option incentives, leverage, and risk-taking. *Journal of Corporate Finance*, *43*, 1–18. doi:10.1016/j.jcorpfin.2016.12.003

Kim, T. K. (2015). T test as a parametric statistic. *Korean Journal of Anesthesiology*, *68*(6), 540–546.

Klapper, L., & Lusardi, A. (2020). *Financial literacy and financial resilience : Evidence from around the world*. doi:10.1111/fima.12283

Klein, T. (2017). Dynamic correlation of precious metals and flight-to-quality in developed markets. *Finance Research Letters*, *23*, 283–290.

Klepáč, V., & Hampel, D. (2017). Predicting financial distress of agriculture companies in EU. *Agricultural Economics*, *63*(8), 347–355. doi:10.17221/374/2015-AGRICECON

Klieštik, T. (2019). *Predikcia finančného zdravia podnikov tranzitívnych ekonomík* [Prediction of financial health of businesses in transition economies]. EDIS.

Kline, R. B. (2016). Principles and practices of structural equation modelling (4th ed.). In Methodology in the Social Sciences.

Knight, F. H. (1921). *Risk, Uncertainty and Profit*. Houghton Mifflin Company.

Koay, K. Y. (2018). Understanding consumers' purchase intention towards counterfeit luxury goods An integrated model of neutralisation techniques and perceived risk theory. *Asia Pacific Journal of Marketing and Logistics*, *30*(2), 495–516. doi:10.1108/APJML-05-2017-0100

Köbberling, V., & Wakker, P. (2005). An Index of Loss Aversion. *Journal of Economic Theory*, *122*(1), 119–131. doi:10.1016/j.jet.2004.03.009

Koopmans, T. C. (1951). Analysis of production as an efficient combination of activities. In T. C. Koopmans (Ed.), *Activity analysis of production and allocation, Proceeding of a Conference* (pp. 33-97), John Wiley and Sons Inc.

Kopczuk, W. (2006). Tax Simplification and Tax Compliance: An Economic Perspective. In M. Sawicky (Ed.), *Bridging the Tax Gap. Addressing the Crisis in Tax Administration* (pp. 111–143). Economic Policy Institute.

Compilation of References

Kováčová, M., & Klieštik, T. (2017). Logit and Probit application for the prediction of bankruptcy in Slovak companies. *Equilibrium. Quarterly Journal of Economics and Economic Policy, 12*(4), 775–791. doi:10.24136/eq.v12i4.40

Kovalerchuk, B., & Vityaev, E. (2000). *Data mining in finance: Advances in relational and hybrid methods.* Kluwer Academic Publishers.

KPMG. (2007). *Tax Governance Institute, Tax Risk Management eSurvey.* http://www.surveys.kpmg.com/aci/docs/surveys/Tax_Riskmanagement_esurvey.pdf

KPMG. (2021). *CEO Outlook Pulse Survey.* https://home.kpmg/xx/en/home/insights/2021/03/ceo-outlook-pulse.html.

Kreander, N., Gray, R., Power, D., & Sinclair, C. (2005). Evaluating the Performance of Ethical and Non-Ethical Funds: A Matched Pair Analysis. *Journal of Business Finance & Accounting, 32*(7-8), 1465–1493. doi:10.1111/j.0306-686X.2005.00636.x

Krishnan, J., & Lee, J. E. (2009). Audit committee financial expertise, litigation risk, and corporate governance. *Auditing, 28*(1), 241–261. doi:10.2308/aud.2009.28.1.241

Kristjanpoller, W., Fadic, A., & Minutolo, M. (2014). Volatility forecast using hybrid Neural Network models. *Expert Systems with Applications, 41*(5), 2437–2442. doi:10.1016/j.eswa.2013.09.043

Kroner, K. F., & Sultan, J. (1991). Exchange rate volatility and time-varying hedge ratios. In Pacific-Basin Capital Markets Research. Elsevier.

Kroner, F. K., & Sultan, J. (1993). Time-varying distributions and dynamic hedging with foreign currency futures. *Journal of Financial and Quantitative Analysis, 28*(4), 535–551. doi:10.2307/2331164

Kruse, T. A. (2002). Asset liquidity and the determinants of asset sales by poorly performing firms. *Financial Management, 31*(4), 107–129. doi:10.2307/3666176

Kukeli, A., Deari, F., & Rocşoreanu, C. (2019). Portfolio composition and critical line: A methodological approach. *International Journal of Risk Assessment and Management, 22*(2), 195–211. doi:10.1504/IJRAM.2019.101289

Kunieda, T. (2014). *Corruption, Globalization, and Economic Growth : Theory and Evidence.* Academic Press.

Kuo, Y.-F., Lin, Y.-M., & Chien, H.-F. (2021). Corporate social responsibility, enterprise risk management, and real earnings management: Evidence from managerial confidence. *Finance Research Letters, 41*, 101805. doi:10.1016/j.frl.2020.101805

Kursa, M. B., & Rudnicki, W. R. (2010). Feature selection with the Boruta package. *Journal of Statistical Software, 36*(11), 1–13. doi:10.18637/jss.v036.i11

Kusnadi, Y. (2015). Insider trading restrictions and corporate risk-taking. *Pacific-Basin Finance Journal, 35*, 125–142. doi:10.1016/j.pacfin.2014.11.004

Kutu, K. (2015). Luxury Fashion Brands: An observation into Johannesburg consumers preferred counterfeit branded products. Vega School of Brand Leadership.

Ku, Y. H., Chen, H. C., & Chen, K. H. (2007). On the application of the dynamic conditional correlation model in estimating optimal time-varying hedge ratios. *Applied Economics Letters, 14*(7), 503–509. doi:10.1080/13504850500447331

Kuzniak, S., Rabbani, A., Heo, W., Ruiz-Menjivar, J., & Grable, J. E. (2015). The Grable and Lytton risk tolerance scale: A 15-year retrospective. *Financial Services Review, 24*, 177–192.

Kweh, Q. L., & Lu, W. (2018). Risk management and dynamic network performance : An illustration using a dual banking system. *Applied Economics*, *50*(30), 3285–3299. doi:10.1080/00036846.2017.1420889

Kwon, K. Y., & Kish, R. J. (2002). Technical trading strategies and return predictability: NYSE. *Applied Financial Economics*, *12*(9), 639–653. doi:10.1080/09603100010016139

L'Haridon, O., & Vieider, F. M. (2019). All over the map: A worldwide comparison of risk preferences. *Quantitative Economics*, *10*, 185–215. doi:10.3982/QE898

Lajili, K., & Zeghal, D. (2010). Corporate governance and bankruptcy filing decisions. *Journal of General Management*, *35*(4), 3–26. doi:10.1177/030630701003500401

Lanz, B. (2012). The large sample size fallacy. *Scandinavian Journal of Caring Sciences*, *27*(2), 487–492. doi:10.1111/j.1471-6712.2012.01052.x PMID:22862286

Laurel, D. (2011). *Socially Responsible Investments in Europe: The Effects of Screening on Risk and the Clusters in the Fund Space* [Working paper]. Politecnico di Milano.

Lavermicocca, C. & Buchan, J. (2015). Role of Reputational Risk in Tax Decision Making by Large Companies. *eJournal of Tax Research*, *13*(1), 5-50.

Lavermicocca, C. (2011). Tax Risk Management Practices and Their Impact On Tax Compliance Behaviour – The Views of Tax Executives from Large Australian Companies. *eJournal of Tax Research*, *9*(1), 89-115.

Lee, C.-C., Lee, C.-C., & Xiao, S. (2021). Policy-related risk and corporate financing behavior: Evidence from China's listed companies. *Economic Modelling*, *94*, 539–547. doi:10.1016/j.econmod.2020.01.022

Lee, C.-C., & Wang, C.-W. (2021). Firms' cash reserve, financial constraint, and geopolitical risk. *Pacific-Basin Finance Journal*, *65*, 101480. doi:10.1016/j.pacfin.2020.101480

Lee, D., Humphrey, J., Benson, K., & Ahn, J. (2010). Socially Responsible Investment Fund Performance: The Impact of Screening Activity. *Accounting and Finance*, *50*(2), 351–370. doi:10.1111/j.1467-629X.2009.00336.x

Lee, H., & Lee, C. (2012). An Analysis of Reinsurance and Firm Performance: Evidence from the Taiwan Property-Liability Insurance Industry. *Geneva Papers on Risk and Insurance. Issues and Practice*, *37*(3), 467–484. doi:10.1057/gpp.2012.9

Lee, T. S., & Yeh, Y. H. (2004). Corporate governance and financial distress: Evidence from Taiwan. *Corporate Governance*, *12*(3), 378–388. doi:10.1111/j.1467-8683.2004.00379.x

Lee, T., Cho, J., Kwon, D., & Sohn, S. (2018). Global stock market investment strategies based on financial network indicators using machine learning techniques. *Expert Systems with Applications*.

Leite, C., Cortez, M., Silva, F., & Adcock, C. (2018). The Performance of Socially Responsible Equity Mutual Funds: Evidence from Sweden. *Business Ethics (Oxford, England)*, *27*(2), 108–126. doi:10.1111/beer.12174

Leite, P., & Cortez, M. (2015). Performance of European Socially Responsible Funds During Market Crises: Evidence from France. *International Review of Financial Analysis*, *40*, 132–141. doi:10.1016/j.irfa.2015.05.012

Lel, U. (2012). Currency hedging and corporate governance: A cross-country analysis. *Journal of Corporate Finance*, *18*(2), 221–237. doi:10.1016/j.jcorpfin.2011.12.002

Lento, C. (2007). Tests of technical trading rules in the Asian-Pacific equity markets: A bootstrap approach. *Academy of Financial and Accounting Studies Journal*, *11*(2), 51-73.

Lento, C., Gradojevic, N., & Wright, C. S. (2007). Investment information content in Bollinger Bands? *Applied Financial Economics Letters*, *3*(4), 263–267. doi:10.1080/17446540701206576

Lester, B., Postlewaite, A., & Wright, R. (2012). Information, Liquidity, Asset Prices, and Monetary Policy. *Review of Economic Studies*, *79*(3), 1209–1238. doi:10.1093/restud/rds003

Levin, A., Lin, C. F., & Chu, C. S. J. (2002). Unit root tests in panel data: Asymptotic and finite-sample properties. *Journal of Econometrics*, *108*(1), 1–24. doi:10.1016/S0304-4076(01)00098-7

Levin, I. P., Snyder, M. A., & Chapman, D. P. (1988). 'The interaction of experiential and situational factors and gender in a simulated risky decision-making task. *The Journal of Psychology*, *122*(2), 173–181. doi:10.1080/00223980.1988.9712703

Levy, M. (2015). An evolutionary explanation for risk aversion. *Journal of Economic Psychology*, *46*, 51–61. doi:10.1016/j.joep.2014.12.001

Liao, C., Lin, H., & Liu, Y. (2010). *Predicting the Use of Pirated Software: A Contingency Model Integrating Perceived Risk with the Theory of Planned Behavior Chechen Liao*. doi:10.1007/s10551-009-0081-5

Liaw, A., & Wiener, M. (2002). Classification and regression by random forest. *R News*, *2*(3), 18–22.

Lichman, M. (n.d.). *UCI machine learning repository*. Retrieved from http://archive.ics.uci.edu/ml/

Li, D., & Xia, Y. (2021). Gauging the effects of stock liquidity on earnings management: Evidence from the SEC tick size pilot test. *Journal of Corporate Finance*, *67*, 101904. doi:10.1016/j.jcorpfin.2021.101904

Li, E. P. H., Lam, M., & Liu, W. S. (2018). Consuming counterfeit: A study of consumer moralism in China. *International Journal of Consumer Studies*, *42*(3), 367–377. doi:10.1111/ijcs.12428

Lien, D., Tse, Y. K., & Tsui, A. K. C. (2002). Evaluating the hedging performance of the constant-correlation GARCH model. *Applied Financial Economics*, *12*(11), 791–798. doi:10.1080/09603100110046045

Lim, E., & McCann, B. (2014). Performance Feedback and Firm Risk Taking: The Moderating Effects of CEO and Outside Director Stock Options. *Organization Science*, *25*(1), 262–282. doi:10.1287/orsc.2013.0830

Lim, N. (2003). Consumers' perceived risk: Sources versus consequences. *Electronic Commerce Research and Applications*, *2*(3), 216–228. doi:10.1016/S1567-4223(03)00025-5

Linsley, P. M., & Shrives, P. J. (2006). Risk reporting: A study of risk disclosure in the annual reports of UK Companies. *Journal The British Accounting Review*, *38*(4), 387–404. doi:10.1016/j.bar.2006.05.002

Lin, X., Liu, M., So, S., & Yuen, D. (2019). Corporate Social Responsibility, Firm Performance and Tax Risk. *Managerial Auditing Journal*, *34*(9), 1101–1130. doi:10.1108/MAJ-04-2018-1868

Liu, P., Li, H., & Guo, H. (2020). The impact of corruption on firms' access to bank loans: Evidence from China. *Economic Research-Ekonomska Istrazivanja*, *33*(1), 1963–1984. doi:10.1080/1331677X.2020.1768427

Liu, Y. (2019). Novel volatility forecasting using deep learning-Long Short Term Memory Recurrent Neural Networks. *Expert Systems with Applications*, *132*, 99–109. doi:10.1016/j.eswa.2019.04.038

Livet, P. (2009). Rational Choice, Neuroeconomy and Mixed Emotions. *Philosophical Transactions of the Royal Society Biological Science*, *365*(1538), 259–269. doi:10.1098/rstb.2009.0177 PMID:20026464

Li, Y., & Zeng, Y. (2019). The impact of top executive gender on asset prices: Evidence from stock price crash risk. *Journal of Corporate Finance*, *58*, 528–550. doi:10.1016/j.jcorpfin.2019.07.005

Loeprick, J., & Engelschalk, M. (2011). Simplified Risk Scoring for SMEs. In M. S. Khwaja, R. Awasthi, & J. Loeprick (Eds.), *Risk-Based Tax Audits: Approaches and Country Experiences* (pp. 45–54). The World Bank Publishing. doi:10.1596/9780821387542_CH04

Lohpetch, D., & Corne, D. (2010). Outperforming Buy-and-Hold with Evolved Technical Trading Rules: Daily, Weekly and Monthly Trading. Applications of Evolutionary Computation, 171-181.

Louche, C., & Lydenberg, S. (2006). *Socially Responsible Investment: Differences Between Europe and United States*. [Working paper]. Vlerick Leuven Gent Working Paper Series 22.

Loukil, N., & Yousfi, O. (2016). Does gender diversity on corporate boards increase risk-taking? *Canadian Journal of Administrative Sciences*, *33*(1), 66–81. doi:10.1002/cjas.1326

Löwen, C., Kchouri, B., & Lehnert, T. (2021). Is this time really different? Flight-to-safety and the COVID-19 crisis. *PLoS One*, *16*(5), e0251752.

Lucey, B. M., & Li, S. (2015). What precious metals act as safe havens, and when? Some US evidence. *Applied Economics Letters*, *22*(1), 35–45.

Lui, Y. H., & Mole, D. (1998). The use of fundamental and technical analyses by foreign exchange dealers: Hong Kong evidence. *Journal of International Money and Finance*, *17*(3), 535–545. doi:10.1016/S0261-5606(98)00011-4

Lukac, L. P., Brorsen, B. W., & Irwin, S. H. (1988). A test of futures market disequilibrium using twelve different technical trading systems. *Applied Economics*, *20*(5), 623–639. doi:10.1080/00036848800000113

Luo, D. (2016). Changes in corporate governance practice of the Chinese commercial banks. In The Development of the Chinese Financial System and Reform of Chinese Commercial Banks. Palgrave Macmillan. doi:10.1057/9781137454669_3

Luo, C., Wu, D., & Wu, D. (2016). A deep learning approach for credit scoring using credit default swaps. *Engineering Applications of Artificial Intelligence*.

Luther, R., Matatko, J., & Corner, D. (1992). The Investment Performance of UK "Ethical" Unit Trusts. *Accounting, Auditing & Accountability Journal*, *5*(4), 57–70. doi:10.1108/09513579210019521

Macedo, L. L., Godinho, P., & Alves, M. J. (2017). Mean-semivariance portfolio optimization with multiobjective evolutionary algorithms and technical analysis rules. *Expert Systems with Applications*, *79*, 33–43. doi:10.1016/j.eswa.2017.02.033

MacKay, D. (1992). Bayesian interpolation. *Neural Computation*, *4*(3), 415–447. doi:10.1162/neco.1992.4.3.415

Magaña, E. C., Ariza, A. C., Palmero, J. R., & Rivas, E. S. (2021). Problematic use of ICTS in trainee teachers during COVID-19: A sex-based analysis. *Contemporary Educational Technology*, *13*(4), ep314. Advance online publication. doi:10.30935/cedtech/10988

Malik, M., Shafie, R., & Ku Ismail, K. N. I. (2021). Do risk management committee characteristics influence the market value of firms? *Risk Management*, *23*(1–2), 172–191. doi:10.105741283-021-00073-8

Malkiel, B. G., & Fama, E. F. (1970). Efficient Capital Markets: A review of theory and empirical work. *The Journal of Finance*, *25*(2), 383–417. doi:10.1111/j.1540-6261.1970.tb00518.x

Mallin, C., Saadouni, B., & Briston, R. (1995). The Financial Performance of Ethical Investment Funds. *Journal of Business Finance & Accounting*, *22*(4), 483–496. doi:10.1111/j.1468-5957.1995.tb00373.x

Manchiraju, S., & Sadachar, A. (2014). Personal values and ethical fashion consumption. *Journal of Fashion Marketing and Management*, *18*(3), 357–374. doi:10.1108/JFMM-02-2013-0013

Mandelbrot, B. (1963). The variation of certain speculative prices. *The Journal of Business*, *4*(4), 394–419. doi:10.1086/294632

Maniraj, S. P., Aditya, S., Shadab, A., & Swarna, S. (2019). Credit Card Fraud Detection using Machine Learning and Data Science. *International Journal of Engineering Research*.

Margaritis, D., & Psillaki, M. (2010). Capital structure, equity ownership and firm performance. *Journal of Banking & Finance*, *34*(3), 621–632. doi:10.1016/j.jbankfin.2009.08.023

Markowitz, H. (1952). Portfolio selection. *The Journal of Finance*, *7*(1), 77–91.

Markowitz, H. (1952). Portfolio Selection. *The Journal of Finance*, *7*(1), 77–91.

Marques, L. D. (2000). *Modelos Dinâmicos com Dados em Painel: Revisão de Literatura*. Universidade do Porto.

Marti-Ballester, C. P. (2019a). The role of mutual funds in the sustainable energy sector. *Business Strategy and the Environment*, *28*(6), 1107–1120. doi:10.1002/bse.2305

Martí-Ballester, C. P. (2019b). Do European renewable energy mutual funds foster the transition to a low-carbon economy? *Renewable Energy*, *143*, 1299–1309. doi:10.1016/j.renene.2019.05.095

Martin, D. (1977). Early warning of bank failure. A logit regession approach. *Journal of Banking & Finance*, *1*(3), 249–276. doi:10.1016/0378-4266(77)90022-X

Martin, J., Mortimer, G., & Andrews, L. (2015). Re-examining online customer experience to include purchase frequency and perceived risk. *Journal of Retailing and Consumer Services*, *25*, 81–95. doi:10.1016/j.jretconser.2015.03.008

Mashrur, A., Luo, W., Zaidi, N., & Robles-Kelly, A. (2020). Machine Learning for Financial Risk Management: A Survey. *IEEE Access: Practical Innovations, Open Solutions*, *8*, 203203–203223. doi:10.1109/ACCESS.2020.3036322

Masters, R., & Meier, R. (1988). Sex-differences and risk-taking propensity of entrepreneurs. *Journal of Small Business Management*, *26*(1), 31–35.

Matta, E., & McGuire, J. (2008). Too Risky to Hold? The Effect of Downside Risk, Accumulated Equity Wealth, and Firm Performance on CEO Equity Reduction. *Organization Science*, *19*(4), 567–580. doi:10.1287/orsc.1070.0334

Mavsar, R., Cabán, A. G., & Varela, E. (2013). The state of development of fire management decision support systems in America and Europe. *Forest Policy and Economics*, *29*, 45–55. doi:10.1016/j.forpol.2012.11.009

Maxfield, S., Shapiro, M., Gupta, V., & Hass, S. (2010). Gender and risk: Women, risk taking and risk aversion. *Gender in Management*, *7*(7), 586–604. doi:10.1108/17542411011081383

Maxfield, S., & Wang, L. (2020). Does sustainable investing reduce portfolio risk? A multilevel analysis. *European Financial Management*, •••, 1–22.

Mcaleer, M., & Medeiros, M. C. (2008). Realised Volatility: A Review. *Econometric Reviews*, *27*(1-3), 10–45.

McAlister, L., Srinivasan, R., & Kim, M. (2007). Advertising, Research and Development, and Systematic Risk of the Firm. *Journal of Marketing*, *71*(1), 35–48. doi:10.1509/jmkg.71.1.035

McKenzie, M. D. (2007). Technical trading rules in emerging markets and the 1997 Asian currency crises. *Emerging Markets Finance & Trade*, *43*(4), 46–73. doi:10.2753/REE1540-496X430403

McNamara, G., & Bromiley, P. (1997). Decision Making in an Organizational Setting: Cognitive and Organizational Influences on Risk Assessment in Commercial Lending. *Academy of Management Journal*, *40*(5), 1063–1088. Retrieved April 3, 2021, from https://www.jstor.org/stable/256927

Mcnulty, T., Florackis, C., & Ormrod, P. (2013). Boards of directors and financial risk during the credit crisis. *Corporate Governance*, *21*(1), 58–78. doi:10.1111/corg.12007

Medeiros, O. R., Van Doornik, B. F., & Oliveira, G. R. (2011). Modeling and forecasting a firm's financial statements with a VAR –VECM Model. *Brazilian Business Review*, *8*(3), 20–39. doi:10.15728/bbr.2011.8.3.2

Meier-Pesti, K., & Goetze, E. (2005). Masculinity and femininity as predictors of financial risk-taking: evidence from a priming study on gender salience. In K. M. Ekstrom & H. Brembeck (Eds.), *European Advances in Consumer Research* (Vol. 7, pp. 45–46). Association for Consumer Research.

Meissner, R. (2010). *The trade in counterfeit goods: What is it, why is it a problem and what is its impact on Africa?* https://www.polity.org.za/article/the-trade-in-counterfeit-goods-what-is-it-why-is-it-a-problem-and-what-is-its-impact-on-africa-2010-08-04

Mendelová, V., & Bieliková, T. (2017). Diagnòstikovanie finančného zdravia podnikov pomocou metódy DEA: Aplikácia na podniky v Slovenskej republike [Diagnosing the financial health of companies using the DEA method: application to companies in the Slovak Republic] [Political economy]. *Politicka Ekonomie*, *65*(1), 26–44. doi:10.18267/j.polek.1125

Mendelová, V., & Stachová, M. (2016). Comparing DEA and logistic regression in corporate financial distress prediction. In *Proceedings of International Scientific Conference FERNSTAT 2016* (pp. 95–104). Slovak Statistical and Demographic Society. http://fernstat.ssds.sk/proceedings/

Menkhoff, L. (2010). The use of technical analysis by fund managers: International evidence. *Journal of Banking & Finance*, *34*(11), 2573–2586. doi:10.1016/j.jbankfin.2010.04.014

Merkle, C., & Weber, M. (2014). Do investors put their money where their mouth is? Stock market expectations and investing behavior. *Journal of Banking & Finance*, *46*, 372–386. doi:10.1016/j.jbankfin.2014.03.042

Merna, T., & Al-Thani, F. (2008). *Corporate Risk Management* (Vol. 2). John Wiley & Sons.

Merton, R. C. (1987). A simple model of capital market equilibrium with incomplete information. *The Journal of Finance*, *42*(3), 483–510. doi:10.1111/j.1540-6261.1987.tb04565.x

Metghalchi, M., Chang, Y. H., & Marcucci, J. (2008). Is the Swedish stock market efficient? Evidence from some simple trading rules. *International Review of Financial Analysis*, *17*(3), 475–490. doi:10.1016/j.irfa.2007.05.001

Metghalchi, M., Chen, C. P., & Hayes, L. A. (2015). History of share prices and market efficiency of the Madrid general stock index. *International Review of Financial Analysis*, *40*, 178–184. doi:10.1016/j.irfa.2015.05.016

Mgammal, M. H., Bardai, B., & Ismail, K. N. I. K. (2018). Corporate governance and tax disclosure phenomenon in the Malaysian listed companies. *Corporate Governance: The International Journal of Business in Society*, *18*(5), 779–808. doi:10.1108/CG-08-2017-0202

Michaelides, A., & Zhang, Y. (2017). Stock market mean reversion and portfolio choice over the life cycle. *Journal of Financial and Quantitative Analysis*, *52*(3), 1183–1209. doi:10.1017/S0022109017000357

Mihalovič, M. (2015). The Assessment of Corporate Financial Performance Via Discriminant Analysis. *Acta oeconomica Cassoviensia. Scientific Journal*, *8*(1), 57–69. doi:10.13140/RG.2.1.4153.7368

Mik, B. (2010). Introduction to Tax Risk Management. In A. Bakker & S. Kloosterhof (Eds.) Tax Risk Management: From Risk to Opportunity (pp. 1–17). IBFD.

Miller, S. (2017). Feasible Generalized Least Squares Using Machine Learning. SSRN *Electronic Journal*, 1–25. doi:10.2139/ssrn.2966194

Miller, K., & Chen, W. (2003). Risk and firms' costs. *Strategic Organization*, *1*(4), 355–382. doi:10.1177/14761270030014001

Mills, T. C. (1997). Technical analysis and the London Stock Exchange: Testing trading rules using the FT30. *Journal of Financial Economics*, *2*(4), 319–331.

Minai, A. A. (1997). Covariance learning of correlated patterns in competitive networks. *Neural Computation*, *9*(3), 667–681. doi:10.1162/neco.1997.9.3.667 PMID:9097478

Minder, R. (2017). Deadly Fires Sweep Portugal and Northern Spain. *The New York Times*. Retrieved from https://www.nytimes.com/2017/10/16/world/europe/portugal-spain-fires.html

Mínguez-Vera, A., & Martin, A. (2011). Gender and management on spanish SMEs: An empirical analysis. *International Journal of Human Resource Management*, *22*(14), 2852–2873. doi:10.1080/09585192.2011.599948

Mitchell, C., & Catalano, T. J. (2021, May 3). *Trading Strategies*. Retrieved from Rules for Picking Stocks When Intraday Trading: https://www.investopedia.com/day-trading/pick-stocks-intraday-trading/

Mitchell, V. (1999). Consumer perceived risk: Conceptualisations and models. *European Journal of Marketing*, *33*(1), 163–195. doi:10.1108/03090569910249229

Miyazaki, A., Rodriguez, A. A., & Langenderfer, J. (2009). Price, scarcity, and consumer willingness to purchase pirated media products. *Journal of Public Policy & Marketing*, *28*(1), 71–84. doi:10.1509/jppm.28.1.71

Modigliani, F., & Miller, M. H. (1958). The cost of capital, corporation finance and the theory of investment. *The American Economic Review*, *48*(3), 261–297.

Moen, P., Pedtke, J. H., & Flood, S. (2020). Disparate disruptions: Intersectional COVID-19 employment effects by age, gender, education, and race/ethnicity. *Work, Aging and Retirement*, *6*(4), 207–228. doi:10.1093/workar/waaa013 PMID:33214905

Mohamad, A., & Jenkins, H. (2020). Corruption and banks' non-performing loans: Empirical evidence from MENA countries. *Macroeconomics and Finance in Emerging Market Economies*, *00*(00), 1–14. doi:10.1080/17520843.2020.1842478

Molnar, P. (2012, June). Properties of range-based volatility estimators. *International Review of Financial Analysis*, *23*, 20–29.

Montinari, N., & Rancan, M. (2018). Risk taking on behalf of others: The role of social distance. *Journal of Risk and Uncertainty*, *57*(1), 81–109. doi:10.100711166-018-9286-2

Morellec, E. (2001). Asset liquidity, capital structure, and secured debt. *Journal of Financial Economics*, *61*(2), 173–206. doi:10.1016/S0304-405X(01)00059-9

Morningstar. (2021). *Global Sustainable Fund Flows Report*. Available at: https://www.morningstar.com/content/dam/marketing/shared/pdfs/Research/Global-ESG-Q3-2021-Flows.pdf?utm_source=eloqua&utm_medium=email&utm_campaign=none&utm_content=27223

Mortimer, G., Fazal-e-hasan, S. M., Grimmer, M., & Grimmer, L. (2020). Explaining the impact of consumer religiosity, perceived risk and moral potency on purchase intentions. *Journal of Retailing and Consumer Services*, *55*(November), 102115. doi:10.1016/j.jretconser.2020.102115

Mühleisen, M., Gudmundsson, T., & Ward, H. P. (2020, August 6). *COVID-19 Response in Emerging Market Economies: Conventional Policies and Beyond*. Retrieved from https://blogs.imf.org/: https://blogs.imf.org/2020/08/06/covid-19-response-in-emerging-market-economies-conventional-policies-and-beyond/

Muller-Kahle, M. I., & Lewellyn, K. B. (2011). Did Board Configuration Matter? The Case of US Subprime Lenders. *Corporate Governance*, *19*(5), 405–417. doi:10.1111/j.1467-8683.2011.00871.x

Mulligan, E., & Oats, L. (2009). Tax Risk Management: Evidence from The US. *British Tax Review*, *6*(1), 680–703.

Muñoz, F., Vargas, M., & Marco, I. (2014). Environmental mutual funds: Financial performance and managerial abilities. *Journal of Business Ethics*, *124*(4), 551–569. doi:10.100710551-013-1893-x

Murphy, J. J. (1999). *Technical Analysis of the Financial Markets: A comprehensive guide to trading methods and applications*. New York Institute of Finance.

Nadarajah, S., Duong, H. N., Ali, S., Liu, B., & Huang, A. (2020). Stock liquidity and default risk around the world. *Journal of Financial Markets*, 100597.

Nahar, S., Azim, M. I., & Hossain, M. M. (2020). Risk disclosure and risk governance characteristics : Evidence from a developing economy. *International Journal of Accounting & Information Mangement*, *28*(4), 577–605. doi:10.1108/IJAIM-07-2019-0083

Nahar, S., Jubb, C., & Azim, M. I. (2016). Risk governance and performance : A developing country perspective. *Managerial Auditing Journal*, *31*(3), 250–268. doi:10.1108/MAJ-02-2015-1158

Nanda, S. K., & Barai, P. (2021). Effect of insider trading on stock characteristics. *Asian Journal of Accounting Research*, *6*(2), 210-227.

National Oceanic & Atmospheric Administration. (2017). *Subject: E11) How many tropical cyclones have there been each year in the Atlantic basin? What years were the greatest and fewest seen?* Retrieved May 28, 2018, from https://www.aoml.noaa.gov/hrd/tcfaq/E11.html

Nau, R. (2020). *What's the bottom line? How to compare models*. https://people.duke.edu/~rnau/compare.htm

Nazário, R. T., Silva, J. L., Sobreiro, V. A., & Kimura, H. (2017). A literature review of technical analysis on stock markets. *The Quarterly Review of Economics and Finance*, *66*, 115–126. doi:10.1016/j.qref.2017.01.014

Nee, V., & Ingram, P. (1998). Embeddedness and Beyond: Instituitions, Exchange and Social Structure. In The New Institutionalism in Sociology. Russel Sage Foundation.

Neelakantan, U. (2010). Estimation and impact of gender differences in risk tolerance. *Economic Inquiry*, *48*(1), 228–233. doi:10.1111/j.1465-7295.2009.00251.x

Neher, A., & Hebb, T. (2016). The Responsible Investment Atlas – An Introduction. In *The Routledge Handbook of Responsible Investment*. Routledge.

Nejadmalayeri, A. (2021). Asset liquidity, business risk, and beta. *Global Finance Journal*, *48*, 100560. doi:10.1016/j.gfj.2020.100560

Nelson, J. A. (2015). Are Women Really More Risk-Averse than Men? A Re-Analysis of the Literature Using Expanded Methods. *Journal of Economic Surveys*, *29*(3), 566–585. doi:10.1111/joes.12069

Nelson, J. A. (2016). Not-So-Strong Evidence for Gender Differences in Risk Taking. *Feminist Economics*, *22*(2), 114–142. doi:10.1080/13545701.2015.1057609

Neubig, T., & Sangha, B. (2004). Tax Risk and Strong Corporate Governance. *The Tax Executive*, (March-April), 114–119.

Neuman, S. S., Omer, T. C., & Schmidt, A. P. (2013). *Risk and Return: Does Tax Risk Reduce Firms' Effective Tax Rates?* https://pages.business.illinois.edu/accountancy/wp-content/uploads/sites/12/2014/10/Tax-2013-Consortium-Neuman.pdf

Neves, E. D., & Costa, N. A. (2017). Investimento racional no PSI20. *European Journal of Applied Business and Management*, *3*(2), 69–91.

Neves, M. E. D. (2018). Payout and firm's catering. *International Journal of Managerial Finance*, *14*(1), 2–22. doi:10.1108/IJMF-03-2017-0055

Neves, M. E., Henriques, C., & Vilas, J. (2019). Financial performance assessment of electricity companies: Evidence from Portugal. *Operations Research*, 1–49.

Neves, M., & Branco, J. (2020). Determinants of R&D on European high technology industry: Panel data evidence. *Management Research*, *18*(3), 285–305. doi:10.1108/MRJIAM-11-2019-0969

Ng'ang'a, P. N., Jayasinghe, G., Kimani, V., Shililu, J., Kabutha, C., Kabuage, L., Githure, J., & Mutero, C. (2009). Bed net use and associated factors in a rice farming community in Central Kenya. *Malaria Journal*, *8*(1), 64. doi:10.1186/1475-2875-8-64 PMID:19371407

Nguyen, M.-H., Nguyen, H.T.T., Le, T.-T., Luong, A.-P. & Vuong, Q.-H. (2021), Gender issues in family business research: A bibliometric scoping review. *Journal of Asian Business and Economic Studies*. ahead-of-print. . doi:10.1108/JABES-01-2021-0014

Nguyen, L., Gallery, G., & Newton, C. (2019). The joint influence of financial risk perception and risk tolerance on individual investment decision-making. *Accounting and Finance*, *59*(S1), 747–771. doi:10.1111/acfi.12295

Nguyen, T., Alpert, K., & Faff, R. (2021). Relative bond-stock liquidity and capital structure choices. *Journal of Corporate Finance*, *69*, 102026. doi:10.1016/j.jcorpfin.2021.102026

Ni, H., & Yin, H. (2009). Exchange rate prediction using hybrid neural networks and trading indicators. *Neurocomputing*, *72*(13), 2815–2823. doi:10.1016/j.neucom.2008.09.023

Nobre, L. H. N., & Grable, J. E. (2015). The role of risk profiles and risk tolerance in shaping client investment decisions. *Journal of Financial Service Professionals*, *69*(3), 18–21.

Noe, C. (1999). Voluntary Disclosures and Insider Transactions. *Journal of Accounting and Economics*, *27*(3), 305–326. doi:10.1016/S0165-4101(99)00014-2

Nofsinger, J., & Varma, A. (2014). Socially Responsible Funds and Market Crises. *Journal of Banking & Finance*, *48*, 180–193. doi:10.1016/j.jbankfin.2013.12.016

Norashikin, N. (2009). *A study on consumers' attitude towards counterfeit products in Malaysia* (Unpublished master's thesis). Graduate School of Business Faculty of Business and Accountancy University of Malaya.

Norton, C. L., & Smith, R. E. (1979). A comparison of general price level and historical cost financial statements in the prediction of bankruptcy. *The Accounting Review*, *54*(1), 72–87. https://www.jstor.org/stable/246235

Noth, F., & Rehbein, O. (2019). Badly hurt? Natural disasters and direct firm effects. *Finance Research Letters*, *28*, 254–258. doi:10.1016/j.frl.2018.05.009

Ntim, C. G., Opong, K. K., & Danbolt, J. (2012). The relative value relevance of shareholder versus stakeholder corporate governance disclosure policy reforms in South Africa. *Corporate Governance: An International Review*, *20*(1), 84-105.

Ntim, C. G., Lindop, S., & Thomas, D. A. (2013). Corporate governance and risk reporting in South Africa: A study of corporate risk disclosures in the pre-and post-2007/2008 global financial crisis periods. *International Review of Financial Analysis*, *30*, 363–383. doi:10.1016/j.irfa.2013.07.001

Nunes, P. J. M., Serrasqueiro, Z., & Sequeira, T. N. (2009). Profitability in Portuguese Service Industries: A Panel Data Approach. *Service Industries Journal*, *29*(5), 693–707. doi:10.1080/02642060902720188

Nyborg, K. G., & Wang, Z. (2021). The effect of stock liquidity on cash holdings: The repurchase motive. *Journal of Financial Economics*, *142*(2), 905–927. doi:10.1016/j.jfineco.2021.05.027

Oberlechner, T. (2001). Importance of technical and fundamental analysis in the European foreign exchange market. *International Journal of Finance & Economics*, *6*(1), 81–93. doi:10.1002/ijfe.145

Odders-White, E. R., & Ready, M. J. (2006). Credit ratings and stock liquidity. *Review of Financial Studies*, *19*(1), 119–157. doi:10.1093/rfs/hhj004

Odean, T. (1998). Are Investors Reluctant to Realize Their Losses? *The Journal of Finance*, *53*(5), 1775–1798. doi:10.1111/0022-1082.00072

OECD. (2004). *Compliance Risk Management: Managing and Improving Tax Compliance*. https://www.oecd.org/tax/administration/33818656.pdf

OECD. (2008). *Study into the Role of Tax Intermediaries*. https://www.oecd.org/tax/administration/39882938.pdf

OECD. (2009). *General Administrative Principles: Corporate Governance and Tax Risk Management, Tax Guidance Series Forum on Tax Administration*. https://www.oecd.org/tax/administration/43239887.pdf

OECD. (2013). *Co-operative Compliance: A Framework: From Enhanced Relationship to Co-operative Compliance*. OECD Publishing. doi:10.1787/9789264200852-

OECD. (2015). *G20/OECD Principles of Corporate Governance*. OECD Publishing. doi:10.1787/9789264236882-

OECD. (2016). *Co-operative Tax Compliance: Building Better Tax Control Framework*. OECD Publishing. doi:10.1787/9789264253384-

OECD. (2021a). *Tax Administration 2021: Comparative Information on OECD and other Advanced and Emerging Economies*. OECD Publishing. doi:10.1787/cef472b9-

OECD. (2021b). Tax Policy Reforms 2021 Special Edition on Tax Policy during the COVID-19 Pandemic. OECD Publishing. doi:10.1787/427d2616-en

OECD. (n.d.). *Competition*. Retrieved from https://stats.oecd.org/glossary/detail.asp?ID=3163

Ohlson, J. A. (1980). Financial Ratios and the Probabilistic Prediction of Bankruptcy. *Journal of Accounting Research*, *18*(1), 109–131. doi:10.2307/2490395

Oliveira Neto, A. M. (2017). *Governance and Risk Management in Taxation*. Springer. doi:10.1007/978-981-10-2297-5

Oliveira, J., Rodrigues, L. L., & Craig, R. (2011). Risk-Related disclosures by Non-Finance companies: Portuguese practices and disclosure characteristics. *Managerial Auditing Journal*, *26*(9), 817–839. doi:10.1108/02686901111171466

Olsen, R. A., & Cox, C. M. (2001). The influence of gender on the perception and response to investment risk: The case of professional investors. *The Journal of Psychology and Financial Markets*, *2*(1), 29–36. doi:10.1207/S15327760JPFM0201_3

Onsongo, S. K., Muathe, S. M. A., & Mwangi, L. W. (2020). Financial Risk and Financial Performance: Evidence and Insights from Commercial and Services Listed Companies in Nairobi Securities Exchange, Kenya. *Int. J. Financial Stud*, *8*(51), 51. Advance online publication. doi:10.3390/ijfs8030051

Oradi, J., & E-Vahdati, S. (2021). Female directors on audit committees, the gender of financial experts, and internal control weaknesses: Evidence from Iran. *Accounting Forum*, *0*(0), 1–34. doi:10.1080/01559982.2021.1920127

Ortiz-Molina, H., & Phillips, G. M. (2010). *Asset liquidity and the cost of capital*. National Bureau of Economic Research. doi:10.3386/w15992

Otten, R., & Bams, D. (2002). European Mutual Fund Performance. *European Financial Management*, *8*(1), 75–101. doi:10.1111/1468-036X.00177

Owens, J., Roy-Chowdhury, C., & Huibregtse, S. (2015). *Tax Risk and Tax Risk Management: How to Mitigate Tax Risk in a BEPS-driven Environment*. CFE Forum 2015, Tax Governance and Tax Risk Management in a post-BEPS World.

Oyelami, B. O., & Sambo, E. E. (2017). Comparative Analysis of Some Volatility Estimators: An Application to Historical Data from the Nigerian Stock Exchange Market. *International Journal of Computational and Theoretical Statistics*, 13-35.

Ozerturk, S. (2006). Managerial Risk Reduction, Incentives and Firm Value. *Economic Theory*, *27*(3), 523–535. doi:10.100700199-004-0569-2

Ozturk, M., Toroslu, I. H., & Fidan, G. (2016). Heuristic based trading system on Forex data using technical indicator rules. *Applied Soft Computing*, *43*, 170–186. doi:10.1016/j.asoc.2016.01.048

Pacula, R. L. (1997). Women and substance use: Are women less susceptible to addiction? *The American Economic Review*, *87*, 454–459.

Pai, P.-F., Hsu, M.-F., & Wang, M.-C. (2011). A support vector machine-based model for detecting top management fraud. *Knowledge-Based Systems*, *24*(2), 314–321. doi:10.1016/j.knosys.2010.10.003

Palazzo, B. (2012). Cash holdings, risk, and expected returns. *Journal of Financial Economics, 164*(1), 162-185.

Palsson, A. M. (1996). Does the degree of risk aversion vary with household characteristics? *Journal of Economic Psychology*, *18*(6), 605–628. doi:10.1016/S0167-4870(96)00039-6

Palvia, A., Vähämaa, E., & Vähämaa, S. (2020). Female leadership and bank risk-taking: Evidence from the effects of real estate shocks on bank lending performance and default risk. *Journal of Business Research, 117*(January), 897–909. doi:10.1016/j.jbusres.2020.04.057

Pantea, M., Gligor, D., & Anis, C. (2014). Economic determinants of Romanian firm's financial performance. *Procedia: Social and Behavioral Sciences*, *124*, 272–281. doi:10.1016/j.sbspro.2014.02.486

Papageorge, N. W., Zahn, M. V., Belot, M., van den Broek-Altenburg, E., Choi, S., Jamison, J. C., & Tripodi, E. (2021). Socio-demographic factors associated with self-protecting behavior during the covid-19 pandemic. *Journal of Population Economics*, *34*(2), 691–738. doi:10.100700148-020-00818-x PMID:33462529

Park, C. H., & Irwin, S. H. (2007). What do we know about the profitability of technical analysis? *Journal of Economic Surveys*, *21*(4), 786–826. doi:10.1111/j.1467-6419.2007.00519.x

Park, H. Y., & Bera, A. K. (1987). Interest rate volatility, basis, and heteroscedasticity in hedging mortgages. *Real Estate Economics*, *15*(2), 79–97. doi:10.1111/1540-6229.00420

Parkinson, M. (1980). The Extreme Value Method for Estimating the Variance of the Rate of Return. *The Journal of Business*, *53*(1), 61–65.

Park, S. H., Goo, J. M., & Jo, Ch. (2004). Receiver Operating Characteristic (ROC) Curve: Practical Review for Radiologists. *Korean Journal of Radiology*, *5*(1), 11–18. doi:10.3348/kjr.2004.5.1.11 PMID:15064554

Park, T. H., & Switzer, L. N. (1995). Bivariate GARCH estimation of the optimal hedge ratios for stock index futures: A note. *Journal of Futures Markets*, *15*(1), 61–67. doi:10.1002/fut.3990150106

Pasiouras, F., & Kosmidou, K. (2007). Factors influencing the profitability of domestic and foreign commercial banks in the European Union. *Research in International Business and Finance, 21*(2), 222–237. doi:10.1016/j.ribaf.2006.03.007

Pástor, Ľ., & Vorsatz, M. B. (2020). Mutual fund performance and flows during the COVID-19 crisis. *Review of Asset Pricing Studies, 10*(4), 791–833. doi:10.1093/rapstu/raaa015

Pata, U. K. (2020, May). *Is the COVID-19 Pandemic a Financial Disaster for G7 Countries? Evidence from a Fourier Cointegration Test.* http://dx.doi.org/ doi:10.2139/ssrn.3603068

Peng, N. (2020). Luxury restaurants' risks when implementing new environmentally friendly programs – evidence from luxury restaurants in Taiwan. *International Journal of Contemporary Hospitality Management, 32*(7), 2409–2427. doi:10.1108/IJCHM-11-2019-0933

Pereira, P. (1993). *Incêndios em Edifícios na Cidade do Porto.* Universidade de Porto.

Perez, E., Castan, R., & Quintanilla, C. (2010). Constructing identity through the consumption of counterfeit luxury goods. *Qualitative Market Research: AnInternational Journal, 13*(3), 219–235. doi:10.1108/13522751011053608

Perez-Gorozpe, J. M. (2020, May 26). *Mexican Toll Roads Remain Vulnerable Amid COVID-19; Recovery Could Come Quickly As Restrictions Ease.* Retrieved from https://www.spglobal.com/: https://www.spglobal.com/ratings/en/research/articles/200204-coronavirus-impact-key-takeaways-from-our-articles-11337257

Pervan, I., Pervan, M., & Vukoja, B. (2011). Prediction of company bankruptcy using statistical techniques. *Croatian Operational Research Review, 11*(2), 158-166. https://hrcak.srce.hr/96660

Petnehazi, G., & Gall, J. (2018, March 19). Exploring the predictability of range-based volatility estimators using RNNs. *Intelligents Systems in Accounting Finance & Management*, 1-11. doi:arXiv:1803.07152v1

Petolick, G. (2010). United States. In A. Bakker & S. Kloosterhof (Eds.) Tax Risk Management: From Risk to Opportunity (pp. 431–468). IBFD.

Petřík, T. (2009). *Ekonomické a finanční řízení firmy* [Economic and financial management of the company]. Grada Publishing.

Pettit, R. R., & Venkatesh, P. C. (1995). Insider trading and long-run return performance. *Financial Management, 24*(2), 88–103. doi:10.2307/3665537

Pham, L. T. M., Vo, L. V., Le, H. T. T., & Le, D. V. (2018). Asset liquidity and firm innovation. *International Review of Financial Analysis, 58*, 225–234. doi:10.1016/j.irfa.2017.11.005

Phau, I., Teah, M., & Lee, A. (2009). Targeting buyers of counterfeits of luxury brands: A study on attitudes of Singaporean consumers. *Journal of Targeting, Measurement and Analysis for Marketing, 17*(1), 3-15.

Phau, I., & Teah, M. (2009). Devil wears (counterfeit) Prada: A study of antecedents and outcomes of attitudes towards counterfeits of luxury brands. *Journal of Consumer Marketing, 26*(1), 15–27. doi:10.1108/07363760910927019

Powell, M., & Ansic, D. (1997). Gender differences in risk behaviour in financial decision making: An experimental analysis. *Journal of Economic Psychology, 18*(6), 605–627. doi:10.1016/S0167-4870(97)00026-3

Powell, M., & Ansic, D. (1999). Gender differences in financial decision-making: A new approach for experimental economic analysis. *Economia, Societa, E Instituzioni, 11*(1), 71–89.

Premachandra, I. M., Bhabra, G. S., & Sueyoshi, T. (2009). DEA as a tool for bankruptcy assessment: A comparative study with logistic regression technique. *European Journal of Operational Research, 193*(2), 412–424. doi:10.1016/j.ejor.2007.11.036

Compilation of References

Premachandra, I. M., Chen, Y., & Watson, J. (2011). DEA as a Tool for Predicting Corporate Failure and Success: A Case of Bankruptcy Assessment. *Omega, 3*(6), 620–626. doi:10.1016/j.omega.2011.01.002

Primo, V. (2008). *Análise Estatística dos Incêndios em Edifícios no Porto*. LNEC-FCTUC.

Prince, M. (1993). Women, Men and Money Styles. *Journal of Economic Psychology, 14*(1), 175–182. doi:10.1016/0167-4870(93)90045-M

Pring, M. J. (2002). Technical analysis explained: The successful investor's guide to spotting investment trends and turning points. McGraw-Hill.

Profeta, P. (2020). Gender equality and public policy. *CESifo Forum, 21*(4), 37-40. Retrieved from www.scopus.com

Profeta, P. (2020). Gender equality and public policy during COVID-19. *CESifo Economic Studies, 66*(4), 365–375. doi:10.1093/cesifo/ifaa018 PMID:34191928

Psillaki, M., Tsolas, I. E., & Margaritis, D. (2010). Evaluation of credit risk based on firm performance. *European Journal of Operational Research, 201*(3), 873–881. doi:10.1016/j.ejor.2009.03.032

Pueschel, J., Chamaret, C., & Parguel, B. (2017). *Coping with copies: The influence of risk perceptions in luxury counterfeit consumption in GCC countries*. doi:10.1016/j.jbusres.2016.11.008

Putri, A., Bunga, M., & Rochman, E. (2021). Financial risk disclosure and corporate governance: Empirical evidence on banking companies in Indonesian Stock Exchange. *Advances in Economics, Business and Management Research, 161*, 32–39.

Putri, A., Bunga, M., & Rochman, E. (2021). Financial Risk Disclosure and Corporate Governance: Empirical Evidence on Banking Companies in Indonesian Stock Exchange. *Advances in Economics, Business and Management Research, 161*, 32–39.

PwC & World Bank. (2020). *Paying Taxes 2020*. https://www.pwc.com/gx/en/paying-taxes/pdf/pwc-paying-taxes-2020.pdf

PwC Indonesia. (2020, APRIL 26). *COVID-19: Considering the potential business impacts for Indonesia*. Retrieved from https://www.pwc.com/id/en/covid-19-potential-business-impact-for-indonesia.html

Qin, Y., Hui Shi, L., Song, L., Stöttinger, B., & Tan, K. (2018). Integrating consumers' motives with suppliers' solutions to combat Shanzhai: A phenomenon beyond counterfeit. *Business Horizons, 61*(2), 229–237. doi:10.1016/j.bushor.2017.11.009

Quah, H., Haman, J., & Naidu, D. (2021). The effect of stock liquidity on investment efficiency under financing constraints and asymmetric information: Evidence from the United States. *Accounting and Finance, 61*(S1), 2109–2150. doi:10.1111/acfi.12656

Quentin, C. (2019). Acceptable Levels of Tax Risk as a Metric of Corporate Tax Responsibility: Theory, and a Survey of Practice. *Nordic Tax Journal, 1*(1), 1–15. doi:10.1515/ntaxj-2019-0001

Quiggin, J. (1982). A Theory of Anticipated Utility. *Journal of Economic Behavior & Organization, 3*(4), 323–343. doi:10.1016/0167-2681(82)90008-7

Quintal, V., Phau, I., Sims, D., & Cheah, I. (2016). Factors influencing generation Y's purchase intentions of prototypical versus me-too brands. *Journal of Retailing and Consumer Services, 30*, 175–183. doi:10.1016/j.jretconser.2016.01.019

Rabbani, A. G., Grable, J. E., Heo, W., Nobre, L., & Kuzniak, S. (2017). Stock market volatility and changes in financial risk tolerance during the great recession. *Financial Counseling and Planning, 28*(1), 140–154. doi:10.1891/1052-3073.28.1.140

Ravi, S. (2020, May 11). *Impact Of COVID 19 On The Indian Stock Markets*. Retrieved from http://www.businessworld.in/article/Impact-Of-COVID-19-On-The-Indian-Stock-Markets/11-05-2020-191755/

Reboredo, J. C., Quintela, M., & Otero, L. A. (2017). Do investors pay a premium for going green? Evidence from alternative energy mutual funds. *Renewable & Sustainable Energy Reviews*, *73*, 512–520. doi:10.1016/j.rser.2017.01.158

Regulation (EU) 2020/852 of the European Parliament and of the Council of 18 June 2020 on the establishment of a framework to facilitate sustainable investment and amending Regulation (EU) 2019/2088. PE/20/2020/INIT, OJ L 198, 22.6.2020, p. 13–43

Rehman, A., Adzis, A. A., & Mohamed-Arshad, S. B. (2020). The relationship between corruption and credit risk in commercial banks of Pakistan. *International Journal of Innovation, Creativity and Change*, *11*(1), 701–715.

Renneboog, L., Horst, J., & Zhang, C. (2008a). Socially Responsible Investments: Institutional Aspects, Performance, and Investor Behaviour. *Journal of Banking & Finance*, *32*(9), 1723–1742. doi:10.1016/j.jbankfin.2007.12.039

Renneboog, L., Horst, J., & Zhang, C. (2008b). The Price of Ethics and Stakeholder Governance: The Performance of Socially Responsible Mutual Funds. *Journal of Corporate Finance*, *14*(3), 302–322. doi:10.1016/j.jcorpfin.2008.03.009

Renneboog, L., Horst, J., & Zhang, C. (2011). Is Ethical Money Financially Smart? Nonfinancial Attributes and Money Flows of Socially Responsible Investment Funds. *Journal of Financial Intermediation*, *20*(4), 562–588. doi:10.1016/j.jfi.2010.12.003

Rensburg, J. (2012). *Tax Risk Management: A Framework for Implementation* (Master's thesis). University of Pretoria, South Africa.

Revelli, C. (2017). Socially responsible investing (SRI): From mainstream to margin? *Research in International Business and Finance*, *39*, 711–717. doi:10.1016/j.ribaf.2015.11.003

Revelli, C., & Viviani, J. (2015). Financial Performance of Socially Responsible Investing (SRI): What Have We Learned? A Meta-Analysis. *Business Ethics (Oxford, England)*, *24*(2), 158–185. doi:10.1111/beer.12076

Rhoades, D.L., Rechner, P.L., & Sundaramurthy, C. (2001). A meta-analysis of board leadership structure and financial performance: are 'two heads better than one'? *Corporate Governance: An International Review*, *9*(4), 311-319.

Riedl, A., & Smeets, P. (2017). Why do investors hold socially responsible mutual funds? *The Journal of Finance*, *72*(6), 2505–2550. doi:10.1111/jofi.12547

Riley, W. B. Jr, & Chow, K. V. (1992). Asset allocation and individual risk aversion. *Financial Analysts Journal*, *48*(6), 32–37. doi:10.2469/faj.v48.n6.32

Rimin, F., Bujang, I., Wong, A., & Chu, S. (2020). The effect of a separate risk management committee (RMC) towards firms ' performances on consumer goods sector in Malaysia. *Business Process Management Journal*. Advance online publication. doi:10.1108/BPMJ-06-2020-0265

Riquelme, H. E., Mahdi, E., Abbas, S., & Rios, R. E. (2008). Intention to purchase fake products in an Islamic country. *Education, Business and Society*, *5*(1), 6–22. doi:10.1108/17537981211225835

Robbins, S. P. (2000). *Administração: Mudanças e Perspectivas*. Saraiva.

Rodrigues, F., & Russo, R. (2011). Heurísticas e Vieses. In *Tomada de decisão nas organizações* (pp. 79–108). Saraiva.

Rodriguez, R. N. (2012, June). Big data and better data. *Amstat News*, 3-4.

Rogers, L. G., & Satchell, S. (1994). Estimating the Volatility of Stock Prices: A Comparison of Methods That Use High and Low Prices. *Applied Financial Economics*, *4*(3), 241–247.

Roháčová, V., & Kráľ, P. (2015). *Corporate Failure Prediction Using DEA: An Application to Companies in the Slovak Republic* [Paper presentation]. 18th Applications of Mathematics and Statistics in Economics, International Scientific Conference. Jindřichův Hradec, Czech Republic. http://amse-conference.eu/history/amse2015/doc/Rohacova_Kral.pdf

Rosillo, R., De la Fuente, D., & Brugos, J. A. (2013). Technical analysis and the Spanish stock exchange: Testing the RSI, MACD, momentum and stochastic rules using Spanish market companies. *Applied Economics*, *45*(12), 1451–1550. doi:10.1080/00036846.2011.631894

Rost, K., & Osterloh, M. (2010). Opening the black box of upper echelons: Drivers of poor information processing during the financial crisis. *Corporate Governance*, *18*(3), 212–233. doi:10.1111/j.1467-8683.2010.00796.x

Roszkowski, M. J., & Grable, J. (2005). Gender stereotypes in advisors' clinical judgments of financial risk tolerance: Objects in the mirror are closer than they appear to be. *Journal of Behavioral Finance*, *6*(4), 181–191. doi:10.120715427579jpfm0604_2

Russo, R. (2010). Risk Management in Taxation. In M. Daelen & C. Elst (Eds.), *Risk Management and Corporate Governance: Interconnections in Law, Accounting and Tax* (pp. 163–190). Edward Elgar Publishing. doi:10.4337/9781849807999.00012

Ryack, K. N., Kraten, M., & Sheikh, A. (2016). Incorporating financial risk tolerance research into the financial planning process. *Journal of Financial Planning*, *29*(10), 51–61.

Rybak, T. N. (2006). Analysis and estimate of the enterprises bankruptcy risk. In *Zborník z 3. Medzinárodní konference Řízení a modelování finančních rizik* [Proceedings of the 3rd International Conference on Financial Risk Management and Modeling] (pp. 315–320). VŠB TU Ostrava. https://scholar.google.com/scholar?cluster=6887450162738206801&hl=en&as_

Saa, L. (2020). *PRI welcomes 500th asset owner signatory*. PRI BLOG. Available at: https://www.unpri.org/pri-blog/pri-welcomes-500th-asset-owner-signatory/5367.article

Sadorsky, P. (2014). Modeling volatility and correlations between emerging market stock prices and the prices of copper, oil and wheat. *Energy Economics*, *43*, 72–81. doi:10.1016/j.eneco.2014.02.014

Saeed, A., Mukarram, S. S., & Belghitar, Y. (2021). Read between the lines: Board gender diversity, family ownership, and risk-taking in Indian high-tech firms. *International Journal of Finance & Economics*, *26*(1), 185–207. doi:10.1002/ijfe.1784

Saeidi, P., Saeidi, S. P., Gutierrez, L., Streimikiene, D., Alrasheedi, M., Saeidi, S. P., & Mardani, A. (2021). The influence of enterprise risk management on firm performance with the moderating effect of intellectual capital dimensions. *Economic Research-Ekonomska Istraživanja*, *34*(1), 122–151. doi:10.1080/1331677X.2020.1776140

Safdar, M.Z., Awan, M.Z., Ahmed, Z., Qureshi, M.I., & Hasnain, T. (2016). What does matter? Liquidity or profitability: a case of sugar industry in Pakistan. *International Journal of Economics and Financial Issues*, *6*(2), 144-152.

Safran. (2019). *Safran Group*. Retrieved from Safran: https://www.safran-group.com/group-0#1

Saggar, R., & Singh, B. (2017). Corporate governance and risk reporting: Indian evidence. *Managerial Auditing Journal*, *32*(4-5), 378–405. doi:10.1108/MAJ-03-2016-1341

Saha, A., Havenner, A., & Talpaz, H. (1997). Stochastic production function estimation: Small sample properties of ML versus FGLS. *Applied Economics*, *29*(4), 459–469. doi:10.1080/000368497326958

Sahin, Y., Bulkan, S., & Duman, E. (2013). A cost-sensitive decision tree approach for fraud detection. *Expert Systems with Applications*, •••, 5916–5923.

Sahni, S., Kumari, S., & Pachaury, P. (2021). Building emotional resilience with big five personality model against COVID-19 pandemic. *FIIB Business Review*, *10*(1), 39–51. doi:10.1177/2319714520954559

Saito, T., & Rehmsmeier, M. (2015). The precision-recall plot is more informative than the roc plot when evaluating binary classifiers on imbalanced datasets. *PLoS One*, *10*(3), e0118432. doi:10.1371/journal.pone.0118432 PMID:25738806

Salisu, A. A., Raheem, I., & Vo, X. V. (2021). Assessing the safe haven property of the gold market during COVID-19 pandemic. *International Review of Financial Analysis*, *74*, 101666.

Salomons, R., & Grootveld, H. (2003). The equity risk premium: Emerging vs. developed markets. *Emerging Markets Review*, *4*(2), 121–144. doi:10.1016/S1566-0141(03)00024-4

Samek, W., Wiegand, T., & Muller, K. (2017). *Explainable artificial intelligence; Understanding, visualizing and interpreting deep learning models*. Retrieved from https://arxiv.org/pdf/1708.08296.pdf

Sandberg, J., Juravle, C., Hedesström, T., & Hamilton, I. (2009). The Heterogeneity of Socially Responsible Investment. *Journal of Business Ethics*, *87*(4), 519–533. doi:10.100710551-008-9956-0

Sandman, G., & Koopman, S. J. (1998). Estimation of stochastic volatility models via Monte Carlo maximum likelihood. *Journal of Econometrics*.

SanobarA. (2012). Business Bankruptcy Prediction Models: A Significant Study of the Altman's Z-Score Model. https://ssrn.com/abstract=2128475

Sapienza, P., Zingales, L., & Maestripieri, D. (2009). Gender differences in financial risk aversion and career choices are affected by testosterone. *Proceedings of the National Academy of Sciences of the United States of America*, *106*(36), 15268–15273. doi:10.1073/pnas.0907352106 PMID:19706398

Saraiva, H. (2020). The disclosure of non-financial information and the possibilities of contribution from management accounting. *Revista de la Asociación Española de Contabilidad y Administración*, *131*, 61–62.

Saraiva, H. I. B., & Carqueja, H. O. (2018). Ensaio sobre o papel da organização das nações unidas no processo de harmonização contabilística - iniciativas durante o período 1953-2009. De Computis. *Revista Española de Historia de la Contabilidad*, *15*(2), 108–132. doi:10.26784/issn.1886-1881.v15i2.336

Sariev, E., & Germano, G. (2020). Bayesian regularized artificial neural networks for the estimation of the probability of default. *Quantitative Finance*, *20*(2), 311–328. doi:10.1080/14697688.2019.1633014

Sarin, R., & Wieland, A. (2016). Risk aversion for decisions under uncertainty: Are there gender differences? *Journal of Behavioral and Experimental Economics*, *60*, 1–8. doi:10.1016/j.socec.2015.10.007

Šarlija, N., & Jeger, M. (2011). Comparing financial distress prediction models before and during recession. *Croatian Operational Research Review*, *2*(1), 133–142. https://hrcak.srce.hr/96658

SBA. (2021). *Nepriaznivý vplyv pandémie koronavírusu na podnikovú ekonomiku SR* [Adverse impact of the coronavirus pandemic on the Slovak business economy]. Slovak Business Agency. http://monitoringmsp.sk/wp-content/uploads/2021/07/Nepriazniv%C3%BD-vplyv-pand%C3%A9mie-koronav%C3%ADrusu-na-podnikov%C3%BA-ekonomiku-SR.pdf

Scherr, F. C., & Hulburt, H. M. (2001). The Debt Maturiry Structure of Small Firms. *Financial Management*, *30*(1), 85–111. doi:10.2307/3666392

Compilation of References

Schneider, C. R., Dryhurst, S., Kerr, J., Freeman, A. L. J., Recchia, G., Spiegelhalter, D., & van der Linden, S. (2021). COVID-19 risk perception: A longitudinal analysis of its predictors and associations with health protective behaviours in the united kingdom. *Journal of Risk Research*, *24*(3-4), 294–313. doi:10.1080/13669877.2021.1890637

Scholtens, B. (2005). What Drives Socially Responsible Investment? The Case of the Netherlands. *Sustainable Development*, *13*(2), 129–137. doi:10.1002d.252

Schröder, M. (2004). The Performance of Socially Responsible Investments: Investment Funds and Indices. *Financial Markets and Portfolio Management*, *18*(2), 122–142. doi:10.100711408-004-0202-1

Schroeck, G. (2002). *Risk management and value creation in financial institutions*. John Wiley & Sons, Inc.

Schubert, R., Brown, M., Gysler, M., & Brachinger, H. W. (1999). Financial Decision-Making: Are Women Really More Risk-Averse? *The American Economic Review*, *89*(2), 381–385. doi:10.1257/aer.89.2.381

Schultheiss, D. E. (2021). Shining the light on women's work, this time brighter: Let's start at the top. *Journal of Vocational Behavior*, *126*, 103558. Advance online publication. doi:10.1016/j.jvb.2021.103558

Schwager, J. D. (1984). *A complete guide to the futures markets: fundamental analysis, technical analysis, trading, spreads, and options*. John Wiley & Sons.

Segal, T., & Maroun, W. (2014). Tax Risk-Management Analysis: Comparison Between the United States of America, The United Kingdom and South Africa. *Journal of Economic and Financial Sciences*, *7*(2), 375–392. doi:10.4102/jef.v7i2.146

Serrasqueiro, Z. (2009). Growth and profitability in Portuguese companies: A dynamic panel data approach. *Economic Interferences*, *11*(26), 265–279.

Setor, T. K., Senyo, P. K., & Addo, A. (2021). Do Digital Payment Transactions Reduce Corruption? Evidence from Developing Countries. *Telematics and Informatics*, *60*(November), 101577. doi:10.1016/j.tele.2021.101577

Shahab, Y., Ntim, C. G., Chengang, Y., Ullah, F., & Fosu, S. (2018). Environmental policy, environmental performance, and financial distress in China: Do top management team characteristics matter? *Business Strategy and the Environment*, *27*(8), 1635–1652. doi:10.1002/bse.2229

Shahzad, S. J. H., Bouri, E., Ur Rehman, M., & Roubaud, D. (2021). The hedge asset for BRICS stock markets: Bitcoin, gold or VIX. *World Economy*. Advance online publication. doi:10.1111/twec.13138

Shammi, M., Bodrud-Doza, M., Islam, A. R. M. T., & Rahman, M. M. (2021). Strategic assessment of COVID-19 pandemic in bangladesh: Comparative lockdown scenario analysis, public perception, and management for sustainability. *Environment, Development and Sustainability*, *23*(4), 6148–6191. doi:10.100710668-020-00867-y PMID:32837281

Sharif, A., Aloui, C., & Yarovaya, L. (2020). COVID-19 pandemic, oil prices, stock market, geopolitical risk and policy uncertainty nexus in the US economy: Fresh evidence from the wavelet-based approach. *International Review of Financial Analysis*, *70*, 1–9.

Sharma, A. (2020, April 13). *Coronavirus impact: India worst hit stock market; China least-affected*. Retrieved from https://www.businesstoday.in/markets/stocks/coronavirus-impact-india-worst-hit-stock-market-china-least-affected/story/400890.html

Sharma, A., & Panigrahi, P. (2013). A Review of Financial Accounting Fraud Detection based on Data Mining Techniques. *International Journal of Computers and Applications*.

Shian-Chang, H. (2011). Using Gaussian process based kernel classifiers for credit rating forecasting. *Expert Systems with Applications*, 8607–8611.

Shier, R. (2004). *Statistics: Paired t-tests*. Mathematics Learning Support Centre. Retrieved from Paired t-tests: http://www.statstutor.ac.uk/resources/uploaded/paired-t-test.pdf

Shropshire, C., Peterson, S., Bartels, A. L., Amanatullah, E. T., & Lee, P. M. (2021). Are Female CEOs Really More Risk Averse? Examining Economic Downturn and Other-Orientation. *Journal of Leadership & Organizational Studies*, *28*(2), 185–206. doi:10.1177/1548051821997404

Shrydeh, N., Shahateet, M., Mohammad, S., & Sumadi, M. (2019). The hedging effectiveness of gold against US stocks in a post-financial crisis era. *Cogent Economics & Finance*, *7*(1). Advance online publication. doi:10.1080/23322039.2019.1698268

Shu, J., & Zhang, J. E. (2003, Jan). The Relationship Between Implied and Realized Volatility of S&P 500 Index. *Wilmott Magazine, 1*, 83-91.

Shukla, P. (2010). Status consumption in cross-national context: Socio-psychological, brand and situational antecedents. *International Marketing Review*, *27*(1), 108–129. doi:10.1108/02651331011020429

Sibilkov, V. (2009). Asset liquidity and capital structure. *Journal of Financial and Quantitative Analysis*, *44*(5), 1173–1196. doi:10.1017/S0022109009990354

Sila, V., Gonzalez, A., & Hagendorff, J. (2016). Women on board: Does boardroom gender diversity affect firm risk? *Journal of Corporate Finance*, *36*, 26–53. doi:10.1016/j.jcorpfin.2015.10.003

Silva, F., & Cortez, M. (2016). The Performance of US and European Green Funds in Different Market Conditions. *Journal of Cleaner Production*, *135*, 558–566. doi:10.1016/j.jclepro.2016.06.112

Simak, P. C. (1997). *DEA Based Analysis of Coporate Failure* [Master Thesis]. Faculty of Applied Sciences and Engineering, University of Toronto. https://tspace.library.utoronto.ca/bitstream/1807/11746/1/MQ29433.pdf

Simon, H. A. (1955). A Behavioral Model of Rational Choice. *The Quarterly Journal of Economics*, *69*(1), 99–118. doi:10.2307/1884852

Simon, H. A. (1960). *A Capacidade de Decisão e de Liderança*. Editora Fundo de Cultura.

Sims, C. A. (1980). Macroeconomics and Reality. *The Econometric Society*, *48*(1), 1–48.

Singh, V. S., Terjesen, S., & Vinnicombe, S. (2008). Newly appointed directors in the boardroom: How do women and men differ? *European Management Journal*, *2*(3), 48–58. doi:10.1016/j.emj.2007.10.002

Sjoberg, L. (2000). Factors in risk perception. *Risk Analysis*, *20*(1), 1–11. doi:10.1111/0272-4332.00001

Sjöberg, L., & Engelberg, E. (2009). Attitudes to Economic Risk Taking, Sensation Seeking and Values of Business Students Specializing in Finance. *Journal of Behavioral Finance*, *10*(1), 33–43. doi:10.1080/15427560902728712

Sláviček, O., & Kuběnka, M. (2016). Bankruptcy prediction models based on the logistic regression for companies in the Czech Republic. In *Proceedings of the 8th International Scientific Conference Managing and Modelling of Financial Risks*. VŠB-TU of Ostrava, Faculty of Economics, Department of Finance. https://dk.upce.cz/handle/10195/67220

Soczo, C. (2003). 2003). Estimation of Future Volatality. *Periodica Polytechnica Ser. Soc. Man. SCI*, *11*(02), 201–214.

Solomon, J. F., Solomon, A., Norton, S. D., & Joseph, N. L. (2000). A conceptual framework for corporate risk disclosure emerging from the agenda for corporate governance reform. *The British Accounting Review*, *32*(4), 447–478. doi:10.1006/bare.2000.0145

Soltani, B., & Maupetit, C. (2015). Importance of core values of ethics, integrity and accountability in the European corporate governance codes. *The Journal of Management and Governance, 19*(2), 259–284. doi:10.100710997-013-9259-4

Song, C. Q., Chang, C. P., & Gong, Q. (2021). Economic growth, corruption, and financial development: Global evidence. *Economic Modelling, 94*(December), 822–830. doi:10.1016/j.econmod.2020.02.022

Son, T. H., Liem, N. T., & Khuong, N. V. (2020). Corruption, nonperforming loans, and economic growth: International evidence. *Cogent Business and Management, 7*(1), 1735691. Advance online publication. doi:10.1080/23311975.2020.1735691

SOSR. (2021). *Statistical Office of the Slovak Republic: DATAcube*. https://slovak.statistics.sk/wps/portal/ext/Databases/DATAcube_sk

Souiden, N., Ladhari, R., & Amri, A. Z. (2018). Is buying counterfeit sinful? Investigation of consumers' attitudes and purchase intentions of counterfeit products in a Muslim country. *International Journal of Consumer Studies, 42*(November), 687–703. doi:10.1111/ijcs.12466

Spence, M. (1973). Job market signaling. *The Quarterly Journal of Economics, 87*(3), 355–374. doi:10.2307/1882010

Sperandei, S. (2014). Understanding logistic regression analysis. *Biochemia Medica, 24*(1), 12–18. doi:10.11613/BM.2014.003 PMID:24627710

Staake, T., Thiesse, F., & Fleisch, E. (2009). The emergence of counterfeit trade: A literature review. *European Journal of Marketing, 43*(3/4), 320–349. doi:10.1108/03090560910935451

Stankovičová, I., & Vojtková, M. (2007). *Viacrozmerné štatistické metódy s aplikáciami* [Multidimensional statistical methods with applications]. Iura Edition.

Startiene, G., & Remeikiene, R. (2009). The influence of demographical factors on the interaction between entrepreneurship and unemployment. *The Engineering Economist, 4*(64), 60–70.

Statman, M. (2000). Socially Responsible Mutual Funds. *Financial Analysts Journal, 56*(3), 30–39. doi:10.2469/faj.v56.n3.2358

Statman, M., & Glushkov, D. (2009). The Wages of Social Responsibility. *Financial Analysts Journal, 65*(4), 33–46. doi:10.2469/faj.v65.n4.5

Stein, J. L. (1961). The simultaneous determination of spot and futures prices. *The American Economic Review, 51*(5), 1012–1025.

Stulz, R. (1988). Managerial control of voting rights. *Journal of Financial Economics, 20*, 25–54. doi:10.1016/0304-405X(88)90039-6

Sultana, N., & Mitchell Van der Zahn, J. L. W. (2015). Earnings conservatism and audit committee financial expertise. *Accounting and Finance, 55*(1), 279–310. doi:10.1111/acfi.12042

Summa, J. (2016). *Option Volatility*. Investopedia. Retrieved from http://www.investopedia.com/university/optionvolatility/default.asp

Sunden, A. E., & Surette, B. J. (1998). Gender Differences in the Allocation of Assets in Retirement Savings Plans. *The American Economic Review, 88*(2), 207–211.

Su, W., Peng, M. W., Tan, W., & Cheung, Y. L. (2016). The signaling effect of corporate social responsibility in emerging economies. *Journal of Business Ethics, 134*(3), 479–491. doi:10.100710551-014-2404-4

Svejnar, J. (2002). Transition economies: Performance and challenges. *The Journal of Economic Perspectives, 16*(1), 1, 3–28. doi:10.1257/0895330027058

Synek, M. (2007). *Manažerská ekonomika* [Managerial economics] (4th ed.). Grada Publishing.

Szado, E. (2009). VIX futures and options: A case study of portfolio diversification during the 2008 financial crisis. *Journal of Alternative Investments, 12*(2), 68–85.

Taffler, R. J. (1983). The assessment of company solvency and performance using a statistical model. *Accounting and Business Research, 13*(52), 295–308. doi:10.1080/00014788.1983.9729767

Tang, F., Tian, V.-I., & Zaichkowsky, J. (2019). Understanding Motivations to Purchase Counterfeit Items in China Understanding counterfeit consumption. *Asia Pacific Journal of Marketing and Logistics*, (March). Advance online publication. doi:10.1007/978-3-319-10963-3

Tanin, T. I., Sarker, A., Hammoudeh, S., & Shahbaz, M. (2021). Do volatility indices diminish gold's appeal as a safe haven to investors before and during the COVID-19 pandemic? *Journal of Economic Behavior & Organization, 191*, 214–235.

Tanyi, P. N., & Smith, D. B. (2015). Busyness, expertise, and financial reporting quality of audit committee chairs and financial experts. *Auditing, 34*(2), 59–89. doi:10.2308/ajpt-50929

Tarca, A. (2012). *The Case for Global Accounting Standards: Arguments and Evidence.* https://papers.ssrn.com/sol3/papers.cfm?abstract_id=2204889

Tarchella, S., & Dhaoui, A. (2021). Chinese jigsaw: Solving the equity market response to the COVID-19 crisis: Do alternative asset provide effective hedging performance? *Research in International Business and Finance, 58*, 101499.

Tavares, F., Santos, E. & Tavares, V. (2021). Risk Categorization in Portuguese Organizations in Times of the COVID-19 Pandemic – an Exploratory Statistical Analysis. *Journal of Entrepreneurship and Public Policy, 10*(3), 306-322. . doi:10.1108/JEPP-03-2021-0033

Taylor, G., Tower, G., & Neilson, J. (2010). Corporate communication of financial risk. *Accounting and Finance, 50*(2), 417–446. doi:10.1111/j.1467-629X.2009.00326.x

Technologies, H. (2020, April 30). *Close-to-Close Historical Volatility Calculation.* Retrieved from http://tech.harbourfronts.com/trading/close-close-historical-volatility-calculation-volatility-analysis-python/

TEG - EU Technical Expert Group on Sustainable Finance. (2019). *Financing a Sustainable European Economy – Report on EU Greenbond Standard - TEG Report Proposal for an EU Green Bond Standard.* Available at: https://ec.europa.eu/info/sites/info/files/business_economy_euro/banking_and_finance/documents/190618-sustainable-finance-teg-report-green-bond-standard_en.pdf

TEG - EU Technical Expert Group on Sustainable Finance. (2020a). *Financing a Sustainable European Economy – Technical Report - Taxonomy: Final report of the Technical Expert Group on Sustainable Finance.* Available at: https://ec.europa.eu/info/sites/info/files/business_economy_euro/banking_and_finance/documents/200302-sustainable-finance-teg-final-report-taxonomy-annexes_en.pdf

TEG - EU Technical Expert Group on Sustainable Finance. (2020b). *Taxonomy: Final report of the Technical Expert Group on Sustainable Finance.* Available at: https://ec.europa.eu/info/sites/default/files/business_economy_euro/banking_and_finance/documents/200309-sustainable-finance-teg-final-report-taxonomy_en.pdf

Teknologi, U., Cawangan, M., & Kampus, K. (2019). Audit and risk committee in financial crime prevention. *Journal of Financial Crime, 26*(1), 223–234. doi:10.1108/JFC-11-2017-0116

Compilation of References

Teodosia, J., Veira, E., & Madaleno, M. (2021). Gender diversity and corporate risk-taking : A literature review. *Managerial Finance*, *47*(7), 1038–1073. Advance online publication. doi:10.1108/MF-11-2019-0555

Thaler, R. (1980). Toward a Positive Theory of Consumer Choice. *Journal of Economic Behavior & Organization*, *1*(1), 39–60. doi:10.1016/0167-2681(80)90051-7

The World Bank Group. (2020, April 16). *The World Bank in Turkey*. Retrieved from https://www.worldbank.org/: https://www.worldbank.org/en/country/turkey/overview

Thi, N., Mai, T., & Linh, N. H. (2017). Antecedents of the intention and behavior toward purchase of counterfeit luxury goods in an emerging economy: A study of young vietnamese consumers. *Organizations and Markets in Emerging Economies*, *8*(2), 207–225. doi:10.15388/omee.2017.8.2.14189

Thornton, P. (2006, March 3). *New E7 nations will overtake G7 by 2050*. Retrieved from https://www.independent.co.uk/:https://www.independent.co.uk/news/business/news/new-e7-nations-will-overtake-g7-by-2050-6107791.html

Ting, H. I. (2013). The influence of insiders and institutional investors on firm performance. *Review of Pacific Basin Financial Markets and Policies*, *16*(04), 1350027. doi:10.1142/S0219091513500276

Ting, M., Goh, Y., & Mohd, S. (2016). Determining consumer purchase intentions toward counterfeit luxury goods in Malaysia. *Asia Pacific Management Review*, *21*(4), 219–230. doi:10.1016/j.apmrv.2016.07.003

Toader, T., Onofrei, M., Popescu, A. I., & Andrieş, A. M. (2018). Corruption and Banking Stability: Evidence from Emerging Economies. *Emerging Markets Finance & Trade*, *54*(3), 591–617. doi:10.1080/1540496X.2017.1411257

Tom, S. M., Fox, C. R., Trepel, C., & Poldrack, R. A. (2007). The Neural Basis of Loss Aversion in Decision-making Under Risk. *Science*, *315*(5811), 515–518. doi:10.1126cience.1134239 PMID:17255512

Topcua, M., & Gulalb, O. S. (2020, July). The impact of COVID-19 on emerging stock markets. *Finance Research Letters*, 12–23. doi:10.1016/j.frl.2020.101691

Torrey, A. (2008). *The Discriminant Analysis Used by the IRS to Predict Profitable Individual Tax Return Audits*. http://digitalcommons.bryant.edu/cgi/viewcontent.cgi?article=1000&context= honors_mathematics.

Transparency International. (n.d.). *What is Corruption?* Retrieved from https://www.transparency.org/en/what-is-corruption

Trejo-Pech, C., Gunderson, M., & Noguera, M. (2015). Corporate Cash Holdings and Economic Crises in Mexico. In A. Gevorkyan & O. Canuto (Eds.), *Financial Deepening and Post-Crisis Development in Emerging Markets.*, doi:10.1057/978-1-137-52246-7_6

Tse, Y. K., & Tsui, A. K. C. (2002). A multivariate GARCH model with time-varying correlations. *Journal of Business & Economic Statistics*, *20*(3), 351–362. doi:10.1198/073500102288618496

Tu, C. A., Rasoulinezhad, E., & Sarker, T. (2020). Investigating solutions for the development of a green bond market: Evidence from analytic hierarchy process. *Finance Research Letters*, *34*, 101457. doi:10.1016/j.frl.2020.101457

Tversky, A., & Kahneman, D. (1974). Judgment Under Uncertainty: Heuristics and Biases. *Judgment Under Uncertainty*, *185*(4157), 3–20.

Tversky, A., & Kahneman, D. (1986). Rational Choice and the Framing of Decisions. *The Journal of Business*, *59*(4), 251–278. doi:10.1086/296365

Tversky, A., & Kahneman, D. (1991). Loss Aversion in Riskless Choice. A Reference-dependent Model. *The Quarterly Journal of Economics*, *106*(4), 1039–1061. doi:10.2307/2937956

Tversky, A., & Kahneman, D. (1992). Advances in Prospect Theory: Cumulative Representation of Uncertainty. *Journal of Risk and Uncertainty*, *5*(4), 297–323. doi:10.1007/BF00122574

U. S. Fire Administration. (2017a). *About the National Fire Incident Reporting System*. Retrieved December 26, 2017, from https://www.usfa.fema.gov/data/nfirs/about/index.html

U. S. Fire Administration. (2017b). *Fire in the United States 2006-2015*. Retrieved from https://www.usfa.fema.gov/downloads/pdf/publications/fius19th.pdf

Ud Din, N., Cheng, X., Ahmad, B., Sheikh, M. F., Adedigba, O. G., Zhao, Y., & Nazneen, S. (2021). Gender diversity in the audit committee and the efficiency of internal control and financial reporting quality. *Economic Research-Ekonomska Istrazivanja*, *34*(1), 1170–1189. doi:10.1080/1331677X.2020.1820357

Ud-Din, S., Khan, M. Y., Javeed, A., & Pham, H. (2020). Board structure and likelihood of financial distress: An emerging Asian market perspective. *Journal of Asian Finance. Economics and Business*, *7*(11), 241–250.

Udin, S., Khan, M. A., & Javid, A. Y. (2017). The effects of ownership structure on likelihood of financial distress: An empirical evidence. *Corporate Governance: The International Journal of Business in Society*, *17*(4), 589–612. doi:10.1108/CG-03-2016-0067

Ugwuanyi, G. O. (2015). Regulation of Bank Capital Requirements and Bank Risk-Taking Behaviour: Evidence from the Nigerian Banking Industry. *International Journal of Economics and Finance*, *7*(8), 31–37. doi:10.5539/ijef.v7n8p31

UK Finance Act 2016 Schedule 19, https://www.legislation.gov.uk/ukpga/2016/24/schedule/19/2016-09-15

UK Financial Reporting Council. (2012). https://www.frc.org.uk/getattachment/e322c20a-1181-4ac8-a3d3-1fcfbcea7914/UK-Corporate-Governance-Code-(September-2012).pdf

Umoru, D., & Osemwegie, J. O. (2016). Capital Adequacy and Financial Performance of Banks in Nigeria: Empirical Evidence Based on the Fgls Estimator. *European Scientific Journal, ESJ*, *12*(25), 295. doi:10.19044/esj.2016.v12n25p295

Utz, S., & Wimmer, M. (2014). Are They Any Good at All? A Financial and Ethical Analysis of Socially Responsible Mutual Funds. *Journal of Asset Management*, *15*(1), 72–82. doi:10.1057/jam.2014.8

Vassalou, M., & Xing, Y. (2004). Default Risk in Equity Returns. *Journal of Finance*, *59*(2), 831–868. doi:10.1111/j.1540-6261.2004.00650.x

Verbeek, M. (2012). *A Guide to Modern Econometrics*. John Wiley & Sons.

Vieira, E., & Neiva, J. (2019). Corporate Governance Board of Directors and Firm Performance in Portugal. In Handbook of Board of Directors and Company Performance: An International Outlook. Virtus Interpress.

Vieira, E. S., Neves, M. E., & Dias, A. G. (2019). Determinants of Portuguese firms' financial performance: Panel data evidence. *International Journal of Productivity and Performance Management*, *68*(7), 1323–1342. doi:10.1108/IJPPM-06-2018-0210

Vintila, G., & Nenu, E. A. (2015). An analysis of determinants of corporate financial performance: Evidence from the Bucharest stock exchange-listed companies. *International Journal of Economics and Financial Issues*, *5*(3), 732–739.

Vipul, J. (2007, Nov). Forecasting performance of extreme-value volatility estimators. *The Journal of Future Markets*, *27*(11), 1085-1105. doi:10.1002/fut.20283

Vochozka, M., Jelínek, J., Váchal, J., Straková, J., & Stehel, V. (2017). Využití neurónových sítí při komplexním hodnocení podniku (11th ed.). Praha: C.H.Beck.

Compilation of References

von Wagner, C., Baio, G., Raine, R., Snowball, J., Morris, S., Atkin, W., Obichere, A., Handley, G., Logan, R. F., Rainbow, S., Smith, S., Halloran, S., & Wardle, J. (2011). Inequalities in participation in an organized national colorectal cancer screening programme: Results from the first 2.6 million invitations in England. *International Journal of Epidemiology*, *40*(3), 712–718. doi:10.1093/ije/dyr008 PMID:21330344

Waddock, S., & Graves, S. (1997). The Corporate Social Performance–Financial Performance Link. *Strategic Management Journal*, *18*(4), 303–319. doi:10.1002/(SICI)1097-0266(199704)18:4<303::AID-SMJ869>3.0.CO;2-G

Walicka, M. (2014). Tax Risks Sources and Consequences as a part of Intercultural Management at Family Companies. *Journal of Intercultural Management*, *6*(4), 191–201. doi:10.2478/joim-2014-0045

Walls, M. R., & Dyer, J. S. (1996). Risk Propensity and Firm Performance: A Study of the Petroleum Exploration Industry. *Management Science*, *42*(7), 1004–1021. doi:10.1287/mnsc.42.7.1004

Wang. (2002). Liquidity management, operating performance, and corporate value: evidence from Japan and Taiwan. *Journal of Multinational Financial Management*, *12*, 159–169.

Wang, F., Zhang, H., Zang, H., & Ouyang, M. (2005). Purchasing pirated software: An initial examination of Chinese consumers. *Journal of Consumer Marketing*, *22*(6), 340–351. doi:10.1108/07363760510623939

Wang, H., & Hanna, S. (1997). Does Risk Tolerance Decrease with Age? *Financial Counseling and Planning*, *8*(2), 27–31.

Wang, Y. H. (2020). Does board gender diversity bring better financial and governance performances? An empirical investigation of cases in Taiwan. *Sustainability*, *12*(8), 1–14. doi:10.3390u12083205

Wang, Y., Stoner, J. L., & John, D. R. (2019). Counterfeit luxury consumption in a social context: The effects on females' moral disengagement and behaviour. *Journal of Consumer Psychology*, *29*(2), 207–225. doi:10.1002/jcpy.1071

Watson, J., & McNaughton, M. (2007). Gender Differences in Risk Aversion and Expected Retirement Benefits. *Financial Analysts Journal*, *63*(4), 52–62. doi:10.2469/faj.v63.n4.4749

Weber, E., Blais, A., & Betz, E. (2002). A domain specific risk-attitude scale: Measuring risk perceptions and risk behaviors. *Journal of Behavioral Decision Making*, *15*(4), 263–290. doi:10.1002/bdm.414

WEF – Worl Economic Forum. (2020). *Global Risks Report 2020*. Insight Report in partnership with Marsh & McLennan and Zurich Insurance Group. Available at: https://www.weforum.org/reports/the-global-risks-report-2020

Wen, F., Li, C., Sha, H., & Shao, L. (2021). How does economic policy uncertainty affect corporate risk-taking? Evidence from China. *Finance Research Letters*, *41*, 101840. doi:10.1016/j.frl.2020.101840

Werbel, J. D., & Danes, S. M. (2010). Work family conflict in new business ventures: The moderating effects of spousal commitment to the new business venture. *Journal of Small Business Management*, *48*(3), 421–440. doi:10.1111/j.1540-627X.2010.00301.x

West, D. (2000). Neural network credit scoring models. *Computers & Operations Research*, *27*(11-12), 1131–1152. doi:10.1016/S0305-0548(99)00149-5

Whaley, R. E. (1993). Derivatives on market volatility: Hedging tools long overdue. *Journal of Derivatives*, *1*(1), 71–84. doi:10.3905/jod.1993.407868

White, R. E., Thornhill, S., & Hampson, E. (2007). A biosocial model of entrepreneurship: The combined effects of nurture and nature. *Journal of Organizational Behavior*, *28*(4), 451–466. doi:10.1002/job.432

Whitmarsh, L. (2008). Are Flood Victims More Concerned About Climate Change than Other People? The Role of Direct Experience in Risk Perception and Behavioural Response. *Journal of Risk Research*, *11*(3), 351–374. doi:10.1080/13669870701552235

WHO. (2020). *Coronavirus disease 2019 (COVID-19)*. World Health Organisation (WHO). Retrieved from https://www.who.int/docs/default-source/coronaviruse/situation-reports/20200327-sitrep-67-covid-19.pdf?sfvrsn=b65f68eb_4

Wikipedia. (2021). *Developing Country*. Retrieved from https://en.wikipedia.org/wiki/Developing_country

Wilcox, J. W. (1973). A prediction of business failure using accounting data. *Journal of Accounting Research, Selected Studies*, *11*, 163-179. . doi:10.2307/2490035

Wilcox, K., Kim, H. M., & Sen, S. (2009). Why do consumers buy counterfeit luxury, brands? *Journal of Marketing Research*, *46*(2), 247-259.

Wilder, W. (1978). *New Concepts in Technical Trading Systems*. Trend Research.

Wiseman, R. M., & Bromiley, P. (1996). Toward a Model of Risk in Declining Organizations: An Empirical Examination of Risk, Performance and Decline. *Organization Science*, *7*(5), 524–543. doi:10.1287/orsc.7.5.524

Wong, W. K., Manzur, M., & Chew, B. K. (2013). How rewarding is technical analysis? Evidence from Singapore stock market. *Applied Financial Economics*, *13*(7), 543–551. doi:10.1080/09603100220000020906

Wooldridge, J. M. (2013). *Introductory Econometrics: A Modern Approach* (5th ed.). South-Western.

World Bank. (2020). *Global Economic Prospects, June 2020*. Washington, DC: World Bank. https://openknowledge.worldbank.org/handle/10986/33748

Wunder, H. F. (2009). Tax Risk Management and The Multinational Enterprise. *Journal of International Accounting, Auditing & Taxation*, *18*(1), 14–28. doi:10.1016/j.intaccaudtax.2008.12.003

Wu, Q., & Zhao, S. (2021). Determinants of Consumers' Willingness to Buy Counterfeit Luxury Products: An Empirical Test of Linear and Inverted U-Shaped Relationship. *Sustainability*, *13*(3), 1194. doi:10.3390u13031194

Wuthrich, M. V., & Buser, C. (2020). *Data Analytics for Non-Life Insurance Pricing*. Swiss Finance Institute Research Paper, 16-68.

Xie, X., Wang, M., & Xu, L. (2003). What risks are Chinese people concerned about? *Risk Analysis*, *23*(4), 685–695. doi:10.1111/1539-6924.00347 PMID:12926562

Yamani, E. (2020). Can technical trading beat the foreign exchange market in times of crisis? *Global Finance Journal*, *100550*, 1–17.

Yang, C. H., & Chen, K. H. (2009). Are Small Firms less Efficient? *Small Business Economics*, *32*(4), 375-395.

Yang, D., & Zhang, Q. (2000). Drift-Independent Volatility Estimation Based on High, Low, Open, and Close Prices. *The Journal of Business*, *73*(3), 477–491.

Yang, S., Ishtiaq, M., & Anwar, M. (2018). Enterprise Risk Management Practices and Firm Performance, the Mediating Role of Competitive Advantage and the Moderating Role of Financial Literacy. *J. Risk Financial Manag*, *11*(35), 35. Advance online publication. doi:10.3390/jrfm11030035

Yao, R., & Curl, A. L. (2010). Do market returns influence risk tolerance? Evidence from panel data. *Journal of Family and Economic Issues*, *32*(3), 532–544. doi:10.100710834-010-9223-2

Compilation of References

Yao, R., & Hanna, S. D. (2004). The effect of gender and marital status on financial risk tolerance. *Consumer Interest Annual*, *50*, 123–124.

Yarrow, E., & Pagan, V. (2021). Reflections on front-line medical work during COVID-19 and the embodiment of risk. *Gender, Work and Organization*, *28*(S1), 89–100. doi:10.1111/gwao.12505 PMID:32837018

Yates, J. F., & Stone, E. R. (1992). The risk construct. In J. F. Yates (Ed.), *Risk-Taking Behavior* (pp. 1–25). John Wiley.

Yazdanfar, D. (2013). Profitability determinants among micro-firms: Evidence from Swedish data. *International Journal of Managerial Finance*, *9*(2), 150–160. doi:10.1108/17439131311307565

Yeap, A. L., & Ramayah, T. (2006). Unraveling perceptions on counterfeit goods: Insights from the Malaysian mindset. *Delhi Business Review*, *7*(1), 47-58.

Yeh, Y.-H., Chung, H., & Liu, C.-L. (2011). Committee independence and financial institution performance during the 2007-08 credit crunch: Evidence from a multi-country study. *Corporate Governance*, *19*(5), 437–458. doi:10.1111/j.1467-8683.2011.00884.x

Yin, R. K. (2003). *Case Study Research. Design and Methods* (3rd ed.). SAGE Publications.

Yordanova, D. I., & Alexandrova-Boshnakova, M. I. (2011). Gender effects on risk-taking of entrepreneurs: Evidence from Bulgaria. *International Journal of Entrepreneurial Behaviour & Research*, *17*(3), 272–295. doi:10.1108/13552551111130718

York, S. (2011). A Risk-Based Approach to Large Businesses. In M. S. Khwaja, R. Awasthi, & J. Loeprick (Eds.), *Risk-Based Tax Audits: Approaches and Country Experiences* (pp. 39–44). The World Bank Publishing. doi:10.1596/9780821387542_CH03

Younas, N., UdDin, S., Awan, T., & Khan, M. Y. (2021). Corporate governance and financial distress: Asian emerging market perspective. *Corporate Governance*.

Yousef, I. (2020). Spillover of COVID-19: Impact on Stock Market Volatility. *International Journal of Psychosocial Rehabilitation*, *24*(6), 18069–18081.

Yuan, R., Sun, J., & Cao, F. (2016). Directors' and officers' liability insurance and stock price crash risk. *Journal of Corporate Finance*, *37*, 173–192. doi:10.1016/j.jcorpfin.2015.12.015

Yu, L., Yue, W., Wang, S., & Lai, K. K. (2010). Support vector machine based multiagent ensemble learning for credit risk evaluation. *Expert Systems with Applications*, *37*(2), 1351–1360. doi:10.1016/j.eswa.2009.06.083

Yu, X., Chen, Z., Xu, W., & Fu, J. (2017). Forecasting bull and bear markets: Evidence from China. *Emerging Markets Finance & Trade*, *53*(8), 1720–1733. doi:10.1080/1540496X.2016.1184141

Zahra, S. A., & Pearce, J. A. II. (1989). Boards of directors and corporate financial performance: A review and integrative model. *Journal of Management*, *15*(2), 291–334. doi:10.1177/014920638901500208

Zalata, A. M., Tauringana, V., & Tingbani, I. (2018). Audit committee financial expertise, gender, and earnings management: Does gender of the financial expert matter? *International Review of Financial Analysis*, *55*(November), 170–183. doi:10.1016/j.irfa.2017.11.002

Zampetakis, L. A. (2014). The emotional dimension of the consumption of luxury counterfeit goods: An empirical taxonomy. *Marketing Intelligence & Planning*, *32*(1), 21–40. doi:10.1108/MIP-10-2012-0102

Zhang, D., Hu, M., & Ji, Q. (2020). Financial markets under the global pandemic of COVID-19. *Finance Research Letters*. Advance online publication. doi:10.1016/j.frl.2020.101528

Zhang, F., Tadikamalla, P. R., & Shang, J. (2016). Corporate credit-risk evaluation system: Integrating explicit and implicit financial performances. *International Journal of Production Economics*, *177*, 77–100. doi:10.1016/j.ijpe.2016.04.012

Zhang, J. (2021). People's responses to the COVID-19 pandemic during its early stages and factors affecting those responses. *Humanities and Social Sciences Communications*, *8*(1), 37. Advance online publication. doi:10.105741599-021-00720-1

Zhong, L. X., & Xiao, J. J. (1995). Determinants of family bond and stock holdings. *Financial Counseling and Planning*, *6*, 107–114.

Zhu, J. (2019). *DEA Frontier software*. Foisie Business School, Worcester Polytechnic Institute.

Zuckerman, M. (1994). *Behavioral Expressions and Biosocial Bases of Sensation Seeking*. Cambridge University Press.

Zumbrun, J. (2014, October 27). *Who owns stocks? It's not just the rich*. The Wall Street Journal, Real Time Economics Blog. Retrieved from http://blogs.wsj.com/economics/2014/10/27/who-owns-stocksits-not-just-the-rich/

About the Contributors

Mara Madaleno is Assistant Professor of Finance and Economics at the Department of Economics, Management, Industrial Engineering and Tourist at the University of Aveiro. Finished her Ph.D. in 2011 at the University of Aveiro in Economics. Director of the Master in Economics – Branches: Finance + Business Economics. Full researcher at the GOVCOPP – Research Unit on Governance, Competitiveness and Public Policies, and Vice-Coordinator of the research line SAD – Systems for Decision Support at GOVCOPP. She is also Vice-Director of the Master in Data Science for Social Sciences and Vice-Coordinator of Continua-UA. Her research interests include financial markets, corporate finance and risk, financial economics, financial energy markets, environmental economics, energy and environment, sustainability. Participates in several research projects.

Elisabete Vieira is Coordinator Professor, ISCA-UA, University of Aveiro. She is researcher at the Research Unit on Governance, Competitiveness and Public Policies (GOVCOPP), being Vice Coordinator of the Competitiveness, Innovation and Sustainability (CIS) Research Group. She has a Ph.D. in Finance from the ISCTE, Lisbon. Her research topics include corporate finance, corporate behavior finance, and corporate governance.

* * *

John Agyekum Addae is a PhD researcher in Finance at the University of Aveiro in Portugal, as well as a Banking and Finance Lecturer at Ghana Communication Technology University. He is a Chartered Banker (ACIB) with a MSc in Development Finance from the University of Ghana and an MSc in Microfinance from the University of Cape Coast, Ghana. His current research interests are on Risk Governance, Bank Risk-Taking Behavior, and FinTech. His work has appeared in journals such as *International Journal of Bank Marketing, Accounting, The Learning Organization, Journal of Hospitality and Tourism Insights and Behavioral Sciences*.

Ezaz Ahmed is the Dean of Division of Business, Entrepreneurship and Technology at Columbia College, South Carolina, USA. Dr Ahmed is a Senior Certified Professional (SCP) by the Society for Human Resources Management (SHRM), USA. Dr Ahmed's research has been published and presented in international journals and conferences. He has been a member of the inaugural Research Advisory Panel of the Australian HR Institute (AHRI), and chair of the Organisational Behavior stream in the Australian and New Zealand Academy of Management (ANZAM).

Feride Bakar Türegün is an Assistant Professor of Fiscal Law at Bursa Uludağ University, Faculty of Economics and Administrative Sciences, Department of Public Finance. Dr. Bakar Türegün is a member of the Publication Committee of the International Journal of Public Finance. Through the scholarship of The Scientific and Technological Research Council of Turkey, she has been at Vienna University of Economics and Business Institute for Austrian and International Tax Law as a guest researcher in 2015. She received her Ph.D. in the public finance department at the Institute of Social Sciences, Bursa Uludağ University in 2017. She took part in tax-related projects and she has authored many articles. In her research, she focuses on taxpayers' rights, tax audits, comparative tax law, taxation of companies and tax risk management.

Cláudio Félix Canguende-Valentim is a Ph.D. student at Doctoral Program in Business and Economics with a specialization in Management at Aveiro University – DEGEIT, Portugal, a MSc in Finance at Portucalense Infante D. Henrique University, Portugal. He is a civil servant in Angola at the Social Security Fund of the Angolan Armed Forces, acting as Coordinator of the Social Support Fund for CSS/FAA workers in Benguela. He is a collaborating Assistant Teacher at the Higher Polytechnic Institutes Jean Piaget and Wonderful in Angola, teaching in economics and management degree courses. His research interests are mainly related to areas such as sustainable consumption and consumer psychology with a focus on consumer emotion and experience and Finance Behavior.

Cristina Casalinho has been Chairman of the Treasury and Public Debt Management Agency since September 2014.

Maria do Céu Cortez is a Full Professor of Management at the School of Economics and Management, University of Minho. She is Associate Editor of the European Journal of Finance. Her research focuses on socially responsible investments and portfolio performance evaluation and has been published in several international peer-reviewed journals.

Özcan Ceylan is Assistant Professor at Özyeğin University in Istanbul. He received his Ph.D. in Economics from Université Paris Ouest Nanterre La Défense. His research focuses on behavioral finance and financial asset pricing. He has several publications in the Journal of Risk, Quantitative Finance, Annals of Economics and Finance, Journal of Applied Economics and Finance Research Letters.

Fitim Deari holds a PhD in Finance and Accounting from the Alexander Moisiu University, Republic of Albania. Since 2020 he works as an associate professor in Finance and Accounting at the Faculty of Business and Economics, South East European University, Republic of North Macedonia. His scientific interests cover financial statements analysis, capital structure, working capital management, risk management, and portfolio management. Fitim's research works as author and co-author have been published in numerous conferences and journals such as: Journal of Construction Engineering and Management, Economic Computation and Economic Cybernetics Studies and Research, International Journal of Risk Assessment and Management, Journal of Economic Studies, Prague Economic Papers, etc.

Luca Di Persio received his PhD in Mathematics by the University of Trento in 2006, jointly with his Doctor Rerum Naturalium title assigned him by the Mathematics Department of the University of Bonn. He spent several years as research assistant for the universities of Verona (Math.Dept.), Trento

About the Contributors

(Math. and Economics Dept.), Bolzano (Economics Dept.), teaching courses spanning from elementary Probability to advanced Stochastic Calculus. He gained a tenure track position within the Dept. of Comp.Science (College of Math.) of the University of Verona in 2012, where he is currently holds an Associate Professor position (starting in 2020), having also received the Italian Scientific Habilitation as Full Professor in 2021. He is currently a member of the College of Math (UniVr), Math. teaching Committee, Comp.Science Dept. Council, and Scientific Committee for Environmental Comp.Science (within Dept.Comp.Science UniVr), PhD College in Mathematics (jointly steered by UniVr and UniTn). He is the Program Director of the Master Degree in Data Science (at UniVr), and co-founder as well as Chief of the R&D section of the UniVr spinoff www.hpa.ai (High Performance Analytics). Luca Di Persio research interests span from Interacting Particle Systems to ML/NNs applications, passing through theory and applications of S(P)DEs, Stochastic Optimal Control and (stochastic) Mean Field Games. He authored 75 Scopus-indexed research papers, about one hundred on ResearchGate/Google Scholar [citations:1510, H-index 16, i10-index 26].

Adnan Gerçek is a Professor of Fiscal Law at Bursa Uludağ University, Faculty of Economics and Administrative Sciences, Department of Public Finance, Bursa, Turkey. Prof. Gerçek is a member of the Turkish Tax Council and an editor of the International Journal of Public Finance. He is also a member of the Scientific Board of International Public Finance Conference/Turkey. He received his Ph.D. in the public finance department at the Institute of Social Sciences, Bursa Uludağ University in 2001. His research focuses on tax law, tax system, tax administration, tax collection procedure, taxpayers' rights, tax responsibility, the discretionary power of tax administration, and the e-taxation system. Prof. Gerçek has considerable experience in the reform of tax system and tax administration in Turkey, development of e-taxation system, and taxation of companies.

John E. Grable, CFP®, teaches and conducts research in the Certified Financial Planner™ Board of Standards Inc. undergraduate and graduate programs at the University of Georgia where he holds an Athletic Association Endowed Professorship. Prior to entering the academic profession, he worked as a pension/benefits administrator and later as an investment advisor in an asset management firm. Dr. Grable served as the founding editor for the Journal of Personal Finance and co-founding editor of the Journal of Financial Therapy and Financial Planning Review. He is best known for his work in the areas of financial risk-tolerance assessment, behavioral financial planning, and psychophysiological economics. He has been the recipient of several research and publication awards and grants, and is active in promoting the link between research and financial planning practice where he has published over 150 refereed papers and co-authored several financial planning textbooks, handbooks, and manuals.

Md. Hasan, having around 12 years of teaching and research experience at the university level, is serving as an Assistant Professor of Business (Finance) in Anwer Khan Modern University, Dhaka, Bangladesh.

Wookjae Heo is an Assistant Professor of Financial Counseling and Planning in the Division of Consumer Science at Purdue University. Prior to join Purdue, Dr. Heo has been a faculty member at South Dakota State University for five years. Dr. Heo earned his Ph.D. degree of financial planning from the University of Georgia in 2016. Prior to earning Ph.D. degree, he had worked for a marketing consulting firm as a Strategic Marketing Planner and Consumer Research Specialist in Korea. Before working at the consulting firm, he received MA and BA degrees from Seoul National University, Korea. His main research interest is broadly about financial consumer welfare including financial behavioral intervention, financial stress, life insurance, and machine learning/data analysis in financial planning and consumer research. With the research interests, he serves a few academic associations as a board/committee member and serves Journal of Financial Therapy as an editorial board member.

Emmanuel Numapau Gyamfi holds PhD in Statistics from the University of Venda in South Africa. He is a Senior Lecturer at the Department of Finance and Accounting at the Ghana Institute of Management and Public Administration (GIMPA). He is a member of the South African Statistical Association (SASA), Ghana Statistical Association (GSA) and a Certified Management and Business Educator (CMBE). His research interests are in applied financial econometrics, market efficiency, financial integration and monetary union, financial markets, and environmental sustainability.

Hai Hong Trinh is a Doctoral Researcher in Finance at the School of Economics and Finance, Massey University, New Zealand. His research areas include financial markets, corporate finance, market microstructure, energy economics, and sustainable development. Hai's research works have appeared in several international peer-review journals such as Pacific-Basin Finance Journal; Regional Studies Regional Science; the International Journal of Housing Market and Analysis; Environment, Development, and Sustainability.

Jarmila Horváthová, is presently working as Associate Professor at Faculty of Management and Business, University of Prešov in Prešov, Slovakia. She completed her Ph.D. study in Branch and cross-section economies at Faculty of Economics of Matej Bel University Banská Bystrica in 1994. She was appointed an associate professor in the field of study Management at the Faculty of Management of University of Prešov in 2020. Within the professional and scientific activities, she focuses on the application of the CAPM model in Cost of Equity valuation and modelling of CAPM inputs, as well as financial health assessment and bankruptcy prediction with the application of financial indicators, prediction models and various mathematical and statistical methods.

Mohammad Irfan is presently working as Associate Professor, CMR Institute of Technology, Bangalore, India. He is MBA (Finance and Marketing) and M.Com (Account and Law). Dr. Irfan has done this Ph.D. from Central University of Haryana. He has qualified UGC-SRF/NET in Management and UGC-NET in Commerce. Dr. Irfan has also qualified NSEs Certification of Financial Market in Capital Market Model and BSEs Certification of Islamic Finance, Banking and Capital Market. Dr. Irfan has been teaching Graduate and Postgraduate Subjects for the last thirteen years in the areas of Financial Management, Security Analysis and Portfolio Management, Management Accounting, Financial Analysis and Decision and Marketing Management. Dr. Irfan has published several research papers in National and International Journals and presented papers in the National and International conferences organized by leading institutions like IIM-A, IIM-C, IIM-Indore, IIM-Shillong, IIT-Roorkee, Bayero University-Kano, Nigeria, Bank of Indonesia, MFAC-Sunway University, Malaysia, Switzerland and many more.

Eun Jin (EJ) Kwak is a Ph.D. candidate in the Department of Financial Planning, Housing and Consumer Economics at the University of Georgia. She holds a Bachelor's degree in Economics and a Master's degree in Business Management with an emphasis in Big Data Analysis. Prior to entering

About the Contributors

the academic profession, she worked at J.P. Morgan and UBS as an operation analyst. Ms. Kwak is the co-author of several peer-reviewed research papers. She was awarded the outstanding financial planning graduate student at the University of Georgia 2021, and the best research award at the Financial Planning Association/Academy of Financial Services 2020 conference. Her research focuses on financial risk-tolerance/aversion assessment, household finance, behavioral financial planning, and machine learning.

Joana Leite is an Adjunct Professor at Coimbra Business School | ISCAC of the Polytechnic Institute of Coimbra (IPC), Portugal. Member of the research unit Centre for Mathematics of the University of Coimbra (CMUC), and a collaborator at Coimbra Business School Research Centre. PhD in Applied Mathematics (Probability and Statistics) from the University of Coimbra. PhD thesis explores the probabilistic structure of a general time series model, the power threshold GARCH model, and an application in statistical process control. Published work are in time series analysis and control charts for time series, recently extending to econometric applications. Research interests are now in time series forecasting, with statistical and machine learning models, and its computational implementation.

Júlio Lobão is an Assistant Professor at the School of Economics and Management of the University of Porto, Portugal, having previously worked as a financial consultant in the wealth management industry. He has authored seven books as well as several dozen articles in the fields of financial markets and behavioral finance.

Martina Mokrišová, is presently working as Assistant Professor at Faculty of Management and Business, University of Prešov in Prešov, Slovakia. She graduated in Finance, banking and investment at the Faculty of Economics, Technical University of Košice. She completed her PhD. at Faculty of Mining, Ecology, Process Control, and Geotechnology, Technical University of Košice in 2012. The areas of her professional interest are accounting, financial analysis, controlling and business performance evaluation. In the current scientific and research work, she focuses on the issue of companies' performance, efficiency, competitiveness, and financial health assessment applying various indicators and models.

Jorge Humberto Fernandes Mota, Ph.D. in Management, specialization in Finance at the Faculty of Economics of Oporto University (Exchange Visiting PhD Student / Research Fellow at the University of Oklahoma Price College of Business, Norman, Oklahoma, in 2011). He received his Master's degree in Accounting and Auditing from the University of Aveiro, Portugal and his Bachelor's degree in Economics from the Lusíada University of Porto (Award as the Second Best Student in the 1996-2001 Economics Course) He has a solid working experience as a consultant in the financial, management control and strategic management (evaluation of investment projects, business valuation, implementation of control management tools - Balanced Scorecard) areas. He was financial and commercial director of two Portuguese firms in the construction and retailing fields. He is a Lecturer at the Department of Economics, Management, Industrial Engineering, and Tourism (DEGEIT), University of Aveiro, Portugal, where he has been lecturing courses in the following areas: Evaluation and Project Management, Economic and Financial Management (especially to the Master in Management course). He published books, proceedings of conferences and articles in international journals in the field of Management and Economics: International Journal of Project Management, South African Journal of Business Management, Energy Policy, International Journal of Energy Economics and Policy.

Elisabete Neves is Adjunct Professor and Coordinator of the Master Degree in Financial Analysis at Coimbra Business School (Polytechnic Institute of Coimbra). She is researcher at Centre for Transdisciplinary Development Studies (UTAD). She received her Ph.D. in Finance from the University of Salamanca (Spain). Her research topics include sustainability, CSR and performance, stock evaluation and performance of investment funds, corporate governance and behavioral characteristics, bank efficiency, and performance. She has several articles published in indexed journals, such as International Journal of Managerial Finance; International Journal of Productivity and Performance Management; International Journal of Accounting and Information Management; Operational Research; Journal of the Operational Research Society, Social Responsibility Journal, etc.

Joana Pena holds a PhD in Management - Finance from the University of Minho since 2018. She is currently a financial consultant.

Helena Saraiva is Adjunct Professor of Accounting and Finance area. Management and Economics Department, in Guarda Polytechnic Institute. Main research areas: Balanced Scorecard, Management Accounting, Entrepreneurship, Finance, Accounting, Accounting History.

Zakir Hossen Shaikh is a Faculty of Islamic Banking and Finance, Commercial Studies Division under Ministry of Education, Kingdom of Bahrain since 2015. Prior to this, he worked more than 15 years in commercial and academic industry. He has published numerous articles in referred journals and presented many papers in various conferences, both local and abroad exclusively in the different area of Accounting, management and Islamic Banking and Finance. He has also participated in a variety of seminars, forums, workshops and international conferences. He obtained his Ph.D. (Islamic Banking and Finance) from India in 2018. His doctoral thesis explored the entrepreneurial phenomenon from an Islamic perspective and argued for profit and loss sharing (PLS) contracts as viable alternatives to conventional interest-based financing instruments. He holds Master degree in Commerce, Business Administration & Finance and Control. He is a member of Chartered Institute of Islamic Finance Professionals (CIIF), Malaysia; Indian Accounting Association; Orissa Commerce Association, India and associated with Accounting & Auditing Organization for Islamic Financial Institution (AAOIFI), Bahrain.

João Teodósio is Assistant Professor in the finance field at School of Management and Techonoloy, Polytechnic Institute of Santarém. He holds a PhD in Management and is a researcher of the Research Unit on Governance, Competitiveness and Public Policies (GOVCOPP) from University of Aveiro. His research interests are in finance and corporate governance.

Index

A

African country 316, 318, 320
Angola 83-84, 86-88, 90, 93-96, 318, 320, 325-326, 332
Artificial Neural Network (ANN) 297, 299-300, 314-315
assets 2, 7, 18-19, 21, 27-31, 40, 49, 66-67, 79, 81, 83, 89-91, 94, 98, 105, 111, 118-119, 129-133, 139-140, 146, 149-150, 162, 185, 188-191, 193, 202-203, 206, 212, 231-236, 240-242, 244-246, 249, 266, 271, 294, 299, 303, 310, 341-342, 344, 349, 355, 360, 363, 365, 379, 383-385, 387, 390, 397-399
attitude 55, 67, 294-295, 316, 318-320, 323-326, 329, 331-334, 338, 396

B

bank performance 15, 17, 20, 96, 99-105, 111-113
banking stability 83, 85-86, 95, 97
bankruptcy 22, 24, 26, 28-29, 32, 34, 57-58, 95, 132-133, 142, 148-154, 163-167, 169-177, 271-272, 389-390
Bayesian Regularized Neural Network (BRNN) 293, 297, 299-300, 303-307, 309, 314-315
bias 74, 76, 109, 120, 130, 141, 144, 146-147, 185, 198, 294, 362, 381
bibliometric analysis 1-2, 4, 19, 21, 24, 38-39, 41, 47, 56-57, 62
big data 293-294, 296, 310-314
boosted decision trees 270, 273, 279, 289-290
Brexit 354-355, 364, 369, 371-372, 375, 379-380, 384, 386, 396-397
Business 2, 6, 10, 12, 16, 20-23, 25-27, 32-36, 42, 46-47, 49-51, 54, 57-59, 61-62, 74-78, 84, 94-97, 112-115, 130, 143, 146, 148-150, 153, 155, 171-176, 180, 182, 193, 196, 198-202, 227-230, 239, 248-257, 260-263, 265-268, 271-272, 334-340, 343-344, 349-351, 353-354, 381-382, 398-400

Buy and Hold 354-355, 357, 380

C

cash holdings 31, 36, 40, 116-118, 139-140, 143-144, 146, 301, 353
consumer behavior 316, 318, 320, 323, 332, 334-336
content analysis 4-5, 7, 24, 41, 62, 336
cooperative compliance 250, 258, 261-262, 264, 266
coronavirus 18, 57, 158, 175, 204-205, 207, 210-211, 224, 226, 228-230
corporate governance 1, 3-4, 6, 10, 15-24, 26-27, 31, 33, 41-42, 49-50, 52, 56-61, 95, 100, 104, 112-114, 150, 172, 182-183, 196, 235, 246, 250-251, 255, 258, 262-264, 266, 268-269, 350-353
correlation 25, 91-92, 109, 119, 137-138, 148, 156, 159, 188-189, 204, 221-222, 224, 226, 327, 347, 384-386, 389-393, 395, 397-399
corruption 83-98, 100, 256
credit risk 2-3, 19, 24, 26, 28, 35-36, 39, 63, 83-86, 88-97, 113, 271-272, 278, 291, 390
credit scoring 270-274, 278, 280, 289-292
cross hedging 388, 401
cut-off 152, 159, 164-165, 167-170, 177, 280, 283

D

debt 7, 28, 34, 36, 40, 49, 51, 116, 129-130, 133, 145-146, 149, 226, 231, 236, 245, 343, 348-349, 389-390, 401
decision-making 39-40, 64-65, 73, 75, 77-78, 102, 119-120, 124, 127, 141, 145, 148, 205, 234, 243, 296, 313, 320, 355
deep learning 291, 293-294, 296-300, 307, 310, 312-315
dynamic conditional correlations 384, 386, 389, 392, 395

E

emerging stock market indices 204, 222, 226
environmental 18, 27, 46, 50, 62, 76, 116, 143-144, 171, 178-179, 182-184, 187, 189, 191-193, 196, 198, 201, 231, 233-237, 239-241, 244-245, 247, 249, 256-257
ESG 18, 21, 56, 179, 183-185, 187, 195-196, 199, 231-237, 240-249
ESG assets 231, 233-235, 241-242, 244-246, 249
European Taxonomy 232, 238-239, 244, 249
Exchange Traded Fund 401
Exchange Traded Note 401

F

Feasible Generalized Least Squares model 83
financial crisis 15, 17-18, 20, 22, 24, 26, 28, 33, 50, 61, 84-85, 100, 113, 116, 132, 134-135, 139, 141-142, 146, 178, 197, 206, 251, 362, 385, 389, 396-400
financial crisis of 2007-2008 17, 24
Financial Derivative 401
financial expert 99-101, 112-115
financial markets 36, 61, 78, 113, 178, 202-203, 226-227, 230-231, 233, 237, 239-240, 249, 270, 353, 355, 357, 378, 380, 382, 384-385, 389-390, 396-397, 400
financial risk 1-4, 15, 17-24, 36, 38-42, 44, 52, 54-57, 59, 61, 63-67, 73-78, 102, 150, 170, 172-173, 175, 270-272, 291, 293-295, 299, 301, 303-304, 307-310, 312-316, 321, 324, 326, 329, 331-333
financial risk tolerance 64-67, 73-76, 78, 293-295, 299, 301, 303-304, 307-310, 312-315
financing 16, 28, 35, 37, 39, 60, 84, 86, 95, 111, 116-117, 128, 130, 132-133, 143, 146, 236, 238, 240-241, 243-244, 248-249, 343
fires 116-118, 122-125, 129-131, 133-134, 136, 139-142, 144-145
firm performance 23, 25-27, 29-30, 32, 34-37, 49, 51, 54, 57, 60, 101, 103, 112-114, 118, 267, 351-353
futures 361, 382-391, 397-401

G

gender 3, 20, 32, 38-42, 44, 49-51, 53-66, 68, 70, 72-80, 104, 114-115, 123, 234, 295, 299, 301, 308, 314-315
gender diversity 3, 20, 32, 38-42, 44, 49-51, 54-63, 114-115
governance 1, 3-4, 6-7, 10, 15-24, 26-27, 31, 33, 41-42, 49-50, 52, 56-61, 86, 88, 95-96, 99-102, 104, 111-115, 150, 172, 178-179, 182-184, 187, 189, 191-193, 196, 201, 231-232, 234-235, 237, 239, 243-244, 246, 249-251, 255, 258, 261-264, 266-269, 314, 350-353
Grable 64-67, 70, 73, 76, 78, 293-295, 299, 311-313
Green Bond Standard 232, 235, 238, 240, 244, 248-249
green bonds 231-232, 235-236, 238, 240, 242, 245, 247, 249, 385, 398

H

harmonisation 232-233, 235, 237-239, 242-243, 245-246, 249
harmonisation process 232-233, 235, 238-239, 242-243, 246, 249
hedge ratio 384, 388-389, 393, 395, 401
hedging 22, 32, 384-391, 393-394, 396-401
heuristic 120, 128, 139-140, 146, 383

I

insiders 340-342, 345, 347-350, 353
investment 3, 7, 15, 24, 31, 37, 51, 57, 61, 63, 65-67, 73-75, 78-79, 81-82, 87, 94, 116, 118, 133, 141, 143, 146, 150, 178-181, 183-185, 187-190, 192-193, 196-203, 227, 231-236, 238-243, 245-249, 264, 272, 290, 294-295, 299, 301, 303-304, 307, 310, 312-314, 326, 342, 352, 354-355, 357, 365-366, 373-375, 378, 382-383, 385, 401

L

large taxpayers 250-251, 258, 261-262
Loss Aversion 51, 116-119, 121-122, 142-147
Lytton 64-67, 70, 73, 76, 295, 299, 312-313

M

MACD 354-357, 359-363, 365-366, 368-370, 372-374, 376, 378-380, 383
machine learning 97, 270, 272-273, 278, 290-291, 296, 299, 309-311, 314
mutual funds 51, 81, 179, 185, 187, 192-193, 195, 198-203

N

Neural Networks 270-272, 290, 311-313, 383

Index

O

optimal hedge ratio 388-389, 393, 401
options 36, 119, 121, 170, 195, 383-384, 386-390, 397, 400-401

P

performance 15, 17-21, 23-27, 29-37, 40, 49-51, 54, 56-57, 59-60, 62, 75, 83-84, 86, 88, 96, 98-105, 111-115, 118, 123, 150, 158, 173-174, 176, 178-193, 195-203, 205-210, 220, 222-224, 230, 235-236, 240, 242, 247, 251, 262, 265, 267, 271, 273, 275, 279-280, 282-283, 285, 293-294, 296-297, 299-300, 303, 309-310, 315, 321, 323-324, 340-345, 347-356, 361-362, 367-370, 372-373, 375, 377, 379-380, 383-384, 389-391, 393, 398-401
portfolio performance 178, 361
Portugal 1, 23, 38, 64-66, 83, 99, 116-118, 122-127, 129-130, 133-136, 139-142, 144-145, 147, 178, 231, 255, 316, 340-341, 348-349, 352, 354, 383
Portuguese companies 340, 343-344, 349, 353
price risk 52, 384, 389, 401
profitability 7, 25, 28, 83, 89-90, 94, 96, 98-99, 101, 104, 109, 111-112, 150, 162, 179, 187, 241, 343-345, 348-351, 353-355, 361-362, 365-366, 373, 375, 377, 380-381, 383
Prospect Theory 74, 118-119, 121-122, 142, 144, 146-147
psychological risk 316, 320-322, 324, 326, 329, 331-332
purchase intention 316-319, 322-327, 329, 331-334, 337

R

Random Forest 296-297, 299, 301, 303, 307, 313-315
risk 1-4, 15, 17-42, 44, 49-71, 73-81, 83-86, 88-97, 99-105, 108-109, 111-115, 117-119, 121, 124, 128-129, 131, 133-134, 139-141, 143-146, 148-150, 153, 170-173, 175, 177, 179, 182, 184, 186, 197, 199-201, 205-206, 209, 226-227, 232, 238, 241, 243-245, 247, 250-272, 274, 278, 291, 293-295, 299, 301, 303-304, 307-327, 329, 331-338, 341, 353, 363, 379-380, 384-386, 388-390, 398, 400-401
risk assessment 15, 25, 27, 35-36, 73, 76-77, 102, 128, 258, 260, 262, 264, 312
risk aversion 35, 51, 64-66, 73-75, 77-79, 119, 209, 227
risk committee 21, 99-105, 108-109, 111-115
risk governance 99-102, 111-115
risk management 15, 18-23, 25-27, 29-30, 32, 34-35, 37, 40, 50-51, 54, 56, 59-60, 85, 99, 101-103, 111-115, 143, 170, 173, 175, 179, 206, 227, 232, 238, 243, 250-252, 257-272, 291, 385
risk tolerance 26, 32, 64-71, 73-79, 102, 293-295, 299, 301, 303-304, 307-315
risk-adjusted returns 178, 180, 186, 189, 192-193, 195-197
RSI 354-358, 361-363, 365-370, 372-380, 383

S

Scopus 1, 4-16, 18, 38, 41-47, 50-52, 54-56, 58, 61
sensitivity 153, 165, 168, 177-178, 210, 282-283, 377
social 6, 12, 17-18, 20, 24, 40, 46-47, 54, 56-58, 60, 62, 66, 74-75, 87-88, 145, 156, 171, 173, 178-185, 187, 189-200, 202-203, 207, 231, 233-237, 243-245, 247-249, 259, 267, 311, 316, 318, 320-327, 329, 331-335, 337, 339, 344-345, 349, 353
Social Bonds 231
social labels 178, 180, 182, 184-185, 195-196, 203
social risk 316, 318, 321-322, 324, 326-327, 329, 331-334
social screening 178-180, 182-185, 190, 195, 197, 200
socially responsible investments 178-180, 183, 185, 190, 197, 200-202
specificity 153, 165, 168, 177, 282-283, 346
structural equation modeling 316, 327, 336
students 26, 64-68, 73-75, 78, 80, 119, 265
Support vector machine 173, 270, 289-291
survey 64-67, 73, 80, 173, 203, 208, 257, 266-267, 269, 291, 298-299, 308, 323
Sustainable Bonds 231
Sustainable Finance 232, 235, 238, 241, 248-249
Symptom 177
Syndrome 177, 235

T

tax compliance 250, 253, 255, 257-258, 260-264, 267-268
tax control framework 250, 257-258, 260-262, 267-268
tax law 250-251, 255
Tax Risk Categories 250, 252-253
taxation 250-252, 254-255, 257, 260-266, 268-269, 365

U

USA elections 354

V

variables 3-4, 7, 17, 25, 27, 29-31, 41, 68, 90-94, 104-105, 109, 118, 121, 124, 129, 131-133, 136, 138-141, 151-152, 162, 166, 187, 189-193, 195, 197, 203, 209, 228, 272, 279, 288-289, 294-305, 308-310, 315, 319, 323, 327, 335, 341-342, 345-348
Volatility derivatives 384, 389-390, 400
volatility estimators 204, 206-208, 210-212, 214-230
volatility risk 28, 209, 227, 384, 386, 390, 401

W

Wildfire 144, 147

Recommended Reference Books

IGI Global's reference books are available in three unique pricing formats:
Print Only, E-Book Only, or Print + E-Book.

Shipping fees may apply.

www.igi-global.com

ISBN: 978-1-7998-1048-3
EISBN: 978-1-7998-1049-0
© 2020; 605 pp.
List Price: US$ 285

ISBN: 978-1-5225-8933-4
EISBN: 978-1-5225-8934-1
© 2020; 667 pp.
List Price: US$ 295

ISBN: 978-1-7998-0357-7
EISBN: 978-1-7998-0359-1
© 2020; 451 pp.
List Price: US$ 235

ISBN: 978-1-7998-0070-5
EISBN: 978-1-7998-0071-2
© 2020; 144 pp.
List Price: US$ 175

ISBN: 978-1-5225-6980-0
EISBN: 978-1-5225-6981-7
© 2019; 339 pp.
List Price: US$ 235

ISBN: 978-1-5225-5390-8
EISBN: 978-1-5225-5391-5
© 2018; 125 pp.
List Price: US$ 165

Do you want to stay current on the latest research trends, product announcements, news, and special offers?
Join IGI Global's mailing list to receive customized recommendations, exclusive discounts, and more.
Sign up at: **www.igi-global.com/newsletters**.

Publisher of Peer-Reviewed, Timely, and Innovative Academic Research

Ensure Quality Research is Introduced to the Academic Community

Become an Evaluator for IGI Global Authored Book Projects

The overall success of an authored book project is dependent on quality and timely manuscript evaluations.

Applications and Inquiries may be sent to:
development@igi-global.com

Applicants must have a doctorate (or equivalent degree) as well as publishing, research, and reviewing experience. Authored Book Evaluators are appointed for one-year terms and are expected to complete at least three evaluations per term. Upon successful completion of this term, evaluators can be considered for an additional term.

If you have a colleague that may be interested in this opportunity, we encourage you to share this information with them.

IGI Global Author Services

Providing a high-quality, affordable, and expeditious service, IGI Global's Author Services enable authors to streamline their publishing process, increase chance of acceptance, and adhere to IGI Global's publication standards.

Benefits of Author Services:

- **Professional Service:** All our editors, designers, and translators are experts in their field with years of experience and professional certifications.
- **Quality Guarantee & Certificate:** Each order is returned with a quality guarantee and certificate of professional completion.
- **Timeliness:** All editorial orders have a guaranteed return timeframe of 3-5 business days and translation orders are guaranteed in 7-10 business days.
- **Affordable Pricing:** IGI Global Author Services are competitively priced compared to other industry service providers.
- **APC Reimbursement:** IGI Global authors publishing Open Access (OA) will be able to deduct the cost of editing and other IGI Global author services from their OA APC publishing fee.

Author Services Offered:

English Language Copy Editing
Professional, native English language copy editors improve your manuscript's grammar, spelling, punctuation, terminology, semantics, consistency, flow, formatting, and more.

Scientific & Scholarly Editing
A Ph.D. level review for qualities such as originality and significance, interest to researchers, level of methodology and analysis, coverage of literature, organization, quality of writing, and strengths and weaknesses.

Figure, Table, Chart & Equation Conversions
Work with IGI Global's graphic designers before submission to enhance and design all figures and charts to IGI Global's specific standards for clarity.

Translation
Providing 70 language options, including Simplified and Traditional Chinese, Spanish, Arabic, German, French, and more.

Hear What the Experts Are Saying About IGI Global's Author Services

"Publishing with IGI Global has been *an amazing experience* for me for sharing my research. The *strong academic production* support ensures quality and timely completion." – **Prof. Margaret Niess, Oregon State University, USA**

"The service was *very fast, very thorough, and very helpful* in ensuring our chapter meets the criteria and requirements of the book's editors. I was *quite impressed and happy* with your service." – **Prof. Tom Brinthaupt, Middle Tennessee State University, USA**

Learn More or Get Started Here:

For Questions, Contact IGI Global's Customer Service Team at cust@igi-global.com or 717-533-8845

IGI Global
PUBLISHER of TIMELY KNOWLEDGE
www.igi-global.com

www.igi-global.com

Celebrating Over 30 Years of Scholarly Knowledge Creation & Dissemination

InfoSci®-Books

A Database of Nearly 6,000 Reference Books Containing Over 105,000+ Chapters Focusing on Emerging Research

GAIN ACCESS TO **THOUSANDS** OF REFERENCE BOOKS AT **A FRACTION** OF THEIR INDIVIDUAL LIST **PRICE**.

InfoSci®-Books Database

The **InfoSci®-Books** is a database of nearly 6,000 IGI Global single and multi-volume reference books, handbooks of research, and encyclopedias, encompassing groundbreaking research from prominent experts worldwide that spans over 350+ topics in 11 core subject areas including business, computer science, education, science and engineering, social sciences, and more.

Open Access Fee Waiver (Read & Publish) Initiative

For any library that invests in IGI Global's InfoSci-Books and/or InfoSci-Journals (175+ scholarly journals) databases, IGI Global will match the library's investment with a fund of equal value to go toward **subsidizing the OA article processing charges (APCs) for their students, faculty, and staff** at that institution when their work is submitted and accepted under OA into an IGI Global journal.*

INFOSCI® PLATFORM FEATURES

- Unlimited Simultaneous Access
- No DRM
- No Set-Up or Maintenance Fees
- A Guarantee of No More Than a 5% Annual Increase for Subscriptions
- Full-Text HTML and PDF Viewing Options
- Downloadable MARC Records
- COUNTER 5 Compliant Reports
- Formatted Citations With Ability to Export to RefWorks and EasyBib
- No Embargo of Content (Research is Available Months in Advance of the Print Release)

*The fund will be offered on an annual basis and expire at the end of the subscription period. The fund would renew as the subscription is renewed for each year thereafter. The open access fees will be waived after the student, faculty, or staff's paper has been vetted and accepted into an IGI Global journal and the fund can only be used toward publishing OA in an IGI Global journal. Libraries in developing countries will have the match on their investment doubled.

To Recommend or Request a Free Trial:
www.igi-global.com/infosci-books

eresources@igi-global.com • Toll Free: 1-866-342-6657 ext. 100 • Phone: 717-533-8845 x100

www.igi-global.com

Publisher of Peer-Reviewed, Timely, and Innovative Academic Research Since 1988

IGI Global's Transformative Open Access (OA) Model:
How to Turn Your University Library's Database Acquisitions Into a Source of OA Funding

Well in advance of Plan S, IGI Global unveiled their OA Fee Waiver (Read & Publish) Initiative. Under this initiative, librarians who invest in IGI Global's InfoSci-Books and/or InfoSci-Journals databases will be able to subsidize their patrons' OA article processing charges (APCs) when their work is submitted and accepted (after the peer review process) into an IGI Global journal.

How Does it Work?

Step 1: **Library Invests in the InfoSci-Databases:** A library perpetually purchases or subscribes to the InfoSci-Books, InfoSci-Journals, or discipline/subject databases.

Step 2: **IGI Global Matches the Library Investment with OA Subsidies Fund:** IGI Global provides a fund to go towards subsidizing the OA APCs for the library's patrons.

Step 3: **Patron of the Library is Accepted into IGI Global Journal (After Peer Review):** When a patron's paper is accepted into an IGI Global journal, they option to have their paper published under a traditional publishing model or as OA.

Step 4: **IGI Global Will Deduct APC Cost from OA Subsidies Fund:** If the author decides to publish under OA, the OA APC fee will be deducted from the OA subsidies fund.

Step 5: **Author's Work Becomes Freely Available:** The patron's work will be freely available under CC BY copyright license, enabling them to share it freely with the academic community.

Note: *This fund will be offered on an annual basis and will renew as the subscription is renewed for each year thereafter. IGI Global will manage the fund and award the APC waivers unless the librarian has a preference as to how the funds should be managed.*

Hear From the Experts on This Initiative:

"I'm very happy to have been able to make one of my recent research contributions *freely available* along with having access to the *valuable resources* found within IGI Global's InfoSci-Journals database."

— **Prof. Stuart Palmer**, Deakin University, Australia

"Receiving the support from IGI Global's OA Fee Waiver Initiative *encourages me to continue my research work without any hesitation*."

— **Prof. Wenlong Liu**, College of Economics and Management at Nanjing University of Aeronautics & Astronautics, China

For More Information, Scan the QR Code or Contact: IGI Global's Digital Resources Team at eresources@igi-global.com.

Are You Ready to Publish Your Research?

IGI Global — PUBLISHER of TIMELY KNOWLEDGE

IGI Global offers book authorship and editorship opportunities across 11 subject areas, including business, computer science, education, science and engineering, social sciences, and more!

Benefits of Publishing with IGI Global:

- Free one-on-one editorial and promotional support.
- Expedited publishing timelines that can take your book from start to finish in less than one (1) year.
- Choose from a variety of formats, including: Edited and Authored References, Handbooks of Research, Encyclopedias, and Research Insights.
- Utilize IGI Global's eEditorial Discovery® submission system in support of conducting the submission and double-blind peer review process.
- IGI Global maintains a strict adherence to ethical practices due in part to our full membership with the Committee on Publication Ethics (COPE).
- Indexing potential in prestigious indices such as Scopus®, Web of Science™, PsycINFO®, and ERIC – Education Resources Information Center.
- Ability to connect your ORCID iD to your IGI Global publications.
- Earn honorariums and royalties on your full book publications as well as complimentary copies and exclusive discounts.

Join Your Colleagues from Prestigious Institutions, Including:

- Australian National University
- Massachusetts Institute of Technology
- Johns Hopkins University
- Harvard University
- Tsinghua University
- Columbia University in the City of New York

Learn More at: www.igi-global.com/publish
or Contact IGI Global's Aquisitions Team at: acquisition@igi-global.com